Report of the Task Force on Broadcasting Policy

Report of the Task Force on Broadcasting Policy

Minister of Supply and Services Canada

Available in Canada through authorized bookstore agents and other bookstores or by mail from
Canadian Government Publishing Centre
Supply and Services Canada
Ottawa, Ontario
K1A 0S9

Also available in French

Printed in Canada

Catalogue No. C022-68-1-1986E
ISBN 0-660-12164-6

Canada	$14.50
Other Countries	$17.40

Price subject to change without notice

Design: Jacques Charette and Associates Ltd.
Publishing Co-ordination: Ampersand Communications Services Inc.

Government of Canada | Gouvernement du Canada

Task Force on Broadcasting Policy | Groupe de travail sur la politique de la radiodiffusion

September 1986

The Honourable Flora MacDonald
Minister of Communications
Ottawa

Dear Miss MacDonald:

We, the undersigned, members of the Task Force established on May 8, 1985 to make recommendations on a cultural and industrial strategy to govern the future evolution of the Canadian broadcasting system through the remainder of this century, have the honour to submit the following report.

Gerald Lewis Caplan, Co-Chairman

Florian Sauvageau, Co-Chairman

Francine Côté

J. Conrad Lavigne

Felix Randolph Blache-Fraser

Finlay MacDonald

Mimi Fullerton

Canada

300 Slater
Ottawa, Ontario K1A 0C8
(613-993-4371)

Contents

Chairmen's Foreword

None of us guessed, when we began our work late in May of 1985, the magnitude of the responsibility we had agreed to assume. In fact the mandate with which Marcel Masse, then the Minister of Communications, entrusted us was vast, encompassing the totality of a broadcasting system infinitely more complex than we yet understood. We embraced our task with an appropriate combination of zeal and trepidation. For all seven of the Task Force members, as well as our staff, it has been a time of great fascination and excitement, challenging always, frustrating occasionally, but an experience neither to have missed nor, as one of our poor predecessors learned, to be so foolhardy as to repeat a second time. As one broadcaster told us, the State had offered us a Ph.D program in broadcasting, and though some of us began the course at the kindergarten level and others were Masters, all of us have been grateful for this singular opportunity to upgrade ourselves.

We learned through several approaches. First, we learned a great deal from each other, seven strangers from across Canada with markedly different backgrounds, experiences and interests. Second, we consulted extensively, holding both public and private sessions in major centres in every province and territory. Our public meetings were invariably dominated by CBC devotees, as often as not anxious to share with us some perceived inadequacy of the poor, put-upon Corporation, maligned, it sometimes seemed, as much by its adherents as its foes. Meanwhile, cynics suggested, most ordinary folk were home contentedly watching American programs on Canadian channels or on American stations carried by Canadian cable companies.

At the same time, the private sessions with representatives of both the private and public broadcasting systems as well as various private and public interest groups allowed us to have lengthier and more in-depth encounters than could have been possible in a large public forum.

In all, we received 253 briefs. At our public meetings we heard 267 submissions and met privately with over 170 people. Mostly we heard from representatives of organizations or groups, but some individuals spoke simply for themselves.

Our third key device for learning was to commission a program of original research to inform more carefully our deliberations. Let us record here a major disappointment. It was our hope, both to save time and money, that we would merely need to fill in gaps and update existing literature. This soon proved wildly optimistic. We found in almost every area we explored a serious paucity of material aiding the development of public policy. Not only did this undermine our honourable intentions with regard to time and the public purse, but it seems unacceptable in principle that the Canadian broadcasting system should operate with inadequate information. We draw attention to this problem in several parts of the text, and make specific recommendations toward its alleviation.

A year (or so) of such intense effort — more, perhaps, than is typically expected from something called a Task Force — necessarily produces many debts, which we are happy to acknowledge. First, we are grateful to the other five members of the Task Force who were chosen as our associates but who became friends and colleagues. To our pleasure, what follows has been approved by each of us. But in the process of seven tough-minded individuals reaching complete consensus on such a multitude of difficult and controversial issues, inevitably each of us feels more enthusiasm for some parts of this Report than for others. That was a price each decided it was worth paying to achieve unanimity.

On behalf of all the members, we pay tribute to our talented and indispensable staff. We cannot here mention each one of them or give them the recognition they deserve. But let it be stated plainly that the dedication to their work of each of them, professional and support staff alike, and their commitment to producing this Report, was equal to that of the seven members. It is as much their report as our own.

We are thankful to the former Minister, to the Deputy Minister of Communications, and to their colleagues for accepting the independent behaviour and thought upon which we insisted from the outset, as well as for facilitating our endless "administrivial" process. While it would be invidious to single out individuals, we at least express to them our gratitude for their co-operation, understanding and patience.

We close on a note of personal concern. We saw our mandate as focussing on general policy matters, not specific issues of program content. We therefore ignored almost completely the debate that currently rages throughout the western world on such vexing questions as the impact of television on our quality of life, how it affects children as they mature or whether it promotes violence. Nor have we made a contribution to the problem of devising criteria by which to judge the quality of programming, although the job must soon be done to assure that broadcasters cannot meet their obligations to the *Broadcasting Act* by quantitative methods alone. It is not enough to show programs that do no more than fulfill formal CRTC Canadian content requirements. We in no way believe that any Canadian program is by definition superior in quality or nature or redeeming social value to any American show. Yet we understand that must appear to be the implication of some of our recommendations, and in that sense we are not satisfied with our own work and hope others can do better.

We recognize too that in certain areas our analysis seems to demand much more drastic and clear-cut recommendations than those we in fact make. This reflects both our determination not to make proposals whose consequences we could not responsibly calculate, as well as the process by which a consensus was able to be reached. But as a result we hope the strong recommendations we do make have an extra credibility and are treated with commensurate seriousness.

Lastly, we share our concern for those inadequacies which we are confident others will discover but which we are blind to see. Reviewing the reports that preceded ours, it is frighteningly easy to perceive the traps into which our predecessors fell without even knowing they were falling. For our inevitable sins of omission and commission, we beg indulgence in advance. This Report emerges from a long process of negotiation among a group of otherwise unconnected individuals, and the final product inevitably reflects the strengths and weaknesses of such a process. A report, we finally understood, is simply not a book.

Let us add a word on process. Nothing was more illuminating to us than the manner in which francophones and anglophones, Quebecois and non-Quebecois, were accommodated in our operations. Of our seven members, five were bilingual. All seven spoke English. We had little choice, therefore, but to conduct our sessions in English. This unavoidable decision added more pressure on certain Task Force members and staff than on others.

Translation of documents bedevilled us from the first to the very last minute. How a multilingual world, let alone a bilingual nation, functions successfully will forever remain a mystery to us. But we were determined, as a matter of principle, that we understand each other clearly, and that our Report says the same things, with the same tone, nuances and spirit, in both languages. Since a significant part of the Report was written originally in French, the anglophones soon learned how difficult this chore was when the French chapters were translated into English.

But the real task came on the French side, in a world where the technical, and often the programming, realities are conceived and first given names in English. We have taken extra steps to assure an appropriate translation, though in the end we simply could not express satisfactorily various technical terms, while at the same time we were dependent on official translations from English to French which often left something to be desired.

The Canadian broadcasting system, as we said, is substantially more complex than most Canadians realize. A number of components are intrinsically in conflict with each other; interests are often in collision; a satisfactory balance has always been impossible to define since the definition of satisfaction depends so greatly on the eye of the beholder. In that sense, our Task Force was fairly representative of the system. There was no more possibility of satisfying fully the positions of each of us than there is, with all the good will in the world, of meeting the expectations of each player in the system.

We have reached our own consensus by meeting at least a significant proportion of the interests each of us held. In so doing, we ended up re-designing the system so that at least part of the "wish list" of each component has been met. No part can function precisely as it chooses without seriously violating the operations of another part, and it is in the spirit of fairly distributing the rights and obligations of each player that we have devised our recommendations. Our overriding goal has been to provide a blueprint for a more truly Canadian broadcasting system for the foreseeable future, one in which public policies and institutional structures allow artistic creativity to flourish. After all, if entertainment is ever truly to become genuine culture, it is the creative aspect of broadcasting that must predominate. Even if we were to devise the perfect policies, in the end it rests with artists and creators to make them work. It is in this spirit that we hope this Report will be received.

Gerald L. Caplan
Florian Sauvageau
September 1986

Part I

THE CONTEXT

Chapter 1

The Development of Canadian Broadcasting Policy

The Development of Canadian Broadcasting Policy

The search for public policy for the Canadian broadcasting system has now gone on for almost six decades. A small but honourable cottage industry, it has been the subject of some dozen reports by commissions, royal or otherwise, committees and task forces. As well, there have been several studies by parliamentary committees and CRTC committees, along with a half-dozen major government statements and the *Broadcasting Acts* of 1958 and 1968. We tread a well-worn path indeed.

At this point some may say enough is enough. Robert Fowler, our distinguished predecessor who chaired both a royal commission and a committee, remarked that he thought it doubtful whether broadcasting could survive many more investigations.

With the utmost respect, we demur. Certainly we sympathize with Mr. Fowler's weariness after two reports in seven years. What he could not know, however, was that those two reports, in 1957 and 1965, would be the only major studies ever undertaken dealing in detail with the entire Canadian broadcasting system until our own. The Massey Commission and the Applebaum-Hébert Committee looked at broadcasting in the larger context of Canadian culture and various studies have reported on specific aspects of the broadcasting system. But there has never been a comprehensive study of the efficacy of the 1968 *Broadcasting Act*, notwithstanding the enormous changes that have affected Canadian broadcasting over the past 18 years.

In short, the widely expressed view that the archives of Ottawa are filled with a succession of largely neglected studies and committee reports is something of a caricature, a symbol, perhaps, of the substantial mythology that envelopes Canadian broadcasting.

If anything, therefore, a study such as ours is long overdue. Existing policy and the legislative framework for the broadcasting system is based in some respects on a rapidly vanishing reality, and in certain inevitable ways is both inappropriate to and inadequate for the emerging era. Our mandate reflects this situation.

The Canadian broadcasting system is one of the great achievements of our nation. In the face of formidable geographical, technical, political, financial and linguistic obstacles; in the face of unparallelled problems inherent in our contiguity with the United States, the greatest purveyor of entertainment (or "culture", as Canadians think of it) in human history; Canada has evolved a radio and television system that, like the country itself, mostly works. There have of course, always been flaws and imperfections, some of them significant, reflecting both the difficulties which had to be met and surmounted and the way the nation has developed.

The Canadian broadcasting system has many strengths and virtues. Our task, however, is not to dwell on these. Formulating public policy is a matter of trying to make what already may be working well work better. That is why our mandate is to investigate the system, to understand its development, dilemmas and failures, in order to recommend ways and means for its improvement.

A Perspective

When this Task Force was created in 1985 it was appropriate for the Minister of Communications to quote the stirring words of Prime Minister R.B. Bennett who introduced public broadcasting to Canada in 1932.

> . . . this country must be assured of complete Canadian control of broadcasting from Canadian sources. Without such control, broadcasting can never be the agency by which national consciousness may be fostered and sustained and national unity still further strengthened . . .[1]

The Minister's citation was appropriate not because of the continuity of party — on the contrary, political partisanship has been the least divisive of the factors affecting broadcasting policy — but rather because of the remarkable continuity of generations. Over and over again we were impressed by the durability of the issues and dilemmas of the broadcasting system. Not even the physical presence of satellites above could constrain us from wondering if there were ever anything new under the broadcasting sun. At the very least, we can say with confidence that the nature of public policy in Canadian broadcasting reflects the constancy of the problems it is designed to solve.

Indeed, our very first predecessor, the Aird Royal Commission on Broadcasting, was appointed in circumstances strikingly like those in which we find ourselves.

The Age of Radio

During the 1920s radio in Canada represented still another manifestation of the waning of British influence and the waxing of American. But there was also a growing sentiment which recognized Canadian culture as being distinct from both British and American. There was already a movement underway to protect Canadian magazines by allowing them tax and postal concessions and by imposing tariffs on American imports. There was also fitful interest in encouraging a Canadian film industry. The Canadian Press news agency was made viable through government subsidy. As the twenties wore on, however, and virtually every city and town established a radio station or two, it was through broadcasting that more and more Canadians felt the constant barrage of American influence — both from stations across the border and from Canadian stations acting largely as relays.

The originator of public broadcasting in Canada was Sir Henry Thornton, president of the Canadian National Railways, who opened a radio broadcasting service for train travellers, hotel guests and employees in 1923. While nearly all the radio stations were privately owned and were broadcasting mostly American material, the CNR service used Canadian performers for concerts, talks and other programming.

Aird

It was in this atmosphere of perceived crisis that Prime Minister Makenzie King created the first inquiry into broadcasting in Canada. The 1928 Royal Commission on Radio Broadcasting was chaired by Sir John Aird, president of the

Canadian Bank of Commerce. Its three members established the pattern for later enquiries — meetings across the country, consultations with key parties, the receipt of written submissions, careful consideration of alternative broadcasting models — and submitted its singularly brief report, a scant nine pages of text, in 1929. The commission had received, the report noted, a considerable diversity of opinion. "There has, however, been unanimity on one fundamental question — Canadian radio listeners want Canadian broadcasting." Yet, it said, "the majority of programmes heard are from sources outside of Canada".[2]

The Aird Commission recommended the adoption of a British or European model of public broadcasting rather than the commercial American one. The Commissioners believed only a national publicly-owned system could achieve a genuinely Canadian broadcasting system. Private broadcasters, they concluded, could not raise sufficient revenues from advertising to satisfy the need for Canadian progamming.

The commission set a coverage goal of "good reception over the entire settled region of the country", an expensive enterprise in a country with the geography of Canada. And it dealt with quality of transmission rather than with quality of content, recommending tougher legislation to deal with sources of interference to broadcast signals.

It was the physical plant and organization of broadcasting that Aird and his colleagues saw as a federal responsibility. Content was to be a provincial responsibility. "It is desirable . . .that provincial authorities should be in a position to exercise full control over the programs of the station or stations in their respective areas", the commission said. But it added, "As to what extent the provinces should participate in effecting this control, of course, is a matter which could be decided between themselves and the Dominion Government authorities."[3]

At the time of the Aird Commission, owners of radio receiving sets were required to pay an annual licence fee of two dollars. Aird and his colleagues suggested increasing fees to cover part of the cost of the proposed broadcasting service, which was the practice followed in Britain and other European countries. They further recommended that sponsorship of programs, but not commercials for particular products, should form another source of financing. Finally, they proposed an annual government subsidy to broadcasting, to be reviewed every five years.

The debate surrounding the Aird report also set the pattern of a remarkably consistent series of recurring issues which have been as much of a challenge to our generation as they were to Aird's. Canadian programming versus American, public ownership versus private, the responsibilities of the public broadcaster versus those of the private sector, the subsidizing of culture versus the protection of commercial interests (often called "cultural industries"), the commercial needs of the private stations versus their national obligations, regulation of content versus freedom of expression, federal authority versus provincial, annual financing of the national broadcaster versus longer-term financing, technology versus programming as the driving force of the system. The long search for sensible public policies for a nation that in some ways defied common sense was well underway by 1929.

Bennett, Spry and Massey

One could scarcely question the devotion to private enterprise of either Sir John Aird or Prime Minister R.B. Bennett, who actually introduced public broadcasting to Canada. Yet both found overwhelming the argument that state control was needed to avoid being swamped by American broadcasting, supported by its mighty domestic market. Public control would also serve the aims of coverage and fair allocation of a scarce natural resource. Bennett laid before Parliament in 1932 three memorable principles:

> First of all, this country must be assured of complete control of broadcasting from Canadian sources, free from foreign interference or influence. Without such control radio broadcasting can never become a great agency for communication of matters of national concern and for the diffusion of national thought and ideals, and without such control it can never be the agency by which national consciousness may be fostered and sustained and national unity still further strengthened . . .
>
> Secondly, no other scheme than that of public ownership can ensure to the people of this country, without regard to class or place, equal enjoyment of the benefits and pleasures of radio broadcasting . . .
>
> [Thirdly] The use of the air. . .that lies over the soil or land of Canada is a natural resource over which we have complete jurisdiction under the recent decision of the Privy Council (and) I cannot think that any government would be warranted in leaving the air to private exploitation and not reserving it for development for the use of the people.[4]

The Aird commission had recommended provincial control of programming, in consultation with Ottawa. By the time of Bennett's speech, broadcasting had been placed firmly in federal jurisdiction. Quebec, supported by New Brunswick, Manitoba, and Saskatchewan, had challenged federal jurisdiction, but the Courts ruled in favour of the Dominion.[5]

With jurisdiction over broadcasting now settled, the creation of a centralized public broadcasting organization proceeded in two stages. The Canadian Radio Broadcasting Commission, established by the Bennett Conservative government in 1932, was remodelled into the Canadian Broadcasting Corporation by the King Liberal government in 1936; because it was a public, not a state, broadcaster, the crucial arm's-length principle was enshrined as a key characteristic. By providing for the inclusion of both publicly owned and privately owned stations, however, the new system institutionalized the CBC's reliance on private stations for distribution, even though Aird clearly hoped such stations would be eliminated as quickly as possible.

By 1936 a number of fundamental assumptions and principles had become the accepted guidelines for Canadian broadcasting. These were:

1. Canada's airwaves are owned by the public, and should be administered by the national government in trust. Transmission frequencies, therefore, may not be owned, but users may be extended the privilege of using one in the public interest.
2. The broadcasting system should be Canadian in ownership.

3. Service should be extended to all Canadians.
4. Payment for the system should come from a blend of public and private sources.
5. Programs should be of high standard and primarily Canadian, but high standard programs should also be obtained from other sources.

The system as it emerged in 1936 followed almost exactly the model devised by the main lobbying organization for public broadcasting, the Canadian Radio League, headed by Alan Plaunt and Graham Spry. "The State or the United States", Spry had proclaimed in one of the great slogans of Canadian history, and indeed the power given the broadcasting arm of the state was mighty. The CBC was called upon not only to provide a national radio service, but also to license and regulate such parts of the national broadcasting system it did not directly own and operate, namely, the private stations.

Predictably this development had been strenuously opposed by the association of the private stations, the Canadian Association of Broadcasters, formed in 1926, and such powerful commercial interests as the Canadian Pacific Railways, which had always objected to CNR radio. The CAB, tending to reflect its larger members, objected to the regulation of private stations by the public broadcaster, which they viewed as a competitor. This attitude was not always shared by the smaller CBC-affiliated stations, which generally had good relations with the Corporation.

Despite the political battles that often swirled around it, the CBC proved the accuracy of the Aird Commission's assertion that Canadians wanted Canadian programming. The Corporation provided it, helped rally the country during the war, and steadily built a constituency that would come to its defence in future challenges. Then, as now, however, the situation was complicated by Canadians' undeniable appetite for American as well as Canadian programming, and providing this service was also a major task for both an under-funded public broadcaster and a commercially-driven private sector.

The Massey Royal Commission, appointed in 1949 under the chairmanship of Vincent Massey, later Governor General, to look into National Development in the Arts, Letters and Sciences, represented a major step forward from the cultural beachhead established by Ottawa after the broadcasting ruling in 1932. It was the first time the federal government had asserted so capacious a responsibility in culture; broadcasting was but a part of the Massey Commission's terms of reference. In brief, the commission rejected the position of the Canadian Association of Broadcasters and strongly endorsed the existing system.

Essentially, the CBC emerged from the Massey examination smelling like roses. The commission's report reaffirmed that the broadcasting legislation called for "one national system". The private stations were licensed only because they could play a useful part in that single broadcasting system, and the CBC properly exercised control over "all radio broadcasting policies and programs in Canada". The report continued:

> The principal grievance of the private broadcasters is based, it seems to us, on a false assumption that broadcasting in Canada is an industry. Broadcasting in

> Canada, in our view, is a public service directed and controlled in the public interest by a body responsible to Parliament.[6]

The Massey report noted that radio coverage had expanded from 50 percent of the population in 1936 to 90 percent in 1950, a considerable achievement in view of the special Canadian coverage problems: two languages, five time zones, and sparse settlement. While Aird had been chiefly concerned with the physical plant and organization for a national system, Massey stressed that "the quality of the programs which the Canadian listener receives must . . . be the test for the justification of a national system of radio".[7]

The theme of cultural sovereignty found strong expression in the Massey report. "Many Canadians in the 1920s . . . began to fear that cultural annexation would follow our absorption into the American radio system just as surely as economic and even political annexation would have followed absorption into the American railway system fifty years earlier."[8] Massey opposed networks of private radio stations because they "would inevitably become small parts of the American systems".[9]

By 1951, the year of the Massey report, the age of radio was giving way to the era of television, and the commission warned presciently about the implications of the imminent ascendance of the magical new medium, pointing out that "The pressure on uncontrolled private television operators to become mere channels for American commercial material will be almost irresistible."[10] What Canada would need in television, it decreed, was a regime similar to the one governing radio.

In its sensible way, the Massey report highlighted both the accomplishments and the inadequacies of the radio broadcasting system and insightfully drew attention to the dilemmas that would plague the television age to an even greater extent.

Fear for cultural sovereignty in the face of American broadcasting penetration has remained a perpetual theme for some six decades, but by Massey's time a certain consensus had emerged that the state had an obligation to support Canadian "culture", however the term had been defined and however Canadians disagreed on the magnitude of that obligation.

The Age of Television

During the period of the Massey Commission, from 1949 to 1951, television was just beginning to build in the United States and its pre-War existence in the United Kingdom was largely unknown in Canada. But its entry into Canada — initially by spilling over the border — altered the Canadian broadcasting scene forever. Just three years after the introduction of television into Canada, a Royal Commission on broadcasting was created, as Massey had recommended.

The first reality to be faced reflected the historic dilemma of broadcasting in Canada. From the beginning, 60 percent of Canadians had over-the-air access to the television programming of the American networks. Throughout the 1950s a distinctive physical characteristic of those Canadian cities within 50 miles of the international border was the proliferation of roof-top television aerials for receiving stations from Plattsburg, Buffalo and Bellingham. It was a veritable peaceful American invasion of the living rooms of Canada — and Canadians welcomed the invaders with open arms.

For the representatives of both the state and the private sector the central issue, as always, was cost. Television posed a far greater challenge than radio to Canadian resources. Television production is vastly more expensive than radio production. Television programs produced in the United States could recover their costs in that market and therefore be available to Canadian broadcasters at very low rates. Private broadcasters had always tried to minimize costs but they now realized that while the capital costs of moving into television were very high, they could draw upon the product of the American networks as well as Hollywood movies at rates much lower than the cost of producing comparable programs in Canada. To do this it was more urgent than ever to shake off the regulatory yoke of the CBC.

The government chose not to provide the CBC with the additional capital investment to build a complete national television network on its own. In the years after the CBC's owned and operated stations in Montreal and Toronto commenced service in 1952, private stations were licenced as affiliates. Thus, the historic pattern was repeated and the national broadcasting system became dependent upon a combination of public and private stations.

At the same time some perceived that the new medium threatened national cultural sovereignty to an unprecedented extent. Whatever its own preferences the CBC was obliged because of both cost and demand to procure some programs abroad, especially for the English-language service. The American networks, in a fierce competition for audience, promoted their programs aggressively and this marketing inevitably spilled over into Canada. As a result, American programs were being marketed in Canada far more effectively than Canadian programs, allowing the private broadcasters to assert that Canadians preferred American programs. But the Canadian desire for Canadian programs, noted by Sir John Aird and every review since, persisted. The Fowler Commission was now formed against a background of considerable dissatisfaction with the existing broadcasting system and a feeling that things had to be sorted out before television developed too far.

The Fowler Commission and the Fowler Committee

Robert Fowler, a lawyer and president of the Canadian Pulp and Paper Association, was appointed to head the Royal Commission on Broadcasting in 1955. In its report issued two years later, the Commission carried over into the age of television the main features of radio broadcasting. It gave the Graham Spry battle cry more formal expression:

> We cannot choose between a Canadian broadcasting system controlled by the state and a Canadian competitive system in private hands. The choice is between a Canadian state-controlled system with some flow of programmes east and west across Canada, with some Canadian content and the development of a Canadian sense of identity, at a substantial public cost, and a privately

> owned system which the forces of economics will necessarily make predominantly dependent on imported American radio and televison programmes.[11]

The Commissioners went right to the heart of the matter:

> . . . if the less costly method is always chosen, is it possible to have a Canadian nation at all? The Canadian answer, irrespective of party or race, has been uniformly the same for nearly a century. We are prepared, by measures of assistance, financial aid and a conscious stimulation, to compensate for our disabilities of geography, sparse populations and vast distances, and we have accepted this as a legitimate role of the government in Canada.[12]

The Fowler report said there was not enough advertising revenue in Canada for a private system that could both cover the country and provide Canadian programming. In the spirit of Aird and Massey, the report concluded that stations on such a system would "necessarily become outlets for American networks and programs".

> This would result not because the private broadcasters are unpatriotic citizens or because they lack a sense of Canadian consciousness or responsibility; it would result from economic pressures on the private operator which make it easy and inexpensive to import American programs and difficult and costly to produce any substantial volume of Canadian programs.[13]

Fowler and his colleagues held that for the foreseeable future Canadian radio and television broadcasting would be a single mixed system of private and public ownership regulated and controlled by an agency representing the public interest and responsible to Parliament. The commission also went to some length to justify regulation of broadcasting content on several grounds: scarcity of frequencies, the absence of a tradition of self-regulation that would create "recognized standards of performance", the influence on programming of commercial sponsors, and the pressure of American economic forces.

> It is not the freedom of the private station operator or the commercial sponsors that is important; it is the freedom of the public to enjoy a broadcasting system which provides the largest possible outlet for the widest possible range of information, entertainment and ideas.[14]

The private broadcasters won partial success in their battle for separate status in Fowler's recommendation that a Board of Broadcast Governors be created which would regulate both the CBC and the private stations. Full recognition of their position came in 1958 from the Progressive Conservative government in legislation providing for regulation of the private sector by the BBG and a continuing CBC board responsible to Parliament. It was the BBG that began the practice of imposing Canadian content requirements on private broadcasters, although it had great difficulty in making them meaningful.

What followed the Fowler report was reminiscent of the beginnings of public radio broadcasting, when the recommendations of a royal commission appointed by the King government were dealt with by the Bennett government and then the Liberals returned to office with amendments. Now, the Diefenbaker Conservatives, after dealing with the recommendations of a royal commission appointed by the St. Laurent Liberals, were succeeded by the Pearson Liberals who, in the nature of things, felt some amendments were needed. In 1964, Robert Fowler was called back into service to act as chairman of an advisory committee on broadcasting which reported the following year.

The heart of the Fowler Committee recommendations lay in its proposal to create a Canadian Broadcasting Authority, to replace both the BBG and the CBC's Board of Directors, with "full powers and authority to regulate, supervise, control and develop the Canadian broadcasting system". Its basic task should be

> . . . to develop a coordinated policy for the provision of broadcasting services to the Canadian people — to all the people, by all the broadcasting stations publicly and privately owned.[15]

Between Fowler's two reports, the BBG had taken the momentous step of licensing CTV, a private English television network, and TéléMétropole, a private French-language television station in the large Montreal market. In one stroke the balance between the public and private sectors had been fundamentaly altered.

The gamble initially seemed shrewd. The new licencees, proud and determined, believed they had major contributions to make to Canadian culture in return for winning their cherished prize and did not hesitate to make grand commitments to fulfil those obligations. Alas, the practical realities foreseen by Massey and Fowler soon exerted their force. The private networks were licenced in 1961; four years later the Fowler Committee was scathing in its comments about the record of private broadcasters.

> . . . the program performance of the private stations . . . bears very little relationship to the promises made to the BBG . . . Undertakings given to obtain the grant of a public asset have largely been ignored, and the program performance has generally fallen far short of the promises made. The BBG has been powerless to deal with this . . . A promise made by a broadcaster to obtain a license . . . should be an enforceable undertaking, and not a theoretical exercise in imagination or a competitive bid in an auction of unrealistic enthusiasm.[16]

The Broadcasting Act and After

It was against this background that the Minister of Communications, Judy La Marsh, drafted the government's 1966 *White Paper on Broadcasting*, which duly led to the *Broadcasting Act* of 1968 (although a key provision of the White Paper, to finance the CBC through 5-year statutory grants, was excluded from the final legislation). The Act, with certain amendments, still governs the Canadian broadcasting system today.

The intent and implications of the Act were perfectly clear: to institutionalize the major principles of and objectives for the broadcasting system as they had been overwhelmingly re-affirmed ever since the Aird report four decades earlier, and as they were supported by all political parties.

Since we examine the contents of the 1968 Act in Chapter 6, we need refer here only to its highlights. It created a new overall regulatory body, the Canadian Radio-Television Commission (today's Canadian Radio-television and Telecommunications Commission), with broad powers including licensing, detailed regulation and the imposition of conditions of licence. The CBC, though it kept its own Board, was put under the jurisdiction of the CRTC. The whole was affirmed as "a single system . . .comprising public and private elements", to be "owned and controlled by Canadians so as to safeguard, enrich and strengthen the cultural, political, social and economic fabric of Canada".[17] But the mandate of the CBC was spelled out with considerable precision while that of the private sector was left quite vague. "The national broadcasting service", as the CBC was described, was to be a "balanced service of information, enlightment and entertainment for people of different ages, interests and tastes covering the whole range of programming in fair proportion". And it was to be "in English and French, serving the special needs of geographic regions and actively contributing to the flow and exchange of cultural and regional information and entertainment".[18]

No comparable obligations were placed upon the private sector, and it was logical to infer that private broadcasters did not carry quite the same burden of state policy as did the CBC. Indeed, the new Act relieved them of the burden established in the 1958 Act to provide programming that was predominantly Canadian in content and character, although they must use "predominantly Canadian creative and other resources". Also, the 1968 Act explicitly stated that where a conflict arose between the public and the private broadcasting sectors, the public element should predominate.

The 1968 Act created the framework within which the broadcasting system has operated for the past 18 years. Invariably, the operations of all the players have been made to seem to be in harmony with the wording of the Act. Over the years, the CRTC has significantly diluted the notion of a "predominantly Canadian" broadcasting system, always in the name of the *Broadcasting Act*. While the private sector acknowledges its responsibility to the national obligations implied in the Act, realistic commercial goals dictate maximum allowable American programming in prime-time. The CBC attempts to be all things to all people, with resources sufficient only to be some things to some people. The Department of Communications and the CRTC have tried to determine how technological change could be accommodated within the confines of an Act passed before some of the new technology had even been conceived. The cable industry has sought justification for its own massive expansion in an Act in which it was a mere afterthought.

In fact the realities of today's broadcasting system would have astonished the framers of the 1968 Act. That is why it is time for a new Canadian Broadcasting Act.

Broadcasting's Changing Environment

The 1968 Act came toward the end of the postwar generation, a period of an expanding world of broadcasting for an expanding country. The large postwar influx of people into the cities from the country, together with the baby boom and heavy immigration, was transforming urban Canada, creating an environment in which mass media flourished. The period was one of rapid growth in real income — more money to buy the goods and services whose advertising supported broadcasting, more money to pay the taxes that supported broadcasting, more money to buy equipment. Television spread to full coverage of the population in Canada faster than in any other country.

In Quebec, CBC's French television service had been moulded into an instrument of social transformation, revealing a people's identity to itself and unleashing a sense of national awareness that would sweep into public life and dominate Canada's domestic politics for a generation — the "Quiet Revolution". In the rest of Canada television spurred nationalism in a reactive way, by serving as the conduit for an increased flood of American pop culture into the Canadian market. But the pressure of inexpensive American programming noted in the first Fowler report drastically curbed the efforts of even the CBC to give English Canada the kind of self-expression that Quebec was enjoying.

The unhappy irony was that Canadian television was booming in a way that reflected less and less the goals set out in the 1968 Act. The Fowler Committee recommended that broadcasting goals be enshrined in legislation to underline the deal between the state and those who had won the privilege from the state of holding a broadcast licence. "All broadcasting agencies", it declared, "both public and private, are recipients of public support in the right to use scarce public assets. They must pay for these valuable rights by giving a responsible performance, and the state is fully entitled to ensure that the trust is honored."[19]

On the other hand there was the implicit demand upon the state to protect Canadian broadcasters in order that they could provide sometimes uneconomic cultural services. In dealing with expanding cable operations, for example, Fowler had warned that cable systems could pose a threat to broadcasters. While cable operations had been brought under the 1968 Act as "broadcasting receiving undertakings" and were therefore an element of the broadcasting system, subject to CRTC regulation, there existed no clear legislative guidance as to the basis on which cable should be regulated. In the years that followed, the CRTC declared that it was obligated to treat the cable industry in such a way as to protect local broadcasting industries and their sources of revenue.

Yet while the Commission would not allow Canadian radio and television stations to affiliate to American networks, it then agreed that cable systems could provide local carriage of the full program schedules of all the American television networks. Thus was born a tension between Canadian broadcasters and cable systems that persists to this day.

Clearly, cable television mattered. The Fowler Committee report demonstrated an appreciation of the new delivery system, assessing correctly the effect cable would have both in bringing yet more American programming into Canada and in segmenting audiences. Technology such as cable, communication satellites, and computer control were gradually changing the nature of broadcasting.

Under the arm's length tradition of keeping control of broadcasting independent from political interference, the CBC and later the BBG and CRTC were formally free of governmental direction. From the start, governments followed instead a policy that might be called direction by inquiry: a parliamentary committee or outside inquiry of some kind made an investigation and submitted recommendations upon which the government acted. Certainly, our own Task Force fits neatly into this pattern.

In succeeding chapters we will examine many of these policy questions in detail as a basis for our own recommendations for change. In the remainder of this chapter we will give a brief summary of important policy developments since the passage of the 1968 *Broadcasting Act*.

The importance of the new communications was given institutional form within the newly-created Department of Communications in 1969, when it took over responsibility for spectrum management and the technical side of broadcasting policy. Two years later the Telecommission, a group appointed by the new Minister to guide policy formation in the early days of the Department, observed in its report, *Instant World*, that:

> . . . the means to implement broadcasting policy are part of the technology of telecommunications and may be improved by new systems and devices. Cable systems, for example, may one day become the predominant broadcasting channels in urban communities, but satellite transmission and new terrestrial modes will also contribute to the effectiveness of national broadcasting policy, and thus to the health of the body politic.[20]

In a 1973 green paper on communications policy commissioned by the DOC, the Liberal government laid the groundwork for combining telecommunications with broadcasting under the mandate of the CRTC. The green paper had offered a sweeping view of communication policy "counter-balancing the strong north/south pull of continentalism" and "fostering national unity and identity in a Canada of admittedly diverse cultural and regional components". More than ever before, it said, "it is clear that the technologies and economic aspects of communications are intimately related with their social and cultural implications".[21]

The 1973 green paper had seen the need for broad policy direction from government to the proposed combined agency for broadcasting and telecommunication policy. This integrated approach was needed because of "the evident and growing tendency for many formerly distinct systems of electronic communications to become interconnected, more integrated, and more powerful". In the atmosphere of the strained federal-provincial relations of the 1970s, this sounded to many provinces, particularly Quebec, like a massive federal bid to move into telecommunication and cultural jurisdiction claimed by the provinces. Ottawa's offers to share control were turned down. The federal government then proceeded to implement its views to the extent possible within federal jurisdiction.

In 1976 the CRTC was expanded to include telecommunications, its initials remaining the same but its name changing from Canadian Radio-Television Commission to Canadian Radio-television and Telecommunications Commission. In 1978 a new telecommunications act covering both broadcasting and telecommunications was introduced in the Commons by the Minister of communications but came to nothing. The bill — Bill C-16 — was notable for taking a broadcast content concept and applying it to the whole of telecommunications in its section 3 (a):

> Efficient telecommunications systems are essential to the sovereignty and integrity of Canada, and telecommunications services and production resources should be developed and administered so as to safeguard, enrich and strengthen the cultural, political, social and economic fabric of Canada.[22]

A Decade of Studies

Reverting to the strategy of leadership by inquiry, the government appointed the Clyne Committee in 1978 to look into the challenges to Canadian sovereignty posed by the new communications. The chairman, J.V. Clyne, was a former justice of the British Columbia Supreme Court. Noting that Canadians were "already being swamped with foreign broadcast programming", Clyne and his colleagues urged an inquiry into making the CBC more effective since its broadcasting services were "the main national instruments for the preservation of Canadian social and cultural sovereignty".

The Committee made 26 recommendations, many of them extremely detailed, but the overall tone of their report may be judged by its final words:

> We conclude our work . . . with an exhortation: with all the force at our command, we urge the Government of Canada to take immediate action to alert the people of Canada to the perilous position of their collective sovereignty that has resulted from the new technologies of telecommunications and informatics; and we urge the Government of Canada and the governments of the provinces to take immediate action to establish a rational structure for telecommunications in Canada as a defence against the further loss of sovereignty in all its economic, social, cultural and political aspects.[23]

While the Clyne Committee took its starting point in integrated communications technology, the Federal Cultural Policy Review Committee, co-chaired by Louis Applebaum and Jacques Hébert, started with the whole spectrum of cultural services and policies as its purview. As an update of the Massey inquiry, Applebaum-Hébert too had broadcasting included in its terms of reference. Indeed, their 1982 report concluded that the CBC was the very heart of Canadian culture, and that private broadcasters must be called upon to make a larger contribution to new Canadian programming on English television. This has been a finding of our own Task Force as well.

In fact there has hardly been an inquiry that has not agreed on the overriding dilemma of the Canadian broadcasting system: how can Canadians be offered a serious choice of Canadian programming in a system in which a) American influences are inescapable, b) market forces dictate American programming, through both production costs and advertising benefits, and c) Canadians themselves want access to Canadian as well as American programming.

On the other hand, the Task Force finds itself in substantial disagreement with many of the recommendations made by the Applebaum-Hébert Committee to resolve this central dilemma. Some of their proposals, notably calling on the CBC to end in-house production of performance programming, would have seriously undermined the very principles they affirmed.

It is the CRTC, under the profound powers granted it by the 1968 Act, that has day-to-day responsibility for regulating Canadian broadcasting. While the federal government has pursued a succession of projects to obtain power of direction over the CRTC, the Commission has continued, as it is entitled, to operate independently, holding hearings on issues, deciding on policy, making regulations, and putting these decisions into effect, with varying degrees of informal consultation with the government and the Department of Communications.

After years of debate, provincial educational television services were licensed in the early seventies and were later given wide latitude as to the programming and policies they could pursue. The beginnings of community broadcasting were approved. Through the late seventies, however, notwithstanding substantial pressure from the DOC to introduce pay-TV, the CRTC kept the door closed against pay on the grounds that it could not operate in a manner consistent with the 1968 Act and that it would be "disruptive" to the existing broadcasting industry.

Eventually the CRTC itself adopted the practice of appointing task forces on major issues, beginning with a committee under CRTC vice-chairman Réal Thérrien on service to native peoples and remote areas — an increasingly vexing issue — and on the introduction of pay television. As pressure grew, the Committee felt it had little choice but to recommend pay-TV when it reported in 1980. But it optimistically persuaded itself that the chief justification for introducing pay-TV was the stimulus it would give to the Canadian program production industry and the provision of new Canadian services. The committee paved the way for both the licensing of the Canadian Satellite Communications (CANCOM) service to remote and underserved areas and the licensing of satellite-to-cable specialty and pay-TV services.

In the meantime, the Trudeau government, after its return to office in 1980, had been pursuing the aim of bringing together policy-making on the means of communication and the cultural content of communication, including broadcasting. Soon the federal cultural agencies and programs of aid to cultural industries were transferred from the Secretary of State's department to the Department of Communications. Cultural policy in this new setting took on a more commercial and industrial coloration, with what some considered an undue emphasis on the economic impact of cultural activities and the desirability of designing Canadian cultural products and services to maximize their export potential rather than recognizing their social and cultural function as a means of Canadian expression. The DOC was particularly anxious to link culture, which it sometimes described as a form of software, to the potential of new communications technologies.

The Department of Communications' 1983 broadcasting strategy for Canada — its very first — consisted of four initiatives. The first suggested a reversal of the CRTC's long-standing emphasis on the role of private broadcasters and the related need to set reasonable limits to cable's impact on fragmenting their market. Cable was to become the state's "chosen instrument", with all programming to be available on cable, described as the "most cost-effective means of significantly expanding the viewing choices of most Canadians". The second was to create a Canadian Broadcast Program Development Fund starting at $35 million and reaching $60 million in its fifth year. The third was to give the government the long-sought power of direction over the CRTC on general policy matters, through Bill C-20. The fourth, reflecting a newly emerging controversy, was to abolish licence requirements for individual satellite reception dishes. Actually, a fifth initiative was an integral part of the strategy but came later in the budget: a new excise tax on cable subscriptions to offset the cost of the program development fund.

Because technological change was multiplying channel capacity, the government concluded that the only way for Canada to compete was to increase its own programming capacity, especially in areas where foreign programming dominated Canadians' viewing time. "As a general principle", the government's 1983 policy statement said, "the Canadian broadcasting system must make available a significant amount of Canadian programming in each program category — for example, the drama, children's and variety categories."[24]

As the first major comprehensive broadcasting initiative since the 1968 Act, this strategy left something to be desired. It overestimated the immediate effects of technological change in expanding channel availability and the related ability to finance attractive programming. It miscalculated in its expectations that DBS — direct-to-home broadcasting satellites — would soon be a reality.

In institutionalizing the status of cable, the Department's strategy was legitimizing cable's overriding function of bringing more American programs to more Canadians. It effectively accepted a class system for broadcast recipients, since some Canadians, for economic or geographical reasons, were in no position to receive cable. (We have had to accept the same reality, but as a challenge to the policy-maker.) In *Building for the Future*, a follow-up document on the CBC,[25] the government imposed greater national obligations on the Corporation without providing commensurately greater funds to do the job. Indeed, in the eight years prior to the release of *Towards a New National Broadcasting Policy*, the government had systematically whittled away the resources of the Corporation. Now it had its mandate expanded on the basis of already diminished funding.

On the other hand, the creation of the Broadcast Fund as part of the Canadian Film Development Corporation, which became Telefilm Canada, was a move adopted from the Clyne and Applebaum-Hébert reports. The purpose of the Broadcast Fund was to meet the programming goals of the broadcasting strategy and to strengthen the Canadian program production industry. The abolition of licences for individual dishes was a welcome acknowledgement of a situation that could not be addressed effectively by prohibition in any event. And the new tax on cable users would offset the cost of producing Canadian programs. Unfortunately, the cable industry has been able to convey the notion that it is the cable operators, rather than the individual subscribers, who are carrying that burden.

The new strategy also reflected the 15-year tug-of-war between the CRTC and the federal government, represented by the Department of Communications, over the formation of broadcasting policy. While the DOC pressed for development of new technology in such applications as communications satellites and the Telidon electronic print services, the CRTC, by its very mandate, naturally gave priority to Canadian broadcasters and programming. To some, it seemed that the CRTC was encroaching on the prerogative of government and Parliament to make national policy, hence the pressure for a power of direction over the regulatory agency. On the other hand, some feared such direction, reluctant to see government interfering in the operations of an autonomous agency dealing in the realm of ideas and freedom of expression.

Within government there was also tension. Those connected with arts and culture felt that the technological side of the DOC, which constituted the whole of the department before arts and culture was added in 1980, was controlling broadcasting policy, which should be essentially cultural in nature. It was only in 1985 that broadcasting policy was made a responsibility of the cultural affairs sector of the department, with consequences yet to be determined.

The Age of Integrated Communication

Over the next few years Canada must overhaul many aspects of broadcasting and telecommunication policies to accommodate a new age of broadcasting. After a first age dominated by over-the-air radio, and a second dominated by over-the-air television, we are already well into a third age characterized by integrated communications. New systems for the delivery, production and reception of programming are greatly expanding the capacity for selectivity, the technical quality, and the scope of service.

Today, improvement in selectivity means for many Canadians a plenitude of channels by satellite and cable; in future it could mean almost unlimited capacity for selection of content, at a price. Today, improvement in technical quality means the arrival of stereophonic, 'smart' television sets — smart because of digital microprocessing capacity that restores the picture to the quality on a studio monitor; in future it could mean high-definition, widescreen TV comparable to 35-mm film, displayed on a flat panel. Today, increased scope of services means new video and specialty services, and the experimental beginning of text, graphics, commercial exchange, and monitoring services; in future, as screen definition and portability improve, it may mean a whole range of electronic publishing in the home. When we explore the technology of the new era in greater detail, we shall see the problem of determining public policy for such an undetermined future.

But whatever kind of Buck Rogers future is in store for us, surely the Canadian tradition demands that we must continue to entrench the Canadian presence in our broadcasting system, and we must adopt policies to do so in a new world in which substantially greater choice may be available to Canadian viewers. More than ever, broadcasting must be seen as a fundamental part of cultural policy. It must be program-driven, not hardware-driven as in its first decades.

While our terms of reference called upon us to look ahead to the year 2000, and while there are major changes on the horizon, we see them coming in stages rather than overnight. The third age of broadcasting, radically different from its predecessor though it may be, is an evolution not a revolution. The ages of broadcasting overlap. Rather than disappearing, old services tend to find new niches. The new age of broadcasting, already partly upon us, brings extraordinary possibilities of conservation as well as innovation. In Canada, we have the skills and talent to be in the forefront of this new age, to make the new technologies work for us.

The members of this Task Force agree with Aird and his colleagues that broadcasting services in Canada, today as a half-century ago, should "continue equal to that in any other country" — and that they should offer, so far as possible, a truly Canadian service for those millions of Canadians who have demonstrated their belief in one.

Notes

1. Prime Minister R.B. Bennett, introducing Bill 94 on broadcasting, *Debates of the House of Commons*, May 18, 1932, pp. 3035-36.
2. Canada, *Royal Commission on Radio Broadcasting* (Aird Commission) *Report* (Ottawa: King's Printer, 1929), p. 6.
3. Ibid., p. 7.
4. Canada, Parliament, House of Commons, *Debates*, May 18, 1932.
5. *In Re Regulation and Control of Radio Communication in Canada*, [1932] A.C. 304.
6. Canada, Royal Commission on National Development in the Arts, Letters, and Sciences, (Massey Commission) *Report* (Ottawa: King's Printer, 1951), p. 283.
7. Ibid., p. 25.
8. Ibid., p. 24.
9. Ibid., p. 287.
10. Ibid., p. 301.
11. Canada, Royal Commission on Broadcasting (Fowler Commission) *Report* (Ottawa: Queen's Printer, 1957), p. 10.
12. Ibid., p. 9.
13. Ibid., p. 11.
14. Ibid., p. 86.
15. Canada, Committee on Broadcasting (Fowler Committee), *Report* (Ottawa: Queen's Printer, 1965), p. 98.
16. Ibid., p. 107.
17. *Broadcasting Act*, R.S.C. 1970, c. B-11, s. 3 (a), 3 (b).
18. Ibid., s. 3 (g).
19. Canada, Committee on Broadcasting, *Report*.
20. Canada, Department of Communications, Telecommission, *Instant World* (Ottawa: Information Canada, 1971), p. 5.
21. Canada, Department of Communications, *Proposals for a Communication Policy for Canada: A Position Paper of the Government of Canada* (Ottawa: The Department, 1973), p. 4.
22. Canada, House of Commons, *Bill C-16*, November 9th, 1978.
23. Canada, Consultative Committee on the Implications of Telecommunications for Canadian Sovereignty, Telecommunications and Canada (Clyne Committee), *Report* (Ottawa: Minister of Supply and Services Canada, 1979), p. 76.
24. Canada, Department of Communications, *Towards a New National Broadcasting Policy* (Ottawa: The Department, 1983), p. 9.
25. Canada, Department of Communications, *Building for the Future: Towards a Distinctive CBC* (Ottawa: Minister of Supply and Services Canada, 1983).

Chapter 2

International Perspective

International Perspective

Sir John Aird would feel very much at home with the issues and dilemmas with which the Task Force has attempted to come to grips. What would truly surprise him, however, is the extent to which satellites and other new technology today make all the industrialized countries susceptible to the problems that have always bedevilled Canadian broadcasting.

It is no exaggeration to say that broadcasting is undergoing a crisis everywhere in the world, particularly in the public sector. In Europe, the trend is towards privatization; all the European public television networks are feeling the effects of government withdrawal of financing. As we were concluding our work, the decision in France to turn one of the public channels, TF1, over to the private sector, caused considerable public outcry. In several countries the monopoly that the public sector had over broadcasting only a few years ago is dwindling. Conrad Winn of Carleton University has commented that virtually all the liberal democracies are currently experiencing a growth in the relative share of the private sector in broadcasting, whether through the establishment of private networks or increased use of independent production. Winn goes on to say:

> There exists a significant cross-national tendency for both public and private broadcasters to contract out more of their program production. Japanese, British, French, Belgian and other national public television broadcasting systems have made conscious decisions in recent years to purchase more programming from independent producers.[1]

News and public affairs are usually excepted, as the Applebaum-Hébert report suggested should be the case in Canada. In Belgium the government recently authorized the French-language RTBF to contract out entertainment programming but emphasized that the network would be required to continue producing all its own news and public affairs programming.

During the winter of 1985-1986 in Britain the Peacock Committee was examining various financing options for the BBC, including the unthinkable possibility of allowing advertising.

> To many, and not least the BBC management, the mere suggestion of the Corporation accepting advertising is akin to taking the Queen Mother off the Civil List and supporting her public duties by sponsorship or other commercial means. The Peacock Committee is now doggedly collecting evidence but its very existence has sharpened debate about the whole ethos of public broadcasting, commercial and ratings pressures, and competitive efficiency.[2]

In the end, however, the Committee rejected the advertising option.[3]

The issues in the Canadian debate are not peculiar to Canada. Not only do budget crises and the reduction of government involvement give rise to the same problems everywhere, but the technological revolution and the ensuing proliferation of channels and options have completely changed the ground rules.

The CRTC's Klingle Task Force on Access to Television Services in Underserved Communities noted the new challenges to the broadcasting system stemming from increased use of satellites:

> The CRTC's policy of promoting Canadian broadcasting services by containing the spread of U.S. broadcast services in Canada which was workable in 1975 is no longer applicable in the changed environment of 1985.[4]

In opening up the skies to satellite dish antennas in 1983, then Communications Minister Francis Fox recognized the limits of regulation as a means of government control in this field. New distribution techniques make content quota requirements used alone problematic because regulation can easily be bypassed by simply shifting to other delivery systems such as videotape recorders. But there is more to it than this.

Every country's production capacity (financial resources and often human resources as well) lags behind the new transmission capacity. As we in Canada know only too well, the programs that are readily and cheaply available are American. The Bredin Report[5] submitted to the Prime Minister of France in May 1985 noted that a program of the production calibre of *Dallas* would cost 12 times as much to produce in France as to buy. National television services everywhere, private and public networks alike, are becoming Americanized, because the public sector gives in to the same temptation to use American programming in order to compete. American products and techniques as well as their universal themes sell well everywhere. The victory of pop culture is complete. "Pop is easy listening, easy watching, easy thinking."[6]

While ten years ago it was the Third World countries that raised the issue at UNESCO, today Europe is invoking national sovereignty to combat a cultural invasion that Canada has faced since the early days of radio in the late twenties, and which has been restored to the headlines by the Canada-United States free trade talks.

In a sense the world is becoming 'Canadianized' as it learns to come to terms with American culture. Canada no longer seems as parochial as it has been painted in the past because of its "standing on guard" for "our home and native land" and for "safeguarding, enriching and strenthening" the country's fabric. A glance at the television programs, movie marquees, newsstands and bookstores in Canada shows just how open we are to foreign cultural products. Moreover Canada has often presented itself in international forums as a model for reconciling opposing points of view in the debate on communications: the preservation of domestic culture on the one hand and freedom of expression and the free flow of information and ideas on the other.

A number of public opinion surveys show that Canadians support access to American culture as strongly as they support government measures to ensure that they have access to

> . . . the creative output of Canadians and information about Canada and the world viewed from a Canadian perspective. It has become almost a commonplace of speeches by Canadian communications ministers that real freedom for Canadians consists of the opportunity to choose between Canadian and foreign content.[7]

This is where government intervention has a key role to play.

Communications today ignores borders. Cultures are becoming homogenized: 'Americanized' or 'internationalized'. Jean-Paul Lafrance, a professor at the Université du Québec à Montréal, and visiting professor at the Université de Paris, writes that

> The evolution of communication systems has seriously compromised the balance of European development in three areas: equipment, networks, programming. It is not a joke to say beware of equipment being entirely Japanese, all programming being American, and network standards being set by the two of them together. When thought is given to what is on TV screens today, there is an industrial threat, a political threat, and a threat to cultural and linguistic sovereignty.[8] (translation)

For the francophone world, the cultural invasion is, in effect, multiplied by a linguistic problem. France even airs American news programs in the original English. Canal Plus, a pay-TV channel, makes the most of the transatlantic time difference to broadcast the previous day's CBS evening news with Dan Rather early in the morning in Paris. This linguistic threat was met by the exceptional measures taken by the French government at the instigation of former culture minister Jack Lang. Grants to cultural activities were substantially increased over a three-year period. The film industry, already being heavily funded by the government, had its grants doubled.

In 1985 Lang appealed in English to the Haute Autorité de la communication audio-visuelle, the French counterpart of the CRTC, to end the invasion of local radio stations by Anglo-American music, said to account for up to 85 percent of air time. This is a familiar development in Quebec, where English has become *de rigueur* in music just a short time after original Quebec songs were thought to have helped shape the social and political renewal of the sixties.

According to journalist Nathalie Petrowski, a critic of the Quebec cultural scene, a new generation of Quebec musicians and composers started singing in English in 1982-1983. In 1984-85 at the "Empire des futures stars" in Montreal, an event organized by CKOI-FM to promote the changing of the musical guard in Quebec, 90 percent of the contestants sang in English. Quebec is not an isolated case. The same thing is happening throughout the Western world, without regard to political borders. From Montreal to Moscow, young people identify with rock music and, more often than not, with songs in English.

> However, geography and a short history make [Quebec] more vulnerable to American culture than older countries like France. The new generation's "sing white" would not be so insidious if young songwriters were using English as no more than a vehicle to describe their own immediate reality and features specific to Quebec. They do nothing of the sort, but rather produce something without identity, interchangeable and devoid of personality, a by-product that bears witness to nothing but an overwhelming urge to be absorbed and assimilated as quickly as possible.[9] (translation)

Some of these young artists reply that they are not solely responsible for preserving the French language, nor do they see any need to save their own culture which they do not see as better than the new 'universal' culture. They feel that cultural identity can be perfectly well preserved while singing in another language. In a remark that sums up the whole issue of culture and the cultural industries, one young Quebec singer said: "I sing in English to make a buck, because it's more profitable, and to increase my chances of making it in markets outside Quebec."[10] (translation)

Easy as it is to understand the legitimate desire of francophone artists to have international careers, the dire consequences of galloping Americanization for the francophone world must also be recognized. The Haut Conseil de la francophonie, chaired by French President François Mitterand, recently registered its alarm by identifying culture and communications as two of the key sectors where French, at the international level, was suffering serious losses. The Haut Conseil said Quebec television deserved attention because its proximity to English-language televison "anticipates what is likely soon to be the situation in many countries of the world as a result of satellite development."[11] (translation)

What can be done? Set quotas? For example, require French-language radio stations to play French-language records in the hope that demand for French songs will be stimulated? This in fact is what the CRTC does and what many singers, musicians, writers, producers and technicians in Quebec would like to see. It should of course be remembered that the cultural community has a vested interest in defending its cultural identity. But quotas without a corresponding production policy are not the solution. According to a study commissioned by the French Ministry of Culture, it is not a matter of imposing restriction for its own sake to give an appearance of national concern, but rather of ensuring that an alternative exists.

> If defending cultural identity is confused with defending a fixed past, it risks becoming no more than conservatism, which immediately produces creeping bureaucracy and self-satisfied mediocrity. Cultural identity is reduced to a sort of smugness and leaves at centre stage 'happy fools born here'. It all adds up to asphyxiating parochialism.[12] (translation)

This is where the concept of the special nature of French-language broadcasting (see Chapter 8) becomes important and the application of uniform rules across the country can create problems. Because of its smaller population, threatened language and limited market French Canada's need for room to breathe is even more pressing than that of English Canada. Hence, Canadian content rules ought not to treat the two communities in the same fashion. In Quebec, quotas mean French-language content, no matter where it comes from. Singers Renaud and Francis Cabrel of France are every bit as important on Quebec rock stations as Martine St-Clair and Daniel Lavoie.

For Quebec, co-operation with other French-speaking countries and communities is a question of survival. That is why the Canadian and Quebec governments, as well as the CBC and Radio-Québec, have in recent years signed numerous agreements and carried out many exchanges with France and other Francophone countries.

The most important agreement and the one best known by Quebeckers is that of approving the introduction of French television into Quebec (TVFQ).

First signed in 1979, it makes an annual volume of 2,300 hours of programming available to Quebec cable operators through France Média International (FMI) and the Société d'édition et de transcodage (SETTE). The vast majority of these programs (2,000 hours) come from the three French television networks (FR3, Antenne 2, TF1). The French foreign ministry and the Quebec international relations department contribute equally toward the technical costs and the purchase of broadcast rights.

The private sector is also showing increased interest in the international francophone community. In June 1984, Télé-Métropole was accepted as a member of the Communauté des télévisions francophones (of which Radio-Canada is a founding member) and now plans to develop its relations abroad. Télé-Métropole, Pathonic, COGECO and independent producers, as well as representatives from the public sector, are members of a Canadian consortium established to participate in TV-5, a satellite-to-cable network whose French language TV programming is distributed to various countries of Europe and North Africa. TV-5, which also includes participation by France, Switzerland, and Belgium, devotes one evening a week to French-Canadian programming.

But the results of all these projects are still minimal and they are being met with significant resistance. Co-operation is in fact often a one-way street. While the agreement for the introduction of television from France into Quebec initially anticipated broadcasting Quebec programs in France, the Quebec programs remained on the shelf and only the French contribution to the exchange remains.

It is therefore important to beware of seeing exports as the miracle solution, as both Ottawa and Quebec City have tended to do in recent years, and to remember that financing for our cultural products must first be found at home. "We export when we give our products away",[13] we were told by Jacques Girard, President and Chief Executive Officer of Radio-Québec. The fact is that there is a tendency to overestimate opportunities in foreign markets and to underestimate resistance.

France is in fact the only potentially profitable market for French-language products. After undergoing a long period when there were few channels and the programming was being produced locally, France now has more channels, including Canal Plus and a fifth private network, and could well begin to welcome French-language programming from Canada. But there are substantial problems facing exports: very few French households are cabled, although major projects are under way; Quebec products also have a language barrier to face — 'Parisian French' does not welcome so-called regional accents with enthusiasm! Pressure from French unions also maintains a ban on foreign programs that are dubbed outside France, except for programs from EEC countries. In spite of all this, both France and Canada now have a better understanding of the need for co-operation and of what is at stake for French culture around the world.

Some exported Canadian programs have been spectacular successes or, to put it another way, exceptions that prove the rule. For example, many countries are interested in Denys Arcand's film *The Decline of the American Empire*, which won the international critics' prize at the 1986 Cannes film festival.

According to the film's director,

> It's very strange. My film is being sold everywhere and yet it's about people from Outremont and Hutchison Street, people who have dinner together on Saturday night. But their regional ways seem to be immediately understandable to everyone.[14]

The journalist who interviewed Arcand concluded:

> It's obvious that the director's comments are intended for all those well-intentioned bureaucrats who by force of circumstances have become the gravediggers of cultural film to the benefit of commercial, international, efficient, soulless, watered-down film with no identity of its own, no character.[15] (translation)

The judgment is harsh but, apart from the tone, not far from the truth, for both motion picture films and some television programs, and for both English and French Canada.

Government has an essential role to play, not in the creative area, but rather to encourage international co-operation. For example, communications will be a central concern at the next Francophone summit, scheduled for Quebec City in 1987. A number of interesting proposals will be considered, including one for the establishment of an international Francophone agency to provide news footage and another for a French-language radio network.

In the aftermath of TV-5, Canada is studying the possibility of proposing a similar project for the Commonwealth, a kind of Commonwealth TV broadcasting network. Member countries would exchange their best programs by satellite. The Department of Communications, in co-operation with the Commonwealth Secretariat, is preparing a feasibility study for this useful project. The English side of TV-Canada, the second public network we wish to see established, could become the primary means for disseminating Commonwealth productions following the model that we recommend in Chapter 13 for French-language productions on TV-5.

Canada's involvement in TV-5 and a possible future Commonwealth network would allow this country to play a greater role in the international debate on communications that we referred to earlier. Canada has also been showing increased interest in the International Program for the Development of Communications (IPDC) established by UNESCO to finance Third World projects. This is one of a number of programs in which Canada contributes technical, financial and advisory assistance in the field of broadcasting to Third World countries. Canada also provides instruction for students and trainees at specialized centres and at the major radio, television and audio-visual organizations.

As examples of this international co-operation, two projects could be considered in the context of the obvious interest Canada has shown recently in Africa and in Third World women.[16] One such project would establish an International Women's Television and Film Network to be distributed by satellite. This project developed out of the Conference on Women held in Nairobi in 1985; it was endorsed at the First International Women's Peace Conference in

Halifax later that year. Another project is the Africa Watch program described by the Honourable David MacDonald in his report on famine in Africa as follows:

> There is a need to provide more continuing media access to Africa as it passes through this critical period in its history. The media often lack the resources to report on important but distant events. CBC-Radio-Canada should combine their efforts with those of Radio Canada International to launch a special "Africa Watch" project to increase coverage of Africa and to provide opportunities for Africans to broadcast to (and about) Canada.[17]

Though it is not appropriate for this Task Force to make recommendation on programming matters, we feel that both projects merit close study.

All these projects, whether exchanges between Quebec broadcasters and the Francophone world or the involvement of Canadians in the development of a women's television network, clearly show that radio and television, like all forms of technology, can become what we want to make of them. Television can shape the future of the global village in different ways:

- Use of television for strictly commercial purposes will certainly ensure the dominance of the American cultural model and its various national clones.
- A more social approach could contribute in unexpected ways to the continuance of various cultural differences and to better understanding between peoples.

When sharp-tongued critics[18] accuse television of having turned politics into show business, thus making it impossible to discuss seriously the major issues of the day, they are too readily confusing media logic with the American commercial model. It is not television that is at issue here, but the use we make of it.

Notes

1. Conrad Winn, "Comparative Broadcasting Policies", study prepared for the Task Force on Broadcasting Policy, Ottawa, 1986, p. 57.
2. John Gainsborough, "Broadcasting in Britain: A Time of Reflection", *Broadcaster* 45 (1) (January 1986), p. 15 and p. 40.
3. Great Britain, Committee on Financing the BBC, (Peacock Committee) *Report* (London: Her Majesty's Stationery Office, 1986), p. 113 et seq. It should be noted, however, that the Peacock Committee, while rejecting advertising as a means of financing for British television, recommended the privatization of BBC Radio 1 and BBC Radio 2, after which advertising could be considered.
4. Canadian Radio-television and Telecommunications Commission, Task Force on Access to Television in Underserved Communities, *The Costs of Choice* (Ottawa: Minister of Supply and Services Canada, 1985), p. 49.
5. Jean-Denis Bredin, *Les nouvelles télévisions hertziennes* (Paris: La Documentation française, 1985).
6. Kurt Andersen, "Pop Goes the Culture", *Time* 127 (24) (June 1986), p. 69.
7. Paul Audley, "Reconciling Balance and Freedom: The Canadian Experience", in *The New International Information and Communication Order*, edited by Hans Kochler (Vienna: International Progress Organization, 1985), pp. 111-112.

8. Jean-Paul Lafrance, "La juxtaposition des territoires", study prepared for the Task Force on Broadcasting Policy, Ottawa, 1986.
9. Nathalie Petrowski, "Du Canadien errant au chanteur sans frontières. Profil de la musique québécoise et de ses rapports avec l'industrie du disque, les diffuseurs et la société", study prepared for the Task Force on Broadcasting Policy, Ottawa, 1986.
10. *Ibid.*, p. 30. Quote by Jean-Marc Pisapia, of the group "The Box".
11. Haut conseil de la francophonie, *tat de la francophonie dans le monde: Rapport 1985* (Paris: La documentation française, 1986), p. 179.
12. Armand Mattelart, Xavier Delcourt et Michèle Mattelart, *La culture contre la démocratie*? (Paris: La Découverte, 1983) p. 35.
13. Meeting of the Task Force on Broadcasting Policy and Société de radio-télévision du Québec, Montreal, August 6, 1985.
14. Denys Arcand interviewed by Nathalie Petrowski, "La renaissance de l'empire québécois", *Le Devoir* (Montreal), May 31, 1986, p. c-1.
15. Ibid.
16. On this matter, see the statement by the Honourable Monique Vézina, Minister for External Relations, to the Special Session of the United Nations General Assembly on the critical economic situation in Africa, New York, May 27, 1986. Also see the News Release entitled "Priority: Women in Development", Ottawa, Department of External Affairs, June 11, 1986.
17. David MacDonald, *No More Famine: A Decade for Africa* (Final Report) (Ottawa: Canadian International Development Agency, 1986), p. 27.
18. See Neil Postman, *Amusing Ourselves to Death* (New York: Viking, Elizabeth Sefton Books, 1985).

Chapter 3

Culture and Industry

Culture and Industry

The Issue

It is our responsibility as a government-appointed Task Force to recommend appropriate public policy for broadcasting. The overriding question throughout our work has been to determine the rationale by which we call for the state either to intervene or to keep its nose out of various aspects of the broadcasting system; what, we needed to understand, was a legitimate role for public policy as opposed to private market forces, or, to complicate the matter, for public policy to bolster market forces?

In practice, grappling with this key conceptual problem led us immediately to the fashionable but complex question of Canada's so-called 'cultural industries'. As the Canada Council asked our predecessors on the Applebaum-Hébert Commission, "Does a cultural industrial policy pursue industrial or cultural objectives?"[1] And, as we learned through repeated examples, the answer remains shrouded in ambiguity and confusion.

The Canada Council was confident of the answer to its question: "In reality, cultural and industrial objectives are usually competitive and often conflicting." Professor Abraham Rotstein of the University of Toronto, one of our research consultants, suggested to us rather more gently that culture and industry interact in a complex manner, sometimes overlapping in a benign way, at times conflicting.[2] But in either case their needs, aims and responsibilities are distinctive and different, and public policy must carefully recognize the discrete interests of each. Indeed, it is precisely in the political arena that the tensions and contradictions which may be present must be faced and resolved.

The goals of industry are normally clear enough. Typically they imply market criteria, with the bottom line being success as judged by the market. In broadcasting that truth has always seemed inadequate. After all, the most profitable broadcasting system in Canada would be one that featured exclusively foreign material, since it is invariably cheaper to buy American production than to produce something new from scratch. But if the bottom line were all, Canada itself would never have been built and would indeed soon cease to have any meaningful existence.

It was two unblemished conservative businessmen, Sir John Aird, president of the Bank of Commerce, and R.B. Bennett, 11th prime minister of Canada, who first decreed that broadcasting was a public trust and a tool to enhance Canadian national consciousness. In principle, private broadcasters have long accepted that only a public system could provide substantial Canadian programming, yet that the private sector had certain social obligations to perform in return for the privilege of being granted a broadcasting licence. The issues from the outset therefore became ones of balance: between the role of the private sector and that of the public broadcaster, as well as between the level of profitability of the private broadcasters and the value of their social and cultural contributions.

Any serious analysis must be based on the reality that private broadcasting as an industry is in the business of selling audiences to advertisers. As CKND

Winnipeg's Donald Brinton noted on behalf of the Canadian Association of Broadcasters, in commercial broadcasting revenues depend directly on audiences and the value of audiences to advertisers. Programming is the commodity that determines the size and nature of the audience, and therefore of the advertising it attracts. Programs are a cost of operations, not an end in themselves.[3]

Most American broadcasting is a far purer example of market economics than our own. In its non-news programming especially, it is substantially uninterested in any non-economic functions — cultural, social or national. Some see it as merely the logical extension of the factory production system of American industry transferred to the mass media. The American critic Dwight MacDonald long ago considered it Mass Culture, "an article for mass consumption, like chewing gum . . . imposed from above. It is fabricated by technicians hired by businessmen . . . producing what might be called homogenized culture."[4] So when we do buy U.S. cop shows and sitcoms and prime time soaps like *Dallas* and *Dynasty*, we buy sheer commodity rather than culture, even if some American programs are undeniably of a higher quality than some Canadian shows.

Television broadcasters buy those programs because they are dramatically cheaper than producing a new show, and because they often attract large audiences; in a word, it is very profitable to do so. And as the CAB underlined in its January 1985 document, *Industry in Transition: A Strategic Plan for Private Broadcasting*, "Above all it must be stressed that private broadcasting is a business . . . By their nature, private businesses are profit-oriented and, cultural objectives of the government notwithstanding, broadcasters will always maintain a strong profit motive . . . ".[5]

Yet the Canadian tradition being what it is, the CAB went on to state that it would yet "continue to support the concept that the private broadcasting sector should make a meaningful contribution towards the achievement of the cultural, social and economic goals of Canada."[6]

The cultural, social and economic goals of Canada: the tools, in short, to forge a national consciousness different from that of the United States. From the first, as we saw in Chapter 1, it has been an article of non-partisan faith that broadcasting had special responsibilities in the Canadian circumstances. It was to play the role of both the railways and the telegraph in binding a geographically absurd entity together. It was to be a key instrument in the never-ending task of affirming a sense of Canadian consciousness.

What evolved was a system that is an exquisite microcosm of the Canadian way. How Canadian was it to be? As Canadian as possible given the economic circumstances. Whose responsibility would Canadian content be? A combination of the private and public sectors. What balance, or proportion, of the nationalist obligation would each sector bear? That would be worked out on an *ad hoc* basis.

The Public Broadcaster

The public sector, the public interest, would be represented by the CBC. Its job was to offer Canadian programming, which in Canada is tantamount to saying Canadian culture, except, of course, when no other broadcaster provided the popular American programs Canadians wanted to watch, or when inadequate government funding made necessary the purchase of popular American programs to assure that advertisers would be interested. The logical notion that only a commercial-free public broadcaster could fulfil the ambitious mandate imposed upon the CBC was never acceptable to any of the governments that have held the purse-strings. Radio, eventually, was allowed to drop advertising, with wonderful ensuing results. But television simply cost too much.

CBC English television especially suffered from its schizophrenic situation. Was it a vehicle for the transmission of Canadian experiences, reflecting our own environment and reality as interpreted by our own creative resources — for the purposes of this Task Force perhaps an adequate enough notion of culture? Or was it to use American-style programs to attract the largest possible audience? How much did its commercial obligations sully its cultural goals?

In 1974, when it was renewing the CBC's licence, the CRTC argued that the marketing environment was inappropriately forcing the Corporation into a mode of operation increasingly based on mass appeal, whereas the range of viewers reached should be much more relevant and important than the numerical size of any particular audience. The CRTC also considered disentanglement of the Corporation from the commercial context to be an urgent priority.[7]

Yet when the CBC proposed non-commercial second television networks in French and English in 1981, the Liberal cabinet refused additional funding, piqued, it was widely believed, by the unproved conviction that Radio-Canada was a hotbed of Quebec separatism. In turn, the CRTC rejected the licence application for CBC-2 since designated funding was not available, instead of joining with the CBC to importune the government to reverse its decision.

CBC television consequently remained a curious hybrid, obligated to offer programming both for advertisers and for demanding fans of public broadcasting, by no means always identical constituencies. At the same time that government funding continued to decline in real terms, new obligations were added. In 1983, for example, the Government announced its expectation that CBC would significantly increase its proportion of Canadian programming, a costly change for which, however, no further funding was offered.[8]

For the main public broadcaster, then, its institutional ambivalence has been a source of never-ending anxiety and perpetual discontent both within the Corporation and among its public supporters. For the private sector, too, the constant attempt to reconcile its obligations to its shareholders with those of the *Broadcasting Act* created a distinct form of schizophrenia. Ironically, however, private broadcasters have on the whole benefited more from their curious situation than has the CBC.

The Obligations of the Private Sector

"The only thing that really matters in broadcasting is programme content," so Robert Fowler, one of our distinguished predecessors, began his committee's report; "all the rest is housekeeping."[9] It is a fine, memorable epigram, but it is wrong. All the rest is in fact a major branch of Canadian industry, and functions accordingly, save for the penalties it pays and the rewards it earns for carrying out certain limited social obligations.

On behalf of the CAB in 1984, Donald Brinton explained one part of the dilemma for private broadcasters. "The private TV licence is an assignment of extensive public service responsibilities to a private, profit-making activity . . . [These are] inherently opposite objectives . . . ."[10]

The following year, Global's Paul Morton angrily scolded a Canadian Conference of the Arts conference consisting mostly of public broadcasting advocates for failing to understand that he could only afford to show Canadian programs if they were cross-subsidized by the profits made on American shows. Global's 1985 submission to the CRTC carefully explained their intention to produce Canadian programs "consistent with our ability to finance the projects on a realistic, business-like basis".[11]

But the private broadcasters hardly have complete freedom of choice. Their social and cultural obligations require that they broadcast certain amounts of Canadian content each day. In fact, the CRTC regulations limit the amount of foreign programming they can broadcast. "One might say", the CAB has said, "that Canadian content is the compromise resulting from the uneasy amalgamation of two conflicting principles, broadcasting as an instrument of national social and cultural policy and as a business enterprise."[12]

In fact, the situation has been even murkier than this. The 'cultural' role of the private sector has not always been overwhelming. Robert Fowler in 1965 described the contribution of private TV to Canadian programming and the support of Canadian artists as "contemptuous". Although CTV representatives have repeatedly re-committed the network to significant amounts of Canadian content, in the 1984 calendar year about one percent of programming on CTV between 7 p.m. and 11 p.m. was Canadian drama, while some 50 percent was foreign drama, overwhelmingly American of course.[13] Herschel Hardin, in his pugnacious and well-documented *Closed Circuits: The Sellout of Canadian Television*,[14] shows the unbroken pattern by which new applicants promise the moon if they receive a television licence, and are invariably back before the CRTC in the briefest possible time seeking relief from their own commitments. As Frank Spiller and Kim Smiley in a report to the Canadian Conference of the Arts neatly put it: "Promises of performance are like campaign promises, glowingly presented by potential licencees but not scrupulously adhered to once the licence is granted."[15]

Even 21 years ago, Fowler was so angry at this process that he insisted that a promise made to obtain a licence should be "an enforceable undertaking". And every one of our predecessors has exhorted the licencing agency to get tough with those licencees who fail to live up to their commitments.

Protecting Private Broadcasting

So regulation, mainly in the form of Canadian content quotas, was imposed on the private sector. Yet this Task force barely heard a single private sector spokesperson call for an end to regulation. We were surprised in two ways: by the unsolicited commitment of the private broadcasters to the aims of the 1968 Act, and by their almost eager acceptance of regulations of some kind. Hoskins and McFadyen provided an answer to this apparent paradox: in a 1980 study[16] they concluded that regulation in Canada had largely operated to the benefit of private broadcasters, who received state protection from American competition in return for undemanding levels of Canadian content "which in any case had not always been met". Let us look more closely at this phenomenon.

In the first place, the Canadian content regulations were not imposed vigorously. Private broadcasters themselves acknowledge the ease of fulfilling the letter but not the spirit of Canadian content regulations. As the CAB explained with notable candour in 1984, their members had been "spreading ever more thinly the level of resources available for original Canadian program production. The net effect of this has often been to reduce the quality of the results while maintaining the quantitative content requirements".[17]

Secondly, the private broadcasters traded their roles as good corporate citizens for substantial legislative and regulatory protection against overpowering American competition as well as against the Canadian cable industry. This can best be demonstrated by an analysis of one piece of federal legislation, Bill C-58, and one regulatory mechanism, simultaneous substitution. As we will point out in the chapters that follow, both function to provide lucrative incentives to Canadian television broadcasters to show popular American programs in prime time. Take simultaneous substitution. In order to protect the rights of Canadian broadcasters to the Hollywood shows they buy each year, if a Canadian and an American station are both telecasting the same program at the same time, the CRTC allows the Canadian broadcaster to have its signal substituted on cable for that of the American broadcaster. In other words, whether you are tuned to the American or the Canadian station, you are watching the Canadian station — and, let it be noted, the commercials being run on the Canadian station. But the catch, of course, is that the purpose is served only if an American program is being shown.

Ralph and Steven Ellis, two Toronto producers, spelled out for us the clear implication of simultaneous substitution as initiated by the CRTC. In a real sense decision affecting prime time in Canada are made in New York, since a Canadian station will buy an American program and create its schedule to match that of the US network showing the same program. Should American executives in New York choose to move its program from Monday at 8 p.m. to Thursday at 10 p.m., the Canadian broadcaster will follow suit.[18]

This may be highly desirable for the commercial needs of television broadcasters. But in setting it up, the CRTC not only chose the interests of broadcasters over the interests of the cable industry — without persuasively indicating why the economic health of the one deserved greater state assistance than that of the other — but chose a form of industrial protection with results inimical to the goals of the *Broadcasting Act*.

Why would the regulatory agency devise regulations which seem directly to contradict its statutory responsibility to implement a "predominantly Canadian" broadcasting system? The CRTC's response to the culture vs. industry dichotomy seems to come in three stages. Initially it acts for the sake of cultural goals. Then it ensures the economic viability of the industry so that the broadcasters will be able to afford to cross-subsidize from their profits on American programming the production and scheduling of Canadian programs. Finally, the CRTC protects the industry for its own sake, as an end in itself. Can this last stage be called anything other than commercial protectionism? The CRTC believes that broadcasting renders a legitimate benefit to the domestic economy with respect to employment, trade balances and foreign exchange investment, benefits which would naturally end were the Canadian system destroyed in head-to-head competition with the Americans.

Is it for the first, second or third of these purposes that the CRTC affords further security to private broadcasters by licence renewal hearings which hear no competitive applications, and by receiving applications for transfers of licence only from the party proposed by the vendor. The Fowler Commission had been unequivocal: "The grant of a new broadcast licence is the temporary and conditional alienation of an important and valuable public asset which, by its very nature, cannot be shared with others."[19] This central principle had been written into the 1968 Act. Yet the CRTC has implicitly institutionalized *de facto* private property rights within the broadcasting system.

This is why our Task Force was not lobbied to end, but merely to modify, the present regulatory system imposed on the private sector. It is also why we rarely heard invoked the grand old entrepreneurial principle of the right to go broke. Whether in the protection of AM radio stations from FM competitors or private broadcasters from cable or cable from satellites, almost everyone involved in the broadcasting system rejects the traditional view of the market as the determinant of economic success, and agrees on the appropriateness of a state agency to protect the various components of the industry from the United States and from each other.

Almost everyone concerned with broadcasting dismisses the unadulterated case for the market to decide, as expressed by economist Steven Globerman: "It is unclear why such ventures [subsidies for cultural projects] should be promoted at public expense any more than Canadians should be expected to subsidize the growing of bananas in Canada."[20] The reason, of course, is not only would there remain as much Canadian culture as Canadian bananas, but the private broadcasting system would perish as well.

That is why little surprise greeted the announcement that "a high-powered committee of cultural industry leaders" had been formed early in 1986 to ensure that "cultural concerns" would not be forgotten in the Canada-U.S. trade negotiations. It included, inter alia, most of the influential private broadcasters in the country. If a broadcasting licence in Canada is often a licence to print money, as a certain Roy Thomson once observed from his own experience with broadcasting, this group controlled the printing presses. Robert Fulford, editor of *Saturday Night*, described them with some cynicism: "Private broadcasters who have made millions mainly by importing cop shows and situation comedies from Los Angeles have been transformed . . . into born-again nationalists, even anti-Americans . . . . The possibility that free trade with the United States will alter or eliminate cultural protectionism and subsidies has brought [them] together . . . ."[21]

Such jadedness has not been the preserve of intellectuals like Fulford; industry insiders have long viewed the public-spiritedness of private broadcasters with much amusement. In the wry words of Wood Gundy analyst Michael Waring, "To win a licence you don't say, 'We're doing this to make a lot of money'. You say, 'We're going to lose a lot of money, but we're doing it for the good of Canadian broadcasting' ".[22]

Nor has it escaped our attention that the interests of many of those who importuned us on behalf of public broadcasting are hurt if the CBC is hurt. In fact we received 60 briefs, over a quarter of the total submitted to us, from sources such as CBC departments, unions within the CBC, producers and talent associations, all extolling the intrinsic virtues of public broadcasting. Of course the sincerity of none of them is in question. But objectively, all have a vested interest in maintaining or enlarging the CBC.

The issue here is not to judge motives but merely to clarify and illuminate interests. For if the state is to intervene, the purposes must be clear, far clearer than they have been thus far.

Assumptions

Our first priority is to make the broadcasting system serve Canadian culture, broadly defined, more effectively in the future than it has done in the past. We want the system to be program-driven, with Canadians able to choose from a substantial number of quality Canadian programs. That is why we call for a significantly expanded public sector.

When we recommend policies to enhance the position of the broadcasting industry — those businesses which produce and disseminate programming — our aim is to induce the private sector to maintain cultural objectives as a serious goal of its operations; that is our second priority, the development of private broadcasting industries as a means to a cultural end, not an end in itself. That is why we call for significant contributions from the private sector to the objectives of the broadcasting system.

Finally, as our third priority we agreed in some instances that, for the sake of economic stability and to preclude economic dislocation, broadcasting industries in their commercial capacities alone merit certain forms of protective intervention by the state. That is why we endorse the continuation of measures such as C-58 and simultaneous substitution. But this must be recognized as simple commercial protection of industries that happen to be in the 'culture business'.

It follows logically from this that the Task Force had little difficulty in reaching its views on the issue of Canada's cultural sovereignty. Only one conclusion is possible under our priorities. We interpret cultural sovereignty to refer to our own control of our cultural destiny, our own control of the instruments of decision-making which determine our cultural future. The broadcasting system has a pre-eminent role to play in both nurturing and reflecting Canadian culture. Governments must therefore not consider measures to achieve the objectives of Canadian broadcasting as mere chips that may be traded across a bargaining table. Canadians must maintain the sovereign right to make whatever decisions we deem necessary to protect our own culture.

Notes

1. Canada Council, *A submission to the Federal Cultural Policy Review Committee*, March 9, 1981, p. 21.

2. Abraham Rotstein, "The Use and Misuse of Economics in Cultural and Broadcasting Policy", study prepared for the Task Force on Broadcasting Policy, Ottawa, 1986.
3. Canadian Association of Broadcasters, *Canadian Content Review, CAB Report on the Montebello Seminar, June 22-24, 1984* (Ottawa: CAB, 1984), p. 14.
4. Dwight McDonald, "A Theory of Mass Culture", in *Mass Culture*, edited by B. Rosenberg and D.M. White (New York: Free Press, 1964), p. 59 et seq.
5. Canadian Association of Broadcasters, *Industry in Transition: A Strategic Plan for Private Broadcasting* (Ottawa: CAB, January 1985).
6. Ibid.
7. Canadian Radio-television and Telecommunications Commission, *Radio Frequencies are Public Property*, CRTC Decision 74-70, (Ottawa: CRTC, 1974), pp. 35-42.
8. Canada, Department of Communications, *Building for the Future: Towards a Distinctive CBC* (Ottawa: Minister of Supply and Services Canada, 1983).
9. Canada, Committee on Broadcasting (Fowler Committee) *Report* (Ottawa: Queen's Printer, 1965), p. 3.
10. CAB, *Canadian Content Review*, p. 14.
11. Global Television Network, "Response to CRTC Decision 85-214", May 29, 1985, p. 10.
12. Canadian Association of Broadcasters, *Canadian Content Review* (English Language Television), Background Paper prepared by the CAB for a Workshop held in Montebello, Québec, June 22-24, 1984, p. 2.
13. Based on availability data reported in Barry Kiefl, Stan Staple, Roger Kain and Jim Stanage, "TV/Radio Audience and Program Trends and the Future", a special presentation to the Task Force on Broadcasting Policy, September 1985.
14. Herschel Hardin, *Closed Circuits: The Sellout of Canadian Television* (Vancouver: Douglas & McIntyre, 1985).
15. Frank Spiller and Kim Smiley, "Regulatory Environment", background paper prepared for the Canadian Conference of the Arts, Conference on the Future of the Canadian Broadcasting System, Ottawa, October 15-18, 1985, (Ottawa: Canadian Conference of the Arts, 1985), p. 9.
16. Colin Hoskins and Stuart McFadyen, *Canadian Broadcasting: Market Structure and Economic Performance* (Montreal: Institute for Research on Public Policy, 1980).
17. CAB, *Canadian Content Review*, p. 16.
18. Ralph C. Ellis Enterprise Ltd. "The Trouble with Simulcasting", study prepared for the Task Force on Broadcasting Policy, Ottawa, 1986.
19. Canada, Royal Commission on Broadcasting, (Fowler Commission) *Report* (Ottawa: Queen's Printer, 1957), p. 102.
20. Steven Globerman, *Cultural Regulation in Canada* (Montreal: Institute for Research on Public Policy, 1983).
21. Robert Fulford, "Blaming the Yanks", in *Saturday Night* 101 (3) (March 1986), pp. 7-9.
22. "CHUM: Out to Show Pay-TV Can Be Lucrative: Rock Videos Mix with Fiscal Conservatism", in *Financial Times* 72 (44) (April 23, 1984), p. 7.

Chapter 4

The Evolution of Broadcasting Technology

The Evolution of Broadcasting Technology

Advances in science and technology determine what is physically possible in broadcasting. Developments now under way will vastly increase technical capacity to provide greater choice of content, higher quality of sound and image, and new telecommunication services such as electronic print and graphics. Following the ages of broadcasting dominated first by radio then by television, broadcasting is entering a third age of integrated communications in which it is becoming a selective and specialized medium as well as a mass medium. More technological capacity does not mean, of course, that everything that can happen will happen.

Technological change brings new challenges to the public policy maker if its benefits are to be extended equitably to everyone. In this chapter, we will review the present state of the broadcasting art. We will consider the prospects of technological advance to the year 2000. And we will take a look at some of the policy issues related to technology.

The Development of Broadcasting

Broadcasting has its beginnings in the use of electromagnetic energy to send messages. The telegraph system promoted by Samuel Morse between Washington and Baltimore in 1844 was based on the electric relay, which passes on the pattern of an electric current from one circuit to another. Messages were sent by a key that turned the current on and off to cause a magnetically activated key at the other end of the line to clack out dots and dashes. Later, Alexander Graham Bell, who carried out some of his work in Canada, found out how to modulate the electric waves passing along a wire in order to carry a signal, analogous to a voice message, which could be demodulated back into voice at the other end.

At the end of the 19th century, the Italian inventor Guglielmo Marconi developed wireless telegraphy, sending messages in Morse code over the air by electromagnetic waves. Working under the sponsorship of the British government, Marconi achieved transatlantic radiocommunication in 1901 when he received the letter *s* at Signal Hill, St. John's, Newfoundland, from a transmitter in Cornwall, England. Later he carried on his experiments in Nova Scotia. In the meantime, a Canadian inventor working for the U.S. Weather Bureau, Reginald A. Fessenden, managed at the end of 1900 to send a voice message over the air for a distance of a mile, thereby inventing wireless telephony. By 1906 he had refined his apparatus sufficiently to make the first radio broadcast — a program of song, violin music, records and Christmas messages — on Christmas Eve 1906, received by ships at sea from an experimental station at Brant Rock, Mass.

When we think of broadcasting technology, it is natural to put transmission and distribution first, as we do in this chapter, since broadcasting originated as a means of transmitting signals. Production and reception depend on the capacity to transmit. When we think of programming, however, it is natural to think in a progression from production to transmission to reception: the creation, sending and receiving of the message. The greater the capacity of transmission and distribution technology, the greater the possibilities for creating program content and the greater the call on technology to develop those possibilities. The more sophisticated the production and transmission technology, the greater the demand on reception technology if listeners, viewers and users are to receive the benefits.

Technology, of course, is only one of the constraints that set limits on the variety of programs that can be produced and transmitted. If the technological limits of spectrum and channel space were to disappear entirely, then broadcasting would be confined instead by economic considerations. In the case of television in particular, the high cost of program production sets limits on the volume and variety of attractive programming that can be generated. These constraints are considered in the remainder of our Report; here, however, our focus is on what is technically possible.

Transmission and Distribution: Proliferation of Channels

Years ago, broadcast transmission gave the language the expression 'being on the same wavelength'. Today's expression for being in touch with people and things that matter, 'networking', gives a better sense of the way broadcasting is developing. Broadcasting began as a linear one-way relationship between the sender and the audience. Today it has the technical potential to become more like the interactive relationship among sharers of a circuit. Broadcasting systems could come to resemble the switched exchange system of the telephone networks. The transmission architecture of broadcasting has become more and more complex. Let us look first at over-the-air transmission and then at newer parts of the distribution system.

Over-the-air Transmission

Radio took its name from the fact that electromagnetic energy is radiated from the transmitter. It travels in wavelike motion at the velocity of light, 300,000 kilometres, or 300 million metres, per second, giving the effect of instant communication over great distances. A radio broadcast requires a source of alternating electric current sufficient to create radio waves. The waves are measured by their length from crest to crest, or by the number of complete wave cycles per second, known as the frequency. The basic unit of frequency is the hertz: one cycle per second. Since electromagnetic waves move at the velocity of light, the frequency multiplied by the wavelength must always equal 300 million metres a second.

Broadcasting requires that sounds or pictures be translated into electrical patterns, or signals, and that these be impressed on radio waves through a process known as modulation. The receiver, tuned to the same wavelength, reverses the process, demodulating the signal and restoring the sounds and images for listeners and viewers. Signals may be impressed on radio waves by modulating — that is, very slightly altering — the wave's amplitude, the vertical distance between crest and trough; this is called amplitude modulation, or

AM. Waves may also be modulated by fractionally altering their frequencies; this is called frequency modulation, or FM.

Electromagnetic waves occupy a spectrum that starts below the frequencies that can carry sound and rises above the frequencies of visible light waves into the realm of ultraviolet radiation, X-rays, gamma rays, cosmic rays as shown in Figure 4.1. The higher the frequency, the greater the broadcast 'load', or amount of information, that radio waves can carry. The adjectival resources of the language have been all but exhausted as higher and higher frequency bands have been brought into use — high, very high, ultra high, super high, extremely high — HF, VHF, UHF, SHF, and EHF. (The top of the EHF band is 300 billion cycles per second, or 300 gigahertz — GHz.) At the bottom are VLF — very low frequency, LF — low frequency; and MF — medium frequency.

A group of radiowaves covering several frequencies is needed to carry the content of a radio signal, but much greater bandwidth is required to carry television, since a television signal carries much more information, that is, electrical information, to convey the complex details of moving video images. The greater the amount of information that must be transmitted in a signal, the greater the bandwidth it requires. One speaks of the width of a band, rather than the height or some other figure of speech, because of the way the electromagnetic spectrum is presented graphically — as a series of horizontal bands. Frequency bands that carry signals are called channels. Radio channels are known by the frequency of their main carrier wave. Television channels are known by their designated channel numbers.

Only a small part of the electromagnetic spectrum is suitable for broadcasting. There is strong demand for allocation of this part of the spectrum for uses other than broadcasting, such as air traffic control and navigation, mobile telephone, police radio and so on. In 1979 the top 14 channels of the UHF television band were re-allocated to the mobile service, including two-way radio for police, fire, taxi and ambulance, as well as cellular radio. Over the years, more precise engineering and improved understanding of the spectrum have permitted the licensing of an increasing number of AM radio channels by national authorities acting under international agreement. After World War II, the development of FM radio in the VHF band further relieved the effect of scarcity, though it was some years before there were enough radio sets capable of receiving FM to make it practical to have distinctive FM programming.

The technical advantage of FM was to offer transmission free of static and with a fuller reproduction of the sounds being broadcast. With a much broader bandwidth than AM radio, FM could carry more information — in this case information conveying musical detail — and thus cover more of the dynamic range of music. FM broadcasting brought high fidelity sound, and stereo sound, to radio. Today FM is threatening the commercial health of the private AM stations. In the autumn of 1985, there were no fewer than 20 applicants for the last available FM frequency in Metropolitan Toronto. A representative of the Canadian Association of Broadcasters told us at a technology briefing that the main challenge to AM broadcasting is to "improve the sound quality of the AM medium and thereby regain audiences lost to FM and to home audio".

Spectrum for all types of telecommunication is allocated under interna-

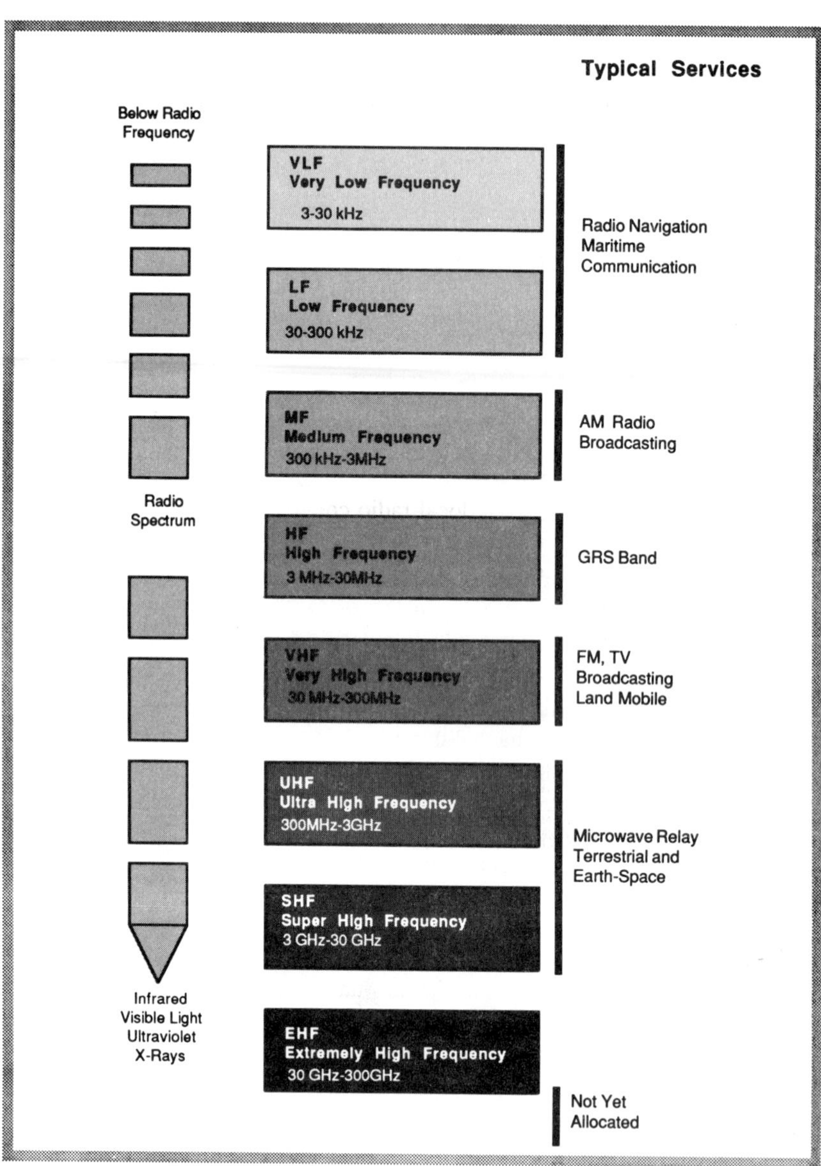

Figure 4.1 Electromagnetic Spectrum

tional agreements reached in the International Telecommunications Union (ITU), an agency of the United Nations, by its World Administrative Radio Conferences (WARC) and Regional Administrative Radio Conferences (RARC). The world is divided into three geographic regions for radio spectrum allocation. Canada belongs to Region II, consisting of North, Central and South America.

Another feature of radio transmission is what is known as a subcarrier channel, that part of the baseband frequency not actually needed for the signal. The AM subcarrier band is so narrow, however, that its exploitation has not yet been undertaken. FM's wider channels permit what are called Subsidiary Communications Multiplex Operation (SCMO) sub-channels. They are starting to be used for such services as delivering background music to stores, minority-language programming, readings for the blind, and teletext. Since 1984, the CRTC has permitted FM broadcasters to develop the commercial potential of SCMO without restriction.

By contrast with television, local radio continues to be received by most consumers over the air, rather than by cable — true broadcasting in direct descent from Fessenden's Christmas Eve broadcast. One reason for the strength of local radio is the popularity of car radio. The spectrum available to radio is all but saturated in most large centres; there is little room for growth.

Television requires much greater bandwidth than radio, and transmits using two different modulations. The television picture is an AM signal, while the sound is FM on an immediately adjacent channel. The greater the clarity and detail desired on the screen of the TV receiver, the broader the bandwidth required for the signal. The present number of over-the-air TV channels was in part determined by the degree of resolution desired for the picture.

The technical standard of television in North America, Japan, and parts of Latin America is the NTSC (National Television Standards Committee) 525-line format. The European PAL and French SECAM systems, with 625 lines, achieve a marginally superior picture. These scanning lines that make up the TV picture are created by an electron beam that causes a phosphoric coating to illuminate as it sweeps across the screen from side to side and top to bottom, covering the 'field' of odd lines and the field of even lines alternately for a total of 60 fields a second.

While the beam is returning from each of its horizontal sweeps, or flying up from the bottom to start sweeping down again, its intensity is suppressed (blanked) to prevent the screen's phosphor coating from being illuminated. During the time it takes for the beam to fly back from bottom to top, known as the vertical blanking interval (VBI), other signals can be transmitted without interference to the video picture.

The VBI is the television equivalent of a radio sub-carrier. In Britain, the public and private networks use the VBI to broadcast teletext, an electronic print service that enables the viewer to access pages of news, weather, sports, and other information on the screen. Such a service was carried experimentally by the CBC in 1983 under the name IRIS, with a special government subsidy, but was dropped when the subsidy ended. Sets must be equipped with special decoders to receive VBI signals. More than two million sets are now so equipped in Britain. Another use of the VBI is to provide closed captioning for the hearing-impaired, which again requires a special decoder.

One of the major current innovations is stereophonic television. It has, in addition to the VBI, a subcarrier capacity in the form of a secondary audio programming (SAP) channel and the possibility of an additional narrowband multiplex channel. Stereo television is already broadcast by hundreds of stations in the United States and is being introduced in Canada, but it requires upgrades of terrestrial microwave links in broadcast and cable systems and may require a change in decoders in the case of pay-TV. The SAP channel provides audio quality as good as AM radio, though not equal to FM. About 50,000 TV sets with stereo capacity were sold in Canada in 1985, and it is estimated that more than 200,000 will be sold in 1986.

Networks

Over-the-air radio and television stations are essentially local because of the characteristics of electromagnetic waves. True, shortwave AM radio, in which the waves bounce back to earth from the ionosphere, can travel vast distances; but owing to the changing conditions of the ionosphere, shortwave transmission is not consistent and reliable enough to carry regular programming services for the mass audience. Thus AM radio for the mass audience is on frequencies which make it a local service. Both FM radio signals and television signals follow line-of-sight paths. This limits their effective coverage with an acceptable signal to a radius of no more than 110 kilometres in most instances.

In order to broadcast programs in many places at the same time, local broadcasting stations have to be linked in networks by means of non-broadcast communication relays or rebroadcast transmitters. A broadcasting network is two or more stations linked to present the same programming according to a schedule. A production network links stations to supply them with program feeds from which they pick and choose to create programs.

The Massey Report of 1951 underlined the technological complexity and cost Canadian geography imposes on radio network broadcasting by contrast with Britain. "Britain reaches a population of 50 million with 975 miles of landline; Canada requires 15,000 miles of telegraph or telephone line to provide a national broadcasting service to her 14 millions."[1]

The establishment of the CBC radio networks in the thirties at least had the advantage of telegraph and telephone lines already in place. When television came to Canada in 1952, its demand for spectrum required the construction of new microwave networks to provide broadband transmission. They were built by the telephone and telegraph companies, and carried voice and other telecommunication traffic in addition to television signals.

Networking introduced one of the fundamental dynamics of broadcast programming, the tension between network control and local station control, between national or regional programming and local programming. The network ambition to be arbiter of taste and fashion confronted the station's ambition to reflect local tastes. The tension was resolved in the balance of each station's local program schedule. Today, satellite networking can aggravate this tension by making prepackaged syndicated programming cheaply available to local stations anywhere in the country, thus displacing local production. Or, by satellite-to-cable or satellite-to-home, local stations can be bypassed.

After the start of television, four new technologies arrived which were to have a profound effect on the balance and scope of networking. We will look at them in the order of their development: microwave relays, cable systems, communication satellites, and optical fibre.

Microwave

Microwaves attenuate or fade so rapidly that for many years they were not considered for telecommunication. Their wavelength goes down to one millimetre and they cover frequencies from 1 billion to 300 billion cycles per second, or gigahertz (GHz), on the spectrum. By concentrating these waves into a narrow beam like a searchlight, however, their power can be increased 100,000 times, and this beam can pierce the atmosphere for a distance of 30 miles or more.

Unlike wires or coaxial cable, microwave relays require no continuous right of way but rather a succession of transmitter-receiver towers. With the advent of television came the national microwave networks which, as we noted above, also carried other telecommunications traffic. Later, microwave relays were to be used to bring signals to cable systems and to transmit television coverage back to TV stations from remote locations.

Cable

Cable systems began in a rudimentary way almost 35 years ago as a means of distributing television broadcasting throughout communities where no stations, or few stations, could be received, and to improve the signals received from local stations. Cable was a broadband relay into people's homes from a receiver of over-the-air broadcast signals. It was called community antenna television (CATV). When TV began, about half the population in Canada could receive American stations over the air. Cable became the means to improve such reception or extend it to centres farther from the border.

Today's cable operations are still the basic tree-shaped delivery systems of 30 years ago (see Figure 4.2). The root of the tree is a headend, where the signal is received and fed into coaxial cable. It passes along a trunk, out into a branch, and eventually through a twig (dropwire) into a leaf (TV set). The signal fades as it passes through the coaxial cable and has to be repeatedly amplified. In the beginning, coaxial cable carried only one or two channels to subscribers, but capacity was steadily increased.

Cable uses a band of frequencies which include the frequencies of the 12 VHF over-the-air television channels. With the introduction of the channel converter, engineers designed cable systems to carry more and more channels at frequencies that were converted into one of the frequencies — usually channel 2, 3 or 4 — that could be tuned on a TV set. Today some North American cable systems are being built to carry more than 70 channels or, with double-cable, twice that number. Engineers are continuing to increase the capacity of single

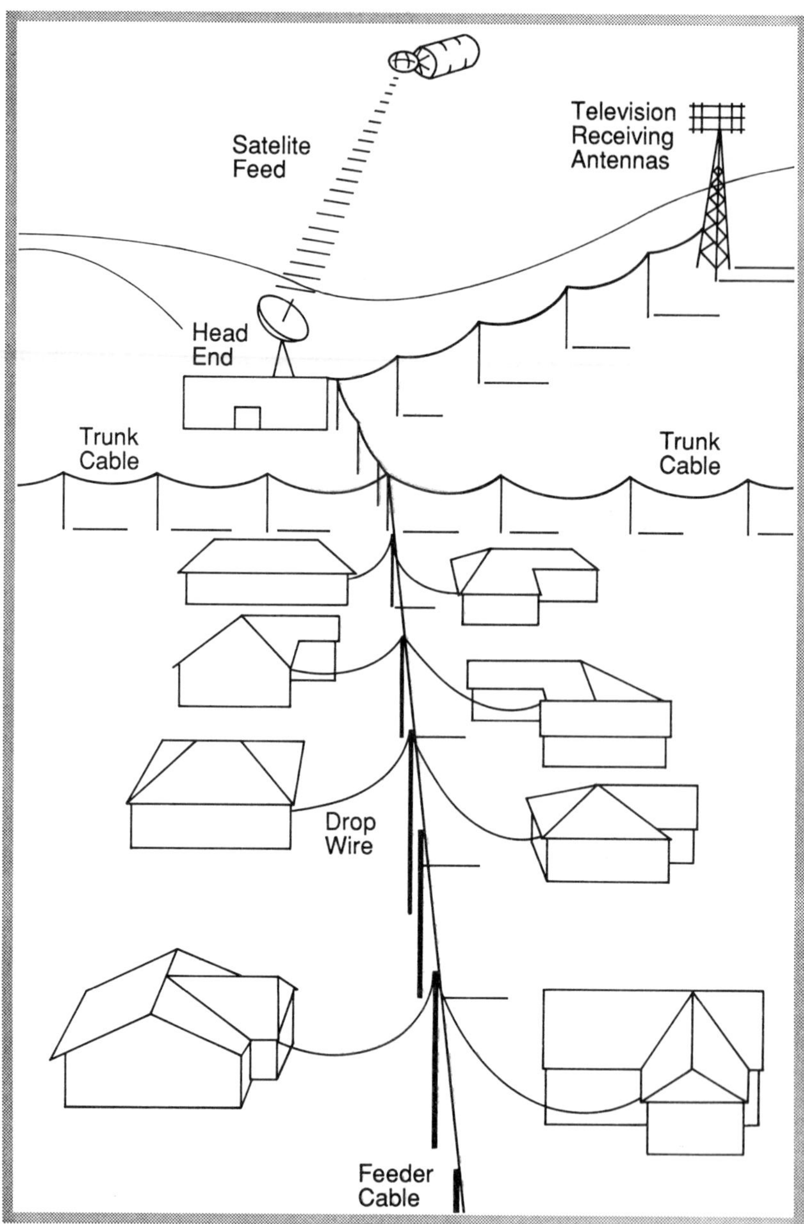

Figure 4.2 The Cable System Tree Network

cable. Terrestrial microwave, and more recently satellite links to cable headends have been used to bring more distant signals to Canadian localities. The constraint on growth is the availability of a sufficient number of attractive television services available to be carried, rather than the technical capacity to carry them.

As systems expanded to comprise scores of thousands of subscribers, microwave links were used to connect headends with remote segments of the system and avoid the distortion of signal caused by repeated amplification. There has also been a beginning of interconnection, or networking, between neighbouring cable systems to provide common programming.

The development of traps and addressable decoders accommodated the arrival of pay television, making it possible for the operator at the headend to control the channels of unscrambled programming received by cable subscribers. With two-way capacity, the subscriber can signal the headend to obtain pay-per-program television, with the transmitting and billing controls being handled by computerized systems. In rudimentary form, the first pay-per-view systems were operated as separate closed-circuit services for hotels by cable companies.

Initially, the advance of cable technology was heavily dependent on the telephone companies, themselves barred from program production since the CRTC does not allow common carriers to control the content of the signals they carry. Some of the coaxial cable is owned by the telephone companies, whose poles and ducts are used to carry it, and leased to cable operators. Regulation requires the cable operator to own the headend, amplifiers and drop wires, with exceptions in Manitoba and Saskatchewan where the provincially owned telephone companies play a more extensive role in cable carriage.

The cable spectrum carries the full range of FM radio frequencies which can be used to carry audio programming, except on frequencies corresponding to those used locally over the air. These FM channels have the SCMO subcarrier mentioned earlier. In addition stereo TV on cable has its SAP subcarrier. The separate audio capacity of cable has been little used except to carry local and distant FM stations and the stereo sound of some pay-TV services.

The advance of cable has been encouraged by the contribution of the space age to telecommunication networks: communication satellites.

Satellites

No transmission technology has been more closely associated with Canadian communications philosopher Marshall McLuhan's vision of the global village than satellite communication, with its ability to bring distant scenes and sounds instantly into the homes of viewers everywhere. While running behind the expectations of its promoters as a means of broadcasting directly to the home, the communication satellite has become a key element in networks linking programmers to local broadcasting stations, cable systems and rebroadcast transmitters.

The communication satellite can be used as a microwave relay or as a broadcast transmitter in space. The concept was envisioned in 1945 by science writer Arthur C. Clarke, who described how a satellite could be placed in position 36,000 kilometres above the equator to complete an orbit every 24 hours, thus seeming to be stationary in relation to the earth, that is, 'geo-synchronous'. Since signals travel a total of 72,000 km out to space and back, satellite communication is said to be cost-insensitive to mere terrestrial distances. Sending a signal from, say, St. John's to Victoria costs no more than from Toronto to Sudbury. The disadvantage is that, even with the velocity of light, there is a .30-second delay in transit which makes telephone conversation awkward.

In January 1973 Canada became the first country to have a domestic commercial geosynchronous communication satellite system in operation. In the joint *Hermes* satellite with the U.S., Canada experimented with direct broadcasting to the home. The Canadian Anik C-3 of 1982 was the first communication satellite in the world with sufficient power to broadcast direct to small home receiving dishes.

The allocation of communication satellite positions and frequencies is negotiated by countries in the manner described for radio. The uplink signal from an earth station must be on a different frequency from the downlink to avoid interference between the two. The uplink signal is at the higher frequency. Hence satellites are referred to in terms of two gigahertz frequencies, such as 6/4 GHz, which is known as the C-band, and 14/12 GHz, or Ku-band. The 6 GHz signal from earth is received by a transponder on the satellite, which converts it to 4 GHz downlink frequency, amplifies it since it has been greatly weakened by the long journey, and transmits it back to earth where it is received by another earth station.

Today's satellites operating in the C-band generally have 24 transponders, each with 36 MHz of bandwidth. Each transponder can carry one colour TV channel, or 1200 telephone-type voice channels, or 16 radio channels, or 1000 data communication channels. A satellite's coverage area, or footprint, can be one-third of the earth's surface, or a smaller area by means of spotbeams.

The size of parabolic antenna, or dish, required to receive the downlink signal depends on the power and frequency with which it is transmitted; the higher the power or frequency, the smaller the dish. Satellites on the C-band require dishes of two metres or more in diametre because their power of transmission is limited in order not to interfere with terrestrial microwave transmission using frequencies in the same range. The 12 GHz downlink in the Ku-band is allocated exclusively to space services, including direct-to-home broadcasting from satellites, so that higher power transmission and smaller dish antennas can be used without fear of causing interference with terrestrial microwave operations. The signals can be received with dishes about a metre in diametre. Canada's 6/4 Anik D satellites cover the whole country, while its 14/12 Anik C satellites have half-Canada or quarter-Canada spotbeams.

At one time, enthusiasts for satellite broadcasting expected direct broadcast satellites (DBS) to supersede network and cable relays. The satellite would have become, in effect, the transmitter in space for the broadcasting station, which thus would have been able to cover all the territory within the footprint of the satellite. In practice, however, the major use of satellites has been in networking.

The development of direct broadcasting from C-Band satellites was nurtured by the backyard-dish movement, not planned by broadcasters. At about the same time in the United States and Canada, highly skilled handymen tapped satellite network relays to obtain regular television and pay-TV programs. Over the past six years, the private TVRO (television receive only) earth station has become big business. More than a million dishes are estimated to be installed in the United States and about 175,000 in Canada, most of them by people unable to receive any, or many, channels off the air. Today that spontaneous movement is being subjected to the scrambling of signals. The days of freely obtaining premium programming services from space appear to be over, but American dish owners will be able, under U.S. law, to receive the programs if they are willing to pay. The Canadian private satellite eight-channel service from Canadian Satellite Communications Inc. (CANCOM) is available on the C-band to dish owners who pay for descrambling.

At the 6/4 GHz level, satellite communication is steadily becoming a more important element in providing television and, in certain cases, radio to Canada's underserved and remote communities either by satellite-to-cable or paid satellite-to-home where cable is impractical. In the built-up areas of the country, however, the potential for direct broadcasting by satellite may be limited by the high penetration of cable TV or another new technology, fibre-optic transmission.

Fibre Optics

A representative of Telesat Canada told us at a technology briefing that "Fibre optics will dramatically increase the carriage capacity of terrestrial facilities without tying up scarce spectrum space. The continuing development of a Canadian fibre optics network will provide direct competition to Telesat's satellite facilities especially in high-volume, point-to-point applications. This will have an effect on the demand forecasting for the next generation of Anik satellites."

Communication by light-wave passing along a glass thread, with a wavelength of around a millionth of a metre, has enormous carrying capacity owing to its extremely high frequency level, far beyond the capacity of the bulkier coaxial cable. In the past 20 years carriage by optical fibre has come out of the laboratory and is rapidly becoming the choice of the telephone companies for long distance transmission — including transoceanic and transcontinental communication — between populous areas.

Saskatchewan's government-owned telephone company, SaskTel, has built one of the first large fibre trunk networks in the world. The system was started with the intention of eventually taking broadband transmission, capable of carrying all types of communication traffic (voice, text, graphics, television and video), all the way to the home. The trunk network, completed in 1985, links 52 of the province's largest communities with 3300 kilometres of fibre installation, distributing both television and other telecommunication services.

Bell Canada reports that by 1989 more than 8500 km of fibre optic cable will be in place in its territory, linking all major centres in Ontario and Quebec along the Windsor-Quebec, Toronto-Winnipeg and Toronto-Buffalo corridors.

Bell began using fibre in local access networks for business in 1985. Telecom Canada, the consortium of the country's major common carriers, plans to complete a 7100-km coast-to-coast fibre network by mid-1990. New Brunswick Telephone has announced plans for an intercity fibre network by the end of the decade. CNCP is also building a trans-Canada fibre connection.

In a field trial at Elie, Manitoba, fibre was used in the local telephone loops to subscribers in a rural community, bringing them voice, data, graphics and television. To become economic, fibre in the local loop — the line that links an individual subscriber to the nearest exchange on the network — must still overcome technological problems of loss of signal in switching from main lines to subsidiary lines and into the home. At present, optical signals must be converted from photonic to electronic energy to be switched or processed. Also, telephone and cable companies have huge investments in copper wire or aluminum cables which will only gradually need replacing.

The recent spurt in adoption of optical fibre for long haul was prompted by a new generation of fibre, monomode, which succeeded multimode. The new type reduced fading of the signal as it passes along the fibre, enabling longer and longer transmission segments without amplification. Optical fibre has the additional advantage over coaxial cable of being virtually immune to electromagnetic interference and does not itself create the possibility of interference with over-the-air transmission. It also makes for a secure communication system, being virtually impossible to tap.

Production: More Sophisticated Tools

Today's broadcasters try to retain a feeling of liveness, spontaneity and shared experience in radio and TV, but increasingly production occupies its own time and space. The first release from the constraints of 'going live' was a storage medium. In radio, almost from the start, sound recordings were an important part of programming; later whole shows would be recorded in advance. Magnetic tape recording added to the flexibility of radio production. Still, a good deal of radio, particularly local, remains live.

In television, although videodisc technology dates from the mid-thirties, there was no high quality storage medium available at the outset. Only when the videotape recorder (VTR) began replacing kinescope (a film recording of TV transmission) in the late fifties did television obtain a versatile medium for storing and editing. Banks of VTRs were used to release programs to Canadians on corresponding schedules in each of five time zones (but half-an-hour later in Newfoundland). The assembling and editing of programs became a steadily more elaborate process, whether commencing on film and then transferred to tape (as with most entertainment programs) or recorded from the camera on videotape (as with informational and sports programming). Relatively light cameras recording on tape in electronic newsgathering (ENG) brought new range and mobility to journalistic programming. The assembling and editing of taped material increased the variety of content that could be crammed into a news or documentary item. Reality became rather tame beside the jolts per minute that could be packed into television programming with the new technology.[2]

Along with improvement of the storage technologies came the development of the computer, bringing with it new electronic control processes. With the computer, too, came the digital language of computer communication.

At present, digital processing is just at the beginning of its sweep through studio equipment and controls. In telecommunication, digital switching speeds the routing of information without loss of quality; some transmission circuits are all-digital. In sound and image broadcasting, digital transmission is replacing analogue. That is, the digitally coded signal replaces the signal coded into a pattern of electromagnetic waves analagous to the sound or image being sent. In analogue transmission the signal loses quality as it is processed. In digital transmission the signal can be regenerated with no loss of quality. Today, analogue signals are converted into digital for limited purposes such as the application of special effects and then re-converted to analogue. Broadcast production has been likened to a few digital islands in an analogue sea.

Computer graphics have entered television production. Artists use an 'electronic palette' to create pictures onscreen to enhance programs. The computer graphic facility at CBC's *The Journal* cost $450,000; it released studio time previously devoted to camera recording of hand-painted graphics, thus helping to make way for production of another current affairs program, *Midday*. Technological advances in production are costly but enable the producer to do far more for the same amount of money.

Current affairs programs like *The Journal* on CBC English television and *Le Point* on CBC French television, and informational programming generally, make heavy use of satellite transmission to gather material. Transmission as part of the production process is well illustrated by *The Journal* and *Le Point* in their use of the double-ender, which is a television interview or panel recorded separately at the different locations of the participants, then edited into a seamless whole. Terrestrial microwave transmission has also been used from mobile units to studio as part of information programming. Today there is increasing use of the term satellite newsgathering (SNG), as mobile news crews with a direct uplink to a satellite send video reports back 'on the bird' from remote locations.

The lightness, mobility and versatility of the new production equipment and transmission links mean that program production is less dependent on expensive studio space.

Reception: Bringing it all Together

Radio led the way toward smaller, multiple-purpose receivers. From the big art deco table-top radios of the thirties, looking like the offspring of a match between a gothic arch and an automobile dashboard, we have come to the minisets of today's solid state technology. Yesteryear's massive radiogramophone, bringing two sources of audio entertainment together to share technology, has become the portable, double-speaker, ghetto-blaster radio with audiocassette tapedeck, or the jogger's delight, the tiny clip-on radio-and-cassette set with earphones. In the course of that evolution, FM reception was added to AM, bringing additional frequencies. The arrival of the pure-sound digital compact disc (CD) has added another audio technology that can be combined with radio reception.

Television reception technology has now started moving in the same multiservice direction. Cable, the converter and satellite transmission have greatly increased the number of channels that properly adapted television receivers can receive. Additional adapters permit the set to receive broadcast teletext, or print, data and graphics services which can come over telephone and cable lines or over the air. Most important of all, magnetic videotape recording has moved downstream from the production to the consumer level, in the shape of the videocassette recorder (VCR), giving the viewer a stronger role in programming. Paul Kaiser, manager of the quality control group at CBC Engineering Headquarters, told us in a technology briefing that ". . . the VCR has been the most important development since the beginning of TV because it has changed viewing habits."

Although the VCR was introduced in North America in 1975, its surge into the marketplace awaited the lower prices of the 1980s.[3] Since 1979 in Canada, VCR penetration has increased from less that 1 percent of households to nearly 40 percent of households, which is estimated to mean about 45 percent of the population. From its beginnings as a movie machine, the VCR is becoming a more interactive technology, whether viewers use its taped programs to exercise, to learn cookery, carpentry, car repair and other skills, to conduct bingo or other games, or to create home movies with a camcorder (camera-recorder). The VCR gives more control over what appears on the TV set by enabling the consumer to reschedule programs (time-shift them, in the jargon of the trade), or to choose quite different programming from a video library or store or from personal video archives.

The VCR is part of the collector technology of reception, bringing together content from different sources — broadcast and non-broadcast — to show on the screen. With music videos, it fosters convergence of sound and visual recording, a trend reinforced by the appearance on the market recently of stereophonic VCRs. With converter attachment, the VCR can become the central control of everything that appears on the screen, whether off cable, off air, or from videocassette. Some TV sets are now available with a VCR built into them. From a technical perspective the VCR capacities for progam choice and time-shifting could in future be built into the broadcasting network.

The Future of Broadcasting: "Far Beyond Its Present State"

Ever since the Aird commission, broadcasting inquiries have had to deal with a medium in transition. The three commissioners of 1929 wrote "We are of opinion that the question of development of broadcasting far beyond its present state, which may include television, is one of great importance and should be closely kept pace with so that the service in Canada would continue equal to that in any other country."[4]

The perils of trying to look ahead are innumerable, but once again not to be avoided, especially by a Task Force whose terms of reference cover "the remainder of the century". Technological predictions tend to be realized later rather than sooner or, as Vannevar Bush, U.S. scientist and adviser to presidents, put it, "We always overestimate the impact of a new technology in the short term and underestimate its impact in the long term."[5]

We have had the benefit of many research reports and other documents, as well as briefings by experts from the public and private sectors, to help us understand technological developments expected in broadcasting to the turn of the century and beyond. The period to the year 2000 is a relatively short time, only 14 years, but it promises to be crammed with technological change.

The expected improvements fall into three categories: quality, selectivity and scope. Leading the technical quality changes will be improvements in display technology including higher picture resolution. Increased selectivity is not just a matter of more channels to choose from but may come to include interactive networks. By greater scope, we mean new informatics services, such as electronic print, commercial exchange, and monitoring, in addition to radio and television programming.

The high-definition television (HDTV) quest in its present form is a Japanese initiative. Even by the turn of the century, however, HDTV is not expected to be the general standard of TV for consumers, according to a survey of broadcasting experts in Japan, North America and Europe.[6]

An end to technological limits on choice is linked to the concept of integrated broadband communications (IBC). As the first section of this chapter showed, the means of distributing broadcast content to the home have been greatly increased; now a new type of broadband network is being developed that could remove the remaining technical limits for most consumers. But it will probably not become generalized until after 2000, according to a study prepared for the Department of Communications[7] and it must be understood that there will continue to be other limiting factors. In the case of television services, for example, unless they are publicly funded, any service must attract a certain level of viewing and a substantial amount of commercial or subscriber support to survive.

The extension of the computer informatics world to the home has long been predicted, although one of Canada's leading authorities on cable engineering, Israel 'Sruki' Switzer, warned the Davey Committee, which reported in 1970, "I think the marketability of many of these services has been drastically overrated".[8] He was right. Since then, however, many informatics services have become well established in business, administration, the professions and industry, but they have fared poorly at the general consumer level. The economic profile of the cable industry prepared for this Task Force by Moss, Roberts and Associates provided an assessment of the financial viability of such services at the present time. They concluded that by the turn of the century they may be doing better, as long as technological improvement is accompanied by lower prices.[9]

Let us look first at quality improvements, then at advances in selectivity, that lie ahead. We will consider new electronic services under both headings.

Toward Higher Quality

The quest for higher resolution of display on television follows the achievement of higher fidelity sound on radio. Higher visual resolution is also critical to the introduction of electronic print and graphics services at the consumer level.

Radio

Although radio has led the way toward higher quality of reproduction it has some positions to defend and some further advances to make. Defensive action is needed to assure radio's quality of sound against what the CBC called an "electronic haze" over our cities. The Canadian Association of Broadcasters (CAB) also drew attention to "increasing electrical noise levels" to which AM receivers are particularly susceptible.

In radio production, progressive digitization will bring sound quality to the level of the new compact discs. Broadcasters will be under competitive pressure from other sources of audio to upgrade their production and transmission standards.

AM radio is fighting for its life against FM by introducing stereophonic sound. Unfortunately, a number of different standards, requiring different tuning, were left to fight for the marketplace in the United States and Canada. The Canadian Association of Broadcasters is now confident, however, that one of the standards will prevail and that this will encourage more consumers to purchase receivers capable of tuning AM stereo. At present, only about 14 percent of Canadian AM stations broadcast in stereo.

The use of satellite feeds and networking can increase the ability of local stations to provide high quality programming. But it can also lead to uniformity and homogenization through the same programming being heard everywhere.

The signal transmitted over the air on the frequencies now being used by FM and AM broadcasters, as formatted at present, will not be able to attain the quality of a compact disc. For that, special analogue formats or digital transmission, which uses more bandwidth than is available on the existing radio allocations of spectrum, would be required. Broadcasters would have to look to re-allocation of the FM broadcast frequencies, special analogue formats, or to satellite or cable for broader-band digital transmission paths, perhaps delivering programs to the home as cable pay-radio.

Some experts consulted by the Task Force noted the possibilities of direct-to-home radio broadcasting via satellite. This could bring the highest quality radio transmission to homes, vehicles and travelers beyond reach of city stations. The Federal Republic of Germany is introducing DBS radio but the cost of receivers is high. The utility of such a system in Canada has not been given much study to date.

Television

High definition television (HDTV), developed in Japan, will be a new viewing experience, bringing the resolution of the cinema's 35-millimetre film to the TV screen.

At the first HDTV Colloquium in Ottawa, Takashi Fujio of the Japanese Broadcasting Corporation (NHK) said:

> Prior to starting research and development of this TV system, extensive studies and tests were conducted regarding characteristics of the human visual system, physical requirements of the TV system needed to satisfy these characteristics, and the future television system expected and desired by viewers.[10]

The outcome is a widescreen television picture of great detail; for example, different actions on the various parts of a football field can be clearly followed without close-up shots. The screen can be a metre or more wide and still produce a high quality picture without discernible lines or impairment even to the closest viewers.

NHK plans to start HDTV broadcasting via satellite in three or four years. The Japanese system requires new technology for production, transmission, and reception. The receiver screen has 1125 lines, or about double the number displayed by the conventional NTSC set. Such a picture demands the transmission of a great deal more information, requiring about four to six times the bandwidth of conventional TV broadcasts. In Japan and elsewhere bandwidth compression and reduction techniques have been developed to lower the load. The camera and other equipment for high definition electronic production (HDEP) can replace film production, since they are of the same standard. The high bandwidth requirement of HDTV means it cannot be broadcast on the existing over-the-air channels, but needs the frequencies available on terrestrial and satellite microwave transmission and coaxial or optical fibre cable, or a combination of them. Two or more conventional cable channels would be needed for the HDTV signal and cable systems would need upgrading to carry them.

The original Japanese concept called for the introduction of an HDTV service that could be received only on HDTV sets. The programs would have to be transmitted separately to standard sets. As HDTV sets spread and services multiplied, the conventional sets providing NTSC services would be phased out, say by early in the 21st century. Most North American and European broadcasters oppose this course and plan for compatibility so that new high resolution broadcasts could be received in conventional form by those without HDTV receivers. This course was followed in the introduction of colour in most countries, with conventional sets able to receive the colour signal in black and white. Advocates of compatibility note that there are 600 million conventional television sets in the world; their owners would not be pleased with being excluded from HDTV programming.

The first step to improved display has already been taken, with the arrival on the market last year of 'smart' TV receivers. These use digital microprocessing to restore the image on the standard NTSC set. Although the first smart sets lack some features, they ultimately will provide a crisp, clear picture without ghosting, shimmer or discernible lines. The picture compares to HDTV in clarity, but not in detail, depth or subtlety, and it is not widescreen.

By 1990 we can expect 'smart' sets to be in widespread use. The likely course seems to be that high definition television itself could come in the period between 1990 and 1995 to mini-theatres, bars, taverns and public meeting places, after having been introduced in specialized industrial and educational applications (such as flight simulators). Then an up-market consumer demand might develop for HDTV using high-definition VCRs or videodisc players.[11]

High-definition display technology is lagging behind production and transmission technology. At present, projector-screens appear to be the best way to display HDTV. Experts are agreed, however, that flat panel displays will be required to make HDTV convenient. While a number of breakthroughs have been made in small-screen liquid crystal, electroluminescent and gas plasma display technology, expert opinion seems agreed that a marketable flat panel display suitable for HDTV will not be available for some years. The breakthrough to the mass market is expected to occur in the period 1995 to 2000, according to the survey of TV technologies mentioned earlier.[12] Technological advance over the next few years will almost certainly alter these projections, but they offer at least a sense of the direction in which technology has been moving for some years.

Both stereophonic sound and higher image resolution will be a challenge to cable transmission systems. A study for the Canadian Cable Television Association has noted that:

> Advances and improvements in receiver display technologies will place an increasing burden on the industry to deliver high quality signals. New technologies such as digital television, high definition television, and stereo audio will force cable systems to make major investment decisions on new distribution technologies. By 1990, these decisions will have to be made not only to obtain a share of new markets but also to maintain the traditional subscriber base.[13]

Nick Hamilton-Piercy, Vice-President Engineering of Rogers Cablesystems Inc., told us in a technology briefing: "In terms of broadcasting technology research and improvements, it is essential that Canadian broadcasters keep up to their American counterparts in introducing new and improved services. Otherwise they will most definitely lose Canadian listeners to superior-quality U.S. programming."

New Electronic Services

Compared to a book, a magazine, a newspaper or almost any other kind of printed matter, a television set is a poor format for reading. This may explain in large part the failure so far of videotex — interactive print, data, and graphics services — at the consumer level. While informatics has transformed the office, the factory floor, newspaper production, and many other activities where productivity and effectiveness can be increased with computer automation, it has yet to make much of a dent in home television. It is a lesson we learned in Canada the expensive way through Telidon. Large enterprises in the United States have also incurred heavy losses through the apparently premature introduction of videotex at the consumer level. The TV screen can carry only about half the data of a home computer screen in relatively low-definition characters. Information that can be found at a glance leafing through printed matter is often slow to access from database indexes. The TV set is also low on portability and flexibility compared to paper reading formats.

The legibility problem will be largely cleared up with higher definition. Display quality will begin to approach that of a magazine. The portability problem will be on the way to solution with flat-panel display. If developers eventually arrive at the 'cordless reading tablet', as it has been called (a wireless, hand-held, flat-panel display), today's paper reading formats may be in danger, which no doubt explains why corporations owning newspapers are major investors in the new technology.

Improvements in display technology come at a time when a new computer-literate, computer-friendly generation is arriving in the marketplace. This probably will give a fillip to introduction of the new technology and services.

Toward Greater Selectivity

The term 'home entertainment and information centre' is often used to describe the larger place in the home and the more elaborate facilities that will be needed to receive all the choices available in the expanding world of broadcasting (see Figure 4.3). With modular equipment, changes in one component do not necessitate changing the whole set; that is, the move to modular would be the reverse of incorporating the VCR in the TV set.

Greater selectivity is based, first, on additional delivery paths on cable, microwave, satellite, fibre-optics, natural spectrum and subcarriers; second, on new distribution architecture in the form of switched networks combining broadband and other services for efficiency, economy and consumer convenience. While technology may eventually be able to accommodate virtually unlimited choice, this does not mean that a corresponding variety of programming will be available.

Let us consider the selectivity question in connection with each of the main cultural services in broadcasting: audio, video and new electronic services.

Audio

New delivery paths and the beginnings of DBS radio and pay radio could expand selectivity in audio programming by the end of the century. It is expected to be some years before the extension of the AM band to 1705 kHz from 1605 kHz by international agreement. New AM assignments have already been made under a Canada-U.S. agreement reducing the protection required for station-coverage areas (contours). The demand for spectrum for AM, however, given its quality and delivery problems, is limited.

Radio broadcasting is still in the early days of exploiting the SCMO subcarriers available to FM stations. The possibility of using subcarriers on AM radio is still being examined. The vertical blanking interval on TV would also be available for audio, as well as data and graphics, if broadcasters wished to use it

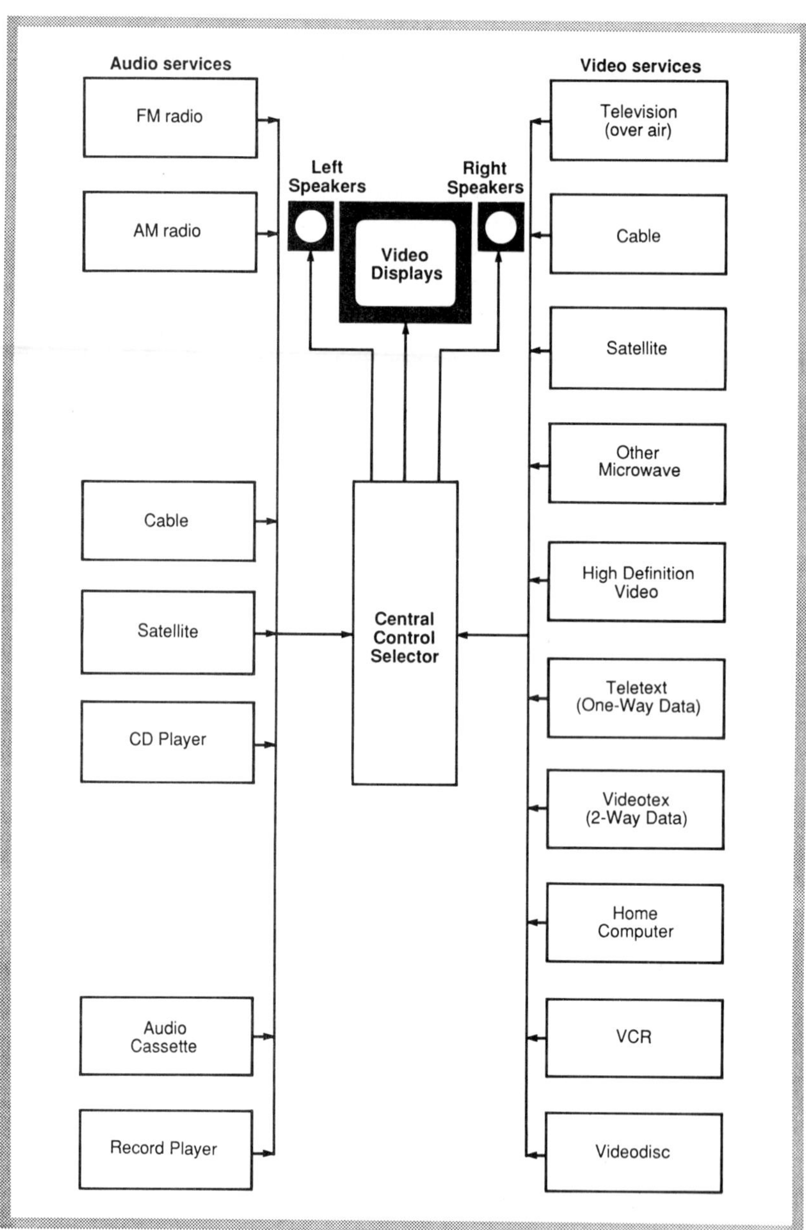

Figure 4.3 Home Information and Entertainment Centre

that way. The SAP channels are only now coming into being with stereophonic TV. Like conventional channels, subcarriers could be networked regionally or nationally for either general or selective audiences.

The major expansion of spectrum available for transmission of radio programming has come at the upper frequency levels set aside for communication satellites. This raises exciting possibilities for multichannel, super fidelity reception — comparable to reception from a compact-disc player — throughout the country. An example is being set by the Federal Republic of Germany where broadcasters are banking on the German taste for classical music to make a success of a DBS radio service due to begin late in 1986. West Germans, using a 60-centimetre dish and digital receiver together costing roughly $400 U.S., will be able to tune in 16 stereo channels of programming gathered from radio stations throughout the FRG. All-digital transmission makes the high quality possible.

The upgrading of cable systems may increase their use for digital or very high quality analogue radio transmission, at least of specialized programming. Digital radio cannot be accommodated on today's allocations on the natural spectrum and must go to either satellite, other microwave, or cable transmission. Assuming that households will tend to obtain modular reception equipment, including components that will do justice to digital and special analogue transmission format sound, wired radio and DBS radio could be features of the home entertainment and information centre. It will depend on the extent of demand that cannot be met by more conventional radio technology — and non-radio technology — at a lower price. Time will tell how important CD sound quality is to the consumer and whether it will erode the popularity of existing FM radio. We expect, however, that the portability of over-the-air radio and the miniaturized equipment that has been developed for its reception will assure it of audiences well past the turn of the century.

Video

The greatest pressure to increase technological capacity for choice has come, not in radio, but in television. There are limits to extending choice through multiplication of TV channels, which can be done by increasing either the number of delivery vehicles or the number of channels each delivery vehicle, such as cable, can carry. Both methods depend, like over-the-air broadcasting, on delivering all available channels to the receiver and using a switch on the receiver — tuner, dial, converter — to display the selected channel. At some point in TV delivery this may come to be seen as an awkward and wasteful method of increasing choice. Economies could be realized by tapping a much larger selection of programming at exchanges available to everyone on the network rather than a range of channels available at the set. This can only be done, however, if the broadband network is a switched system like the telephone network.

By contrast with the tree-structure of the cable system, the star-switched network of the telephone has lines which radiate from an exchange to the subscribers (like a star), and interexchange connections that radiate from main

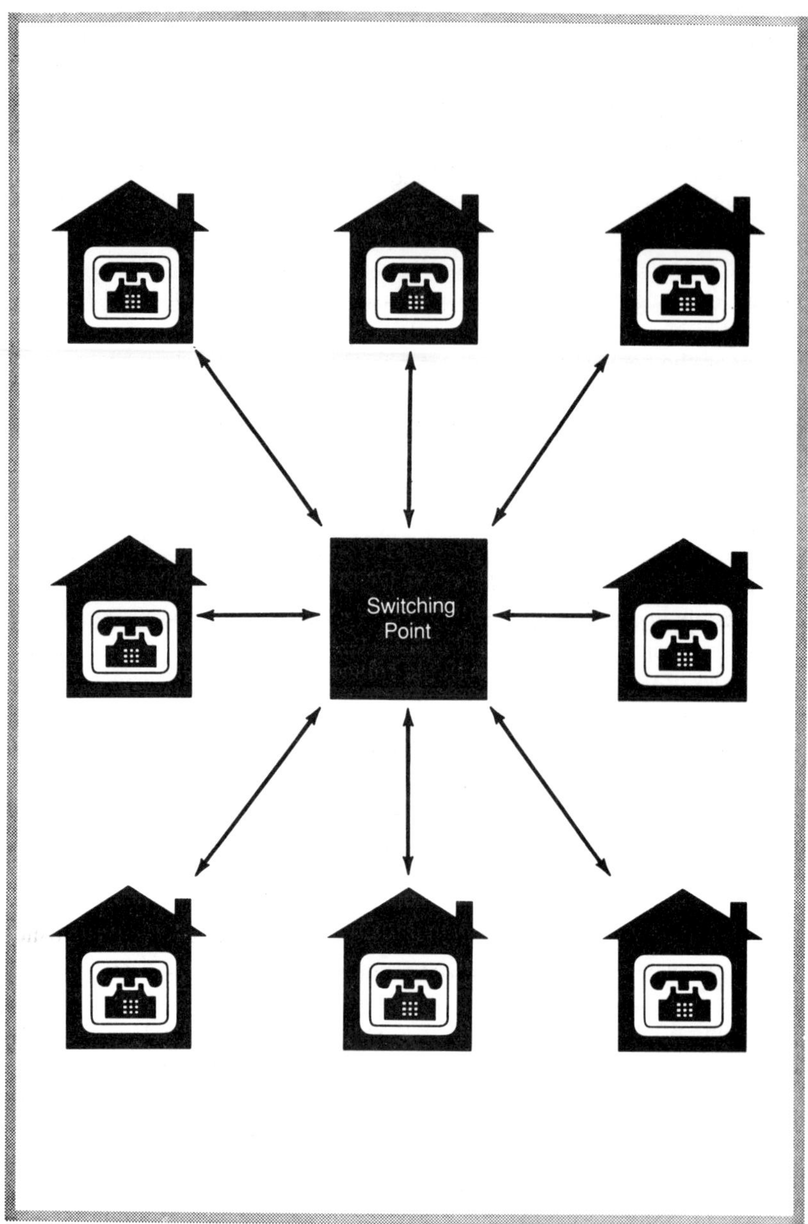

Figure 4.4 Telephone System Star–Switched Network

to subsidiary exchanges as shown in Figure 4.4. Together, all the exchanges on a telephone network make up an almost infinite number of circuits. The network is interactive, in the sense of giving subscribers access to each other. But at present it is not broadband; it cannot carry TV.

The broadband star-switched network could remove technical limits on choosing programs, thereby obviating the need for costly scrambling and descrambling as a means of controlling reception. Although demand for two-way, or interactive, service is at present limited, it may increase with variety of content, especially if new electronic services are added. By retrieving programs on the network, the recipient would trigger microprocessing controls that handled billing; there would be no need for scrambling, since retrieval by one person on the network would not mean that the signal was available to all.

Comparing switched networks and over-the-air broadcasting, the 1971 report of the Telecommission, *Instant World*, said, "Whereas the capacity of a switched network can always be increased by adding circuits and switching apparatus, the number of radio frequencies is limited by the nature of the radio-frequency spectrum."[14]

Broadband networking all the way to the home has long been forecast, but only with the development of fibre optics and associated technologies did actual experiments and field trials begin. Only with the concept of aggregating all services — voice, data, text, graphics and video — in digital format, affording economies of scale, did confidence develop that interactive broadband networks might someday reach most or all homes. Saskatchewan was the first large jurisdiction in the world to start translating principle into practice.

Cable networks have been under some pressure from VCRs, potential satellite services, and the minicable services known as MATVs (master antenna television) and SMATVs (satellite to master antenna television) to offer more services. These issues are addressed later in our proposals concerning the redefinition of broadcasting and in the review of public policies affecting the distribution system. Cable capacity for interactive operation, under which subscribers would be able to send messages upstream to the headend to receive services, is expected to be introduced by many major cable companies by 1990. Upgrading of amplifiers and other equipment could accommodate stereo and high quality video transmission. In cooperation with the telephone companies, cable systems have the potential to simulate the advantages of the star-switched network.

In the United States, multichannel multipoint distribution systems (MMDS) and low power television (LPTV) have been used to provide additional variety or a substitute for cable. A multipoint distribution system uses terrestrial microwave to broadcast several channels directly to receivers equipped with special converters; its range is limited to about 15 miles. It has been suggested that high definition television might be introduced in some Canadian centres by MDS; for example, from the CN Tower in Toronto. Low power TV is used in the United States as a distinct form of licensed service.

The possibility of a distinct programming system delivered by satellite-to-home has often been discussed. The extensive series of studies on DBS completed for the Department of Communications in 1983 concluded, however, that even a distinctive service would probably be received by most urban dwellers over cable, rather than direct from the satellite.[15]

Invitations for comment on the report brought strong opposition from nearly all quarters to the possibility of government backing for a distinct DBS programming service to compete with existing public and private services. Most objected also to putting a DBS service on the 14/12 GHz, or Ku band, in addition to existing services on the 6/4 GHz, or C band. A departmental working group agreed with the main thrust of the representations: that DBS should be supported as a complementary service reaching sparsely settled areas, not as a new programming service for the whole country.[16]

Expert opinion is divided on the future of point-to-multipoint satellite relays within the broadcasting networks. On one side, this is seen as the ideal way to bypass complex routing and switching of program signals by transmitting them directly from studios to local broadcasting stations or cable headends. On the other side, the carrying capacity of fibre optics is seen as undercutting this advantage. The Task Force received briefings from experts in Bell Canada, Bell-Northern Research, and the Department of Communications, and in addition gathered documentation on plans for fibre optic systems. Considering all these sources together, it appears that the telephone companies will have overcapacity of long distance and interexchange fibre links by the early 1990s. They may also have access to optical switching systems which would further improve the capacity of fibre to carry video. The reduction of telecommunication traffic on the satellites is already leaving satellite systems with unused capacity. Fibre and satellite systems may be competing in a few years to sell unused capacity to broadcasters.

In Canada, satellite relays will always be important to take broadcast programming and other communications to places where the cost of extending optical fibre or any other kind of cable would be prohibitive. Some parts of our population will always be dependent on DBS, rather than satellite-to-cable, if they are to have multichoice broadcasting at all.

To sum up the evidence we have received on present trends, some applications of the switched star network in broadband video transmission to the home seem likely in the 1990s. Business and institutions appear likely, because of their heavy use of telecommunications, to be the first to be 'fibred up'. A universal broadband network to all subscribers is not expected until after the turn of the century. In the meantime, cable seems likely to continue increasing its share of TV transmission to the home, carrying more channels and acquiring limited two-way capacity for greater selectivity. These trends toward interactive broadband transmission will be reinforced by the introduction of new electronic services. Satellite communication will be important to broadcasters in reaching remote and underserved communities, in program production, perhaps in direct-to-home radio broadcasting, and at least for some years in network distribution. But it would require some new development to resuscitate earlier predictions of extensive direct-to-home TV broadcasting by satellite.

New Electronic Services

The new electronic services have tended to be always the bridesmaid, never the bride at the numerous marriages of communication and computer technology in broadcasting.

We suggested earlier that improved display quality in TV receivers and a more computer-friendly generation may give electronic publishing and other text and graphics services a better run than they have had so far. As the trend to having two or more TV sets in households continues, extra sets might become increasingly available for the new electronic services. They could be used in conjunction with the broadcasting system or, with a modem (modulator-demodulator), they could be used to tap databases available on the telephone system. The disadvantage of the phone network is that, unless the subscriber has two lines, the phone is tied up by using it for text and graphics services. Owing to its relatively narrow bandwidth, the phone system can be annoyingly slow in transmitting all but the simplest graphics. These shortcomings have been overcome in telecommunication facilities for business premises in the integrated services digital networks (ISDN) which are being built. The ISDN offers considerably more bandwidth than the ordinary phone line. It is by extension of these networks to the home and their eventual conversion into broadband that technically unlimited video choice will be offered to the home.

Cable operators expect that only the larger cable systems will introduce some of the new informatics services by 1990. Young professional people are showing interest in information services downloaded to home computers, which use the storage capacity of the PC and are periodically updated. Other types of services are classified ads, other information services, security and alarm monitoring, transactional services, and electronic mail. Cable operators have tended to regard informatics as small potatoes in the near future but nevertheless a potentially important contribution to operating margins. The CRTC's proposed cable regulations, removing most restrictions on advertising on non-programming services, should encourage development.

Introduction of teletext is problematic. Teletext is a one-way technology, making about 150 to 200 continuously broadcast pages available to be grabbed and held on screen by viewers with decoders, if the vertical blanking interval is used; or it may be broadcast on a full channel, making a much bigger selection available. There is now a North American standard for teletext and the prospect that new receivers will be equipped to tune in the VBI. Television broadcasters may come to see teletext as a useful supplementary print and graphics service for giving program information, sport scores, news, weather, and other information.

The term videotex covers the interactive services, some of which, such as games, could be downloaded to the viewer in the manner of full-channel teletext; that is, the viewer selects from a continuously broadcast series of programs which then require home computer power to operate if they are interactive. Such a service has so far not enjoyed financial success. The more conventional videotex model involves the use of databases from which viewers can retrieve the information or software they seek, whether it be flight schedules, cooking recipes, or advertisements for big ticket items like houses and cars, which can be described and pictured on the screen, or smaller items shown in less detail. Transactional services are a natural extension from classified ads, enabling the viewer to order goods or services.

Competition between telephone and cable videotex services could spur their development. But the brightest future for such services at the consumer level probably awaits the availability of high quality, convenient display devices on a universal, switched, broadband network at the right price.

Implications of Third-age Broadcasting

The third age of broadcasting may eventually release us from the constraints of channel and schedule. The VCR has shown the way to consumer choice beyond channels and scheduled times; the switched network, with its banks of current and stored programming, could incorporate this capacity in broadcasting itself. Videobases and audiobases could take their place beside databases on the broadband network. Scheduled programming would come on stream as it does now, but be receivable either at the scheduled time or later; there would be no need to delay one type of program in order to show another in real time, as happens now with news and sports events.

What we do know is that at present technology has already broken the link between the provision of scheduled programming services by electronic means and their transmission over the air. The services we have traditionally referred to as broadcasting, drawing our terminology from the earliest technology, now need to be redefined. This redefinition which is necessary to ensure clarity and fairness in the regulation of the Canadian broadcasting system is addressed in Part II of this Report.

Should the public's two-way power of control and selectivity increase so much in the future that the role of broadcasters in scheduling services is fundamentally altered, it will be necessary to review again the basic premises of broadcasting policy. In the meantime, what lies ahead is evolution rather than revolution. We cannot be sure today what new turns that evolution may take by the end of the century.

Coverage: People and Geography

Broadcasting service of some kind now reaches virtually all Canadians by radio and television. The introduction of new delivery technologies and services increases costs, fragments audiences, and introduces user payments. In broadcasting, as in other domains of the information society, the gap is widening between those who can afford to take advantage of the new technology and those who cannot; between the information rich and the information poor. As a result, coverage issues have become social, as well as geographical.

Broadcasting technology policy has to be reconsidered in light of the continuing public interest in ensuring "to the people of this country, without regard to class or place, equal enjoyment of the benefits and pleasures of broadcasting", to recall Prime Minister Bennett's remark quoted in Chapter 1.

A system of highly differentiated services which may be paid for in bulk (basic cable service) or in detail (pay-per-channel or pay-per-program) makes the payments system of broadcasting more flexible. Future choices of technology in such a system, in combination with regulatory policy, will help determine how accessible broadcasting services are to remain to all Canadians.

So-called free broadcasting, supported entirely by revenue from taxes or advertising, predominates in radio and likely will continue to do so; but it now accounts for a minority of television viewing, if one takes into account payment for cable service, and probably will continue to diminish in importance. As cable displaces over-the-air, we see the introduction of a new balance of financial support between revenues from taxes, advertising, and users, together with uneven coverage. While 80 percent of Canadian households were in cabled areas in 1984, only 76 percent of that group actually subscribed, corresponding to just under 61 percent of the whole population.[17] A portion of the 25 percent who did not subscribe may simply not have wanted cable or any other additional service. Another, albeit very small proportion, may have had satellite dishes, MATV or SMATV, or illegal hookups. But it also must be assumed that a portion simply could not afford cable, an assumption which is supported by survey research.[18] Within the cabled group there are further gradations according to number of channels provided, and different tiers of paid service.

The incidence of cabled homes in Canada is quite uneven, ranging from 40 percent of households in Newfoundland to 82 percent in British Columbia, and from 50 percent in Quebec to 68 percent in Ontario.[19] There are many reasons. French-speaking Quebec tended to be less cabled in part because it did not have the same thirst for American programs as English-speaking areas. More sparsely settled provinces are less cabled than more urbanized provinces. Other technological advances, such as satellite service and VCRs, offer some compensations to non-cabled areas. Nevertheless, part of the differential in coverage between different parts of the population must be ascribed to income level, even for basic service.

Eventually, if switched-star configurations were to succeed today's tree-structure systems, the degree of deprivation of people excluded from the network — or from broadcasting service on the network — could be greater. On the other hand, if the reach of the new broadcasting network were to correspond to the reach of the telephone network, then coverage would be almost universal and the only issue would be at what cost to consumers.

Representatives of Bell Canada told us that CRTC regulations on cable technology at present hinder the extension of fibre optics to the home. In other countries, such as the United States and Britain, telephone companies can lease bandwidth to cable companies. In Canada the telephone companies must lease the whole cable to cable companies and cannot lease any of it back. Under another regulation, the cable companies must own amplifiers and dropwires on the cable system, even when they lease the cable itself from a telco. These rules stand in the way of joint telephone-cable ventures to combine video and other telecommunication carriage on the same optical fibre into the home. Bell contends that without such economies of scale it would not pay to go the last mile into the home with fibre.

Another approach is the creation of hybrid systems linking the switching capacity of the telephone network to the broadband transmission capacity of cable systems. An example is a type of pay-per-program television now coming into operation in the United States — known as automatic number identification (ANI) — in which subscribers can order the scheduled showing of a movie by dialing a special number.

As more and more television and video services are available only on cable, policy regarding basic service — how it is to be assured, what it is to include, what it is to cost — will become increasingly important if Canada is to retain Prime Minister Bennett's goal of TV broadcasting coverage "without regard to class or place". Many billions of dollars — consumers' and taxpayers' dollars in the end — are at stake in coming decisions as to the kind of networks we should have.

Quality: Producer and Consumer Interests

A considerable range of public policies affect technical quality at the production, transmission, and reception levels of broadcasting: standards requirements, consumer protection laws, research, technology assessment, industrial development, spectrum conservation and management, and regulatory requirements imposed on licensees. The advances in both quality and selectivity of the third age of broadcasting will impose heavier demands on the policy maker: there are more services to be maintained at high quality standards.

Broadcasting and other types of telecommunication have become more entwined. Broadcasters leasing their subcarrier channels are in the telecommunications business. Cable carriers providing community channels and organizing new electronic content services are in the broadcasting business. Telesat Canada wants to be in the broadcasting business by organizing a direct-to-home satellite service. Fibre optics in the telephone system would tend to bring broadcasting into the carriage regime of the common carriers; that is, the broadcaster would be a programmer and perhaps distributor, but not a transmitter of programs.

At the same time as the various technological media of communication are converging, the different cultural media have begun to make use of the new networks. That is, print (newspapers, magazines, books, and so on), art reproduction, all types of imaging systems from cinema to the whole range of video are, or are becoming, in part broadcast or electronically transmitted media.

This technological and cultural convergence may be followed by an expansion of new technical and cultural services. A combined political and managerial effort by governments, broadcasters and interested parties will be needed to sort out the problems and give effect to both a strong Canadian presence and freedom of expression.

The problem of standard-setting, basically the problem of assuring that what is sent can be received, is becoming more complex. If standards are set too soon, they may curb optimum development. If they are not set soon enough, the marketplace may be plunged into confusion and standards may simply be imposed by the biggest firm.

In the case of AM stereo, the Federal Communications Commission in the

United States refused to set a standard in view of industry disagreement on the best system. Various technologies were left to fight it out in the marketplace, which meant that receivers for AM stereo were either incompatible with one another or had to be capable of receiving several different types of signals. In either case the marketplace — the consumer — was left with the expensive, time-consuming and difficult task of deciding among the contenders on highly technical matters. The same confusion slopped over into Canada, with the DOC deciding to regard AM stereo as being still at an experimental stage. Today two contenders are still in the ring, one standard having been adopted by North American car manufacturers, the other by American broadcasters serving the largest audiences. Failure to agree on an AM stereo standard has been a setback to the effort of the AM stations to compete with FM, hence to the public interest in diversity of sources of programming.

The adaptation of television sets to receive signals off cable is a difficult area of standard-setting. Today, many subscribers have up to three converters if they receive all possible types of service. Subscribers have often found unexpected limitations, such as inability to tape a pay-TV program while watching an off-air program, and so on. Duplications are costly and foul-ups annoying to the consumer. As systems become more complex, with more elements to be made compatible with one another, greater effort will have to be devoted to agreeing on standards. High definition television will introduce its own standard-setting issues.

Standard-setting is also important from a production point of view. Agreed standards give smaller firms, and countries, a chance to compete in a world which otherwise would tend to allow big firms to corner markets by imposing their own standards. A standard for high definition electronic production, for example, is of particular interest to Canada. It would encourage exchange of programming with many countries rather than leave this country to share common standards with only the United States. Without a world standard, Canadian production has to be converted to foreign standards to sell abroad, and foreign production has to be converted to be sold in Canada, adding to the expense and thus limiting the flow.

There are, of course, limits on what Canada can achieve, owing to its inability to compete in the manufacture of consumer products in the electronic field. Nevertheless, there are areas of strength in the Canadian transmission and production equipment industries. The Canadian market for consumer products is by no means negligible. These strengths can be played in international standard-setting if the Canadian effort is concerted.

Spectrum conservation and management constitute a long established service which formed part of the core of the new Department of Communications when it was established in 1969 and remains one of its most important components. Our interest, because of our terms of reference, is in seeing that broadcasting receives its proper share in spectrum allocation. We have noted in technical documentation and in our consultation with experts that there has been a good deal of speculation about releasing spectrum from broadcasting to other purposes as television transmission tends to move from natural spectrum to microwave relays (terrestrial or satellite), to cable, and to optical fibre. This movement away from the airwaves will continue. Indeed, many stations or rebroadcast transmitters now appear to be on the air only to be picked up by cable, since for jurisdictional reasons they wish to be considered broadcasters under federal regulation. This is a wasteful practice. But broadcasters will tend to stick to the present regime until an equally stable one, respecting their interests, is designed to replace it.

Economic and Industrial Policy

The expansion of third-age broadcasting services could involve billions of dollars of investment in production, transmission, and reception equipment and software. The home entertainment and information centre, including non-broadcast equipment, may soon represent the equivalent of the investment in an automobile if the centre is fully equipped with micro processing, aural, and visual elements. Like automobiles, the home centres will come in a range of prices and models.

Virtually all broadcast reception equipment sold in Canada is imported. There appears little prospect that HDTV receivers will be manufactured in this country. At the other end, Canada's production equipment industry, which has some small but important niches in the market and exports the larger part of its production, faces the challenge of digitization. In the middle, Canada's industrial presence in transmission equipment, through giants such as Northern Telecom and Bell-Northern Research, as well as other world class companies, is strong but also faces strong competition. Important employment, trade, and balance-of-payments problems will thus be associated with the third age of broadcasting.

The introduction of new production equipment sometimes brings with it industrial relations problems. The ENG camera is an example, with jurisdiction being claimed by both the union that holds jurisdiction in film production and a different union which holds jurisdiction in the use of electronic equipment. Complicating matters, opposite managerial decisions were made by the largest French-language private station, on the one hand, and the CBC English network, on the other. The issue is being studied by the Canadian Labour Relations Board.

Putting New Technology to Work

We have tried in this chapter to take a look at technology in a more hard-eyed than wide-eyed way. So many futuristic scenarios have been put forward as sure things in the past generation, only to evaporate in face of reality, that we felt it best to err on the side of caution. It appears obvious that some federal policies in recent years have sought to press technology on the public before there was a call for it. Such was the case with Telidon, which started out as a world-leading transmission code for sending graphics but was over-extended into a whole consumer videotex system. Canadian leadership in the development of direct broadcast satellites (DBS) may have prompted governmental over-optimism, or at least premature optimism, about their coming into service, although a number of countries made the same error. There is always the danger that enthusiasm for a particular technology — interactive cable, satellite-to-home, broadband switched network — will lead to the premature use of a technology, or to the use of an inappropriate balance of technology, at a particular time.

Technology will always raise dilemmas. On the one hand, policy makers in broadcasting may want to put the emphasis on program content. Especially they may not want to see money diverted from programming to equipment, since Canada is at a disadvantage in meeting costs of program production by comparison with the United States. On the other hand, this country cannot afford to lag far behind the United States in adopting new technology; otherwise, it would abandon to the United States the provision of services based on the new technology. This was the case in television itself, again in colour television. In the same way, Canada has to start planning now in order not to leave Canadians dependent on the United States for high definition television when it comes.

We have been able to consult a large number of studies of broadcasting technology undertaken in recent times for the Department of Communications and for various industrial groups. The government will also have the advantage of the Telecommunications Policy Review in considering the technological side of broadcasting policy. We would like to identify two challenges that we feel should be addressed by additional policy initiatives in the near future.

Cultural Impact of New Broadcasting Technology

The DOC has made considerable recent progress toward giving priority to cultural considerations in the formulation of broadcasting policy. Nevertheless, the body of knowledge on which it can draw is limited. There could be merit in an initiative that would bring together the various governmental and non-governmental interests in broadcasting with a view to creating an independent research program to investigate, assess, and advise upon problems in cultural communications, including broadcasting.

It is one thing for the *Broadcasting Act* to declare that "the regulation and supervision of the Canadian broadcasting system should be flexible and readily adaptable to scientific and technical advances".[20] It is another to make sure that all the relevant authorities connected with broadcasting have sufficient grasp of the implications of scientific and technical advances to carry out the intent of the legislator.

The importance of such a culture-and-technology initiative is only heightened by the distinct characteristics of our French and English and Native peoples communities, and the special needs of our multicultural society. In several parts of this Report it will be seen that the new channels of radio and television broadcasting that are becoming available will be of particular importance in meeting the wishes of minorities in taste, culture, heritage, ethnic origin and so on — minorities to which all Canadians belong in some measure.

Regional and Political Impact of New Broadcasting Technology

Readers will notice that the spirit of this Report is to treat the federal and provincial governments and local communities as partners in broadcasting, all with roles to play and the right to participate in the formulation of broadcasting policy. The government has already embarked upon a process of consultations with the provinces. Our only purpose here is to urge that the eighties and nineties must not, like the seventies, be characterized more by confrontation than progress when the various orders of government get together to consider telecommunications and broadcasting. Too much is at stake in the technological renovation on which our telecommunication systems are already embarked.

Conclusion

For Canadian broadcasting, technology has always been a two-edged sword. On the one hand, it has allowed instant communication across this astonishing landmass. On the other, it has allowed the broadcasting system of another nation almost unlimited access to Canadians.

The present exotic level of technological development, and especially the science-fiction-like future that is predicted by many, is sometimes seen as the end of the road for national control of broadcasting. Has technology become the ultimate de-regulator? The technologically-induced challenge to the cultures of the entire globe by American programming is unquestionably real; but does it follow that those who dare resist it have not learned the lesson of King Canute?

We are not prepared to agree. To understand the implications of technology is one thing, to surrender to it another. The fact that culture is at stake cannot be overlooked. If anything, the decades-old responsibility of the Canadian broadcasting system to help Canadians remain Canadian is more crucial than ever.

In fashioning the response that is needed now to the new wave of foreign programming borne by satellites, we must be wise enough to use both the same old-fashioned tools and the new ones. The technologies which have flooded Canada with foreign programs can also be turned to the Canadian purpose. We cannot keep American programming out of Canada, and it would be futile to try. In the past, beginning with the early days when the CBC alone brought U.S. shows to Canadians in remote parts of the country, we have absorbed the American programming into our broadcasting system and we will continue to do so. What we must concentrate on now is making realistic, effective provision for more high quality Canadian programming to be produced and exhibited by our broadcasters and, through new satellite distribution mechanisms, to be distributed to every corner of this country.

The appropriate objective for public policy in the face of the technological challenge from American television is to offer all Canadians compelling home-made alternatives so that they will choose to resist the foreign seduction. It is to this end that most of this Report is addressed.

Notes

1. Canada, Royal Commission on National Development in the Arts, Letters and Sciences, (Massey Commission) *Report* (Ottawa: King's Printer, 1951), p. 27.
2. For discussion of 'jolts' in TV programming see Morris Wolfe, *Jolts: The TV Wasteland and the Canadian Oasis* (Toronto: James Lorimer, 1985).

3. Nordicity Group Ltd., *Film/Video Retail Study*, research study prepared for the Department of Communications, Ottawa, 1985.
4. Canada, Royal Commission on Radio Broadcasting, (Aird Commission) *Report* (Ottawa: King's Printer, 1929), p. 8.
5. Quoted in Carrol Bowen and Michel Guite, "Program, Products and Services", in *High Definition Television Colloquium '82 Proceedings*, vol. 2 (Ottawa: Department of Communications, 1982), pp. 3.1–3.3.
6. For a major survey of higher resolution TV, see Nordicity Group Ltd., in association with CBC Engineering Headquarters and Kalba Bowen & Associates, *An Assessment of Current and Future TV Technology and Its Impact on Canada*, research study prepared for the Department of Communications, Ottawa, 1985.
7. T.L. McPhail and B.M. McPhail, *Telecom 2000: Canada's Telecommunications Future* (Calgary: The University of Calgary, 1985).
8. Canada, Senate, Special Senate Committee on Mass Media, *Report*, (Davey Committee), vol. I, *The Uncertain Mirror* (Ottawa: Information Canada, 1970), p. 215.
9. Moss, Roberts and Associates, Inc., "An Economic Profile of the Canadian Cable Industry", study prepared for the Task Force on Broadcasting Policy, Ottawa, 1986.
10. Takashi Fujio, "High Definition Television System of NHK", in *High Definition Television Colloquium '82 Proceedings*, vol. 2 (Ottawa: Department of Communications 1982), p. 1.3.
11. Scenarios derived from an international survey of experts are to be found in the Nordicity study *Current and Future TV Technology*.
12. Ibid.
13. Nordicity Group Ltd. in Association with Moss, Roberts and Associates, *Project 90: New Directions* (Ottawa: Canadian Cable Television Association, 1985), p. 11.
14. Canada, Department of Communications, Telecommission, *Instant World*: (Ottawa: Information Canada, 1971), p. 12.
15. Department of Communications, *Direct-to-home Satellite Broadcasting for Canada* (Ottawa: Minister of Supply and Services Canada, 1983), c. 5, "DBS System Models".
16. Canada, Department of Communications, Working Group on Direct-to-Home Satellite Broadcasting for Canada, "Report", Working Paper (Ottawa: The Department, 1984).
17. Statistics Canada, *Cable Television*, cat. no. 56-205 (Ottawa: Statistics Canada, annual publication).
18. Paul Audley & Associates, *Viewer Choice of TV Services in Ontario* (Toronto: Ontario Ministry of Transport and Communications, 1984).
19. Canadian Broadcasting Corporation, *TV and Radio: Figures that Count, 1985* (Ottawa: CBC, 1985).
20. *Broadcasting Act*, R.S.C. 1970 c. B-11, s. 3(j).

Chapter 5

Programs and Audiences

Programs and Audiences

Ever since the founding of public broadcasting in 1932 our federal government has tried to make sure that audiences receive a variety of programs of high standard and of predominantly Canadian origin, first on radio, later on television. As a result, Canadians have always attached cultural value to television and radio programming, nowadays treating their own sitcoms and rock music as though they were significant statements of national purpose.

In Chapter 3, we describe the paradoxes of a major activity that must be treated for some purposes as cultural, but for others as industrial. A similar kind of tension runs through our examination of programs and audiences — what is "culture" to one person is mere "entertainment" to another. Our American neighbors, the most prolific producers of pop culture in history, have often found the attitude of Canadians baffling. In the United States, federal policy and the broadcasting business only intersect at the margins of program-making.

The American treatment of all commercial television and radio as essentially entertainment adds a particular poignancy to Canada's principal regulatory problem — maintaining a reasonable balance between foreign content and domestically made programs. It simply is not a problem Americans have to think about. One of the more difficult things about writing this Report has been to find a sensible way to interpret what programming of "high standard" means, and how it differs from less rewarding or lower quality material. We have a pretty good sense of the differences when period drama is compared to a game show. But there is a large grey area in between, and judgements fall easily into the subjective and impressionistic.

Our primary purpose in this chapter is to provide a descriptive profile based on both commissioned and existing research of what programming is available on Canadian television and radio and how audiences respond to this programming — their 'tuning behavior'. We take a brief look at the types and sources of programs and factors affecting program supply or availability. On the audience side we look at the size of audiences for certain kinds of programs, as well as at their demographic makeup — age, gender, education and so forth.

However, it is impossible not to be struck by the patterns our data reveal about TV viewing in Canada. Almost half of all English television viewing is of 'drama' — and by drama we mean here not just 'serious' plays, but most of what is usually considered entertainment programming, — movies, situation comedies, soap operas, police shows and so on. And yet only two percent of the drama seen on English-language television is Canadian in origin. (In this chapter, references to English-language television include American as well as Canadian stations.) There is too little such programming and as a category it is therefore too little watched. Other Canadian programs do get heavier viewing. But even so, only 29 percent of viewing of English-language television is spent on Canadian programs, and that drops to only 24 percent in prime time. English Canadians, in other words, are virtual strangers in television's land of the imagination.

What has sometimes been described as a crisis in English television programming must not however be allowed to eclipse important developments in French television and in radio in both languages. Although the French television stations have been more successful at getting their dramatic act together, even here the majority of viewing is of foreign drama. Most francophone viewing of programs of all types is of Canadian programming, although about one-fifth of this is of English-language programming.

In documenting these and other facts we have been forced to be selective. Program and audience research is a vast and complicated field and we of course have not had the space to provide a complete review even of our own commissioned research on the topic. However, we take a general look at how broadcasters define and assess both their audiences and their programming, and then deal separately with issues in television and radio respectively.

First of all we can gain some sense of how quickly each generation of consumers accepts new broadcast technologies by referring to Figure 5.1. Penetration expressed as percentage of households is plotted against the time line by decade. Television, FM radio and colour television all show initial introduction quickly followed by very rapid growth, almost to saturation, when growth levels off. Cable grew very quickly through the 1970s but its growth has slowed somewhat in the 1980s. In the projections given for the period from 1985 to the year 2000, converters and especially pay-TV grow at a modest rate compared to the optimistic growth rate predicted for VCRs.

Measurement: The Yardsticks of Success in Broadcasting

The basic measure of success in commercial broadcasting is popularity — sheer audience size. The more listeners to a station or viewers of a program, the more advertisers are willing to pay. Determining audience size sounds simple enough but in fact requires a sophisticated battery of statistical techniques based on information from small samples of just a few hundred or a few thousand people, much like public opinion surveys. Audience measurement has become a big business in itself and the information it provides to broadcasting clients is as precious as stock market quotes are to investors.

Audience measurement differs from public opinion surveys in that audiences are normally measured not for their opinions or attitudes to programs but for their recorded behavior — what they actually listened to or watched during a particular period, along with the respondent's personal characteristics. The traditional method of measurement is to ask people belonging to a representative sample to record their listening and viewing in diaries. While this continues to be the preferred method in radio, television diaries are being supplanted by electronic metering. TV sets in selected homes are connected to a microprocessor and through the telephone line to a mainframe computer which can monitor viewing every few seconds.

Whether these headcounts are derived from diaries or meters, they provide broadcasters with three kinds of yardstick: ratings, shares and reach. Researchers sample audiences to find out what percentage of the whole population

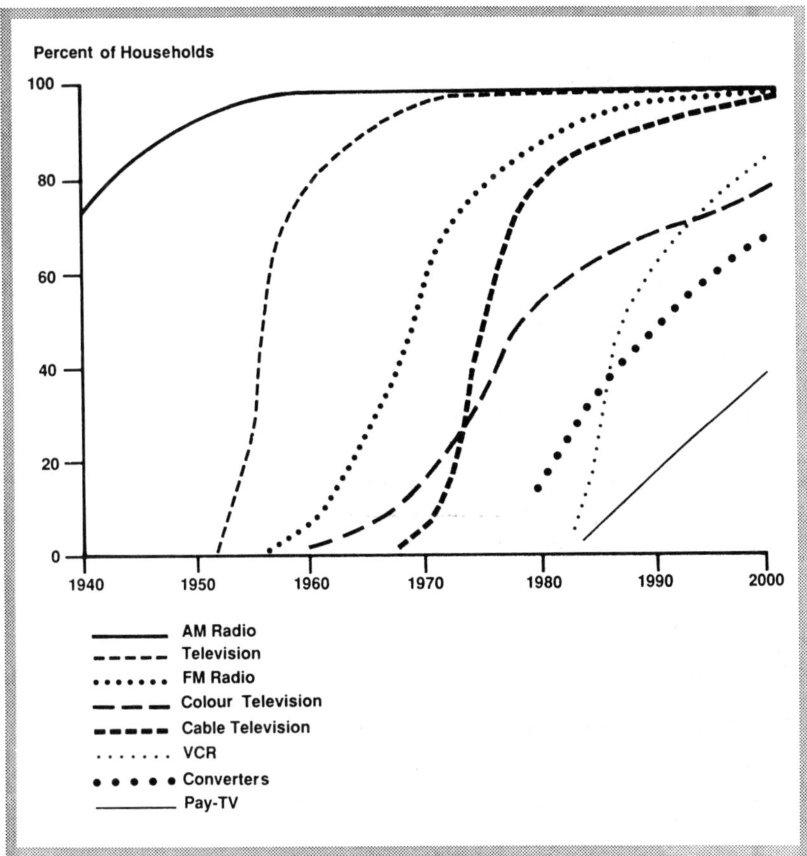

Figure 5.1 Growth in the Penetration of Viewing and Listening Equipment

Note: All material in figures in this chapter is based on information compiled by Barry Kiefl, Stan Staple, Roger Kain and Jim Stanage of CBC Research, and reported in" TV/Radio Audience and Program Trends and the Future", a report prepared for the Task Force on broadcasting policy,September 1985. Raw data for these compilations were supplied by A.C. Nielsen, with additional data from BBM and Statistics Canada. Interpretation of these data in the present chapter does not necessarily reflect the views of the original authors.

is tuned to a particular station, network or program, thereby establishing its rating. The same sets of figures also serve to measure audience share, the percentage of all those actually listening or viewing who are tuned to a particular program. Finally, a broadcaster's reach is expressed as the number of people who tune to a program, station or network at least once in a specified period, say a week.

In the past few years, television broadcasters and their advertisers in particular have become somewhat dissatisfied with these methods. For even when audience figures are broken down by gender, age group, education and occupation, they still tell us little beyond the fact that the television has been tuned to a certain channel for a certain length of time. They do not say whether audiences actually watched the set, or whether they chatted, did the dishes or made telephone calls. They certainly do not say whether audiences enjoyed the program; they do not indicate whether the program with the second or third rating at a particular time might have placed first if scheduled some other night. Nor do they explore the possibility that audiences might want programs entirely different from those they receive, only watching what is on because they prefer television to homework or walking the dog.

Much more attitudinal research is now being done in both the public and private sectors to answer these 'qualitative' questions. Public broadcasters in particular are concerned with a broader range of information than has been available in the past about what selected groups think of their programming. Public broadcasters also want to know about year-round television viewing patterns, not just those measured in the fall and spring 'sweeps' — the periodic surveys of selected television households to determine the sizes of audiences to particular stations and networks carried out by audience measurement companies.

But private broadcasters have also shown a renewed interest in understanding not only the numbers of viewers they are attracting, but also the values and lifestyles of their viewers, especially the values they attach to certain consumer commodities. As a result, one of the most studied groups in the viewing (and listening) population is the baby-boomer generation (roughly 25 to 40). They are part of a significant demographic trend — the relative aging of the Canadian population. By the year 2000, for example, the over-50s will have risen to 29 percent of the overall population from today's 25 percent. More and more, broadcasters will have to take account of the priorities of this aging population in their programming decisions.

Several broad patterns in audience behaviour continue to remain fairly stable. One of the most important of these is the average weekly consumption of radio and television. As shown in Figure 5.2, total radio and television weekly tuning has changed very little over the period from 1976 to 1984, when Canadians on average listened to 19.9 hours a week of radio and watched 23.6 hours of television. In television, these fall sweep averages are a little higher than those for the full year, which include the summer season when viewing usually drops off.

In this same period, a much larger number of television stations became available in most parts of Canada through widespread cabling, extended off-air coverage and the appearance of several newly licensed stations. Because the average viewing hours have remained stable, many individual stations have seen their viewing shares reduced by the increased competition. This is the phenomenon usually referred to as 'fragmentation'.

On the radio side, the picture of stability conceals a striking shift in listening from AM to FM radio. In the 1976-1985 period, the AM listening share dropped from 83 percent to 59 percent, while the FM share rose from 17 percent to 41 percent.[1] Among the reasons most often cited are the more stable signal quality of FM, and its ability to transmit music in high fidelity stereo. The

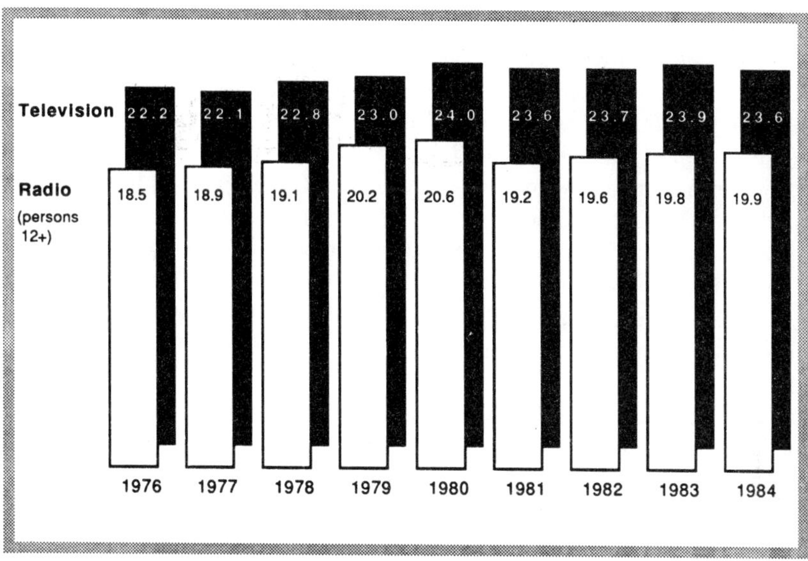

Figure 5.2 Weekly Hours Spent Listening to Radio and Watching Television 1976–1984

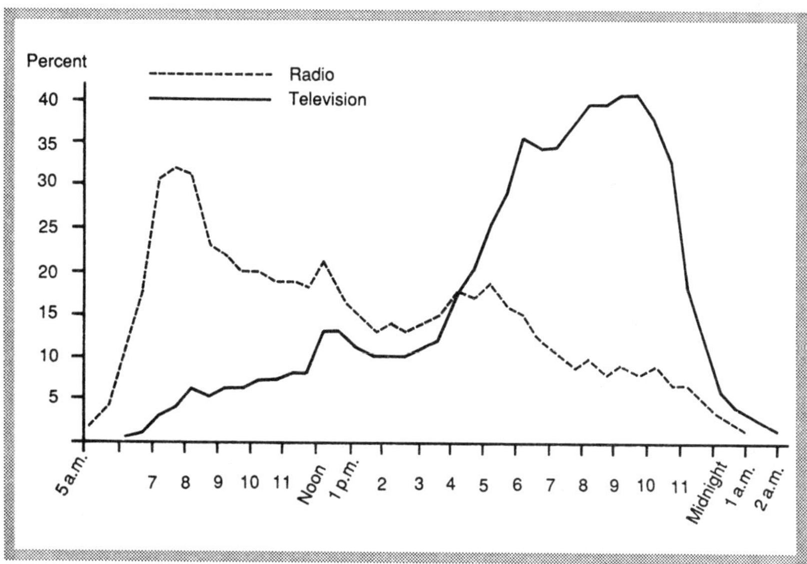

Figure 5.3 Fluctuations in the Size of Audiences on Average Weekday 1983–1984

financial repercussions of this shift are explored further in Chapter 16.

In Figure 5.3 we see one of the fundamental differences between the way Canadians use radio and the way they use television. Radio's peak and off-peak listening periods are almost the mirror-image of those typical of television. Radio captures its biggest audiences as people start their day — getting up, eating breakfast, driving to work — and has secondary peaks at lunchtime and in the late afternoon. Almost one third of all radio listening takes place outside the home, much of it in cars — hence the reference to the late afternoon peak as the 'drive' period.[2]

Television use, by contrast, climbs rapidly after 4 p.m., when children tune in, and on into evening prime time. The peak period from 7 p.m. to 11 p.m. when the entire household may be watching accounts for 45 percent of the total time TV sets are turned on. The CRTC's definition of prime time — 6 p.m. to midnight — is not the period when peak viewing is normally measured for research purposes.

The CRTC uses this extended definition for its calculation of Canadian content quotas. This eases the burden on television broadcasters, who can average their Canadian contribution over the six hours and still schedule a great deal of American entertainment programming in what we use in this Report as the peak viewing period, namely 7 p.m. to 11 p.m. (unless otherwise indicated). This is more than just a semantic difference, since the 6 p.m. to 7 p.m. time slot is devoted by almost all stations to the local or 'supper hour' news which of course counts as Canadian content. The 11 p.m. to 11:30 p.m. time slot is also frequently devoted to news, and helps boost overall content averages, although total viewing drops off very sharply after 11 p.m.

Consequently, the availability of Canadian programming cannot be examined without taking two factors into account: the kinds of programming at stake and the times when programs are scheduled. An objective presentation of the facts and figures about Canadian programming runs some risk of obscuring these points. Despite regulatory treatment that minimizes such distinctions, a game show cannot be said to have the same cultural weight as a comedy, drama or adventure series. And a program scheduled when few people are watching — though it may provide a service for a certain minority — has much less significance than if it is scheduled in peak viewing time.

The established peak-time radio and television tuning periods may be changing slowly under two separate influences. The first, primarily affecting TV, is the impact of new technologies like the videocassette recorder or VCR. The VCR allows viewers to record programs off-air at one time and view them at another, a technique known as 'time-shifting'. There is some dispute about the long-term effects of time-shifting, although its use is still marginal, accounting for only 2.2 percent of all TV viewing time.[3]

Demographic change, and particularly shifts in occupational and leisure time patterns, may ultimately have a more lasting effect on tuning behavior. Staggered hours, increased ability to work at home, the changing age and family structure of the population and the changing roles of the sexes will all play a part. However, the most recent data show that women, who are still more homebound than men, tune to both radio and television 25 percent more each week than men. This fact combined with the greater consumer spending discretion of women has traditionally made 'women 18 to 49' the favored audience target of advertisers.

Fitting Programs into Formats and Categories

If the measurement of audiences is a complex undertaking, the classification of programs and the analysis of their content pose even greater problems. On the one hand the way programming is segmented and presented on radio and television has been changing over the years. On the other hand there is little uniformity in the way program categories are defined for purposes of research, regulation and commercial sales.

In the early days radio and television broadcasters addressed a diverse audience with a wide range of different programs at scheduled times. Each type of program — news, public affairs, comedy and so on — was distinct and came on air at the promised time. A move away from the traditional program patterns started on private radio in the 1950s. Broadcasters realized they could reach target audiences for their advertisers more effectively if they programmed according to a specific musical format — top 40, easy listening, middle-of-the-road (MOR) and so on — which would suit a segment of the general audience. Private radio thus became almost entirely formated. Formated radio guarantees that listeners interested in a certain kind of music can tune to a station at any point in the schedule and find satisfactory content.

When formating is left under market control the tendency of radio stations is still to program for the largest audience: on private AM radio, the MOR musical format is prevalent. In an attempt to increase the range of musical formats on private radio the CRTC requires FM licensees to program according to a distinctive format differing as much as possible from other stations in the same market. Even with these restrictions individual stations in the less popular formats will choose music with the greatest appeal.

Television has more recently followed the example of radio with the advent of satellite-to-cable services. Many of these subscriber-based services — such as MuchMusic and TSN, the Sports Network — are called 'specialty services' because they concentrate on a particular kind of program content, rock music and sports in this case, even though they try to appeal to a fairly wide cross-section of the audience. Wide appeal is more typical of general interest cable networks such as movie channels. Canadians also have access to third-language services such as Chinavision and Telelatino. They contain a number of different kinds of program content, although they are targeted to a particular minority audience. The practice of programming a service to appeal specifically to a demographic, ethnic or linguistic minority is often referred to as 'narrow-casting'.

Major differences still exist between the conventional station and the satellite-to-cable network, just as differences are quite audible between 'easy listening' and rock radio formats. But the audience fragmentation created by increased competition, and the huge losses suffered even by many of the larger American satellite-to-cable networks, exert a steady pressure on the specialty networks to look for ways to win market segments that would normally lie outside their target audience.

The major broadcasting institutions — the CRTC, CBC and others — use different schemes for classifying news, situation comedies, soap operas, sports and so on, which seldom match one another. These discrepancies, which can make comparing viewing data difficult, are not the result of lack of good will or ingenuity. Different users have different reasons for classifying programs in a certain way: CBC's set of 15 or 16 categories used for budget control as opposed to research are based on administrative distinctions, unlike the much more complicated CRTC typology that was developed for research purposes.

Many programs, moreover, do not lend themselves to straightforward classification. A program intended for children may have elements of both current affairs and drama or variety, and therefore fit logically into two or three categories. A documentary with dramatized portions is more than just a documentary, but not on the same footing as a dramatic series. This then opens up a new category, the docudrama. The term 'drama' itself, as we noted earlier, is used in the television context to denote far more than just plays. On the expanded definition, police shows like *Night Heat* and sitcoms like *Snow Job* are usually classified as drama, along with virtually all movies.

Research data involving program types or categories should therefore be treated with circumspection. In tackling this problem, we have relied on some broad and generally accepted distinctions. Television programs can be divided into the two generic categories of information programming and performance programming, designed to cover everything but sports. These are more or less self-explanatory — news and current affairs go under information; drama, comedy, variety and music under performance. This still leaves some grey areas, such as religious programs and documentaries made outside the context of news and current affairs. Still, the components of journalism on the one hand and artistic endeavor on the other make the basic idea clear.

This broad distinction also corresponds to the areas of greatest success and greatest concern in television: Canadian information programming is not only in plentiful supply but also gets large regular audiences, whereas in most of the performance areas, especially serious drama, both availability and viewing are very low. Other program categories will be described below as necessary.

Television

Two basic measures are used to analyze consumption patterns in television: these are the availability of programs and viewing of programs, which correspond to the notions of supply and demand. Availability is usually expressed as either number of broadcast hours, or a percentage of total broadcast hours, indicating the amount of a certain kind of programming made available by a given station or network. Viewing is also expressed in terms of hours or a percentage of total hours devoted to a program type, or to all the programming available from a certain source (such as a Canadian station or all American networks).

Program Availability and Viewer Choice

The number of available hours of television can be looked at from the point of view of a typical or average viewer (usually understood to be at least two years of age — "two-plus" in the jargon — unless otherwise indicated). Networks or classes of stations (CTV affiliates, CBC owned stations, the three commercial US networks, etc.) — usually termed 'station groups' — each transmit a certain number of hours of programming in a given period. But each station group is of course not available in every part of Canada. Global, for example, is pretty much restricted to southern Ontario, TVA stations to Quebec. Furthermore, individual viewers do not all have the same means at their disposal for capturing signals. Those who have basic cable usually have more channels at their disposal than those who view strictly off-air, and those with a cable converter usually have more available again than basic cable subscribers.

By calculating the number of viewers who can receive the various station groups in each locality, we can derive two interesting averages. One is the average number of English-language stations, including American stations, available to all Canadians. Based on data for the 1984 calendar year, the average Canadian receives 7.5 stations.[4] The other is the total number of hours of television available to the average viewer in a given year, on a full-day basis. Based again on data for 1984, Canadians have available to them on average about 52,000 hours of programming of all types from English-language station groups. A corresponding average of 20,700 hours of French-language programming is available to francophone Canadians. (see Chapter 8).[5]

Like all averages, these figures conceal as much as they reveal. First of all, there are significant variations in the average number of English-language stations available on a provincial basis. In 1984 residents of only two provinces, Ontario and British Columbia, were able to receive more stations than the national average. Residents of Newfoundland, Prince Edward Island, New Brunswick and Quebec had the least choice, with only about four stations from which to choose. Generally speaking the larger the market the more stations are available. This is both because larger markets are more heavily cabled and because they can support more local originating stations.[6]

The second factor that deserves comment is the total number of broadcast hours available to the average viewer in a year. Some Canadians can of course receive considerably more than this total, others have considerably less available, depending on where they live and whether they have cable and converter. Now, we noted earlier that the average Canadian watches 22 or 23 hours of television a week. That means about 1100 hours over a full year. It would appear therefore that the proverbial average Canadian has a wealth of English-language programming from which to choose, by comparison with the time actually devoted to viewing — a ratio of about 50 to 1.

What this figure conceals, however, is the huge amount of duplication of programming in the 50,000 or so hours, and the great discrepancy in availability between various types of programs. Duplication occurs *within* station groups. That is, when viewers in a single market can receive, say, two CTV affiliates, or both a CBC owned station and a CBC affiliate, then all the hours from both stations are counted as available to that group of viewers, even though the schedule on the one CTV or CBC station may be almost identical to the schedule on the other.

Duplication also occurs *between* station groups, as when CTV carries the same mini-series as ABC or NBC at exactly the same time. It is no coincidence that viewers so often find this kind of overlap in the TV schedule, especially in peak time. The reason is a CRTC cable regulation referred to as 'simultaneous substitution'. The CRTC requires of the larger cable operators that whenever a local station and a distant station carried on any one system are both transmitting the same program at the same time, the operator must substitute the local signal for the distant one so that subscribers receive the local signal over both affected channels.

Subscribers also receive over both channels all the commercials that go with the local broadcast. This is crucial, because part of the rationale for this 'simulcasting' rule is protection of the commercial revenues of local broadcasters. Broadcasters have turned this very much to their advantage by deliberately scheduling their procured American programming as much as possible at the same time as the scheduled US network telecasts of this programming (even though the CRTC rule is not specifically aimed at foreign distant signals).

In most larger Canadian markets, where cable penetration is high and the three commercial U.S. networks are available, simulcasting injects a great deal of duplication into the total available program hours on English-language television. One index of this is the discrepancy between the proportion of program hours available from American stations across Canada — 47 percent of the total — and the proportion of viewing time, which is only 33 percent of the total.[7] The difference between these two figures is largely accounted for by the fact that much of that same American programming was actually watched (unwittingly in many cases) by cable subscribers on a Canadian station.

Clearly, then, a substantial difference exists between the sheer number of hours available to viewers and the actual choices they can exercise among different programs. And if we further sub-divide the total available hours by program type and by nationality we find still other constraints operating on viewer choice. These factors will be discussed below.

Program availability can be considered from another perspective: in terms of the relationship between diversity of programs and choice of channels or stations in a given market. It would seem logical to assume that the greater the number of stations the greater the diversity of programs and therefore the greater the choice to the viewer. This is not, however, the case. Apart from the reasons just noted, the nature of commercial television is such that as more stations enter a market and competition increases, broadcasters tend to respond by relying more not less on mass-appeal entertainment programming. A 1980 study found that program diversity measured using a specially devised index did not increase in proportion to increases in the number of stations in a market. Instead, as additional stations were added each new one tended to add less to diversity. In short a kind of law of diminishing returns set in. It was also found that the addition of an American station to a market was the least effective way of increasing program diversity. The study concluded that CBC stations and affiliates provided greater diversity and a more even balance of each type of program than the private station groups.[8]

Availability and Viewing by Program Category and Nationality

One important measure of the success of a particular program type or category is the relationship between the proportion of broadcast time devoted to it and the proportion of tuning or viewing time devoted to it. Figures 5.4 and 5.5 indicate this balance for the major program categories in English and French television. From this we can see that TV is essentially an entertainment medium: in calendar year 1984, 54 percent of the 51,900 English hours available to the average Canadian and 50 percent of the 20,700 hours of French-language programming available to the average francophone viewer, were in the performance category: drama (i.e. adventure, comedy, soaps, etc.), variety, music and quiz shows.

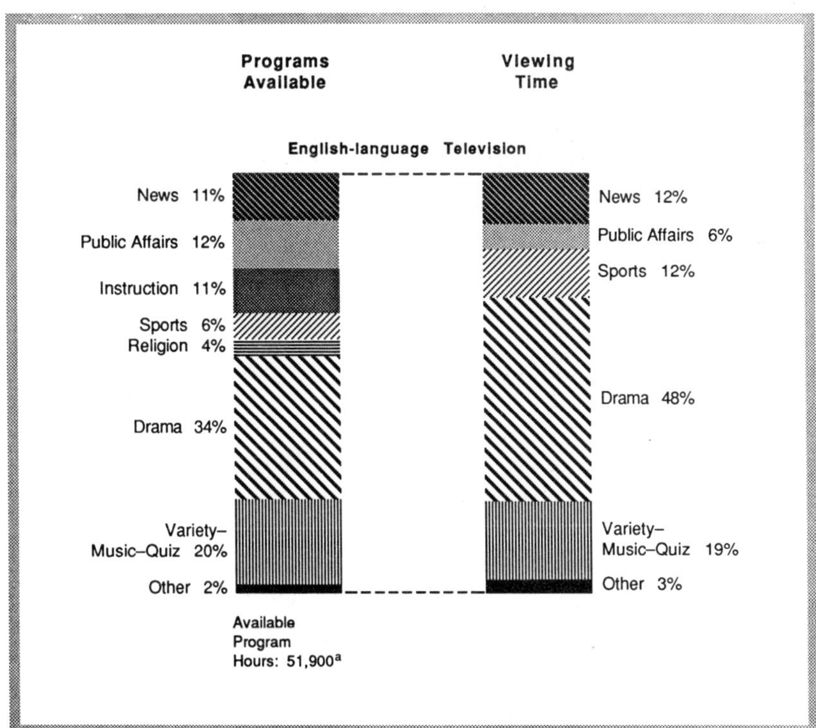

Figure 5.4 Availability and Viewing of Various Types of Programs, 6a.m.–2a.m., Monday–Sunday, Calendar 1984

Note: a. Available hours of English–language television refers to the aggregate of programs aired by all English–language television stations available in Canada during the 1984 calendar year. Programs carried by individual stations or networks are weighted according to the number of anglophone and francophone Canadians, aged 2–plus, able to receive them.

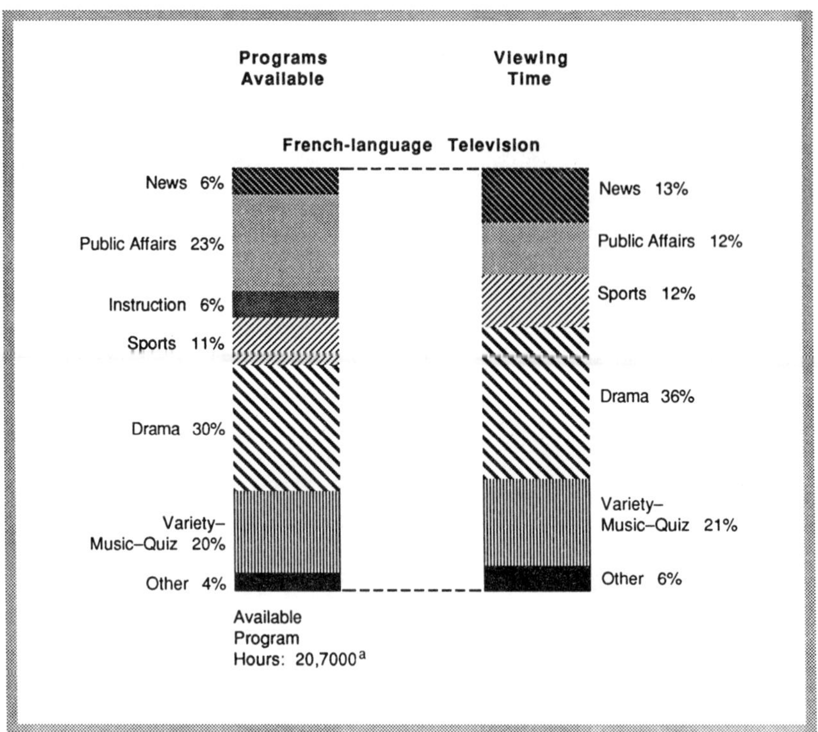

Figure 5.5 Availability and Viewing of Various Types of Programs, 6a.m.–2a.m., Monday–Sunday, Calendar 1984

Note: a. Available hours of French–language television is defined as in Note a. to Figure 5.4, except that programs aired by individual French–language stations or networks are weighted according to the number of francophones only, aged 2–plus, able to receive them.

Apart from the extent to which drama dominates all other categories, the most striking thing about what we see here is the extent to which actual viewing of drama exceeds the proportion of available drama programming — 48 percent versus 34 percent in English and 36 percent versus 30 percent in French. Viewing of news and sports is equal to or exceeds availability but at 12 percent of viewing, sports is still overwhelmed by drama. On the English side, religion and instruction account for 15 percent of all broadcast hours but were barely measurable as a percentage of viewing.

These contrasts are even more marked if we look at the other two most important considerations to the broadcaster and policy-maker — availability in the peak period from 7 p.m. to 11 p.m. and nationality of the available programs. Figures 5.6 and 5.7 show that the availability and popularity of drama both go up sharply in peak-time viewing of both English and French stations. Fully 60 percent of peak viewing of English and 49 percent of peak viewing of French is accounted for by drama.

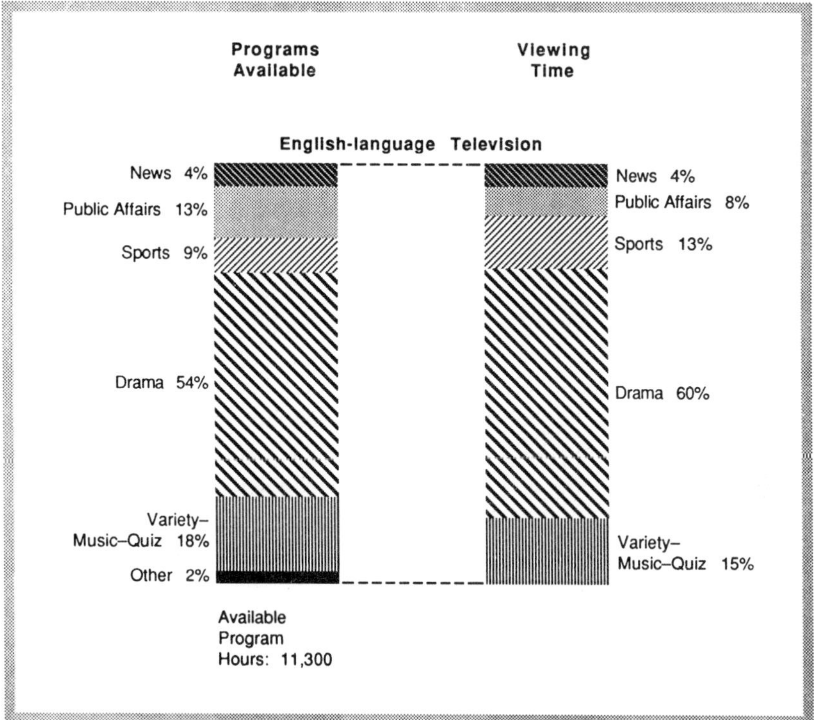

Figure 5.6 Availability and Viewing of Various Types of Programs, 7p.m.–11p.m., Monday–Sunday, Calendar 1984

the primary entertainment medium are foreign. Although some foreign programming shown in Canada originates in Britain, France and other European countries, by far the most common source is Hollywood or the three American commercial networks, ABC, CBS and NBC. Canadian access to American commercial programming is unique in the world. In fact, owing to the duplication of American programming between originating American stations and Canadian stations which also carry it, Canada's largest anglophone cities have more American TV on tap than comparable cities within the United States itself.[9]

Figures 5.8 and 5.9 show the balance between Canadian and foreign programming across the full viewing day, again for 1984. The figures for all programs indicate that on English-language television, the viewing of Canadian program content corresponds closely to its availability. That is, Canadian-origin content captures 28 percent of programming hours available and 29 percent of the actual viewing hours. On French-language television, Canadian viewing outstrips Canadian availability by a considerable margin: 57 percent of the programs available are Canadian, but 68 percent of the viewing is of Canadian content.

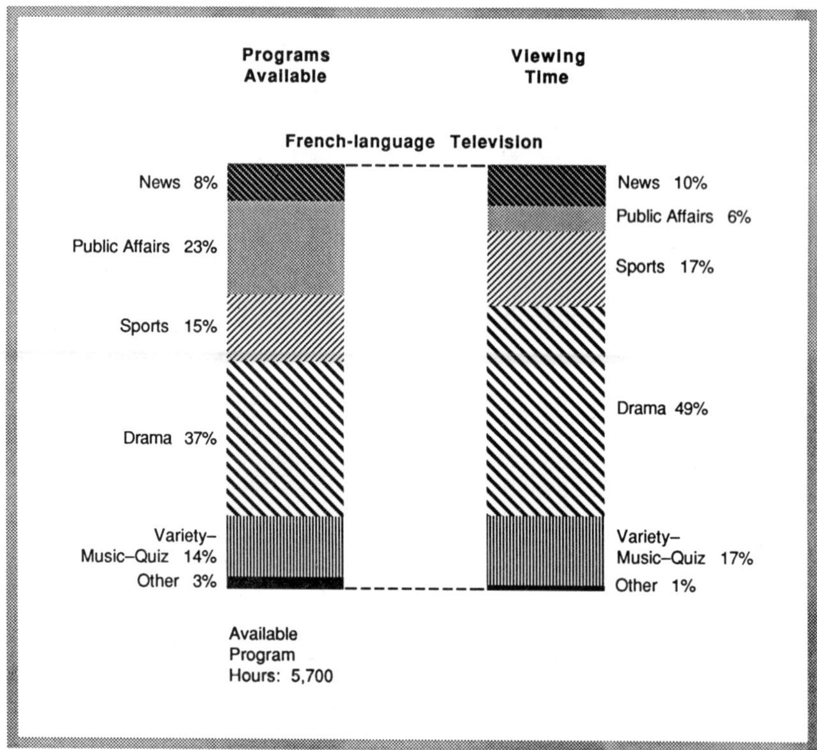

Figure 5.7 Availability and Viewing of Various Types of Programs, 7p.m.–11p.m., Monday–Sunday, Calendar 1984

A more revealing picture emerges when we look at individual program categories. Under English drama we see that no less than 98 percent of all available programming is foreign. This corresponds one-to-one with the viewing side, where 98 percent of time spent with drama goes to foreign programs.

As we suggested earlier the idea persists that this wholesale allegiance to foreign drama is an English-Canadian issue, that with the tradition of homegrown product like the téléromans, Quebec's answer to the 'soap' and the sitcom, French-speaking Canadians are somehow insulated from foreign influences. As Figure 5.9 shows, this is not the case. Francophone viewers watch proportionately twice as much Canadian drama as availability would suggest — that is, 20 percent of their drama viewing is of only 10 percent of the available programs. What this means, however, is that francophones are still spending 80 percent of their all-day drama viewing of French stations watching foreign programs, many of which are dubbed in French.

The peak-time ratios for English drama (Figure 5.10) are not all that different from the all-day ratios. Francophone viewing of Canadian drama (Fig. 5.11) maintains its two-to-one ratio over availability, while viewing of foreign programs decreases; but francophones still spend well over two-thirds of their peak-time viewing of French stations on foreign drama. This is a good deal lower than the corresponding 96 percent for English, but it is a far cry from the

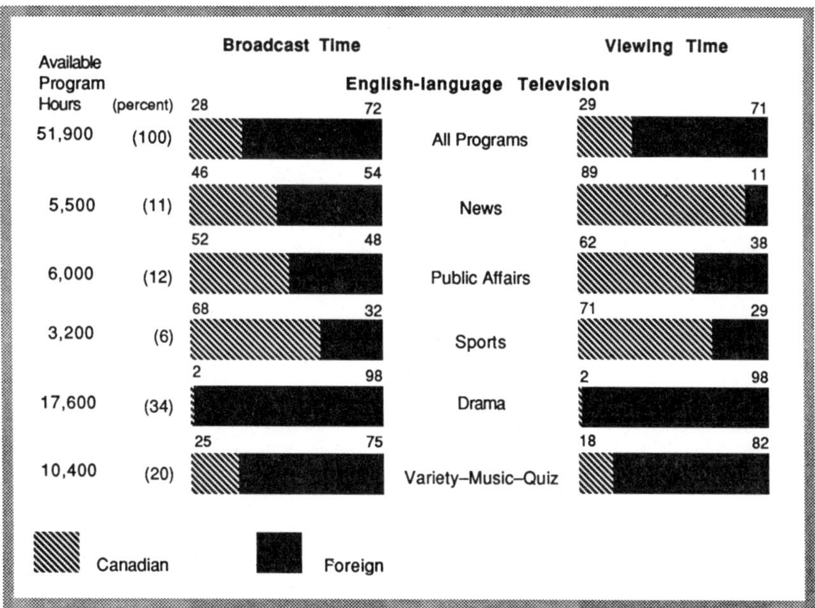

Figure 5.8 **Proportions of Broadcast and Viewing Time for Various Types of Canadian and Foreign Programming 6a.m.–2a.m., Monday–Sunday, Calendar 1984**

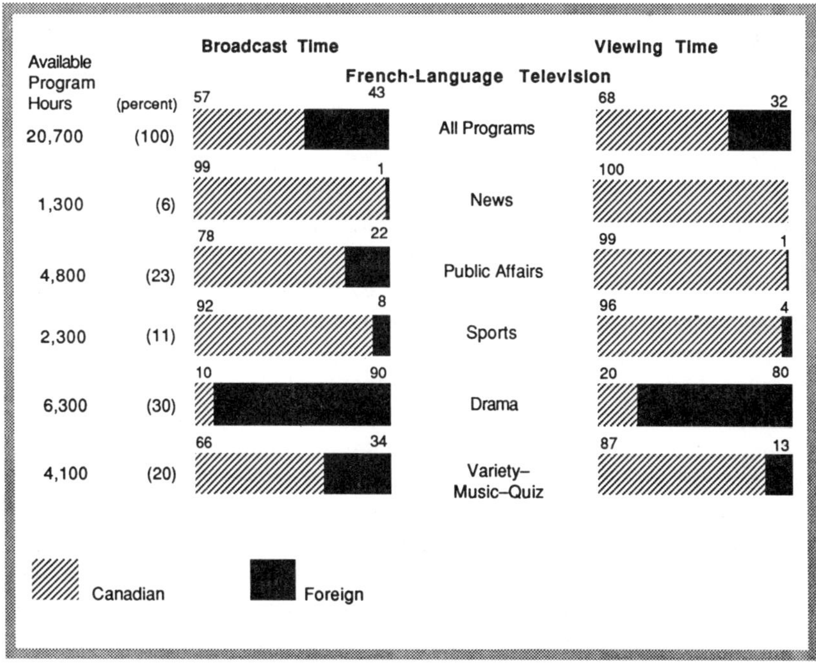

Figure 5.9 **Proportions of Broadcast and Viewing Time for Various Types of Canadian and Foreign Programming, 6a.m.–2a.m., Monday–Sunday, Calendar 1984**

idea that Quebec is so enthralled by its own téléromans as to have no interest in *Dynasty* or *Dallas*. It should also be noted, however, that almost half of this francophone viewing by adults of foreign drama is accounted for at present by movies, largely American movies, rather than by soaps like *Dallas*.

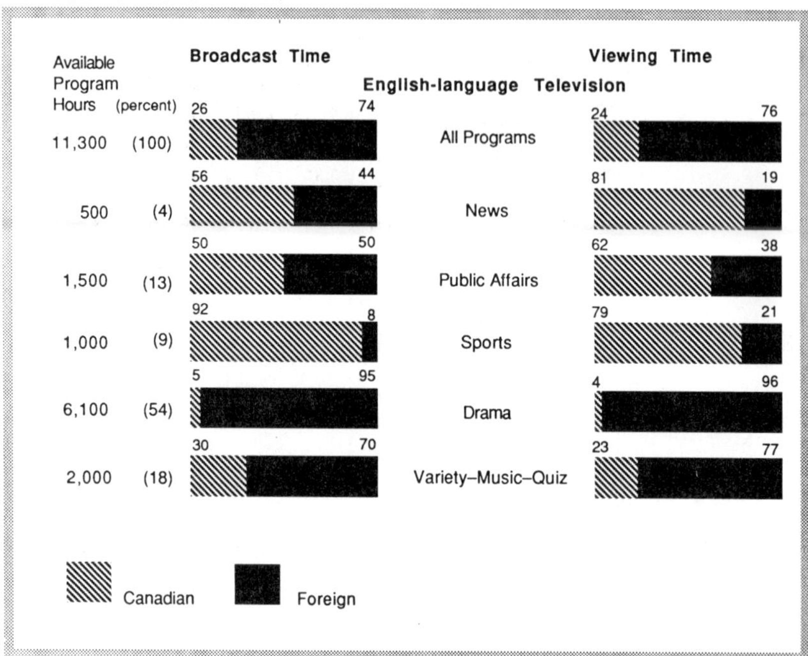

Figure 5.10 Proportions of Broadcast and Viewing Time for Various Types of Canadian and Foreign Programming, 7p.m.–11p.m., Monday–Sunday, Calendar 1984

It is important to distinguish between the viewing of French television and francophone viewing of television in general. Although 68 percent of all tuning to French television stations is to Canadian programs (compared to 29 percent mentioned above for English), only 57 percent of all tuning by francophones is to Canadian programs. The reason is that francophones watch a good deal of English television. Teenage francophones (aged 12 to 17), who watch a lot of American drama and rock video clips, give only a 48 percent share to Canadian programs. Francophones over 50, on the other hand, give a 66 percent share to Canadian programs, watching significantly more Canadian information programming.

Figures 5.8 to 5.11 also reveal the great Canadian TV success story — news and public affairs. For both English and French, all-day and peak time, in both categories, Canadian supply matches or exceeds foreign supply (with the single exception of all-day English television news where the foreign content reaches 54 percent (see Figure 5.8). Even more remarkable is the jump in viewing of Canadian news and public affairs compared to their availability: English peak-period news gets 81 percent of viewing to 56 percent of broadcast time. On the French side, American news faces the barrier of language, as well as a Canadian preference for local rather than imported daily information.

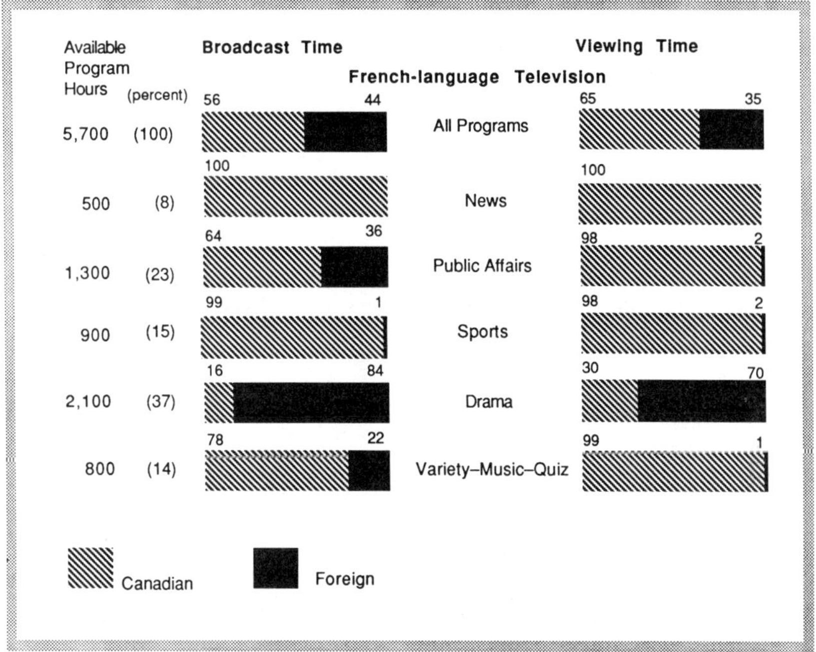

Figure 5.11 Proportions of Broadcast and Viewing Time for Various Types of Canadian and Foreign Programming, 7p.m.–11p.m., Monday–Sunday Calendar 1984

English television also plays on this journalistic advantage — few Canadian viewers are interested in local American newscasts. Other factors to be considered are the preference Canadians have expressed in opinion polls for television as a source of news, and the generally high quality of Canadian television journalism.

Program Availability by Station Group

There are wide differences in both the proportion of Canadian programming supplied by each of the different television station groups and the share of the total audience for Canadian programming that each group obtains. Historically the total audience share of the main station groups has been reasonably stable, at least over the eight-year trend reported in Figures 5.12 and 5.13. Generally, CTV, CBC English and CBC French have lost some share over this period, while both American commercial networks and Canadian independents have gained.

Discrepancies also exist between the total hours broadcast by each station group and the proportion of viewing they capture as indicated in Figures 5.14 and 5.15. Both CBC and CTV capture a proportion of viewing time higher than their proportion of broadcast time, whereas stations in the United States capture a much lower proportion of viewing — 33 percent versus 47 percent of available programs. This difference is explained in large part by the practice of simulcasting, as we noted earlier, by which any viewer who has tuned in to a simulcast

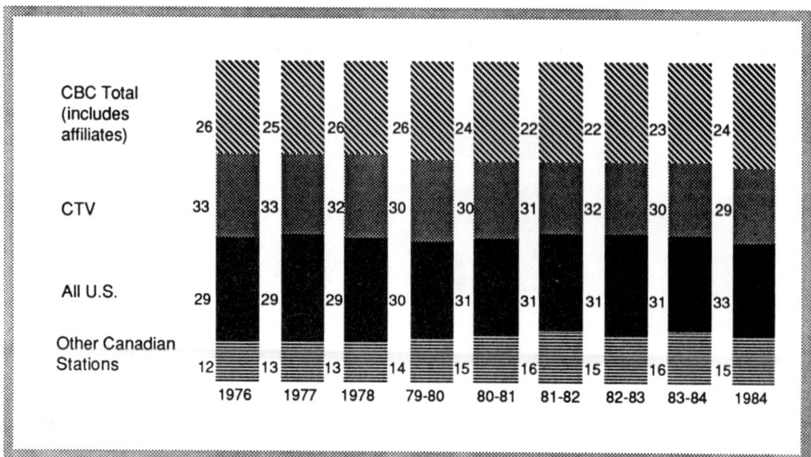

Figure 5.12 Station Group Shares of Total Audience for English-language Television, 1976–1984 (percent)

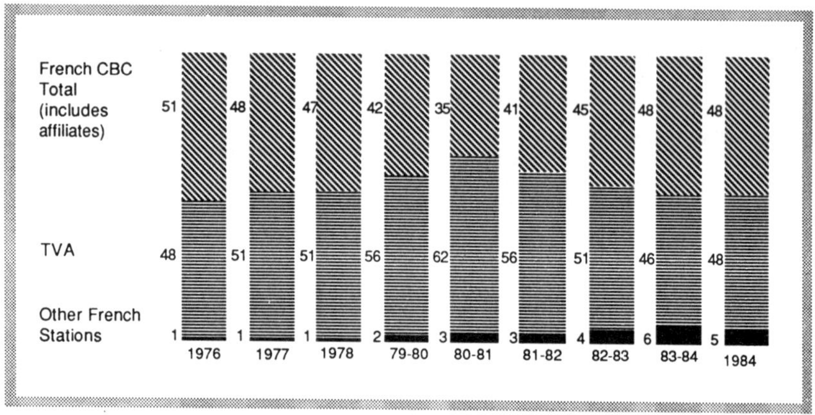

Figure 5.13 Station Group Shares of Total Audience for French-language Television 1976–1984a (percent)

program on an American network would actually view the signal from the Canadian station or network which was simulcasting. That viewer would thus be credited in surveys to the Canadian broadcaster in question. The figure of 33 percent for the United States does not therefore reflect the true number of people who tuned in to an American network. Because there is no limit on simulcasting, Canadian broadcasters try to schedule as many of these programs as possible in peak time during the fall and winter seasons, ghettoizing Canadian shows into off-peak hours and low-audience summer runs. American scheduling therefore tends to dictate Canadian scheduling. Canadian broadcasters are discouraged by this practice from programming material from countries other than the United States, including their own, thereby limiting viewer choice.[10]

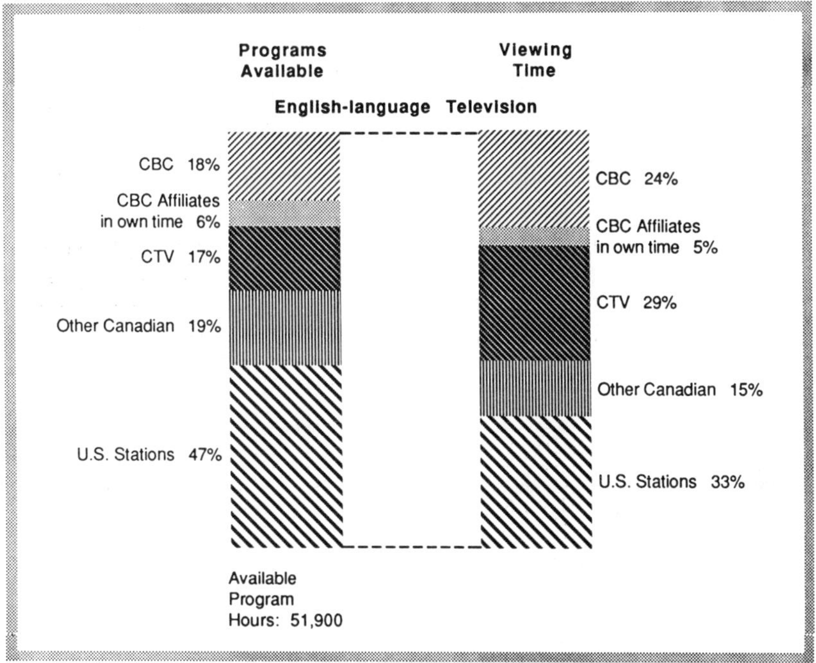

Figure 5.14 Availability and Viewing by Station Group 6a.m.–2a.m., Monday–Sunday, Calendar 1984

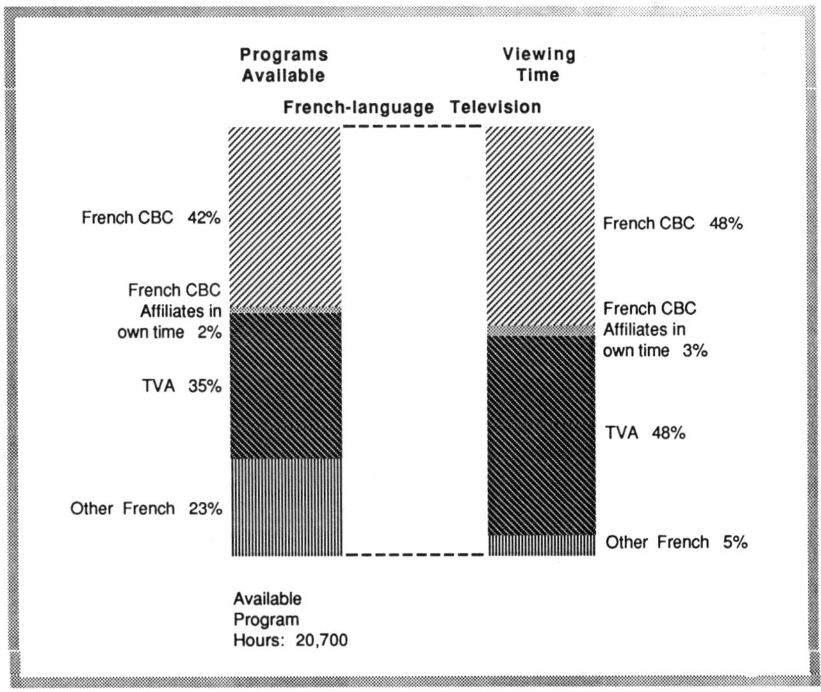

Figure 5.15 Availability and Viewing by Station Group 6a.m.–2a.m., Monday–Sunday, Calendar 1984

Within the viewing shares of each group, wide disparities also exist as to the nationality of programs viewed. Table 5.1 shows the proportion of viewing of Canadian programs by English and French station groups.[11] We see that the highest proportion of Canadian viewing is enjoyed by CBC's owned and operated French stations (or 'O and O's'), and that the proportion rose over the three fall seasons in question. The lowest proportion among the Canadian groups went to the English independents at 27 percent and Global at 32 percent. In the fall of 1984, they each received less than half the proportion of viewing of Canadian programming that the CBC O and O stations did, namely 65 percent.

Table 5.1 Portion of TV Viewing of Canadian Programming 1982-1984, All persons 2-plus

(percent)

System	1982	1983	1984
CBC French Owned & Operated	62	67	72
Radio Québec	82	72	72
CBC French Affiliate	51	57	60
CBC English Owned & Operated	62	61	65
TVA Affiliate	60	62	52
CBC Affiliate	41	42	46
CTV Affiliate	34	35	37
TVO/Knowledge Network	36	39	39
Global	29	31	32
English Independent	23	24	27

Source: Based on information in Harrison, Young, Pesonen and Newell Inc., "Canadian TV Viewing Habits", a report prepared for the Task Force on Broadcasting Policy, Ottawa, January 1986.

The Canadian-foreign balance by station group shifts again when we look at availability and tuning in the peak 7 p.m. to 11 p.m. period (Figures 5.16 to 5.19). As we can see, the CBC provides about half the Canadian programming on both the English and French sides — 55 percent of the English, 51 percent of the French. English CBC captures 64 percent of the tuning to Canadian programming. French CBC captures 54 percent of the tuning to Canadian programming.

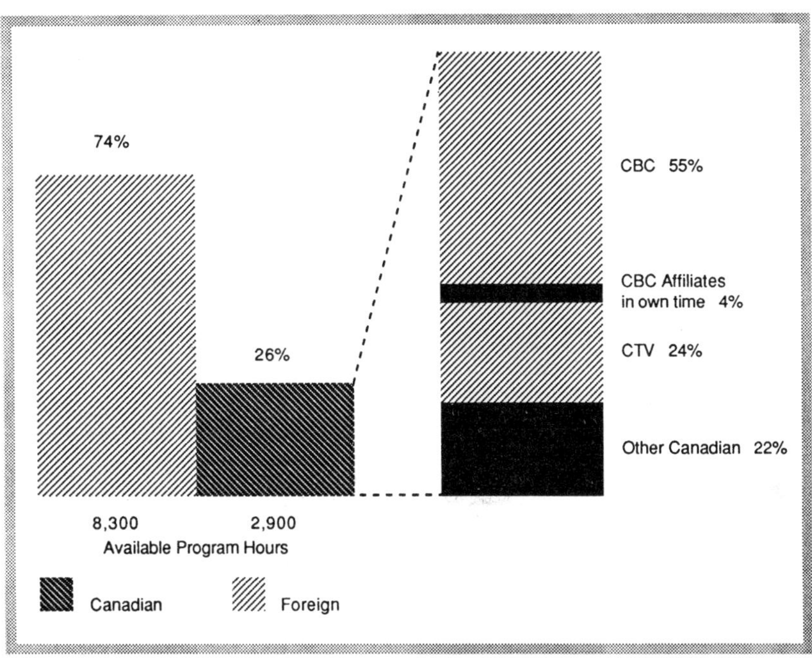

Figure 5.16 Availability of Canadian and Foreign Programs on English-language Television 7p.m. – 11p.m., Monday–Sunday, Calendar 1984

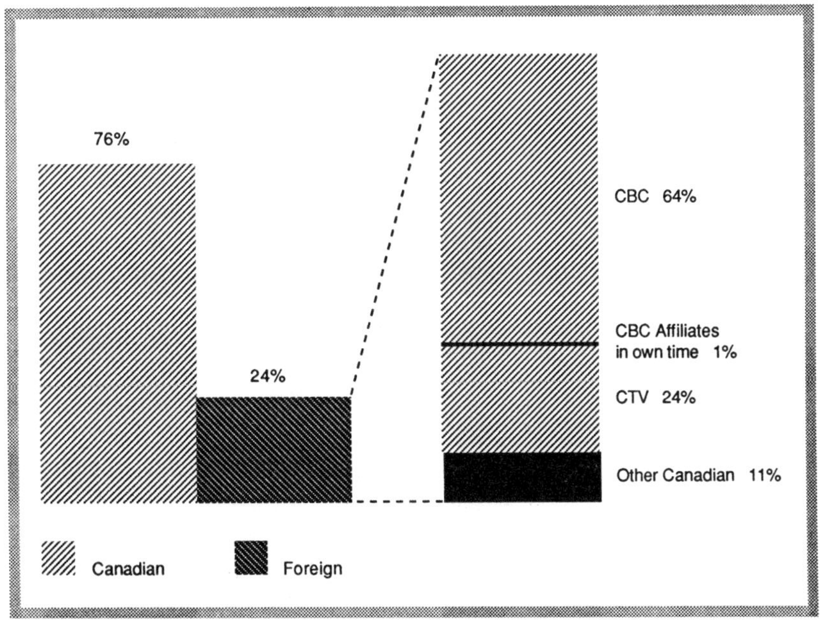

Figure 5.17 Viewing of Canadian and Foreign Programs on English-language Television 7p.m.–11p.m., Monday–Sunday, Calendar 1984

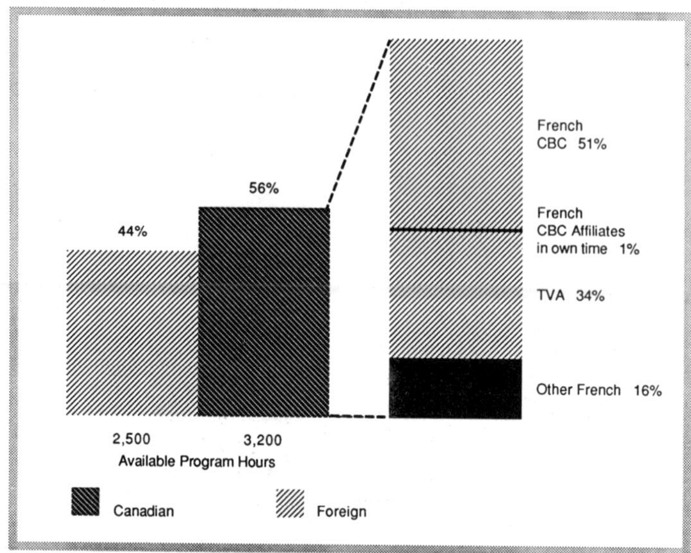

Figure 5.18 Availability of Canadian and Foreign Programs on French-language Television 7p.m.–11p.m., Monday–Sunday, Calendar 1984

The CTV network accounts for 24 percent of the supply of English-Canadian programming and the same percentage of the tuning to it. The French TVA stations supply 34 percent of French-Canadian programming but obtain 41 percent of tuning. The tuning to Canadian programming on other stations and networks in the peak period is very low.

The amount of Canadian programming available in the peak period from 7 p.m. to 11 p.m. compared to the full-day schedule varies significantly by station group. CBC English drops from providing 55 percent of all available Canadian production during the peak period to 37 percent throughout the day. CTV's 24 percent of available Canadian production in peak time compares with 31 percent throughout the day. Global produces 4 percent of Canadian peak-time programming and 8 percent during the day. Independents account for 10 percent of Canadian peak time, 14 percent of Canadian full-day programming.

Our research revealed an important relationship between the proportion of Canadian programming available on English-language television and the number of stations available in individual counties outside the province of Quebec. It shows that in English Canada there is a strong negative correlation, or inverse proportion, between Canadian programming and number of stations. For all Canada, excluding Quebec, in those counties with only three stations available, 43 percent of the available programming broadcast over the whole day is Canadian whereas in those counties with nine or more stations, only 28 percent of the available programming is Canadian (based on 1984 data). This

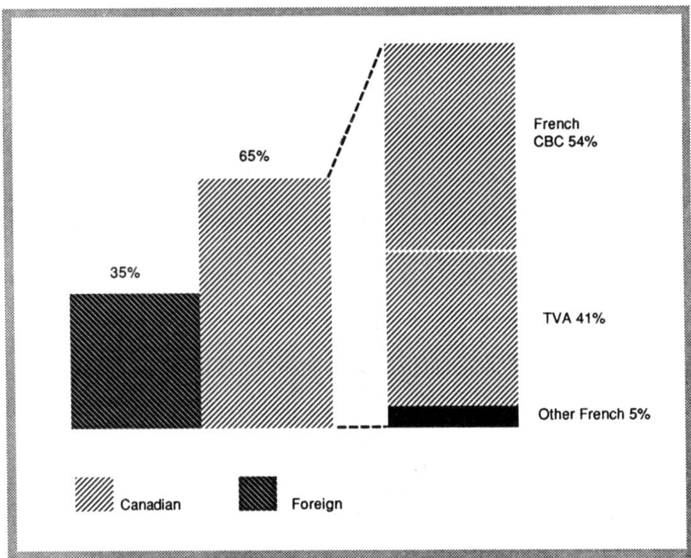

Figure 5.19 Viewing of Canadian and Foreign Programs on French-language Television 7p.m.–11p.m., Monday–Sunday, Calendar 1984

disproportion is even more pronounced in peak time. As far as English Canada is concerned it is clear that increased channel choice has meant and continues to mean a decline in the proportion of available programming that is Canadian.[12]

It is useful to bear these facts in mind when we consider the role of cable in bringing more channels to Canadian subscribers. Both operators and subscribers measure the value of cable service in terms of the sheer number of channels a system makes available for a given price. Both parties are bound to see better value in more channels (see Chapter 24 for further analysis). Once again, however, we must be careful not to assume that better value in terms of this consumer transaction translates of necessity into a proportionately greater choice of programming (as opposed to channels).

The research data show among the effects of cable, that cable households watch far less CBC television than non-cable households, as indicated in Figures 5.20 and 5.21: on the English side, roughly 19 percent as opposed to 31 percent, and on the French side, 32 percent versus 39 percent. Viewing of CTV and TVA also drops sharply in cable households. This finding is consistent with the common sense expectation that as more channels become available any individual channel will account for a smaller share of viewing.

Because the additional channels made available by cable are largely foreign, the viewing of these channels tends to be higher in cabled households. Viewing of the American commercial networks roughly doubles in English households. However, the viewing of Canadian independents and Global (most

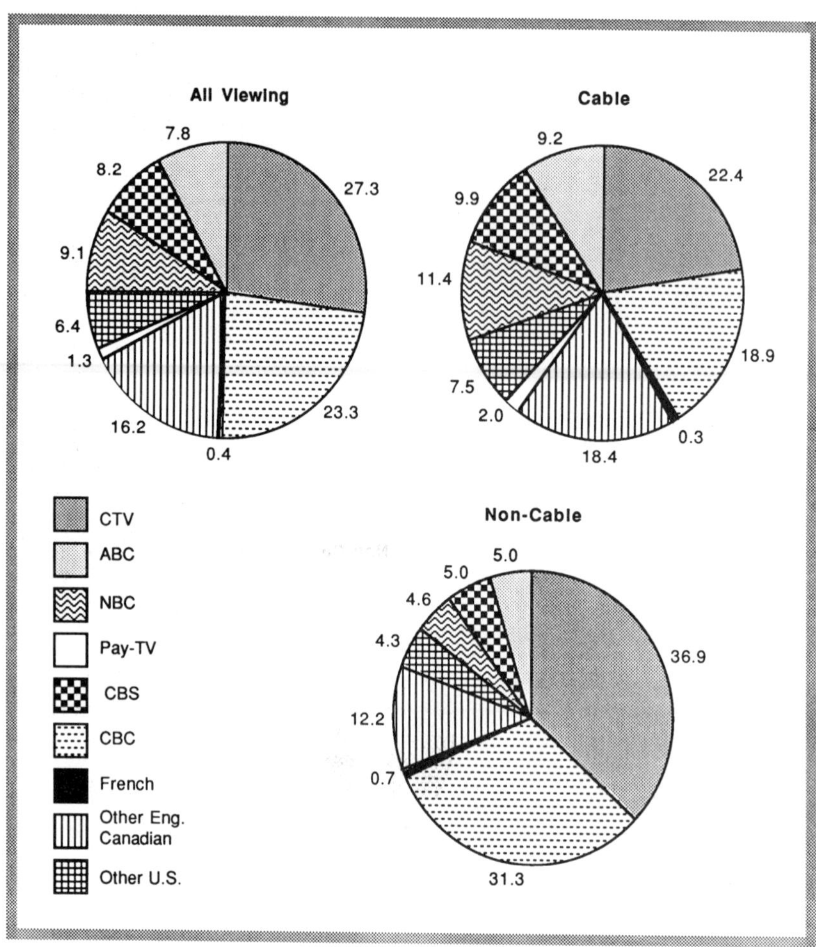

Figure 5.20 The Effect of Cable on Anglophone Viewing Choices by Station Group

of what is measured under 'Other English Canadian') also increases by 50 percent, reflecting the fact that in many communities these channels are not available off-air and can, therefore, only be received in cabled households.

As we have already noted, the American networks and Canadian independents contribute least to program diversity. The Canadian independents also contribute least to the viewing of Canadian programming for all day parts and in all program categories. CBC, on the other hand, contributes most to both program diversity and the availability of Canadian fare. We therefore conclude that cable does not at present increase program diversity in proportion to the increased number of channels it makes available, and that cabled households have a lower proportion of Canadian programming available. The viewing of

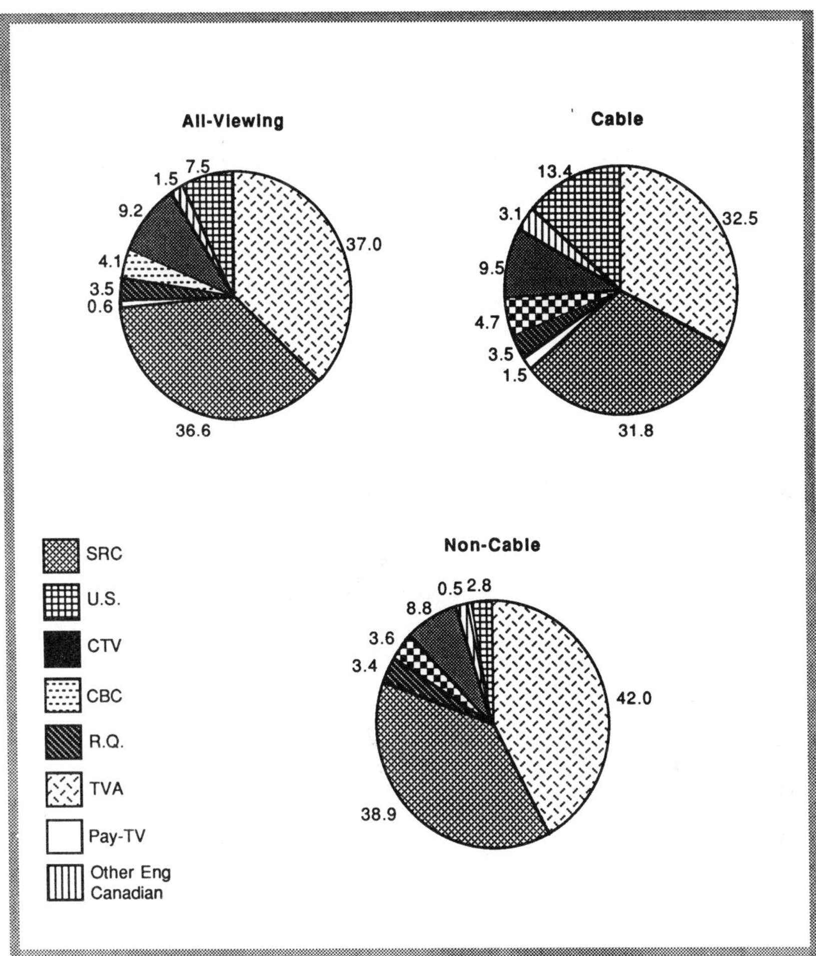

Figure 5.21 The Effect of Cable on Francophone Viewing Choices by Station Group

French-language stations is also lower among francophones who receive cable television.

Program Content

Turning now to a brief look at various program categories, we should bear in mind how individual programs are delivered and the conditions under which they are viewed. Because of the constraints of scheduling, promotion, regulation and technology, programs are seldom appreciated by the ordinary viewer or even critic for their own intrinsic merits.

What particular viewers have available for viewing is affected by their geographic location; their willingness and financial ability to pay for cable or converter service; and the actual channel choice made available by the cable operator on individual systems, restricted by both regulation and plant capacity.

Conventional wisdom has it that technology has liberated viewers from some of these constraints and given them more control over their viewing. Two of the most important new devices are the VCR and the remote control. The first of these allows viewers both to see material on cassette that is not available to them on a scheduled program, and to 'timeshift' regularly scheduled programs by recording them off-air for viewing at a later time. The remote control device has given rise to greatly increased viewer manipulation of the incoming or recorded TV signal, in the form of so-called 'zapping', 'zipping' and 'muting', which are all intended primarily to avoid commercials. Zapping is the practice of switching channels rapidly to sample other programs, especially when a commercial comes on. Zipping consists of putting a VCR into fast forward to avoid commercials recorded off-air with a program, or simply to shorten viewing time. And muting refers to turning the volume down or off during commercial messages.

As far as the VCR itself is concerned, it accounts for only 2.2 percent of total TV viewing time in Canada though this will undoubtedly rise in the future. Producers and programmers have, however, reacted with a good deal of alacrity to the zapping phenomenon. Entertainment programs have long resorted to gimmicks and razzle dazzle to hold viewer attention and keep them away from the competition: carefully constructed 'teaser' openings, suspenseful commercial breaks, expensive production values such as spectacular explosions and car crashes (which Morris Wolfe has referred to as American television's culture of the 'jolts per minute' or JPMs).[13]

More recently, such production techniques have become even more prevalent while broadcasters press every moment of their advantage with such devices as promotional inserts read over the end credits of one program to advertise another. Advertisers too are adopting new strategies to hold the restive viewer. These include the 15-second commercial; commercials that tell a story or make their point in a very graphic or humorous fashion; and placement of commercials on programs which are viewed for their topicality, like news and sports, and are therefore less likely to be recorded on a VCR.

Indeed, many of the production values that were once confined to entertainment programs have found their way into information programs. The development of new production technologies such as computer graphics has made such an approach to news programming possible; the slow erosion of the network share of total viewing in favor of pay and other new services has made this approach necessary. The handling of news like a form of entertainment has been referred to as 'infotainment'. In the next section we look more closely at news and information as a programming category, before turning to the children's and performance categories.

News and Information

As we have seen, news and public affairs constitute one of the strongest Canadian-content drawing cards on the TV schedule. Information programming and sports are the two kinds of Canadian programming consistently preferred over American. In recent years information programming has come to be seen in North America not just as a social responsibility of the broadcaster, but also as an increasingly important source of revenue. Some news people rise to the kind of star status accorded popular performers in other types of programming. Particularly in the larger markets, "local newscasts on private stations have improved immeasurably over the years, and often compare favourably with network newscasts in terms of studio production and quality of news reports", writes Peter Desbarats in a commissioned study of news programming.[14]

For many years in both Canada and the United States opinion surveys have shown that people rely more on television than any other medium for their news. In Canada, for example, a survey conducted in 1981 for the Royal Commission on Newspapers showed that 67 percent of respondents regarded television as the most influential of the news media, and 54 percent regarded it as the most believable. Television was the preferred medium for obtaining international, national and provincial news; newspapers were preferred only for local community news.[15]

In its submission to this Task Force, the CBC pointed out that

> the single most important service the CBC provides is its journalistic service, and especially *The National* and *Téléjournal* with their partners *The Journal* and *Le Point*, *Midday* and the regional supper-hour programs. They are the informational spinal column for the nation and with their huge audiences must use only the highest possible professional and socially responsible standards, as must all our information programming.[16]

The Corporation has launched strong initiatives in news in recent years, starting with the twinned news and public affairs shows on English and French television at 10 p.m., which began on the English side in early 1982 and on the French side in 1983. Highly successful in building audiences, these shows were followed by a review of English regional television programming in 1984, while a refurbishment of the French-language supper hour news shows began in 1986. The result on the English side has been a consolidation of regional programs and a renovated series of supper hour shows across the country — newsier, livelier and making better use of network material and exchanges among the regional stations on the network.

Our researchers found a mixed reaction in the private sector to the CBC's aggressive bid for local news audiences. Off the record, many news directors welcome it because they have been able to argue for better equipment and more personnel in order to compete. At the same time many of them reflect the view of private TV licensees that the CBC, subsidized by the taxpayer, is mounting unfair competition. Commercial broadcasters tend to regard the CBC not simply as a state-owned network but as a commercial competitor in the area of news.

There have been demands that CBC leave local TV news to the private stations. These have come not only from the private broadcasting sector but also from commentators who feel the CBC should concentrate its efforts in other areas where it is more needed, such as national and international news.

The question of whether the CBC duplicates private-station TV news or offers a distinct alternative can only be answered by looking at the philosophy, approach and organization of the competing broadcasters, the content of the news they provide and the audiences they attract. First it must be noted that one of the reasons for diversity of sources of news is for each organization to keep the other on its toes, to offer an alternative source of employment for TV journalists so they will not be dependent on a single employer. There is bound to be a certain amount of duplication in content because the different news organizations are covering the same array of situations and circumstances in the life of the community.

News philosophy and organization This is perhaps the most significant area because of its influence on content and audience appeal, but it is difficult to define. Studies of electronic journalists in the public and private systems have indicated that CBC journalists tend to be older, better paid, more highly educated and more experienced than their counterparts in the private sector. There is a tendency for journalists who want more time and scope for in-depth journalism to gravitate to the CBC, but this is not the case everywhere, according to information gathered by our researchers in some 70 interviews with both French and English news directors and journalists in every region of the country. Our research also found that

> . . . unlike newspaper publishers, who often enjoy the status and influence of their position, commercial broadcasters tend to be schizophrenic about their news operations, regarding them as a constant drain on financial resources as well as essential factors in attracting and retaining local audiences.
>
> Within the CBC, on the other hand, the importance of news and current affairs programming has always been recognized as a major part of the Corporation's job, although money available for news and other forms of programming ebbs and flows as tidal currents within the bureaucracy shift and as the CBC responds to changing external demands.[17]

Content of newscasts The Task Force commissioned a study of content, covering both CBC and private network and local news, in English and French, in the fall of 1985.[18] The results indicated little discernible difference between CBC and CTV network news in English, or between CBC and TVA network news in French, but certain variations between public and private station news at the local level.

At the network level, the differences between CTV and CBC lay mainly in the fact that CTV carried commercials, while CBC did not; CBC carried more stories than CTV of a hard, spot news character; and CBC carried more of both short items and those over two minutes, while CTV scheduled more stories in the mid-range. In French, CBC also had more hard news than TVA, but there was not the same distinction between the two networks in length of items.

At the local level, on the English side, the comparison of CBC and private stations revealed, in summary, these variations: CBC items were longer, more often presented by a reporter as well as a studio anchor, more often presented by female anchors, originated less often than private station items in the broadcaster's own community, more often contained film or videotape while private stations were more apt to use still photos or graphics.

At the local level, on the French side, CBC items were longer than on private stations, more often had the combination of a reporter in the field with an anchor in the studio, originated more often from local sources while private stations more often used network and other sources. A majority of CBC anchors were women while a majority of private station anchors were men. By contrast with the English side, French CBC stations focused more on local community news while private stations focused more on U.S. and Canadian-American news, and French CBC items were less apt to use film or videotape.

Making allowances for the fact that a different selection of stations in each category, or a different time sample, might have led to somewhat different results, the content-analysis study nevertheless makes evident that there are distinctions between CBC and private local newscasts on television.

Audiences There is much evidence from public opinion surveys that the different types of newscasts of CBC and private stations attract different audiences. A 1982 survey of 1,447 Toronto viewers for CBC Research showed that CBC supper hour news viewers show somewhat more interest in international and national news than do CTV viewers, with interest in local news about the same, and CBC viewers show slightly less interest in sports news than do CTV viewers. This study and a number of others have indicated that the typical CBC viewer is older, more highly educated and has a substantially higher interest in information programs, international and national news, and generally in cultural programs than has the population at large. The CBC also attracts a larger audience among the managerial and professional group — by a wider margin in French than in English — and among people who have retired from the work force.

It would appear, then, that the public does get the benefit of an alternative in news by supporting a public as well as a private TV news system at the local level. A number of CBC journalists interviewed for this Report were concerned, however, that head-to-head commercial competition in news with private broadcasters could undermine what they considered to be the Corporation's non-commercial mandate. As we have mentioned, the private broadcasters feel that a publicly funded service is one thing, but a public service that goes out after advertising dollars for its newscasts is unfair competition with stations that must rely totally on commercial revenues.

Children's Programming

Responding to the developmental and recreational needs of young viewers has always been a difficult task. Canadian children (whom we define here as being between the ages of two and 17) watch a good deal of adult and so-called 'family' programming, such as sitcoms, in part due to a dearth of interesting material made specifically for children. Children's average viewing time is, however, roughly 25 percent less than that of adults.

Here, availability is caught in a kind of three-way squeeze involving imports, commercial constraints and the financial priorities of our public broadcasters.[19] First, most of the American imports for children are cartoons with a penchant for strident, often violent action and jingoistic values ('foreigners' are often given funny accents and treated as outsiders). Even imports such as *Sesame Street* have been criticized for their reliance on 'jolts per minute' to transmit educational values, compared to the more serene approach of Canadian programs such as *Friendly Giant*, *Mr. Dress-Up* and *Polka Dot Door*. As far as viewing by francophone children is concerned, animated programs from Japan seem to have been gaining ground on similar material from the United States.

Second, children's programming is not a reliable source of profits for broadcasters, particularly given the more or less severe restrictions placed on ads directed at children. In Quebec, provincial law prohibits broadcasters entirely from advertising to children. At the behest of the CRTC, the CBC has not allowed advertising on its children's programs since 1975, although older children are certainly a target for advertising carried on rock video shows, sitcoms and other programs that may also be intended for older viewers. Other scheduling and demographic restrictions, including the complexities of marketing to a group which in itself has little or no discretionary income, have prompted most private broadcasters to regard children's programming as primarily a task for the public broadcaster.

As a third and final point, however, we note that chronic shortage of funds — or other priorities — has hampered the development of children's programming in the public sector, especially at CBC. Availability by province varies considerably, in any case, with Ontario and Quebec enjoying the widest variety of programming because of the efforts of TVOntario and Radio-Québec in addition to CBC. The Knowledge Network in British Columbia and Access in Alberta have even more limited resources.

In order to provide a rough idea of the nature of children's programming and its audience, our researchers used BBM data to study typical weeks in francophone Montreal and anglophone Toronto in the fall of 1985. As with any such sampling the results obtained are not representative of other Canadian cities since the configuration of station groups is unique in each region of the country. Nevertheless, the survey shows that the state of Canadian children's programming leaves much to be desired even in the two largest markets in the country which we would expect to be well endowed compared with smaller markets.

Seven stations provide children's programming in the Toronto market, including CBC, CTV and several independents whose schedules are typical of what is available in other anglophone cities across Canada. In Toronto, TVOntario and Global each generate 25 percent of the available hours. CBLT (CBC) follows with 15 percent, CHCH (the Hamilton independent) provides 13 percent and CFTO (CTV) produces 9 percent. An average of 14.2 hours is available every weekday, from a high of 26 hours on Saturday to a low of 10.5 hours on Sunday.

In the prime viewing hours of 7 a.m. to 12 noon and 3 p.m. to 7:30 p.m., 45 percent of the programs are Canadian and 47 percent are American. CITY and TVO have the highest Canadian content (67 percent and 65 percent), CBLT has 59 percent, Global has 20 percent and CHCH 14 percent. Over 90 percent of

Global's programs are animated cartoons, many of foreign origin. The most popular format, however, is the combination of live action and puppets which constitutes 60 percent of the programming on CBLT and TVO.

The 6-to-11 age group is by far the worst served by television: virtually no material on the private stations is addressed to this sector leaving them with American cartoons targeted at the 2-to-11 group overall. On the other hand, two-thirds of all programs on TVO and CBLT are for pre-schoolers (2-to-5). Still, most of the programs children watch are not intended for them exclusively: the exception is TVO, where 86.5 percent of the children's audience share goes to children's programs. The figures for CBLT, CHCH and Global range from 40 percent to 50 percent, while for CFTO only 5.5 percent of children's tuning is to children's programming.

In recent years, CBC English television has gradually withdrawn from the key weekend morning viewing times except for *Sesame Street* on Saturday and occasional showings of *Switchback* for the 12-to-17 age group. On Saturday mornings, therefore, when children's tuning is highest, the Toronto schedule is occupied with CFTO's live action shows with American cartoons on Global and the independent stations. Throughout the week American cartoons with their high production values consistently draw higher audiences than the cheaper Canadian live action and puppet shows. *Polka Dot Door* achieves a high rating at 6 p.m. partly because its competition on the other channels is news. *Sesame Street* is repackaged by CBC to include about 20 minutes of Canadian segments which are produced at several regional centres across the country. The Canadian version is now carried by TVOntario as well.

Although the number of available hours of children's programming per week has risen from 76 in 1976 to 109.5 in 1985, new production is declining. In 1976, there were 247 hours of new programming; by 1985 the figure had dropped to 237 reflecting cutbacks at the CBC which reduced new production there from 100 hours in 1976 to 60 hours in 1985. The rise in overall hours available therefore indicates an increased use of repeats and material from outside resources.

Most new shows involve live action series and entertainment specials for children between two and twelve. There is little new programming for teen-agers, apart from video clip series, and no information programming which appeals to the entire family so that children can benefit from the presence of adults while watching — an important consideration for dealing with social issues as they arise in programs.

French-language stations in the Montreal area provide an average of 49 hours of children's programming a week: CBFT (CBC) supplies 44 percent, CFTM (TVA) provides 25 percent and CIVM (Radio-Québec) 31 percent. TVOntario's French programming (17 percent of its total) is also available on cable in Montreal, as is TVJQ, the all-day children's channel on Vidéotron, the area's largest cable company.

CBFT is the most popular station, capturing 72 percent of all tuning to French-language stations. CFTM is next with 21 percent and CIVM has 7 percent of the audience share. When viewing of English stations is also included, figures show that crossover tuning to anglophone stations accounts for

16 percent of overall tuning by francophone children. The most popular programs are live action and puppet shows such as *Passe Partout* and *Bobino* (now only in repeats) which are predominantly Canadian. Animated shows are a distant second, with Japanese programs such as *Candy* and *Tao Tao* drawing higher audiences than American cartoons. As in the English-language market, only part of children's tuning is to children's programs. On CBFT children's programs account for 58 percent of their viewing, but on CFTM the figure is only 16 percent.

Over 60 percent of the programming for children in the Montreal market is Canadian in origin. The next most common country of origin is Japan with 11 percent, followed by the United States with 7 percent. On the two stations which account for over 90 percent of all viewing (CBFT and CFTM), each has 48 percent Canadian content. Animation is much more common than in Toronto. Almost half the programs on CBFT and CFTM are animated and on CIVM the figure rises to 77 percent. Furthermore, the 6-to-11 age group is better served in French than in English with 18 percent of all programs aimed at this group. An additional one-quarter to one-third is directed at pre-schoolers, with over half of the total production accounted for by *Passe Partout*.

As in English Canada, however, the production of new programs is gradually declining because of Radio-Canada cutbacks. CBFT produced 5.25 hours in 1976 and 4 hours in 1985. Overall hours at CFTM have dropped from 15.75 to 10.5, but its original production has remained at 5 hours.

Performance Programming

The category of television performance programming gets more attention from policy-makers and social critics than any other. There are two reasons for this. One is the sheer quantity of programs available. As we saw, drama, variety, music and quiz shows accounted for 54 percent of all available English programming in 1984, and 50 percent of French programming (with viewing shares of 67 percent and 57 percent respectively). The other reason is the supposition that dramatic programs, broadly construed, help to shape cultural values or at least reflect them for large numbers of people.

There is some danger in putting too much stock by this very heterogeneous group of programs. First, to the extent that television shapes or merely reflects values — from the limits of political satire to the most acceptable methods of conflict resolution — news and other information programming certainly have a part to play alongside drama, variety and so on. Second, the program types we group together for purposes of analysis have many divergent purposes. Little of what one might wish to say about a production of *As You Like It* would apply even remotely to an episode of *Snow Job*. In the opening paragraphs of this chapter we drew a contrast between differing perceptions of programming as culture for some and entertainment for others.

These problems naturally take on a greater intensity when we turn our attention to Canadian-produced material. Despite the CRTC's forbearance over the regulation of actual program content, the Canadian content quota system has had its impact on Canadian performance programming. Because program categories are not specified in the regulations (although they can and have been in conditions of licence), and because dramatic programs (as distinct from variety, music and quiz) are relatively expensive to produce, the volume of Canadian serious drama, sitcoms, movies, adventure series and so on is remarkably small.

Thus, in 1984, the average Canadian could have received a total of roughly 370 hours of English-language Canadian 'drama' out of a total of nearly 52,000 hours of television programming. Francophone viewers on average had available about 630 hours of French-language Canadian dramatic programs. Even these figures do not reflect the actual number of hours of Canadian dramatic programs produced, because they contain both repeat showings and duplication between stations. And since these are all-day figures, some of the programming included falls outside the peak 7 p.m. to 11 p.m. period when most Canadians are watching television.[20]

Perhaps the most difficult part of the attempt to make our voices heard lies in something we have taken for granted so far — not how much Canadian content nor at what times of day — but what is Canadian about a program in the first place. In broadcasting, a good deal hangs on just how 'Canadian' is defined.

When we speak of 'Canadian television programming' in regulatory terms, we are using the definition used since 1984 by the CRTC for official purposes. (It is different from the one we have used elsewhere in this chapter that treats as Canadian only those programs actually produced in Canada). The official definition is similar to that used by the Canadian Film and Videotape Certification Office to certify productions as Canadian for purposes of eligibility under the special Capital Cost Allowance provisions in the *Income Tax Act*.

First of all, a Canadian program is defined as one in which the producer is Canadian. Six points must then be earned on the basis of 2 points for a Canadian director, 2 points for a Canadian writer and 1 point each if the following are Canadians: leading performer, second leading performer, head of art department, director of photography, music composer and editor. Regardless of the number of points amassed either the director or the writer and at least one of the leading performers must be a Canadian. However, upon application, either one of these last conditions can be waived, provided "all other key creative functions are filled by Canadians". Finally, at least 75 percent of all payments to individuals, with the exception of the participants listed above, must be to Canadians, as must 75 percent of the cost of processing and post-production services.

The CRTC also accepts as Canadian all productions certified by the Canadian Film and Video Certification Office in the Department of Communications, including those which qualify under Canada's official co-production treaties with other countries. These treaties are negotiated by the Department of Communications and administered by Telefilm Canada. The purpose of such treaties is to have the two countries involved consider the resulting co-productions as domestic programs in both countries thereby qualifying them for access to the financial assistance programs and treatment as national content in relation to quota requirements in both countries. The target in negotiating such treaties is to establish terms which ensure a fair balance of both cultural and economic benefit to each country, an objective which in the past has not always been successfully achieved by Canada.

The most controversial and important element in the CRTC's Canadian content definition is that it accepts what the Commission refers to as "co-ventures" as though they were official treaty co-productions. Co-ventures are productions involving producers in Canada and in some other country, almost always the United States. These productions are not based on the kind of negotiation which goes on in the case of official co-production treaties in order to ensure that both countries involved share equally in the cultural and economic benefits.

In co-ventures some of the producer functions are performed by Canadians. To ensure that the Canadian producer involved has something more than a passive and minor role, the CRTC requires that the Canadian production company have an equal measure of decision-making on all creative elements of the production and administer at least the Canadian element of the production budget. Such formal requirements, however, cannot guarantee an equal division of real creative control in cases where the foreign producer has brought in most of the funding through a pre-sale to a broadcaster in the United States.

Co-ventures normally must qualify under the rules defining Canadian productions described above. This at least ensures that economic benefits flow to Canada from these productions. The Commission will, however, accept as Canadian all of a 'production package' of two or more co-productions or co-ventures, as long as each foreign production in the package, which may have only minor Canadian involvement, is matched with a Canadian production having only minor foreign involvement. Sports programs qualify as Canadian if a Canadian licensee or production company has production control and the event takes place in Canada or if production control rests with Canadians and the event occurs outside Canada as long as Canadian teams or athletes participate. Any foreign program which is dubbed into English, French or a native Canadian language also qualifies for one-quarter Canadian content credit, a provision with practical implications at present mainly for French-language television.

We discuss the merits of this definition of 'Canadian' in Chapter 10 on The CBC, Chapter 14 on The Broadcast Fund and Chapter 17 on Private Television. It is worth noting here that although this system has the advantage of providing explicit and objective guidelines it is at present a highly complex one with many special provisions which affect especially the area of performance programming.

Unfortunately, as in any such regulatory structure, the minimum requirements tend to serve also as the maximum standard. The present content quota system has thus given rise to a kind of 'regulatory tokenism' in Canadian television. In other words, a great deal of programming today qualifies technically as Canadian without there being much distinctly Canadian about it, and the criteria seem designed to permit that.

In a specially commissioned study of performance programming based on the 1984 schedule,[21] we grappled with the question of how to distinguish 'Canadian' programs that meet the minimum technical definition concerning production of the program from those which have distinctive Canadian features as part of their actual content. Our researchers developed a system of qualitative 'cultural markers' designed to identify certain themes, locales, personalities and so on as more-or-less typically Canadian.

It is true that a well-known Canadian landscape or political figure is easy enough to identify. Nor is it too difficult to demonstrate the consistent differences between the resort to violence in Canadian as opposed to American adventure series. We acknowledge, however, that putting dozens of such symbols or features together into a composite definition of 'distinctively Canadian' is a very complicated and sometimes subjective task.

As might be expected, our study found a strong tendency for the producers of Canadian performance programs to manipulate distinctive Canadian symbols, either by suppressing them or introducing them artificially into the program context. We found a number of programs that removed all references to the Canadian setting, in order to make them acceptable to their American co-producers.

Current examples of such TV dramas are *Night Heat*, the crime program on CTV, and *Danger Bay*, the adventure program on CBC. Although both shows qualify as Canadian content and originate in Canada they could be mistaken for American productions and seem to have been made on the assumption that references to their Canadian origin would hurt their appeal to audiences outside Canada, particularly in the United States. The strategy has apparently worked for the producers of *Night Heat*, who have been asked by CBS to produce two more series for network use in 1986-87.[22]

As we might also expect, our examination of 45 performance programs revealed significant differences concerning the presence of certain cultural symbols, as between English- and French-language programming. The French programming showed greater evidence of a common cultural heritage and a stock of more pervasive cultural reference points than did the English. Some of these features of French-language programming can of course be accounted for by the simple lack of a large foreign market, part and parcel of Quebec's relative cultural and linguistic isolation, obviating appeal to potential foreign buyers.

While French-language quiz and talk shows were found to aspire to the production values of their American counterparts, often successfully, they were distinguished by references to Quebec society and history and the presence of Quebec personalities. Quebec has its own star system, in which personalities move between their roles as actors, singers, comedians and so on, and their roles as media personalities on the talk shows. English programming lacks the same degree of recognition of show business and media personalities. While French performance programming in general is marked by a reliance on North American commercial formats, it reflects an indigenous community to a greater extent than English programming.

The few Canadian situation comedies on English TV did not show a significant preoccupation with Canadian themes, although most had obvious Canadian settings. Quiz, variety and filmed stage performance programs were those in which an effort to avoid reference to time and place was evident. These programs appeared to be directed to a general North American or international audience and strove for an absence of explicit acknowledgement of their Canadian settings.

Francophone audiences respond strongly to domestic variety shows which constitute 66 percent of the French-language variety available but draw 87 percent of the tuning to variety. Canadian audiences are on the other hand, less enthusiastic about English-language variety, as shown by the ratio of 25 percent availability and 18 percent tuning. Although a program such as the CTV's *Don Herron Show* qualifies as Canadian variety it features American television personalities. The CBC has little variety programming apart from the *Tommy Hunter Show*, although music video shows like *Good Rockin' Tonite* are achieving some prominence. Whereas regional variety shows have consistently drawn loyal and enthusiastic audiences, *Country West* is now an isolated phenomenon.

The French networks have succeeded in drawing mass audiences to relatively inexpensive programs, but viewers do complain about low production values. These programs have relied on the identification of the Québécois with their own culture to avoid competing with large amounts of expensively packaged American programming. Today, however, this cultural security is being challenged by the increasing availability of American programs on cable and shifting tastes within the francophone community. A more detailed discussion of these developments will be found in Chapter 8.

A concern about whether programs produced in Canada are distinctively Canadian — distinct for example from similar kinds of American programs — springs in part from a concern over ensuring that Canadian viewers have a real diversity of programs to choose from. Given that real program choice is a desireable goal in itself, we undertook in our study of performance programming to look at this question in another and somewhat more objective way. This concerned the relative balance given to the various types of Canadian performance programming by each of the major Canadian station groups. It also included measurement of the degree to which individual station groups or networks rely on repeat showings. We thus compared the number of individual program titles produced in Canada for telecast with the total number of program hours, including repeats, actually telecast in 1984.

The results of our analysis are shown in Tables 5.2 and 5.3. They include all performance programming produced for network telecast in 1984 (they exclude local production by affiliated stations). The programs were divided into 12 categories as listed. All are more or less self-explanatory, except perhaps for Documentary, which includes only programs produced and telecast outside a regular current affairs series (this category includes a special series such as *War*).

Among the four English-language networks listed — and concentrating first on numbers of different programs shown on the left side of Table 5.2 — we can see that CBC is the only network with titles in all the performance categories. CBC also counts more separate titles under Classics, Drama, Documentary and Variety than the other three networks combined, by a factor of almost two-to-one in each case. TVOntario's heaviest contribution to performance programming is in Documentary, with 25 titles.

Both CTV and Global produce more in the talk, quiz and game show categories combined than either of the public broadcasters. The differences in these latter categories are not very great when measured in terms of program titles. The differences are imposing, however, when we move to the right side of Table 5.2 and look at the extent to which the private networks rely on these formats to fill their schedules. In 1984 CTV filled no less than 324 hours of its schedule with three talk shows and 260 hours with two quiz shows. These five shows, therefore, account for 82 percent of the total broadcast hours of the CTV schedule devoted in 1984 to Canadian performance categories (this, of course, excludes CTV's other Canadian programs in news, sports, etc.). Global for its part ran 11 such program titles a total of 371 hours, representing 72 percent of its total broadcast hours devoted to Canadian performance categories.

When measured in broadcast hours, CBC again makes far more hours available across the categories than the other networks (except in the Talk, Quiz and Game categories). CBC telecast more hours than the other three networks combined in the categories of Classics, Drama and Documentary. It also telecast more hours than CTV and Global combined in the composite Variety category.

When we turn to the three major French-language station groups, a somewhat different picture emerges as Table 5.3 shows. Once again, CBC (i.e. CBC's French television network) is the only network of the three represented in the six major categories, also producing more titles in each of the first four categories (though not in the Talk and Quiz categories).

Once we take broadcast hours into account, some of the differences between networks noted for English television tend to be less marked in French television. TVA stations scheduled significant amounts of dramatic programming in all sub-categories except Crime Drama. As Table 5.3 shows, none of the three networks produced any programming in this sub-category in 1984, leaving the field wide open to the American police and adventure shows. The provincial public broadcaster (Radio-Québec) also ran 51 hours of Drama (15 titles), considerably more than TVOntario.

The CBC French network ran less than half the number of hours of Variety featured by its English counterpart (70 hours as opposed to 155). Here French CBC was overwhelmed by the 370 hours of Variety broadcast by TVA based on 13 program titles, a much higher reliance than for any other network. One striking difference between CBC's English and French networks lies in the latter's use of 187 hours of one Talk Show title, compared to 11 hours of CBC English. On the other hand, French CBC broadcast only 11.5 hours in the quiz category whereas TVA broadcast no less than 223 hours in this category, nearly twenty times as many hours.

Generally speaking, the TVA stations telecast a considerably larger number of Canadian performance hours in 1984 — 965 — than either CTV (708) or Global (517). TVA relied on the talk and quiz categories for 49 percent of its broadcast hours compared to 82 percent and 72 percent for CTV and Global.

One of the major lessons to be learned from this kind of analysis is that total logged telecast hours are never a sure guide to either overall diversity or to quantity of actual production. The degree to which individual productions are distinctively Canadian remains the major qualitative regulatory problem. The degree to which station groups rely on repeats certainly stands out as a major quantitative problem.

Table 5.2 Canadian Performance Programming[a] Number of Programs and Total Broadcast Hours by Station Group and Program Type (English-language – 1984 Calendar Year)

	Number of Programs (Titles)[b]				Total Hours[c] (Original and Repeats)			
	CBC	CTV	GLOBAL	TVO	CBC	CTV	GLOBAL	TVO
1. Classics	4	1	0	1	9.17	1.5	0	0.5
2. Drama								
– Domestic[d]	13	3	6	2	40.5	21	7	9.5
– Crime	2	3	0	0	11	28	0	0
– Socio-Hist.	18	2	4	0	64	4	32.5	0
– Sitcom	4	1	1	0	58	21	2	0
Subtotal (Drama)	37	9	11	2	173.5	74	41.5	9.5
3. Documentary[e]	44	0	1	25	73	0	3	62.67
4. Variety[f]								
– Comedy performance	1	1	1	0	1.5	21	32	0
– Musical performance	33	3	9	5	73.17	3	67.5	24.5
– Comedy and musical performance	12	3	1	1	22.67	24.5	1	13
– Music Video	4	0	0	1	58	0	0	0.5
Subtotal (Variety)	50	7	11	7	155.34	48.5	100.5	38
5. Talk Shows	2	3	4	1	11	324	58.75	25.5
6. Quiz and Game Shows	2	2	7	0	24	260.5	313.03	0

Source: Bruck et al. "Performance Programming in the Canadian TV-Broadcasting System", study prepared for the Task Force on Broadcasting Policy, Ottawa, 1985

Notes: a. Network only (excludes local production).

b. Individual program titles may be single or multi-episode.

c. Total broadcast hours by program category do not reconcile with total hours available to average viewer because of different methods of calculation.

d. Refers to dramatic content, not nationality.

e. Excludes regular current affairs series.

f. Categories 4, 5 and 6 classify programs somewhat differently from the system used elsewhere in this chapter.

Table 5.3 Canadian Performance Programming[a] Number of Programs and Total Broadcast Hours by Station Group and Program Type (French-language – 1984 Calendar Year)

	Number of Programs (Titles)[b]			Total Hours[c] (Original and Repeats)		
	CBC (Radio Canada)	TVA	Radio-Québec	CBC (Radio Canada)	TVA	Radio-Québec
1. Classics	2	0	0	3	0	0
2. Drama						
– Domestic[d]	15	3	8	118.67	55.5	40.17
– Crime	0	0	0	0	0	0
– Socio-Hist.	3	3	7	17	11	10.83
– Sitcom	5	3	0	52.5	57	0
Subtotal (Drama)	25	9	15	191.17	123.5	51
3. Documentary[e]	15	0	7	22.5	0	24.67
4. Variety[f]						
– Comedy performance	4	1	2	9.17	86	21
– Musical performance	15	4	3	26.17	92.5	32.67
– Comedy and musical performance	7	6	1	29.67	146.3	128
– Music Video	1	2	0	5	45.75	0
Subtotal (Variety)	27	13	6	70.01	370.55	181.67
5. Talk Shows	1	4	4	187	248	83.5
6. Quiz and Game Shows	1	5	0	11.5	223	0

Source: Bruck et al. "Performance Programming in the Canadian TV-Broadcasting System", study prepared for the Task Force on Broadcasting Policy, Ottawa, 1985

Notes: a. Network only (excludes local production).

b. Individual program titles may be single or multi-episode.

c. Total broadcast hours by program category do not reconcile with total hours available to average viewer because of different methods of calculation.

d. Refers to dramatic content, not nationality.

e. Excludes regular current affairs series.

f. Categories 4, 5 and 6 classify programs somewhat differently from the system used elsewhere in this chapter.

Radio

In the past generation radio has become more a delivery system for sound recordings than a generator of programs. But some distinct radio program types or genres such as the open-line show, various kinds of talk show, and news and information programming continue to have impact.

FM radio, with its high fidelity and stereophonic sound capabilities, has reached roughly a 40-percent share of nationwide radio listening and has surpassed AM in some cities.[23] FM's sound transmission capability has fostered the dominance of music programming on radio. In the past few years the FM growth curve has tended to flatten by contrast with FM growth in the United States where it now captures over two-thirds of all listening. Shares of listening for AM and FM stations in Canada from 1976 to 1984 are shown in Figures 5.22 and 5.23.

Private broadcasters dominate the market more in radio than in television, accounting for a 90 percent share of audience in both English and French Canada, the remainder going to CBC AM and FM stations on the English and French networks and a number of community and educational stations. The contrast in programming between private and public sectors has been stronger in radio than television since CBC radio dropped commercials in 1975.

In private radio, individual stations are more in charge of their own programming and less dependent on station groups or networks than is the case in television. In public radio, by contrast, network programming continues to be an important element of CBC French and English stations. Increasingly in English Canada, however, the private stations are turning to syndicated programming delivered by satellite especially in the field of news and public affairs. Quebec stations have a longer history of radio networking. The past generation has also seen the introduction of a new kind of radio broadcasting, community radio. Community broadcasting is the subject of Chapter 19.

Coverage

Virtually everyone in Canada is reached by radio; that is, they can pick up at least one radio station with an AM or FM receiver, and usually several. By contrast with television, few radio stations in Canada today reach mass audiences, partly because there are more than 500 of them and partly because the use of networking in radio is so rare. By Canada's centennial year of 1967, 66 percent of the population could receive nine or more stations. By 1977, that proportion had risen to 80 percent. Nearly all English Canadians could receive four or more English-language stations that year, and most Quebecers were also covered by at least four French-language stations.[24]

There remain wide variations in the number of stations available to different communities, depending on their size or proximity to other centres. In the spring of 1983 Montreal had 22 stations, Toronto 24, both being metropolitan areas with roughly 3 million population each. Metropolitan Vancouver, with less than half their population, had 18 stations, while at half Vancouver's population level Ottawa had 17 and Calgary 14 stations.[25] Halifax County in

Figure 5.22 Trends in the National Share of Listening to English-language Radio Fall 1968 – Fall 1984

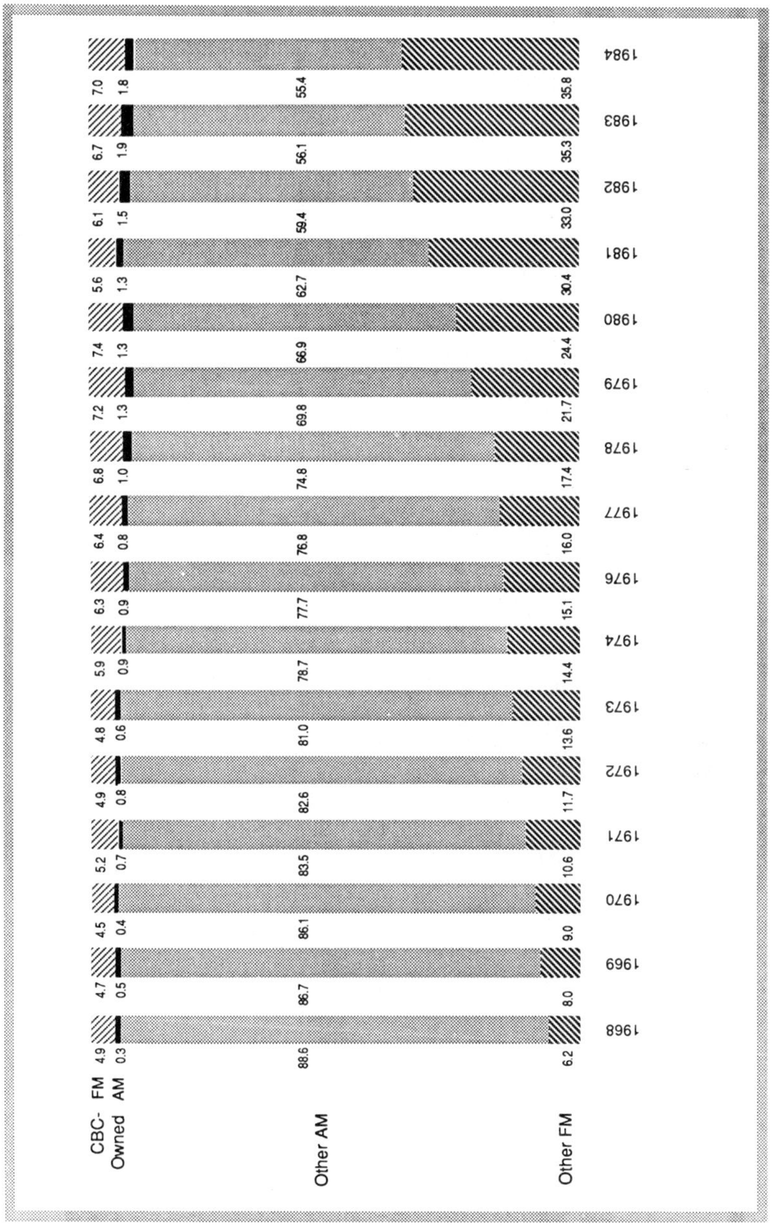

	1968	1969	1970	1971	1972	1973	1974	1976	1977	1978	1979	1980	1981	1982	1983	1984
CBC-Owned FM	4.9	4.7	4.5	5.2	4.9	4.8	5.9	6.3	6.4	6.8	7.2	7.4	5.6	6.1	6.7	7.0
CBC-Owned AM	0.3	0.5	0.4	0.7	0.8	0.6	0.9	0.9	0.8	1.0	1.3	1.3	1.3	1.5	1.9	1.8
Other AM	88.6	86.7	86.1	83.5	82.6	81.0	78.7	77.7	76.8	74.8	69.8	66.9	62.7	59.4	56.1	55.4
Other FM	6.2	8.0	9.0	10.6	11.7	13.6	14.4	15.1	16.0	17.4	21.7	24.4	30.4	33.0	35.3	35.8

Nova Scotia and Kitchener in Ontario, both with populations of 268,000, illustrate the significance of proximity to other population centres. Halifax is covered by 8 stations while Kitchener, where some Toronto and American stations can be received, is covered by 24 Canadian stations. The number of originating stations located in a particular area does not, of course, always coincide with the number of stations receivable. AM stations can sometimes be picked up sporadically across great distances, depending on topography, time of day, weather and so on.

No matter the number of stations, individuals tend to stick to the few they like best. To take a couple of examples, those who listen to radio in St. John's tune an average of 2.4 of its 8 stations; that same average applies to the Durham region of Ontario with 19 stations. Listeners with higher income and educational levels tend to tune a somewhat higher average number of stations, but dial-spinning on radio does not match channel-hopping on television. Nevertheless, most radio listeners are 'duplicated', that is, tend to listen regularly to more than one station.

Listening

In the fall of 1985, 94 percent of Canadians over the age of seven listened to radio at least once in the average week. As with other media, a large proportion of total use is accounted for by a more limited proportion of listeners. The most recent surveys showed 40 percent of the population accounting for three-quarters of the listening; this rough proportion has not changed over the past 10 years.[26]

Children and teenagers are disproportionately low users of radio. Teenagers listen for 13.6 hours a week, compared to the average 19 hours for everyone. There is a slight tendency for older adults to be heavier listeners, but there are no significant differences by educational level or by labour force status; that is, radio's appeal cuts across demographic groupings. But different stations appeal to different segments of the population with different formats.

The major change in radio listening over the past 15 years, the shift to FM listening, is illustrated in Figure 5.22 and Figure 5.23. Private English AM stations have seen their audience share drop to 55 percent in 1984 from 89 percent in 1968, private French AM to 56 percent from 85 percent. The private FM share in both languages has risen to 36 percent from 6 percent. CBC FM shares have also increased, but while CBC's French AM share has gone down, English CBC's has gone up. Since 1984, however, the French AM share has increased again.

According to fall 1984 BBM data, 13 percent of radio listening by francophones is to English stations. The figure is influenced by the heavy English listening of francophones outside Quebec; the 1985 fall data indicated 62 percent of their listening was to English stations. In Quebec the figure was only 8 percent. Tuning by anglophones to French stations is negligible.

While Canadian viewing of television stations in the United States is significant, Canadian listening to American radio stations is not. Although many American stations can be received in the Toronto and Vancouver metropolitan areas, for example, the American station share of audience in Toronto is

Figure 5.23 Trends in the National Share of Listening to French-language Radio
Fall 1968 – Fall 1984

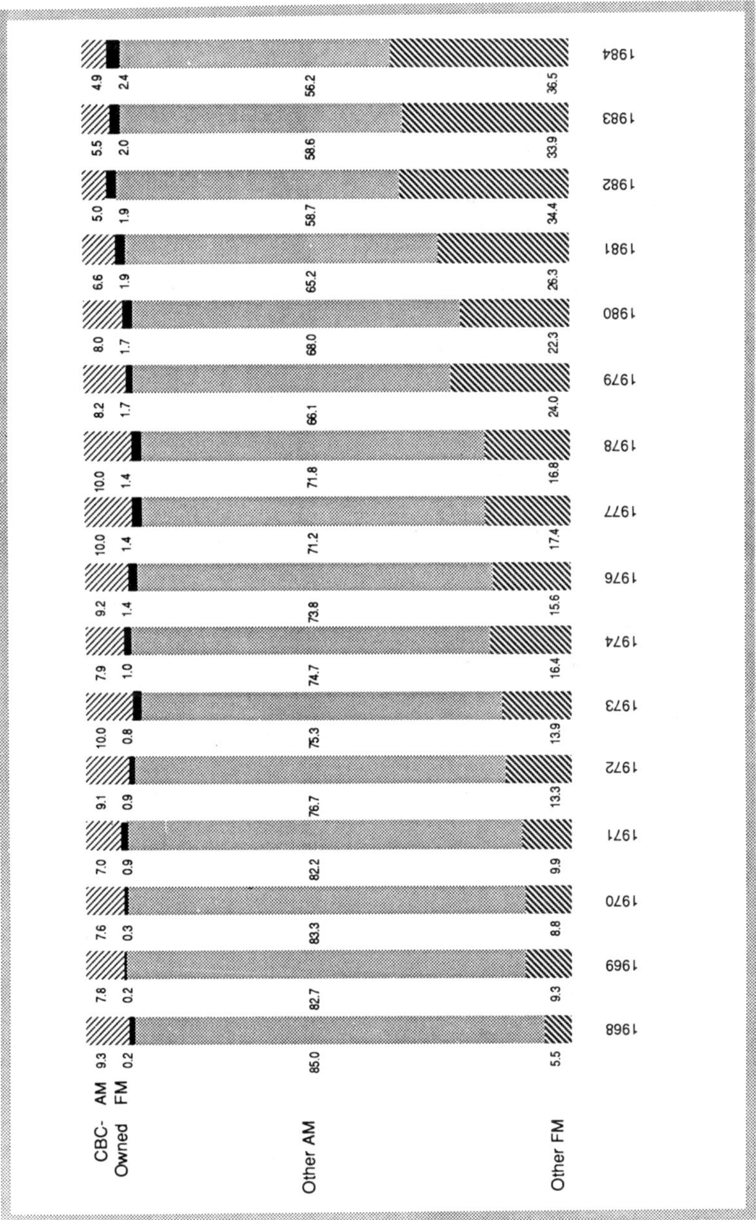

only 4 percent and in Vancouver only 6 percent. In the whole country, it is a little under 4 percent and has remained at that level for the past five years. A few border communities, however, have high listenership to stations in the U.S. — almost 60 percent in Windsor and just over 25 percent in the St. Catharines area.[27]

Radio stations in the major centres serve as magnets to listeners in the surrounding areas. While the three large urban areas in Canada — Toronto, Montreal and Vancouver — account for 30 percent of the population, their radio stations draw 43 percent of tuning. Stations in the medium-sized markets, containing 21 percent of the population, get 28 percent of the audience. Aside from pulling in listeners from rural areas and communities too small for their own stations, the city and metropolitan stations attract listeners with more focused and specialized programming than their small-town counterparts who have to try to suit all tastes.

Formats

Most private radio stations are known by their music, although there are exceptions, the most striking being all-news radio. The CRTC has established a number of music categories in order to lend variety to the various private-sector stations in a given market. CBC stations are not subject to the same system of classification.

The CRTC starts with a large, umbrella category for popular music called 'music — general', which includes just about everything since the beginning of mass produced recordings, provided it has had fairly wide appeal. A second umbrella category is called 'music — traditional and special interest' and includes such music as classical, opera, and authentic folk and jazz. Each category is broken down into sub-categories. It is chiefly the sub-categories of 'music — general' that concern us here because they are the basis of the formats of most private radio stations.

For FM radio, the four popular music formats defined by the CRTC require that 70 percent of the station's popular music programming be devoted to one of the following:

- Group I — Softer music, ranging from instrumental to middle-of-the-road (MOR) and soft rock; includes 'easy listening', also known as 'beautiful music'.
- Group II — Rock, hard rock and harder popular music.
- Group III — Country music.
- Group IV — Other kinds of popular music, such as folk-oriented and jazz-oriented.

The CRTC does not impose a system of musical formats on AM stations. An applicant for an AM licence or licence renewal has to cite the content categories into which the application falls but he is not bound by his choice as a condition of licence, as an FM operator is, and he does not have to have a minimum of 70 percent in one given category.

Since the CRTC introduced its FM policy in 1975, some private stations have been required to include in their programming a certain number of hours of out-of-format music which otherwise would be under-represented in their area. Usually this meant music from the 'music — traditional and special interest' category. More recently, the CRTC has relaxed these special requirements.

Radio Music and Canadian Content

Almost all the records played by private stations in Canada are produced by a few international recording giants: Capitol EMI (British), Polygram (German-Dutch), and CBS, WEA, RCA, MCA (American). With a few notable exceptions, these companies do little to develop Canadian music or talent. CRTC Canadian content rules have served to counteract this pressure toward international conformity. The CBC and independent producers bear a disproportionate burden of the recording and promoting of Canadian musical talent.[28]

For both AM and FM radio, musical content is defined as Canadian by the CRTC if it meets any two of the following four criteria:

1. The music was composed by a Canadian.
2. The lyrics were written by a Canadian.
3. The instrumentation or lyrics were principally performed by a Canadian.
4. The live performance was wholly performed in Canada and broadcast live in Canada, or wholly recorded in Canada.

On AM radio, 30 percent of the musical content must be Canadian. In addition, at least five percent of all selections must be of music composed or lyrics written by a Canadian. On FM, the CRTC has made adjustments to keep quotas in line with the supply of Canadian recordings in the various formats. Thus, in early 1986 the Canadian content rules applied to FM promises of performance in the different categories were: Group I — 20 percent when more vocal than instrumental music is played, otherwise 10 percent; Group II — 20 percent; Group III — 30 percent; Group IV — varies between 20 and 30 percent depending on the mix. The regulator has also given FM stations a 'maximum repeat factor' of 18 plays of one composition a week.

The Commission does not regulate the distribution of Canadian content through the broadcast day, saying only that it should be "scheduled in a reasonable manner". In some highly competitive markets, such as Toronto, concentrating Canadian content in off-peak listening periods is common. In 1985 the CRTC censured CFTR and CHUM-AM for dumping Canadian content into the after-10 p.m. slot.[29]

Diminishing variety is becoming a problem in both English and French record production in Canada, but it reflects reduced diversity everywhere. Investors in the recording industry tend to focus on 'one song, one video, one hit'. Radio station playlists include a smaller choice of songs and more repetition, trying to exploit stars to the maximum profit possibility while avoiding burnout. Canadian content rules may help boost rock singers such as Bryan Adams and Corey Hart to rapid stardom. But stars may then be overplayed and burned out by stations using them to meet content quotas and maximize ad revenues at the same time.

In a musical world dominated by international distributors and a limited number of live-concert stars, a rich tradition such as Canada's country music can get pushed into the shade. Canadian country has recognized subdivisions — traditional, Maritime, Ottawa Valley and Prairies. These indigenous cultural forms have a hard time reaching their own regional audiences, let alone national audiences and the kind of exposure that would give them a crack at recording and radio playlists.

While francophone Quebec had a stronger indigenous tradition of popular culture and performers than anglophone Canada, it too has been affected by the universal impact of Anglo-American music exports. The popular singer-songwriters or chansonniers have suffered. The predominance of rock, which many consider a form of music best suited to English, has encouraged Quebec artists to write and record music in English, as noted in Chapter 2.

The CRTC guideline requiring that 65 percent of vocals on French radio be in French reinforces the notion that self-expression should be in one's mother tongue. There was an outcry from many cultural quarters when the quota was reduced to as low as 55 percent early in 1986 owing to pressure from the broadcasters. Many broadcasters said they had been driven to using old records to meet the quota and were even finding that these were in too limited supply. Record industry spokesmen disputed this view. But there has been general agreement in recent years that there was an inadequate supply of records in some categories such as rock and rock-oriented music.

Background and Foreground

Aside from music formats, the CRTC has also laid down formats governing the balance of music and spoken-word and general presentation. These originated in the desire that radio should not become completely a background accompaniment to other activities. As the CRTC saw it in the 1975 FM regulations, radio should continue to have some 'foreground' programming which demanded the listener's attention and rewarded it.

The CRTC's 'gramophone' and 'rolling' formats cover essentially background programming of musical records with introductions at varying intervals. The 'foreground' format includes live or taped concert performances, magazine and public affairs programs, and human interest presentations related to a particular theme. Foreground segments are required to run at least 15 minutes without commercial interruption. Finally, 'mosaic' format is a format of presentation other than gramophone, rolling or foreground format.

News and Information Programming

The eighties have so far been a difficult time for radio news in the private sector owing to competition from television and a revitalized print sector (particularly magazines), and the effects of the recession on radio broadcasting. In the CBC, on the other hand, news and information programming has been the centrepiece of efforts to put new vigour and appeal into the radio service.

Owing to the 1981 deregulation of radio in the United States it is estimated that only about half that country's 9,000 radio stations still carry news.[30] When they do, the programs tend to be shorter and carry less local news, more network or syndicated news. In Canada, where stations are required by CRTC regulation to carry news, there has not been such a decline in radio news programming.

The Canadian Association of Broadcasters (CAB) reported that in 1984 the cost of news programming to radio stations ranged from a low of 19 percent to a high of 34 percent of total program expenses. As a rule, the larger the station, the higher the proportion of revenue devoted to news. More than half the stations surveyed by the CAB had increased their news budget in the previous five years.[31]

On the whole, CBC radio journalists, French and English, are more highly paid than those in the private sector who usually do not belong to unions, except in Quebec. CBC journalists also as a rule have more time to develop their reports. CBC radio devotes more time and money to recruitment and professional development than does the private sector. A study for this Task Force of francophone radio and TV journalism found that journalists with private French radio stations are usually novices with little experience.[32] This is particularly true outside the major centres. The same can be said for many smaller radio stations outside the major markets in English Canada.

A feature of English radio is the all-news radio network, CKO. It consists of eight FM stations from Vancouver to Halifax, a series of news bureaus, and more than 100 editorial and program personnel, about half of whom are radio journalists. The network has been fighting an uphill battle for survival.

The movement to FM may affect radio news and information in a number of ways. In most major markets, the leading news station is on AM, where it is allowed 250 minutes a day of commercials compared with 150 for an FM station. Thus listeners are switching to a technology that, because of regulation, offers less potential revenue for news and other programming.

Another technological development with a strong influence on news programming is the increasing use of satellite transmission for national and regional radio networks. The radio subcarriers of TV channels are being used to provide relatively cheap service to radio stations. By the end of 1985, Broadcast News, the broadcast subsidiary of the Canadian Press news agency owned by Canada's newspaper proprietors, had installed 100 receiver dishes and was distributing several different channels of service with superior audio quality under an agreement with Canadian Satellite Communications Inc. (CANCOM). These subcarrier channels are also used to move English and French text at high speeds.

Satellite transmission has facilitated creation of regional networks, such as Western Information Network originating in CKNW Vancouver and covering 15 B.C. stations and their rebroadcasters. This type of service offers automated newscasting to local stations and may result in reduction of news staff at these local stations. A major nationwide grouping to facilitate satellite transmission of both radio and TV news and challenge the dominance of BN has taken shape in the form of Electronic News Group Inc., an alliance of major TV and radio interests. The outlook thus appears to be for increasing reliance on syndicated news and information programming.

Conclusion

From among the thousands of discrete pieces of data this chapter has cited or alluded to, a good many patterns begin to emerge. But for those interested in formulating public policy, a much smaller number of clear and critical generalizations can be drawn. It seems to us that those would include the following propositions:

- Canadians watch Canadian performance programming in proportion to its availability.
- They are insatiable consumers of Canadian news programming.
- Canadian children are ill served by what the broadcasting system offers them.
- Private broadcasters have powerful incentives to import American programs and to put Canadian programs at a disadvantage in terms of budgets, scheduling and promotion. The larger private English station groups (CTV, Global) have a better record of support for Canadian programming than do the independent stations as a group.
- Cable has contributed not only to the fragmentation of local broadcaster revenues, but also to a sharp reduction in the proportion of programming available that is Canadian. The viewing of Canadian programs declines in cabled households, as does the viewing of French-language programming in cabled francophone households.
- Increased channel choice is at present not resulting in proportionate increases in program diversity, nor in proportionate increases in the availability of Canadian programming.
- In Quebec, viewing of both English-language television and American programs in particular remains relatively high.
- FM radio continues to take listening share from AM radio.

Much of what follows in this Report is based on those observations. In general, we can see that certain components of the system make only minor contributions to Canadian programming, and that certain categories of Canadian programming are all but absent from our television screens. A great many of the recommendations we make will, we hope, serve to reverse some of these findings.

Notes

1. BBM Bureau of Broadcast Measurement, "A Review of Trends in Canadian Radio Listening, 1976-1985", study prepared for the Task Force on Broadcasting Policy, Ottawa, January 1986.
2. BBM Bureau of Broadcast Measurement, "Trends", p. 7.
3. Ken Purdye, *Temple of Doom . . . or Empty Pew*? (Toronto: Bureau of Broadcast Measurement, 1985), p. 3. Media analysts are not agreed as to whether the amount and effects of VCR time-shifting are over-estimated.
4. Stan Staple, "Supply and Demand: English-language Television in Canada during 1984", study prepared for the Task Force on Broadcasting Policy, Ottawa, 1986.
5. Barry Kiefl, Stan Staple, Roger Cain, and Jim Stanage, "TV/Radio Audience and Program Trends and the Future", report prepared for the Task Force on Broadcasting Policy, Ottawa, 1986.
6. Stan Staple, "Supply and Demand", pp. 1–2.
7. Based on 1984 data. The relationship between availability and viewing is explained in more detail in the next section. See also Figure 5.14.
8. See Stuart McFadyen, Colin Hoskins, and David Gillen, *Canadian Broadcasting: Market Structure and Economic Performance*, (Montreal: The Institute for Research on Public Policy, 1980).
9. Conrad Winn, "The Relative Accessibility of Canadians to American Commercial Programming", study prepared for the Task Force on Broadcasting Policy, Ottawa, 1986.
10. R. Stephen Ellis, "The Trouble with Simulcasting", brief submitted to the Task Force on Broadcasting Policy, Ottawa, 1986.
11. As this table is based on BBM fall sweeps for the three years indicated, it is not directly comparable to other tables based on A.C. Nielsen full-year data.
12. Staple, "Supply and Demand", p. 8.
13. Morris Wolfe, *Jolts: The TV Wasteland and the Canadian Oasis* (Toronto: James Lorimer, 1985).
14. Peter Desbarats, "Radio and Television News: The Role of Public and Private Broadcasters, and Some Other Critical Issues," study prepared for the Task Force on Broadcasting Policy, Ottawa, 1986. The information in this section is largely drawn from the Desbarats study.
15. Canada, Royal Commission on Newspapers, (Kent Commission) *Report* (Ottawa: Minister of Supply and Services Canada, 1981) p. 36.
16. Canadian Broadcasting Corporation, *Let's Do It*!, brief submitted to the Task Force on Broadcasting Policy, Ottawa, 1986 (Ottawa: CBC, 1986), p. 19.
17. Desbarats, "Radio and Television News", p. 120.
18. Walter Romanow, Stuart H. Surlin, and Walter C. Soderlund, "Analysis of Local TV News Broadcasts", study prepared for the Task Force on Broadcasting Policy, Ottawa, 1986.
19. David Nostbakken and André Caron, "Children's Television: Programs, People, Policies", study prepared for the Task Force on Broadcasting Policy, Ottawa, 1986. This section is drawn from the Nostbakken study.
20. Kiefl et al., "Audience and Program Trends".
21. Peter Bruck, Will Straw, and Dennis O'Sullivan, "Performance Programming in the Canadian TV-Broadcasting System", study prepared for the Task Force on Broadcasting Policy, Ottawa, 1986. Much of the information is drawn from this report.
22. *Toronto Star*, June 16, 1986.
23. BBM Bureau of Broadcast Measurement, "Trends".
24. Canadian Radio-television Telecommunication Commission, *Special Report on Broadcasting in Canada, 1968–78*, vol. 1, pp. 61–64.
25. BBM Bureau of Broadcast Measurement, *Special Report* (Toronto: BBM, 1983).
26. Canadian Broadcasting Corporation, *How People Use Radio*, research document (Ottawa: CBC, 1983).

27. Data sources same as Ibid.
28. John Roberts, Denis Bergeron, and Brian Chater, "Music and the Electronic Media in Canada", study prepared for the Task Force on Broadcasting Policy, Ottawa, 1986.
29. Roberts et al., "Music".
30. Desbarats, "Radio and Television News".
31. Canadian Association of Broadcasters, *1984 Analysis of Financial Statistical Data for All Private AM, FM and TV Stations* (Ottawa: CAB, 1985).
32. Bernard Cleary and Michel Cormier, "La presse électronique au Québec", study prepared for the Task Force on Broadcasting Policy, Ottawa, 1986.

Part II

TOWARD A NEW BROADCASTING ACT

The 1968 *Broadcasting Act,*[1] contains most of the provisions that govern broadcasting in Canada. Part I of the Act, which is the key to its distinctiveness, sets out the fundamental principles and establishes the general objectives of Canadian broadcasting policy. Part II assigns the implementation of this policy to the CRTC, which is given broad regulatory powers (the authority of the CRTC over telecommunications falls under a different Act). Part III establishes the Canadian Broadcasting Corporation and states both its objectives and responsibilities.

Few statutes contain this kind of policy statement. Those that do incorporate a great deal of hard-won experience which it is important to preserve.[2] The principles and objectives governing Canadian broadcasting must therefore not be considered a mere preamble: they have normative and symbolic importance of which we are very much aware.

While the CRTC is subject to the stated policy in the sense that each of its decisions must be grounded in policy,[3] it has a great deal of latitude in interpreting the policy, which gives it broad jurisdiction indeed. The independence of the regulatory body is a dominant feature of the existing *Broadcasting Act*. While Parliament may be said to have chosen the point of departure and the destination, the CRTC, and in some instances the government, are free to decide the route. This gives the broadcasting system flexibility to adapt the rights and obligations of licensees, where required, to rapid changes in circumstances.

But everything depends on the principles and objectives stated at the outset in Section 3 of the Act. It is these principles and objectives that define the various components of the system: the CRTC, the Canadian Broadcasting Corporation, the private broadcasters and the rights of viewers and listeners. They state clear choices about Canadian society and it is on these choices that our study will initially focus in Chapter 6.

Whenever these principles need to be modified to reflect current circumstances, the regulatory apparatus designed to implement them must also be reviewed as we show in Chapter 7. The Canadian Broadcasting Corporation is considered separately in Chapter 10.

Notes

1. R.S.C., 1970, c. *Broadcasting Act*, B-11, amended, c. 16 (1st supp.), s. 42 and c. 10 (2nd supp.), s. 65 (item 2), subsection 261; S.C. 1973-74, c. 51; S.C. 1974-75-76, c. 49; S.C. 1984, c. 40, s. 8; S.C. 1984, c. 31, s. 14, schedule 14, no. 6.
2. R. Grant Hammond "Embedding Policy Statements in Statutes: A Comparative Perspective on the Genesis of a New Public Law Jurisprudence" (1982) vol. 5 *Hasting International and Comparative Law Review*, 323, and Jacques Frémont, *Study of Objectives and Principles Proposed and Adopted Concerning the Canadian Broadcasting System*, study prepared for the Task Force on Broadcasting Policy (Montreal: Public Law Research Centre, 1985).
3. Like any agency with powers delegated by Parliament, the CRTC has no inherent powers; it has only the authority recognized implicitly or explicitly in the Act.

Chapter 6

Principles and Objectives

Principles and Objectives

Some of the basic principles of the Canadian broadcasting policy are now included in the Constitution. We shall consider these first because they limit other principles embedded in ordinary statutes.

Principles Guaranteed by the Constitution

The *Canadian Charter of Rights and Freedoms*, which is a part of the *Constitution Act, 1982*[1] guarantees the rights of all Canadians. Since the Charter became law we are the first to attempt an in-depth review of the Canadian broadcasting system, and it is therefore incumbent upon us to examine the extent to which the Charter affects the constitutional basis of the broadcasting system.

The Charter is not merely a statement of intent. It is an integral part of the Constitution and takes precedence over other statutes by limiting their scope. Section 52 of the *Constitution Act* states it as follows: "The Constitution of Canada is the supreme law of Canada, and any law that is inconsistent with the provisions of the Constitution is, to the extent of the inconsistency, of no force or effect."

Section 1 of the *Constitution Act*, however, states that the rights and freedoms guaranteed under the Charter are not absolute. They can only be restricted by "such reasonable limits prescribed by law as can be demonstrably justified in a free and democratic society".[2]

Parliament can thus pass legislation to limit rights and freedoms but not if such limits cannot reasonably be justified, as we shall see in connection with broadcasting.

The Constitution guarantees a number of fundamental rights, of which the most frequently invoked in connection with broadcasting are freedom of expression and, in recent years, the right to equality.[3] The Constitution also recognizes equality of status for English and French in all institutions of the Government of Canada, as well as aboriginal rights, and at the same time states the general objective of preserving and enhancing Canada's multicultural heritage. All rights and freedoms guaranteed under the Charter are, moreover, guaranteed equally to males and females.

Parliament must in the normal course of events provide a legal framework for broadcasting that does not conflict with these fundamental rights. But broadcasting is so complex and plays such an important role in the lives of all Canadians that it sometimes gives rise to conflicts among rights. That is why in setting out a policy Parliament must put forward provisions that reconcile the rights in question, sometimes at the price of placing reasonable limits on the exercise of each.

Freedom of Expression

"Freedom of thought, belief, opinion and expression, including freedom of the press and other media of communication"[4] is clearly the foundation of broadcasting as we conceive it in Canada. The principle has always been the cornerstone of the regulatory system. Moreover, the 1968 Act states that the right to freedom of expression is unquestioned.

There are two opposing views as to how best to interpret this basic freedom in the broadcasting sector. The first is that all persons licensed to operate broadcasting undertakings have a right to express their points of view, which assumes the right to broadcast what they choose subject only to criminal and civil liability. This traditional view generally prevails in print media. According to the second view, licensees are instead considered to be trustees of a public asset, the airwaves, and that far from expressing only the view-points of the owner, their role is surely to make possible, in the name of freedom, the balanced expression of the differing view-points to which any question of public interest gives rise.[5]

Because it is not absolute, freedom of expression cannot be defined once and for all. Rather, it must be based on the reasonable limits, related to the Charter, upon its exercise, whether to extend it from the few to the many, or to make room for other rights. The provisions governing broadcasting are such limits: they must therefore be reasonable and justifiable in a free and democratic society, as laid down in the *Canadian Charter of Rights and Freedoms*.

That most democratic countries have found greater restrictions on freedom of expression in broadcasting than in print media to be acceptable validates the concept under which radio and television undertakings are regarded as public trustees.

On the other hand, one must be careful not to impose restrictions on broadcasters that are so strict that they will no longer be able to make genuine programming decisions. Doing so could certainly not be considered reasonable and justifiable limits on freedom of expression under the Charter.

To establish that a restriction is reasonable and that it can be justified in a free and democratic society, the courts, which are the ultimate arbiters in such matters, verify compliance with the rights and freedoms stated in other provisions of the Charter. According to the Supreme Court,[6] an objective must be of real and urgent social concern in a free and democratic society if it is to be considered important enough to infringe upon a right. Also, the methods chosen to limit a right or freedom guaranteed by the Constitution must be equitable and carefully designed to achieve only the desired objective and be logically linked to it. The Supreme Court recently recalled that the burden of proof in demonstrating that a restriction of a right guaranteed by the Charter is reasonable and that it can be justified in a free and democratic society falls to the party requesting that the restriction be maintained.[7]

It was in this spirit that the Task Force worked on revising the obligations of broadcasters. Broadcasting regulation calls for the development of sophisticated measures to ensure the rights and freedoms of all in the use of a public asset, radio waves. A balance among the various rights and freedoms at issue must be sought and taken into consideration in all important decisions.

Equality Rights

The right to equality in broadcast programs has led to vigorous debate because it has been claimed that it conflicts with freedom of expression. Some want the promotion of equality among various social groups to become one of the objectives of programming. Bill C-20 proposed the following amendment to the *Broadcasting Act*:

> The programming provided by the Canadian broadcasting system should respect and promote the equality and dignity of all individuals, groups or classes of individuals regardless of race, national or ethnic origin, colour, religion, sex, age or mental or physical disability[8]

This proposed amendment was met with misgivings. The Consumers Association of Canada considered that such a provision, by obliging the CRTC to foster human equality and dignity, would place an even heavier burden on the Commission than is placed on censors.[9] The Canadian Cable Television Association saw it as an unhealthy form of interventionism, as did the Canadian Association of Broadcasters, who feared that the CRTC would be in a position to exercise absolute control over program content.[10]

Other groups, however, want the amendment strengthened to eliminate unequivocally discriminatory stereotypes on the grounds that television is a determining factor in the development of such stereotypes and attitudes.

It is clear that the *Canadian Charter of Rights and Freedoms* affects the regulation of the use of public airwaves. The embryonic state of research on freedom of expression, the right to equality and appropriate methods of regulation hampers discussion of such issues. It should not deter us, however, from giving careful consideration to the relationship between the right to equality and broadcasting activities.

Current debate on this aspect of Bill C-20 centres on the question of whether radio and television programs should promote equality or reflect the various groups in an equitable manner.

It is frequently argued that it is not up to the media to promote equality. The media, whose purpose is to reflect reality, would become censors if they were to take on a task of righting wrongs. From this point of view, the idea of obliging the press to promote a cause, however legitimate it might be, is incompatible with freedom of expression.

According to advocates of the promotion approach, however, section 15 of the *Canadian Charter of Rights and Freedoms* not only prohibits Parliament and the provincial legislatures from passing discriminatory measures, but also requires them to act in such a way as to encourage and protect the right to equality.[11]

Recognizing that the Constitution now prohibits discrimination, other groups have argued that programs need only adequately reflect the presence of women and minority groups. Obviously many Canadians, including the Task Force members, agree that stereotyped discrimination or portrayals that could lead to prejudice and discriminatory behaviour are unacceptable. But while it is easy to recognize the promotion of equality as praiseworthy in itself, to impose it on broadcasting by a provision with the force of law raises many problems, not the least of which is the contradiction with the freedom associated with the very concepts of creativity and a free flow of information.

Our concern is to achieve compliance with both freedom of expression and the right to equality without doing so at the expense of either. Freedom of expression exhorts us to intervene as little as possible in what is broadcast while the right to equality imposes on broadcasters a responsibility for the messages they broadcast in that respect.

Administering a legislative provision calling for the fostering of equality would clearly require a highly developed system for monitoring and analyzing all programming. A code of professional ethics is a more desirable alternative; however, the efforts of the CRTC and the broadcasting industry to combat stereotypes have thus far yielded results that some consider inadequate.

In 1984 the CRTC amended its regulations on AM broadcasting, FM broadcasting, television broadcasting and cable to include a prohibition of the broadcast of

> any abusive comment or abusive pictorial representation that when taken in context, tends or is likely to expose an individual or a group or class of individuals to hatred or contempt on the basis of race, national or ethnic origin, colour, religion, sex, age or mental or physical disability.[12]

The purpose of this provision is to prevent the most obvious forms of discriminatory programming. It can be shown to be a reasonable and justifiable limit on freedom of the press and other media because the abusive representations targeted by the provisions are similar to those for which Canadian courts have admitted that freedom of expression may be limited.[13]

The new provision also covers stereotyping or at least the most reprehensible examples. Stereotypical representations must, however, be distinguished from abusive programming.

Stereotyping

In 1979 the CRTC, at the request of the Minister of Communications, established the Task Force on Sex-role Stereotyping in the Broadcast Media. The Task Force's report *Images of Women* explained that it was the cumulative effect of stereotyped portrayals that was likely to lead to discriminatory behaviour:

> It is not the isolated incident of portraying a woman in a stereotyped role that is at the center of public criticism. When a program or commercial presents a stereotyped image of a woman or a man in a certain role, it may be acceptable for that particular role in that particular script. Rather, it is the cumulative effect of associating women and girls with certain roles, products, and behaviour that is the source of concern. For example, when too many portrayals show the man as the breadwinner and the woman as the homemaker, the cumulative effect is that men and women become associated exclusively with those roles. An identical problem occurs when men and women appear again and again in traditional "male" or "female" jobs, perform only "male" or "female" tasks, and consistently display sex-stereotyped behaviour.
>
> The constant repetition of these images tends to reinforce their perceived reality, thus influencing the attitudes of women, men, and children, and encourages both women and girls to limit their horizons both socially and professionally to those roles which they see portrayed.[14]

The same is true of ethnic stereotypes. In its Public Notice entitled *A Broadcasting Policy Reflecting Canada's Linguistic and Cultural Diversity*, dated July 4th, 1985, the CRTC stated that:

> Representatives of cultural and visible minority groups and organizations across Canada felt that many broadcasting undertakings do not accurately portray ethnic groups. Such portrayal ranges from classic stereotyping to instances where biased treatment of ethnic and racial minorities is involved.[15]

The struggle against discrimination therefore requires that we pay close attention to the stereotypes found in the media if we are to ensure that they do not give rise to prejudices that will lead to discriminatory behaviour against women or minority groups.

In a research study prepared for the Task Force, Mahoney and Martin[16] argue that section 15 of the *Canadian Charter of Rights and Freedoms*, which guarantees equality rights to every individual, can be used to justify regulations prohibiting stereotyping. Such regulations would be a justifiable limit on freedom of expression because their purpose would be to protect the equality rights guaranteed by the Constitution. The absence of regulation and the proliferation of images which depict stereotypes could even be considered a form of discrimination prohibited by the Constitution. It could also be asserted that all the other rights and freedoms guaranteed by the Constitution are themselves reasonable and justifiable limits on freedom of expression, and were formulated specifically to set such limits.

These arguments support the provision in Bill C-20 which states that "the programming provided by the Canadian broadcasting system should respect and promote the equality and dignity of all individuals".[17]

While recognizing the legitimacy of the objective, which is the elimination of stereotypes, the wording opens the door to an interpretation that would allow intervention by the public authorities in programming decisions to achieve the desired goals. Such interference seems to us altogether incompatible with freedom of expression. That is why the provision stated in section 3 of Bill C-20 should be rejected.

There would also be further problems for the CRTC in administering such a provision. It would, for example, have to develop sufficiently precise criteria to make it possible to distinguish clearly what is allowed from what is not. So accurate, adds Marie Finklestein in her study for the Task Force, that they "must quantify in percentage terms the type of programming required". Hence the problem of attempting to quantify the obligations needed to promote equality. Finklestein states:

> The problem is how the CRTC can possibly quantify the amount of programming required to meet stated equality objectives. How many black program hosts, for example, is enough to promote the equality of blacks in Canadian society? It is submitted that any such determination would be completely arbitrary and would effectively cast the CRTC rather than the broadcaster in the role of programmer.[18]

The CRTC ought not to be allowed to become so deeply involved in programming decisions.

Thus far, the CRTC's efforts to develop standards for decreasing stereotyped portrayals have taken a different approach, more respectful of civil liberties. The approach, called self-regulation, involves voluntary compliance by broadcasters with a code of ethics.

Following the publication of the *Images of Women* Report, the CRTC established a self-regulatory program with its industry partners. The evaluation of the program has just been completed. According to the CRTC's 1986 report on the program, there has been a decline in sex-role stereotyping, although many forms of stereotyping remain. The Canadian Association of Broadcasters (CAB), in co-operation with advertisers, amended its Code of Ethics to include clauses addressing sex-role stereotyping in programming, adopted its own self-regulatory guidelines, and established a standing committee to receive complaints from the public. The CBC, for its part, monitored its own programming and concluded that stereotypical representations of women and conventional role portrayals were still numerous.

The same trend is taking shape to prevent ethnic stereotypes. At the CRTC hearing on ethnic broadcasting policy in March 1985, the Canadian Association of Broadcasters announced that its committee on ethical and social issues was planning to develop guidelines on ethnic program content.

The approach does appear to be yielding results for sex role stereotyping. Although one might wish for more rapid progress, some changes have taken place in the portrayal of men and women on television and radio. The question is not so much whether more changes are needed; it is clear that the complete elimination of discriminatory representations and sex-role stereotypes is the objective. The important point at issue is rather how to go about achieving it. Would a higher level of interventionist regulation have led to any better results? It will no doubt always be extremely difficult to define general standards to be applied to creative endeavour, partly because creativity is inherently difficult to measure and partly because measurement of this kind is largely subjective, depending on changing perceptions. Much remains to be done in exploring regulatory approaches that will respect these features, at least in the Canadian context.

Thus far, common sense has always been the best way of identifying stereotyping in the broadcast media. The right to equality is not necessarily denied by the broadcast of any particular program, no matter how full of stereotypes it may be. Problems begin to arise when all of a licensee's programming tends in the same direction. It is up to the broadcaster to ensure that programming generally strikes an appropriate balance. Also, nothing can replace the role of the public itself. It is the public that listens and watches. With appropriate mechanisms allowing individual and group complaints to be taken into account, it would be possible to determine which sorts of programming encourage stereotypes. In the next chapter we recommend the appointment by the CRTC of public advocates in its regional offices. By receiving and following up such complaints and intervening at licence renewal hearings, the public advocates could help to ensure that a licensee's overall programming complies with the right to equality.

All such measures, appealing to personal responsibility, attempt to reconcile the right to equality with freedom of expression. They will no doubt not please those who believe that one or other of these two rights must take precedence. The rest, ourselves included, recognize that the rights and freedoms upon which our society is based must be balanced and that this balance takes shape in broadcasting within the regulatory process.

Recommendation

When licences are renewed, the CRTC should ensure that the overall programming offered by licensees does not conflict with the right to equality.

Participation of Women and Minorities in Broadcasting

However successful a policy based on a self-regulatory approach and increased public awareness may be, it cannot alone guarantee equitable representation for women and minority groups on radio and television. Only increased participation of women and individuals belonging to minorities in broadcasting will bring about change.

Stereotypes are a manifestation of a deeper problem; women and minorities are under-represented in most broadcasting jobs. Equality of employment opportunity at all levels of broadcasting is a fundamental objective here as elsewhere, because changes have to come about before they can be portrayed: the frequency of stereotypical portrayals will diminish if more women and members of minorities contribute to the development and production of programs and to broadcast programming decisions.

The Employment Equity Bill[19] proposes requiring licensees to report annually on the number of women hired in each employment group. The figures should include the number of vacant positions, the number of persons hired and the number of promotions. Statistics like these, which are not available at the moment, would make it possible to measure progress. Broadcasting undertakings should also be required to implement programs to encourage increased hiring of women and members of minorities in strategic positions. We recommend that this requirement be made a condition of licence. The equal employment opportunity programs would require a commitment to a significant increase in the number of women and the number of members of minorities at all employment levels. Like any other condition of licence, they could vary to suit the specific conditions of each undertaking.

In order to increase their influence in broadcasting, the government should take appropriate action to ensure that more women and representatives of minority groups are appointed to bodies like the CRTC and the boards of directors of the Canadian Broadcasting Corporation and Telefilm Canada.

Finally, there is a need for more programs prepared by women. There is no longer any need to prove that women can produce quality programs. In the seventies, Radio-Canada produced and broadcast *Femmes d'aujourd'hui*, which greatly influenced the movement to redefine the role of women in society. At the National Film Board, Studio D has produced many very interesting films that were well received by the public, including *Not a Love Story*, *If You Love this Planet*, *The Way It Is*, and *Dream of a Free Country: A Message from Nicaraguan Women*, to name only a few. Just as the excellent work of Studio D — which, to Canada's credit, is the only experiment of its kind in the world — deserves praise, it is deplorable that there are so few productions by women; many more should find their way to our screens. We would like to see all institutions involved in program production grant women and minorities equal opportunities to produce and disseminate their works.

Recommendations

> Broadcasting licences should include an obligation to establish an equal employment opportunity program. Such programs should provide for efforts to increase significantly the number of women and members of minority groups at all levels within each undertaking and be adjusted to suit the specific conditions of each undertaking.
>
> The Government should appoint women and members of minority groups to the CRTC, to the Board of Directors of the Canadian Broadcasting Corporation and to other decision-making positions in sufficient numbers to reflect their relative numbers in society.
>
> All broadcasters should ensure that women and minority groups have equal opportunity to produce and disseminate their works.

Essential Public Services

In addition to guaranteeing these fundamental rights, the Canadian Constitution refers to the rights of Canadians to essential public services of "reasonable quality".

> Without altering the legislative authority of Parliament, or of the provincial legislatures, or the rights of any of them with respect to the exercise of their legislative authority, Parliament and the legislatures, together with the government of Canada and the provincial governments, are committed to . . . providing essential public services of reasonable quality to all Canadians.[20]

Although the wording of this provision is far from clear, analysts have not given it the attention it deserves. It is unusual for a constitutional instrument to refer merely to the "commitment" of Parliament and the legislatures. It would appear that it involves neither an obligation to act nor any changes in their respective jurisdictions. In fact, it raises more questions than it answers. The one thing that is certain is that the commitment stops at "essential public services" without ever defining them.

Do the meaning and scope of this provision provide all Canadians with a right to essential broadcasting services? Is this constitutional commitment of Parliament and the legislatures intended to cover the public broadcasting sector?

Could it be invoked to prevent any dismantling of such services? Without going to such an extreme, does a provision of this kind provide a constitutional basis for the principle, heretofore well established in Canadian tradition, of the independence of the CBC?

While the answers to the questions raised by this provision of the Constitution may not be obvious (it is up to the courts to decide them), the fact remains that for a large number of Canadians, public broadcasting services are deemed to be essential. That is why Parliament must take this constitutional commitment into consideration. Although it is clear that it is up to our elected representatives to determine the means to be used, the conditions under which public broadcasting services are organized and provided cannot be considered 'acceptable' without taking qualitative considerations into account. It has been argued that there is a minimum level below which the resources devoted to public broadcasting cannot be reduced without affecting the quality of programming. We limit ourselves in this instance to reporting the facts: just as the Constitution guarantees a number of rights and freedoms, the principle stated in section 36 (a) circumscribes, to an extent not yet clearly established, Parliament's freedom of action with respect to public broadcasting services.

Principles Stemming from the Act

The unique aspect of the *Broadcasting Act*[21] is that it begins with a policy statement followed by a delegation of powers.[22] It was the Fowler Committee (1965) that first suggested including a policy statement in the Act. The Fowler Report attributed the problems of Canadian broadcasting to an inadequate formulation of the goals set forth by Parliament. That is why it recommended:

> Parliament should state firmly and clearly what it expects the boadcasting system to be and do; and should set explicit goals for both the public and private sectors of Canadian broadcasting in the Broadcasting Act and more fully in a White Paper on broadcasting policy . . . [23]

The 1968 *Broadcasting Act* was the first to receive this addition. It carefully set forth the principles and objectives of the system and then assigned to the CRTC the powers to regulate and control it.

Critics of the Act have not called the model itself into question. What they argue about is the relevance of the objectives. Section 3 is criticized for not including the whole field of broadcasting, cable operations for example, which has sometimes led the CRTC to hand down decisions without a firm principle upon which to base them.[24]

The way in which the system is organized, requiring objectives from Parliament and the implementation of these objectives through an independent authority, assigns enormous decision-making powers to the authority. The advantage of this method is that it can deal with a variety of situations and interests in a flexible manner. But its effectiveness depends entirely on the regulatory body so established, which is expected to be able, without betraying the general objectives, to adapt the system to circumstances by using innovative approaches and yet remain fully aware of its responsibilities. As we consider what principles and objectives to define in the new act, we are also assuming, before even providing for it, that there will be an effective regulatory authority capable of basing its decisions on Parliament's policies.

Some have been tempted to see the prescriptions of Parliament as being opposed to the laws of the marketplace and technological progress, as if they were mutually exclusive. However, if the objectives already included in the Act as well as those we are putting forward are reviewed, it becomes clear that they do not imperil the commercial viability of the broadcasting undertakings as demonstrated by the performance of broadcasting compared to other industries. If these objectives are to be achieved, the industry must be healthy and dynamic.

What some people perceive to be constraints are values that are inherent in the mixed nature of broadcasting, which is both economic and cultural. These values encourage the use of Canadian talent and imagination to develop a strong and dynamic Canadian industry to reflect the creative output of Canadians, wherever they may live and whatever language they may speak.

We believe we must once again gamble that the Canadian broadcasting system will stand a far better chance of prospering by remaining true to its own traditions rather than indiscriminately copying foreign models.

Recommendation

The *Broadcasting Act* should continue to state the fundamental principles upon which Canadian broadcasting policy is based. This policy statement should be the basis for decisions by the government and the broadcasting regulatory authorities respecting the undertakings which make up the broadcasting system.

The Public Character of Radio Frequencies

To the best of our knowledge, the radio frequencies used for broadcasting are considered to be public property in every country of the world, even though they are subject to many different forms of control, ranging from government monopolies to commercial operations with varying degrees of regulation.

It has often been claimed that the rules governing broadcasting activity ought to be liberalized because the basic justification for existing regulations — the scarcity of frequencies — no longer holds true. According to this line of argument, although radio frequencies have in the past been considered public property because of their scarcity, such frequencies, including those used for broadcasting, are no more scarce than other goods.[25] Moreover it is argued that alternative methods for carrying broadcasting signals have been developed, notably cable and satellites. Scarcity is being replaced by a proliferation of channels.

Nevertheless, the radio frequencies that can be used for broadcasting are not unlimited; nor does the availability of a large number of channels guarantee access to them. It is unlikely that the time will come when anyone who happens to have the appropriate resources will be able to broadcast at will, just as written materials are printed and published. The government has a number of other reasons for maintaining control over the airwaves, including its international responsibilities in the assignment of frequencies in order to avoid technical interference. A degree of regulation is also needed to define broadcasting countours within boundaries. Radio frequencies are also needed for purposes other than broadcasting. For example, UHF frequencies are used for both television and land mobile radio[26] and they can interfere with one another. This too makes public intervention necessary.

If Parliament wishes to continue to have a different regulatory system for broadcasting than for other forms of communication, it should provide reasonable arguments in favour of doing so. Otherwise the courts might determine that the regulations are incompatible with freedom of the press and other media. Although the scarcity of radio frequencies was for a long time the main justification for restrictions, it has never been the only one.[27] The social and cultural importance of broadcasting, the still little-known effects of broadcasting on audiences, and the need to protect certain minorities have been added to scarcity of frequencies and to the need to co-ordinate transmission sources[28] as reasons for regulating broadcasting.

Unlike American communications legislation which was designed primarily for co-ordination purposes, Canadian broadcasting policy has always pursued social and cultural objectives. It was never just because radio frequencies were scarce, but also because the Canadian presence on the airwaves was weak, that since 1929 commissions of inquiry into broadcasting have recommended strengthening the system. The assignment of radio frequencies for broadcasting in Canada is an essential component of national sovereignty.

Because of the urgency of the issue, Canada has always expected broadcasting to reflect the country's identity. From the outset radio and television were considered instruments for creative expression, education and information by and for Canadians rather than simply as entertainment media. The availability of a larger number of channels will do little or nothing to guarantee access or to ensure that the airwaves will reflect the Canadian identity and culture.

There are therefore still very good reasons for maintaining the public character of the radio frequencies used for broadcasting. It is not so much on the ground of the scarcity of radio frequencies that this policy is justified, but rather because of the importance of broadcasting in maintaining our national identity and expressing the values upon which our society is based.

Those who are granted the right to use radio frequencies are given an important responsibility. Contributing to the dissemination of Canadian culture is a duty inherent in the privilege they are granted as a public trust on behalf of Canadians.

Recommendation

The *Broadcasting Act* should continue to include the principle that radio frequencies used for broadcasting are public property. All persons authorized to use radio frequencies should be considered trustees of the Canadian public.

Broadcasting Undertakings Considered as a System

The present Act states that undertakings authorized to broadcast in Canada constitute a single system comprising both public and private elements. It states that the broadcasting undertakings are to be considered as a whole because the objectives referred to in the Act are assigned to the whole. The White Paper that preceded the passage of the Act stated that:

> The Canadian broadcasting system, comprising public and private sectors, must be regarded as a single system which should be regulated and controlled by a single independent authority.[29]

It is nevertheless a whole made up of many parts and in which are found not only French and English as well as public and private elements but also general services and specialty services, commercial stations and community stations, urban areas and virtually unpopulated regions. It is unrealistic to hold the same expectations for each of the many elements in the broadcasting system. The Government of Nova Scotia noted in its brief to the Task Force that:

> Although the Broadcasting Act states that private and public broadcasting undertakings constitute a single Canadian broadcasting system, we would argue that there are, in fact, two systems — one private and one public. The expectations, mandate and role each takes should be premised on this assumption.[30]

The Canadian broadcasting system does in fact consist of undertakings with different goals. Private undertakings clearly have profit motives while the mandates of public broadcasting services are defined by Parliament or the provincial legislatures. Depending on the region, the roles of community stations vary considerably.

These differences are not incompatible with the pursuit of the national objectives defined by Parliament for broadcasting. That is why the broadcasting undertakings should henceforth be considered a composite system. Each must contribute in its own way to the achievement of the public-service objectives assigned to the Canadian broadcasting system.

Recommendation

> Within the meaning of the Act, broadcasting undertakings should be considered part of a composite system, each contributing in its own way to the achievement of the objectives assigned to the Canadian broadcasting system.

Definition of Terms

Because it states policy, the *Broadcasting Act* is demanding of individuals and undertakings involved in broadcasting. If responsibilities are to be shared equitably, it is important to have an unambiguous statement of what is included in the broadcasting system.

Because of developments in broadcasting and telecommunications, two concepts must be redefined: "broadcasting", to cover the provisions of all scheduled television programming services, and the transmission and distribution of such services by whatever means; and "broadcasting undertaking" to reflect network structures.

Broadcasting

The *Radio Act* and the *Broadcasting Act* define broadcasting as "any radiocommunication in which the transmissions are intended for direct reception by the general public". This definition covers only the activities of undertakings that broadcast their programs free of charge to anyone who has equipment capable of receiving the signals. It is based on the assumption of program transmission by Hertzian waves, which was the dominant configuration in 1968 when the *Broadcasting Act* was passed.

Because it covers only radiocommunication in which the broadcasts are intended for "direct" reception by the "general" public, the definition appears to ignore the many program services such as specialty services transmitted by point-to-point satellites that are distributed to subscribers only. It was determined that such services are not intended for reception by the general public and therefore are not broadcasting services within the meaning of the Act. Nevertheless, pay-television is intended for the general public insofar as it is prepared to pay.

In its brief to the Task Force, Allarcom Limited expressed the need for a new and broader definition of broadcasting as follows:

> There is a definite need to revise the legal definition of broadcasting so as to clearly encompass the various forms of broadcasting operations that have resulted from technological advances in the field of telecommunications. For the purposes of a national broadcasting policy, broadcasting should include origination, transmission, distribution and reception of signals through various configurations, and the use of any combination of telecommunications means for the purpose of providing programming to the viewing public, whether any consideration is involved or not.[32]

The important thing is to include all forms of transmission, distribution and reception of signals containing programs intended for the public, whether in scrambled form or not.

It is not fair for individuals or companies involved in activities that very closely resemble the activities of companies considered to be part of the broadcasting system to be able to avoid the obligations incumbent upon the latter simply because the definition of broadcasting in the Act is too narrow to include them.

Defining a Broadcasting Undertaking

The definition of a broadcasting undertaking should of course tally with the definition of broadcasting. It should cover not only the transmission and reception of broadcast signals, but also any other form of program distribution by telecommunication, whether or not there is a charge for the service, as well as networks. All undertakings involved in such activities would, within the meaning of the Act, be considered broadcasting undertakings. Only common carriers such as telephone companies should be exempted because their role is limited to relaying messages.

The network concept requires special attention because broadcasting networks have grown dramatically over the past 20 years. The 1968 Act defines the word "network" as:

> . . . any operation involving two or more broadcasting undertakings whereby control over all or any part of the programs or program schedules of any of the broadcasting undertakings involved in the operation is delegated to a network operator.[33]

The definition implies a delegation of authority. The broadcaster assigns to the network operator control over all or part of his programming. The network is therefore an entity distinct from those it controls for specific purposes.

In Canada today there are three major network categories: radio networks, television networks, and satellite-to-cable networks. The *Broadcasting Act* covers only the first two. The introduction of satellite-to-cable networks came much later, and the Act has not yet been amended to accommodate them in explicit terms.

Radio and television networks decide what programs will be offered to their affiliates and are therefore responsible for the programming and regulated accordingly. Since one of the objectives of the Act is to apply certain standards to all undertakings that have a degree of control over the programs broadcast in the interests of Canadians, it is clear that undertakings which distribute programs, even though they may not have produced them, have ultimate control over access to these programs by the Canadian public. There is therefore no reason to exempt undertakings that operate satellite-to-cable networks from the meaning of the act.

These networks are nevertheless operated differently from conventional radio and television networks. Their relations with cable operators are more like a transmission contract than the typical affiliation contract. Since the definitions in the current Act do not make such distinctions, they should be amended before the regulatory concepts become distorted as a result of trying to squeeze services based on new technology into categories formulated for another era.

If all the activities and undertakings that make programming available to the public through electronic means are to be covered by the Act, then we recommend new definitions for three concepts: broadcasting, broadcasting undertaking, and network. There are some activities and undertakings that will be subject to little or no regulation. Such decisions should be the responsibility of the regulatory authority and be based on consistent reasons rather than on the inadequacy of the definitions given in the Act.

Recommendations

> The Act should cover all undertakings involved in broadcasting in the widest sense, that is, those that decide what programs to carry, as well as those that are involved in program dissemination to the public and thus in determining program accessibility to Canadians.

> The Act should broaden the definition of broadcasting and related concepts to cover all types of program reception and distribution whether by Hertzian waves or through any other technology.

Canadian Ownership of the System

The *Broadcasting Act* states that "the Canadian broadcasting system should be effectively owned and controlled by Canadians so as to safeguard, enrich and strengthen the cultural, political, social and economic fabric of Canada".[34] Following the adoption of the Act in 1968, the regulatory authorities ensured that undertakings owned by non-Canadians were sold to Canadians in compliance with the Act. All broadcasting undertakings operated in Canada are now in the hands of Canadians. This is a situation which must be maintained, because it makes it possible in principle to carry out the next step, which is to encourage them to "safeguard, enrich and strengthen the cultural, political, social and economic fabric of Canada". The Canadian ownership requirement, while it is essential, cannot by itself "Canadianize" the airwaves, as experience has shown, because it does not address the content issue. This is an objective that will best be achieved through a careful regulatory approach.

Recommendation

> The Act should reaffirm the principle that only Canadians may own and control broadcasting undertakings in Canada.

A Broadcasting System for Canadians

The idea that the Canadian broadcasting system should contribute towards "safeguarding, enriching and strengthening the cultural, political, social and economic fabric of Canada" is not a new one. Many commissions of inquiry into broadcasting have supported the idea and nothing would appear to be more legitimate than to count on Canadian broadcasting to serve first the interests and needs of Canadians.

In an area where cultural considerations are also at stake, one cannot restrict debate to purely economic concerns. For example, it is difficult to argue that costly Canadian products should be replaced by lower-cost foreign goods in the field of broadcasting because if Canadians do not produce works that reflect their own culture, no one will do it for them; it is only when the market has a reasonable share of Canadian creative works that Canadians will find a reflection of themselves.

To this extent, we subscribe to Parliament's objective. But taken in isolation as formulated in the Act, it invokes the idea of undue political pressure, "national promotion", that would in some way be applied to programming. At this stage, the important point is to put the objective back in its proper context to allow us to understand its meaning correctly. It is now in the section that requires Canadian ownership of broadcasting undertakings so as to "safeguard, enrich and strengthen" etc. This means that it is intended to support a measure designed to regain control over the system and we have already seen that regaining ownership of the system is not enough to guarantee that Canadians will find their proper place on Canadian airwaves.

This, then, goes some way toward explaining how the Act was a reaction to a powerful and recurring trend present from the very inception of Canadian broadcasting: left to itself, Canadian broadcasting slips out of the hands of Canadians. The intent is not to promote something but rather to redress a specific state of affairs. The purpose is to establish conditions that give Canadians access to a medium of expression that has a complex and ponderous infrastructure.

The expression "safeguard, enrich and strengthen the cultural, political, social and economic fabric of Canada" may appear to be mere rhetoric, even to some members of the Task Force, but placed in a broader perspective that clearly shows it to be an objective of Canadian policy, it becomes forceful again. The current French version of the Act uses the word "structure" for the English "fabric". The word "tissu" would be a more appropriate translation. It would be a good idea to make this linguistic amendment.

The objective requires that the Canadian broadcasting system should play an active role in fostering a greater awareness of Canada and make available a greater variety of Canadian programming to allow the expression of the Canadian identity. It binds those involved in the Canadian broadcasting system to make their operations consistent with these objectives. The objective may on occasion conflict with the short-term interests of some participants. But it would tend in the long run to make a reality of the principle of Canadian broadcasting for Canadians, whatever region they may live in and whatever their culture. A concern for regionalism is one of the things that sets Canada apart. The broadcasting system must therefore be open to aspiring artists from across Canada who wish to have their work distributed and meet particular regional needs. Its programming must by the same token reflect Canada's cultural diversity as urged by many minority groups (see Chapter 22).

Recommendation

In both its organization and operation, the Canadian broadcasting system should serve the interests of all Canadians and their need to express themselves, in order to "safeguard, enrich and strengthen the cultural, political, social and economic fabric of Canada".

The Canadian broadcasting system should play an active role in developing an awareness of Canada, reflect the cultural diversity of Canadians and make available a wide range of programming that is Canadian in content and character and that provides for a continuing expression of Canadian identity. It should serve the special needs of the geographic regions and actively contribute to the flow and exchange of information and expression among the regions of Canada.

Access to the Broadcasting System

Although Canadians have access to innumerable radio and television programs, comparatively few Canadians manage to express themselves through radio and television. The problem remains one of providing an equitable place for everyone in the broadcasting system: Canadians in general; producers, workers and artists in various regions or representing various views; finally, aboriginal peoples, minorities, women, and local communities. All these groups stated in our consultations that they had little or no access to the system. The introduction of a new multi-channel environment increases the number of doorways but does not necessarily open them. Paradoxically, the proliferation of channels contrasts with a drought in programming as creative talents remain untapped. The challenge of the coming years will therefore be to provide increased access to the airwaves for a diverse range of Canadian communities and interest groups.

There has been a failure to anticipate that once Canadians in every remote corner of the country had been provided with radio and television programming they would want to play a more active role. It must not be forgotten that the art of communication is itself communicative. Access to the airwaves, which has for so long faced technical barriers, is now within reach and the new technologies have given a renewed impetus to demands for such access, spurred on by the apparent realization of the old dream of a universal forum in which people in isolated villages become part of the bustling "global village".

Although the reality is perhaps not on such a grand scale, many new forms of access are indeed appearing and it is up to the state to decide how to allot these. Local communities (city neighbourhoods, small towns, isolated villages, northern communities) have needs for expression and information that no national service will ever be able to meet. The low power stations that were established in many communities were testing grounds, classrooms for the people, public markets and community centres, and it was here that community broadcasting developed.

Canada played a pioneer role in community radio and television. Under CRTC regulations, most cable operators include a community channel in the basic service offered to subscribers. Community radio stations, especially in Quebec, broadcast over-the-air.

Community broadcasting has proved to be very useful on occasion in providing access to the system. That is why we recommend that it should be recognized in the Act as a distinct sector in the system, on an equal footing with the public and private sectors which it complements. Although the standards and objectives may not be the same, it is precisely the grass roots foundation of community radio and television that allows them to take different forms depending on the community and the projects. Too much control over community broadcasting would change its nature and perhaps stifle its spontaneity. It is nevertheless important to give community radio and television a statutory basis to allow it to fulfil the role of granting access to the system, a responsibility which the other two sectors, with other calls on their services, have been unable to fulfil.

Recommendations

The right of access of all Canadians to the broadcasting system should be affirmed.

Community broadcasting should be recognized for this purpose as one of the components of the system.

The Right of Persons to Receive Broadcasting Service

Like the right to freedom of expression, the right of persons to receive programs is recognized as "unquestioned" in subsection 3(c) of the *Broadcasting Act*, "subject only to the generally applicable statutes and regulations".

The wording of this right reflects the general view of broadcasting when it was more or less limited to transmission by Hertzian waves. With over-the-air transmission, the programs broadcast in a particular area are intended for direct reception by anyone with the appropriate receiver. Since then, new distribution methods have come into general use, including cable or satellites which are not public property and whose technical characteristics lend themselves to reception by subscription. The right of persons to "receive" programs has therefore been subjected to a number of conditions by operators. Canadians without the means to subscribe or who live in areas that are not served by cable now feel abandoned by a system in which everyone else has abundant choices. A new class division has appeared between the information rich and the information poor.

This new state of affairs has given rise to conflicts. Clearly basing themselves on a right which appears to them to be recognized in subsection 3(c), individuals began to receive by means of their own dish antennas satellite signals intended for cable operators. Others connected their television sets to cable themselves or rigged up a decoder to unscramble programs intended for subscribers without paying subscription fees. Television piracy was born.

Of course all radio and television services must be paid for in the long run. Whether they earn their revenues from the government, from advertising or from subscriptions, the consumer pays in the end. Consumers should thus have the right to receive broadcasting services just as freedom of expression gives them the right to any publications they wish as long as they are willing to pay for them. Geographical happenstance and the current state of technology impose further limits.

The principle of the right to broadcasting service is, moreover, already recognized in the *Cable Television Regulations*[35], which require every licensee, on receipt of the amount of the installation fee, to install equipment for the provision of service to all homes situated in any residential area within its licensed area. The many configurations now available for the delivery of broadcasting services prompt us to state explicitly the right of persons to receive such services. Unless provided for under generally applicable statutes and regulations, broadcasting services ought not to be available to some residents of a given area and denied to others without legitimate reason.

Recommendation

> The Act should state the right of persons to receive broadcasting services, subject only to generally applicable statutes and regulations, rather than stating the right to receive programs.

The Right of the Hearing Impaired to Receive Broadcasting Service

In order that the right of Canadians to receive broadcasting services does not knowingly exclude anyone, we wish to stress that the rights of groups like the hearing impaired need to be given special consideration. In its brief, the Canadian Captioning Development Agency pointed out that:

> For close to 2.2 million Canadians, television is a picture puzzle. They all get the picture, but only a few get the message. To be denied access to television is considered a hardship by many. For someone who is hearing impaired, it is a double handicap.[36]

Until quite recently not much could be done. Beginning in 1980, however, closed captioning began to be more widely used. Like movie subtitles, the captions are part of the picture but they are invisible to those who are not equipped with a special decoder.

Reacting to the recommendation of the Special Parliamentary Committee on the Handicapped in its report *Obstacles*, the Department of Communications supported the establishment of the Canadian Captioning Development Agency, a non-profit agency that provides broadcasters with closed captioning services for the hearing impaired. The CBC and, to a lesser extent, the private television networks now include closed captions on a number of programs. With an estimated 30,000 decoders now in use in Canada, large numbers of hearing impaired viewers are able to understand what is being said on these programs. Further, more than two hundred companies are now providing captions for their advertisements.

Although the *Obstacles* report recommended that closed captioning should be made a condition of licence, the CRTC and the Department of Communications have clearly stated their preference for a voluntary approach. Many broadcasters have promised to increase the number of captioned programs. They are to be congratulated for this commitment and the CRTC should be encouraged to consider it in issuing and renewing licences.

Recommendation

> At the time of licence renewal the CRTC should take into consideration the licensee's willingness to increase the number of programs with closed captioning for the hearing impaired.

The Right to Broadcasting Service in English and French

Subsection 3(e) of the Broadcasting Act states that ". . . all Canadians are entitled to broadcasting service in English and French as public funds become available".[37]

It may safely be said that this right has become a reality: except for a few isolated pockets, all of Canada is provided with broadcasting service in both languages. This is no mean achievement, especially since some of the areas covered — in English and French — are among the most inaccessible in the world.

Clearly, it is up to the CBC to cover the whole country. Although some private broadcasters have extended their service to areas remote from the major centres, a policy cannot be based on intermittent action. Private enterprise should not be required to broadcast in all regions in both official languages unless there is an appropriate market. In all other instances the right of Canadians to broadcasting services in French and in English requires action by the public sector.

Recommendation

The Act should reaffirm the right of all Canadians to broadcasting service in French and in English, to be implemented if necessary by means of concerted action by the public sector.

Broadcasting in Quebec

As we see in Chapter 8, French-language broadcasting in Canada faces a number of special problems. The differences stem not only from language and culture, but also from the characteristics of the French-speaking audience, 90 percent of which is concentrated in Quebec and which thins as it moves westward. Although it gains in consistency what it lacks in size, the French market remains too small to have its needs served through normal commercial television and radio.

A realistic and effective Canadian policy cannot ignore the facts. A distinctive Quebec broadcasting system exists and lacks only recognition in law and in appropriate institutions, in order that the CRTC, the CBC, Telefilm Canada and others be able to tailor their decisions to it where they are not already doing so.

Recommendation

Canadian broadcasting policy should recognize the special character of Quebec broadcasting, both in itself and as the nucleus of French-language broadcasting throughout Canada.

Consultation with the Provinces

It is often forgotten that the Aird Report recommended in 1929 that provincial authorities should exercise jurisdiction over the programming of stations broadcasting on their territory. The 1932 Act provided for somewhat less — the appointment by the provincial authorities of assistant commissioners who would in turn appoint provincial and local consultative committees following agreement with the provincial authorities. It was the Privy Council's 1932 decision on broadcasting[38] that put a stop to this process. Since that time, the role of the provinces has been officially ignored, at least in the Act.

The 1968 *Broadcasting Act* is thus silent on the role of the provinces. In 1973, however, then Communications Minister Gérard Pelletier recognized a degree of legitimacy for the provinces by proposing that they and the Government of Canada should consult with a view to co-ordinating their respective policies. Bill C-16 (1978) included federal-provincial consultation as one of the principles of the system; it was never adopted. Following the debates of the seventies on the role of provincial government broadcasting undertakings, the Clyne Report in 1979 and the Applebaum-Hébert Report in 1982 both recommended that existing provincial broadcasting undertakings should continue. The CRTC was allowed to continue to issue licences to provincial broadcasting undertakings.

More recently, the report *The Future of French-language Television*, stated the wish that it would "mark the beginning of fruitful consultations" between the governments of Canada and Quebec. A co-operative agreement for consultation and harmonization in the development of the French-language television system was signed soon thereafter.[39] We welcome this initiative to improve co-operation in the field of Canadian broadcasting between the provincial governments and the federal government.

The time has come to establish a clear position on this issue. Broadcasting raises too many questions in too many different areas for the federal government to ignore the concerns of the provinces. Provincial jurisdictions often come into play in broadcasting, as we see with the development of educational television and provincial networks which, by carrying out their respective functions, also contribute to increasing Canadian content on the airwaves. Intergovernmental co-operation can only strengthen Canadian broadcasting policy. That is why we recommend that the principle be included in the Act.

It must be remembered that the principle should not infringe upon the autonomy of the various institutions involved and ought not to be used as a pretext for government intervention in the decisions of regulatory authorities or public broadcasting agencies.

Recommendation

The principle of federal-provincial consultation should be part of the Broadcasting Act but it should not interfere with the autonomy of broadcasters or regulatory authorities.

Broadcasting in Native Languages

The Constitution specifically recognizes the rights of Canada's aboriginal peoples, who generally were late in gaining access to the communications media essential to the preservation of their threatened cultural heritage. Much remains to be done, however. Each of the aboriginal peoples has its own culture, which it is important to preserve, enrich and further develop.

Justice would be done if the very factor that accelerated the assimilation of aboriginal peoples in the past were henceforth to foster their development. We therefore recommend including in the Act the right of aboriginal peoples to broadcasting services in representative native languages (see Chapter 20). "Representative languages" means the most widely used languages that the aboriginal peoples themselves would like to see survive.

The Inuvialuit Communications Society's brief to the Task Force described the role played today by the Inuit language:

> Language is the heart of a culture, and the keeper of people's heritage, but our language is in serious trouble . . . When English is the predominant language in more than four out of five homes, it is imperative to offer young people opportunities to hear and use Inuvialuktum, and to emphasize its worth.[40]

The Northern Native Broadcasting Society emphasized the close link between the economic well-being of native populations and their use of their own languages:

> Many northerners still speak their native languages. For those people whose first language is not English, they find much of the public affairs and news programming available from the mass media unintelligible. Yet the events and the decisions portrayed in such programming demand the participation of these same people, if they are to be successful contributors to the socio-economic development of their homelands.[41]

There is no shortage of reports illustrating the degree to which the survival of many native languages is threatened. Broadcasting policy cannot by itself ensure their survival. It can, however, play a role in helping to redress the current state of affairs.

Recommendation

> The Act should include the right of aboriginal peoples to broadcasting services in representative native languages, where numbers warrant and as public funds become available.

The Responsibility of Broadcasters for the Programs they Broadcast

The principle of the responsibility of persons licensed to carry on broadcasting undertakings for the programs they broadcast is one of the basic principles of Canadian broadcasting. The Act states that "all persons licensed to carry on broadcasting undertakings" have such a responsibility. The principle makes a clear distinction between these persons who are in practice the management of the undertaking from all others involved in the broadcast of programs.

Anything said on the airwaves, no matter who says it or what program it is said on, is the responsibility of the broadcasting undertaking. It is the broadcaster, for example, that is responsible before the courts for any prejudicial statements for which the person whose rights have been infringed is claiming restitution. It is therefore up to the management of each broadcasting undertaking to ensure that there are no prejudicial statements made in the programs broadcast. A broadcasting undertaking may use this principle as ground to refuse access to the airwaves to a person who wishes to express a point of view.

The concern for legal responsibility therefore threatens to restrict access to the system, which would be contrary to the objectives stated elsewhere in the *Broadcasting Act*. There is nevertheless a way of reconciling responsibility and accessibility if legal responsibility is adjusted to the actual roles played in the broadcasting of programs. A careful examination of the concept of responsibility or liability in Canadian law is therefore in order.

According to civil law in Quebec, a person's liability for a prejudicial act depends on the behaviour leading to the injury. If the behaviour is at fault, whether voluntarily or as a result of negligence, and a sufficient link can be established between the injury caused and the individual's behaviour, there is liability and hence an obligation on a person to compensate for the injury. Behaviour is considered to be at fault if it demonstrates an error of judgment, negligence or intent to cause injury that would not have been committed by a reasonable, prudent and diligent person placed in the same circumstances.[42]

Under common law in all provinces except Quebec, libel or damage to a person's reputation is covered by a system of strict liability. The person held responsible is the one who decided to publish the information, regardless of intent. The injury caused is the determining factor. An undertaking involved in disseminating a defamatory libel in the course of its operation may only avoid liability by demonstrating that it took every care to ensure that the material broadcast was not defamatory, and can prove it did so.[43]

On the basis of these criteria, a broadcasting undertaking cannot be held responsible for injury unless its behaviour is at fault, by intervening or failing to intervene in the content or transmission of the program in question. It is because the undertaking excercises under the law the power to broadcast that it is ultimately responsible for what is broadcast.

Where a radio or a television station uses its own facilities to broadcast programs that it produces or has chosen to broadcast, the responsibility is clear: the undertaking is responsible for the messages transmitted because it is constantly involved in the decisions that create or retain contentious matter. On the other hand, carriers whose role is simply to relay programs on behalf of broadcasters have no authority over these programs and hence escape any liability for program content. Their position is similar to that of a telephone company which no one would think of holding responsible for any slanderous statements exchanged between callers.

There is, however, one category of undertaking whose activities cover both broadcasting and telecommunications, and do not call for equal degrees of responsibility. This leads to confusion. When the 1968 Act was passed the legislators could not have guessed at the expansion that was to take place in cable and therefore gave it no special consideration.

Some cable television channels are used exclusively to distribute in a particular area programs that belong to other undertakings. The cable operator is restricted to receiving and distributing the signals that section 18 of the *Cable Television Regulations*[44] prohibits it from altering or curtailing, in whole or in part. Such activity excludes any responsibility for content.

The issue becomes more complex when the cable operator also offers different types of services, for example when the operator programs the content distributed. Here there is reason to recognize the cable operator's responsibility for content. But the Act includes cable operators under broadcasting undertakings and this automatically makes them responsible for all programs they carry, even if they are doing no more than redistributing the programs of others.

If this appears to go beyond the intent of the legislation, it is because it was necessary to use verbal agility in the *Broadcasting Act* to cover cable television without naming it. Thus the Act states that "broadcasting undertaking includes a broadcasting transmitting undertaking, a broadcasting receiving undertaking and a network operation . . .". Because another section of the Act associates traditional broadcasters with "transmitting undertakings", it was determined that "receiving undertaking" was intended to cover cable operators. Then again, elsewhere in the Act it is stated that those who operate broadcasting, now deemed to include cable operators, are responsible for the programs they broadcast. The verbal web leaves no room for variations. A new Act should provide for them.

There are other circumstances that prompt such amendments. For example, most cable operators, as required by CRTC regulations, set aside a special channel for community programs which are either produced by or submitted to the operator. The channel is to be used strictly for community programming, but the choice of programs is up to the cable operator who, as a result, becomes solely responsible for the program content.

This appears to us to be less than very compatible with the idea of community broadcasting because the power to decide on the programs distributed, which in turn determines legal responsibility, does not lie with the community or its representatives. The resulting problems are not serious, but the community representatives who work on such programs are forced into a kind of official irresponsibility and do not have the autonomy they want.

The essence of community broadcasting is that program content should depend entirely on the local or regional community. If cable operators are to keep to their primary function of merely providing transmission facilities, then it is up to those who produce the programs to take full responsibility for them, including any implications resulting from broadcasting them.

We therefore recommend that the status of broadcasters' responsibility for programs broadcast be adjusted to reflect the nature of their operations within the framework of the legal criteria we establish elsewhere for cable television and community broadcasting. Once cable operators drop responsibility for programs they limit themselves simply to carrying, the responsibility must be shifted to another undertaking: this is the opening which will accommodate the development of autonomous community undertakings.

Recommendation

The Act should consider persons authorized to operate all categories of broadcasting undertakings responsible for the programs they distribute except when they have no decision-making power, in whole or in part, over the messages distributed.

The Search for Balance

The central principle of Canadian broadcasting policy is a striving for balance on which many of the system's principles and objectives are based. Thus in describing the range of programming to be provided to Canadian audiences, the *Broadcasting Act* specifically requires a balance among types of programs and points of view.[45]

Balanced Types of Programs

The present Act requires broadcasters to offer a varied and comprehensive range of programming to suit the interests and tastes of all viewers. Until the introduction of pay-television and specialty services, it was up to each broadcaster to devise a selection of programming that would comply with this balance in types of programming. A limited number of undertakings were licensed to broadcast and what was expected of the system was required of each of them. The proliferation of channels makes it possible from now on to allow a degree of specialization without reducing the choice offered by the whole system: the diversity lost to the system because of specialization by one channel is replaced by the gamut of specialized channels.

It is therefore important to continue to ensure a balance in the types of programming offered by adapting the principle to the new circumstances. It is up to all general and specialty services as a whole to achieve the balance required by the Act and up to the regulatory authority to see that it occurs in issuing licences and renewals.

Recommendation

> The Canadian broadcasting system should offer a range of programming that is varied and comprehensive, providing a balance of information, enlightment and entertainment for people of different ages, interests and tastes.

Balance of View-points

The balanced expression of differing points of view has in fact always been more or less explicitly tied to the principles of Canadian broadcasting. Hence the controversy which led to the first inquiry into broadcasting in 1929.[46] The Minister of Marine had revoked the licence of the International Bible Students Association and the Jehovah's Witnesses were subjected to what looked very much like censorship. Broadcasting, which had until then been primarily concerned with technical matters, shifted its focus to ideas. And ever since, the authorities have been reluctant to grant broadcasting rights to religious or political groups whose purpose would be primarily the promotion of a single point of view.

In 1939, the Canadian Broadcasting Corporation, which was the authority over broadcasting at the time, published a statement of principles on controversial programming.[47] The statement rejected censorship and recommended that radio should be used to discuss controversial subjects because the critical expression of differing points of view was the best way to protect civil liberties. It was here that the Canadian Broadcasting Corporation noted for the first time that radio would evolve along with its listeners and that the ways of presenting arguments over the airwaves would change accordingly. The use of any predetermined formulas would be a waste of time and would quickly become obsolete.

The statement emphasized tolerance and flexibility. In 1961, the Board of Broadcast Governors restated the principle as follows:

1. The air belongs to the people, who are entitled to hear the principal points of view on all questions of importance.
2. The air must not fall under the control of any individual or groups influenced by reason of their wealth or special position.
3. The right to answer is inherent in the doctrine of free speech.
4. The full interchange of opinion is one of the principal safeguards of free institutions.[48]

Almost a decade later, the CRTC in its turn reinforced the tradition. The special committee established to study the controversial program *Air of Death*[49] stated that in discussing matters of public interest, the role of broadcasters was to allow the statement of a number of points of view and the privilege of audiences was to select from among them. It then reiterated the importance of flexibility, stating that the quality of Canadian broadcasting would not be improved by over-regulation or restrictive interpretations of the Broadcasting Act.[50]

Over the years the CRTC stated its views on this subject on a number of occasions.[51] Decisions of the CRTC and its predecessors provide everything needed to establish a code of ethics which we believe can be used to deal with what is meant by "opportunity for the expression of differing views on matters of public concern".

What are we to make, however, of the argument that such a limitation is incompatible with freedom of expression because it constrains the statement of opinions by the press? It may reasonably be argued that providing for differing points of view, which goes beyond the freedom of expression that broadcasters claim for themselves alone, complies with the right that the Constitution guarantees all Canadians. In the United States, where the First Amendment guarantees freedom of the press, the Supreme Court has ruled that far more restrictive measures than these are compatible with freedom of the press.[52]

Balance of points of view does not mean the same thing for a small community with a single radio station as it does for a large city with a wide range of broadcasting services. A small community station with a restricted territory, which states points of view rarely expressed on major stations, ought not to be forced to broadcast opinions that are already widely circulated. Under such conditions, the CRTC should act with circumspection.

Measures to put such objectives into practice should stop short of censorship. Also, the CRTC's supervision of the application of such measures should be exercised as it is now, after the fact, at arm's length, and in a measured way. One way to describe it would be with subtle moral authority. There are already well-established mechanisms — analysis of public complaints, restatement of basic principles, requesting broadcasters to explain certain actions, outlining remedial steps to be taken in the future. The advantage of this method is that it recognizes that prime responsibility rests with the broadcaster. It is up to the broadcaster to present programming that is, on the whole, balanced.

This method is in fact based on the voluntary compliance of broadcasters with a professional code of ethics. There is not yet any general trend in this direction, but in Quebec, for example, despite the frustrations that result from a scarcity of resources, the Press Council's increasingly important role, with broadcasters as members, is becoming the envy of many.

Recommendation

> The programming of each broadcaster, in keeping with its circumstances in the community served, should be designed to present a balanced opportunity for the expression of differing views on matters of public interest. The principle applies to each broadcaster's overall programming and not to every program broadcast.

Programming of High Standard

While it is relatively easy to obtain general agreement that the programming offered by the Canadian broadcasting system should be of a high standard, there is a great deal of disagreement about what is meant by "high standard".

Despite some progress, the research carried out over the past twenty years has not developed program evaluation tools for determining whether the broadcasting system as a whole complies with the high standard requirement. The high standard criterion has been invoked under many different circumstances, notably to justify, sometimes with a number of strange twists, various CRTC decisions.

For example, the CRTC has prohibited the broadcast of telephone conversations over the air without prior permission from the person in question unless the person telephoned the station with the intention of participating in a program. Both the Ontario Court of Appeal and the Supreme Court of Canada have handed down majority decisions stating that the CRTC has the power to make this regulation pursuant to the section on the high standard requirement.[53] This meant that both courts recognized that the CRTC prohibition aimed at implementing the high standard objective by making a rule condemning inappropriate procedures.

This is not too surprising, especially when one recalls that the only powers the CRTC has are the implementation of the policy stated in the Act and that all decisions must be based on one or other of the concepts contained in it.

The CRTC itself has had occasion to refer to the wording of the Act. In its *Notice Concerning a Complaint by Media Watch with Respect to CKVU Television, Vancouver*, it commented as follows on the inflammatory statements made about a public interest group:

> The responsibility imposed on each broadcaster for the programs it broadcasts includes the requirement that the programming provided on its undertaking be of high standard.[54]

To determine whether the broadcaster has met this responsibility, the CRTC considers the precautions that should have been taken under the circumstances. For example, following the shooting that took place at the Quebec National Assembly, the CRTC received numerous complaints against radio station CFCF in Montreal. In its notice on this matter, the CRTC ruled that the use of spontaneous "telephone surveys" of events bearing on a vital component of public order do not meet the high standard requirement.[55] The CRTC concluded that by using an inappropriate method, the station served its listeners and the public at large poorly.

As we can see, the high standard requirement sets an ideal standard somewhere in never-never land. Nowhere is the concept defined. Although the definition is always left implicit or expressed poorly, it authorizes the CRTC, with all the attendant risks of arbitrariness that the courts complain about, to make value judgements on programs. More discretion could be hoped for from the CRTC. If, on the other hand, programs were subjected to "recognized professional standards", this would provide criteria independent from the CRTC. But can one prevent the debasing of such standards if they are to be established by the industry itself, and how are they to be prevented from being lowered? This is the dilemma of evaluation; broadcasters are being asked to use their own resources to raise their standards and to renew them wherever necessary in ceaseless cycle of progress.

It is obvious that "recognized professional standards" will have to vary depending on the category of the undertaking. Flexible standards are needed to allow proportionately more to be required of all undertakings, whether large or small, without allowing them to attempt to escape from the low end ("the small companies won't be able to follow suit") or the high end ("only the big companies have the appropriate means"). Seen from this standpoint, the high standard requirement has merit. If the high standard criterion is to be prevented from becoming a dead letter, it should be closely linked to a regulatory authority requirement for firm commitments from broadcasters as described in the model we put forward in the following chapter.

Recommendations

Programs aired on Canadian radio and television should be of high standard, pursuant to firm commitments by broadcasters when their licences are issued or renewed and for which they are accountable before the regulatory authority.

The concept of high standard should be based on recognized professional standards, depending on the category of the undertaking.

The Principles and Objectives of Canadian Broadcasting

The principles and objectives that we have just described are those we recommend for inclusion in a new Canadian broadcasting policy to replace the existing provisions of section 3 of the *Broadcasting Act*. They are summarized in the following list (except for those concerning the CBC, which are provided in Chapter 10):

- The radio frequencies used for broadcasting are public property.
- All persons authorized to use broadcasting frequencies should be considered trustees of the Canadian public.
- An independent body should continue to regulate the undertakings which make up the broadcasting system in accordance with principles set out by Parliament.
- Broadcasting undertakings in Canada form a composite system. Each in its own way should contribute to the achievement of the objectives assigned to the Canadian broadcasting system.
- Only Canadians may own and control broadcasting undertakings in Canada.
- In both its organization and operation, the Canadian broadcasting system should serve the interests of all Canadians and their need to express themselves, in order to safeguard, enrich and strengthen the cultural, political, social and economic fabric of Canada.
- The Canadian broadcasting system should play an active role in developing an awareness of Canada, reflect the cultural diversity of Canadians and make available a wide range of programming that is Canadian in content and character and that provides for a continuing expression of Canadian identity. It should serve the special needs of the geographic regions and actively contribute to the flow and exchange of information and expression among the regions of Canada.
- All Canadians have a right of access to the broadcasting system. Community broadcasting should be recognized for this purpose as one of the components of the system.
- All Canadians have a right to receive broadcasting services, subject only to generally applicable statutes and regulations.
- All Canadians have a right to broadcasting services in French and in English.
- The special character of Quebec broadcasting should be recognized, including its role as a nucleus for French-language broadcasting throughout Canada.
- The principle of federal-provincial consultation is fundamental and should be pursued without interfering with the autonomy of broadcasters or regulatory authorities.
- Aboriginal peoples have a right to broadcasting services in representative native languages, where numbers warrant and as public funds become available.
- All persons authorized to operate broadcasting undertakings and retransmission undertakings are responsible for the programs they distribute except when they have no decision-making power, in whole or in part, over these programs.
- The Canadian broadcasting system should offer a range of programming that is varied and comprehensive, providing a balance of information, enlightenment and entertainment for people of differing ages, interests and tastes.

- The overall programming of each broadcaster, in keeping with circumstances in the community served, should provide a balanced opportunity for the expression of differing views on matters of public interest.
- Programs aired on Canadian radio and television should be of high standard, pursuant to commitments made by broadcasters and in keeping with recognized professional standards appropriate to the category of the undertaking.

Any new broadcasting act should obviously be founded in respect for the rights and freedoms now guaranteed by the Constitution. It should deal with all broadcasting services in Canada, including the Canadian Broadcasting Corporation.

Notes

1. Enacted in the *Canada Act*, 1982, c.11.
2. Section 33 of the *Canadian Charter of Rights and Freedoms* also provides that: 33.(1) Parliament or the legislature of a province may expressly declare in an Act of Parliament or of the legislature, as the case may be, the Act or a provision thereof shall operate notwithstanding a provision included in section 2 or sections 7 to 15 of this Charter.
3. *Constitution Act*, 1982, s.15.
4. Stated in section 2 of the *Constitution Act*, 1982. We shall hereafter refer to this freedom by the term "Freedom of Expression".
5. The two views are not as irreconcilable as they may appear. Both print and broadcast media have the same key limitation: financing. Not everyone can afford to operate even a small newspaper. It is also important in the print media to distinguish between information and opinion. The avowed purpose of the latter is to defend a single social, political or religious standpoint while the former requires reporting all the relevant facts from more than one point of view.
   The print media have tended towards the view that freedom of information means the right to inform. They therefore usually express differing points of view to a greater extent than statutes and regulations require of the electronic media.
6. *The Queen v. David E. Oakes*, Supreme Court of Canada, February 28, 1986, no. 17550.
7. Ibid., reasons given by the Right Honourable Brian Dickson, p. 49 ff.
8. Canada, House of Commons, *Bill C-20, An Act to amend the Canadian Radio-television and Telecommunications Commission Act, the Broadcasting Act and the Radio Act*, First Session, Thirty-third Parliament, 33-34 Elizabeth II, 84-85-86.
9. Canada, House of Commons, Standing Committee on Communications and Culture, *Minutes of Proceedings and Evidence*, Issue No. 22, (Ottawa: Queen's Printer, 1985). Testimony of K.J. MacDonald from the Consumers' Association of Canada.
10. Ibid, Issue No. 21. Testimony of Michael Hind-Smith from the Canadian Cable Television Association.
11. See Kathleen Mahoney, Sheilah L. Martin, "Broadcasting and The Canadian Charter of Human Rights and Freedoms: Justifications for Restricting Freedom of Expression", study prepared for the Task Force on Broadcasting Policy, Ottawa, November, 1985. Section 15 of the *Canadian Charter of Rights and Freedoms* reads as follows: 15. (1) Every individual is equal before and under the law and has the right to the equal protection and equal benefit of the law without discrimination and, in particular, without discrimination based on race, national or ethnic origin, colour, religion, sex, age or mental or physical disability.
    (2) Subsection (1) does not preclude any law, program or activity that has as its object the amelioration of conditions of disadvantaged individuals or groups including those that are disadvantaged because of race, national or ethnic origin, colour, religion, sex, age or mental or physical disability.

12. Canadian Radio-television and Telecommunications Commission, *Amendments to Radio (AM), Radio (FM) and Television Broadcasting Regulations*, CRTC Public Notice 1984-274 and *Regulations Respecting Pay Television Broadcasting Undertakings*, CRTC Public Notice 1984-275 (Ottawa: CRTC, 1984).
13. *Q. v. Keegstra* (1984) 14 W.C.B. 112 (Alta. Q. B.); *C.H.R.C. v. Taylor* (1984) 20 A.C.W.S. (2d) 430.
14. Canada, Task Force on Sex-Role Stereotyping in the Broadcast Media, *Images of Women* (Ottawa: Minister of Supply and Services Canada, 1982) pp. 5-6.
15. Canadian Radio-television and Telecommunications Commission, *A Broadcasting Policy Reflecting Canada's Linguistic and Cultural Diversity*, CRTC Public Notice 1985-139 (Ottawa: CRTC, 1985), p. 7.
16. See Mahoney and Martin, "Broadcasting and the Canadian", p. 5.4 and 5.5.
17. Canada, *Bill C-20*.
18. Marie Finklestein, "Selected Social Issues in Programming: The Legal, Constitutional and Policy Implications of the Equality Provision in Bill-C-20", study prepared for the Task Force on Broadcasting Policy, Ottawa, November 1985, p. 162-163.
19. Canada, House of Commons, *Bill C-62, An Act Respecting Employment Equity*. First Session, thirty-third Parliament, 33-34 Elizabeth II, 1984-85-86.
20. *Constitution Act*, 1982, s. 36.
21. *Broadcasting Act*, 1968, R.S.C. 1970, c. B-11.
22. Like any agency with powers delegated by Parliament, the CRTC has no inherent powers; it has only the authority recognized implicitly or explicitly in the Act.
23. Canada, Committee on Broadcasting, (Fowler Committee) *Report* (Ottawa: Queen's Printer, 1965), p. 94. See also R. Grant Hammond, "Embedding Policy Statements in Statutes: A Comparative Perspective on the Genesis of a New Public Law Jurisprudence", (1982) Vol. 5, *Hastings International and Comparative Law Review*, p. 323.
24. See David Ellis, *Evolution of the Canadian Broadcasting System* (Ottawa: Minister of Supply and Services, 1979), p. 88 and Claude Jean Devirieux, "Réflexions sur le statut de la radio-télévision publique", brief to the Task Force on Broadcasting Policy, Montreal, 1985.
25. See also, J.R. Minasian, "Property Rights in Radiation: An Alternative Approach to Radio Frequency Allocation", *Journal of Law and Economics*, Vol. 18, no. 1, 1975, p. 221-272.
26. See Craig Leddy, "Land Mobile Affecting UHFs", *Broadcaster*, May 1986. p. 45.
27. See Gaétan Tremblay, "Le Service public: principe fondamental de la radiodiffusion canadienne", study prepared for the Task Force on Broadcasting Policy, October 1985, p. 10.
28. For a review of the arguments concerning the limits on freedom of expression, see Marie Finklestein, "Social Issues in Programming".
29. Canada, Department of Secretary of State, *White Paper on Broadcasting* (Ottawa, Queen's Printer, 1966), p. 8.
30. Government of Nova Scotia, brief to the Task Force on Broadcasting Policy, Nova Scotia, August, 1985, p. 3.
31. *Q. v. Shellbird Cable Limited* (1982) 38 NFLD and P.E.I. R. 224, 108, A.P.R. 224. (NFLD C.A.). See also Jay A. Herringer, Ram S. Jakhu and Cliff Arnold, "Options for a New Legal Definition of Broadcasting for Canada", study prepared for the Task Force on Broadcasting Policy, Ottawa, November 1985, p. 3.
32. Allarcom Limited, brief to the Task Force on Broadcasting Policy, Edmonton, August, 1985, p. 2.
33. *Broadcasting Act*, 1968, s. 2.
34. Ibid., s. 3(b).
35. *Cable Television Regulations*, C.R.C., c. 374, s. 16.
36. Canadian Captioning Development Agency, "Broadcast Policy and Closed Captioning for Hearing Impaired Television Viewers", brief to the Task Force on Broadcasting Policy, Toronto 1985.

37. *Broadcasting Act*, 1968, s. 3(e).
38. *Regulation and Control of Radio In Canada*, (1932) A.C. 304.
39. Canada, Department of Communications and Quebec, Department of Communications, "Canada-Quebec Memorandum of Understanding on the Development of the French-language Television System" (Ottawa, Quebec, February 13, 1986).
40. Inuvialuit Communication Society, brief to the Task Force on Broadcasting Policy, Edmonton, September 1985, p. 1.3.
41. Northern Native Broadcasting, Yukon, brief to the Canadian Radio-Television and Telecommunications Commission, Vancouver, December, 1982, p. 4-5.
42. See Nicole Vallières et Florian Sauvageau, *Droit et Journalisme au Québec*, (Montreal: Editions GRIC-FPJQ, 1981) and Pierre Trudel, *Droit de l'information et de la communication*, (Montreal: Editions Thémis, 1984) p. 59.
43. Allan M. Linden, *Canadian Tort Law*, 3 Ed (Toronto: Butterworths, 1982), p. 694.
44. *Cable Television Regulations*, C.R.C., c. 374.
45. Section 3(d) of the *Broadcasting Act* was interpreted in this manner in *National Indian Brotherhood v. Juneau*, (1971) C.F. 498
46. David Ellis, *Evolution of the Canadian*, p. 1.
47. See Peter Geoffrey Cook, "The Concept of Balance in the Supervision and Regulation of Canadian Broadcasting. Public Issues and CRTC Policies", M.A. Thesis, Simon Fraser University, Burnaby, 1982, p. 14.
48. Board of Broadcast Governors, "White Paper on Political and Controversial Broadcasting Policies, - Circular 51", in P.S. Grant, *Broadcasting and Cable Television Regulatory Handbook*, (Toronto: Law Society of Upper Canada, 1973).
49. This concerned a controversy raised by a CBC report on the problem of pollution in an Ontario farming community. See Ronald Squire and Steve Stepinac, "The CRTC Hearing into 'Air of Death': Comments on the Regulation of Controversial Broadcasting", in (1969) 1 Can. Com. L.R., 132.
50. Canadian Radio-Television and Telecommunications, *Report of the Special Committee Appointed in Connection with the CBC Program "Air of Death"*, (Ottawa: CRTC, 1970).
51. See Canadian Radio-television and Telecommunications Commission, *Controversial Programming in the Canadian Broadcasting System - Report on issues raised by CFCF's anti Bill-22 Campaign*, (Ottawa: CRTC, 1977) and Robert V. Morriss, "The CHNS Case: An Emerging Fairness Doctrine for Canada?" (1974) in Can. Com. L.R., and Pierre Trudel, op. cit., p. 440.
52. *Red Lion Broadcasting v. F.C.C.* (1969) 395 U.S. 367.
53. *CKOY v. The Queen*, (1979) 1 R.S.C. 2 which confirmed the decision of the Ontario Court of Appeal.
54. Canadian Radio-television and Telecommunications Commission, *Notice Concerning a Complaint against CKVU Television, Vancouver, British Columbia by Media Watch* CRTC Public Notice 1983-187 (Ottawa: CRTC, August 1983). A commentator appearing on a CKVU program said the following about Media Watch, an agency designed to keep the public informed about how women are and ought to be depicted in the media: "If there is ever another conventional war, it's my hope that Media Watch and its army of snoops will be found in the front line where they can be raped by the Russians."
55. Canadian Radio-television and Telecommunications Commission *Controversial Broadcasting — Complaints Against Radio Station CFCF, Montreal*, CRTC Public Notice 1984-159 (Ottawa: CRTC, 1984).

Chapter 7

Policy-making and Regulation

Policy-making and Regulation

A sound broadcasting policy requires a number of delicate balances. For example, it should be both flexible and capable of adapting to technological development, while at the same time effectively fostering Canadian cultural expression. Similarly, in the area of programming, particularly news, it should avoid partisan political intervention while allowing those politicians responsible for legislating and governing to exercise effectively their responsibility for public policy.

It is appropriate to review the actions of public authorities at each stage in policy-making. The authorities in question are Parliament, the government, the Department of Communications and the CRTC. The roles of the provinces and the Canadian Broadcasting Corporation, while very important in other respects, do not extend to the whole system and are considered elsewhere in this report. In this chapter, we will discuss only those institutions that are responsible for the *Broadcasting Act* and the Broadcasting Regulations.

Sharing of Responsibilities

There are four major operations in policy-making: defining ends, choosing means, carrying out decisions and evaluating results. As Professor Vincent Lemieux of Laval University notes, these functions are not necessarily carried out in this order but are inextricably bound up with one another.[1] We nevertheless distinguish between them for analytical purposes because they highlight the division of the various roles of policy-making.

A government's policy consists of directing certain activities, in this instance broadcasting, to certain objectives. It is therefore essential to begin by defining the ends, which amounts to imagining the activity in its desired state. Ends are therefore general and long-lasting: they point the way. It is Parliament that establishes broadcasting ends, for it is in statutes and regulations passed in Parliament that not only the major principles of the system are defined but also the responsibilities of the government, the CRTC and the broadcasters in making the system work. The government, which in our tradition introduces bills in Parliament, is clearly the driving force in the formulation of ends.

Once the ends have been established, the means by which to adapt the system to them remain to be determined. The government and the CRTC play the determining role at this stage. The government amends legislation or takes direct action, where required, to make the required adjustments. The CRTC defines the regulatory obligations. Everyone must then comply with the decisions made, and such compliance requires controls.

None of these regulations can be regarded as immutable, however. Their effectiveness must be evaluated, and if the results are unsatisfactory, it will be because of problems with regulations, behaviour, the solutions or the ends themselves and appropriate action will have to be taken. The task of review and evaluation is often assigned to committees, commissions of inquiry and task forces.

In this interplay of authorities, how is the role of each to be clearly defined? For often they share the same responsibility. As Professor Peter Lown of the University of Alberta Faculty of Law notes:

> Overlapping authority can mean complementary regulation (which in itself may be an inefficient use of resources), but overlapping authority also allows the possibility of inconsistent and conflicting policies. The answer to such potential conflict has been to look merely to the question of who has jurisdiction to regulate rather than to look at the policy itself.[2]

The separate jurisdictions must therefore be identified, with particular attention paid to preserving, wherever powers granted by Parliament are to be exercised, the independence that is needed to ensure freedom of expression.

Parliament

Parliament has always played an active role in the development of broadcasting policy, as evidenced by the many reports produced from time to time by Parliamentary committees assigned the task of studying the problems of broadcasting. In 1968 Parliament established the broadcasting legislation in effect today. The Standing Committee on Communications and Culture regularly calls the minister of communications and witnesses from other major public bodies subject to the *Broadcasting Act* during its study of the spending estimates and mandates for which they are accountable to Parliament.

We believe that Parliament should continue to follow the development of broadcasting closely, respecting the independence that the Canadian Broadcasting Corporation and the CRTC have enjoyed thus far and which has made our broadcasting system one of the freest in the world.

Government

The 1968 Act limits government involvement in broadcasting policy: it is Parliament that sets objectives and the CRTC that translates these into regulations. Subsection 3(j) states: "The objectives of the broadcasting policy for Canada . . . can best be achieved by providing for the regulation and supervision of the Canadian broadcasting system by a single independent authority."

The government nevertheless has authority over CRTC budgets and appoints CRTC members. More important for us is that the Act allows the government to intervene in two ways in the operations of the CRTC. Under section 23, it can set aside or refer back to the CRTC any decision concerning the issuing, amendment or renewal of a broadcasting licence. Under section 22, it may issue directions to the CRTC on a specified number of matters.[3]

Over the past ten years, the CRTC and the government have diverged on a number of issues such as the policy of substituting advertising in American programming distributed by cable, the introduction of pay television in Canada and a number of issues involving the CRTC's authority in telecommunications. Jurisdictional disputes have led to unhealthy confusion that is still with us today. It is unclear that the drafters of the 1968 legislation envisaged the importance of the place government and the Department of Communications would come to occupy in broadcasting.

Broadcasting is difficult to compare with any other industry. Its responsibilities in producing and disseminating information are such that it cannot be exempted from the usual provisions protecting freedom of expression against outside pressures. The CRTC's independence must therefore be protected.

These considerations do not, however, remove the duty of an elected government, which is responsible before Parliament, to determine policies and to adjust them to the circumstances, in broadcasting as in other areas. How is this power to be exercised without encroaching where an arm's length relationship is called for? Opinion on this issue is divided.

It has been argued that the government is entitled to propose and Parliament to pass legislation to amend existing policies at any time. Others say that statutory action is too slow; however, there is nothing to prevent members of Parliament from acting rapidly, as they have done on numerous occasions in the past.

The Power to Set Aside or Refer Decisions back to the CRTC

The government may, within 60 days, refer back or set aside CRTC decisions by order (section 23) on its own initiative or upon request. Many have viewed this provision as an appeal mechanism, because it can be used to reverse an unwanted or harmful decision. It is not, however, strictly speaking an appeal. There is a right to appeal legal and jurisdictional issues, but it is to the Federal Court.[4] Cabinet action is criticized rather because it is a form of political intervention.

This power to set aside or refer decisions back to the CRTC can have far-reaching implications even if the government does not avail itself of it. It could keep the CRTC from relying on its own judgement or cause the CRTC to try to anticipate what the government wants, thus avoiding interference with its own authority. Moreover, the wording of the Act says nothing about the procedure to be followed. There is also nothing that requires the Cabinet to hold hearings, to explain its decisions or to acknowledge requests.[5] In fact, the existing mechanism of resort to the Cabinet favours those who are adept by skill, interest, or experience at influencing government.[6]

If the Cabinet's power to set aside or refer decisions back to the CRTC is to be kept, a number of guarantees are needed to ensure equitable treatment of all parties. Even with such guarantees the question remains of whether it is compatible with Cabinet functions in our political system. Cabinet is a body that makes political decisions which, while they comply with the law, need not take into consideration the rules of justice that are found in the courts.

Section 23 has nevertheless given the government the opportunity to recommend to the CRTC adjustments in how it interprets its mandate. Such recommendations do not have the legal force of directives, but some commentators agree that they are important in terms of policy in so far as they make the wishes of the government clear.[7]

The Power to Issue Directions to the CRTC

The government may, however, issue directives — formally called 'directions' — to the CRTC with respect to three subjects specified in section 22: the maximum number of frequencies and channels in the same region, the reservation of frequencies and channels for the use of the CBC or for any "special purpose", and the classes of applicants ineligible for licences such as non-Canadians. Some would like to see even greater government powers to issue directions to the CRTC to allow it to impose general policy directions on the regulatory authority.

Bill C-20, which the present government inherited and reintroduced in part, gives it precisely this power.[8] It is a procedure that has caused a great deal of concern, however, and many briefs have described the various dangers involved. The wording of Bill C-20 appears to be intended to authorize the use of the power to issue directives only on matters of general policy and to exclude government intervention in specific decisions, such as the renewal or revocation of a licence. Nevetheless, Bill C-20 would authorize intervention that would discredit the regulatory process by making it appear arbitrary.

The level of independence that would remain with the CRTC if the government were to be granted such power without qualification would be considerably diminished, especially since the power to set aside or refer back provided in section 23 has already raised concerns about its independence. It would allow the government to reject CRTC decisions and dictate decisions to it. The question arises whether it would be worth while to maintain an agency which could be pre-empted by government in so many respects.

However, as the Institut canadien d'Éducation des adultes (I.C.E.A.) notes:

> Legislators have always been unanimous on the need to assign the power of monitoring broadcasting to an independent authority because of the particular nature of this sector.[9]

If the government reserves the right to intervene, some way of placing restrictions on partisan political decisions must therefore be found. The I.C.E.A. continues:

> In Bill C-20, the power to issue directions is not restricted to broad policies; it also includes regulation. The danger of partisan political intervention is all the greater because the Bill does not state how and on what basis such new directions would be formulated. Nor does it provide conditions that would allow true democratic debate to take place prior to their adoption.[10]

The above analysis suggests the following conclusion. If the CRTC's independence is to be preserved at the same time as ministerial responsibility for policy, there ought to be only one intervention mechanism in the Act. Either the government should have the power to veto (1968 Act, section 23), or it should have the power to issue directives (Bill C-20); if veto power is retained, it should not have the power to issue directives except the strictly limited matters set out in section 22 of the 1968 Act. If the power to issue directives is kept, cabinet should lose the power to set aside or refer decisions back to the CRTC. We prefer the latter alternative.

If our preference carries the day, a number of precautions are still in order. The Law Reform Commission's Report No. 26 on independent administrative agencies[11] considers the power to issue directives and recognizes that there are dangers: it leads to fear of political intervention, especially in the decisions of a regulatory body. The Commission therefore recommended that this power be limited.

One of the most important of the Law Reform Commission's recommendations is that an appropriate consultative process should take place before any directives are issued, especially where major policy changes are called for. We believe that it should be up to the CRTC to conduct such a consultative process. On the request of the government, the CRTC would hold hearings on the subject of the directive and report back on its findings. The CRTC already follows this practice when it plans to amend regulations. In view of the regulatory nature of directives, it appears appropriate that they should be subject to the same test. The principle of ministerial accountability would be protected.

As the Law Reform Commission observes, however, the use of directives interferes with the normal administrative process and using them repeatedly would offset any benefits they may have. Allowing them does not mean that their use should be made common.[12] The two important rules should be public consultation and moderate use. The Law Reform Commission also formulated a number of other rules, which we agree are essential if the government is to issue directives to the CRTC:

- directives should take the form of regulations and be subject to the provisions of the Statutory Instruments Act;
- directives cannot be retroactive;
- only the Government, and not ministers, may issue a directive;
- directives shall be formulated in general terms, like regulations, and the regulatory authority is responsible for interpreting them and monitoring their application.

Recommendations

The Act should recognize government entitlement to intervene with the CRTC according to one or other of the following methods, but not both: either it can set aside or refer decisions back to the CRTC, or it can issue directives to the CRTC. The Task Force prefers that government have the power to issue directives.

If it is decided to grant government the power to set aside or refer decisions back to the CRTC, such power should be exercised so as to comply with the principles of due process.

Cabinet, prior to issuing a directive, should be required to consult public opinion in the way the CRTC does when it plans to make or amend a regulation. The CRTC should be responsible for such public hearings.

Directives should be used in moderation so as to leave the regulatory authority free of intervention in exercising its day-to-day mandate, and the following rules should be observed:

- directives take the form of regulations and are subject to the provisions of the Statutory Instruments Act;
- directives cannot be retroactive;
- only the government, and not ministers, may issue a directive;
- directives shall be formulated in general terms, like regulations, and the regulatory authority shall be responsible for interpreting them and monitoring their application.

The CRTC

It is the CRTC that regulates and supervises broadcasting in Canada. The CRTC was established under the 1968 Act to replace the ten-year-old Board of Broadcast Governors. Initially called the Canadian Radio Television Commission, the *Canadian Radio-television and Telecommunications Commission Act* (1975) extended its authority to include telecommunications falling under federal jurisdiction and added "Telecommunications" to the name of the authority without changing the initials. Its dual mandate has made the CRTC one of the most important administrative tribunals in Canada and there has been widespread criticism of the extent of its powers.

In broadcasting, the part of the Commission's mandate we are dealing with, the powers of the Commission remain so broad that it has been derisively referred to as the "Parliament of broadcasting".[13] The 1968 Act assigns it the power to regulate and supervise all aspects of the Canadian broadcasting system with a view to implementing the broadcasting policy enunciated in section 3 of the Act. Any regulatory instruments must therefore refer to this policy within which the Commission interprets and exercises its powers. Since the policy is expressed in general and sometimes vague terms, it leaves the CRTC a great deal of latitude in interpreting its mandate.

In the 18 years since it was established, the CRTC has interpreted its mandate in various ways. From 1968 to 1975, when telecommunications[14] was not yet among its responsibilities, the Commission acted as an independent authority whose mission was to translate the principles of the Act into concrete terms. During this time it oversaw the Canadianization of broadcasting undertakings, formulated Canadian content regulations, developed cable television and FM radio policy and prepared community broadcasting and northern broadcasting policies. In short, the Commission attempted to implement Parliament's will in broadcasting. It was also during this period that the Commission, setting its sights even higher, attempted to define criteria for program quality, especially in news and information, where it was concerned with journalistic integrity and the handling of controversial subjects.

Beginning in 1975, the Commission, which had been assigned telecommunications regulation without adequate resources, relinquished its activism bit by bit and opted to oversee the smooth working of the system from a distance.[15] This was also the period during which the communications explosion raised yet again the problem of our neighbour to the south in a new form: the invasion of Canada by American channels delivered by cable. With rapid growth in distribution technologies the CRTC moved still further from hands-on control and confirmed its fallback position of reacting to the various pressures of the broadcasting environment.

The cable television industry and part of the Canadian public began increasingly to claim a right that was nowhere to be found in the Act: the right to receive equivalent services anywhere in the country.[16] This led the Commission to pursue two apparently contradictory objectives: to increase the Canadian presence on the airwaves and to open Canada to many additional services from the United States. How are two such objectives to be reconciled?[17] It seems to us clear that access to more services has won out thus far over a stronger Canadian presence. There are many contributing factors: the increased use of satellite dish antennas, the ambiguous status of cable television and pay television, and the emphasis placed by the Department of Communications on the development of infrastructure rather than on program content. The Department's policy during this period may well have something to do with the ambiguity of the CRTC's approach.

Since 1982, after pay television's initial failures, the CRTC has emphasized supervision. It relies increasingly on the responsibility of the industry for day-to-day activities and responds to requests in other matters.

The CRTC justifies this change of direction in two ways related to the expansion of broadcasting: increased competition among broadcasters and the dramatic increase in its own workload. By emphasizing supervision, rather than regulation, which reduces the CRTC's workload, the Commission avoids a bureaucratic and inflexible approach that would, according to CRTC Chairman André Bureau, require "hordes of increasingly interfering inspectors".[18] By remaining more flexible "to deal with the often abrupt and unforeseen requirements often imposed on licensees by technological change, the economy and a fickle public"[19] the Commission in return expects licensees to comply with regulations and conditions of licence.

The CRTC has been criticized from many quarters. It has been accused of being a captive of the regulated undertakings and at the same time of being too slow to take an interest in industry innovations; it has been accused of producing fussy regulations like those for FM radio and also of giving in too often to the interests of those it regulates. Some have complained that the cost of holding public hearings is much too high while others, who believe that the hearings are essential, complain that not enough is covered at the hearings, that the procedures impede the disclosure of many facts, and that the general conditions under which they are held discourage public participation.

Those who accuse the CRTC of collusion with broadcasters submit as evidence practices that appear to them to be otherwise inexplicable: for example, that the CRTC refuses to regulate certain areas such as advertising aimed at children; that the CRTC authorizes the purchase of stations on the basis of anticipated earnings at the expense of the public good; that the CRTC approves cable subscriber rates without establishing any criteria, in order to make it easier to agree to the claims of the operators. In short, that the CRTC has turned the broadcasting licence into proprietory ownership of the airwaves. Above all, it is criticized for doing nothing when undertakings repeatedly fail to meet their commitments (promises of performance).[20]

For their part, of course, broadcasters complain of red tape, of petty regulations and of instances of different treatment for comparable undertakings.

A close look at the internal workings of the Commission shows that it has not developed any clear strategy to ensure compliance with regulations and licensing conditions. Many critics have also deplored the fact that an authority which is called upon to determine so many complex issues, whether technical, difficult or simply new, should have abandoned the research work so necessary to its independence.

Any public perception that the CRTC is inequitable or inconsistent leads to a loss of confidence that it is free from political influence. Some of the accusations against it would not hold if the Commission were to make an effort to inform the public of the principles that guide it. Even then, it would never be able to satisfy everyone, especially those who are refused a licence.

The many criticisms of the CRTC, especially by consumer protection groups, raise serious questions. Is it worth keeping a regulatory authority? Some have suggested that conditions of licence be replaced by a market-based mechanism. It is argued that this is a viable alternative because the CRTC is in any case tending towards privatization of the use of radio frequencies.

In a May 1985 report published in early 1986 the Task Force on Government Programs[21] suggested replacing broadcasting licences with a system of "negotiable licences". Radio frequencies, which are public property, would be sold and the proceeds would go to public broadcasting. Private ownership, it argued, would benefit the most efficient operations and eliminate from the market those whose programs do not appeal to the public or whose operating expenses are too high.[22] Free competition would separate the efficient broadcasting undertakings from the less efficient as it does for industries providing other goods and services.

There are objections to this optimistic picture. It is certain that market forces alone would not ensure compliance with the broadcasting principles established by Parliament or even lead to the diversity which is usually considered to result from competition. Since audiences generally receive programs without paying any direct costs, there can be no price-based competition for attracting audiences.[23] It is rather by attempting to attract mass-market audiences and hence by imitating one another that stations would attempt to increase their market share to attract more advertisers. They would tend to neglect secondary audiences. Even strictly economic arguments do not lead to the conclusion that the market, left to itself, would produce programs attractive to all audiences.[24] On the contrary, we fear that both programming diversity and the number of Canadian programs would suffer.

Adopting a market approach to Canadian broadcasting would assume that the task of producing varied and Canadian programming is the sole responsibility of the public sector. Without a firm resolve to make broadcasters comply with the objectives stated in the Act, this viewpoint makes more and more sense. Thus The Friends of Public Broadcasting recommend dropping the requirement on private broadcasters to carry Canadian programs and instead taxing their revenue to finance public broadcasting services.[25] We believe that this compartmentalized approach would do a disservice to the objectives of Canadianization. We believe the public, private and community sectors must share responsibility for serving the tastes and interests of all Canadians.

Under such conditions, what could be substituted for a regulatory authority? For obvious reasons, the task of deciding among broadcasting licence applicants cannot be left up to the government. We believe that it would be better to profit from the CRTC's experience. We are now able to identify the dangers faced by the CRTC, the first of which is being perceived as a captive of the regulated broadcasters. Powerful lobbies exert constant pressure on the institutions that control broadcasting. The practice is better understood today, and it is up to the CRTC to beware of it. More than resolve is needed. We shall explain later what action ought to be taken.

Structure of the CRTC

According to section 3 of the *Canadian Radio-television and Telecommunications Commission Act*, the CRTC has a maximum of nine full-time and ten part-time members, appointed by the Governor in Council.

The former are appointed for a term of seven years and the latter for a term of five years. The powers of the Commission are exercised by its Executive Committee, which consists of the full-time members. For some decisions, such as the making or amending of regulations or the revoking of licences, consultation with part-time members may be required. Part-time members have the right to vote in matters dealing with the making of regulations and the revocation of broadcasting licences, but their role is strictly advisory in matters such as the issuing, renewal or amendment of a licence. That part-time members should be able to attend public hearings without being allowed to vote is puzzling. We recommend the elimination of part-time members. The current number of Commission full-time members is sufficient to allow it to carry out its mandate. The same number should be kept and the government should be careful to ensure a balance between men and women as well as reasonable minority representation.

Part-time members are expected to represent regional interests in CRTC deliberations. It might be possible to achieve the same objective in other ways. To bring the Commission closer to the public, the powers and the duties of its regional offices could be broadened to have them work closely with representative groups in each region. Regional communities would thus be more involved in important decisions than if they continue to rely on part-time members who are remote from them and deprived of a vote. A public advocate would be appointed in each regional office to oversee public participation and represent the public interest at licence renewal hearings.

The Commission's membership also reflects the country's linguistic duality. French-language broadcasting has its own special personality in the Canadian system. It has a right to be treated differently. But English and French broadcasting are nevertheless part of both an overall system of domestic principles and common resources and an international environment in which they have every advantage in cooperating with one another. We recommend that the current francophone proportion, four of nine members, become the rule and that the practice of calling upon francophone members to hear matters arising from Quebec be continued.

Recommendation

The CRTC should consist of nine full-time members appointed for a term of five years. There should be equitable representation for women and minorities; and the present proportion of francophone members should be adopted as the rule.

Regulation

Regulation consists of all the rules of conduct that must be followed to comply with the broadcasting policy set forth in the Act. It includes not only regulations in the strict sense, but also other forms of commitment, whether prescribed or voluntary, such as conditions of licence which establish the rights and obligations of the broadcaster, policy statements in which the CRTC states its policies on certain issues, and rules of behaviour adopted by the undertakings themselves (self-regulation).

Policy discussions in recent years have centred on deregulation, with the United States often being given as an example of a country which has wholeheartedly gone in this direction. Although debate has been heating up, arguments are often exchanged which betray only a superficial understanding of what is happening in the United States.

Some people believe that deregulation means eliminating useless regulations or regulations that could prove harmful to efficient resource management. Others think it involves withdrawing certain industries from special forms of regulation and subjecting them only to common law.[26]

A briefing paper from the Deputy Prime Minister's office states that the word 'deregulation' is frequently used and abused in discussions of change in regulatory policy.[27] Although changes have been made to the regulatory process in the United States, broadcasting, as well as many other industries, are still regulated.

It would therefore be more accurate to speak of regulatory reform than to use the buzzword 'deregulation'. Any regulatory regime needs to be reviewed regularly because with the passage of time regulations go out of date. It is therefore to be expected that the review process should lead to the repeal of certain obsolete regulations and the introduction of new rules to solve new problems.

Regulations are made to deal with problems that exist at the time they are approved. An effective regulatory policy allows for the elimination of regulations that have outlived their purpose.[28]

That said, regulation does more than just create obstacles; it also provides regulated industries with a number of benefits. Broadcasters are in fact handed a share of a protected market and are carefully shielded from competition. Taken too far, however, regulatory protection can promote inefficiency.

Regulations are therefore not ends in themselves but rather a means to achieve objectives included in an act of Parliament. A regulation that does not contribute to these objectives has no reason for existing. It should be either eliminated or replaced with a more appropriate regulation.

In broadcasting as elsewhere, regulations are not the only source of obligations. They are part of a hierarchy of statutory instruments that set standards. At the top of the pyramid are constitutional precepts that no other law may infringe and hence that all of the other statutory rules must comply with. Following the Constitution are acts, including the *Broadcasting Act*, and then government directives to the CRTC, which are subject to the Act and the Constitution. Then come, in the following order, CRTC regulations, conditions of licence, self-regulation by broadcasters and internal corporate regulations (by-laws). Figure 7.1 illustrates the overlapping of standards that govern the behaviour of all those involved in broadcasting.

Despite what the skeptics say, it is not unusual for undertakings to comply willingly with the principles of broadcasting policy stated in law. Self-regulation generally succeeds when the undertakings see clearly that it is in their own interest. Self-regulation is widespread. For example, advertisers and broadcasters have joined in agreements on self-imposed standards disallowing offensive commercials. Government intervention, that is, regulation, is only needed when broadcasters feel that something that is in the public interest is not in their own interest. This very important distinction can be most useful in helping to determine which model ought to be followed: where self-regulation is adequate, the government should restrict itself to encouraging undertakings to adopt self-regulation and to supervising such self-regulation. This approach would improve relations between undertakings and regulation: freed from odious regulation, they would be much readier to comply with essential regulations. With the burden of control better shared in this way, the whole system of standards would be more economical to run.

The approach we advocate is different from the CRTC's. The Commission was obliged to adapt to the supervisory approach because any other regulatory regime would have required resources that were not available. The sole justification of a regulatory approach, however, is compliance with the principles and objectives defined by Parliament. If competition leads undertakings to comply with the broadcasting policy out of self-interest, then constraints are unnecessary; self-regulation and supervision can be used instead.

Not everything can be covered by such an approach, however. Where broadcasting policy and business interests diverge, regulatory measures appropriate to the circumstances are called for. From our standpoint, self-regulation and supervision are simply aspects of a broader compliance strategy.

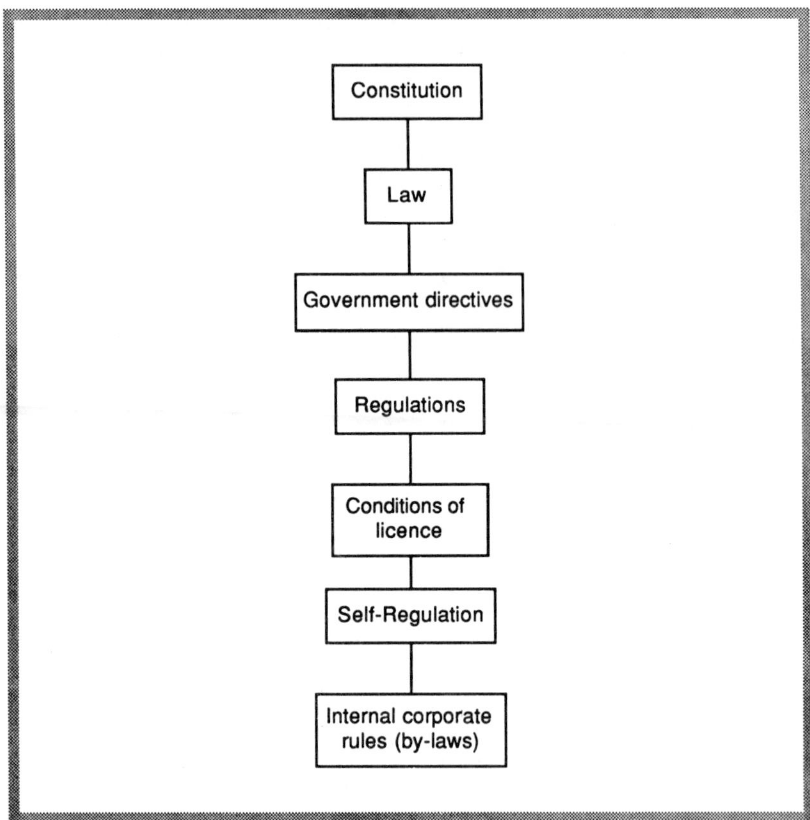

Figure 7.1 Broadcasting Norms

Regulation is nonetheless costly for both government and business. The costs do not always show because they are spread among so many different budgets and cover long periods. Thus the tendency is to regulate rather than exercise forbearance. The result is that regulations accumulate as problems arise and as public pressure is felt. Once the concern has subsided, regulation comes into force and brings costs with it. This is because ensuring compliance with regulation requires supervision, monitoring, compiling, comparing, assessing, certifying, and penalizing. The licensees interpret, calculate, record, arrange, and report.

When government resources are scarce, supervision slackens and infractions tend to increase, causing the regulations to lose some of their legitimacy. A lack of supervision results in delinquency because compliance with regulation often means behaving in a manner which is perceived to be contrary to or at least not in one's own interest. There is advantage, then, in regulating less but ensuring full compliance.

The situation may be summarized as follows. Over time, the regulatory apparatus becomes encumbered and weighed down, sometimes seizes up. Its effectiveness declines, it is expensive to administer, and resources become scarcer. This is the time for reform. Out-of-date regulations ought simply to be eliminated. Others that are widely accepted should be left to self-regulation, with the regulatory authority's role restricted to supervision, that is, control at arm's length without going into detail. Others again are too general to be effective: while they require virtually nothing from the larger undertakings, they are often capable of crippling small ones. In areas like these, greater use ought to be made of conditions of licence, which may be seen as 'made-to-measure regulation', and which could adjust the regulatory burden to the revenue of the undertaking, to regional characteristics and to general economic conditions. The regulations that would remain would be those considered to be indispensable; it is on these that the greatest effort ought to be concentrated: they should be applied strictly across the board without any exceptions; and above all the necessary means to do so should be supplied.

These are the components of our regulatory reform. We now address ourselves to the measures necessary to put it into effect.

Recommendations

> In regulating the broadcasting system in a way that ensures that all components contribute to meeting the objectives of the Broadcasting Act, tailor-made conditions of licence should be used when they are preferable to overall regulations. Self-regulation may be used when doing so is consistent with the public interest.
>
> Regulation should be reviewed regularly to ensure that the burdens do not outweigh the potential benefits, keeping in mind the broadcasting principles enacted by Parliament.

Conditions for Effective Regulation

Research

Ineffective regulation is useless regulation. Hence the need for continuing evaluation. It is here that research is essential. Parliament, government and CRTC are all responsible, within their respective jurisdictions, for the operation of broadcasting. They are the decision-makers. But it is impossible to make decisions without having the required information on which to base them. Otherwise the licensees, or any other parties involved, are likely to be placed in awkward situations. It is impossible to formulate broadcasting policy without solid research; and if policy is to be continually updated, access to current information about the system and its evolution is needed.

Although Canada has undertaken advanced research on communications methods and technology, it has neglected the fields that concern us: policy analysis and policy development in broadcasting and related cultural industries. Little original work or follow-up has been done in these areas. The inclusion of fundamental rights in the Constitution, especially freedom of the press and other media of communication, requires the various public authorities to examine their decisions carefully. This is yet another area where there is a shortage of research. Beyond the tyranny of audience ratings, there are few qualitative audience and program studies available to those who want to look beneath the surface. Likewise, studies on regulatory methods and compliance strategies are lacking.

It is not by creating new structures that the absence of research on cultural activities and broadcasting will be set right. There are other more appropriate ways: taking stock of and using more effectively the often abundant resources of existing organizations, notably the universities; cultivating excellence in the disciplines related to communications; encouraging exchanges and cooperation among interested groups. These sorts of initiatives would encourage the kind of expertise needed to increase the level of information available on the state of Canadian broadcasting.

All those who are involved in broadcasting policy would benefit from sharing the task of conducting appropriate research. For it is impossible to make enlightened decisions without having full knowledge of the facts. While most basic research falls naturally to the Department of Communications, the CRTC also needs to carry out research work, especially in connection with issuing licences, where lack of information leaves the Commission at the mercy of the broadcasters.

Licence applicants appear before the CRTC in competitive circumstances that encourage them to overstate their case. Carried away by enthusiasm, they often make rash promises, only to beg to be released from them several months later when they are faced with financial problems. Applicants inevitably present figures and arguments in a favourable light. The CRTC's task is to stick to the facts. The Commission's job is to assess accurately the assumptions that are hidden from it as well as those loudly advertised for its benefit. For factual research, the CRTC must rely on itself alone. It is not being asked to master the imponderable but should try to outline the foreseeable. Inattention to unfavourable conditions, as in the initial licensing of pay-TV, leads undertakings up dead-ends from which they are retrieved by allowing them to drop their commitments and stated principles. The contradictions in the behaviour of the undertaking have almost become the rule: they promise the CRTC the moon and come back with much less. What suffers in such cases is the credibility of the regulations.

This problem has existed too long for the CRTC not to base its future decisions on independent research. Research has a valuable role to play in the compliance strategy that we describe later. The CRTC should therefore maintain an up-to-date and meaningful data base on the broadcasting industry and its components.

Recommendations

The Department of Communications and the CRTC should support the development of research in communications-related disciplines on all aspects of Canadian broadcasting, especially regulatory policies and methods. Instead of concentrating on establishing new structures, their research support should emphasize centres of excellence that already exist, particularly in the universities.

In order to be able to carry out independent assessments of the broadcasting industry, the CRTC should reactivate its research department and consult specialists in all appropriate disciplines to establish and maintain a meaningful and up-to-date database on the broadcasting industry.

Access to Documents and Public Participation

Self-regulation, conditions of licence and a compliance strategy are methods that call into play broadcasters' responsibility and public vigilance. If these interested parties are to work together in the way we hope, the regulation should be readily understandable and support given for groups of concerned citizens to make themselves heard.

Whether dealing with licence renewals or rate increases, the CRTC hands down many decisions each year (73,000 since 1968), all of which are collected in the archives without being properly filed or indexed.[29] How is it possible to understand the development of regulation without ready access to the documents describing it? If, as we recommend, licensing conditions become increasingly important in the regulatory process, there will be less and less reliance on general regulations applicable to all licensees. A method must be found to keep track of the contractual variations from one licence to another, in order to identify trends and understand the general direction that is being followed. It is imperative that some way of keeping the various parties up-to-date on such matters be found. Our view is that there ought to be a database for referencing CRTC decisions and perhaps the decisions of councils set up to hear public complaints on matters left to self-regulation.

Recommendation

The government and the CRTC should work together to establish a readily accessible database on regulatory and self-regulatory processes and decisions.

It is not enough to make the regulations and decisions available. They must also be understandable. Those who have had to deal with them can confirm that CRTC decisions and other related documents are written in a jargon that is both inaccessible to the lay person and self-defeating because there is no resemblance whatever to ordinary language. Yet they are documents whose substance is not intended for a private group or a circle of initiates. The public has an interest in understanding the meaning of their contents and whether they are being observed. A simple concern for effectiveness requires that they be made readable. As if this were not enough, the hazardous process of translation or simply inadvertent error introduces doubtful language that makes them even less clear.

Recommendation

Regulatory instruments should be drafted clearly and simply in English and French.

We emphasize the need for regulatory instruments to be accessible, that is, both available and understandable because public participation depends upon it. If the CRTC's shift towards more individualized regulation is not to give rise to imbalances, there must be further opportunities for public comment.

There is of course a technical side to the broadcasting industry and the issues can only be fully understood with time and effort. Our consultations have nevertheless convinced us that many Canadians, both individuals and groups, agree that the public has a part to play. We have also examined with interest their points of view on the direction the system should take. To strengthen this link, we believe that permanent mechanisms to extend and simplify their participation should be set up. This is especially true when issuing or renewing a licence, which from our made-to-measure regulation approach will become excellent opportunities for adjusting the obligations of broadcasters to the needs expressed.

That is why we would like the federal and provincial governments to support citizens' groups interested in monitoring broadcasting. There is no need to establish any standard patterns for such associations, because they will certainly vary by region and circumstances. Our role is simply to establish conditions to help them organize and operate effectively.

Recommendation

> The federal and provincial governments should support the efforts of representative citizens' groups for the purpose of monitoring broadcasting.

Careful Application of the Rules

Policy will only succeed if the government has the resolve to apply the law in full: that is, to ensure that the statutory rights and obligations designed to implement the policy are observed. Regulation constantly flouted or enforced haphazardly is self-defeating. Worse still, it is harmful: its costs are greater than its benefits and it tends to discredit the very objectives it is intended to protect.

Words must be backed up with actions. Those who choose to ignore the law and its regulations must be prepared to suffer the consequences. Otherwise, the majority who do comply are penalized and the government may appear to condone civil disobedience.

The fact that a rule is considered unsuitable is no justification for breaking it. The best way to deal with rules becoming obsolescent is to monitor systematically their application and establish a mechanism that provides for them to be kept up to date. Flouting the law for whatever reason is unacceptable behaviour. Any broadcasting policy must therefore include compliance and updating mechanisms.

We therefore recommend that the government and the CRTC adopt a three-part regulatory compliance strategy: First, constant study and updating of regulation to adapt it to the rapidly changing world of broadcasting; second, a system of penalties designed to reduce costs substantially for those who comply with the rules and increase costs substantially for those who flout them; third, helping licensees understand the rules. It goes without saying that we feel that the departments of justice and communications should be closely involved in preparing the strategy.

We do not agree with those who see revocation of a licence as a panacea. There is a wide range of intermediate sanctions available to adjust the penalty to the offence without losing sight of the objective that the rules should hold sway. We believe that such measures are more effective in practice, provided clear cases of infringement are consistently reprimanded. For example, the CRTC can renew a defaulting undertaking's licence for a shorter term, as it is increasingly doing, or require it to justify its action. The CRTC can thus make judicious use of such measures to penalize all serious shortcomings. Also more effective than fines and licence revocation, the traditional penalties, are pressures from within the broadcasting environment itself. Financial markets, broadcasters, associations, insurance companies, advertisers and public interest groups can all apply pressure to comply. If the CRTC itself is vigilant, strict and equitable, it will find in them the natural allies it needs to dissuade and curb effectively those who are tempted by the rewards of non-compliance.

Realistic regulation and rigorous enforcement are inseparable aspects of our strategy. If we reduce the burden on undertakings to a few essential obligations based on attainable objectives, it is precisely with a view to basing broadcasting policy on rigorous compliance with the rules needed for the achievement of broadcasting objectives. What we are searching for is not less effort but rather a shift in effort.

The CRTC itself has already begun to reduce the regulatory burden. But this is only part of the task. The more difficult part still remains: to ensure that the increased leeway given the undertakings benefits Canadian broadcasting and that the conditions of licence be tailored to their resources and carried out in full.

Debate on broadcasters' failure to comply has often been diverted to the rules themselves, on grounds of relevance or precision. It is in fact easier to argue about whether or not a rule is appropriate than it is to reflect upon ways of ensuring that undertakings comply with them. Many studies of regulation fall into this trap. They begin by concluding that rules are ineffective because they are not complied with and then claim that the rules should be eliminated. Nevertheless, our public and private meetings indicate that Canadians and the industry hold strongly to the principles that govern broadcasting.

The question is therefore not whether one ought to deregulate or regulate but rather, a matter of deciding how principles are to be enforced once they are approved. In other words, if the problem is the ineffectiveness of the existing rules, the solution is not to eliminate all rules but rather to devise effective ones.

Regulatory reform assumes that the compliance mechanisms as well as the rules themselves be reviewed. It is useless to expend energy on establishing sophisticated regulations, whether general or made-to-measure, without taking into consideration how they are to be applied and the reasons for compliance. Because the principles are not being called into question, extra attention to the regulations and hence a strategy is called for. Unfortunately, neither the CRTC nor anyone else has expended much effort on devising a compliance strategy for broadcasting.[30] We will try to identify the main components of such a compliance strategy.

The strategy does not itself establish any new rules, but is rather an extension of existing rules. It does not call for automatic compliance with irrelevant, equivocal or outdated rules; it continually assesses their merits, including costs and benefits, with a view to facilitating compliance. It requires the cooperation of each participant, but also recognizes the need to discourage non-compliance by means of penalties.

Everything would be simpler if it were analogous to administering the highway code, with one eye on the speed limit and a pen at hand to write out tickets. In broadcasting, regulation is more complex and its objectives are not readily measurable. The various undertakings involved in broadcasting operate in very different markets in which the rules are demanding for some and easy for others. Thus, we recommend greater recourse to made-to-measure regulation using conditions of licence. That is a key element of our compliance strategy.

Adjusting the rules to the facts is not enough, however, to guarantee the compliance which we have made the ultimate goal of regulatory reform. The CRTC's compliance strategy should clearly take into account the various causes of non-compliance and provide effective protection against the various sorts of pressure that try to undermine its authority.

There is no single explanation for non-compliance. A study by Kagan and Scholz identified three major non-compliance behavioural models:

> In the first image, business firms are pictured as amoral calculators. Motivated entirely by profit-seeking, they carefully and competently assess opportunities and risks. They disobey the law when the anticipated fine and probability of being caught are small in relation to the profits to be garnered through disobedience. Non-compliance stems from economic calculation.
>
> The second image pictures the business firm as a political citizen, ordinarily inclined to comply with the law, partly because of belief in the rule of law, partly as a matter of long-term self-interest. That commitment, however, is contingent. Business managers have strong views as to proper public policy and business conduct. At least some law breaking stems from principled disagreement with regulations or orders they regard as arbitrary or unreasonable.
>
> In the third image, the business firm is seen as inclined to obey the law but as a potentially fallible or organizationally incompetent entity. Many violations or regulations are attributed to organizational failure — corporate managers fail to oversee subordinates adequately, to calculate risks intelligently, to establish organizational mechanisms that keep all operatives abreast of and attentive to the growing dictates of the law.[31]

In short, businesses fail to comply with the law for reasons of profit, conviction, or incompetence. Although most Canadian commentators on broadcasting policy have argued that callous sizing-up of the relative costs and benefits is the main reason for non-compliance, it does not account for all cases. A compliance strategy limited to this model alone would fail to correct the situation. In fact, much delinquent behaviour corresponds more closely to two or three alternative models and the CRTC should include the whole range in its strategy. We will review the models and describe the main components of a compliance strategy that could be developed for each.

The first model assumes that business undertakings calculate the costs of compliance before acting. Subject to market pressures, they break the law unless they believe they will lose more than they will gain. For firms that operate from such a standpoint, authors Kagan and Scholz suggest that heavy penalties are immediately required to make compliance with the law profitable.[32]

In broadcasting, the punitive approach creates as many problems as it solves. The cost of legal action is high and fines are generally low. Many of the offences are not serious or not perceived to be serious, and repeated non-compliance creates considerable damage. Moreover, emphasizing a system of penalties pays greater attention to the form of the rules rather than their content and creates a climate of mistrust between business undertakings and the regulator. It is possible to avoid such undesirable consequences by making use of a judicious selection of graduated sanctions, as we noted earlier.

According to the second non-compliance model, business firms refuse to comply with the law when they disagree with or call into question the value of the laws in question. Kagan and Scholz note:

> Corporate officials we interviewed, and many scholarly studies as well, repeatedly referred to instances of governmental arbitrariness: ill-conceived and conflicting regulations; officious and poorly trained government inspectors, unreasonable paperwork requirements; bureaucratic delay; governmental indifference to the disruption or inefficiencies in productive processes caused by literal enforcement of regulations.[33]

This kind of behaviour invites us to view regulation as reciprocal relations between responsible citizens and regulatory authorities who are sensitive to their concerns. Thus, the effectiveness of the regulatory process requires a commitment from the businesses involved to build regulatory requirements into their management process. One cannot expect rules on matters of small detail, which are applied inconsistently and which take long periods of time to be settled, to be complied with.

Business undertakings do not resist rules that appear to them to be legitimate because they generally recognize the need for rules. We therefore encourage the CRTC, with a view to simplifying the regulatory process, to use conditions of licence as a made-to-measure form of regulation, that is adjusted to the undertaking's profile and suited to its circumstances. This co-operative approach to regulation would overcome problems with those undertakings that currently do not comply because of the inadequacies of the rules.

The third model of non-compliance includes businesses that do not know how to comply with regulations. They neither understand nor study them. Here, management incompetence leads to non-compliance. We must admit that the complexity of regulation bears some responsibility, the more so because the CRTC is not the only source of problems. It shares this responsibility with taxation, labour and other administrative authorities. Broadcasting itself touches on so many issues that managerial competence alone does not cover them all. Complying with regulation is no easy task because it involves the specific principles of Canadian broadcasting, which must be understood in their entirety.

When non-compliance is due to incompetence, the best response for a compliance strategy is assistance to the undertaking. Providing expertise, organizing seminars and maintaining close contacts with professional organizations are all forms of assistance that are well known to the Canadian broadcasting industry. The CRTC may also test the undertaking's knowledge of the regulations when it issues or renews a licence; it can also improve the situation by making the rules readily understandable and accessible to all those who will have to comply with them.

This review of the three non-compliance models shows that there is no miracle formula for regaining compliance and that it is even somewhat dangerous to use only one such model:

> One implication of the diverse sources of non-compliance is that indiscriminate reliance on any single theory of non-compliance is likely to be wrong, and when translated into an enforcement strategy, it is likely to be counterproductive. . . . The relevant question, therefore, from the standpoint of regulatory strategy, is not which theory to use, but when each is likely to be appropriate.[34]

The important point is that the compliance strategy should be an integral part of all regulatory decisions. Whenever the CRTC makes a regulation, amends a provision or sets a condition of licence, it must at the same time assess the likelihood of success and the methods available for ensuring it; in other words, it must become expert in regulatory methods and evaluation.

Recommendation

The CRTC should make greater use of conditions of licence to define the obligations of each undertaking, adapting them to the circumstances of each.

The CRTC should adopt a compliance strategy as part of its regulatory and supervisory role, a set of coordinated measures to ensure that it costs less for licensees to comply than not to comply. The CRTC should establish appropriate enforcement measures in conjunction with setting conditions of licence or drafting new regulations.

Powers of the CRTC

The powers of the CRTC consist of a set of rights and mechanisms identified by the Act to ensure that individuals and undertakings involved in the Canadian broadcasting system act so as to comply with the principles stated in the Act. Here again, a compliance strategy appears to be called for if CRTC decisions are not to be a dead letter. With that in mind, we examine the powers of the CRTC and recommend appropriate changes.

The Power to Make Regulations

The *Broadcasting Act* gives the CRTC the power to make regulations on any matters falling within its jurisdiction, including programming standards, allocation of air time to various types of programs, types of advertising and the amount of allowable advertising time, assignment of time allowed for partisan political broadcasts, rights and obligations of stations involved in network operations, and the information to be provided to the CRTC by licensees on their financial position and their programs. These regulations are intended for all licensees or for certain classes of licensees depending on the case.

The regulatory powers of the CRTC can readily be seen to be broad indeed, and their extent has been confirmed by the Supreme Court. The powers are in fact almost as broad as the subject matter of section 3 of the Act, which sets out Canada's broadcasting policy. The majority decision of the Supreme Court was that a CRTC regulation, to be valid, need only refer to one or other of the subjects stated in section 3.[35]

According to the *Third Report* of the Special Committee on Statutory Instruments,[36] a regulation is a "rule of conduct, enacted by a regulation-making authority pursuant to an Act of Parliament, which has the force of law for an undetermined number of persons".[37]

Contrary to the case in licensing conditions, which like the clauses of a contract bind only one licensee, the provisions stated in regulations apply to all licensees. For example, paragraph 5(1)(b) of the *Radio (AM) Broadcasting Regulations*, which prohibits the broadcast of abusive comment, applies to all AM broadcasters regardless of their specific financial circumstances or geographical location.

There are many differences, however, among the various undertakings, notably profitability. Generally, regulations cannot make distinctions. They lead to procedures which are costly for some undertakings and insignificant for others. Hence there are limits to the usefulness of regulations. Not all issues can be dealt with using solutions that are appropriate for the 'average' undertaking. An average is, after all, an abstraction with which few undertakings correspond. Furthermore, even when a regulation sets reasonable obligations for an average company, it can be far too harsh on companies below the average and too soft on those above. This does not prevent the regulation from contributing to certain ends like preventing abusive subject matter.

Unable to deal with specific instances, regulations also do not have the flexibility to deal with the rapid evolution of broadcasting. When there are infringements, dealing with offenders becomes as slow as dealing with offenders under the Criminal Code. It is extremely difficult and time-consuming to establish evidence and the courts hesitate to assess heavy fines for actions rightly or wrongly deemed to be isolated incidents that have not resulted in identifiable damage.

Thus a regulatory approach is not always the most appropriate way to implement broadcasting policy. It is suitable for dealing with matters that affect all undertakings equally or that affect their relations with third parties. For other matters, however, we prefer conditions of licence, which can be tailored to specific circumstances.

Recommendation

The *Broadcasting Act* should keep the CRTC's extensive powers to make regulations on all matters within its jurisdiction.

The Power to Set Conditions of Licence

The CRTC has the power to issue, renew, suspend or revoke a broadcasting licence. It is also empowered to exempt undertakings from the requirement to hold a licence.[38]

When the CRTC issues a licence, it gives an undertaking the right to use a public resource for its own benefit. In return, the licensee is committed to operate in a manner compatible with the principles defined by Parliament.

The power to issue a licence is not linked to specific criteria. The CRTC studies the applicant's file and decides the case on its merits. The Act in fact specifies that the power is to be exercised "in furtherance of the objects of the Commission", that is, in accordance with the role of the CRTC, which is to implement broadcasting policy. This vague provision gives the CRTC great freedom of action[39], which it can use as it sees fit.

The CRTC is free to adjust its requirements for each undertaking; in other words, to take into account distinctions the regulations disregard. The use of conditions of licence thus opens the way to 'made-to-measure' regulations.

Every broadcasting undertaking operates in an environment that is different because of its geographical location, the language of its audience and the market for cultural products. The CRTC and its predecessors misunderstood the language situation in Quebec when they issued a disproportionate number of English AM and FM radio licences in Montreal, given the linguistic composition of the population. In television, the CRTC recently attempted to reduce the language imbalance by authorizing cable carriage of programs from other French-speaking countries under the auspices of La SETTE, a consortium of cable operators formed for this special purpose.[40] The special character of French-language broadcasting in Canada places Quebec broadcasters in a situation without equivalent in English Canada. It justifies a number of special licensing conditions, as would any other economic or cultural factors that differentiate the various undertakings.

Among the conditions of licence are sometimes the 'promises of performance' commitments made by a licensee in support of the licence application. Conditions of licence are in a sense the terms of contract entered into between the broadcaster and the public authorities. It is therefore to be expected that the undertaking should, on the basis of its capacities, specify what it intends to do to contribute to the objectives of the system. These are discussed at a public hearing, where participants may require that the commitment be more specific or more extensive.

The CRTC has considerable leeway to determine conditions of licence. The Supreme Court, in its *CRTC v. CTV* decision, even recognized the validity of a licensing condition imposed upon the CTV network requiring it to broadcast a specified number of hours of original drama programs over two seasons. As the

CRTC has then, under the current Act, the power to set a condition of licence that requires the licensee to spend specified amounts for specific purposes, then it should be clearly stated in the Act to eliminate any doubt on the matter.[41]

Because licensing conditions specify the commitments made by undertakings, it makes them enforceable and makes it possible for the CRTC to supervise them. This is another advantage over regulations.

Although there is nothing in this regulatory approach that is contrary to the freedom of expression guaranteed by the Constitution,[42] it would, to say the least, be unwise to use conditions of licence to control program content. It is better to restrict conditions of licence to the general conditions governing programs and the resources to be used.

Clearly and accurately worded conditions of licence are indispensable for later evaluating the broadcaster's record at the time of licence renewal. This leads again to the main concern of our proposed reform: the effectiveness of regulation. Like any regulatory measure, conditions of licence will be effective only if they are complied with. Hence, conditions ought not to be imposed unless a method has been provided to ensure compliance. Monitoring mechanisms spring to mind, but they are not advisable when it is obvious that they will be complex and costly. There are other more economical ways to ensure compliance, such as the participation of consumer groups and attention to individual or group complaints.

Licence renewals are the key to the approach, because it is at the time of renewal that the undertaking is assessed in terms of its commitments and its contribution to the achievement of the general broadcasting policy objectives. It is at renewal that the undertaking must show its willingness to correct any shortcomings. Since the CRTC has the power to suspend the undertaking's licence, it is able to exert the required pressure. If it were demonstrated to the undertakings that non-compliance with their licensing conditions would lead to stricter conditions at renewal, they would tend to adjust their behaviour accordingly. This is yet another component of our compliance strategy.

Recommendation

The *Broadcasting Act* should continue to provide for broad CRTC power to set conditions of licence on each licensee, including conditions that oblige the licensee to spend specified amounts for specific purposes.

Policy Statements

The CRTC's practice is to publish in a policy statement the direction it intends to take on particular issues, usually after public hearings. As Raoul Barbe stresses, "a policy statement has no legal force or effect; it merely suggests a form of behaviour in individual decision making".[43] The CRTC's policy statements can nevertheless guide broadcasters.

A policy statement does not have the rigidity of a formal regulation. It states intent; it does not prescribe obligations. A policy statement can neither validly contradict a regulation[44]; nor bind the regulatory authority when it decides an individual case. It is therefore not a substitute for regulations. Its standard-setting effect is indirect because the regulatory authority reveals the reasoning that it will base its decisions upon, for example in issuing licences, and because undertakings are obviously interested in preparing themselves accordingly.

The principles set forth in a policy statement will therefore take shape in promises of performance and conditions of licence. We believe that the policy statement is an appropriate way of informing undertakings what the CRTC expects of them and suits the made-to-measure approach to regulation.

Supervision

The *Broadcasting Act* assigns the CRTC a dual responsibility: to regulate and to supervise the system. For a number of years the CRTC has emphasized supervision, so that broadcasters respond appropriately to the requirements of competition, changing audience tastes and the evolution of cultural products.

This position requires the CRTC to assume that the industry itself will guarantee that the public and the objectives of the Act will be properly served. In Public Notice 1986-66 *Draft Regulations Respecting Radio (AM and FM)*, the CRTC notes that "there already exist industry codes in the area of sex-role stereotyping and children's advertising". The CRTC therefore shares with broadcasters themselves the responsibility for regulating: it encourages them to regulate themselves, supervises the self-regulatory approach and retains the right to use more coercive measures if it considers that the broadcasters have not lived up to their responsibilities.

We feel that this experiment should be encouraged. If the approach is to work it is essential that the self-regulatory process be accepted. Hence we recommend public participation in the formulation and application of the standards the broadcasters adopt. The CRTC should therefore work with representative groups towards this goal. It should also state clearly what it expects of self-regulation by identifying the areas that lend themselves to this form of regulation and by including industry standards in conditions of licence where appropriate.

Supervision of this kind, however, will not do the whole job. It can only be effective if research allows the CRTC to assess the state of the industry and to have at its disposal all the facts it needs to set licensing conditions, including a compliance strategy.

Complaints

The CRTC's supervisory role is also exercised by receiving public complaints. The handling of complaints, in addition to providing a service to users, brings to the attention of the CRTC a number of programming problems. As Salter and Anderson note in a report prepared for the Department of Communication:

> Public comment and complaint is just another type of audience survey, tapping the responses of minority audiences in most cases . . . the broadcaster council or agency that receives no complaints is one [that] has little impact upon the audience or one whose activities have provoked cynicism or quiescence.[45]

The ordinary consumer can generally only be heard by complaining. The more the CRTC emphasizes its supervisory role, the more it will need public support. The ongoing analysis of complaints would give the CRTC the added benefit of voluntary monitoring by the public.

After a sorting process, substantive complaints are forwarded to the broadcasters by the CRTC. Complaints are dealt with on the basis of the principle that broadcasters are responsible for the programs they broadcast.[46] It is not a matter of censoring programs. Even if the CRTC wanted to act as a censor it would be unable to do so, especially since the adoption of the *Canadian Charter of Rights and Freedoms*.[47] The CRTC can, however, consider the concerns expressed when a licence is renewed or amended. That is why, since 1982, it has been placing complaints in the public examination file of the broadcaster, as it explained in notice 1982-36:

> To ensure that all complaints and replies thereto become an integral part of the licensing process and that significant issues arising from public complaints are fully considered in assessing the overall performance of a licensee, correspondence relating to complaints will form part of the public record. At the time of licence renewal, complaints received during a term of licence will be placed in the public examination file along with the licensee's application for licence renewal.[48]

The CRTC forwards complaints to the broadcasters concerned and they are required to look into them and report back. In some cases, the complaints give rise to public hearings, at the discretion of the Commission,[49] although such action is relatively rare.

The CRTC sometimes publishes a notice warning broadcasters who are at fault.[50] Such action has generally been taken as the result of exceptional incidents involving failure to provide programming of high standard or balanced points of view, or the broadcast of abusive material.

It is at the time of licence renewal that current shortcomings are studied. While including complaints in the broadcaster's file makes the system more workable, the users themselves have been lost in the shuffle. To remedy this state of affairs, we recommend that the CRTC appoint, in each of its regional offices, a Public Advocate who is responsible for receiving complaints and who will follow them through to their conclusion.

The Public Advocate will have the authority needed to demand an explanation from a broadcaster and to submit serious cases to the Commission for consideration. The Public Advocate would make sure complaints were fully dealt with. He would provide liaison with groups wishing to intervene at renewal hearings and would enter on the agenda any problems that have arisen since the previous examination. At the hearing itself, the Public Advocate would be the spokesperson for any concerns expressed and would present recommendations to the Commission on the conditions of licence and the term of renewal.

The presence in each region of a Public Advocate responsible for ensuring public participation would bring the Commission closer to Canadians and represent an alternative to having part-time members. The Public Advocates will have to show in-depth knowledge of broadcasting and of the regulations and be secure for the term of their appointment.

Recommendation

> The CRTC should appoint a Public Advocate in each of its regional offices. The Public Advocate would be responsible for ensuring public participation. He or she would receive and investigate public complaints. The Public Advocate would have the authority to demand, if necessary, explanations from broadcasters and to submit serious cases to the Commission for consideration. The Public Advocate would maintain liaison with groups wishing to intervene at licence renewal hearings and express any concerns identified as well as make recommendations to the Commission on conditions of licence. He or she would be appointed for five years and not be removable from office except for cause.

Public Hearings

The CRTC is required to hold a public hearing before issuing, suspending or revoking a licence. For other decisions, it is required to hold a hearing only if it deems that it would be in the public interest to do so.[51] The hearing procedure is very flexible, as Christopher Johnston notes:

> Applicants appear and speak to their applications and are questioned by the Commissioners and Commission Counsel on their written and oral presentations. Interveners then appear to make their oral presentations and questions are similarly addressed to them. Applicants are permitted to reply. In all of this, the evidence given is not sworn and there is no cross-examination beyond the questioning of the Commission. Evidence is not 'led' by counsel for applicants. Parties generally read their oral submissions from a prepared text.[52]

The CRTC's objective has been to attempt to avoid the legal formalities typical of courtroom hearings, which are often believed to encourage confrontation. Because the courtroom ritual is so alien to the uninitiated, the CRTC has abandoned any rules that resemble court proceedings. But for these burdensome rules another set of rules, equally burdensome, has gradually been substituted. For example, the CRTC limits the length of interventions and allows the right of reply only in relation to questions raised at the hearing. Only members of the Commission examine applicants and participants. The information obtained at a hearing therefore depends entirely upon the amount of preparation that has been done.

It has been argued that this procedure encourages members of the public to take part in the hearings and to express their opinions to the CRTC because there is no risk of being vigorously cross-examined. The result, according to Johnston, is that sometimes "conflicting statements on the same point have sometimes been left unchallenged on the records or have not been sufficiently clarified".[53] There have even been hearings where questions have been asked at random, without any accuracy or consistency. Such a procedure does not provide for a thorough search for the facts. This type of hearing may be appropriate for political debate, but it is unsatisfactory where specific interests conflict. It needs to be reviewed.

We have recommended making increased use of conditions of licence. The CRTC should therefore study the financial position of applicants, evaluate their production capacity and assess their plans. How is this possible without the required facts? This is where cross-examination is useful and also where it would fit in well with our compliance strategy. If broadcasters were required to give a public explanation under this procedure, they would be less inclined to break their promises.

To accelerate the process without sacrificing information, we also suggest preparatory conferences, at which the parties would submit their questions in writing to the CRTC beforehand; the Commission would decide which were relevant and require the undertaking submitting an application to answer them. If the written answer is inadequate, the same question would be raised at the public hearing.

Section 20 of the *CRTC's Rules of Procedure* gives the Commission the authority to withhold specific financial information where it deems it preferable.[54] The CRTC has shown itself increasingly willing in recent years to avail itself of this provision. However, it is impossible to hold a real public hearing if basic information on the question under consideration is withheld from the public. To encourage the greatest possible openness in consideration of the issuing or renewal of a licence, we recommend keeping confidentiality of information to a strict minimum. For example, it would be unthinkable to keep secret information on an undertaking's ability to produce Canadian programs. In practice, the only information that should be allowed to remain confidential is information that identifies and could potentially harm individuals.

Recommendations

The CRTC should authorize cross-examination by parties with opposing interests wherever the possibility exists that contradictory statements could impair the proceedings.

The CRTC should respect the rights of all parties to all useful information on applicants and licensees, and drop existing confidentiality practices that hinder the evaluation of applications at public hearings.

Notes

1. Vincent Lemieux, « Le rôle des différents acteurs dans les politiques de radiodiffusion » study prepared for the Task Force on Broadcasting Policy, Ottawa, December 1985, p. 4.
2. Peter J. Lown, "A Reflection on the Roles and Responsibilities of the Major Actors in the Broadcasting System", study prepared for the Task Force on Broadcasting Policy, Ottawa, December 1985, p. 6.

3. Section 22 of the Broadcasting Act states that:
   22. (1) No broadcasting licence shall be issued, amended or renewed pursuant to this Part
   (a) in contravention of any direction to the Commission issued by the Governor in Council under the authority of this Act respecting
   (i) the maximum number of channels or frequencies for the use of which broadcasting licences may be issued within a geographical area designated in the direction,
   (ii) the reservation of channels or frequencies for the use of the Corporation or for any special purpose designated in the direction, or
   (iii) the classes of applicants to whom broadcasting licences may not be issued or to whom amendments or renewals thereof may not be granted and any such class may, notwithstanding section 3, be limited so as not to preclude the amendment or renewal of a broadcasting licence that is outstanding on the 1st day of April 1968,
4. *Broadcasting Act*, R.S.C. 1970, c. B-11, s. 26. See also, Pierre Trudel, *Droit de l'information et de la communication: notes et documents* (Montreal: Éditions Thémis, 1984), p. 309.
5. Jacques Frémont and Pierre Trudel « Étude des relations entre le C.R.T.C., la Société Radio-Canada et le gouvernement à l'occasion de la détermination des conditions de licence relatives au service national de radiodiffusion », study prepared for the Department of Communications, Ottawa, February 1986, p. 37. See also Donna S. Kaufman, "Cabinet Action and the CRTC: An examination of Section 23 of the Broadcasting Act", (1985) 26 *C de D*. 841.
6. See H.N. Janisch, "Policy-Making in Regulation: Towards a New Definition of the Status of Independent Regulatory Agencies in Canada" (1979) 17 Osgoode Hall, *L.J.* 48, 66; and Jacques C. Frémont, "Protection of the Public interests in Communications Regulations: The Canadian Radio-television and Telecommunications Commission", Masters thesis submitted to Osgoode Hall Law School, Toronto, August 1978, p. 104.
7. See Patrick Kenniff, Denis Carrier, Patrice Garant and Denis Lemieux, *Le Contrôle politique des tribunaux administratifs*, Québec, PUL 1978.
8. Bill C-20 proposes adding the following provision to the CRTC Act:
   14.1 (1) Without limiting any power of the Government in Council under any other Act of Parliament to issue directions to the Commission, the Government in Council may, of his own motion or at the request of the Commission, issue to the Commission *policy directions* concerning any matter that comes within the jurisdiction of the Commission and every such direction shall be carried out by the Commission under the Act of Parliament that establishes the powers, duties and functions of the Commission in relation to the subject-matter of the direction.
9. Canadian Institute for Adult Education, "Broadcasting in Canada: A Public Service", brief submitted to the Task Force on Broadcasting Policy, Montreal, October 1985, p. 58-59.
10. Ibid.
11. Law Reform Commission of Canada, *Report No. 26: Independent Administrative Agencies* (Ottawa: Minister of Supply and Services Canada, 1985).
12. Ibid., p. 31.
13. Daniel Jay Baum, "Broadcasting Regulation in Canada – The Power of Decision" (1975) 13 *Osgoode Hall Law Journal*, 693.
14. Liora Salter, "Issues in Broadcasting", study prepared for the Task Force on Broadcasting Policy, Ottawa, December 1985.
15. Ibid.
16. Ibid.
17. Ibid.
18. André Bureau, "Cancon in Turbulent Times", speech by the Chairman of the Canadian Radio-television and Telecommunications Commission to the Broadcast

Executives Society in Toronto (Ottawa: CRTC, March 1984), p. 2-3.

19. André Bureau, "Remarks to the House of Commons Standing Committee on Communications and Culture" (Ottawa: CRTC, May 1984), p. 2.
20. See Hershell Hardin, *Closed Circuits: The Sell-out of Canadian Television* (Vancouver: Douglas and McIntyre, 1985).
21. See A Study Team to the Task Force on Program Review, *Management of Government: Regulatory Programs* (Ottawa: Minister of Supply and Services Canada, 1986), p. 190.
22. In the United States, this point of view was supported by Mark S. Fowler and Daniel L. Brenner in "A Marketplace Approach to Broadcast Regulation", (1982) 60 *Texas Law Review* 207.
23. See Timothy J. Brennan, "Economic Efficiency and Broadcast Content Regulation" (1983) 35 *Federal Communications Law Journal*, 117; and Todd Bonder, "A 'Better' Marketplace Approach to Broadcast Regulation" (1984) 36 *Federal Communications Law Journal*, 27.
24. See Bruce M. Owen, "Regulating Diversity: The Case of Radio Formats" (1977) 21 *Journal of Broadcasting*, 305; Peter O. Steiner, "Program Patterns and Preferences, and the Workability of Competition in Radio Broadcasting", (1952) 66 *Quarterly Journal of Economics*, 194.
25. Friends of Public Broadcasting, brief submitted to the Task Force on Broadcasting Policy, Toronto, September 1985.
26. Office of the Deputy Prime Minister, "Background to the Regulatory Reform Strategy" (Ottawa: the Department, February 1986), p. 3.
27. Ibid.
28. For example, the AM and FM radio regulations as well as those for television broadcasting include a prohibition against broadcasting "any program on the subject of birth control unless that program is presented in a manner appropriate to the medium of broadcasting". This regulation was made a very long time ago, following controversy on the issue. Since the regulation has never been revised, it remains on the books despite the fact that it is out of date.
29. See Marie Phillipe Bouchard, Michèle Gamache and Mireille Beaudet, "Étude du Statut juridique des entreprises de radiodiffusion au Canada", study prepared for the Task Force on Broadcasting Policy, Ottawa, 1986, p. 284.
30. Most important work on the problem of compliance with regulation and policy implementation has been carried out by the Law Reform Commission of Canada. It is striking to note that the many studies that have been carried out in Canada on regulation, often from an economic standpoint, say nothing about the problems of compliance. See J.C. Clifford, "Content Regulation in Private FM Radio and Television Broadcasting: A Background Study about CRTC Sanctions and Compliance Strategy", study prepared for the Law Reform Commission, Ottawa, 1983.
31. Robert A. Kagan and John T. Scholz, "The Criminology of the Corporation on Regulatory Enforcement Strategies" in *Enforcing Regulation*, by K. Hawkins and J. Thomas (Boston: Kenver – Nijhoff, 1984), p. 67.
32. Ibid., p. 69.
33. Ibid., p. 75.
34. Ibid., p. 85.
35. *CKOY v. The Queen* (1979), S.C.R. 2.
36. Special Committee on Statutory Instruments, *Third Report*, (MacGuigan Report) (Ottawa: Queen's Printer, 1969), p. 14.
37. See Gilles Pepin and Yves Ouellette, *Principes de contentieux administratif* (Montreal: Yvon Blais, 1982), p. 84 and, in general, Raoul P. Barbe, *La Réglementation* (Montreal: Wilson and Lafleur, Sorej, 1983).
38. See the *Broadcasting Act*, s. 17 (1)(e)
39. This was determined by the Supreme Court in *CRTC v. CTV* (1982) S.C.R. 530.
40. See Canadian Radio-television and Telecommunications Commission, *Decision 79-460* (Ottawa: CRTC, August 8, 1979). The decision approves applications from

cable operators who are members of SETTE.

41. See Henri Brun, « Opinion juridique concernant le pouvoir du CRTC d'assortir les licences qu'il émet de certains types de conditions », study prepared for the Task Force on Broadcasting Policy, Ottawa, April, 1986, Brun contends:
"In my opinion, the current wording of subsection 17(1) of the *Broadcasting Act* nevertheless, from an administrative law standpoint, provides sufficient authority to the CRTC to require broadcasters to use some of their assets for specified broadcasting purposes. This could only be considered not to be the case if the renewal conditions could reasonably appear to be indirect expropriation measures, which, *prima facie*, is difficult to imagine. To avoid any possible disputes, it would nevertheless be preferable, to meet the criterion of the Payne decision, that 17(1) should be amended to specifically provide for the power to impose such conditions of licence." (translation)
42. That at least is the conclusion of the Federal Court of Appeal in its decision *CJMF-FM Ltée v. CRTC*, March 29th,1984, No. A-398-84.
43. Barbe, supra Note 27, p. 24.
44. *Capital Cities Communications Inc. v. CRTC* (1978) 2 R.S.C., p. 141.
45. Liora Salter and Peter Anderson, "Responsive Broadcasting: A Report on the Mechanism to Handle Complaints About the Content of Broadcast Programs", study prepared for the Federal Department of Communications, Ottawa, August 1985, 2, p. 7.
46. *Broadcasting Act*, s. 3(c).
47. People are generally very wary of prior restraint because it assumes suppressing the message prior to its broadcast, which makes any decision about the alleged dangers that are likely to result from broadcasting it. The approach which is generally considered to be compatible with freedom of information is based on the idea that it is better to punish after the fact those who have disseminated libellous messages than to restrain *a priori*.
48. Canadian Radio-television and Telecommunications Commission, *Complaints and the Public Examination Files*, CRTC Public Notice 1982-36 (Ottawa: CRTC, 1982) and Salter and Anderson, op. cit., p. 8.
49. This is the Commission's Executive Committee. See the *Broadcasting Act*, s. 18.
50. See Canadian Radio-television and Telecommunications Commission, *Concerning a Complaint Against CKVU Television, Vancouver, British Columbia, by Media Watch*, CRTC Public Notice 1983-187 (Ottawa: CRTC, August 17, 1983).
51. *Broadcast Act*, s. 19.
52. C.C. Johnston, *The Canadian Radio-television and Telecommunications Commission: A Study of Administration Procedure in the CRTC*, study prepared for the Law Reform Commission of Canada, Ottawa, 1981, p. 26-27.
53. Ibid., p. 44.
54. *CRTC Rules of Procedure*, s. 20, reads as follows:
20. The Commission may, at the request of an applicant, if in the opinion of the Commission the public interest will best be served by so doing, treat as confidential the following material or information, if such material or information can be separated from the application and is marked "Confidential", namely
(a) financial statements of an applicant who holds a licence;
(b) evidence of the financial capacity of any person participating in an application; and
(c) the names of prospective employees of an applicant.

Part III

FRENCH-LANGUAGE BROADCASTING

Chapter 8

The Distinctiveness of French Broadcasting

The Distinctiveness of French Broadcasting

We recommend in this Report that the distinctive character of Quebec broadcasting be recognized both in itself and as the nucleus of French-language broadcasting throughout Canada (see Chapter 6). We do so not only because of recent pressing concerns, but also because Quebec has developed a broadcasting system with its own special history, methods, programs, audiences and problems. Moreover, it is a system that needs its future development to take place within a framework that is made-to-measure for its aspirations.

During our consultations this distinctive character of French-language broadcasting in Quebec was mentioned by a number of representatives from the industry itself, including the President of the TVA network, Claude Blain.[1] According to him, the language factor is so important in Quebec television that TVA's basic problems are closer to those of the CBC than those of CTV (for example, the loss of viewers to English networks) and solutions appropriate to the English networks do not work for the French networks (for example, the substitution of Canadian for American signals on cable television when the Canadian channel carries an American program in the same time slot).[2]

When this basic difference has been ignored, as in the imports of pay-TV and music formats on FM radio, a uniform policy or regulation applied to the French sector as a solution more often than not becomes a new source of problems. It was to reverse this trend that a joint committee of the Canadian and Quebec governments recommended in May 1985 that French-language television in Canada should be recognized as a distinct entity and that appropriate policy and regulations should be formulated for it.[3] In February 1986 the approach recommended resulted in Ottawa signing a formal agreement with Quebec linking the province to the development of French television.[4] We extend the principle to the whole system, including radio.

The language difference leads to many other differences. With respect to Canadian content, for example, a continuing weakness in the Canadian broadcasting system, Quebec television is remarkably successful and the envy of English Canada. Viewers of French-language stations spend 68 percent of their time viewing *Canadian* productions (almost all of which are made in Quebec), while viewers of English-language stations spend 71 percent of their time watching *foreign* programs.[5]

If we were to stop there, francophones could rightly celebrate. But the picture changes considerably when other variables are introduced, because francophones do not restrict themselves to French-language stations. About 20 percent of total francophone viewing in 1984 was of English-language (Canadian and American) stations. Total viewing of Canadian productions on all stations dropped to 57 percent and if viewing is broken down by age group, it drops still further to 48 percent among teenagers.[6]

All of this goes to show that there are two important things to note about French-language television in Canada. First, linguistic isolation (the well-known "two solitudes") has created a breeding ground for creative works in

Quebec. However, pressures of all kinds threaten not only these works but the language itself. The problem of Canadian content is therefore very different from that in English Canada: French-language viewers are subjected to a dual acculturation process.

This has a number of consequences for us. From a strictly linguistic standpoint, the increasing number of English channels available to francophone viewers represents the same danger whether they are American or Canadian. Conversely, an increase in French-language services would solve part of the problem, whether the programs were imported, dubbed, or produced here. When the need is filled primarily by imported and dubbed programs, French-speaking viewers are faced with the same problem as their English-Canadian counterparts: too many foreign programs in their own language. But at least the language, which is the key to audiences and programming on French language television, will have been preserved.

That is how the language difference affects the problem of Canadian content on Quebec television. When combined with economic factors like a small market, it determines the audience, programs, viewing habits, network organization, resource sharing and program creation; it explains the direction taken by educational television, the development of community stations, the popularity of téléromans (serial dramas), FM radio music quotas and the disparities in programming available to minorities: all of which places French-language television in Canada in a different world.

The Indicators of Distinctiveness

Audiences

The 1981 census counted 6,249,095 Canadians whose mother tongue was French, or 25.7 percent of Canada's population as shown in Table 8.1. They represent the current and potential market for French-language radio and television.

What is different about this market is that 97 percent of it is concentrated in Quebec or in areas close to Quebec: 85 percent in Quebec itself and 12 percent in the bordering provinces of Ontario (8 percent) and New Brunswick (4 percent).

Other disparities appear when one looks at the real audience, that is, the audience share of French-language stations. Hence, everywhere in Canada and increasingly as we move away from Quebec, the audience share for French-language television drops below the percentage of francophones in the population (see Table 8.2). French-language television stations capture 21 percent of television viewing across Canada with francophones accounting for 25.7 percent of the population. In Quebec, where the percentage of francophones is 82.4 percent, viewing of French-language stations is much higher (72 percent); but in New Brunswick, French-language stations capture only 14 percent of total viewing, even though francophones represent 34 percent of the population. In the other provinces French-language stations never capture more than 1 percent of total viewing, even where francophones represent 5 percent of the population, as in Ontario and in Manitoba.

Table 8.1 Distribution of Francophone Population in Canada (Mother Tongue French)

	Francophone Population		Percent of total Francophone population
	No.	%	
Canada	6,249,095	25.7	100
Quebec	5,307,015	82.4	84.9
Outside Quebec	942,075	5.26	15.1
Ontario	475,605	5.5	7.6
Atlantic Canada	278,795	12.5	4.5
New Brunswick	234,030	33.6	3.7
Nova Scotia	36,025	4.25	0.6
Prince Edward Island	6,085	4.9	0.1
Newfoundland	2,655	0.5	0.04
West	185,860	2.66	3.0
Alberta	62,145	2.7	1.0
Manitoba	52,555	5.1	0.8
Saskatchewan	25,540	2.6	0.4
British Columbia	45,620	1.6	0.7
Northwest Territories	1,235	2.7	0.02
Yukon	580	2.5	0.009

Source: Canada, Statistics Canada, *1981 Census of Canada, Mother Tongue*, Catalogue No. 92-902.

These discrepancies lead to economic and cultural choices. In the private sector there are no French-language television stations outside Quebec and only six radio stations: four in Ontario and two in New Brunswick. Although there are 22 French-language television stations in Quebec and eight outside Quebec, the latter all public, 89 percent of programs produced in French in Canada are produced in Quebec.[7]

As a result of Canada's linguistic distribution, therefore, production, stations and audiences for French-language radio and television in Canada are almost entirely in Quebec. The Canadian content of programs is essentially Quebec content.

Programs

French-language radio and television schedules have always had a high percentage of Canadian programs. An unexpected consequence of linguistic isolation was that French-language television had to rely on its own resources and produce the programs it needed because it did not have an abundant supply of readily available French-language programs from nearby foreign sources. The distance from France was physically and culturally too great. Even if it had been possible to overcome it, television developed slowly in France. Even today, with a population one-tenth that of France's, Quebec produces more programs: 300 hours per week compared to 275.[8]

When television was introduced in Canada in 1952, the English-language network had an apparent advantage over the French in having a supply of

Table 8.2 Viewing of French-language Stations in Each Province as a Percent of Total Viewing (Monday to Sunday, 6 a.m. – 2 a.m., 1984-1985 Season)

	Nfl'd.	P.E.I.	N.S.	N.B.	Que.	Ont.	Man.	Sask.	Alb.	B.C.	CANADA
Viewing of French-language stations (%)	0.1	0.3	0.1	13.8	71.7	0.8	0.4	[illegible].1	0.1	0.1	20.7
Francophone Population (%)	0.5	4.9	4.25	33.6	82.4	5.5	5.1	[illegible].6	2.7	1.6	25.7

Sources: For the viewing share, Canadian Broadcasting Corporation, CBC Research, raw data from A.C. Nielsen. For the population, Canada, Statistics Canada, *1981 Census of Canada, Mother Tongue*, Catalogue No. 92-902.

American programs available. This advantage was also a risk because all it had to do to win over viewers was to tap the American networks. E.A. Weir, who worked for the CBC in its early days, recounts in *The Struggle for National Broadcasting in Canada*, that this was precisely what CBC radio had done in the thirties. In 1938, ten of the sixteen sponsored evening programs on the national network were American. They were to be the driving force for Canadian programs, contributing to establishing a large network audience, generating the advertising revenues needed for Canadian production.[9]

In television, this strategy of reliance on the U.S. led to important gaps in program production. The CBC developed news and information, where it excels, and neglected by comparison production of drama, the popularity of which has today captured large segments of the Canadian audience for American programming.

The French-language network had to develop variety, drama and children's programs from scratch. CBC followed the lead of the successful radio serials and developed what was to become one of the great successes of French-language television, the "téléroman" (a combination of the French words for 'television' and 'novel'), by drawing on the best of Quebec literature — Guèvremont, Lemelin, Grignon, Choquette — or by developing original scripts. In variety programming, it began by putting on nightclub stars before adopting the American *Ed Sullivan Show* format in the program *Music-Hall*; and in the 60s, it became the natural extension of the "boîtes à chanson" in giving exposure to the new generation of modern Quebec "chansonniers" (singer-composers). In news and public affairs, no one needs reminding that Radio-Canada was at the heart of all the debates, all the liberalising movements that have stirred Quebec society over the past 30 years. As the years went by, CBC was to produce all kinds of programs, reflecting all aspects of life in French in this country. When the first private television station went on the air in Quebec, it was well aware of the significance of these efforts and planned accordingly.

Viewing Patterns

An important feature of French-language television that has often been commented upon is the large audience for its original productions. In all program categories, Canadian programs have a proportionally higher number of viewers than their foreign competitors (see Table 8.3). In all but one category, they fill at least two-thirds of air time and capture nearly nine of ten viewing hours.

Oddly enough, it is the drama programs that cause the average to drop, despite the number and popularity of téléromans. However, the drama category dominates air time with 30 percent of total programming and also includes motion pictures, which are almost entirely foreign-produced, as well as American series. Thus, for each episode of an American series (one hour) and for each feature film presented (one and one-half hours or longer), there would have to be, respectively, two or three téléromans (one-half hour). Canadian drama nevertheless remains the most popular program category (20 percent of tuning compared to 10 percent of air time), which corroborates the survey results.

Table 8.3 Availability and Viewing of Canadian Programs (%) (Monday to Sunday, 6 a.m. – 2 a.m., Calendar 1984)

Types	French TV[a]		English TV[b]	
	Broadcast Time	Viewing Time	Broadcast Time	Viewing Time
All	57	68	28	29
News	99	100	46	89
Public Affairs	78	99	52	62
Sports	92	96	68	71
Drama	10	20	2	2
Entertainment	66	87	25	18

Notes: a. Includes TVFQ.
b. Includes American channels
c. For methodology, see notes to Figures 5.4 and 5.5 in Chapter 5.
Source: Canadian Broadcasting Corporation, CBC Research, raw data from A.C. Nielsen.

Table 8.4 The Most Popular Programs in Canada (Week of January 16-22, 1986)

French channels	English channels
1. Le temps d'une paix (SRC)	1. Cosby Show (CTV)[a]
2. Peau de banane (TVA)	2. Family Ties (CTV)[a]
3. La bonne aventure (SRC)	3. Miami Vice (CTV)[a]
4. L'âme soeur (TVA)	4. Dallas (CBC)[a]
5. Montréal en direct (TVA)	5. Simon and Simon (CTV)[a]
6. Poivre et sel (SRC)	6. Walt Disney (CBC)[a]
7. Épopée rock (TVA)	7. CBC National News (CBC)
8. Paul, Marie et les enfants (SRC)	8. Hockey Night in Canada (CBC)
9. Dallas (SRC)[a]	9. The Nature of Things (CBC)
10. Entre chien et loup (TVA)	10. Scarecrow and Mrs. King (CTV)[a]

Note: a. American programs.
Source: BBM Bureau of Broadcasting Measurement, Survey of television networks (total of French and English networks, all public, age 2-plus).

The ratings for the English- and French-language Canadian networks in Table 8.4 are revealing. In French Canada nine of the ten programs with the highest ratings are domestic productions (compared to only three in English Canada). Eight of the nine Quebec productions are téléromans, even though popular American series such as *Dynasty* and *Dallas* are shown dubbed into French; *Dynasty* is not even on the list for this particular week and *Dallas* is ninth. Both networks are represented approximately equally in the list of most highly rated programs (five TVA versus four CBC).

In radio, a public affairs show called *l'Informateur*, which runs at mid-day on CKAC in Montreal, was the most popular program in the country in June 1986, despite being in a time slot that is generally less popular for this type of program than the morning.[10] The station that airs the program often has over one million listeners. In March 1986 it was the most listened-to AM radio station in the country; in 1985 it came in second in total weekly number of hours of tuning.[11]

The Cultural Background

Two of the most popular téléromans from the early days of television, *Les belles histoires des pays d'en haut* by Claude-Henri Grignon and *La famille Plouffe* by Roger Lemelin, had already been radio serials and, before that, novels adapted by the authors themselves for the new media, where a larger audience could be found. Both were later made into movies and two of the most colourful characters, Séraphin and Le Père Gédéon, developed stage careers of their own in the form of comic monologues performed by the actors who played the roles on TV.

Broadcasting and the art forms it drew upon worked so well together because everyone was part of the postwar cultural boom in an extremely homogeneous Quebec society in which Quebeckers remembered their roots as they underwent urbanization. "Les belles histoires" reminded people of the life on the soil of days not long gone by; the Plouffe family was new to city life. The Quebec novel was beginning a development that would bloom in the 60s, along with poetry, music and theatre, at the same time as book publishers and record companies were springing up everywhere to distribute them and universities, after having wondered for a long time whether there were such things as Quebec novels, poetry, music and theatre, began to study them in earnest.

No matter what the literary form, radio and television were already established when this cultural flowering began. Quebec theatre pioneer Marcel Dubé got his start writing plays for television. The "father" of Quebec chansonniers, Félix Leclerc, started in radio and, long before the appearance of the "boîtes à chansons", Radio-Canada was organizing and broadcasting song competitions in an attempt to find worthy successors to him. Among the winners who were later to become stars was Robert Charlebois, who added the influence of American music to Quebec's, which was primarily based on folk music, the French tradition and poetry.

The common denominator in all the arts was the French language, which itself benefited from this intermingling. Francophones are well aware of the importance of radio and television in strengthening the language. The best known example is the sports vocabulary, which was almost completely anglicized, even in France. Two Radio-Canada announcers, Michel Normandin and René Lecavalier, had to develop new terms to describe the games they were announcing and the French equivalents they developed were adopted so wholeheartedly that competing private broadcasters, print media and sports fans gradually began to use them, and they eventually became an accepted part of the language.

In technical matters, in news and elsewhere, the same need was felt and each field had its own innovators. In 1960, Radio-Canada finally established its language committee, which today is known throughout the French-speaking world for the high level of its terminological work. The committee is widely consulted and works closely with the Office de la langue française and many international organizations; private industry has imitated it in recent years.

Everyone is aware that the CBC's concern for the French language has been its trademark and this concern has spread to other broadcasters. We mention this here because it is clear that broadcasting played a key role in the evolution of French even though that development went far beyond broadcasting because it stemmed from Quebec society itself. Even though it did not always adopt the same solutions, society as a whole had the same requirements as broadcasting. It had become important not only to return to a French that was free of Anglicisms, but also to Canadianize (or "Quebecize"), that is, to adapt French to life in North America without waiting for all the answers to come from France. In novels, theatre and song, artists found in the French spoken by ordinary Montrealers expressive linguistic forms that could be moulded to the mass media and the rhythms of rock music.

The language issue has always been closely associated with broadcasting and related arts in one form or another. Today a number of new challenges are a source of surprise and concern: for although Quebeckers remain faithful to Quebec performers and works, francophones are nevertheless consuming more cultural products in English. The trend is strongest in Montreal.

However, according to a CROP survey conducted in May 1986 for the Union des artistes and *La Presse*[12], Quebeckers feel that their cultural products are better than or as good as their American counterparts: songs (56 percent vs 33 percent), records and cassettes (47 percent vs 34 percent), and television programs (45 percent vs 44 percent). Only in motion pictures do they feel that Quebec products are inferior (58 percent vs 27 percent).

According to the same survey, Quebeckers are "very much" or "somewhat" in favour of government intervention to set minimum Quebec content quotas for cultural products such as music played on radio (77 percent), television programs (78 percent) and motion pictures (67 percent).

The fact is that Quebec broadcasting, culture, language and society grew up together. This is not surprising, because it is only in Quebec that francophones are a majority and hence able to run their own political and social institutions. According to the Macdonald Commission, this is the key to the special character of Quebec:

> Above and beyond this recognition of the distinctive nature of Quebec society, it is the existence of the whole francophone community, in other words, of Canada's basic duality, which is at stake. Notwithstanding such recognition, the fundamental linguistic isolation of this community will endure. The essential question for Quebec and for francophones outside Quebec will remain unchanged: How can the French element of our populations retain its identity in North America?[13]

The Role of the Quebec Government

The Government of Quebec has always played an active role in communications because the all-important areas of language and culture fall within its jurisdiction and also because of its moral responsibility to provide leadership, as the only government in Canada representing a French-speaking majority.

The milestones in the Quebec government's involvement in broadcasting over the years have been as follows:

1929 – Quebec Broadcasting Act

The Quebec Legislature was eager to get a broadcasting act on the books. The Taschereau Government wished in this way to declare vigorously that Quebec had jurisdiction over radio because of provincial jurisdiction over education and culture.

1945 – Establishment of Radio-Québec

An act passed on 20 April 1945 established a provincial broadcasting service, Radio-Québec, whose purpose was to make Quebec, its resources, its culture and its aspirations known. The act remained on the shelf until 1968 when it came into force by proclamation of the Government. In 1969, it was replaced by a law creating the Office de la radio-télévision du Québec (ORTQ) with a mandate to establish, own and operate a broadcasting service for educational purposes. Radio-Québec's earliest programs were delivered by cable in 1972 and three years later it launched its first two broadcasting stations in Montreal and Quebec City.

1969 – Establishment of the Quebec Department of Communications

The act establishing the Department of Communications assigned it a mandate to formulate and enforce communications policy for Quebec, to supervise communication networks on Quebec territory and to establish communication services for government departments.

1972 – Regulation of Cable Television

Maintaining that cable television is a public service falling within provincial jurisdiction, Quebec assigned its Régie des services publics the power to regulate cable, which the federal government had assigned to the CRTC. Among other things, Quebec was attempting to give priority to French-language programs in the allocation of channels. The conflict between the two authorities led to a 'cable war' which ended when the Supreme Court of Canada decided against Quebec's claims in 1977. It confirmed the authority of the federal governement over cable television on the grounds that cable was part of broadcasting, which had been placed under federal jurisdiction in 1932. The Régie des services publics immediately ceased to issue operating licences.

Other Measures

Despite these Court decisions, Quebec never stopped wanting to make its presence felt in communications. It is against this background that we must understand the mandate assigned to Radio-Québec, which is more cultural than strictly educational, the technical and financial support given by the Quebec Government to community media, which have prospered in Quebec, and the establishment of agencies like the Société générale du cinéma (SGC) and the Société de développement des industries de la culture et des communications (SODICC).

Established primarily to provide assistance to motion picture production, the SGC allocated approximately 10 percent (almost $1 million) of its budget in 1984-1985 to television programs.[14] SODICC, which was established in 1978, intervened in 1984 to assist financially troubled Super-Écran (the trademark of Premier Choix-TÉVEC) with $3 million in investment and a loan guarantee of $1.3 million.[15]

As Jean-Paul l'Allier, a former Quebec communications minister, commented, the Government of Quebec, whatever the party in power, would like to control communications in the province for as long as the media are perceived not only as a vehicle for culture but also as a direct influence on culture that continually and directly affects viewers and listeners.[16]

The co-operation agreement signed this year between the governments of Canada and Quebec does not change the distribution of jurisdictions but recognizes the need to work together to support the progress of a culture that history has already subjected to all sorts of centrifugal pressure.

Organization and Shortcomings of the System

The geographical distribution of the French-speaking audience across Canada opens up only very small markets to advertisers in most regions. Of the 15 largest French-speaking population centres in Canada, 13 are in Quebec and 12 have a population of less than 150,000 (see Table 8.5). The 15 largest English-language population centres, on the other hand, from Toronto to St. John's, are spread over seven provinces and every one of them has a population of over 150,000. Thus the word 'region' refers to something different in each of the official languages. This helps to explain the distortions that arise in network configurations, which francophones in Quebec and outside Quebec complain about.

To fulfill its mandate, the CBC had to extend its network outside Quebec to serve isolated and often very small audiences. This has led to there being more CBC stations outside Quebec than inside; there are still large Quebec population centres that do not receive the full CBC radio and television schedules.

There are no private television stations outside Quebec because it would not be economically viable to operate one. In Quebec, the only private network, TVA, has affiliates in six markets with a population of 100,000 or more, as well as in a number of small regional centres (see Table 8.6). Compared with the big English-speaking cities, these affiliates provide hardly any contribution to programming.

Radio-Québec attempted to overcome the shortcomings of the other networks by placing stations in Quebec's ten administrative regions, with the intention of decentralizing production to these regions. But four of its nine regional production centres outside Montreal have just been closed to save money and these large cities – Quebec City, Hull, Trois-Rivières and Sherbrooke – will no longer contribute to Radio-Québec programming.

The losers will be primarily small towns in more remote areas and medium-sized cities located on the periphery of the regions: it is in such communities that community television stations have flourished, with the assistance of the government, which sought to extend French-language service throughout Quebec.

Table 8.5 Distribution of French-language Television Stations in Major Urban French-speaking Centres in Canada (1981)

Francophones		Urban Centres	CBC owned[a]	CBC aff.[a]	TVA	Radio-Quebec
No.	%					
1,936,200	68.5	Montreal	X		X	X
554,775	96.3	Quebec	X		X	X[b]
253,925	35.4	Ottawa-Hull[c]	X		X	X[b]
132,545	98.1	Chicoutimi-Joncquière		X	X	
108,235	97.1	Trois-Rivières		X	X	X[b]
105,780	90.2	Sherbrooke		X	X	X[b]
61,300	97.8	Shawinigan				
57,120	94.1	St-Jean-sur-Richelieu				
53,375	97.6	Drummondville				
46,605	98.2	St-Hyacinthe				
45,745	97.3	Sorel				
45,455	1.5	Toronto	X			
45,405	30.3	Sudbury				
43,070	94.3	Granby				
42,305	96.6	St-Jérôme				

Notes: a. CBC owned: Stations owned by CBC.
CBC affiliate: Private stations affiliated with CBC.
b. Offices closed August 31, 1986.
c. In Ontario, 113,065 (20.7 percent); in Quebec, 140,865 (82.6 percent).

Sources: Canada, Statistics Canada, *1981 Census of Canada*, Census Metropolitan Areas and Census Agglomerations with Components, Catalogue No. 95-903, vol. 3.

Table 8.6 Other French Television Stations in Quebec

Francophones		Urban Centres	CBC owned	CBC aff.	TVA	Radio-Québec
No.	%					
36,965	98.7	Rimouski	X		X	X
27,275	90.8	Sept-Iles	X			X
26,905	93.9	Rouyn-Noranda		X	X	
20,270	98.8	Rivière-du-Loup		X	X	
–10,000	–	Matane	X			
–10,000	–	Carleton			X	X
–10,000	–	Alma				X
–10,000	–	Amos				X

Source: Canada, Statistics Canada, *1981 Census of Canada*, Census Metropolitan Areas and Census Agglomerations with Components, Catalogue No. 95-903, vol. 3.

The Public Sector

Canadian Broadcasting Corporation

Only the CBC has radio and television stations across the country capable of reaching all francophones (99 percent).

Television CBC owns thirteen French television stations, five in Quebec and eight outside. To extend its network westward, despite restricted markets, CBC established stations in provincial capitals, where the CBC English network already had facilities.

The network also has five affiliates, all in Quebec, serving Saguenay-Lac St-Jean, the Eastern Townships, the St. Maurice region, Abitibi and the Lower St. Lawrence (see Table 8.5 and Table 8.6). The total population of these centres includes at least 500,000 francophones who do not receive full service because the affiliates can fill much of the air time with programming of their choice (see Chapter 10). This is particularly disconcerting in view of the fact that in Eastern Quebec, CBC has two stations only a few miles apart serving a much smaller population. Uneven network configuration leads to imbalances in program content, especially in news (see below).

Radio CBC has 21 French radio stations, 15 AM (Mono) stations — six in Quebec and nine outside — and six FM (Stereo) stations — four in Quebec and two outside.

It was in 1970 that CBC French radio began to take its present form by equipping its regional Mono stations for production, and setting aside peak time slots for their programming. With the development of FM, CBC gave a specialized role to each network, with a community service and news role on Mono and a cultural and classical music emphasis on Stereo.

Some regions have only one Radio-Canada station. Where this is the case, CBC offers a composite schedule (the 'service de base') consisting of Mono programming during the day and Stereo cultural programs during the evenings. By selecting from both Mono and Stereo programs, the basic service ensures that listeners are not deprived completely of one or the other. But once again, substantial parts of the population in the very heart of Quebec get less than full service and in some instances they are the same regions that receive poor television service: Sherbrooke, Trois-Rivières and Abitibi, for example, must content themselves with an affiliate on television and the basic service on radio.

This composite, or third service is a compromise, CBC acknowledges.

> As soon as possible, all the population should be provided with a choice of two complementary schedules; 82 percent of francophones from Moncton to Ottawa already have such a choice. But unfortunately, these two full networks still miss, even in Quebec, important population areas: Central Quebec (Mauricie, Bois-Francs, Eastern Townships), North-East and Gaspe areas. Elsewhere, in northern New Brunswick and the Sudbury region, there still are quite a few francophones receiving the third service.[17]

The autonomy of French-language services The CBC French-language service has been virtually autonomous for a long time. The delegation of authority came about partly for reasons of administrative efficiency, because a television network is difficult to manage at a distance. It did not take place without problems.

It was as a result of the 1966 CBC Headquarters decision to discontinue the program *This Hour Has Seven Days*, then at the height of its popularity, that the decision was made in 1968 to establish two divisions within the Corporation, the French Services Division and the English Services Division. The decentralized structure made the existence of the two networks official and gave them all the autonomy they needed for their development. All that remained in Ottawa was regional station management, which in any event went to Montreal or Toronto within three years. For nearly 15 years, there was in fact not one CBC, but two separate CBC networks "at the service of distinct societies". Marc Thibault, former News Director of CBC's French Services, explained the arrangement as follows:

> Under these conditions, where disparities between the English- and French-language services were much greater than their similarities, it is not surprising to find that relations between them had primarily to do with administrative rather than programming problems, except for a number of areas like music and sports, some documentary productions, special events like elections, political conventions, and royal or papal visits, which called for exchanges and a sharing of responsibilities and resources.[18]

In all other respects, the two networks developed independently of one another: programming, production and regional stations. Until 1983 each had all the powers it needed to carry out its operational responsibilities: finance, personnel, engineering, technical services, and so on.

The structure of the CBC was radically changed in the spring of 1983. The reorganization concentrated most of the powers previously exercised by the two networks, including regional and auxiliary services, in Ottawa, where Headquarters is ultimately accountable to Parliament. It also separated radio and television network operations.

The centralization in Ottawa of decisions concerning the French network was far from popular. Decisions made in Ottawa are often English-network-oriented. But the English and French networks are not identical twins. The French network has its own special character, both in television and radio. For instance, the relations that may be expected between the network and the local French-language stations scattered outside Quebec are clearly different from those that would be suitable between the Toronto headquarters of the English network and stations in other Canadian cities.

French Canada has been able to develop a separate, inventive and popular broadcasting system. This is an achievement that must be preserved at a time when new problems require Radio-Canada to strengthen its ties with the constituency that supports it.

Recommendation

> The autonomy of French-language services (radio and television) within the CBC should be recognized, and French-language CBC should be allowed to develop distinctly from English-language CBC. The two sectors, serving distinct societies, should be allowed to take different approaches to meeting the objectives assigned to public broadcasting, without prejudice to the ultimate responsibility of the Corporation under the Act.

Radio-Québec

Although Radio-Québec is educational television within the meaning of the Act, its programming and the audience it attempts to reach during prime-time are not at all like audiences and programming normally associated with a television 'classroom'.

The service was born, as we saw earlier, out of the need that the government of Quebec has always felt to intervene in an area that affects culture. Education is the only area of provincial jurisdiction in Canada's Constitution that could open the door to such involvement and in Quebec, traditionally, education, language and culture are inextricably bound together. Radio-Québec's mandate is in fact specifically 'cultural'.

Radio-Québec describes itself as the "other" television, that is, different and complementary. It must be seen as part of a whole that includes the two networks that preceded it in the market when it went on the air in 1972. They were often criticized for neglecting Quebec's 'regions', especially in news and information. Radio-Québec's mandate is therefore also regional

It is no doubt in this light that Radio-Québec's long-standing intention to produce its own news programs from a Quebec viewpoint should be seen, with the way being prepared by including current affairs segments in the schedule. According to Radio-Québec President Jacques Girard, public expectations revolve around entertainment programming and news, the two major program categories.[19] These are two types of programs that are expensive to produce and for the present, Radio-Québec does not have the resources to fulfil its ambitions, as indicated by the closing of four regional offices following budget cuts in the Spring of 1986.

Radio-Québec's programming in 1984-1985 was 30 percent educational programs, generally presented during the day, and 70 percent cultural programs aimed at the general public during prime time.[20] Virtue is rewarded as it is a children's program in the former category, *Passe-Partout*, that is Radio-Québec's most popular program. Produced by the Department of Education in cooperation with TVOntario and also broadcast on the CBC, the program is so popular that strong protests have prevented its withdrawal from the schedule in the past. A private sector spokesman recently complained that they were losing their audience for the local news program aired in the same time slot.

Radio-Québec's modest beginnings in 1972 restricted it to two hours of programming a day in two cities for a small number of cable subscribers. Today it serves 92 percent of Quebec's population and its overall audience share among all French Quebec stations is 5.6 percent, a higher share than any other educational television network in Canada in its own market.[21]

The Private Sector

Television

In 1961, long before Radio-Québec and to a much greater extent, Télé-Métropole (Channel 10) had radically altered French-language television in Montreal. CBC, which until then had been like Adam in the Garden of Eden, now had to share the television screen with a competitor whose rapid rise would soon force it to change direction. Since then, the programming on channel 10, which from the very outset adapted successful formats from the American networks and aired dubbed versions of some of their popular programs, has usually had the lion's share of the BBM's top-rated television programs. To avoid losing too much of its audience and revenue, CBC was forced to adjust. Survival meant capturing viewers. Thus the too uniformly cultural television of the 50s, with its weekly theatre, concerts and windows on the world, had to come to terms with entertainment television.

In 1971 Télé-Métropole joined forces with private stations in Quebec City and Chicoutimi to establish the TVA network. The purpose of the arrangement was to share the high cost of news production. It was later extended to include public affairs coverage of events like political conventions and elections, as well as some sports events. Today the TVA network consists of ten stations that broadcast ten hours per week of common programming. Most production is carried out by one or another of the affiliated stations, usually Télé-Métropole, the network's flagship station.

Unlike the CTV network, which is based in a number of major Canadian cities, the TVA network consists mainly of stations in medium-sized cities, most of which are unable to depend on sufficient advertising revenue to be able to produce expensive programs locally. These stations therefore broadcast many other programs, especially drama, obtained from Télé-Métropole or its subsidiaries. These arrangements have nothing to do with the network agreement, although the difference does not show on the screen.

On 6 September, 1985 the CRTC licensed a new French-language private station to operate in Montreal: Quatre Saisons. In its first year (1986-1987), it will broadcast 77 hours of programming per week, of which 40, according to its commitment to the CRTC,[22] will be Canadian (11 hours of in-house productions and 29 hours purchased from independents which could be produced with the assistance of Telefilm Canada).

The need for a third French-language television network in Quebec was hotly disputed between those who wanted to increase the number of French-language channels available and those who feared the Americanization of the airwaves. Opponents argued that market fragmentation would lead competing stations to depend increasingly on popular American product available at lower cost. When Télé-Métropole and Quatre Saisons announced their 1986-1987 schedule in the Spring, a Montreal newspaper described it as the most American television season ever. But CBC and Radio-Québec will continue to pursue their traditional objectives, and Quebeckers in many large cities (affiliates will relay Quatre Saisons programming outside of Montreal) will henceforth be able to choose from among five French-language channels, only one of which (TVFQ) is not Canadian.

Radio

Private AM radio in Quebec, unlike its counterpart in English Canada, is dominated by two major networks — Télémédia and Radiomutuel.

Télémédia, the largest network, consists of 34 AM stations, some of which are also affiliated to CBC. The network offers its members news and public affairs, sports and other programs such as the *Festival de l'humour*. The

Télémédia group, which operates the network, itself owns nine French-language stations in Quebec: five AM, all network affiliated (O and O) stations, and four FM, which are currently planning to work together in news production.

The Radiomutuel network, which is older but also more modest, has 15 AM member stations. The network offers its affiliates a generous 38 hours of programming per week, including news, telephone call-in shows and music. The Radiomutuel group, which operates the Radiomutuel network, owns four of the affiliates.

Alongside the major networks are regional groupings that offer their member stations common programming and are themselves affiliated to one or more major networks for national and international news. Thus six stations in the Bois-Francs region make up the Appalachian group, a Télémédia affiliate. And in the Abitibi region the four stations of Radio-Nord (in Rouyn, Val d'Or, la Sarre and Amos) also form a regional group, wholly owned by Radio-Nord and affiliated with both CBC and Télémédia.

Network affiliation certainly allows small stations to save considerable amounts of money. However, they risk losing their individuality. If diversity is lost, there are a number of dangers in store, especially in news (see below).

Community Broadcasting

A new form of broadcasting is thriving in Quebec, arising from pooling of resources by the audience itself. We emphasize in Chapter 6 how important we feel community broadcasting is in ensuring a right of access for communities neglected by the major networks.

It was in Normandin (Lac St-Jean) that community television appeared in 1970. Under the NFB Challenge for Change/Société nouvelle program, members of the community were given a one-week session introducing them to the basics of television production. The programs produced were carried on a channel of the local cable television system. It was also in the Lac St-Jean region, at St-Félicien, that those working in community television began to join forces. The first Community Council was established, paving the way for its many successful followers.

Community television spread rapidly in Quebec. Most community television channels, the old as well as the more recent, are strongly rooted in small communities — such as Cabano (1981), Cap-à-l'Aigle (1974), and Mont-Laurier (1978); in communities on the edge of big cities — such as Laval (1977), Repentigny (1982), and Vaudreuil (1981); and in a number of medium-sized towns — such as Alma (1979), Valleyfield (1973), Victoriaville (1974). There are 37 community television stations in Quebec today, six of which are located in the pioneer Lac St-Jean region.

Community radio, on the other hand, developed in the cities. The first community radio station, CKRL-FM, originated as a Quebec City student station in 1973. It was followed two years later by CINQ-FM a multilingual community station broadcasting in downtown Montreal. There are now 22, mainly in small and medium-sized centres, although there are two in Montreal and two in Quebec City (see Chapter 19).

Cable Distribution and Specialty Services

In the early years of cable television in Montreal, the Rediffusion Company made Muzak available to its subscribers as well as the programming from a number of Montreal radio and television stations, in addition to original television programming consisting of feature films, public affairs and news.[23]

From the outset, the features that continue to set French-language cable television in Quebec apart were already in evidence: original programming from the cable operators themselves and various forms of in-house filler. While this can be seen as a virtue, it was also a necessity owing to the paucity of appropriate French-language programs to feed the voracious cable systems and their many channels.

There is no doubt some connection between these 'home made' early programs and the reluctance of Quebeckers to become cable subscribers. In 1984, cable service was available to almost as many households in Quebec (79.6 percent) as in Ontario (82.4 percent); yet 67.8 percent of Ontarians were subscribers, compared to only 47.5 percent of Quebeckers.[24]

At a time when cable operators in English Canada were attempting to attract new subscribers by adding more American channels, Quebec cable operators had to devote a great deal of additional effort to developing French-language programming. It was Vidéotron, today Quebec's major cable operator, that first had to deal with the situation when it installed 36-channel cable on the south shore of Montreal in the early 70s. At the time, the Régie des services publics forced the company to include a converter in the base subscription price, thus providing universal access to 36 channels immediately. To fill all these additional channels, the management of Vidéotron provided a 5,000-title video library from which subscribers could call up titles on eight channels set aside for the purpose.

Vidéotron ended this form of distribution but it now offers a dozen "theme channels", which are included in the cable subscriber fee, thus allowing the operator to claim that 60 percent of the channels are French. They are mostly non-professional services developed with limited resources, some in alpha-numeric or teletext form, and used so little that even taken together they do not figure in the ratings. They include: an ethnic channel, an educational channel, a local sports channel, a youth channel, as well as a weather channel, classified advertising, a channel providing program listings for other channels, and so on. To distribute these programs, cable operators established regional consortia called "Inter-Vision networks" for the production, distribution and exchange of programs.

Since 1979, most cable operators also carry TVFQ, a selection of programs from France. The channel is distributed from Montreal by satellite. Although the quality standard is higher than that found on existing theme channels, the TVFQ programming reaches Montreal with a delay of several weeks, including news reports. Quebeckers are left to wonder how useful it is to know what the weather was like in Toulouse last month.

These channels — Parliamentary debates, community television, TVFQ, theme channels and conventional stations — were all that was available on cable in original French-language programming until the arrival of pay-television in 1982. The theme channels were developed as a stop-gap measure to make up for the lack of genuine French-language specialty channels — music, sports, news, and other. They demonstrated resourcefulness, but could never be more than a makeshift measure.

Thus on 13 May 1986, the CRTC issued a network licence to Vidéotron for the distribution to a group of cable operators of a special programming service called "Télé des jeunes" (Youth TV). The Commission nevertheless made the renewal of the licence conditional upon possible future specialty services of the same kind, thus illustrating the temporary and stop-gap nature of theme channels. The CRTC added that it would have to evaluate Vidéotron's role as a programmer.[25]

Even though theme channels are a compromise, all things considered, specialty-channel policy suited to the specific needs of Quebec could be based on them.

The introduction of French-language specialty channels in Quebec has been delayed because of the small size of the market. The federal-provincial committee on the future of French-language television recommended that this difficulty could be overcome by authorizing the inclusion of French specialty services in the basic cable subscription, with a possible slight increase in the fee, in order to reach the maximum number of viewers.[26] On this model, the guarantee of a substantial audience would facilitate the introduction of French specialty services, which could be substituted for some of the existing Inter-Vision theme channels. Many Quebec cable operators already charge an additional fee for these channels. The practice of increasing the subscription fee in order to extend basic service is therefore well established.

A study carried out by the Quebec Department of Communications in March 1986 estimated that the advertising base was large enough to support on its own one or two specialty channels with annual operating expenses of between $5 million and $10 million each.[27] If financing were to come not only from advertising but also from cable subscribers, it would be possible to finance from four to six specialty channels with operating costs of between $5 million and $7 million per year. According to the Quebec study, all it would take would be an increase in the annual basic cable subscription rate of less than 2 percent a year until 1990. A study done by Moss, Roberts and Associates for this Task Force shows that the market reacts well to increases in the monthly fee within specified limits (described in economic terms as elasticity).[28] For us, however, there is one factor which moderates the optimism in the figures: there can only be a limited number of channels if there are to be sufficient resources to provide high quality programs.

The CRTC obviously did not see the need to give serious consideration to the conditions necessary for viable French-language specialty services. In its decision of 2 April 1984 the Commission noted merely that there were no specialty services in the French language and encouraged suppliers of English specialty programs and cable operators to consult one another![29] This is an example of the unhappy consequences produced in the Canadian system by the tendency to make decisions without taking the special character of Quebec broadcasting into account. In this case, the discretionary approach would lock francophone Quebeckers into a model in which French services would only be viable with support from their English-language counterparts.

The CRTC policy in this matter created a political and artistic storm in early 1986. On 13 March the CRTC licensed MuchMusic, the discretionary English specialty channel, to establish a francophone portion on which all announcing and a minimum of three percent of music would be in French. The new service would carry eight hours of programming a day, from 8 p.m. to 4 a.m., half of which would be repeats. The Commission said that it was satisfied with these arrangements since MuchMusic had met its wishes.[30]

The Quebec music video network (MTVQ) appealed the decision to Cabinet and started legal proceedings before the Federal Court. MTVQ felt it had been injured because the CRTC had not even studied its own proposal to provide all Quebec cable subscribers with a French service specializing in popular music. The Quebec Minister of Communications, Richard French, also opposed the precedent, stating: "A partly bilingual service, controlled outside Quebec, cannot be a satisfactory and definitive response to the cultural needs of Quebec francophones."[31]

Cabinet did not reverse the CRTC's decision on MuchMusic, but Marcel Masse, then Minister of Communications, asked the Commission to hold a public hearing on the question of specialty channels that could be included on the basic tier.

Our analysis of the French-language specialty channel issue suggests a strategy other than the one followed thus far by the CRTC. In Chapter 13, we recommend as part of a revised approach that a new public, non-commercial service, TV Canada, be created which would be carried on basic cable and paid for by cable operators on a per-subscriber basis.

The program schedules of TV Canada in French would differ from those of its English counterpart, reflecting the different needs of French and English broadcasting. The premise of the new service is that there must be public broadcasting services, as well as commercial services, if Canada's own production and programming needs are to be met. While this is true of both English and French television it is even more urgently needed in French.

Nevertheless, there is also room for the development of more effective commercial specialty services in French. With the smaller market in Quebec, it is difficult to see how these can be more than just slight adaptations of their English counterparts unless they are carried on basic service and reach most of the relatively small Quebec market. Even so, the potential revenues from advertising and cable are limited and a very selective approach should be used in deciding which commercial specialty services ought to be licensed to be carried on basic cable.

Recommendations

A public French-language channel Télé-Canada (TV-Canada in English) should be created which will repeat existing Canadian programs and provide new Canadian programs in a number of areas including, among others, children's, news and public affairs, documentaries and arts programs.

Carefully chosen specialty channels should be licensed to operate in French on the basis of both advertising revenue and a per-subscriber charge to cable system operators, and these services should be carried as part of basic cable service.

Specialty services should be provided by companies distinct from cable television undertakings.

Priority carriage should be given to services in French on systems that serve primarily francophone subscribers. (See Chapter 24.)

Francophones Outside Quebec: a Special Case

Francophones living outside Quebec have an even more limited range of programming than francophones in Quebec. There are many groups of francophones in Canada who have no programs or very few programs available in French on cable television. Cable operators are not required to provide them and argue that they cannot make such services available because of the small number of francophones in most regions.

Francophones outside Quebec are isolated, usually living in small communities geographically remote from one another and lost in a sea of English, with very few opportunities for them to express their culture.

A Problem of Content

Francophones outside Quebec complain above all about the absence of choice. However, they also emphasize that there is very little programming available that reflects them and their communities, because CBC programming is, they find, too oriented to Montreal or Quebec. The Task Force received a dozen briefs from associations of francophones outside Quebec which made this observation. According to the Société des Acadiens du Nouveau-Brunswick, "It is recognized in practice that when you talk about CBC you are talking about Montreal and Quebec and that's it."[32] The Association canadienne-française de l'Alberta added:

> What we clearly recommend above all is a change in CBC attitude . . . We believe that this change should involve more flexible and individualized policies concerning the programs that CBC provides (or one might say inflicts on) its network stations, programs which often mean just about nothing to communities that are 3,000 kilometres away from Montreal and which certainly do nothing to develop any sense that francophones belong to their respective communities.[33]

Francophones outside Quebec say they are turning increasingly towards English-language media because they cannot find what they need in French: in fact they spend only 27 percent of their television viewing and 36 percent of their radio listening tuned to French-language stations.

Even during the period when francophones operated their own radio stations as they wished, however, the problem was already felt, as the tale of radio station CKSB (St-Boniface) illustrates:

> At the general meeting of April 1960, the Director noted a degree of indifference to the station. During the following decade, surveys showed disaffection with it, specially on the part of the younger generation.[34]

Francophones outside Quebec recognize the all-important role played by CBC and more than anything else would like to see its service improved. CBC is primarily criticized for not using local resources and talent and for overlooking its own audiences. They feel that CBC should have a different policy for francophones outside Quebec, one that would take into account their status as minority francophone groups in an English environment, their need for a sense of identity as a distinct community and their need to communicate with those who share their lot. There is a great deal at stake for francophones outside Quebec, because in the absence of appropriate means to express themselves, assimilation is inevitable.

The Fédération des francophones hors-Québec (FFHQ) has recommended a number of options for improving service to French-speaking communities, based on the use of existing or readily available resources.[35]

CBC Service

The Fédération makes two main requests of CBC: that French-speaking communities be sent the signal of their province's French-language station rather than the signal of the closest French station, which is often in another province; and that for the same reasons greater autonomy from the network be granted to regional stations.

The Fédération also feels that only small and inexpensive programming changes would be required to express this autonomy: news reports based on local interests; replacement of French-language versions of American foreign films, which they already receive on the English networks, by other films in French; more leeway for local announcers and acceptance, notably, of regional expressions and accents; and integration of the everyday life of francophones outside Quebec into drama programming, among others.

Community Radio Stations

The Fédération des francophones hors Québec supports the project proposed by the Association des jeunes Canadiens français for the establishment of a network of local radio stations with flexible programs suited to community requirements and preferences, oriented towards local events and open to local accents.

Market studies commissioned by the Fédération des jeunes Canadiens français in Winnipeg, Edmundston-Grand Sault and the Acadian peninsula (Gloucester County) were encouraging: French-speaking communities would welcome the presence of a community radio station; financial support from the francophone community and community organizations and from advertising would be sufficient to operate a community radio station. The Fédération hopes to obtain the co-operation and technical assistance of CBC to establish such community radio stations.

Program Choice in French

Finally, the FFHQ recommended exploring all avenues for increasing the supply of French programming outside Quebec. It specifically asked for changes to current broadcasting policy and regulations to require cable operators to provide several French channels.

Conclusions

The Task Force makes a number of recommendations in this Report that respond to the legitimate expectations of francophones outside Quebec.

The extension of CBC's FM network to all provincial capitals (Chapter 10) and the new television service we recommend in Chapter 13 would significantly improve the choice of programming available in French. We recommend in clear terms in Chapter 26 that a reasonable number of French-language services be made accessible throughout the country.

The proposed reorganization of news and information on the CBC's French-language network (see Chapter 10) would also lead to services better suited to the everyday life of francophones outside Quebec. Finally, the new community sector that we recommend be recognized serves the same objectives.

Like it or not, however, francophones outside Quebec will always have to depend to a great extent on Quebec for French-language programming and this is particularly true for television, which requires costly equipment and plentiful skilled labour. Jean-Paul L'Allier observes in his study for this Task Force:

> The continuance and even the development of electronic media of high quality by and for French-speaking communities outside Quebec cannot be completely dissociated from policies formulated to deal with the requirements of Quebeckers.[36]

But francophones outside Quebec should not be reduced to being simply consumers of Quebec products. They also need media that allow them to express themselves directly for their everyday survival. That is the dual solution we recommend.

Cross-over Tuning and Imports of American Programs

Even though all kinds of expedients have been tried to broaden the range of French-language programs available on television, competition from the English channels remains very strong. The success of téléromans and other popular Quebec programs hides two disturbing phenomena: the cross-over of francophone viewers to English-language stations and the massive importation of American programs by the French networks.

There is more to broadcasting in Quebec than the French system. There are three English-language television stations and 12 radio stations. In the Montreal region, where three-quarters of anglophone Quebeckers live, the percentage of English-language stations has always been higher than the anglophone proportion of the population.

Quebec audiences in addition have cable access to a wide range of English-language programs from elsewhere: the three-plus-one American networks, pay television (First Choice) and a few Canadian and American specialty channels (five or fewer, depending upon the cable system). The only French-language specialty service, Musique Plus, will only be partially French.

Francophone Quebec is often considered a market with a captive audience protected from American influence by a language barrier, while the English-Canadian markets are usually seen as being invaded by the American networks. In fact, a significant and, until recently, growing share of television viewing by Quebec francophones is captured by American television channels despite the language. Another problem specific to Quebec is tuning to English-Canadian radio and television stations by francophones. On the other hand, only one percent of anglophone total viewing is of French-language television.

Particularly in the Montreal market, listening by francophones constitutes a significant share of total listening to English stations: one-third of the audience for Montreal English-language TV stations, 41 percent for FM radio stations and 10 percent for AM stations (see Table 8.7).

Although the problem would appear to be resolved when francophones return to French-language stations, the fact is that the French-language stations themselves have been changing. For in order to regain their audiences and lost advertising revenues, French stations have been increasing the percentage of Anglo-American songs on radio and dubbed American programs on television.

That at least appears to be the meaning of recent data on programs and audiences, which we shall now analyze.

Cross-over Tuning in Television

Greater Montreal

The share of francophone viewing captured by English-language television stations in the Montreal market grew steadily until 1983 (see Table 8.8). Whereas 14.2 percent of viewing by francophone Montrealers was to English-Canadian and American stations in 1976, the figure reached 26.3 percent in 1983. While the long Télé-Métropole technicians' strike (from late 1982 until early 1984) may partly explain the pronounced increase in audience transfers in 1983, that increase was nevertheless part of a long-term trend.

The growth in the share of francophone viewing accounted for by English-language stations can be explained both by increased average viewing by individual francophones of the programs broadcast by these stations (average of 3.4 hours a week in 1976 and 5.7 hours a week in 1983) and also by an increase in the percentage of francophone viewers tuning to English television. From 1976 to 1983, the reach of English-Canadian stations increased from 52 percent

Table 8.7 Francophone[a] Viewers of English Stations, Montreal Market, Fall 1985 (%)

	Proportion of each station in total listening/ viewing	Proportion of francophones in listening/viewing of each station
Television		
CFCF (CTV)	15.6	34.0
CBMT (CBC)	7.0	28.0
Total	22.6	32.0
American stations		33.0
Radio		
CBM	1.6	6.0
CJAD	6.9	4.0
CFCF	2.2	7.0
CKGM	3.1	29.0
Total AM[b]	13.8	10.0
CBM-FM	1.5	23.0
CFQR-FM	3.8	36.0
CHOM-FM	6.8	56.0
CJFM-FM	5.1	33.0
Total FM	17.2	41.0
Total AM and FM	31.0	28.0

Notes: a. Whose usual language is French.
b. Includes CKO.

Source: Canadian Broadcasting Corporation, CBC Research, raw data from BBM Bureau of Broadcast Measurement.

Table 8.8 Share of Viewing by Francophone Montrealers Accounted for by English Television (%) (Monday to Sunday, 6 a.m. to 2 a.m., Fall 1976-1985)

Stations	1976	1978	1979	1981	1982	1983	1984	1985
English Canadian	9.6	11.6	12.5	12.8	14.0	16.6	12.3	11.2
American	4.6	6.1	4.8	7.7	8.0	9.7	7.3	7.4
Total	14.2	17.7	17.3	20.5	22.0	26.3	19.6	18.6

Sources: L. Giroux and A.H. Caron, *Les Québécois francophones et l'écoute de la télévision de langue anglaise : 1976-1984*, study prepared for the Federal-Provincial Committee on the Future of French-language Television (Ottawa: Department of Communications; Quebec, Department of Communications, 1985). Data updated for 1985 by CBC Research.

Data in the Giroux-Caron study are taken from the BBM fall surveys. The use of these surveys to measure viewing by broadcast language encounters methodological problems which are mentioned by the authors themselves (op.cit. pp. 13 and 148).

to 63 percent of the French-language Montreal population and the corresponding increase for American stations was from 22 percent to 38 percent.[37] (Reach is defined as the number of people or percentage of a population who tune in to a station for a minimum of 15 minutes per week.)

The trend reversed in 1984: the English stations' share of francophone viewing dropped significantly from 26.3 percent to 19.6 percent, the lowest since 1979. This downward trend was confirmed in 1985 with a further decline (to 18.6 percent), shown in both the declining proportion of francophones tuning to English stations (their reach) and in the reduced average number of hours spent viewing these stations.

Despite this, it would be incorrect to believe that the problem has been cleared up. The recovery is real but brittle. This is partly because francophone Montrealers' viewing of English-language television remains significant, but primarily because the renewed popularity of French-language stations is the result of restructuring the French-language schedule to include more American series, a problem we will return to later.

Quebec Excluding Montreal

Cross-over tuning is far less pronounced among Quebec francophones living outside Montreal (see Table 8.9). In 1985, the share of francophone viewing accounted for by American and English-Canadian stations was only half the share found in Montreal (9 percent versus 18.6 percent). Although the cross-over tuning to English-language stations outside Montreal is lower than that of the Montreal area, it has steadily increased, paralleling the trend in Montreal. The cross-over tuning outside Montreal has nearly doubled, rising to 10.6 percent in 1983 from 5.7 percent in 1976. After a drop to 7 percent in 1984, it rose again to 9 percent in 1985.

As far as the number of viewing hours is concerned, Quebec francophones outside Montreal were spending a weekly average of 1.5 hours watching English TV in 1976 and 2.5 hours in 1983.[38] This dropped to 1.7 hours weekly in 1984 and then rose to 2.5 hours in 1985.[39]

Outside Montreal, the reach of English-Canadian stations increased from 26 percent to 36 percent of the francophone population in 1978 but has not risen since then. On the other hand, the reach of American stations doubled from 1976 to 1985, rising from 12 percent to 24 percent of the French-speaking population.

Language Mobility Factors

The ability to understand English and subscribing to cable are the determining factors in the language mobility of francophone viewers. Outside the Montreal region, where bilingualism is less widespread, cross-over viewing levels are lower. Understanding English is, however, not enough to gain access to English stations; cable makes the difference.

For example (see Table 8.10), although over one-third of the viewing time of bilingual French-speaking Montrealers subscribing to cable television was spent watching English-language stations in 1985, the figure for unilingual viewers without cable was barely 5 percent. Cable subscriptions particularly

Table 8.9 Share of Viewing by Francophone Quebeckers Outside Montreal Accounted for by English Television (%) (Monday to Sunday, 6 a.m. to 2 a.m., Fall 1976-1985)

Stations	1976	1978	1979	1981	1982	1983	1984	1985
English Canadian	3.9	5.4	5.7	5.7	5.4	5.9	3.6	5.4
American	1.8	2.8	2.1	3.4	3.5	4.7	3.4	3.6
Total	5.7	8.2	7.8	9.1	8.9	10.6	7.0	9.0

Sources: L. Giroux and A.H. Caron, *Les Québécois francophones et l'écoute de la télévision de langue anglaise : 1976-1984*, study prepared for the Federal-Provincial Committee on the Future of French-language Television (Ottawa: Department of Communications; Quebec, Department of Communications, 1985). Data updated for 1985 by CBC Research.

Data in the Giroux-Caron study are taken from the BBM autumn surveys. The use of these surveys to measure viewing by broadcast language encounters methodological problems which are mentioned by the authors themselves (op.cit. pp. 13 and 148).

increase the share of viewing captured by American stations, which are inaccessible almost everywhere without cable (from 3.6 percent to 16 percent for bilingual and French-speaking Montrealers).

French-speaking Montrealers who have access to more English stations, including some without cable, are greater consumers of English-language television than other Quebeckers. In short, the greater the exposure to English stations, the more people view them especially if they have mastered English. Even unilinguals without cable tune to them more in Montreal than outside.

Table 8.10 Viewing Share of English Television for Unilingual and Bilingual Francophones in Quebec: Cabled and Uncabled Households (%) (Monday to Sunday, 6 a.m. to 2 a.m., Fall 1976-1985)

	Unilingual without cable	Unilingual with cable	Bilingual without cable	Bilingual with cable
Montreal				
English Canadian	4.2	5.5	15.8	18.4
American	1.0	5.9	3.6	16.0
Total	5.2	11.4	19.4	34.4
Outside Montreal				
English Canadian	1.8	3.4	12.7	15.0
American	0.5	3.0	3.3	14.2
Total	2.3	6.4	16.0	29.2

Source: Canadian Broadcasting Corporation, CBC Research, raw data from BBM Bureau of Broadcast Measurements.

Foreign Programs on French-language Stations

Cross-over viewing takes a more subtle form when viewers can find on the French stations an abundant supply of the foreign programs that draw them to the English networks. In 1984, 43 percent of French-language programs shown in Canada were of foreign origin, chiefly American, 38 percent if France's TVFQ is excluded. This is shown in Table 8.11. Although on English television, 72 percent of the programs aired were foreign, that percentage drops sharply to 49 percent on the English-Canadian stations (this reflects the fact that American stations, account for 47 percent of all available English-language programming).

Table 8.11 Availability and Viewing Share of Foreign Programs (%) (Monday to Sunday, Calendar 1984)

	Availability(%)[a]		Viewing(%)	
	6 a.m.-2 a.m.	7p.m.-11p.m.	6 a.m.-2 a.m.	7p.m.-11p.m.
French-language Television				
French Canadian stations and TVFQ	43	44	33	35
French Canadian stations only	38	39	32	35
CBC, owned	35	22	24	25
CBC, affiliate	35	24	34	27
TVA	42	45	38	43
Other[b]	58	69	29	43
English-language Television				
English Canadian and American stations	72	74	71	76
English Canadian stations only	49	53	57	64
CBC, owned	41	28	34	26
CBC, affiliate	47	34	53	46
CTV	47	63	61	79
Others[c]	56	70	73	84

Notes: a. For methodology, see notes to Figures 5.4 and 5.5, Chapter 5.
b. Includes Radio-Québec, TVFQ and pay-TV.
c. Includes Global, independent stations, TVO/Knowledge and pay-TV.

Source: Canadian Broadcasting Corporation, CBC Research, raw data from A.C. Nielsen.

In other words, if we compare the percentage of foreign programs included in the programming of the Canadian channels only, the proportion is not that much lower in French television than in English (38 percent compared to 49 percent). This is particularly noticeable when the two major private television systems are compared: 42 percent on TVA and 47 percent on CTV. The difference — which is not negligible — is that CTV concentrates its foreign programs in prime-time: 63 percent of the programs it offers in prime time are imported. However, twice as many foreign programs are shown in prime-time on TVA stations as on Radio Canada's own stations (45 percent vs 22 percent).

It has been said that it is primarily cost considerations that lead broadcasters to acquire certain American programs instead of producing them in-house or having them made by independent producers in Canada. On the one hand, producers of American series and films have very large budgets and are able to export programs at low cost because they have been amortized in the American market. On the other hand, Canadian broadcasters can buy these programs at a price which is under their production cost. The makers of the téléroman *Le temps d'une paix* have to work miracles with their budget of $180,000 an episode to compete with *Dallas*, with its budget of $1.1 (U.S.) million an episode. Yet, *Le temps d'une paix* has the highest budget of any téléroman produced by CBC.

It is thus not surprising that the French stations should rely more on imported drama than any other type of program: 90 percent of drama programs aired in French in 1984 were foreign, while 22 percent of public affairs, eight percent of sports and one percent of news was imported.[40]

Although the French networks rely more on foreign programs than might have been expected, the fact remains that Canadian programs are much more popular than on the English networks. In 1984, as shown in Table 8.11, only 33 percent of all viewing time for programs broadcast in Canada in French was spent watching foreign programs (35 percent during prime-time), while on the English side 71 percent of viewing is of foreign programs (76 percent during prime-time). There is no doubt that the availability of American channels is one of the key reasons explaining the difference. Nevertheless, even if only Canadian stations are considered, the difference persists: a moderate 35 percent of viewing time for French-Canadian stations during prime-time is of foreign programs while the corresponding percentage for English-Canadian stations is a high 64 percent.

At this stage of our analysis, it is important to make a distinction. As we have shown, Quebec francophones spend a significant part of their viewing hours watching English-language stations (13 percent in 1984). Cross-over viewing has become extreme for francophones outside Quebec, accounting for (73 percent) of viewing. Francophones therefore view foreign programs on English-Canadian and American stations, as well as French channels. If we look now at all programs aired in Canada, regardless of language, 43 percent of francophones' viewing time in 1984 was spent watching foreign programs — lower than the anglophones (70 percent), but nevertheless surprising.

We have already noted that viewing of English television reached a peak among francophone Montrealers in 1983 and that it has declined since then. It would be gratifying to be able to attribute this return to French-language stations to the increased popularity of Canadian programs. However, a number of indicators lead us instead to ask the following question: have francophone Montrealers not forsaken the English networks (Canadian and American) for American series aired in French on the French stations?

A Strategy to Recover Viewers

CFTM (channel 10), which until 1986 was the only private French-language station in Montreal, has in recent years been giving an increasing share of its schedule to American movies and series (see Table 8.12).

Until 1983, American programs filled an average of one-third of CFTM's fall prime-time schedule. The amount rose suddenly to over 55 percent in 1984 and 1985. Of all types of American programs, the greatest increase was for series: until 1983, American series represented less than 20 percent of the schedule; the figure increased to 30 percent in 1984 and to 48 percent in 1985.

Table 8.12 Proportion of American Programs in CFTM Fall Programming (%) (Saturday to Friday, 7 p.m. - 11 p.m.)

	4-11 Sept. 1976	17-23 Sept. 1977	9-15 Sept 1978	15-21 Sept. 1979	13-19 Sept. 1980	20-26 Sept. 1981	11-17 Sept. 1982	17-23 Sept. 1983	20-26 Oct. 1984	21-27 Sept. 1985
American programs[a]	37.5	46.4	41.1	33.9	19.6	30.4	23.2	33.9	55.4	55.4
American dramas	14.3	26.8	19.6	21.4	14.3	17.9	16.1	19.6	30.4	48.2[b]

Notes: a. Among the films presented each week are a greater or lesser number of American films. This is the major reason for variations in percentage from year to year.
b. This week in September was not necessarily representative of the entire season due to the large number of American mini-series shown at the beginning of this season.

Source: Gilles Marotte "La programmation de Télé-Métropole (1964-1984): influence américaine au Québec", Master's thesis, Department of Sociology, Université Laval, 1986.

These results are based on a single broadcast week. They do not necessarily reflect accurately the proportion of American programs over an entire season. They do say a great deal, however, about CFTM's programming strategy.

In 1984 CFTM restructured its entire evening programming schedule. The news was moved to 11 p.m., outside prime-time, and the variety show *Michel Jasmin* was withdrawn from the schedule. The empty slots were filled by American series like: *Dynasty, Hotel, Magnum P.I. and The Dukes of Hazzard.*

In 1985, while keeping the most popular regular series, CFTM provided viewers with a veritable flood of American mini-series, one of which, *V*, is memorable because when it was withdrawn before completion, it caused such a commotion that the station had to do an about-face and bring it back.

CFTM's strategy was a winner: its viewing share in the Montreal market went from 22 percent in the fall of 1983 to 27 percent in 1984 and 26 percent in 1985.[41] The decline in cross-over viewing among francophone Montrealers is therefore largely attributable to CFTM's strategy. CFCF (CTV) on the other hand showed a reduction in its share of viewing in Montreal from 22 percent to 16 percent during the same period.

The highest percentage of viewing of foreign programs aired by French-language broadcasters is of drama programs and, to a lesser extent, variety. The amount of viewing of foreign news, public affairs and sports broadcast in French is negligible. These viewing patterns contrast sharply with English-language stations, where news is the only type of foreign program that does not attract a substantial share of viewing.

Table 8.13 shows that in 1984, 80 percent of the viewing time for drama series broadcast in French was spent watching foreign programs (70 percent during prime-time). Since this program category is very popular, accounting for 49 percent of viewing during prime-time, this finding is significant. It is even more significant when one considers that the great popularity of Quebec téléromans often leaves the impression that massive viewing of foreign drama productions (primarily American) is to be found only in English Canada. A significant factor is the fact that roughly 40 percent of francophone drama viewing is of movies, most of them foreign.

Table 8.13 Viewing Share of Foreign Programs on Television, by Type (%)
(from Monday to Sunday, Calendar Year 1984)

Programs	News	Public Affairs	Sports	Drama	Variety	Total Programs
French language						
6 a.m. - 2 a.m.	0	1	4	80	13	32
7 p.m. - 11 p.m.	0	2	2	70	1	35
English language						
6 a.m. - 2 a.m.	11	38	29	98	82	71
7 p.m. - 11 p.m.	19	38	21	96	77	76

Source: Canadian Broadcasting Corporation, CBC Research, raw data from A.C. Nielsen.

Cross-over Listening in Radio

In Canada, cross-over listening to American radio stations is not a problem. In 1984, barely 4 percent of radio listening by Canadians was to American stations. For Quebec francophones, the percentage was negligible. However, a significant number of francophones are drawn to English-Canadian radio. In 1985, 12.4 percent of listening by Montreal francophones was to English-Canadian stations, while 4.4 percent of francophone listening elsewhere in Quebec was to English radio. But the cross-overs were concentrated on FM radio. In 1985 FM stations accounted for 80 percent of listening by francophones to English radio in Montreal and 67 percent outside Montreal.[42]

However there has not been a steady increase in listening to English radio. In recent years it has been on the decline outside Montreal, where the listening share of English-Canadian stations has dropped steadily since 1980. In Montreal there was a steady increase in cross-over tuning until 1982, but there has been a decline ever since (see Table 8.14).

Table 8.14 English Radio's Share of Listening by Francophones (%) (Fall, 1980-1985)

Stations	1980	1981	1982	1983	1984	1985
Montreal						
English Canadian	13.5	14.7	16.4	13.1	12.6	12.4
American	—	0.1	0.3	0.2	0.1	0.1
Total	13.5	14.8	16.6	13.3	12.7	12.5
AM	3.0	5.0	2.8	2.5	1.9	2.1
FM	10.5	11.8	13.8	10.8	10.9	10.4
Outside Montreal						
English Canadian	6.3	5.8	5.7	5.1	4.4	4.4
American	—	0.1	0.2	0.2	0.1	0.2
Total	6.3	5.9	5.9	5.2	4.5	4.7
AM	2.7	2.2	1.7	1.3	1.3	1.4
FM	3.7	3.8	4.2	3.9	3.2	3.3

Source: Canadian Broadcasting Corporation, CBC Research, raw data from BBM Bureau of Broadcast Measurement. In 1981, BBM changed its methodology.

In 1980, the average French-speaking Montrealer spent 3 hours each week listening to English-language radio. This reached a peak in 1982 at 3.5 hours per week, and then declined to 2.7 hours per week in 1985. Outside the Montreal area, listening to English-language radio decreased slightly but steadily, dropping from 1.2 hours per week in 1980 to just under one hour per week in 1985.[43]

Another difference is that the proportion of francophone listening to English-language AM radio also declined considerably in recent years while the reach for FM radio has remained relatively stable. In Montreal, the reach of English-language AM stations declined from 13 percent of the French-language population in 1980 to 8 percent in 1985. A similar trend can be seen outside Montreal: from 8 percent in 1980 to 4 percent in 1985.[44] Over the whole period, the reach of English-language FM stations was significantly more extensive and stable: about 28 percent for Montreal francophones and 9 percent for francophones in the rest of Quebec.

Listening to French Radio with Strong English Content

Beginning in 1983, cross-over listening in Montreal began to decline (see Table 8.13). But, once again, this cannot be interpreted as a victory for French programming, because the French FM stations, making the most of the latitude granted by the regulations, were broadcasting a great deal of Anglo-American music.

In Montreal, the two French-language rock music stations, CKMF-FM and CKOI-FM saw their Montreal listening share double from 8 percent in 1977 to 16 percent in 1985. Similarly, CJMF-FM, the Quebec City rock station nearly doubled its listening share, from 7 percent in 1979 to 13 percent in 1985.[45] In this connection CKOI-FM obtained CRTC permission to reduce its French music quota substantially in 1983. The same permission was obtained in 1984, by CJMF-FM in Quebec City.

We have already seen that the private television stations reacted to the increased availability and popularity of American television by airing more American programs dubbed into French. Faced with a rising tide of American records and the resulting audience infatuation with them, radio reacted in much the same way; but since it is impossible to dub records, the French-language radio stations simply present songs in English and commentary in French. This situation will be discussed in the following section.

Radio and Television Programming

Radio, Music and Records

Although the broadcasting of Anglo-American music is spread throughout French radio, it comes mainly from FM radio, where music accounts for 75 percent of air time.[46] FM stations use the same argument as television stations to make their case: American content is more popular and audiences would otherwise switch their allegiance to English-language stations. There is the further paradox in radio, however, that to keep French-speaking listeners from going over to English radio, French radio is being partly transformed into English radio. What is being saved is the audience, not the language.

The attraction of Anglo-American music is widespread in the Western world and beyond. In Quebec, it is one more factor added to a number of other linguistic pressures in communications and elsewhere, which contributes to the erosion of the francophone community.[47] It also hits hard at the Quebec recording industry, a young industry (less than 25 years old) and still struggling (145 albums in 1980 but only 72 in 1985). In fact, some fear the recording of Quebec artists could virtually cease within two or three years.[48]

Minimum French Song Content

It was in 1972 that the CRTC took up the problem. Studies showed that on some stations, less than 50 percent of the songs aired were in French. The following year, the Commission set a minimum quota of 75 percent for broadcasters at peak hours (between 6 a.m and 6 p.m) with a weekly average of 65 percent.[49] Giving in, later, to the complaints of producers about the relative lack of French records in certain types of music, the CRTC reduced its requirement, and again brought it down in March 1986 for songs in French for all AM stations to 55 percent and for FM stations upon their request.[50]

This minimum applies to songs in French, without regard to their origin. In any case, stations remain subject to the Canadian content requirement which varies between 10 percent and 30 percent, depending on the case. Some French broadcasters find this double requirement (for both French content and Canadian content) unfair. Certainly English stations do not need to be regulated to play English songs!

In May 1985 the CRTC created the Advisory Committee on French Music which had a mandate to measure the availability of French records in all types of popular music, both in Quebec and elsewhere in the world. The Committee had also

> to examine the most efficient way for French broadcasters, together with the record industry and other interested parties, to foster and promote new French-language musical talent.[51]

The Committee recommended keeping the requirement at 65 percent, but four out of the five radio representatives — all but Jean-Pierre Coallier, the chairman — dissented and the requirement was lowered.

If past trends continue, as the chronology of events reveals, all indications are that the downward pressure will continue and that in a few years the quota levels run the risk of being well below 50 percent:

1. Rock stations, which lead the movement, already want a lower quota. CJMF-FM (Quebec City), whose percentage stood at 60 percent in 1984, asked the CRTC for approval to set a new level for French-Canadian songs at 30 to 35 percent. And CKOI-FM (Montreal), which had been at 55 percent since 1983, asked the CRTC in 1984 to drop it to 40 percent (the CRTC refused).[52]
2. The AM stations, which are falsely believed not to face the same problem, also told the CRTC that they have trouble in meeting the quota and asked that it be lowered. The CRTC noted the problem as early as 1980 when it renewed the licences of a number of Montreal stations and mentioned it again in 1985 when it established its committee.[53]
3. The CRTC has always yielded to industry pressures on quotas. Thus, of the three proposals put forward by its own committee, the first two of which recommended keeping the quota at 65 percent, the CRTC chose the third option, the one put forward by the broadcasters. The broadcasters, in a letter dated January 30, 1986, agreed to a "predominance" of French songs. On March 19, the CRTC set the quota at 55 percent, with a number of minor variations.[54]
4. Whatever the prevailing quota may be, it does not illustrate the real state of affairs because recalcitrant stations air a percentage of French songs which is very frequently below the required level. For example, CKMF in Montreal with a quota of 65 percent, actually broadcast at the following levels, according to CRTC surveys: 1980, 29 percent; 1981, 51 percent; 1982 to 1984, from 48 to 62 percent.[55]
5. The problem is most acute in Montreal, where there is fierce competition between English and French stations. The English stations are required to play 5 percent French songs as a "contribution" to the francophone milieu. They tend to play less than this or at least ask for less and the French stations tend to ask them to play more.[56] On the other hand, the English stations are opposed to a lower quota for the French stations[57] and two of them, CHOM-FM and CKGM, regularly ask for approval (1976, 1980) to have more French spoken on their stations, which is always refused by the CRTC because the French stations are opposed.[58] The inconsistency is more apparent than real. The stations are competing in a highly fragmented francophone market for young listeners who like rock music and especially on stations that "sing English" and speak French.

The introduction of the French-language MuchMusic specialty channel on cable television will increase both competition and downward pressure on the quota because the network is required to air only 3 percent French videos.

At all licence renewals the CRTC has consistently emphasized the need for broadcasters to commit themselves to encouraging young talent so as to increase the supply of French records. And the broadcasters have in fact been spending significant amounts of money on contests, programs and recording sessions for young musicians. On the one hand, however, the CRTC encourages the stations to foster the works of young people of both languages, whatever the language of the station.[59] On the other, in many song contests young francophone musicians sing in English.[60] The CRTC effort neither identifies correctly nor solves the particular problem faced by the French recording industry.

Market surveys have shown that consumers buy records first because of hearing them on the radio, a fact recognized by the CRTC.[61] Not hearing a record therefore reduces demand and ultimately dries up production. It follows that every time the quota is lowered, whether at the request of broadcasters or in practice by the stations or with the approval of the Commission, there is a cause-and-effect relationship: lower quotas serve to induce the shortages that are used to justify them. This trend must be reversed by the introduction of a higher quota, and creating an upward pressure. Production assistance is necessary but not enough. Abandoning quotas in favour of promotional contests,on the excuse that French records are in short supply, is like sawing off the branch on which you are sitting because it is too short, then stretching it to make it longer.

Music Formats

In its conclusions the Committee identified a number of major problems, including a shortage of French-language records, which formulates the problem in the same terms as the stations and confuses the effect with the cause. It also noted another apparently innocuous problem, over-specialization of radio stations in narrow music formats.

A moment's consideration shows, however, the determining effect that has been exercised on the development of music in Quebec by this specialisation, decreed by the CRTC without study, in musical formats conceived for American production and arbitrarily superimposed on French vocals.

Quebec Vocals

Although it reached new heights during the 60s as part of the nationalistic movement, modern Quebec song, which goes back to the 30s, has always been pulled in two directions by the tradition of France and the influence of the United States.

In the 50s, Quebec songwriters were few and far between and the production system was virtually nonexistent. Quebec singers sang songs from France or French versions of American songs. But it was the golden age of French vocals and celebrated voices like Trenet, Piaf, Bécaud and innumerable others dominated the Quebec airwaves. When Félix Leclerc appeared on the scene he was first recognized in France. This was the tradition upon which the Quebec songs of the 60s were based, born as they were in the "boîtes à chansons" which spawned Gilles Vigneault, Jean-Pierre Ferland, Claude Gauthier and Pauline Julien.

But the American influence was also present. French-speaking Quebeckers, depending on how old they were, bought records by Frank Sinatra or Elvis Presley. And the Montreal station CKVL, basing itself on the American top 40 concept, presented the "Hit Parade of French Music" with various disk jockeys following one another without a break throughout the broadcast day. It was nevertheless in the 60's, once again, that the American trend became firmly established, with popular groups like Les Baronnets and Les Classels and singers like Pierre Lalonde and Ginette Reno, who sang the big Anglo-American hits translated into French and became TV idols on programs for young people based on the hit parade format.

It was to supply these two trends in Quebec music that Quebec production and distribution houses proliferated during this period. The Quebec record industry hit the marketplace and radio gradually took it up and played its product.

Beginning in 1970, Quebec songwriters sought to incorporate American music trends. Robert Charlebois and Jean-Pierre Ferland led the way, followed by Diane Dufresne and groups like Offenbach, Octobre, Harmonium, Beau Dommage, the Ville Émard Blues Band and Maneige — all now disbanded — that developed the various directions taken by French-language Quebec rock. At the same time, performers of "French versions" of American songs were able to include Quebec songs in their repertory.

Faced with foreign influence, there are only two possible responses: incorporate it or copy it. Quebec music had freed itself from French music and was attempting to assimilate the American influence. It was creative. But as the 80s approached, the movement fell apart: the strength of the Anglo-American trend swept young listeners, the recording industry, broadcasting, and the CRTC along with it. No wonder rock music came increasingly to be written and sung in English in Quebec! What happened?

American Popular Music

Until the arrival of television in the early 50s, most radio stations presented a variety of programs very much the way television stations do today — something for everyone. But television dealt radio a harsh blow and it had to adjust, which it did by specializing. In the United States, some stations began to play only the 40 most popular songs all day long with a minimum of talk. The so-called 'top-40' format was born. As radio stations proliferated in the same market, particularly when FM became widespread, other formats emerged to appeal to different segments of the potential audience — 'easy listening', 'progressive rock', 'beautiful music', 'MOR' (Middle-of-the-Road), 'contemporary adult' and so on.[62]

In choosing a format, radio station operators relied on market research: based on the figures showing the tastes of a specified target population, they decided whether to compete directly with others or to offer a new product. Take for example 100 listeners broken down as follows:

Audience group	1	2	3
Number of listeners in the group	60	25	15
Category of music preferred	A	B	C

If there is only one station, the station operators will choose music category A (60 prospective listeners). If there are two, the operators of the second station will also choose category A, because market A, even divided in two (30), is still larger than market B (25). If there are three stations, the choice will surely be a type B station, because market A (60) divided into three parts (20) is smaller than market B (25).

Though logical, this model has many weaknesses. The music formats are assumed to be watertight compartments and listeners attracted to but one format. In reality there are many musical compositions that could fall into more than one format and a person can like both Bob Dylan and Tina Turner.

In major markets like New York, Chicago and Los Angeles, the model leads to extreme specialization. An American publication has identified 24 basic formats which can be broken down differently, redefined or reorganized ad infinitum, the way colours can be isolated or mixed, and which establish formats based on sound, ethnic origin, rendition, era, duration, popularity, or rhythm of the music played: Pop/Adult, Top 40, MOR, Ethnic, Album-Oriented Rock (AOR), Contemporary Rock, Gold/Oldies, Blues, Nashville Sound, Progressive, Gospel, etc. Trade papers like *Billboard* publish ratings of the most popular categories of songs and the whole industry jumps on the bandwagon: programmers, record companies, managers, advertisers.

Superimposing the American Model

It was in its policy on cable carriage of FM radio signals (1976) that the CRTC, basing itself on prevailing commercial practices, itself adopted the format system for protecting local stations (for example, CJMF-FM in Quebec City) against competition from stations outside its area (for example, CKOI-FM in Montreal) that broadcast the same type of music (progressive rock).[63] These formats were then used to prevent stations from competing for the same audiences in a market.

In adopting the format system, the CRTC entrenched a classification that was designed for American music production and imported into Canada. Some French-language Quebec radio stations had already jumped on the bandwagon, but by incorporating this commercial practice in the regulations, the CRTC forced all stations to conform. At no time did the CRTC do any research indicating concern with adapting the model to Quebec, to the French-language, or to Quebec music. It made no attempt to base the formats on Quebec traditions.

Superimposing a foreign music structure on a different tradition forces it to copy the other system and this means always being behind the original, which evolves at its own pace. It also encourages music trends to follow the imported model with which the whole industry — creativity, production, radio and the trade press — is already integrated in line with the chosen blueprint.

Flung onto this modern-day Procrustean bed, three-quarters of French vocals, according to the 'specialists', fall into the MOR category and the distinctions typical of French songs are not put forward. If a station decides to specialize in Michael Jackson type music, it is obviously going to have trouble obtaining appropriate French records unless it finds imitators.

The fact is that designations like 'Adult Contemporary', 'Beautiful Music' and 'Middle-of-the-Road' (MOR) make no sense in French. They are not so much different types of music as marketing categories. The only conceivable translation of MOR into French, for example, would be "neither fish nor fowl".

And in fact, even in a category as broad and with as many subcategories as MOR, the result is homogenization more than diversity, since stations always tend to try to please the largest number of listeners. To return again to the classical marketing model, if 40 listeners like subcategory A, a station will select it rather than others because even though the other categories taken together form the majority, they are broken down among a number of different subcategories, for example with 30 preferring B, 20 C and 10 D. To reach a majority audience the extremes are left out of the picture: from subcategory A, stations will play songs that will be most similar to B or to C and D together, in other words, "neither fish nor fowl".

That is how a system devised to ensure diversity leads to standardization. The records that are played most frequently on radio either have a mainstream sound or are simply insipid. In such a marketing system, artistic creation in a non-mainstream format has no real place at all.

Remedies

There are three possible ways to set things right and they should be used in conjunction with one another: formating that takes French songs into consideration, an immediate increase in the quota, and production assistance.

Former communications Minister Marcel Masse allocated $25 million spread over five years to his recording industry development strategy. The program includes the production and marketing of quality records, music videos[64] and high-quality radio programs in English and in French.

In view of the special situation in Quebec, where French-language record production has dropped 45 percent since 1978, 40 percent of the amounts allocated under each part of the program are earmarked for the French industry. The purpose is to increase the supply of French product and to lead radio stations to air a higher percentage of French songs.

The broadcasters have committed themselves to financing a foundation, MusicAction, the Quebec counterpart of FACTOR-CTL, which is designed to provide assistance to young musicians. In the first year, 80 percent of the funds collected ($98,000) have been allocated to support French-language vocals. It will be a source of new works which will contribute to the general effort to fill the need for French records in the French-speaking world community allowing broadcasters to follow trends outside of those set by the American multinationals (see Chapter 16).

A second remedy, linked to broadcasting policy, would be a complete review of the music formats being used by the CRTC and broadcasters. To what extent does the existing classification and fragmentation of market stifle the broadcasting of French songs from the start? Couldn't other models be examined and, for example, formats be defined taking into account French music, which includes, need we say, an element of rock? We are not advocating imposing older trends in French music against the will of the audience but rather adjusting the regulatory regime to its contemporary characteristics so that it will flourish. The classification should fit the product and not vice versa.

In view of all these proposed approaches, the quota for French songs on radio should be raised again to 65 percent. If problems arise in finding enough French records in certain categories, the CRTC could lower the quota in the licence conditions of specific stations while requiring the broadcaster to invest in the category in short supply.

Recommendations

Independent research should be carried out on the application of the American music format system to French-language radio, including the impact on the French record industry of a model imported uncritically, and adjustments that would be needed to take French and Quebec traditions into account.

Production support systems should have the participation of all interested parties in the radio and recording industries (see Chapter 16).

The quota for French-language songs on radio should be set at 65 percent. When, in specific instances, it is shown that it is impossible to achieve this percentage in the station's music format, an exception may be made, provided that a specific obligation to invest in the production of records or programs appropriate to the station's format be required.

Drama Programming

Drama programs (serials, series, theatre and motion pictures) indisputably dominate television viewing. The United States, with abundant production and powerful resources, has hit French-language television hardest in this sector.

Francophones continue to see themselves reflected in the characters found in *Le temps d'une paix*, *La bonne aventure* and *Peau de banane*, but American production tends in sheer numbers to overwhelm the téléromans, as has been evident on Télé-Métropole in recent years.

In the spring of 1986, Télé-Métropole's schedule included only five Quebec téléromans for a total of 2.5 hours, only 8.9 percent of prime time, compared to the 10 American series such as *Dynasty, Magnum P.I.*, and *Fantasy Island*, for a total of nine hours, or 28.6 percent of prime-time (see Table 8.15 and Table 8.16).

Programming on CBFT (CBC) reverses the Télé-Métropole pattern. In the spring of 1986 it included ten Quebec téléromans — twice as many as on Télé-Métropole — for a total of 5.5 hours, or 20 percent prime-time viewing. CBFT

Table 8.15 Télé-Métropole Prime Time Programs for the Week of March 22 - 28, 1986[a]

	Saturday	Sunday	Monday	Tuesday	Wednesday	Thursday	Friday[b]
7 p.m.	« V »	L'île fantastique	L'âme soeur	Peau de banane	Épopée rock	Arnold et Willie	Cinéma du vendredi « Le roi des rois »
7:30 p.m.			K-2000	Deux font la paire	Le hockey TVA	Magnum	
8 p.m.	Cinéma du samedi « Valentino »	R.S.V.P.					
8:30 p.m.			L'or du temps	Entre chien et loup		Chacun chez soi	
9 p.m.		Cinéma « Appelez-moi docteur »	En chanson. . . Nicole Martin	Made in Quebec		Cinéma du jeudi « Resurection »	
9:30 p.m.							
10 p.m.	Justice pour tous		Dynastie	Pour l'amour du risque	Politique Québec		Contexte
10:30 pm.	Sur la colline						
11 p.m.							

Notes: a. In this sample week, chosen at random, all of the movies shown were American. This is, of course, not always the case.
b. The usual Friday night programming also includes the British series "Arme et charme" from 9 p.m. to 10 p.m.

Table 8.16 Distribution of Programs According to Origin (%)
Télé-Métropole Programs in Prime Time for the Week of March 22-28, 1986

		Number of programs	Broadcast Time	% of Canadian hours	% of Foreign hours	% of Total hours
Canada	*Téléromans*	5	2.5	22.7		8.9
	Variety	3	3	27.3		10.7
	News/Public Affairs	4	3	27.3		10.7
	Sports	1	2.5	22.7		8.9
	Sub-total	13	11	100		39.3
U.S.A.	*Series*	9	8		47.1	28.6
	Films	4	9		52.9	32.1
	Sub-total	13	17		100	60.7
	Total	26	28			100

also scheduled only two American series (one hour each), *Dallas* and *Walt Disney World*, representing only 7 percent of its prime-time programming.[65]

As we pointed out earlier the fact that Quatre Saisons and Télé-Métropole will be competing with one another beginning in September 1986 will tend to strengthen the trend toward showing American programs since audience fragmentation and revenue splitting leads broadcasters to cut production costs. Since young viewers like American programs, the temptation to do so will be all the stronger. Francophone teenagers in particular (see Table 8.17) consume more American programs than other francophones (53 percent of their viewing), and they even watch a large part of those programs on English stations.

Table 8.17 Viewing Share of Canadian and Foreign Programming, According to Language and Age Group (%)

	Age 2-5	Age 6-11	Age 12-17	Age 18-49	Age 50 and over	All, age 2-plus
Francophones						
Canadian Programs	60	53	48	54	66	57
Foreign Programs	40	47	53	46	34	43
Anglophones						
Canadian Programs	22	19	20	27	39	30
Foreign Programs	78	81	80	73	61	70
Canadians						
Canadian Programs	32	26	26	34	46	36
Foreign Programs	68	74	74	66	54	64

Source: Canadian Broadcasting Corporation, CBC Research, raw data from A.C. Nielsen.

Francophone teenagers watch English TV to learn English (80.6 percent) and also to see 'more interesting programs' (77.9 percent). They are also well versed in American pop culture, including movies and records, where they find an international camaraderie of youth and a reliable model of modernity.[66]

The Effects of Being Poor

It is obvious that television viewers are increasingly choosing among programs rather than choosing a channel to watch. Since the resources of French-language television are paltry compared to those available for the production of major American series, it will become increasingly difficult to compete with them. This relative poverty hinders the development of ideas. A téléroman has to be produced with only eight actors, a maximum of two minutes of location shooting, and only three sets, which moreover have to be amortized by making the téléroman run as long as possible. Lise Payette, author of *La bonne aventure*, who argued for giving up location shooting altogether, noted that when the two minutes of location shots were not used one week they could not be used the following week.[67] Maurice Falardeau complained that with only two minutes of location shooting all he could do in his new téléroman *La clé des champs* was show that the action was taking place somewhere in the Eastern Townships.[68] Apart from major coproduction series on which the network 'blows a bundle', such as *Lance et compte* or *Laurier* ($6 million for 7 episodes), one of the few big budget téléromans is *Le temps d'une paix*. The author, Pierre Gauvreau, gives an interesting account of what happens to the others, like *Monsieur le ministre*:

> Is a Prime Minister we never see in the National Assembly, because it costs too much to pay the extras to sit in the Assembly and the visitors gallery, really a credible character? Solange Chaput-Roland (the writer) has to talk about the life of politicians without ever showing them in the places that symbolize them best.[69] (translation)

The search for new scripts is totally haphazard because it is impossible to include them in the budget. Richard Martin, Director of Drama at CBC explains that they very rarely commission a script because there is no money. Martin goes on to say that he has no budget that allows him to pay writers to develop ideas and then move on to the production stage. "The script has to be good right away." And, according to him, there is no room whatever for luxuries like enrichment courses for producers or training replacements. What is true for CBC applies even more to Télé-Métropole, where a larger number of programs is produced with fewer producers. Programs are mass produced, with all the risks of standardization that this entails.

Renewing the Tradition

To the shortage of resources is added the lack of renewal. Although audience ratings remain high for téléromans, surveys have shown that television viewers are also dissatisfied with certain aspects: emphasis on the past, kitchen-party settings, and propensity for talk rather than action.

Young writers in particular are critical of television dramas for their mindless content, their facileness and especially their neglect of Quebec theatre, so inventive and open to international currents. "Out of touch" is an expression they use frequently. CBC is cut off from contemporary theatre and creativity. According to Suzanne Aubry, a playwright and television writer, young writers are never in demand at CBC even when they have proved themselves in the theatre.[70]

Claude Maher, a freelance producer (*Poivre et sel* and *Manon*) is equally harsh. He deplores the fact that two major artists who gave Quebec theatre new life in the 70s and whose works are among the most frequently produced in Quebec and abroad, cannot be found on television.

> I find it frightful that Jean Barbeau has never worked for television. I find it frightful that Michel Tremblay has been produced only very rarely on television . . . There are all kinds of young writers who are doing interesting things in theatre. Why shouldn't we seek them out? Why don't we ask them to do a one-and-a-half hour special? These are people who could use a few dollars for their craft and they are also the people who speak to today's society.[71] (translation)

As with music, the much needed renewal is already knocking at the door. This year, CBC drama will lose five of its twelve producers. "There goes 150 years of experience", says Richard Martin. The fact is that a large number of CBC managers and producers were hired in the 50s. It would have been desirable to have constant renewal of creative staff, if only to allow the newer generations to express themselves. The small amount of renewal there was came from internal promotion instead of outside hiring of younger staff. Pierre Gauvreau sees in this one of the shortcomings of permanent staff. "It is inconceivable that someone can be an adequate interpreter of a society for 30 years." This is no doubt one of the reasons why young viewers are losing interest in home-grown programs.

That neither CBC nor Radio-Québec nor Télé-Métropole should have recruited staff from successive generations does not mean that creation came to a standstill in Quebec. It simply was channelled elsewhere. Gauvreau again:

> There is a gap in television technical expertise. But there is no gap in terms of creation. Those who couldn't find work in television went elsewhere — to work in the theatre for example. And theatre developed a great deal. There are thus many young theatre producers who could be good television producers and who will make the transition in greater numbers in years to come. It is sure to happen.[72] (translation)

But how is it going to take place? We believe that it will be, among other ways, by making greater use of independent producers. The young people our researchers met were generally in favour of privatizing production because it is their only chance to find work, the administration and union structures at CBC being too inflexible. But CBC must remain a centre, a permanent place where skills are practised and grow, because creative people need a solid centre, a core, from which they can then spread. We must therefore beware of throwing out the baby with the bath water by abandoning in-house production, especially in a society which tends to use community effort to compensate for its modest resources. We are proposing, rather, to develop linkages between CBC and the outside and to require private broadcasters to reinvest a reasonable proportion of their profits in production (see Chapters 10 14 and 17).

News and Information

Comparison of Private and Public Sector Production

French-language television news in Quebec was for many years the prerogative of CBC. Télé-Métropole entered the field of news and information so slowly that ten years after it was established it had only ten journalists who were given no support whatever and who had to use ancient equipment; the possibility of sending correspondents to Ottawa or Quebec City, let alone abroad, was never even considered.[73]

It was in the early 70s that Télé-Métropole finally recognized the importance of news for its credibility and even its ratings, and equipped itself to compete with CBC. Today, TVA news is often comparable to CBC news. Its weekly public affairs programs have not, however, followed the same course. Little money is spent on them and they are scheduled at poor viewing times.

A Statistics Canada survey conducted for the Task Force showed that in

1984-85, stations of the TVA network spent $2.7 million on public affairs, CBC French network (not including affiliates), spent $16.3 million, and CTV and its affiliates $17.6 million.[74] Although CTV's and CBC's overall programming expenditures are naturally higher than TVA's because they are richer organizations, the difference is nevertheless noteworthy because CTV and CBC spend a higher proportion of their total programming expenditures — twice as much as TVA — on public affairs.

As in television, CBC French network radio dominates the private radio sector in terms of the resources and time devoted to news and information. In 1985-1986, 24.7 percent of all programs aired, excluding regional programs which also have their own significant news and information component, fell into this category.[75]

The Télémédia network, on the other hand, is by far the leader in number of affiliates and audience share for information programming. CKAC, the flagship station, is one of the very few stations to have increased its journalist staff during the recession of the 80s.

Disposing of fewer resources, Radiomutuel's news service is undergoing a complete restructuring. The flagship station, CJMS in Montreal, wants to emphasize Montreal news and produce news reports of more general interest for its affiliates in the province.

Shortcomings of Private Stations in Local News

Joining a network allows independent stations to offer their listeners news programs broader in scope than they could produce on their own. In principle, combining resources to produce higher quality material is an excellent idea. However, such arrangements do have a number of pitfalls, like making news uniform, centralizing the selection of topics to be covered in Montreal and excluding local and regional news.

Whatever their association — with a news network or with the agency Nouvelles Télé-Radio (Broadcast News) — independent radio stations tend to depend on them for their news. A typical independent station has a too small, inexperienced staff that is provided with little support and is overloaded with work. All of which makes such stations dependent on formal handouts. Where they exist, the local CBC stations serve as a model or as an incentive to higher quality.

The same comments apply to television. Thus Télé-Métropole's news is given by far the largest segment of *Les Nouvelles TVA*, the TVA network daily news program. According to data submitted by the network to the CRTC, news from the regions accounted for only 13.7 percent of *Les Nouvelles TVA* in 1982-83 and 20.1 percent in 1983-84 (see Table 8.15). When it renewed TVA's licence in 1985, the CRTC obtained a commitment from the network to remedy the situation. The CRTC expects an equitable contribution from all the affiliated stations in view of their favourable position in the markets they are licensed to serve.[76]

We have already noted (see Chapter 5) the low emphasis placed by some private stations on local news. An analysis of the 6 p.m. news reports broadcast

Table 8.18 TVA Network News — Items from Affiliated Stations

	1982-1983[a]		1983-1984[a]	
	No.	%	No.	%
Quebec	225	9.5	213	10.1
Rouyn	5	0.2	17	0.8
Rimouski	13	0.5	20	0.9
Carleton			7	0.3
Trois-Rivières	59	2.5	75	3.5
Sherbrooke	18	0.8	60	2.8
Hull/Ottawa			20	0.9
Rivière-du-Loup	0		1	
Chicoutimi	2	0.1	12	0.5
Sub-total	322	13.7	425	20.1
Parliament/Ottawa	345	14.7	410	19.4
National Assembly/Quebec	324	13.8	288	13.6
Sub-total	669	28.5	698	33.0
Montreal	1,358[b]	57.8	993	46.9
Total	2,349	100	2,116	100

Notes: a. The 1982-83 season lasted only from September to June, the 1983-84 season ran from September to August.
b. Includes reports from abroad and texts read over images from abroad.
Source: TVA data supplied to CRTC, 1985.

in October 1985 by Télé-Capitale in Quebec City and Télé-Métropole in Montreal confirmed that these stations, at least during this period, presented less local news than the CBC stations.[77] Télé-Capitale, majority owned by the Pathonic Group, at the time devoted approximately 70 percent of its 'regional' news to Canadian and American stories (35 percent each). Journalists who produced local and regional news for Télé-Capitale prior to its acquisition by Pathonic were then assigned to translating reports from the Atlanta Cable News Network (CNN). Paul Vien, the owner of Pathonic, describes the situation as follows:

> In 1982, we pirated the Turner Broadcasting signal (we informed him ahead of time of our intent to do so). With this international news footage available, we then went ahead and bought the technology we needed to show our own journalists on film and programmed an hour-long daily news program . . . [78] (translation)

Pathonic operates stations in Quebec City, Rimouski, Trois-Rivières and Sherbrooke. In the Spring of 1986 it submitted a network licence application for these stations to the CRTC and proposed reducing the local content on each station. The applications produced strong reactions from unions and other groups in the regions concerned.

The Supervision of News Programming

These are the sorts of frustrations in news programming that lead people to call for the intervention of authority. A number of briefs to the Task Force maintain that the CRTC is not playing its true role and should force private stations to expend more effort on regional news.

Thus the Fédération nationale des communications (FNC), which represents most unionized journalists in Quebec, asked the Task Force to examine how much of their budgets private broadcasters devote to news. The FNC also suggested that guidelines on news and information should be specified for broadcasters and that they should be required to adopt a specific news policy to be included in their promises of performance.[79]

We recommend the greatest caution here. Certainly it would be wrong to ask the CRTC to do what it cannot and should not do. Freedom of the press prevents the regulatory authority from making news coverage decisions on behalf of broadcasters. But it also seems to us obvious that a number of private stations are not serving their communities appropriately. What the CRTC could well do, without intervening in news-program content itself, would be to use conditions of licence to require the private stations to devote resources to news and information that are commensurate with their financial resources and with generally recognized professional broadcasting practices. The regulatory strategy described in Chapter 7 advocates this approach.

Because this is a delicate area where government intervention is unwelcome, should an increased role perhaps be recommended for agencies like press councils? This approach seems to be indicated in the case of Quebec, where by contrast with the other provinces, the Press Council has from the beginning included electronic media.

All these problems of news coverage are not specific to Quebec; they could just as well apply to English Canada.

CBC Shortcomings in News

Our emphasis on the private sector in this section does not indicate the CBC is above criticism. Francophones outside Quebec complain that CBC news is too closely tied to Quebec, and Quebeckers complain that the network reports a fire in Vancouver but it neglects important regional events in Quebec regions. A CBC journalist, Claude-Jean Devirieux, explained in a brief to the Task Force that:

> Sherbrooke, Trois-Rivières, Gaspé and Rouyn-Noranda have no Radio-Canada correspondent; when needed, reporters are sent from Montreal, for example when a mine caves in on workers or when the local police kill carpet layers.[80] But Radio-Canada's *Téléjournal* receives and broadcasts regularly, several times per week, coverage from Winnipeg or Vancouver. Thanks to permanent East-West communications links, this coverage comes in from Saskatoon or Edmonton every day almost instantly; if coverage is to be sent to Montreal from Chicoutimi or Rouyn-Noranda, it has to go by plane or bus.[81] (translation)

In radio as in televison, there are whole regions of Quebec, lively and dynamic though they may be, that are served only by affiliates or rebroadcasters. There was no doubt a need in the early stages to link all the country's francophones, and it was also to be expected that CBC should establish stations first where private stations were not viable. But has the time not come to adapt the French network to social realities in which, numerically, Québec regions are the major regions of French Canada?

When Quebeckers emphasize the need to develop regional news, it is not because they have none at all: each station (O and O or affiliate) produces its own regional news of variable quality and receives Canadian and international news from the network. But each region receives only the regional news for its own region: except in cases of disaster, the people of Chicoutimi do not know what is going on in Quebec City, Sept-Iles or Trois-Rivières; and the people of Montreal are no better off. In the French network news structure, Quebec regions do not exist.

It is not a matter of inflicting upon CBC audiences news that has no journalistic interest for them simply because it is regional. We only wish to emphasize strongly that the network configuration imposes unacceptable distortions on news. We take up this issue and possible solutions in Chapter 10 on the CBC.

The Budgets of the CBC's French Network

French-language television production in Canada will generally continue to depend more on public funds than its English-language counterpart. With the opening of Canada's borders to enormous American production resources, the only way we can aspire to a comparable cultural life, in quality if not in volume, is to receive support from the government. The programs produced by the major American corporations have a market of 250 million consumers. Policy debate will have to adjust to this reality.

Although we expect a greater contribution from the larger private stations, the small Quebec market makes it impossible for them to provide all the essential television services required by Canada's francophones.

It is already very expensive for the public sector to provide service both to the Quebec audience and to francophone communities elsewhere in Canada. As in all French-language radio and television in North America, there is also the permanent problem of providing news in a minority language. It is often impossible to have direct access to sources because they are unilingual English.

Because the task of providing news and information is more expensive and more complex for francophones, one might expect the CBC's French network to have more resources than the English network to carry out its journalistic responsibilities. The truth is something else again. Let us take the example of *le Point* and *The Journal*, the major evening news background programs on the French and English networks. According to CBC data, the budget for *le Point* in 1984-85 was $61,500 per hour, and for *The Journal* $111,000 per hour. This is a significant gap and it is typical of the general gap between the per-hour production budgets of the English and French networks (see Table 8.19).

Several of the French network's employee unions told the Task Force that they were worried about this budget gap, because they believed it was widening at the expense of French production. Our research showed, however, that the gap between *The Journal* and *le Point* narrowed considerably between 1984 and 1985.

Table 8.19 Average Hourly Cost of CBC Television Programs ($ thousands)

	French Network[a]			English Network[b]		
	1982-1983	1983-1984	1984-1985	1982-1983	1983-1984	1984-1985
News/Current Affairs	38.6	45.6	51.1	71.1	75.1	75.7
Daily newsmagazines (*Le Point/The Journal*)	44.2	44.2	61.5	91.3	117.3	11.0
Total Network programs	21.7	22.2	27.3	37.7	41.7	41.0

Notes: a. The Montreal station fulfills a network role which is integrated with its metropolitan role; it serves both the populations of metropolitan Montreal and the French Network. Consequently, because of the integrated practice of the service, the news and Public Affairs operations cannot be broken down to distinguish between the types of News/Public Affairs services provided.

b. Unlike Montreal, the Local and Network operations are not integrated in Toronto. Consequently the News/Current Affairs figures reflect only the network hours and costs.

Source: Canadian Broadcasting Corporation, data compiled at the request of the Task Force on Broadcasting Policy.

Overall, the difference continues, and the CBC provides various explanations:[82]

- First, program acquisition rights are three to four times higher for American programs in English than in French because there are many more English stations and viewers. The United States also considers Canada to be part of the U.S. market, where competition is stiff and raises prices, while the French network can buy dubbed programs at lower-cost residual rights.
- Second, the CBC argues that bigger budgets are needed for the English network to compete directly with American networks. For example, the U.S. networks are willing to pay enormous fees to the performers they want and much larger salaries to lure top English-Canadian journalists to the U.S. Francophone stars obviously do not have the same prospects and their pay reflects this.

The CBC goes on to say:

> The English and the French Networks address different audiences with different tastes. Drama in the French Network consists mainly of "téléromans" which can be produced at approximately $107,000 per broadcast hour. The English Network audience is exposed to American series and super-productions which are substantially more expensive program types. Thus English Network drama is produced at an average cost of $231,000 per hour.[83]

This argument is not convincing. French-speaking viewers also watch American television and are able to compare it to the other programs they watch. They, too, want productions that use the most modern techniques and therefore have the highest budgets. The producers of téléromans, who are faced with small budgets for sets and no budgets for location shooting, will not be able to compete with American-style programs for long, and are already competing less, as statistics are showing. Francophone producers cannot be required to perform the daily miracle of producing original, varied and popular programs on a shoestring.

Recommendation

The Task Force recommends that CBC French network budgets be reviewed to establish hourly production costs that reflect the role assigned to the French network in the new television environment.

Notes

1. Meeting of the Task Force on Broadcasting Policy with Management of TVA, Montreal, August 9, 1985.
2. While the practice of simultaneous substitution or simulcasting benefits English-Canadian broadcasters by increasing their advertising revenues and audiences, this regulatory protection of program rights does not benefit French-language broadcasters.
3. Canada, Department of Communications, Quebec, Department of Communications, *The Future of French-language Television*, Federal-Provincial Committee Report (Ottawa: The Department; Quebec: The Department, May 1985), p. 85.
4. Canada, Department of Communications, Quebec, Department of Communications, *Canada-Quebec Memorandum of Understanding on the Development of the French-language Television System* (Ottawa: the Department, Quebec: the Department, February 13, 1986).
5. Canadian Broadcasting Corporation, CBC Research, raw data from A.C. Nielsen.
6. Ibid.
7. Canada, Quebec, Federal-Provincial Committee, op. cit., p. 11.
8. Ibid., p. 25.
9. E.A. Weir, *The Struggle for National Broadcasting in Canada* (Toronto: McClelland and Stewart, 1965), p. 229.
10. Louise Cousineau, " Les BBM du printemps à Montréal: Pascau et Suzanne, toujours n° 1, parleront plus fort en septembre ", *La Presse* (Montreal), June 13, 1986, p. E-1.
11. BBM Bureau of Broadcast Measurement, Spring Survey 1986 and Autumn Survey 1985.
12. CROP Inc., " Sondage sur la pratique des activités culturelles et le statut de l'artiste ", research survey prepared for Union des Artistes and *La Presse*, Montreal, May 15, 1986.
13. Canada, Royal Commission on the Economic Union and Development Prospects for Canada (Macdonald Commission), *Report*, vol. 3 (Ottawa: Minister of Supply and Services, 1985), p. 333.
14. Budget information provided by the Société générale du cinéma, 1986.
15. Information provided by the Société de développement des industries de la culture et des communications, 1986.
16. Jean-Paul L'Allier et Associés Inc., " La spécificité québécoise et les médias électroniques ", study prepared for the Task Force on Broadcasting Policy, Ottawa, 1986, p. 41.
17. Canadian Broadcasting Corporation, *La Radio publique – Les réseaux français de Radio-Canada Passé, Présent, Avenir* (Montréal: CBC, 1984).
18. Marc Thibault, "Radio-Canada : des structures et des hommes", study prepared for the Task Force on Broadcasting Policy, Ottawa, 1986, p.14.
19. Meeting of the Task Force on Broadcasting Policy with Management of the Société de radio-télévision du Québec, Montréal, August 6, 1985.
20. Société de radio-télévision du Québec, Rapport annuel 1984-1985 (Montreal: the Société, 1986), p. 23
21. Canadian Broadcasting Corporation, CBC Research, raw data from A.C. Nielsen.

22. Canadian Radio-television and Telecommunications Commission, *Télévision de Montréal, Télévision de Québec Inc., Télévision Saint-Laurent Inc., Four Seasons Television Network Inc.*, CRTC Decision 85-733 (Ottawa: CRTC, 1985).
23. Bernard Benoist, "Un brin d'histoire : la télévision à péage dans le contexte des systèmes de communication et de diffusion" in *La télévision payante : jeux et enjeux*, ed. J.-P. Lafrance and C. Gousse (Montreal : Éditions coopératives Albert Saint-Martin, 1982), p. 44.
24. Canadian Radio-television and Telecommunications Commission, Statistical Analysis Division, Ottawa.
25. Canadian Radio-television and Telecommunications Commission, *Vidéotron Ltée*, CRTC Decision 1986-214, (Ottawa: CRTC, March 1986).
26. Canada, Quebec, Federal-Provincial Committee, op. cit., p.73.
27. Jean-Marc Veilleux, *Le développement des canaux spécialisés au Québec : une évaluation économique*, (Quebec: Department of Communications, March 13, 1986), p. 38.
28. Moss, Roberts and Associates Inc., "An Economic Profile of the Canadian Cable Industry", study prepared for the Task Force on Broadcasting Policy, Ottawa, 1986, p. 90.
29. Canadian Radio-television and Telecommunications Commission, *Speciality Programming Services*, CRTC Public Notice 1984-81 (Ottawa: CRTC, April 1984).
30. Canadian Radio-television and Telecommunications Commission, *CHUM Ltd (MuchMusic Network)*, CRTC Decision 1986-215 (Ottawa: CRTC, March 1986).
31. Canada, Department of Communications, Quebec, Department of Communications, *French-language Speciality Music Channels Masse and French are Pleased about Upcoming Public Hearings*, Press Release (Ottawa: The Department, May 12, 1986).
32. La Société des Acadiens du Nouveau-Brunswick, brief submitted to the Task Force on Broadcasting Policy, Saint John, N.B., August 1985, p. 2.
33. Association canadienne-française de l'Alberta, brief submitted to the Task Force on Broadcasting Policy, Alberta, October 1985, p. 3.
34. Rossel Vien, *Radio française dans l'Ouest*, cahiers du Québec (Collection Communications) (Montreal : Hurtubise/HMH, 1977), p. 128.
35. Fédération des francophones hors Québec, brief submitted to the Task Force on Broadcasting Policy, Ottawa, November 1985.
36. Jean-Paul L'Allier et Associés, op. cit., p. 28.
37. Luc Giroux and André H. Caron, *Les Québécois francophones et l'écoute de la télévision de langue anglaise : 1976-1984*, study prepared for the Federal-Provincial Committee on the Future of French-language Television (Ottawa: Department of Communications, Québec: Department of Communications, 1985).
38. Ibid.
39. Canadian Broadcasting Corporation, CBC Research, raw data from BBM Bureau of Broadcast Measurement.
40. Canadian Broadcasting Corporation, CBC Research, raw data from A.C. Nielsen.
41. Canadian Broadcasting Corporation, CBC Research, raw data from BBM Bureau of Broadcast Measurement.
42. Ibid.
43. Ibid.
44. Ibid.
45. Ibid.
46. Canadian Radio-television and Telecommunications Commission, *FM Radio in Canada: A Policy to Ensure a Varied and Comprehensive Radio Service*, Policy Statement (Ottawa: CRTC, 1975), p. 3.
47. According to the 1981 Census, there were 100,000 linguistic transfers among Quebec francophones. See also Daniel Monnies, *La perception de la situation bilinguistique par les québécois*, (Québec : Conseil de la langue française, 1986), p. 45.

48. Denis Bergeron, Brian Chater and John Roberts, "Musiç and the Electronic Media in Canada", study prepared for the Task Force in Broadcasting Policy, Ottawa, 1986, pp. 102-D and 102-H.
49. Canadian Radio-television and Telecommunications Commission, *Report of the Advisory Committee on French-language Music*, (Ottawa: CRTC, 1985), p. 2.
50. Canadian Radio-television and Telecommunications Commission, *French-language Popular Music*, CRTC Public Notice 1986-67 (Ottawa: CRTC, March 1986).
51. Canadian Radio-television and Telecommunications Commission, *Task Force on French-language Popular Music*, CRTC Public Notice 1985-100 (Ottawa: CRTC, May 1985).
52. Canadian Radio-television and Telecommunications Commission, *Radio Futura Ltée*, CRTC Decision 1985-356, (Ottawa: CRTC, May 1985)
53. Canadian Radio-television and Telecommunications Commission, *Renewal of Broadcasting Licences for AM and FM Stations in Montreal and Surrounding Areas*, CRTC Public Announcement (Ottawa: CRTC, September 1980).
54. Letter from David Bond, President of the Canadian Association of Broadcasters to André Bureau, Chairman of the CRTC, Ottawa, January 30, 1986.
55. Canadian Radio-television and Telecommunications Commission, *Supravox Corporation Ltée*, CRTC Decision 80-638 (Ottawa:CRTC, 1980); *Supravox Corportion Ltée*, CRTC Decision 82-586 (Ottawa: CRTC, 1982); *Mutual Broadcasting Canada Ltd.*, CRTC Decision 84-844 (Ottawa: CRTC, 1984).
56. Canadian Radio-television and Telecommunications Commission, *CFCF Inc.*, CRTC Decision 83-842 (Ottawa: CRTC, 1983); *Maisonneuve Broadcasting Ltd.*, CRTC Decision 84-820 (Ottawa: CRTC, 1984).
57. Letter, supra, note 54.
58. Canadian Radio-television and Telecommunications Commission, *Maisonneuve Broadcasting Ltd.*, CRTC Decision 80-639 (Ottawa: CRTC, 1980).
59. CRTC, Public Announcement *Renewals*, supra, note 53. See also *CHUM Limited*, CRTC Decision 85-666 (Ottawa: CRTC, 1985).
60. For example: Following a musical competition, radio station CJFM-FM of Quebec City produced a long-playing record entitled *Studio Rock FM 93* on which half of the young musicians sang in English.
61. CROP Inc., op. cit., p. 6.
62. On the subject of different radio formats and music categories, see Theodore Glasser, "Competition and Diversity Among Radio Formats: Legal and Structural Issues", *Journal of Broadcasting*, vol. 8 (2), 1984, pp. 127-142; Frank J. Kahn, "Radio: Regulating Format Diversity", *Journal of Communications*, vol. 32 (1) 1982, pp. 181-191; Ervin G. Krasnow and William E. Kennard, "Competition and Diversity Among Radio Formats: A 1984 Response", *Journal of Broadcasting*, vol. 18 (2), 1984, pp. 143-145; Bruce Owen, "Regulating Diversity: The Case of Radio Formats", *Journal of Broadcasting*, vol. 21 (3). 1977, pp. 305-319; and, Peter O. Steiner, "Program Patterns and Preferences and the Workability of Competition in Radio Broadcasting", *Quarterly Journal of Economics*, vol. 66, 1952, pp. 194-223.
63. Canadian Radio-television and Telecommunications Commission, *Policy Regarding the Carriage on Cable Television of FM Signals*, CRTC Public Announcement (Ottawa: CRTC, July 1976).
64. Canada, Department of Communications, *Marcel Masse unvails a $25 million development strategy for sound recording*, Press Release (Ottawa: the Department, May 9, 1986)).
65. For the week of March 22-28, 1986 on CBFT, Radio-Canada in Montreal.
66. Pierre Bouchard and Henri Tremblay, *Avoir 15 ou 16 ans en 1985 : inventaire des activités socio-culturelles des jeunes* (Quebec: Department of Education, 1985), p. 33. See also Henri Tremblay, *L'Adolescence et la télévision, c'est un monde à observer*, (Quebec: Department of Communications, 1985), p. 38.

67. Lise Payette as quoted by Normand Cloutier in "La télévision au jour le jour (entrevues avec artisans)", study prepared for the Task Force on Broadcasting Policy, Ottawa, 1986.
68. Maurice Farladeau as quoted by Normand Cloutier, op. cit., p. 8.
69. Pierre Gauvreau, Ibid., p. 8.
70. Suzanne Aubry, Ibid., p. 15.
71. Claude Maher, Ibid., p. 20.
72. Pierre Gauvreau, Ibid., p. 20.
73. Gilles Constantineau, "La concurrence, Keusséça?" in Bernard Cleary and Michel Cormier, "La presse électronique au Québec", study prepared for the Task Force on Broadcasting Policy, Ottawa, 1986, p. 10.
74. Canada, Statistics Canada, "Special Survey of Television Programming Expenses", Ottawa, 1986.
75. The data includes news, current events and public affairs programs broadcast in Quebec between 6 a.m. and 12 a.m., but excludes the political addresses such as "La Politique fédérale" and "La Politique provinciale".
76. Canadian Radio-television and Telecommunications Commission, *Le réseau de télévision TVA Inc.*, CRTC Decision 85-653 (Ottawa: CRTC, 1985).
77. Walter I. Romanow, Stuart Surlin and Walter Soderlund, "Analysis of Local TV News Broadcasts", study prepared for the Task Force on Broadcasting Policy, Ottawa, 1986.
78. Meeting of the Task Force on Broadcasting Policy with Pathonic Communications Inc., Montreal, August 8, 1985.
79. Fédération nationale des communications (Confédération des syndicats nationaux–CSN), brief submitted to the Task Force on Broadcsating Policy, Montreal, August, 1985.
80. The author is referring to an incident which occurred at Rock Forest in December 1983. While pursuing suspects of a crime, a team of police officers burst into a motel room and mistakingly shot an innocent carpet layer.
81. Claude Jean Devirieux, "Réflexions sur le statut de la radio-télévision publique", brief submitted to the Task Force on Broadcasting Policy, Montreal, 1985.
82. Canadian Broadcasting Corporation, "Program Costs", research document prepared for the Task Force on Broadcasting Policy, Ottawa, 1986.
83. Ibid.

Part IV

THE PUBLIC SECTOR

Chapter 9

Principles of Public Broadcasting

Principles of Public Broadcasting

Introduction

Europe and Britain had already introduced broadcasting through the public sector when the CBC was created in 1936, and much of its inspiration came directly from the most famous public broadcaster in the world, the BBC. Given the North American tradition, the private sector was allowed from the beginning to become a significant player within the structure of the CBC and the system as a whole. This peculiarly Canadian hybrid was once viewed sceptically by broadcasters in Europe, but recent international developments, as we note in Chapter 2, have made us seem rather less unworthy.

In a quintessentially Canadian manner new layers of the public sector were added over the years. Never couched in any terms other than the pragmatic, they nevertheless underlined the widespread conviction that the public had certain legitimate needs that could not be fulfilled by the private sector. Creation of the National Film Board was deemed a necessary function of the government not long after the CBC was founded, and although it had no relation to radio broadcasting and has so far contributed insufficiently to television, it has a significant role in our blueprint for a broadcasting system.

Much later, after years of disputes and endless meetings, the provinces were authorized to develop so-called educational broadcasting, under which guise the new institutions broadcast pretty much what they chose. More recently, when the perceived crisis in Canadian programming for television was deemed sufficiently acute, the Broadcast Fund was created, a thoroughly Canadian phenomenon providing government funds to public sector institutions and private entrepreneurs alike.

Following in this grand tradition, we have identified further public needs which, in our view, can be best served by the public sector. In what follows we call for an all-news and information channel to be run by the CBC and a new public network to fill a number of gaps we perceive in our broadcasting system.

This brief summary indicates the charming lack of ideological rigour with which the public sector in broadcasting has developed over the decades. It is true, of course, that Canadians are not always given to philosophical discourse on the phenomena that surround them, and public broadcasting seems an indisputable example of this generalization. We thought it useful, nonetheless, to sketch a rationale for a public broadcasting system.[1]

The concept of public broadcasting can be characterized in half a dozen principles. The first three all stem from one overriding idea — that public broadcasting provides radio and television programs for everyone, regardless of social status, place of residence or aesthetic preference. Commercial broadcasting, like any other commercial enterprise, will not cater to everyone, since some of the potential audience will always be too marginal to be worth reaching.

Thus, the first duty of the public broadcaster is to provide service to the entire sovereign territory of the nation where there are inhabitants to be served. Making transmission arrangements to serve sparsely populated areas is naturally not cost-effective, and the rationale for the CBC's Northern Broadcasting Service, to take a Canadian example, must be based on grounds other than audience ratings. Public broadcasting is a valuable service providing worthwhile experiences from which no citizens should be disenfranchised just because they do not live in a large built-up urban centre. In fact it is precisely those most remote from media of cultural expression, as in the far North, who most deserve an electronic window on the world beyond the confines of their own community. In this way public broadcasting is really no different from other basic social services such as education and health care, paid for at least in part out of general revenues.

The second duty of the public broadcaster is to provide programs that will appeal to all tastes. This is a highly controversial proposition, by no means universally supported by devotees of public broadcasting. In our view, it is properly interpreted to mean that a body of programs should appeal to the largest possible number of viewers or listeners, but not necessarily at the same moment. We disagree with those who argue programs should distinguish themselves from mainstream popular fare by appealing exclusively to minority audiences. At its best, public broadcasting should achieve both these objectives, yet must not be the captive of either extreme. Nor, one trusts, should it be axiomatic that a popular program cannot be a quality program, nor a quality one popular.

By the same token, audiences are not compartmentalized according to taste. In other words, watching a classical play one day does not prevent one from watching a serial situation comedy the next, or vice versa. So the public broadcaster should not treat the audience as though it were one homogeneous group wanting one kind of fare to the exclusion of all others. On the contrary, few viewers and listeners are the exclusive consumers of minority or majority interest programming all the time. And the public broadcaster must behave not only as though different members of the audience have different tastes, but as though each individual member has a range of tastes to be satisfied.

The third duty of the public broadcaster is to make programs that reflect the experience of all significant groups in society — women, visible minorities, natives and others who may be disenfranchised for social or economic reasons. Television, for example, must not be a medium that is mostly about well-to-do, white middle-class professionals, just as radio must not be a medium that is exclusively a vehicle for top-ten hits. This same principle extends to the provision of service, technically speaking, to those who might be disenfranchised because of some handicap, such as hearing impairment. Television is not therefore an eminently democratic medium just because it brings handsome doctors, rich lawyers and macho detectives into every living room in the land. Public television must strive to do more, by bringing a broad cross-section of society into the cultural mainstream.

A related but somewhat different principle, the fourth in this enumeration, concerns the contribution of public broadcasting to national consciousness or nation-building. This takes several forms. The most obvious expectation is that the public broadcaster will act as a rallying point for national sentiments, not by espousing any specific cause, such as national unity, but by providing shared experiences simultaneously to large numbers of people and by defining, exhibiting and explaining national events and trends, from sports finals to election coverage. It is an essential part of such activities that they utilize program production from different regions of a nation, so that individuals in disparate communities can learn about each other and communicate more effectively with one another. The public broadcaster is also expected to be the showcase *par excellence* for the nation's culture. In many cases this means acting as an agent of cultural development by providing work and exposure for talented performers, writers, producers, craftspeople, journalists and others.

Finally, in addition to these duties or responsibilities, the public broadcaster has an important privilege without which the notion of service to the public would be altered beyond recognition: that is, freedom from control by vested interests, whether political or financial. This privilege clearly includes the freedom to express certain opinions, especially journalistic ones, without fear of reprisal from politicians who would rather not hear themselves or their party taken to task for bad policies or acts of mischief.

But even a mature democracy can give no iron-clad guarantees that such reprisals will never be attempted, both because politicians are never happy to be criticized and because freedom of expression is never absolute. The restrictions on freedom of expression, and the related principle of operating at arm's length from the government of the day, are made even more complicated for the public broadcaster by the need to be accountable for the wise use of public funds. A public television or radio network cannot thus act capriciously or irresponsibly, not only because of the usual constraints on libel, obscenity and so forth, but also because such a network is a public institution, funded by the taxpayers who can, through their elected representatives, insist on an accounting from those who make the programming decisions. But the principle must be clear: it is a public broadcasting system we are discussing, not a state or government system.

The tension between the privileges of autonomy and the duties of accountability can never of course be resolved in the abstract. Such tension is an ever-present fact of life, and its management requires much vigilance and democratic goodwill. But the public broadcaster's freedom to program in a professionally responsible way brings with it more than just the right not to be a propaganda tool of government. In a more positive vein it is also intended to make room for a diversity of voices and opinions on the airwaves, by providing liberating working conditions for artists and program-makers.

Commercial broadcasting, driven by the profit motive and thus the need to attract the largest possible audiences, has an inevitable tendency to homogenization in its programming. Public broadcasting, which serves the audience rather than the advertiser, is free in theory from these commercial constraints, which tend to discourage experimentation, controversy and, above all, diversity. These constraints are not necessarily expressed in the form of direct control or outright censorship of programs by sponsors. Rather, they are usually expressed in more subtle form as the by-product of competition for the same audience and the same sources of funding.

Whether subtle or not, the absence of commercial constraints leaves the public broadcaster free to accommodate a whole range of minority interests — in terms of both who produces and who consumes — that would be shunned by the private broadcaster. Naturally this freedom is more, not less, difficult to manage, since it entails that neither profit nor sheer ratings can be applied as a measure of quality or success in program-making. Inevitably, then, the public broadcaster must fall back on the creative personnel who make the programs for inspiration and guidance. While this gives rise to the many problems of what former CBC President Laurent Picard once referred to as "the management of creativity"[1], with their two opposing sets of values, it also fosters excellence in programming, as well as a measure of real choice for the audiences.

We would be surprised to discover a single national public broadcaster that has successfully realized all these principles. Because of historical or political circumstance, public broadcasters have different sets of operating principles and objectives. The CBC differs from other major broadcasters such as the BBC in that it has never been able to raise all its revenues from a single, independent source (the receiver licence fee), but rather has been obliged to rely on a problematic combination of parliamentary appropriations and earned commercial income. We can glean some idea of the importance of this difference in Great Britain by noting the tremendous controversy that has been stirred up by the appointment of the Peacock Committee to examine — and ultimately reject — the feasibility of requiring the BBC to offer air-time for commercial sale.

While a single, independent source of funding is a privilege the CBC has had to do without, it has instead certain duties from which other national broadcasters are exempt. One of the most unusual of these springs from Canada's demographic makeup, which includes two founding linguistic groups whose languages, French and English, are both officially sanctioned. It has always been an integral part of the mandate of the national service that the CBC provide all its services in both official languages.

But the single defining feature which sets the CBC apart as a public broadcaster is that it has developed over half a century as a hybrid, not a fully fledged public broadcaster. This is in part because it has always been only one element in a wider North American context dominated by commercial radio and television. This relationship with commercial broadcasting, whether cooperative or competitive, has had a profound effect on every facet of CBC's activities — financing, distribution, program content.

The CBC is therefore an institution with very mixed values, faced by an environment which has been intermittently unfriendly and has for a decade or more been going through dizzying change. All of this has made the process of adapting to changing times an often awkward and uncomfortable one. The CBC, after all, does not face the challenge of adaptation as a monolithic organization with one set of goals and a clear-cut set of achievements. For in truth there is not one CBC, but many. As we see below in relation to the programming mandate, it is often difficult even to attempt a general analysis that has a bearing not only on radio but also on television; not only on English-language services but also on French. It is part of the conventional wisdom that most of CBC's policy-related problems have to do with English television, and that revenue or content or image problems in that particular service should not be allowed to obscure the successes — or different kinds of problems — typical of radio and French television.

But this truism should not in turn be allowed to obscure the fundamental observation that the CBC is a vast organization with a staggering burden of responsibility comprising network functions mandated in legislation, non-mandated program and technical functions, and obligations to staff, affiliates, a large pool of creative talent and the taxpayer. We have had to ask ourselves if the CBC is not over-extended.

In retrospect, it would hardly be surprising if the CBC were anything other than over-extended. On the one hand, it has been Canada's single national public broadcaster for the past six decades. On the other hand, the burdens it is expected to carry have increased by geometric proportions. On the one hand, the need (in television especially) for a second public network to exhibit Canadian programming has been evident for years. On the other hand, when the CBC sought government funding for this network it was turned down flat. On the one hand, Canadians acknowledge their dependence on the contribution to Canadian culture made by the CBC. On the other hand, the CBC has not been given the tools to do its job — its many jobs — in the optimum manner.

This Task Force has had fun with the problems of being Canadian. How Canadian do we wish our brodcasting system to be? As Canadian as possible — under the circumstances. How public must our broadcasting system be to be as Canadian as possible? As public as possible — under the circumstances. The circumstances include an acceptance of the role of the public sector that is far more pragmatic than philosophical; an understanding that the cost of public broadcasting, one way or another, falls to the public; and a reluctance by politicians to be especially supportive of a public broadcaster whose various media often exercise their absolute right to expose the limitations of politicians.

Nonetheless, the broadcasting responsibilities for which the public sector is the best agency are significant. That is why, notwithstanding the constraints just noted, this Report calls for a substantially expanded public sector in broadcasting, with the CBC as its major component. We therefore begin our discussion of the various elements of this sector as we envision it with a long and detailed analysis of its key component.

Notes

1. Especially useful in this connection was Broadcasting Research Unit, *The Public Service Idea in British Broadcasting: Main Principles* (London: BFI Publishing, 1985).
2. Speech by Laurent Picard, at "Le Colloque sur la gestion moderne en radiotélévision", organized by la Radiodiffusion-Télévision Belge for l'Union Européene de Radiodiffusion, Brussels, May 17 — 19, 1972.

Chapter 10

The Canadian Broadcasting Corporation

The Canadian Broadcasting Corporation

The CBC and Canadian Programming

This is an appropriate year to submit a report on the state of broadcasting in Canada because 1986 marks the fiftieth anniversary of the CBC, the centerpiece of our broadcasting system. This year many Canadians, both inside and outside the CBC, will sing the praises of our largest and most important cultural institution. Our Report is intended to focus on problems — and certainly the CBC has enough of them.

Over the years, the CBC has become the kind of institution that every Canadian has something to say about. Both its friends and foes feel and speak strongly about the CBC, as we have learned in our public and private meetings across the country. Yet far too often in our experience gossip, rumour or myth is asserted as fact. For this reason we have come to see as one of our important duties the effort to make this debate as informed as possible.

We begin by affirming our high regard for the CBC and our conviction that it continues to be indispensable. Further, we are proud to be voicing these sentiments as part of a tradition of public broadcasting advocacy that stretches back to the founding of the CBC in 1936, and back still further to the first Canadian royal commission on broadcasting, which reported in 1929.

We have already devoted space to these historical antecedents, but it is useful to repeat here what Prime Minister Bennett expressed as his primary concern on second reading of the 1932 broadcasting legislation.

> First of all, this country must be assured of complete control of broadcasting from Canadian sources, free from foreign interference or influence. Without such control radio broadcasting can never become a great agency for communication of matters of national concern and for the diffusion of national thought and ideals, and without such control it can never be the agency by which national consciousness may be fostered and sustained . . .[1]

Subsequent events have not unfolded as Mr. Bennett would have wished, especially with regard to the inroads of foreign influence, but he would be pleased with the "great agency" which public broadcasting has become in the hands of the Corporation which he helped to found. The CBC has accomplished the mission outlined in Bennett's speech with remarkable success, and in the face of enormous geographic, financial, political and demographic obstacles. The CBC has built one of the finest radio services in the world and has mounted a television service that competes directly with the most prodigious, influential and heavily financed entertainment industry ever created.

The keynote of this chapter is Canadian programming. The broadcast distribution technologies, particularly cable and satellite, have opened Canadian channels to precisely the foreign influence that Bennett feared. Specifically, Canadian viewers are now subject to an influx of American television programs that are a permanent fixture of our system. The situation in radio is different and somewhat less alarming, but the fact remains that we need a national instrument to redress the existing programming imbalance. All of our publicly funded broadcasters, and to some extent private broadcasters as well, must share in achieving this goal. Nevertheless, the major burden will inevitably fall to the CBC and it is upon the CBC that we must rely for an abundance of compelling radio and television programs — by, for and about Canadians.

The first requirement of the *Broadcasting Act* is that the CBC be "predominantly Canadian in content and character". As a Task Force we reaffirm our support for this objective. Thousands of talented Canadians have laboured over the years to bring a distinctive Canadian character, as well as 'Canadian content', to the programs of the CBC. Millions of Canadians appreciate CBC news, current affairs, sports and serious television drama. We know too that many policy-makers and pundits, as well as bodies of inquiry like ours, want CBC to make more good Canadian programs.

If there is general agreement on the goal, there is little agreement on the means to achieve it. In fact, few Canadian institutions attract such vehement and bitter disagreement, or such conflicting sets of expectations, as does the CBC. We had ample evidence of this during our deliberations, not only from direct consultations, but also from outside events. In 1985 one group of Canadians, alarmed by what they saw as drastic budget cuts at CBC, formed the Friends of Public Broadcasting, who in an open letter to the Prime Minister published in February 1985 expressed dismay over CBC's bleak and uncertain future. Others, alarmed instead by what they saw as profligate overspending at CBC, suggested Draconian measures such as turning over certain functions of the English television service to private enterprise, an idea promoted briefly by a group consisting largely of business people calling itself "The Committee for the Responsible Privatization of CBC Television".[2]

The CBC, in fact, finds itself in a classic love-hate relationship with Canadians: even those who love it love to complain about it, and those who denounce it most vehemently would be loathe to do without it. For example, The Friends of Public Broadcasting deliberately declined to call themselves the Friends of the CBC, while Allan Slaight, who was chairperson of the privatization committee, assured a public gathering that he and his colleagues "care about the CBC and accept the idea that public broadcasting has an important role to play in telling Canadians about themselves".[3]

It is true, of course, that stories of CBC mismanagement, bureaucratization, inefficiency and insensitivity are legion. And our researchers, seeking the views of craftspeople and artisans who either worked for or had dealings with the CBC, passed on to us identical stories. Whether in Quebec or English Canada, creative people who are dedicated to the ideals which the CBC is supposed to represent in broadcasting express frustration and dismay at their perception that those ideals were being undermined either by poor management or by an antagonistic budget-cutting government. At times it seemed as though the CBC produces its endless stream of quality programs almost in spite of itself.

Some argue that more structural problems must be faced. Professor François Baby of Laval University, for example, a former Radio Canada suggested to us that the Corporation had developed

> . . . according to a highly centralized model, complete with a huge bureaucratic and technocratic infrastructure and superstructure, which have progressively crushed creativity and spontaneity.[4] (translation)

Certainly there can be no doubt the CBC is in a difficult situation. Whether that situation is more critical than other rough passages the Corporation has traversed over the years is, of course, impossible for us to say. It must also be clear that any large and complicated organization, whether creative or not, whether public sector or not, is grist for the rumour mill. However, we are satisfied that at least part of the present "crisis" of the CBC has roots that are not all that difficult to trace. In the first place, some of it arises from a budget that for the past decade has not kept pace with its expanding obligations while competition has increased steadily.

But the CBC's troubles would not be over if it suddenly had more money and less competition. For one thing, it is clear that CBC's performance as a broadcaster and a bureaucratic institution will not be improved by adjusting its appropriation — unless we pay careful attention to what it is we want the CBC to do for us.

All the research and consultations in the world, however, will never forge a permanent consensus on how the CBC ought to carry out its mandate. No legislative provision for the operations of a creative institution can foretell the artistic and technological future. In a large, publicly owned journalistic organization, any attempt to determine more than the most general goals would threaten the exercise of free expression. But the price to be paid for flexibility and free expression is controversy — controversy over how to interpret the CBC's mandate.

One provision of CBC's programming mandate more than any other has been responsible for making the CBC try to be all things to all people. This is the provision that the national service should "be a *balanced service* of information, enlightenment and entertainment for people of different ages, interests and tastes covering the *whole range of programming* in fair proportion" (our emphasis). While this applies to both radio and television, the historical development of the two services was quite different. Private radio began in 1919, some 13 years before the creation of the public system by the Bennett government, and flourished from the beginning. In radio, CBC does not in fact — properly we think — cover the whole range of programming.

On the other hand, for the first several years of public television CBC developed its French and English networks at a faster pace than the private sector. The CTV network and Télé-Métropole, flagship of the TVA network, were not licensed until 1961. This meant that CBC was assumed to have two responsibilities that loomed much larger for television than for radio. First, it had to provide services to as many Canadians as possible and, second, it had to provide all kinds of programming, for all kinds of audiences, because commercial broadcasters were either unwilling to produce unprofitable kinds of programming (current affairs, drama, children's, religious, etc.), or simply did not broadcast their signals to every part of the country.

The job of CBC television, in other words, was to offer real viewing choice which, in the circumstances, became an obligation to show both American and Canadian programming. American programming has, of course, since become a common commodity for most Canadians, and as our examination of local schedules has shown, Canadians in many towns and cities actually have a wider choice of American programming on their local cable system than do typical cable subscribers even in Manhattan and other large American markets![5]

The Task Force does not see American, or American-style, programming in itself as a threat to our cultural survival. American programs are well crafted, often exciting and occasionally satisfying to watch. We see American television as a threat only when it discourages Canadian self-expression by leaving few financial incentives for domestic production. This is where the CBC has a role to play.

We have not approached our deliberations about CBC with a predetermined view that it must retrench or expand. Rather, we have tried to fit CBC's operations to our vision of the national service, and then to calculate the cost of achieving certain objectives. In programming, we see the CBC paradoxically having to retrench and expand at the same time. Retrench because it no longer has to provide all the American programming Canadians want: this task can be shared with others. Expand because much remains to be done, above all in Canadian performance programming on television.

Like so much else in Canadian broadcasting, the efforts of the CBC are shaped too much by physical resources and technology, and not enough by programming. We do not necessarily mean by this that CBC owns too many buildings or too much studio equipment (in fact a case can be made that in some locations the CBC's plant is inadequate or obsolete, or both). What this does mean is that the CBC's resources were originally designed and deployed in an era when the driving force was distribution rather than production. In a much less competitive or technologically sophisticated environment, CBC's first responsibility was to provide equality of service, a criterion not of program quality but of geographical coverage.

Times have changed. Even if the deployment of physical resources has changed at CBC, especially after two years of severe budget cuts, the outlook and expectations of many staff have perhaps not kept pace. That is why we argue below not for another round of resource reduction, but for a consolidation of resources, especially in the regions, along with a much more realistic appraisal of what it is that the CBC's stations should be expected to produce in the future.

Structure and Organization of the CBC[6]

The Distribution Infrastructure

Canadians are more than casually aware of the CBC. Most feel they 'know' it through the programs they hear and watch on radio and television. Transmission to the home or car receiver may be the last stage in the programming link for the broadcaster, but it is the only stage that really counts for the audience.

The individual stations that bring local, regional and network programming to their audiences are, of course, more than just transmission centres. They also do duty as production centres for purposes of local programming, and they contribute items, episodes or whole series to network schedules. On the other hand, the radio and television stations actually owned and operated by CBC (the so-called O and Os) are far from sufficient for delivery of the CBC's six main networks, which are English television, English mono radio, English stereo radio, French television, French mono radio and French stereo radio.

We can glean some idea of the relative complexity of production and distribution facilities by making the following comparison. The four CBC media, English television and radio, French television and radio, which operate the six networks just noted, currently have about 75 production points across the country. This figure includes all locations where at least some program origination occurs (many locations, of course, house two or more services under one roof). At the same time, the CBC maintains a system of over 1600 transmitters to transmit all its programming in the four media, including both mono and stereo radio in both languages.

These transmission points are essentially of three different types: transmitters which form part of a CBC-owned station; those which form part of an affiliated station; and rebroadcast transmitters (often termed 'rebroads'), which are normally isolated from a station operation. All of these points are interrelated in a very complex way through branching structures comprising network, regional and sub-regional distribution centres, the most important and costly of which are the owned stations.

The Affiliates

With the exception of the two stereo networks, CBC depends on a number of commercial stations with which it has affiliate agreements to distribute its signals in various parts of the country. The reasons for this partnership lie in CBC's historical primacy in the broadcasting system, as well as in the need to use public funds. Until 1958, CBC effectively controlled all technical and operational aspects of broadcasting in Canada, since in addition to its role as national public broadcaster, it acted as regulator of the private sector.

Because of the enormous expense of providing radio and television coverage to all parts of the country, and the assumed alliance between public and private sectors in a 'single system', the CBC found it necessary to make its national coverage as complete as possible by calling on the collaboration of several dozen commercial stations. This alternative was far less costly than building stations or transmitters of its own.

At present CBC has an individually negotiated arrangement with 31 private television stations (26 English, 5 French) and 17 private radio stations (10 English, 7 French). The radio affiliates no longer play a major role and have been greatly reduced in number over the last several years under the Radio Affiliate Replacement Plan (RARP). In television, however, the affiliates continue to have a major impact in three areas: audience coverage, network schedules and revenues.

The affiliates cover collectively both a large 'unduplicated' audience, i.e. an

Table 10.1 CBC Stations Operating – June, 1986

	Television		Radio		
	English	French	English		French
	18	13	31	Mono	15
			16	Stereo	6
Total	31		68		

audience not otherwise reached by CBC itself, and a smaller 'duplicated' audience, i.e. one which is already covered by CBC's own transmitters. The unduplicated television audience delivered by the affiliates amounts to nearly one-third of the total French and English audience — some 29 percent.

This proportion of the audience does not, however, see the same network schedule as do viewers of the owned and operated stations. The affiliates must carry that part of the schedule known as 'reserved time', but can then pick and choose among remaining programs in the balance of the schedule, the 'available time'. No affiliate carries either the French or English schedule in its entirety. Out of a total of 84 hours on the English schedule, individual affiliates carry roughly 50 to 80 hours. Out of 119 hours on the French side, the range is from 88 hours at the low end to 117 at the high end. Some of the affiliates also make it a practice to 'timeshift' certain of their CBC programs to off-peak periods of their schedules, and then fill these peak slots with more popular American programming.

Use of Satellite Transponders

The single most crucial and yet least apparent link in this complex distribution chain is undoubtedly the nine satellite transponders leased by CBC on the Anik D1 satellite. The satellite is utilized for release of all the main networks to regional distribution centres, a task greatly complicated by the fact that all the feeds have to be transmitted across five different time zones by the use of delays.

A good deal of the satellite capacity is also devoted to distribution of the Northern Service, discussed in more detail below. The satellite has made possible live television broadcasts to the Far North, greatly facilitated development of native language programming and generally allowed improvements in both quality and availability.

In addition to the dramatic impact of satellite delivery on remote audiences, the creation of new program formats was also made possible by the satellite. This includes the introduction of the so-called 'double-ender' interview in programs such as *The Journal* and *Le Point*, in which the host appears to be face-to-face with a guest who may be thousands of miles away. A number of the CBC's French and English current affairs shows make substantial use of three of the transponders for shunting segments back and forth through the system as program material is assembled each day.

Over and above these satellite applications across the main networks, the CBC distributes two other networks, the French and English Parliamentary channels, by satellite to all cable systems in the country. They are therefore available to a smaller segment of the viewing public, since they are not distributed off-air and most cable subscribers require a cable converter to receive them.

Despite the CBC's heavy and increasing reliance on satellite technology, with its clear advantages, regional and sub-regional distribution still relies on a substantial commitment to terrestrial facilities, both owned by the CBC as in the case of its off-air transmitters, and leased from common carriers as in the case of the microwave networks provided by Telecom Canada, the telephone consortium.

These terrestrial facilities, the off-air transmitters and microwave networks, are more expensive than the satellite services — a little over $20 million each versus a little less than $20 million. The CBC pays as much as all three of these items taken together — well over $60 million — for maintenance of presentation and time zone delay facilities at its production centres across the country. Total distribution costs for all networks amount to about $145 million annually, including the roughly $16 million paid to affiliates for their services.

Program Production and Procurement

Whereas the program delivery system may be taken for granted by the audience, this is less apt to be the case with the programs themselves, the actual vehicles of entertainment, enlightenment and information. Even here the seamless flow of daily programming masks another set of complexities — the structures in place at CBC for making, buying and scheduling individual radio and television programs.

Virtually all broadcasters, both public and private, must strike a balance between making and buying programs on the one hand and satisfying national and local needs on the other. In the case of the CBC the situation is further complicated by the sheer number of networks and production centres which it operates. By and large, however, the programming seen or heard on any given CBC station comes from one of five sources:

- *network production* (broadcast on network)
- *local production* (broadcast in local or regional coverage area, or on network)
- *regional exchange* (produced at one centre, broadcast by one or more stations in other regions)
- *domestic supplier* (procurement from Canadian independent, may involve buying rights, equity participation or other form of co-production)
- *foreign supplier* (distributor, production house or other broadcaster).

Because of the major differences in the balance of these sources between radio and television, the two media are examined separately.

Television

French and English television are both organized in essentially the same fashion, with a network vice-president operating from headquarters in Montreal and Toronto respectively, each one having responsibility for programming at all levels while the regional operations report to corporate headquarters in Ottawa. French television's Montreal flagship station is complemented by 12 regional stations in Quebec and across Canada while their English counterparts number 17, in addition to the Toronto station.

Both the networks themselves and the individual stations produce programs. Naturally, since they have more substantial resources as well as overriding responsibility for a balanced daily schedule, the networks produce the lion's share of the programming, particularly that seen during prime time. What the stations produce depends on their size and location and thus varies enormously from one to another.

The three smallest English locations produced well under 60 hours each in 1985-86, while Toronto produced over 1000 hours.[7] About half the English stations produce between 400 and 500 hours a year of their own programming. This disproportion is more pronounced in French television since more than half of its stations are located in areas with a relatively low francophone population. The regional stations produced less than six percent of the programming telecast on the French network in 1984-85.

The balance between network and regional production is as follows. On the English side, about 3000 hours are produced by the network as opposed to some 11,000 hours by the regions, most of them news shows. On the French side, the proportions are almost reversed with the network producing about 3,500 hours compared to 2,500 hours in the regions. As noted above, some of the programming produced in the regions is telecast in local coverage areas only, whereas certain programs or program segments are seen in other regions, under the auspices of regional program exchange. Others still are produced regionally for telecast on the national network. Although this latter practice is not widespread, it is gaining ground as efforts are made to concentrate regional television resources.

Canadian Content

All Canadian broadcasters are required under the CRTC's television regulations to broadcast a certain minimum of Canadian-originated programming. A more stringent quota is imposed on the CBC than on private broadcasters: it must offer no less than 60 percent Canadian content averaged throughout the entire broadcast day on its main networks and no less than 60 percent averaged during prime time (defined for the CRTC's purposes as 6 p.m to 12 midnight), while the respective figures for the private sector are 60 percent and 50 percent.

In actual practice the CBC has long exceeded these minimum requirements. Even during peak time viewing, from 7 p.m to 11 p.m, Canadian content of both French and English networks reaches over 75 percent. Since 1983 it has been CBC and government policy to aim at a gradual increase, over five years, in the Canadian content of prime-time television. An increase to over 80 percent Canadian content is to be accomplished, particularly on English television, by the removal of commercial American programs in favor of domestic productions. The CBC has maintained in its public statements that the success of this initiative will depend to a large extent on the availability of incremental funding.

Independent Production

Public broadcasters in many of the Western democracies have been adjusting in recent years to increased collaboration with independent producers. In line with this general trend the CBC has adopted as a major corporate policy the long-term goal of increasing the proportion of independent production, outside of sports and information, to 50 percent by 1988. At the same time the CBC is committed through its union agreements, notably with its principal technical union, NABET (the National Union of Broadcast Employees and Technicians), to maintaining a minimum level of in-house production staff. By gradually increasing the level of independent production at the expense of foreign programming, CBC can afford for the time being to maintain existing levels of in-house production.

The CBC's relationship with the independents is different from that typical of other Canadian broadcasters. For many years the CBC was virtually the only steady Canadian customer for much of the independently produced programming in current affairs, variety and drama. Private broadcasters have traditionally preferred purchasing American programs at greatly reduced prices, or, for purposes of meeting the content quota, producing in-house or through a vertically integrated production company.

The CBC's cultural mandate did create outlets for certain kinds of programming for which there was no demand from the private sector. But CBC, virtually a monopoly buyer, operated with a large capacity for in-house production in a very small market. And it paid 'licence fees' — a negotiated payment to a program rights holder to 'licence' one or more airings of the program — that were more reflective of the low costs of acquiring foreign programs than what it cost the CBC to produce Canadian programs internally. Often they represented less than 20 percent of program budgets with the balance having to be found from other sales, whether domestic or foreign.

This may be contrasted with the situation in the United States, where the networks have typically paid 80 percent or more of program costs in licence fees. This reflects a number of major differences. First, the market is much larger and more competitive. Secondly, on the basis of anti-trust precepts prohibiting vertical integration, the Federal Communications Commission effectively prevented the networks from producing or co-producing entertainment programming, and the only way to get domestic programs from outside sources was to pay licence fees that cover a substantial proportion of their production costs. Ironically, while the rest of the world moves towards a greater use of independent productions, those constraints in the United States are now loosening and American networks are being allowed to produce their own entertainment programming.

The Broadcast Program Development Fund

In 1983, partly as a consequence of the unsatisfactory relationship between the CBC and the independent sector, the Minister of Communications elected to create a fund to promote independent television program production, to be administered by the Canadian Film Development Corporation (CFDC), known informally as Telefilm Canada (see Chapter 14). According to the original provisions of the Fund, CBC-related projects were to have access to up to half the total monies available.

In fact, the CBC became by far the major participant, accounting for no less than 85 percent of all broadcaster investments in Fund projects in its first year. Because of the 2-for-1 financing formula of the fund, CBC investments could now be levered into much higher total program budgets. In 1984-85, CBC was able to double the number of broadcast hours devoted to independent production to over 500 hours. The long-neglected category of Canadian drama was the main beneficiary of the new funding.

The Fund gave the CBC, as well as the private broadcasters, much more budget leverage for a given level of investment. Yet the system depended on stability in broadcaster investments, especially on the part of the CBC, which by year two (1984-85) accounted for roughly two-thirds of both number of projects and total production budgets. It was a system that was therefore potentially very sensitive to reductions in the Corporation's budget.

The $85 million budget cut announced in the fall of 1984 threatened to curtail these activities very seriously. The resulting slowdown in production, combined with a concern about other issues such as a growing imbalance between French- and English-language production resulted in several basic changes in the rules governing the Fund. The most significant of these was that for certain categories of production, and in particular for fully Canadian productions, Telefilm could now invest not one-third but up to 49 percent. This was a move intended in part to increase the Corporation's budget leverage.

At the time of writing, a number of questions have been left in suspension, particularly concerning the future relationship of the CBC and the Broadcast Fund, the evolving mandate of the Fund and the prospects for continued growth of CBC-sponsored independent production. The Broadcast Fund is looked at separately in Chapter 14.

Television Expenditures

It has traditionally been difficult to compare costs by network and regions, French and English, or television and radio, because of CBC's system of budget accountability and the practice of 'hosting' or cross-subsidizing between the main services at many locations. The difficulties inherent in calculating programming costs are compounded by the structural and financial relationships between programming *per se* and other functions such as operational support (engineering, finance, human resources, etc.) and transmission. Still other complications are introduced by budget cuts. A new real cost accounting system for regional broadcasting has recently made this job considerably easier.

In order to put some observations on expenditures in perspective, it is helpful to understand the basic size and sources of the CBC's budget. In the 1986-1987 fiscal year, the total budget is $1.1 billion which reflects adjustments for recent reductions. Not all of this total comes from the taxpayer. Over 22 percent is accounted for by revenues earned by the CBC, which are forecast for each year as budget planning proceeds. This amount is then subtracted from planned, government-approved expenditures and the balance of roughly 80 percent (which naturally varies from year to year) is then raised from CBC's annual parliamentary appropriation. The current appropriation is $848 million dollars. (For additional information on CBC financing see also Table 29.2 in Chapter 29).

In real costs, adjusted for cross-subsidization between services, regional television is expected to cost a little more than $130 million on the English side in 1986-87, and some $45 million on the French side, exclusive of support services, transmission and outside procurement. No exactly comparable figures are available for the corresponding network program production operations. In rough terms, however, the English network spends about $220 million and the French network about $170 million. Notice that these figures reflect the fact that the French network budget includes costs related to the flagship station, CBFT, whereas the English network budget excludes the Toronto station, CBLT.

Radio

CBC radio in almost all its aspects presents a less complicated operational picture than does television. This is particularly true of program production and procurement, which in radio is not buffeted by the same high costs, regulatory constraints and supplier relationships. This section will offer a brief look at the structure of the radio networks, the make-up of the schedules and salient expenditures.

Network Structures

Reference to the English or French radio service in a given CBC location may include either or both of the two main networks, i.e. Mono and FM Stereo. Confusion often arises because the two networks do not correspond neatly to the services provided through the AM and FM bands respectively. This is because financial constraints have required the CBC to deliver its English Mono service via the FM band in certain areas.

Moreover, in some areas where distribution of the French networks is limited to one network, a third program stream, known as the 'service de base', is made available, combining daytime programming from Mono and evening programming from Stereo. To add still further to the confusion, CBC seems poised to adopt the titles Radio 1 and Radio 2 for the Mono and Stereo networks, though this usage is not yet current.

CBC radio is strikingly different from the television services in several ways. The first of these is that the programming on all networks, with the singular exception of recorded music, is overwhelmingly Canadian and virtually all of the spoken-word programming, current affairs, features and drama are produced in-house. No private-sector radio program industry exists as a counterpart to the independent television production sector.

This is not to say that the creative talent utilized in radio production are all permanent staff. On the contrary, most of the performing, writing and producing talent is freelance, often long-term contract employees, while most of the technical and support staff is permanent. Most personnel, in any case, operate from CBC facilities, with CBC organizational support.

Secondly, regional production centres have a much more important role to play in radio than they do in television. Both the Mono networks cut away for several hours each day to local stations, which deliver news, interviews and other information and 'survival' programming, like weather, to their local audiences. In contrast to television prime time, which is largely network controlled, it is precisely the radio peak listening periods — early morning and late afternoon — which are devoted to local concerns, at least in Mono.

The French Stereo network transmits exclusively from its Montreal headquarters, without local time periods. All told, however, the hours broadcast annually by French radio include some 42,000 hours produced by the regions, whether for direct transmission or retransmission through Montreal. English radio boasts an even greater dependence on its regional centres. Thus, of a total program output of some 71,000 hours (reflecting the greater number of English stations), over 60,000 are regionally produced, while regional programming accounts for approximately 60 percent of the Mono schedule and 70 percent of the Stereo schedule.

Finally, CBC's radio services are much more distinctive compared to their commercial competitors than is CBC television in its market environment. CBC radio stations are virtually the only ones in the system not dependent on commercials. CBC television, for its part, runs commercials, as well as a certain amount of programming, notably American serials, that are widely available on other station groups. On the other hand, CBC radio operates in a much more fragmented market — i.e. one in which a large number of stations are competing for a given audience. The CBC's overall share of the radio market is about 13 percent, or a little more than half the overall audience share enjoyed by CBC television and its affiliates.

Program Schedules

Both French and English radio have carried out a particular strategy in the way they program each of the two main networks. The Mono networks are designed to appeal to a somewhat broader audience than the Stereo networks by concentrating on information programming, light music and conversation. Their topical nature fits well with the audience coverage they achieve, which is now 99 percent of the population in both languages.

While the Mono networks stress high information content and a local public service orientation, the Stereo networks have specialized in performance programming — i.e. music, both recorded and in concert, and features and documentaries. Thus, the balance favors more serious cultural fare, with less attempt to keep audiences abreast of local or practical information. This program mandate is also in keeping with the audience coverage enjoyed by Stereo, which is considerably more limited than Mono coverage, at roughly three-quarters of the anglophone and francophone audiences respectively. Since 1984, however, the CBC has transmitted the Stereo networks to all cable systems in conjunction with satellite delivery of the Parliamentary Television Network, thereby raising potential coverage by roughly 10 percent.

Radio Expenditures

The greater number of English radio stations and the greater reliance by English radio on regional production are reflected in the balance of expenditures by Toronto and Montreal. Keeping once again to approximations for the sake of clarity, French radio spends almost twice as much for network programming as it does for regional programming (about $40 million compared to about $20 million). English radio, on the other hand, spends approximately $37 million for network programming and $53 million for regional programming.

In terms of programming expenditure for each of the four radio networks, French and English radio both spend about five times as much on Mono as they do on Stereo. Among anglophones with access to full CBC radio service, the Mono audience share is about four times the Stereo audience share, i.e. roughly eight percent versus two percent. The difference is less marked on the French side, where the audience shares are about six percent and two percent for Mono and Stereo respectively.

A high proportion of these program expenditures go directly to the development of Canadian artistic talent. Relatively speaking, more funds are available for this purpose in radio than in television, since radio spends so little outside for program procurement. One of the mechanisms used by radio is talent competitions for performers, composers and writers, as well as commissions, workshops and co-operative ventures with performing arts organizations. Talent development also operates through agreements such as the contract with the American Federation of Musicians (AF of M), whose members are guaranteed a certain annual minimum level of expenditure. The French Stereo network devotes approximately half of all its direct program expenditures to AF of M members through this agreement. However, CBC's once extensive network of orchestras has been reduced to a single ensemble, the CBC Vancouver Orchestra.

Other Broadcast and Non-Broadcast Activities

As was suggested at the beginning of this section, CBC engages in a much broader range of activities than is obvious to the casual observer. This is in part because the Corporation is a large, diversified organization operating over thousands of miles of sovereign territory, as well as in many other parts of the globe. But its complexity is more than just a function of sheer size. It is also a function of a mixed pedigree: a public service mission combined with constraints imposed by having to compete in the commercial television marketplace.

Few of the activities outlined below are unusual in themselves. Along with the main network services described above, most of them are typical of either commercial broadcasters or other public broadcasters. What is unusual is that they are all combined together under one corporate roof, not always in easy co-existence. Even a rough sketch of some of these activities provides a hint of what makes the CBC unique, in both its strengths and its weaknesses. The enumeration below includes selected activities from general operations, as well as from non-mandated broadcast services.

Engineering Headquarters

CBC operates a large engineering establishment (known as 'EHQ') for all corporate needs from a Montreal-based facility. Its annual budget is approximately $10 million. It is responsible not only for on-going operations and maintenance of a huge investment in production, post-production and transmission equipment, but also for the design and construction of new physical plant, such as transmitters or entire station and studio complexes.

All broadcasters must of course have access to engineering support services, since broadcasting is a technology-intensive business. In the case of the CBC engineering expertise is not only a support function but also a commodity now marketed by the CBC. Early in 1986 EHQ received ministerial approval to sell its technical planning and design services to foreign clients, especially developing nations. This 'profit-centre' function is intended to develop in close conjunction with Canadian private sector suppliers.

CBC Enterprises

Apart from the sale of commercial time on the television networks, the main sources of CBC's earned revenues are channeled through the Enterprises division. Enterprises sells CBC products to a number of different kinds of customers, not unlike its counterparts at other national broadcasting organizations. The original impetus for creating such divisions has usually been the desire to sell programs to foreign broadcasters. CBC Enterprises is a corporate division housed in Montreal which represents both French and English services.

Its main activities can be grouped into three areas: program sales, consumer products, and pre-sale and co-production agreements. Thus, Enterprises acts in three rather different capacities, as distributor, retailer and co-producer. Gross revenues are projected at about $7 million in the current fiscal year. This includes both foreign program sales and domestic syndication such as sales to Canadian educational broadcasters.

The sale of consumer products, the merchandising function, realizes only about half the revenues of program sales but is somewhat more diversified. It includes the sale to the public of musical recordings such as the SM5000 classical music series, spoken-word recordings, publications and transcripts, right down to promotional items such as coffee mugs bearing the CBC logo. But the strongest growth area in retailing may turn out to be direct sales of prerecorded video cassettes, a line which was non-existent only a couple of years ago.

Special Events and Activities

Every year brings special events of wide public interest which it is the responsibility of the national broadcaster to cover. These include both planned and unplanned events. The planned events can be routine, such as political conventions and elections, or unique, such as the papal visit or Expo 86. Unplanned events calling for the mobilization of CBC journalistic resources on a large scale include natural disasters and conflicts such as wars, uprisings and, some might argue, unanticipated election campaigns.

Certain of the planned special events require an extra measure of effort on the part of the CBC. Because of its special position, the CBC is sometimes called upon to act as 'host broadcaster' to its foreign confrères and thus supply not only images and commentary to Canadians but also facilities and broadcast feeds to visiting broadcasters. This role was such a large-scale and expensive undertaking in the case of the papal visit, for example, that a special appropriation of $9 million was set aside for the purpose.

The CBC has from time to time engaged in other *ad hoc* or experimental activities not directly related to its broadcast services. One of the most interesting such examples was its participation in a pilot application of Canada's Telidon technology. This experiment, known as IRIS (Information Relayed Instantly from the Source), ran from 1981 to 1986 and was designed to give both CBC journalists and trial subscribers a chance to use a CBC-operated teletext information service.

Non-Mandated Broadcast Services

Over the years the CBC has had to look beyond the confines of its main networks, even beyond Canada's borders, in fulfilling the entire range of its responsibilities. The so-called 'non-mandated' services are undertakings which are not explicitly provided for in CBC's enabling legislation. The three most important of these are the Parliamentary Television Network, Radio-Canada International and the Northern Service, described later in this chapter.

CBC's Statutory Mandate

The *Broadcasting Act* of 1968 establishes a corporation — the CBC — charged with providing a national broadcasting service. As we shall argue below, some of the provisions of the mandate for this national service should be shared with other parts of the broadcasting system. At least one of the provisions — dealing with national unity — seems to us inappropriate for any broadcaster, public or private.

The several provisions of the mandate, part of section 3 of the Act, are spelled out in a scant two dozen lines. Seven distinct propositions are advanced. Five flow from the general concept of public broadcasting we discuss in Chapter 9, while two are more typical of the Canadian system. The seven are as follows (arranged for ease of presentation rather than by order of appearance):

- i That the service be "predominantly Canadian in content and character", and "provide for a continuing expression of Canadian identity".
- ii That it "contribute to the development of national unity".
- iii That it "be a balanced service of information, enlightenment and entertainment for people of different ages, interests and tastes covering the whole range of programming in fair proportion".
- iv That it "be extended to all parts of Canada, as public funds become available".
- v That it serve "the special needs of geographic, regions, and actively [contribute] to the flow and exchange of cultural and regional information and entertainment".

vi That it "be in English and French".

vii That "where any conflict arises between the objectives of the national broadcasting service and the interests of the private element of the Canadian broadcasting system, it shall be resolved in the public interest but paramount consideration shall be given to the objectives of the national broadcasting service".

It is clear that the first two provisions regarding Canadian identity and national unity can for some purposes be considered as facets of the overriding principle that a public broadcaster ought to contribute to nation-building. Similarly, the balance provision in (iii) is an expression of the principle of universal appeal (sometimes expressed in terms of programs, sometimes in terms of audiences). The provisions in (iv) and (v) for coverage and regional reflection constitute two different aspects of the principle of geographic universality.

Although all five of these provisions, especially the last two concerning linguistic duality and public sector priority, flow from widely accepted principles and by and large have served well as part of the broadcasting policy for Canada, the Task Force believes that several should be adjusted to the changing realities of the 1980s. The admonitions to contribute to national unity and be identifiably Canadian are very different in the means by which they are apt to promote a sense of nationhood. Much ink has been spilt over the elusive Canadian identity. There is, however, no doubt in our minds about the value of treating the national service as an instrument of Canadian cultural expression. This must remain the special mission of the national service and the ultimate justification for the substantial expenditure of public funds it represents. Canadians do not need to agree on what the Canadian identity consists of, or even if there is one, in order to want to turn on their radios and televisions and be able to recognize their own distinctive national service.

The insistence that the national public broadcaster promote national unity is another matter. It suggests constrained attachment to a political order rather than free expression in the pursuit of a national culture broadly defined. To Canadians the concept is also weighted down with unpleasant historical and political baggage. An indication of how it could be misused can be found in the 1983 federal strategy, "Building for the Future: towards a distinctive CBC". The fourth policy initiative described there concerning the CBC's national unity role, interprets the phrase "contribute to the development of national unity" as meaning that CBC must be "consciously partial to the success of Canada as a united country with its own national objectives" — an interpretation taken from the 1974 CRTC decision to renew CBC's licences. In the very same passage, however, the CBC is enjoined to maintain "the highest standards of professional journalism", — which presumably includes the privilege to operate without CBC's journalists having to be consciously partial to anything except scrupulously responsible journalism.[8]

Confronted with this conflict, we question whether the national unity provision adds anything to the neighboring provision for a "continuing expression of Canadian identity". Given the historical background, it would appear to restrict rather than enhance this broad cultural mandate by placing a prior obligation on CBC journalists to practice in a certain way — as a propaganda service, a cynic might say.

Recommendation

The provisions that the national broadcasting service be predominantly Canadian in content and character, and that the service provide for a continuing expression of Canadian identity, should be left intact in new legislation. The provision that the national service contribute to the development of national unity should be rescinded and replaced by a more socially oriented provision, for example, that the service contribute to the development of national consciousness.

We have already discussed the background to the 'balance' question in radio and TV. American programs and American program styles, in both radio and television, are more than adequately represented. Indeed, the balance has for many years weighed heavily against Canadian programming. No amount of regulation or incentive applied to the private sector will effectively redress the balance in favor of domestic program-making. We are therefore led inexorably to the conclusion that the CBC must henceforth give Canadians balance and diversity across not the whole range of programming, as previously required, but rather across the whole range of *Canadian* programming.

Recommendation

The Act should require the CBC to cover the whole range of Canadian programming in fair proportion, while offering Canadians the best of international radio and television that is not normally available.

The third broad principle, that of geographic universality, embodies two objectives — extension of coverage and regional reflection — which conceal a host of operational complications. For example, the question of coverage in itself seems pretty straightforward, but on closer examination there are at least five issues which, taken together, would seem to indicate the need for a recasting of the coverage provision: the availability of public funds; the financing of new, satellite-delivered specialty services; the technical means of signal distribution; the differences in the status of radio and television; and the role of CBC's affiliated stations.

The expression "as public funds become available" in section 3 (g) (ii) has been treated for some years as bureaucractic paraphrase of *Waiting for Godot*. All of the policy objectives that constitute the CBC's mandate have depended on the availability of public funds, and in many cases additional funding has not been forthcoming, even for initiatives proposed by the government itself such as increasing Canadian content on television.

Expansion based on availability of public funds is also out of step with the development of certain new CBC services as we envisage them. The original idea behind the coverage provision was that Canadians had the right to receive basic radio and television service regardless of place of residence (but in such a huge country with its scattered population even this right was not fiscally unqualified). As noted earlier, the CBC's six basic or main networks are: English television, Mono and Stereo radio, and French television, Mono and Stereo radio.

Over the next several years, the CBC may introduce one or more new services in both radio and television, intended for reception not by the general population but rather by individual subscribers through cable systems or perhaps direct broadcast satellites. It is our view that new services such as cable-audio classical music or all-news television should be sharply distinguished from the basic or main networks as far as financing and right of reception are concerned. New services will entail an additional expense to the consumer to help make them self-sustaining, but the objective should be to make such services as widely available as possible.

Such services should not be expensive or unduly limited in their potential coverage. There are circumstances where signals must be scrambled in order to obviate payment or rights problems but the principle of reasonable access should still hold good.

We believe that the national service should be encouraged to exploit the newest distribution technologies whenever this will result in wider coverage, better reception or financial savings. This would extend the sense of the provision in section 3 (j) that "the regulation and supervision of the Canadian broadcasting system should be flexible and readily adaptable to scientific and technical advances".

The differences between radio and television coverage, and the issue of the CBC affiliates, are discussed in detail in a later section. The present coverage provision does not recognize the contrast between television coverage, which is very nearly at saturation, and radio coverage, which falls well short in both English and French stereo services and leaves much to be desired on the mono side, in terms of reception quality and accessibility by means of cable. The role of the television affiliates, and the few remaining radio affiliates, has a bearing on coverage. While in some respects this constitutes an operational rather than a legislative problem, we think there is an important principle at stake, namely the ability or willingness of all affiliated stations to transmit the full network schedules to their audiences, another issue we take up later.

Recommendation

The Broadcasting Act should require that the national service be extended to all parts of Canada, by the most appropriate technical means, and in a way that brings the full schedules of the six basic networks as close as possible to full audience coverage. The CBC should also be allowed to develop new specialty services for both radio and television as both opportunity and Canadian audience needs dictate.

We referred earlier to a second aspect of geographic universality, namely regional reflection, which is distinct from the coverage principle in that it promotes the idea of programming originating in the regions as well as flowing to the regions from the centre. It is linked in the Act and operationally as well to provision of service in both languages. Thus section 3 (g) (iii) provides that the national service should "be in English and French, serving the special needs of geographic regions, and actively contributing to the flow and exchange of cultural and regional information and entertainment". By and large the regional issues — the future deployment of plant and human resources, access to the network and so on — are operational in nature and do not necessitate any substantive change in the provision as it stands. There seems no reason, however, to drop "enlightenment" from its association with "information and entertainment" when we speak of the regions, as the Act now does.

The Act should enshrine certain rights of service for speakers of Canada's major aboriginal languages. For many years, the CBC has performed a valuable public service in the operation of its Northern Service by broadcasting in several Amerindian languages and Inuktitut. This service addresses a relatively small population and is somewhat limited by the availability of production funds, technical resources and personnel.

But for the native audiences in question, these broadcasts are not only a link to other similar communities and to the outside world, but a bulwark against the erosion of their languages and cultural values. Assurance must be given that reasonable service will continue in the representative languages. This means that explicit provision should be made for native-language broadcasting in the mandate of the national service.

Recommendation

> The Broadcasting Act should affirm the right of native peoples to broadcasting services in aboriginal languages considered to be representative where numbers warrant and to the extent public funds permit (see also ch. 20).

We come finally to the seventh proposition in the CBC mandate, that "where any conflict arises between the objectives of the national broadcasting service and the interests of the private element of the Canadian broadcasting system, it shall be resolved in the public interest but paramount consideration shall be given to the objectives of the national broadcasting service". This is a provision to which we react with a certain ambivalence. On the one hand, it embodies an important principle, whose expression in the legislation has in a number of contentious cases obliged the regulator or the courts to put the interests of public broadcasting first. On the other hand, it is widely recognized that in many other instances the principle has been ignored or even flouted. We are, however, reluctant to forego at least the degree of protection afforded by this provision.

We draw two conclusions concerning the "paramount consideration" provision. On the one hand, the spirit of this provision will have to be realized in large measure through structural and regulatory changes, rather than through a mere redrafting of the provision. On the other hand, however, a slight recasting could reinforce the encouragement afforded Canadian programming.

Recommendation

The Broadcasting Act should provide that "paramount consideration" be given to the objectives of the national broadcasting service, and in particular the funding, production and scheduling of Canadian programming of all types whenever these are in conflict with private interests.

To sum up, we suggest that the CBC's mandate be cast in the following manner:

- The CBC's services should remain predominantly Canadian in content and character, but should not be expected to be partial to the development of Canadian unity.
- The CBC should offer a balance from the whole range of Canadian programming. It should not be expected to provide foreign programming that is readily available from other Canadian broadcasters, but it should provide the best of foreign programming not otherwise accessible to Canadians.
- The six core CBC radio and television networks should be made available to as many Canadians as possible by technical means that enhance quality and coverage while minimizing costs.
- The CBC should provide the fullest possible service to official language minorities, as part of its functions as broadcaster of last resort. These functions should also explicitly include provision of broadcasting services in representative aboriginal languages.
- Policy and regulatory decision-making should give paramount consideration to the role of the national service in the production and exhibition of Canadian programming.
- In a later part of this chapter, we argue for inclusion of two other provisions: that CBC radio and television services be allowed to develop separately; and that the three main 'non-mandated' services (Parliamentary Network, Radio Canada International, Northern Service) be given explicit mention in the legislation. Finally, in Chapter 8 we urge that CBC's French services be recognized as having a special role to play, different from that of CBC's English services, and that CBC's French and English services therefore be allowed to develop separately.

The Radio Networks

Like many other Canadians, we applaud the achievements of CBC Radio. The CBC radio networks perform a unique and irreplaceable service for the nation. In part because it has traditionally faced no competition from American radio and in part because program costs are relatively modest, CBC Radio is cast in a flattering light when compared to its beleaguered television counterpart. In fact, radio has been successful in doing what television, English television at least, has not — creating a service that is unmistakeably Canadian and celebrated for being as good as any radio service in the world. It has achieved that most elusive of goals: striking a balance between popular programming, including survival information, comedy, sports and so on, and programming for a range of minority tastes, in classical music, jazz, documentaries and drama. Despite these achievements, however, CBC Radio must cope with dwindling resources, imperfect coverage of the country and uncertainties about its program mandate and administrative structure.

Before examining these more detailed issues, we would make one general point in relation to support for CBC Radio. CBC Radio has achieved a kind of motherhood status — heaping praise on the national radio networks is the rule rather than the exception. The 1985 revamping of some of the radio services, especially English Stereo, may have weakened long-standing loyalties. Some harsh words were directed at CBC management by members of the public and others for attempting to create a more popular program schedule, appealing to a younger audience. We too are concerned that the CBC preserve the distinctive and unique qualities of all its radio services so that choice is not diminished, even though we do not wish to intervene in matters of taste.

Our examination of CBC documents shows that in many regions, radio operations have been cut progressively closer to the bone. Praising CBC Radio while reducing its resources puts the decision-makers in an awkward position. CBC Radio needs more than lip service paid to its virtues; it also needs some reasonable assurances that it will be allowed to maintain at least its present levels of service, rather than risk becoming the poor cousin to television, which gets lavished, if not with praise, at least with the devout attention of the policy-makers.

Recommendation

> The main CBC radio services should at a minimum be spared any further budget cuts, in order to allow CBC radio to function to the highest creative and technical standards.

The Radio Mandate

The different treatments of television and radio are ironic, given that the present mandate of the national broadcasting service makes no distinction between them. Whatever the original intentions of the legislator may have been, the apparent assumption that the goals of radio should be indistinguishable from those of television now makes little sense. It would make even less sense to chart a course for CBC Radio over the next 10 to 15 years that took no account of the differences between it and CBC Television.

These differences can be summarized as follows:

Centralization vs regionalism Television production by its very nature is a more centralized activity, requiring a certain level of both technical resources and personnel — often referred to as the 'critical mass'. Radio, being both less costly and less technically complex, and a portable medium at the listener end, is much better suited to covering local concerns. As a result, CBC Radio incorporates regional production and utilizes regional resources to a much greater extent than CBC television. Almost 70 percent of the English radio schedules and 25 percent of the French radio schedules depend on regional production centres. The proportions of regional television production broadcast either locally or on the networks are much lower.

Independent vs in-house production Television production lends itself more readily to contracted-out or collaborative production, and the independent television production sector has become an important source of drama and documentary programming. This is not the case in radio because, apart from the CBC, there are simply no profitable markets for the specialized radio programming the CBC does, nor are the requisite production resources always available in the private sector, except for musical recording facilities.

Competitive environment The single greatest obstacle to the creation and acceptance of Canadian television programming is the presence on a massive scale of American television programming (this is a problem for French television as well as English because of the reported loss of Francophone viewers to English station groups and the viewing of dubbed American programs). CBC Radio suffers from no such competition. Although there is tremendous demand for American musical content on Canadian commercial radio stations of almost every type, the CBC's non-commercial format and unique programming have largely insulated radio from the competition television experiences in the marketplace. The CBC's spoken-word programming is almost exclusively Canadian. It serves an audience, or audiences, that represent only a minority share of the listenership but have proven loyal over time, and the CBC can continue to serve these interests economically because production costs are only a small fraction of costs for the production of television dramas and documentaries. If a Canadianization issue exists in radio, it has to do with the high levels of European content in the serious recorded music programs heard on the CBC networks.

Coverage CBC Television is available to about 99 percent of the viewing public even though problems exist in both local services and distribution through affiliates. The television service is also made available as a priority, by regulation, on every cable system in the country. Radio does not enjoy the same privilege. Stereo coverage falls well short at 72 percent of anglophones and 76 percent of francophones. The stereo networks are now available by satellite to all cable systems in the country, increasing potential coverage of English stereo radio to roughly 86 percent of all Canadians and French stereo radio to about 83 percent. No reliable figures are available for the audiences to CBC Stereo captured by cable, as opposed to off-air, but it would appear that there is little increase in the audience.

The CBC Mono services present a different problem. Techically they too cover 99 percent of the population, like television, but CBC's AM signals face two obstacles. First, in built-up areas an electronic fog created by microwave and other broadcast signals, data transmission and so on, has made it increasingly difficult to assure clear off-air reception from local CBC transmitters. The presence of high-rise buildings can make interference so serious that in Toronto, Canada's largest English market, a significant proportion of potential listeners cannot receive CBC-AM clearly off-air. Second, cable operators are not required by regulation to carry local AM signals as a priority, which means CBC Mono often cannot take advantage of the improved reception afforded by cable carriage.

A further complication arises from deployment of the 'service de base', the mixed French radio service described earlier. It attempts to make up for the stereo coverage shortfall by adding a package of stereo programming to the mono service in the evenings (broadcast on the AM band in mono). Both the problem and the solution are of course unique to CBC Radio.

We have therefore concluded that the role of CBC Radio in the provision of a national broadcasting service must be viewed as substantially different from that of television, at least as the system is presently constituted. But more important, we believe that the differences we have highlighted between radio and television, as well as certain consequences of these differences, should be reflected in a new mandate for the CBC.

Recommendation

New broadcasting legislation should specify that the CBC is responsible for providing both radio and television services. The legislation should provide scope for CBC radio and television, English and French services, to develop on the basis of different program mandates, audiences and financial needs.

Over and above these special differences, we do not wish to lose sight of one basic idea. As we noted above, the CBC has succeeded in serving a series of minority audiences with specialized programming. While it is a difficult challenge, we feel strongly that CBC radio must continue to program to a wide range of minority audiences. We therefore agree with the CBC's general strategy to concentrate information programming on what is termed Radio 1 — the Mono network — and musical and dramatic performance programming on Radio 2 — the Stereo Network.

Radio Affiliate Replacement

Reliance on the CBC's affiliated commercial stations has created problems for both radio and television, though to a much greater extent in TV. This is in part because the CBC implemented the Radio Affiliate Replacement Plan (RARP) over a decade ago, whereby dozens of affiliates were replaced with transmitters. Because of budgetary restraint, however, the RARP has been suspended, leaving only ten English radio affiliates and seven French.

Affiliate replacement has had its disadvantages, apart from capital and maintenance costs for new transmitters. The most noteworthy is the significant loss of audience caused by the disappearance of local service in those communities where affiliates have been replaced by transmitters. Some disruptions were also caused by the fact that FM transmitters were chosen as replacements because of their technically superior performance and lower cost compared to AM transmitters. According to the CBC, much of the lost audience has now been recaptured; and, as explained in Chapter 5, the FM share of listening has been rising sharply over the past several years. The CBC estimates that the total capital cost of replacing the remaining 17 radio affiliates with transmitters would fall between $5 and $6 million.

The Task Force believes it would be wise to complete the RARP. Although the erection of transmitters is not a perfect solution in itself, we have evidence not only of improved service to CBC listeners once they are able to get the full Mono network on the FM band, but also of improved operating conditions for many of the affiliates once they are released from their CBC service obligations.

Recommendation

Both English and French CBC radio services should receive sufficient funding to allow them to proceed with completion of the Radio Affiliate Replacement Plan.

Cable Distribution

CBC stereo signals are now available by satellite to all cable systems in Canada. CRTC Cable Television Regulations require that cable operators carry the local CBC FM signal in the majority language as a matter of priority, but do not require that they carry the local or regional CBC AM signal when both signals are in the same language. In a large cable system in southern Ontario, for example, about half of more than 30 FM stations delivered by the operator are of local origination, including CBC FM. Of the rest, a little more than half are regional Canadian signals, and a little less than half, or one-quarter of the total, are American FM stations. The main urban market served by this same operator, who does not carry CBC AM, is Toronto where, as noted earlier, a significant proportion of the population is deprived of adequate reception of CBC AM because of interference. These signals could be remodulated at cable head-ends for distribution with other signals on the FM band. If carriage of CBC AM signals were assured by regulation in all areas served by cable, quality of coverage would be greatly enhanced in densely populated areas suffering from interference problems, and in other areas not served, or poorly served, by the mono services using conventional transmitters. Consideration should be given to including regional signals in such a requirement, in addition to local signals, as defined in the regulations.

Recommendation

The CRTC should amend its Cable Television Regulations to require cable operators to carry as a priority not only the CBC Stereo (FM) signal, but also the CBC AM Mono or Stereo signal, along with appropriate subcarriers, regardless of whether these signals are available from a local or regional source, or by satellite.

CBC and Private Radio

The suggestion that the local presence of CBC Radio service should be enhanced by cable carriage may not sit well with some of Canada's private radio broadcasters. A number of them made representations to the effect that CBC was competing — unfairly — with AM radio in many markets and cutting into profits by taking away listeners. The Task Force was therefore asked to recommend that CBC radio be required to withdraw local services such as news and weather during peak radio listening hours and to adopt a less commercial, less locally oriented format in order to reduce alleged duplication of service.

As noted in Chapter 5, the Task Force does not conclude that CBC radio is duplicating local AM service in any significant way. In the first place the nature of the CBC's programming is, by and large, qualitatively different. Moreover, it is possible that the presence of CBC news and information services, particularly in smaller markets, acts as an incentive to the private radio broadcasters to keep their own news departments operating to a high standard. Research commissioned by the Task Force found significant differences between the importance accorded news on CBC and private radio stations, and demographic differences between their respective audiences.[9]

It should also be noted that a listener to CBC is not necessarily a listener 'lost' to private radio, as was suggested during some of our consultations. This assumes that a listener to one station never listens to any others. While many radio listeners do have a favorite station to which they may tune almost exclusively, research examined by the Task Force clearly demonstrates that in the case of CBC stations this exclusive audience is very small, compared to the 'duplicated' audience which listens to commercial stations as well. In the fall of 1985 this exclusive CBC audience ranged from 2 percent to 18 percent of CBC listeners, depending on the market.[10]

Another suggestion brought to our attention was that the CBC syndicate some of its spoken-word radio programming to commercial station groups for rebroadcast.[11] As far as we are aware, no details have been worked out for such a scheme, but in principle it would seem to have distinct advantages. It would give Canadian commercial radio stations access to a much wider variety of current affairs, documentary and dramatic programming than is currently available outside the CBC. It would also raise the public profile of the CBC among audiences which might otherwise never tune to CBC radio. Finally, it would give greater exposure to the creative personnel involved in the production of any such syndicated programs.

Depending on pricing arrangements, production personnel could also realize greater income from syndication, in the form of step-up or residual payments. We believe the principle of cost recovery should be applied. The CBC should recover all incremental costs entailed in releasing a radio program into syndication, rather than subsidizing its use by the private sector. Some distinction might also be made between re-use with commercials and re-use without.

One other consideration is the timing of re-use. It would be counter to the Corporation's interests to have its local market competitor run topical programming such as a newscast in the same general time-period as a CBC station, let alone simultaneously. Some safeguards would have to be built in to prevent competitive use of syndicated programs. The CBC has gained a little experience at giving other broadcasters the opportunity to use its programming by making a non-commercial arrangement with American Public Radio, the publicly-funded American network, which distributes *As It Happens* to over 30 public radio stations in the United States and *Sunday Morning* to over 45 stations.

Recommendation

> The CBC Radio service should study the potential for syndicating some of its best radio information and performance programs to commercial stations for rebroadcast in markets where a demand exists. The scheme should be planned on a cost-recovery basis, with the best possible financial terms being negotiated for the personnel whose work is to be re-used.

The 'Storefront' Solution

The CBC English service proposes to enhance its information coverage in areas that may receive the Mono signal, but are unable to receive local news because they are served not by a CBC station but only by a transmitter. A small news staff would be assigned to a particular locality with facilities to produce a few weekly hours of news and information programming centered on that locality.

An operational proposal from English radio identifies 19 critical areas where this improved service would be warranted. They were selected by considering population, public expectations, alternative media services and so on. CBC has estimated that the total capital costs would be about $5.4 million over five years. Production costs over the same period would be about $7.6 million — in other words, about $13 million to bring local information services to English Canadians in 19 underserved areas of the country in the initial five-year operational period. A similar strategy for French radio is discussed below.

Recommendation

> Funding for CBC English radio should be sufficient to allow it to proceed with its proposed storefront strategy.

Stereo Extension

We have already noted that the CBC stereo networks fall well short of full coverage of either the French-speaking or English-speaking audience. Stereo extension, like many other expansion plans, has a high priority. The costs are substantial, but would bring benefits to many Canadian communities. The CBC does not propose to create new stations — this would be prohibitively expensive — but rather to ensure local distribution by either conventional methods or, in many cases, by satellite transmission to local transmitters. This technique is increasingly available and has helped reduce costs of distribution.

For its part, English radio has a long-range plan for 139 new transmission projects costing some $37 million. Distribution would range from centres as large as Victoria, B.C. to those as small as Corner Brook, Nfld. Taken together, these projects would achieve over 96 percent coverage, meaning that every community of at least 5,000 people of the appropriate mother tongue would be covered.

To start, the CBC has proposed a five-year implementation plan, involving only 31 projects for a total capital cost of about $10 million. It is estimated that these new transmitters would increase coverage from 72 percent to 82 percent or more. (Exact targets are difficult to specify, because of complex federal requirements concerning physical siting of equipment, operating power and methods of calculating audience covered.) The Task Force regrets the fact that centres as large as Victoria and Charlottetown are without the English stereo service.

Recommendation

Funding for CBC English radio should be sufficient to allow it to extend the Stereo service gradually over a five-year period, with a view to ensuring as complete a coverage pattern as is practicable, utilizing satellite technology to the fullest possible extent.

The 'Service de base'

As described earlier, the 'service de base' offers a mix of information and cultural programming to francophone listeners who receive only one of French radio's two main networks. It is referred to as the 'basic service' ('service de base') because it contains at least a sampling of almost every program type produced by the CBC, and is transmitted throughout most parts of Canada. Programming is from the Mono network during the day and from the Stereo network in the evening, but the service is not delivered simply by switching between the two network feeds. It is built up program-by-program and thus differs from each of the main networks.

There are only six centres which receive both French radio networks: Moncton, Rimouski, Chicoutimi, Quebec City, Montreal and Ottawa-Hull. In all other regions, listeners receive the 'service de base', but they may do so on either the AM or FM band depending on local conditions. As we have noted, the AM service is distributed in some regions through FM transmitters, which are less expensive to build and maintain than AM transmitters.

The CBC's attempt to bring a reasonable level of radio service to francophones throughout Canada is admirable. We believe, however, that it is an appropriate and justifiable use of public funds to bring CBC's full core services to linguistic minorities of a certain minimum size. We believe further that the French Stereo service should be extended at the earliest possible time to the dozen or so major centres having a francophone population of 40,000 or more.

These projects are contemplated in the CBC's Five-Year Capital Plan. Together, they would require a capital outlay for transmitters of some three million dollars and annual operating costs of about $265,000. A number of smaller FM stereo projects for settlements of at least 5,000 inhabitants have been discussed as part of a long-term extension plan.

Recommendation

Funding for CBC French Radio should be sufficient to allow it to extend the Stereo service gradually over a five-year period, with a view to dismantling the 'service de base' as the full two-network service becomes available in each region.

Extension of both French and English radio service has been in abeyance for some time because of budgetary restraint. We would not therefore expect any of the smaller projects, or all of the major projects, to be carried out in the very near future. We are fully aware that the CBC's capital priorities have focussed on plant and equipment obsolescence in major facilities, and that existing services, whether in French or English, cannot be put at risk for the sake of coverage expansion projects.

Nevertheless, we wish to have it plainly established as a matter of principle that the CBC is responsible for providing basic service as widely as possible, including service to linguistic minorities, despite the uneconomic nature of such efforts. We are reluctant to propose incremental funding for what the CBC itself cannot make a first priority, but we feel the gradual extension of FM Stereo should not be pushed aside while the CBC and the central federal agencies grapple with the accelerating problems of obsolescence at existing facilities across the country.

The Television Networks

Canadianizing CBC Television

As we have noted elsewhere, we believe that CBC's English and French networks must both be part of a programming renaissance in Canadian television. We argue in Chapter 8 for a new perspective in French-language television, one which acknowledges that Quebec, too, has been experiencing some concern over the share of viewing hours devoted to Canadian-made programs. In the perennial struggle for a self-respecting Canadian culture, however, the most visible battleground is English television. It is here that the American cultural invasion has left its mark most clearly. It is here that our policy-makers have tried continually to shore up Canadian strength in both supply and demand. We therefore concentrate in the next several sections on the policy and financial issues relating particularly to English television. In Chapter 29 we recapitulate the whole question of the costs of our CBC-related recommendations, including those to be incurred by the further Canadianization of CBC's French television network.

We have already discussed the principle that public funds should not subsidize the presence of popular American television programs that are already available from other station groups on Canadian screens. The CBC suggested in its brief to us that it should aim to remove the remaining 5½ hours of mainstream American shows from the English weekly prime-time schedule by September 1987.[12]

We are in general agreement with this proposal, but with one or two reservations. First, policy-related discussions inevitably focus on prime time, at the expense of other times of day which tend to get overlooked when program philosophies are being analyzed. We would point out that there are other significant periods, such as the late afternoon when many children are watching television, for which little appropriate Canadian fare has been made available. The great obstacle here, as elsewhere, seems to be cost.

Before examining costs, which the CBC's submission to this Task Force unfortunately does not do, one more general comment might be appropriate concerning how we interpret a balanced range of Canadian programming. When we suggest that the CBC ought not to make a special effort to supply programs that are abundantly available elsewhere, we refer in particular to American programs. We do not mean to suggest that CBC should necessarily withdraw from program services that happen to be duplicated by the private sector. Some commentators would like to see sports programming, among other things, pulled from the CBC networks so that the CBC can concentrate on more specialized forms of programming. We believe that both professional and amateur sports play a legitimate cultural role in our society and therefore deserve to be part of a mainstream public television service. The CBC has done a creditable job of bringing Canadians a wide cross-section of sports some of which, such as a college or regional events, are not commercially profitable.[13] The CBC should not be steered away from this service role in any rewritten mandate. A number of broadcasters have also expressed alarm about what they see as encroachment on local news services by both CBC radio and television, to the detriment of private sector profitability.

We remain convinced, however, that CBC television must continue to provide all Canadians with free, off-air services of wide popular appeal — programming that offers a balance of Canadian fare to suit all tastes. This means CBC television should not be asked to confine itself to whatever minority material would fill in the gaps left by private television. Such a 'by default' program philosophy would be a disservice to the public, as well as to CBC programmers, whose plans would be subject to the whims of the commercial marketplace.

What, then, would be distinctive about CBC television if it did basically what the privates do, with the exception of importing American shows? In large measure, of course, what would be distinctive would simply be that CBC offered primarily Canadian rather than foreign programs at all times of the day, including peak viewing time. However, this raises as well the question of whether the CBC should strive to be as popular as possible, programming for what is sometimes referred to as the lowest common denominator. We are resolutely opposed to a philosophy that would drive out specialized or limited appeal programming such as theatre or symphony performances on the grounds that the audiences for such programming are small and would force down CBC's ratings. On the contrary, a balanced service must include minority as well as popular programming. The success or failure of the CBC cannot be measured strictly in audience numbers. The Corporation must dare to be different and distinctive by tackling all kinds of program challenges — Canadian program challenges.

The Costs of Canadianizing

The costs of Canadianizing the English television schedule must be looked at in three ways. First, how much of the schedule is to be Canadianized: prime time only or the entire schedule? Second, what kind of programming replaces the American: expensive drama or less expensive current affairs or variety? Third, what is the impact on advertising: must CBC sustain large losses or can attractive Canadian shows keep rates up?

According to our calculations, Canadianizing even prime time alone will be expensive. Our calculations are based on several assumptions. The first is that the prime-time programming in question will in most cases be drama (in the broad sense) or other material produced by independents and eligible for Broadcast Fund funding. While this will appear to reduce the incremental cost of the replacement Canadian programs, the subsidy from the Broadcast Fund is of course a further charge on the taxpayer, even though it does not appear as part of the CBC's own budgets.

Another aspect of this cost-sharing is the ratio of the contributions of the CBC, the Broadcast Fund and the producer. Although this matter is taken up again in the chapter on the Broadcast Fund, we should point out here that we find the prevailing ratio unsatisfactory. Historically, the CBC has paid very low licence fees — the fees, as we explained earlier, paid by a broadcaster to 'licence' the telecast one or more times of a procured program or series. Before the Broadcast Fund, CBC fees typically represented about 20 percent of total program budgets, a figure that the industry considered completely unsatisfactory. By contrast, typical network licence fees in the United States have run traditionally around 80 percent of budgets.

The CBC's problem was that neither its appropriation nor its earned revenues could justify consistently higher fees, at least not for a substantial volume of independent production. Even with the Fund in place, the CBC's contribution during its involvement has, according to our figures, held steady at roughly 20 percent of budgets averaged over all CBC productions subsidized by Telefilm. We consider this unacceptably low, for two reasons. First, it sets a poor standard for broadcasters participating in the Fund and diminishes the importance of the first sale in the Canadian market. Second, even with Broadcast Fund participation at 49 percent for designated projects, producers are still left to find roughly one-third of their budgets elsewhere. The implications of this pattern of financing are looked at in more detail in Chapter 14. We have concluded that sound public policy requires that the average CBC licence fees for projects receiving support from the Broadcast Fund rise to 40 percent, with matching funds provided from the Broadcast Fund up to 35 percent, leaving on average only 25 percent for the producer to raise from 'second windows' and international sales.

To return to the question of Canadianizing English prime time, we assume that the CBC's licence fee or cost will be $300,000 per program, with average budgets at $750,000 per hour (this may be higher for mini-series and TV movies). We further assume that a full season comprises 22 original hours, with 22 repeat showings.

Each additional hour will then cost the CBC about $6.6 million per season, less the saving realized by discontinuing American purchases at about $2.5 million. The net additional cost per hour per season is therefore about $4 million (but could rise to $5 or even $6 million for material with particularly high — read 'expensive' — production values). The replacement of five full hours would total at least $20 million in program costs alone.

The real imponderable here is the potential foregone ad revenue. No one is in a position to predict this with certainty, but we feel that $30 million is a reasonable guess. Some analysts put the potential much higher — $50 million or even more. The actual outcome depends on several unknown factors such as the kind of material to be produced, how it is scheduled, how it is promoted and what the competition happens to be up to in the same time slots. The net annual cost of Canadianizing prime time could, therefore, be a minimum of $50 million, at least in the first year or two. Taking an optimistic view, ad sales might recover after an initial phase-in period, although increased ad revenues might have to be won at the cost of higher production budgets. However, if the tax incentive recommended in Chapter 29 is accepted it should substantially mitigate the loss of advertising revenues.

As for programs outside prime time, these could be replaced by similar Canadian programs for a total incremental cost of $5 million to $10 million, plus a possible revenue loss of about the same amount. None of these costs, however, takes into account the charges to the public purse associated with Telefilm Canada budget subsidies. These are discussed later.

We suggest that in any decision to phase out American programming on the English television schedule, the following points be considered:

- The phasing-out should not aim at the elimination of *all* foreign programs; room should be left in the schedule for some prime-time foreign programming to which Canadians normally do not have access.
- The replacement Canadian programming should not necessarily be designed to imitate American shows it replaces. CBC stands to defeat the whole purpose of the exercise if their Canadian productions are nothing more than surrogates for the American fare. Yet, to win audiences from the American competition they must be of high quality and may therefore be relatively expensive.
- The CBC should not be bound to September 1987 as a deadline for the phase-out. Availability of both funds and programming, as well as commitments to American suppliers, might make this unrealistic. Moreover, allowance must be made for the phase-out of non-prime-time programming as well, which could affect the overall timetable.

Recommendation

The CBC should gradually phase out the use of commercial American television programs which are readily available on other networks, but only when adequate funds are available to permit their replacement with attractive and distinctive Canadian programming.

The Multi-Channel Strategy

One of the principal aims of our deliberations has been to find ways to increase the availability of Canadian programming. We have approached this question from two angles: improving the proportion and scheduling of Canadian programs on existing services, and creating new services designed to be predominantly Canadian in content.

The advent of communications satellites has made the new services objective compelling. While entry costs are very high, particularly costs associated with satellite distribution, they are far lower than the distribution costs associated with a conventional network using broadcast transmitters. Nevertheless, even with special reductions or deferments on Telesat transponder rates the financing of satellite-delivered specialty or premium services on a commercial basis remains problematic in a market as small as English Canada, let alone French Canada. Despite the much-heralded technological miracles being wrought in communications, significant constraints also remain on the delivery of such services, because of cable plant capacity and the great uncertainties surrounding direct reception of satellite signals by the consumer.

In its submission to this Task Force, the CBC suggested half a dozen new projects as part of what is described as the 'multi-channel strategy'. These include CBC-2 and Radio-Canada 2 networks; a children's channel; a superstation to cover the United States, possibly out of Windsor; a "closer working relationship" with The Sports Network (TSN); and a Canadian news channel. Many of the programming ideas discussed as part of CBC's strategy are worthwhile, and promote the goals of increased choice and Canadianizing the airwaves. Unfortunately, any strategy involving so many new satellite services seems to us extravagant, particularly in light of the tug-of-war between resources and services that is already threatening the fabric of the Corporation.

We need to ask two questions about these proposed services. What would they cost? How important are they in fulfilling the CBC's mandate?

In Chapters 8, 13 and 18 we conclude that there is a limit to the number of specialty Canadian services that can provide a substantial proportion of well-funded, attractive Canadian programming as well as service in both English and French. For this reason we reject, for example, the idea of a dedicated Canadian children's channel on basic or extended basic service. Instead, we propose new non-commercial networks in both English and French which would include children's programming, but also other kinds of Canadian programming.

Other CBC proposals introduce financial questions of a different order. With regard to the TSN partnership idea, the CBC seems to have overlooked the fact that the cost of the rights to many sports properties would be prohibitive if TSN were distributed on basic or extended basic cable.

The CBC has also proposed a Canadian 'superstation' to be delivered by satellite to American cable operators, featuring Canadian programs from the CBC, the commercial broadcasters and independent producers. We are not aware of all details of this project, which is in development under the title of Northstar, the North American Television Network, but we would raise two cautions based on the information we do have.

We agree with the general principle of promoting Canadian programs in the American market and generating the best return for all participants. We note, however, that many traditional avenues exist for selling Canadian programs in the United States through licensing deals with established American independent and network broadcasters rather than through a separate satellite-to-cable network structure. We question whether these traditional avenues may not ultimately be more profitable than the proposed network and result in more viewing of Canadian programming in the United States.

Second, CBC resources are stretched thin and if our recommendations are followed the CBC will have still further responsibilities. The history of American cable networks is full of well-financed and well-promoted networks such as CBS Cable, which failed outright, and others which have had to accept mergers or a major repositioning in the market. Even the successful ones, such as CNN, lost tens of millions of dollars for several years before showing a profit. We are concerned about how much risk the CBC should be prepared to take. At the very least, the whole proposal needs a careful weighing of priorities among the CBC's many existing responsibilities. We wonder whether programming to the United States should be a very high priority for the Corporation at this time when many Canadians still cannot receive existing CBC services.

We do believe that Canada can afford two of the suggested new services. Indeed, we cannot afford *not* to have them. These are a second public noncommercial service and the news channel. We do not, however, recommend that both of them be developed as part of the CBC. We believe that the resources and energies of the Corporation must be dedicated primarily to making the existing television networks even better. We are persuaded that beyond this overriding responsibility, the only extra obligation that makes sense is the all-news channel, since the Corporation's experience and existing production capacity in this field are already so great. To add responsibility for two entirely new French and English networks, particularly the kind of networks we envision, seems to us an unreasonable extra burden to ask the CBC to assume. This by no means indicates, of course, that the CBC would not be an important program supplier to the new service. But we believe that the new public network should be independent and should be created by a consortium of its key players. This central element of our Report is elaborated on in Chapter 13.

The All-News Channel

The news channel, for its part, presents a whole other set of possible costs and benefits. We consider it unfortunate that the only round-the-clock news services available on Canadian cable systems — CNN and Headline News — are supplied out of Atlanta. These give virtually no coverage to Canadian news or points of view. Even Canada's own broadcast news services rely heavily — for the usual reasons of cost — on content from foreign networks and agencies. We agree with the CBC that "sovereignty in a country's information is critical to the conduct of its political culture".[14] We also agree with the CBC that it is well positioned to supply and operate such a service. The research discussed in Chapter 5 shows convincingly that Canadians are avid viewers of Canadian news.

There are many arguments for catering to this taste with another channel, particularly in English Canada. The CBC's existing news and current affairs services, *The National* and *The Journal*, often get pre-empted in their regular time slots by major league sports matches, especially during playoff periods. This is a scheduling dilemma that creates ill-will among at least some CBC viewers, no matter how the problem is handled. The all-news channel would assure viewers their news at its scheduled hour.

A news channel by definition does not have to compete with other kinds of programming that appeal to a different segment of the audience. On the other hand, all-news television has a related advantage in that it can interrupt its own regular programming to cover live breaking stories such as major accidents, crimes or natural disasters. It can also stay with lengthy planned events such as hearings or leadership conventions, giving greater coverage than the conventional networks.

A news channel would make a good complement to the existing CBC news structure. CBC reporters often have more material at their fingertips than their editors can use in ordinary newscasts. These reporters could double file by preparing short items for the regular news and then longer items from the same research or interviews, including perhaps an on-screen debriefing with an anchor or editor, for the news channel. While in no way wishing to impose production ideas on the CBC, we feel it is useful to give some indication of what an all-news service could add to the regular service.

The news channel could also act as a catalyst of change within the existing CBC services. It would give far more substantial openings to the regions than are currently available on the English network. Such a service could run successive news packages, perhaps parts of the supper-hour newscasts, from each of several regional centres over the course of the day. Such opportunities would allow the stations to develop new formats and program ideas, while providing a valuable second window for network current affairs programs like *The Journal*, *Venture* and *fifth estate*. By playing an active role in programming the new service, the smaller O and O stations — whose real strengths and budget commitments are presently in news — could operate on a more cost-effective basis. All of this could only boost morale at the CBC and enhance its service to Canadians.

One reason for the relative success of CNN in the United States has been its ability to cover international stories in many parts of the globe, thanks to an extensive network of foreign bureaus. Canadian television viewers have many windows on the international scene, but unfortunately a large number of them are foreign-supplied or foreign-controlled. The CBC cannot now afford to expand its foreign coverage by putting more of its own reporters in the field, thereby purchasing fewer items from the American networks and international agencies. We believe that a CBC all-news channel could provide the incentive and the funds to allow the CBC to expand foreign coverage.

Indeed, Canada's ability to field and maintain foreign correspondents has reached something of a crisis, according to testimony given to the Joint Commons-Senate Committee on External Affairs. Mark Starowicz, Executive Producer of *The Journal* and *Midday* told the Committee that no Canadian television network has a permanent correspondent in the Middle East, Africa or anywhere in this hemisphere south of Washington, D.C. The situation is little better in print journalism, at least in French, where, as Paul-André Comeau, a former CBC foreign correspondent, now Editor-in-Chief of *Le Devoir*, explained to the Committee, the number of foreign correspondents in the French-language media has dropped from 15 to four since the early 1970s. Ironically, over this same period Canadians appear to have taken a greater interest in international affairs, and business and tourism have both seen Canadian contact with the outside world growing.[15]

A CBC all-news channel should be planned and promoted not as another charge to the taxpayer but as a self-sustaining exercise. Our look at some preliminary models convinces us that this can only be achieved if the service is financed by both advertising and a small 'pass-through' charge to subscribers of no more than 25 cents per month. A fairly ambitious news channel could be operated on this basis for about $30 million a year, given ready access to existing CBC resources. But it should receive no funding beyond that which accrues from advertising and the pass-through charge.

Our scheme assumes that while the bulk of resources would be devoted to the English side of the service, which would be distributed on a dedicated channel, an appropriate share of the funds raised would also help create and sustain a partial French-language news service, to be distributed as part of the French Télé-Canada network. As we have argued at length in Chapter 8, Quebec's broadcasting problems, even when they resemble those of English Canada, do not necessarily call for precisely the same solutions.

A major reason behind this proposal is to provide an important new outlet for regional reporting. In the province of Quebec, regional journalistic resources are under-developed by comparison with those in the regions of English Canada. Our option has been to give priority to restructuring and consolidating the CBC's existing news resources in Quebec, with an emphasis on quality and equitable coverage. We think this is a necessary first step for Quebec. It is entirely possible, however, that once the consolidation of news resources in Quebec has been carried out along the lines suggested in both this chapter and Chapter 8, the French component of the news service might be allowed to develop more fully.

In the meantime, we would suggest that the fees invested in the all-news channel could be directed to the benefit of francophone viewers in two ways. First, a fair proportion of the news channel fee revenue should be reinvested in a daily French-language news service to operate on Télé-Canada. Second, we further suggest that the all-news channel should be the basis for an expanded network of foreign correspondents. They should all be bilingual, whether anglophone or francophone. These correspondents could, by mutual agreement, file stories or features with the CBC's main French news services and perhaps even documentary or magazine programs on the French TV Canada network. This would help amortize costs and would continue a trend started by the CBC at its Peking news bureau in which anglophone and francophone correspondents alternate, reporting in both languages.

Recommendation

CBC should seek from the CRTC a licence to operate an all-news and information channel, to be delivered by satellite to basic cable subscribers, and financed by both advertising revenue and a small pass-through fee to subscribers. This service should be operated by the CBC as a self-sustaining enterprise.

A New Balance in Regional Television

We came away from our consultations convinced that finding an appropriate role for regional television broadcasting is the most vexing single question in the current debate on the role of the CBC. It is also one of the most important. We began by examining the current state of affairs. The CBC made us aware of the manpower complements and budgets allocated to its various regional operations, as well as the volume of local, regional and network programming produced in each centre. Having reviewed these figures, we believe that resources must be concentrated not only by shrinking smaller stations, but also by rationalizing the operations of the key regional stations, though not necessarily by reducing their budgets or output.

In their submission to this Task Force the CBC asserts that "the regions must move more fully to the national stage". We agree. But to make their move the regions must get rid of some baggage. It is not enough simply to scale down the smallest stations and let the remaining ones carry on as though it were still 1970. The provincial or regional centres must help the CBC strike that elusive happy balance between the appeal of the centres of excellence, which would only stifle the CBC's regional roots, and regional demands to maintain or even extend costly physical plant. The time has come for the CBC to send out a psychological message — that it is prepared to re-examine its commitments to a certain level of facilities and even to certain kinds of programming for the sake of fewer hours of something more distinctive with higher production values and lower cost per viewer.

Local and Regional Production Centres

Most CBC TV stations were built as production centres with the expectation that when funds are available they will produce a range of programming beyond news and information, and sports. In the performance field, very few programs are actually produced at these stations. Reallocation of budget resources and changes in management structure in recent years — in other words, a continual whittling away of the regions as a priority in the CBC's diminishing world — have resulted in a CBC whose regional stations produce programs which are rarely seen on the national network.

This seems to us unsatisfactory. We express often in this Report our commitment to redressing the imbalance in both regional access to the broadcasting system and the obligation of the system to reflect the Canadian regions. It was an idea voiced repeatedly during our hearings across the country. The

Canadian regions may never be the full partners in the network system that they yearn to be, given realities of financing, production resources, and programming and scheduling needs, but we are determined they have a better share. While TV Canada, the all-news channel, Telefilm and the NFB all have a contribution to make towards this end, the role of the CBC itself must be central.

If further nibbles are taken from the regions, they will soon not be able to deliver even their supper-hour news shows. The pattern of more or less even cuts from each station whenever the knife next falls may seem equitable in theory but makes no sense for program production. By spreading already limited resources so thinly, it becomes impossible for the CBC regions to fulfil their mandate to reflect the regions to themselves and to one another.

We go further. We believe the regions must have access to more of the time now allocated to the network schedule. There must be more regional performance programming produced for the region itself. We eschew recommending precise scheduling or number of hours, since we have no intention of becoming programmers, and we understand too the financial implications of losing network time and therefore possible advertising revenues. But we want the principle of significant time for the purpose of telecasting regional performance programming to be firmly established. For too long have the regions had to live with empty promises. The fact that we do not choose to put a precise figure on the number of hours that must devolve to the regions must not be used as an excuse for tokenism by CBC decision-makers.

These regional changes cannot be accomplished without concentrating resources and putting into place administrative and financial structures which will allow meaningful regional production to develop. It is not possible for every CBC station to function as a large-scale production facility. It is possible, however, for every CBC station to continue providing local news, both supper-hour and late-evening versions.

As a Task Force we wrestled with a variety of scenarios which might make CBC English television more effective. We ran the gamut from considering the 'critical mass' or centres-of-excellence theory and centralizing production in Montreal and Toronto, to making the CBC a regional organization with establishment of a major production centre in the capital or principal city of each province, with a mandate to program for the network and to reflect the region it served. We looked at closing stations in some parts of the country, and even at various ways of creating centres of specialization across the country.

After much deliberation, we concluded that none of these alternatives was realistic. We therefore rejected them in favor of another scheme whereby the CBC's television resources across the country would be reorganized into a three-tier structure around the concepts of local, regional and national service. We believe that the existing O and O television stations should concentrate their resources into five major English production centres and four major French production centres. We describe these as 'regional', although they of course include the network centres in Toronto and Montreal. While the network centres would continue with their national programming responsibilities, they would be joined by the seven other English and French centres, identified below, in the production of major programs of all types, primarily for regional but also for national exposure. Other existing television operations would continue to provide a local news and information service, on a basis to be determined by CBC on journalistic grounds.

The question is how to determine the number of regional production centres that can do the regional job, and where they should be situated. The answers are to some extent arbitrary. There is no scientific formula which can be applied. But a number of criteria should be taken into account: cultural identity, demographics, population, CBC plant resources, CBC creative resources, other community resources and regional communication.

There are major political and emotional obstacles to our recommendation. People in every province want the CBC to produce all kinds of programs there. Politicians, even those often highly critical of the CBC, shout blue murder at the prospect of a station in their bailiwick being cut back, let alone cut out. That is why the CBC has never made these tough decisions. Nor would it be in any way appropriate for the government to do so. It seems, in the end, that it is a policy only a group like ours can advocate.

Our conclusions will not satisfy many legitimate arguments we have heard and wish we could have accommodated. We can see a case, for example, for a full scale production centre in Newfoundland, and equally a case for not lumping together B.C. and Alberta. In the end, however, our deliberations have led us to conclude that the least unacceptable method of rationalizing the production resources of English CBC TV would lead to the creation of five major production centres in five regional divisions.

Recommendation

The CBC's English television service should be reorganized into five regions: Alberta-British Columbia, Manitoba-Saskatchewan, Ontario, Quebec and Atlantic. Responsibility for all programming and production other than news and information, and sports — and the related facilities, management and infrastructure — should be concentrated in one centre in each region: Vancouver, Winnipeg, Toronto, Montreal, and Halifax, with each centre having responsibility to reflect its entire region. Other stations in each region should be limited to the production of news and information programs on a basis to be determined by the CBC on journalistic grounds, as well as for sports production in appropriate centres.

New Brunswick forms an exception to this pattern of consolidation, since it is the only province in Canada which does not have at least one English-language CBC television station. The CBC does have production facilities in Fredericton and maintains ENG crews in Saint John and Moncton, from which items can be fed to the Fredericton facilities.

The problem then lies not in production capacity, but in distribution. Under current arrangements, the CBC broadcasts a supper-hour news program from CHSJ, the affiliated station in Saint John. Since it has no other transmission facilities in the province, it can neither provide full coverage nor supply the full network service to the areas covered at present.

This unsatisfactory state of affairs poses a dilemma much like that concerning the extension of FM service. Anything less than full coverage for the CBC's main networks is unacceptable. Yet with the severe budget-cutting experienced by the regions in the last two years, extension of coverage cannot be treated as an absolute priority. Obsolescent facilities in many CBC locations cannot be ignored year after year. And in the particular case of New Brunswick, an upgraded English televison service has been something of a political football over the years with factors such as the number, location and cost of new transmitters being in dispute.

We feel it is our job to make a case for an upgraded service in New Brunswick, even if we cannot argue that it should take precedence over other technical projects, which is a job for the CBC and the central federal agencies. The CBC maintains that one desirable configuration would see 17 transmitters installed at a cost of anywhere from $10 to $13 million, with an additional $15 million needed for improvements to the Fredericton studio facilities. Annual operating costs for transmission would be roughly $1.5 million, which might be offset by the savings realized in terminating the present distribution agreement. Both supper-hour and late-night news shows could be produced under this new arrangement without the need for any new production personnel.

Recommendation

Every effort should be made by the CBC and other appropriate public agencies to support the upgrading of CBC's English television service in New Brunswick through the construction of new transmitters and facilities. The goal should be to ensure high quality local and regional newscasts and the widest possible availability of the full English television network service.

The principles we have applied to the English production centres would apply in the same fashion to their French counterparts, while taking into account the distinctive nature of French language broadcasting. Even though 90 percent of the French-speaking audience is concentrated in one province, the present configuration of CBC resources has meant that Quebec is poorly served in certain regions while some other provinces enjoy better French production facilities.

On the other hand, francophones outside Quebec have complained that the CBC's programming is too tied to life in Quebec and fails to address their own concerns adequately. The Task Force believes that the reorganization it has proposed will meet the expectations of all concerned as well as respect the integrity of the CBC's French network.

We believe these principles can be put into practice by concentrating production in four francophone centres in Eastern Canada, while maintaining a French news production capability elsewhere. The French supper-hour news programs across the country should be packaged from a syndicated feed from Montreal, along with local material. Newscasts could then be tailored to the needs and interests of each region, a process we understand is already underway at the CBC.

We would point out that our suggested rationalization of facilities will not result in large savings in most places. This is because in a number of centres certain staff, such as technicians, whose salaries are posted to French service budgets, actually spend much of their time working on English-language production, such as the supper-hour news. If staff such as these were released or transferred, costs would appear to drop in French television; but there would be a corresponding rise in many cases on the English side when departing French staff had to be replaced. Some of our other suggestions for French operations will entail new expenditures, in particular to achieve equitable French news coverage throughout Quebec and the Atlantic provinces. In any case, the provision of service to minority linguistic populations cannot be judged solely on factors such as ratings and cost per viewer.

Recommendation

The CBC's French television service should be concentrated in four centres, namely Montreal, Quebec City, Moncton and Ottawa. No major production other than news and information programming should take place in other centres. News coverage of the Atlantic provinces should be improved, out of Moncton, by opening some news bureaux in other parts of the region. Centres outside Quebec should be encouraged to provide a service more suited to local conditions.

CBC television operations within Quebec should also be improved in a number of ways. First of all, in order to concentrate production resources and clarify the role of the Quebec stations, non-journalistic television production at Matane, Rimouski and Sept-Iles should no longer be contemplated. Full production facilities should be maintained at the Quebec City station, in addition to Montreal. Operations in Eastern Quebec should be reorganized so as to make most efficient use of resources, and to improve news coverage in Gaspé.

Second, resources should be allocated to allow news coverage in three other important regions of Quebec which are currently not served by full-time journalists. These are Abitibi, Mauricie and Estrie (Eastern Townships). We would like to see funds devoted to the establishment of news bureaux in these three regions, on roughly the same scale of operations as the 'storefronts' suggested above in connection with English services.

Third, Chicoutimi has a CBC radio station but the surrounding region is not served by a CBC television newscast. A CBC-produced newscast could be prepared for transmission by the local affiliate on the model developed for the English service in New Brunswick. Radio news staff could be reassigned for this purpose without, we assume, a very large outlay for the necessary equipment and technical staff. All of these proposals should be developed as three- to five-year experiments subject to periodic review and renewal.

Recommendation

CBC's French television service should be reorganized within Quebec. The objective should be to maintain less ambitious facilities in all program areas except news and information, which should be supported by a more extensive and equitable network of journalistic staff throughout the main regions of the province.

Impact on Programming

The consolidation of regional centres has implications for future CBC service to small communities such as Corner Brook or Matane, which under our scheme might lose some of their present facilities. We have already suggested, however, that the sub-regional stations should in most cases operate on a reduced scale rather than be shut down. As news programming is the most important and cost-effective local station service, the reduced operation should concentrate more-or-less exclusively on news-gathering and presentation, along with the necessary master-control and transmission facilities.

English television already broadcasts regional news in this kind of format, reducing both cost and duplication of effort. Unfortunately, the sense of community that typifies a Maritime newscast out of Halifax is not likely to be achieved in the 'Ontario' region newscast that links Ottawa, Windsor and Toronto on weekends. It is, in other words, very difficult to introduce change in the structure of regional broadcasting by trying to apply one set of goals or principles across all regions, let alone across the two official language groups.

By redirecting resources from the operation of full stations the CBC might be able to provide better coverage of suburban and rural communities whose concerns often lie beyond its news-gathering capabilities. Improved coverage might be afforded by more reporters or by storefront news bureaus in small localities which do not now have a CBC O and O or affiliate. No local audience, under our scheme, would lose CBC television service. On the contrary, we think that our recomendations taken as a whole will make for a higher quality, more attractive service.

We have concluded that better production values, higher program quality, more economical use of resources and an improved image of the CBC as an institution that is willing to change with the times outweigh any possible disruptions that might happen to local television service or audiences.

The Toronto Broadcast Centre

Since we have had to grapple at some length with the problem of existing CBC plant, we would be remiss if we did not offer at least a brief comment about the Broadcast Centre, the proposed new CBC complex intended to consolidate all existing English and French radio and television facilities in Toronto. Anyone familiar with the CBC's plant in Toronto understands the reason for this project. Technical and administrative facilities, many of them woefully outdated and substandard, are dispersed across nearly two dozen sites, many of them widely separated. This Task Force has no capacity to judge either the priority the project deserves or the financial or architectural details of its execution. We are, however, concerned about how a project being developed on such a large scale is apt to be perceived by friends and critics of the CBC alike.

In a world where perceptions count for a great deal this idea could hardly have come at a less opportune moment, whatever its real merits. Across the country the CBC is being forced to cut back staff, services and new production because of budgetary restraint. This Task Force, for its part, is calling for a leaner physical infrastructure rather than unchecked growth. The two are not, of course, incompatible: a new centre could co-exist with a rationalized regional plant such as we have recommended. Yet, the perception may still persist that the CBC is racing in opposite directions at the same time.

This Task Force also has questions about the number and size of studios to be contained in the new facility. If the CBC's commitment is to transfer 50 percent of production to outside producers, where will that production be done? Private sector producers report that union agreements make it difficult or impossible to work in CBC facilities, particularly with outside technical staff. Indeed, if ways can be found to make CBC facilities available on competitive commercial terms to private sector producers, what will be the impact on existing and potential private sector services and facilities? We urge that these questions be given full and careful consideration.

Recommendation

The proposed Toronto Broadcast Centre should be considered in a way that is consistent with the revised mandate and operational principles recommended in this Report.

The Television Affiliates

For historical reasons discussed earlier, 31 French and English private television stations have an affiliation agreement with the CBC.[16] As with any similar affiliation agreement, the CBC pays these stations a certain proportion of network revenues in return for the valuable service of delivering almost 30 percent of the CBC's total television audience. Arrangements vary from station to station, but in 1985-1986 the CBC paid a total of $16 million to the affiliates from its network commercial sales revenue.

A second, non-financial cost of doing business with the affiliates is that no station carries the entire CBC service, on either English or French networks. In fact, some stations turn down as many as 30 hours of programs a week. The programming most likely to be rejected is innovative Canadian drama or current affairs. Some of the affiliates believe they can make higher profits by showing instead commercially oriented programming, normally American series. As business undertakings, their first responsibility is to their investors, not to Canada's social or cultural goals.

Thus the more the television schedule (particularly the English schedule) is Canadianized, the less attractive the CBC service will be to the affiliates, even if no attempt is made to rid the schedule of commercial breaks (which would be enough in itself to destroy the relationship). Hence the affiliates, though they are delivering a substantial audience, are not exposing it to the full Canadian schedule. Since this situation can only get worse if our other recommendations are followed, we must examine ways of mitigating the undesirable consequences of the affiliate agreements.

The least expensive way to replace the affiliates outright without loss of signal coverage would be by erecting rebroadcast transmitters. The capital cost of doing so is reported by the CBC to be $113.5 million. Operating costs would rise by $9.3 million annually, but at the same time CBC estimates its retained advertising revenues would rise by $27 million. This would leave a net operating surplus of nearly $18 million against which to amortize the required capital investment. In purely financial terms this does not seem a high price to pay for bringing the full CBC schedule to more than one in four of its viewers. (The proposal would thus cost about $14 per viewer in capital outlay.)

Unfortunately, the scheme has two serious drawbacks. One is the possibility that some of the smaller stations would fail if they disaffiliated, since they tend to be located in smaller and commercially marginal markets. The other is the certain loss of the local programming now provided by the affiliates. Few of the affiliates do any appreciable amount of their own programming but the one area where they do — news and 'survival' information, such as weather — would virtually disappear as a local service, since 19 of the 31 affiliates serve one-station markets.

No sweeping solution will be appropriate in all 31 of the markets at issue. As it happens, it is the largest of the English affiliates that transmit the lowest number of CBC network programs and therefore impair coverage to the greatest degree. These are the stations most likely to thrive on their own. At the time of writing, at least one had requested the CRTC to terminate its affiliation.

We therefore believe the only option is to approach the problem case by case, insisting that affiliates either carry the full network schedule at an agreed cost or have their agreement with the CBC discontinued. Several criteria should be used in applying this principle:

i Maximize coverage of the full network service. If an affiliate shows a willingness to negotiate a basis for phasing in the full service, this should be pursued. Otherwise, the relationship should be considered contrary to the public interest.

ii Minimize the cost to the taxpayer. The affiliates are, or will eventually be, a net drain on CBC's commercial revenues. This long-term cost must be weighed against the capital cost of providing other distribution, or purchasing distribution hardware from the affiliates themselves.

iii Protect local service. This valuable goal depends on preserving some relationship with the local affiliate. In the case of the few larger stations that have already indicated a desire to disaffiliate, this is not an issue.

iv Balance coverage of the public networks against the financial health of private stations. The public interest must in general take precedence. In practice this means the CBC might well strike short-term or even long-term agreements that benefit the affiliates. But this must not be at the expense of reasonably priced, full network coverage.

Recommendation

CBC should negotiate with its television affiliates to have them all phase in over time the full network schedule, without time-shifting, for what both sides deem to be reasonable compensation. Whenever an affiliate declines to do so, CBC should consider ensuring distribution by whatever means it sees fit, according to local market conditions.

Television Advertising

Advertising on CBC television militates against its being distinctive in a sea of look-alike commercial networks. This is not a new concern. In its 1974 CBC licence renewal decision, the CRTC wrote that "the CBC's commercial posture was not in keeping with its mandate to provide a national broadcasting service primarily supported with public funds". The Commission reported that intervenors at the renewal hearings had identified two major problem areas: "public annoyance at the frequency and inappropriate nature of commercial interruptions in programming, and the influence of commercial considerations on the selection and scheduling of programs for purposes of maximizing audiences".[17]

In a move that was ultimately to enhance both program quality and listener loyalty, the CBC ended the sale of commercial time on its radio networks in 1975. Although there have since been calls for CBC television to do the same, as by the Applebaum-Hébert Committee in 1982, we in fact received remarkably few submissions that saw the presence of advertising as a central concern. The simple truth, we concluded, was that few people believed it any longer realistic for the CBC to surrender its advertising revenues when no replacement revenues could be counted on.

Nevertheless, the advertising issue places the Task Force in something of a quandary, for we are concerned about the influence of commercial sales on production and programming decisions. As part of the merchandising strategies whose purpose is to expose the largest possible audiences to commercial messages for the lowest possible cost, television advertising often has an undesirable impact, such as formula program-making and avoidance of controversy.

We are, as the note of ambivalence must suggest, uneasy about perpetuating for the CBC all the dilemmas inherent in being a hybrid broadcaster, part public, part commercial. We do not wish to put temptation in the way of CBC programmers, since there is a natural tendency to want to increase advertising time in the expectation that the resulting increased revenue will eventually redound to the benefit of the program-makers. CBC itself fell victim to this very influence in 1984 when it ran the prestigious miniseries *The Jewel in the Crown*, and was discovered to have cut several minutes from the program in order to sell proportionately more commercial time. The program-maker's job, as we have already noted, is to make programs, not money. The CBC should thus observe the strictest possible separation between production decision-making and revenue decision-making.

Our surmise is that there have been real victims of the commercial ethos at the CBC. One of the most worrisome instances concerns the sharply declining coverage of live performing arts productions. We can only assume that this is directly related to the need to increase commercial revenues and cut costs. A case in point is the apparent failure to take any real advantage of the hundreds of annual performances by Canadian actors and musicians at the National Arts Centre in Ottawa. After managing to broadcast only five events for English television in 1982, the peak year, the level has fallen to a sole performance in all of the current year. In all, English and French television will each present no more than 20 arts telecasts in the 1986-87 season, only some of them original productions. We also note that in news and current affairs, there has been pressure to introduce ads or increase the number of commercial availabilities.

Despite our misgivings about possible harm to programming, we too believe it is unrealistic in today's circumstances to expect tax revenue to support the entire cost of the CBC's activities. Removal of all advertising would not only reduce net revenues by perhaps $150 million, but it would also cost several million dollars to fill the holes left in the schedule.

It is also worth noting that some kinds of programming would be difficult or even impossible to schedule without their advertising component. This is particularly true of professional sports, in which telecast rights or even teams are often owned by large advertisers such as the breweries. From a still wider perspective, a public broadcaster is perfectly free to pursue the best of both worlds in all kinds of programming, particularly drama, by combining high professional standards with popular appeal. Just because a program gets a large audience does not mean it cannot also be good. And if it gets a large audience it can, if properly sold to advertisers, bring in good ad revenues as well. Almost all program-makers, no matter how difficult or refined their material, usually want their programs seen by as many people as possible. Finally, it may be desirable to stipulate that additional earned revenues be earmarked for further Canadian production. We also believe the tax treatment of advertising on certified Canadian programs should be allowed an accelerated tax write-off, at a rate of 150 percent for example. These questions are explored further in Chapter 29.

Recommendations

The CBC should continue to generate commercial revenue by selling airtime on its television networks.

However, through policy statements, administrative structuring or other means, the CBC should exercise its best efforts to insulate production, programming and scheduling decisions from attempts to maximize commercial revenues.

Through its commercial acceptance policy and commercial scheduling practices, the CBC should also exercise its best efforts to minimize the disruptive qualities of on-air commercials, and to exclude or minimize them where appropriate, such as in children's programming.

The CBC and the Independents

We are pleased to note that the CBC's relationships with independent producers are much less fractious than they were even four or five years ago, when they profoundly influenced the recommendations of the Applebaum-Hébert Committee. We are also pleased to note that the long-standing controversy over whether the CBC or the independents are more 'efficient' seems to be a non-issue.

The Task Force consulted production departments in both English and French television and compared several sample productions, half in-house, half independent. At our initiative, we held two meetings in Montreal attended by representatives from both the CBC and the independent sector. We found throughout that difficulties stand in the way of making meaningful comparisons. No two dramatic or variety shows are the same in all respects. Moreover, the way CBC attributes indirect costs for its own overheads, as opposed to cash expenditures, is not analogous to the accounting categories used in private industry.

To the extent comparisons could be made, we saw no evidence of the private sector producing drama or variety specials, TV movies or series more 'efficiently' than the CBC — if by this is meant producing a certain kind of program at less cost. By the same token, we saw no firm evidence of the opposite — that the CBC was consistently more efficient thanks to alleged economies of scale. We conclude that decisions as to whether programs should be produced in-house or outside should be based on criteria other than the undemonstrated assumption that either party will manage production cost-control in a superior way.

We believe the still somewhat competitive relationship between the CBC and independent producers stimulates creative efforts. This advantage should not however, be allowed to obscure the goal of producing more and better Canadian television programs and bigger and better Canadian audiences for them. Otherwise, the CBC might be viewed not as the broadcaster of Canadian programs *par excellence* — surely its first responsibility — but merely as an instrument of industrial development, responsible for fostering the growth of the program production industry. Nothing in the CBC's current mandate suggests that the Corporation has any such responsibility. This is no reason, however, why producing more quality programming cannot strengthen the program industry and we believe the CBC should play a role towards that end.

It has been both government and CBC policy for some time that CBC television strive to procure more of its programs from independent producers, the ultimate goal being 50 percent of programming apart from information and sports. We agree that 50 percent is appropriate, and we note that the CBC intends to reach this goal by September 1987 (it has achieved a level of about 35 percent in English television at the time of writing).

It is essential that independent producers contribute, as the CBC mandate puts it, to a "continuing expression of Canadian identity". One of the unwelcome consequences of a purely quantitative or industrial approach to Canadian content is that television programs which qualify technically as Canadian under the CRTC point system are often indistinguishable from the American genres upon which they are modeled. We are confident that the CBC, when commissioning or licensing programs, will keep in mind that neither Canadian crews nor Canadian locations themselves necessarily imbue a television program with Canadian values or concerns.

Finally, we anticipate that new opportunities will be created for both the independents and the CBC by the advent of TV Canada, the second public network discussed in Chapter 13. Our proposal for TV Canada should go a long way to solving the dilemma of having only one domestic buyer for certain types of programs, provided also that the suggested arrangements for the CBC's collaboration with the private sector are put in place for a guaranteed minimum period of time, which in our view should be no less than 10 years. This arrangement should also have the happy consequence of providing a certain stability to the CBC in place of the insecurity that cutbacks and the consequent lay-offs and threats of lay-offs have created in recent years. That, in turn, should unleash the creative powers of the Corporation's staff which, in the end, are the real justification of public broadcasting.

Recommendation

> The CBC should pursue its policy of cooperation with private producers whereby 50 percent of television programming apart from information and sports will eventually be independently produced.It should be understood that the goal is the creation of a diversity of genuinely Canadian programs, not merely pursuit of an industrial policy aimed at fostering the growth of the production industry.

Non-Mandated Program Services

The *Broadcasting Act* does not specify that the national service must operate any particular configuration of networks nor does it indicate how many services there should be in each medium. Nevertheless, a clear distinction has developed between the main radio and television services in the two official languages and the so-called non-mandated services. The distinction is misleading to the extent that none of the CBC's services is explicitly given a mandate in the legislation. But the real issue is whether it is wise to allow national programming functions to develop without legislative provision. This tends to create two kinds of problems.

First, if a service such as the Parliamentary Television Network is not explicitly provided for by law, it becomes easier for those who fund or operate such services to downgrade or discontinue them. Second, and this is certainly the more pressing problem, the CBC has been expected to take on more and more responsibilities over the years, often without additional funds from government to pay for them. It is our view that adequate resources must be forthcoming once CBC's responsibilities have been defined.

Logic would therefore indicate two general measures. On the one hand, several non-mandated functions should be enumerated in amended legislation. On the other hand, some of these same functions should be continued under the budget of an agency or department other than the CBC, though we would naturally count on the existing personnel and resources of the CBC for actual operation of the services. The three principal services which should be accorded explicit mandates are: the Parliamentary Television Network, Radio Canada International and the Northern Service.

The CBC Parliamentary Television Network

The CBC's Parliamentary Television Network, often referred to as the 'House of Commons Channel', has the distinction of being Canada's first national satellite-to-cable network, featuring 100 percent Canadian content, with signal delivery in both official languages. It was originally licensed by the CRTC in 1980. While it is technically available free as a public service to all Canadian cable systems, not all systems carry it; of those that do, the vast majority make it available to subscribers only on the mid-band or converter service. As a result fewer than four million Canadian households are able to receive the service, whether in French or English.

Certain conditions imposed by the Speaker, as well as financial constraints, mean that the service contains only a minimum of contextual and explanatory material. Sessions are transmitted without interruption and no special or supplementary use is ordinarily made of the service's two leased satellite transponders during recesses, evenings, holidays and other downtime. The largest cost item in the roughly $4 million budget of the service is the leasing charge for the two transponders.

Despite these constraints and a relatively limited viewership, the Parliamentary Network makes a valuable contribution to public understanding of our most important national institution. We believe that the network could be put to even better use in the service of both Parliament and the people. Numerous suggestions have come from the CBC itself and from the Special Committee on Reform of the House of Commons. Our conclusion is that the service should be expanded in two ways: first by devoting more of the available time to transmission and second by broadening the range of its content.

An expanded service at a certain additional cost would certainly be in the public interest. The crucial point is that both the existing service and any future expansion should, in our view, be paid for entirely from the budget of the Speaker of the House. If the Speaker were to assume financial responsibility then it would only be reasonable that plans for future growth of the service would be kept within the Speaker's own discretion. Naturally the Speaker would want to take full advantage of the CBC's production and technical expertise, and to consult both the CBC and the political leadership of the House before proposing any significant changes.

Recommendation

> The cost of providing the Parliamentary Television Network should be borne by the Speaker of the House of Commons, with the Speaker responsible for determining the scope and nature of that service. The CBC should be compensated in full for continued use of its technical and human resources.

Radio Canada International

Radio Canada International (RCI), Canada's foreign shortwave radio service, now broadcasts in 12 languages to Europe, South America, the Middle East and, most recently, Japan. RCI also distributes recorded program material on disc and tape. It is believed that RCI's 160 weekly hours of broadcasts reach about 10 million listeners, including Canadians overseas.

RCI is unusual among national shortwave services in that its program content is not controlled by government. It is the prerogative of the Department of External Affairs to select RCI's languages of broadcast and geographical target areas. But once policy decisions are taken at this level, it is the CBC alone that determines program content and editorial policy.

The annual budget for RCI is about $16 million. We believe this is money well spent, given how widely it allows informative programming about Canada and world events to be broadcast. We further believe that two changes are called for, analogous to those proposed in the preceeding section on the Parliamentary Network: RCI should be allowed to expand its services, and all operating costs should be borne by External Affairs, with CBC providing all resources on a fee-for-service basis. As well, we are persuaded that to protect the future of the service, RCI should be included in the formal mandate of the CBC.

The CBC notes in its brief to this Task Force that both it and External Affairs have certain priorities for expansion of service. These priorities are of two kinds: increased broadcast hours to certain high priority areas and a substantial expenditure on new shortwave technical facilities to serve new priority areas, particularly the Pacific Rim. According to the figures provided in the CBC brief, full implementation of the projects discussed would cost some $40 million over four years — a doubling of RCI's present budget in each year. The CBC itself should not be expected to fund such an ambitious expansion. While we cannot comment on the details of the proposed projects, we believe that External Affairs should consider carefully what advantages may be lost if at least some additional funds are not found to keep this valuable service growing.

Recommendation

The cost of operating of Radio Canada International should be assumed by the Department of External Affairs, with the department deciding on the scope of the service provided. The CBC should continue to provide all necessary human and technical resources for a fee and retain full editorial control over program content, without being journalistically answerable to the Department or its officials. External Affairs should be urged to place a high priority on consolidating and expanding RCI, according to priorities established in consultation with the CBC.

The Northern Service

The CBC Northern Service, which was created in 1958, provides services across a vast region stretching from the Alaskan border to the James Bay area of northern Quebec. It operates sub-regional radio stations at Whitehorse, Inuvik (Western Arctic), Yellowknife, Rankin Inlet (Keewatin) and Frobisher Bay (Eastern Arctic). A television production centre has been established in Yellowknife, while a television field production unit is being created to operate from Whitehorse. Other operations include a Cree radio and television unit in Montreal, radio bureaux in Ottawa and Kuujjuaq (Arctic Quebec), and administrative and support offices in Ottawa.

The Northern Service significantly expanded both its radio and television coverage during the 1970s, thanks to the Accelerated Coverage Plan which was designed to place transmitters in all communities of more than 500 inhabitants. This was supplemented by installations in most smaller communities funded by the Yukon and Northwest Territories governments.

While terrestrial distribution is used extensively for radio in the Yukon, most communities in the Northern Service region receive both radio and television signals by means of Telesat's Anik D satellite. As the Northern Service does not produce its own daily news and current affairs programs for television, northern audiences are provided with regional productions from St John's and Vancouver.

The Northern Service is heavily committed to radio production, such that the number of program hours produced often exceed those produced at southern regional centres. This is necessary to provide sufficient outlets for service in aboriginal languages. This commitment also acknowledges that the Northern Service provides the only regional radio network in many communities, and in some the only radio signal at all.

By contrast, television production is minimal — about 10 percent of the amount of regional origination achieved by CBC in other parts of Canada. Although production and distribution facilities are limited, the Northern Service does provide coverage of events such as elections and the Arctic Winter Games.

The CBC also plays an important role in assisting community and native access programming within the Northern Service region. Communities with predominantly native populations can ask for help in establishing a community radio station with access to CBC transmitters under agreed-upon conditions. Community programming is undertaken in other settlements having community-owned transmitters. Such locations relay CBC programming much of the day, supplemented by local content. The Northern Service also assists native communication agencies operating under the Northern Native Broadcast Access Program with distribution of both radio and television programming in the North.

The operations of the Northern Service described above have a staff of approximately 180 people and a budget of about $14 million. The general point we wish to make is that the Northern Services like the other two services described here, must be brought under the broadcasting legislation as a specific part of the mandate of the national service.

Recommendation

The three main non-mandated services — the Parliamentary Network, RCI and the Northern Service — should be written into the broadcasting legislation either within the mandate of the CBC or in some other appropriate context, in order to confer official recognition and continuity of service.

Financing, Accountability and Arm's Length

We have devoted much of this chapter to arguing for changes in the CBC's programming mandate, as well as in the deployment of its existing resources. We have recommended that the CBC's responsibilities be clarified and we have seen that carrying out this new mandate will involve substantial costs. This is occasioned in particular by the renewed emphasis we feel must be put on Canadian programming.

A careful examination of expenditures undertaken in cooperation with CBC did not suggest to us that the funds we feel are required could be freed up through savings resulting from consolidation of physical resources or redirection of funds. Some $32 million will have been cut from regional broadcasting operations alone in the last two fiscal years, across all services. In our recommendations for a reorganization of the CBC we were motivated by reasons other than cost-cutting — a clearer sense of mission at the station and regional levels, more equitable coverage in terms of population served, more efficient use of existing resources and reduced likelihood of even the perception that CBC resources are being utilized in a wasteful or inefficient manner.

Neither our wish to see increased funds go to the CBC for certain purposes nor our conviction that little fat remains to be cut, especially from program operations, should imply that we can find no room for improvement in how the CBC gets or handles its money. On the contrary we believe that the present system of financial controls and the matching of mandate to resources leaves much to be desired.

Part of the problem lies in having to serve both commercial and non-commercial masters. The CBC receives about 80 percent of its monies from Parliament and earns the other 20 percent or so mainly from the sale of commercial time on its television networks. Because the budget is raised from different sources, the CBC must answer to both its commercial clients and the elected representatives whose function it is to account for the expenditure of public funds.

Since the CBC is accountable to Parliament for its appropriation, its relationships with advertisers, affiliates and audiences might appear to have no bearing on whether public funds are being spent wisely by the Corporation. But the uncertain nature of the mandate produces unavoidable dilemmas for CBC programmers. From the perspective of Parliament, for example, the CBC has a clearly defined role in the realization of national cultural goals, which includes certain costly activities as broadcaster of last resort. The provision of cultural or sustaining programming on the television networks, however, sometimes works against the effort to increase commercial revenue, since success is associated, rightly or wrongly, with commercial American programs.

It can also be argued that the CBC's accountability to Parliament overrides all other considerations, both because the CBC is a legal creature of Parliament and because Parliament is by far the CBC's major source of revenue, even if it is not exclusively so. This may be perfectly true, but it is a generalization that conceals a Byzantine network of accountability relationships within the confines of the public sector. It is our firm conviction that the CBC is now answerable to so many bodies — Parliament and its committees, the Department of Communications, Treasury Board, the CRTC, the Auditor-General — that it is encouraged to behave as if it is answerable to none.

Paradoxically, no other Crown corporation carries such a heavy burden of supervision. This is demoralizing for the CBC and costly for the taxpayer. Far from ensuring effective controls on spending and meaningful measures of performance, the present system is a source of frustration for all parties — programmers, politicians and bureaucrats alike. Even if the CBC were not so over-supervised it would still pose special problems of accountability as a public agency engaged in creative and often controversial activities.

There is at least an argument that, in the words of one critic, it is not

> just as easy to analyse and quantify the activities of a ballet company as it is to explain the cost of a post office . . . Cultural organizations . . . if they are to be any good, are incapable of being fitted into the flow-chart mentality that dominates government . . .Nevertheless, politicians and bureaucrats cling to the idea that they will someday find a system for making culture behave in a way that suits Ottawa.[18]

Although it is no doubt excessive to suggest that "managing creativity" is an oxymoron, we must at least agree it is problematic. Laurent Picard, a former president of the CBC whose job it was to try, certainly felt the tension between the two concepts, but had no doubt which should predominate:

> . . . managing a broadcasting enterprise amounts first and foremost to managing creativity. And managing creativity means resorting to unorthodox management methods.[19] (translation)

Nevertheless, there must be accountability by a billion-dollar public agency and we have several suggestions for achieving a better balance between the legitimate needs for controls and for creative autonomy. First, however, we look at CBC's current relationship to government.

The CBC's Status as a Crown Corporation

Like other Crown corporations, the CBC has been created to administer certain goods and services on behalf of the Crown. In order to do so in the most efficient manner, such public agencies are expected to operate in the marketplace more in the style of a commercial concern than like a government department — even though it is equally necessary to have them account to Parliament for their use of public resources through their responsible minister.

This arrangement is reflected in the structure of the CBC's Board of Directors, which comprises the president and 14 other members, who collectively constitute the Corporation. Though they are appointed by the government and can be removed for cause, they are not employees of the Crown and do not receive directives concerning their day-to-day operations from the Minister of Communications, who is responsible to Parliament for the CBC.

So far nothing in these arrangements makes the CBC unique. It is widely recognized, however, that the services provided by the CBC play a special role in the creation and distribution of programs which reflect Canadian expression, including the often controversial work of broadcast journalists. The free circulation of ideas and information in our society is regarded as too important to be subjected to undue outside pressures. In recognition of the essential differences between the CBC and agencies such as Air Canada, as well as in order to protect the CBC's special role, it has been set apart from its fellow agencies in a number of respects. One of the most notable of these is that the CBC was exempted from new provisions of the *Financial Administration Act*, embodied in Bill C-24, which were designed to strengthen ministerial control as part of an attempt to improve their accountability.

This arm's length relationship is balanced by other accountability arrangements. The national service provided by the CBC is heavily subsidized from public funds. It is therefore only reasonable that those responsible for the wise use of these funds — i.e. ministers of the Crown — should have some means at their disposal for holding the public broadcaster to account. This is a responsibility which ministers share with other members of Parliament, who are also concerned to see that the CBC spends its appropriation in conformity with the statutory mandate and any other policies in force. Thus, members of Parliament may seek out information about CBC operations through questions put to the Minister of Communications. Members of the CBC Board and senior management may also be asked to give evidence to parliamentary committees, particularly the House Committee on Communications and Culture.

Regulation: The CBC's Status as a Broadcaster

As we have discussed elsewhere in this Report, the *Broadcasting Act* sets out a broadcasting policy for Canada whose various provisions address both public and private broadcasters, including the CBC (though not in the same way as other broadcasters). The Act stipulates that the objectives of this policy "can best be achieved by providing for the regulation and supervision of the Canadian broadcasting system by a single independent public authority". This authority is of course the CRTC.

The CBC is given funds by Parliament to carry out certain national policy objectives, as established by Parliament. But it is up to this other body, the CRTC, to set all the detailed conditions of licence which determine the operational means by which the CBC realizes these parliamentary objectives. The CRTC is empowered, for example, to ask the CBC to meet a higher Canadian content quota than private broadcasters. On the other hand, the CRTC is not empowered to finance or subsidize in any way the program activities, such as increased domestic production, necessitated by conditions it has imposed.

The CRTC's legal relationship as regulator of the CBC is significantly different from its relationship to private broadcasters. While the Commission has some sanctions it can apply to the CBC, the CRTC power to suspend or revoke licences under sections 24(1) and 24(2) of the Act does not extend to licences held by the CBC. Also, unlike private broadcasters, the CBC has its own mandate directly from Parliament and its own direct reporting relationship to Government and Parliament as well. From time to time a condition of licence may be disputed by the CBC. If this happens and the Commission and Corporation cannot resolve their differences, the Minister of Communications must be called upon to adjudicate. The minister may, after consulting both parties, issue a written order to the Commission which imposes a resolution of the dispute.

In practice this formal arbitration procedure has never been utilized. In those few instances where disputes between the two agencies have had to be resolved, the procedures invoked have shown remarkably little consistency. This is symptomatic of the uncertain relationship between the national broadcaster and the regulator.

Accountability and Policy-Making

The CBC is held formally accountable through a number of processes, which include submission of an annual report tabled before Parliament, and reports of the Auditor General, who examines the accounts and operations of the CBC and may make recommendations for change as he sees fit. Moreover, estimates of CBC's operating and capital expenditures must be approved by Parliament each year. Parliament cannot, however, exercise continuing or detailed control of expenditures. This is partly because the CBC is protected from public scrutiny of certain expenditures, and partly because it is too large and complex for any but full-time specialists.

Real scrutiny of the CBC takes place under the auspices of the Department of Communications (DOC) and the Treasury Board. In the public arena, supervision is largely confined to the issuance of broad statements of policy by the Minister of Communications. Such statements do not normally deal with operational or program-related issues. In this relationship, techniques such as informal, closed-door meetings and the application of moral suasion count for a great deal in the guidance of the CBC's conduct. Often these *ad hoc* techniques pose a greater threat to the arm's length relationship than do formal directives.

We are sensitive to the need for safeguards to be built into the relationship between the CBC and the minister through whom it reports to Parliament. Yet we are equally sensitive to the need for rational policy-making. If there is anything problematic about the CBC's relationship to the government, it lies not so much in opportunities for political control as in the singular lack of coordination among the various players concerning the CBC's mandate and how it must be adapted to meet changing times.

One aspect of this lack of coordination is the gulf that seems to separate strategic policy-making on the part of the government and the five-year cycle of CBC licence renewals. In 1983, for example, the then Minister of Communications issued a major policy document on the CBC, entitled *Building for the Future: towards a distinctive CBC*. What is problematic about this document is the fact that it was released at a time when public hearings on the renewal of CBC's network licences were still some way in the future. This is unfortunate because licence renewal hearings are designed to provide an opportunity for interested parties to comment on the applicant's past performance and on its plans for the coming five years. It is in precisely such a forum that a government-initiated revision of the CBC's mandate ought to be discussed. Otherwise debate over the government's policy-making becomes more diffuse and less effective, while the CRTC licensing process is apt to appear like a duplication of effort.

The 1983 policy document illustrates another weakness in the present system. It called for a number of initiatives whose realization appeared to be dependent on additional funding. Yet nowhere in the document was provision made for such funding, and no commitments were forthcoming in other statements. In the section devoted to increasing Canadian content levels to 80 percent, we find the statement that "achievement of this target will be expensive and will require continued improvement in CBC efficiency, the reallocation of CBC's internal resources and perhaps additional funding".[20]

Certainly nothing is wrong in principle with funding a new programming initiative internally, through the redirection of funds. Yet without a clear accompanying statement on whether or not funds were available, and if not what specific alternatives could be entertained, the 80 percent target could hardly be subjected to public scrutiny and debate. In the event, the CBC did manage to plan for redirection of the funds it thought it needed to embark on an ambitious program of independent production in 1984. Later that year, however, the Corporation's budget was cut by $85 million in the government-wide deficit reduction scheme.

Financial Controls

We have noted that the ongoing supervision of the CBC by the minister, acting in the interests of both Cabinet and Parliament, takes the form of broad policy statements, at least as far as public actions are concerned. Behind the scenes, as we also suggested, a great deal of give and take goes on between officials of the CBC and those of the central agencies, much of it naturally concerning money.

Our consultations and research have indicated that the present system of financial controls, the operational tools that give meaning to accountability, are not working. One flaw in this system on which the parties seem to agree is its unpredictability. This is a two-way street (two-edged sword might be a more appropriate figure). It has often been observed in studies of the CBC's resourcing framework, looking at things from the CBC's perspective, that unpredictable annual budgets wreak havoc with CBC's strategic planning. For all that the CBC may be protected from partisan or vested interests, there is no practical limit to how far the government of the day may reduce (or increase) the CBC's budget, except perhaps for common sense and the weight of public opinion. And drastic changes in the budget from one year to the next, to take but one example, make it difficult for television programmers to develop writing and performing talent for a medium in which critical and public acceptance must often be measured over years rather than months.

From the perspective of the central government agencies, other kinds of uncertainties have plagued the planning process. Some of these have been of the CBC's making, others lie beyond its control. The first category includes a number of methods the CBC has used for determining both shortfalls in its revenues and unforeseen increases in committed costs. In addition to annual changes in the approved level of the CBC's expenditures, fluctuations occur in the annual level of earned commercial income, usually because of competitive and market factors over which the Corporation has little or no control.

Under the present system, the annual appropriation is calculated by subtracting projected commercial revenue from the approved expenditure level. In the last three fiscal years, the CBC projected a drop in anticipated commercial revenue and requested an upward adjustment in its appropriation to compensate for this. In the event, CBC actually will have earned significant revenues on an annual basis in excess of its original revenue targets. Our review of pertinent Treasury Board documents indicates that these additional revenues have been successively absorbed into the operating base, along with the incremental appropriations that were to compensate for an expected shortfall.

Even if CBC has gained on the revenue swings, it has, it claims, lost on the expenditure roundabouts. CBC notes that over the last several years its budgets have declined in constant dollars when inescapable cost increases are factored into the calculations. Losses in the millions of dollars are ascribed to factors such as increases in utility rates, municipal taxes and the currency premium paid by the CBC when it buys goods and services from the United States. The Corporation has asked to be compensated for these costs, but it has not been.

We are not so much concerned with how to apportion responsibility for this state of affairs as we are with how to cure its ill effects, which are felt by all those involved. The bureaucrats who supervise the CBC's budgets are stymied in their attempts to impose objective controls, whereas many CBC staff members have found the financial roller-coaster of the last two years completely demoralizing.

Here we can only reiterate our basic principle that it is not sufficient to pacify either party by arbitrarily raising or lowering budgets. What looms behind all these uncertainties is the larger problem of the poor match between resource levels and the levels of service anticipated by the existing mandate and new policy initiatives. We believe the proper match can be achieved only by a new approach that ties together financial controls, revenue generation, and the periodic preparation and approval of the CBC's plans for execution of its mandate.

We have no illusions that a corporate plan, more elaborate financial controls and the panoply of other management tools will act overnight to banish 'inefficiency' from the CBC, let alone inspire more sublime programs. Many large cultural organizations are faced with special problems in the management of their creative resources, a group that includes CBC's fellow agencies such as the National Film Board, Canada Council, National Arts Centre and so on. Hence the importance of looking at administrative changes in the accountability régime against the wider backdrop of stability and consensus.

Our approach to this question is divided into three stages or strategies. The first concerns the matching of resources to mandate through a mechanism for drawing together the government, the CRTC and the public in a forum whose purpose is to seek consensus on periodic changes to the strategic plans of the CBC, as well as to ensure that government funds the services it expects from the CBC at an appropriate level. The second part of the strategy would introduce a long-term resourcing framework that would give the CBC a more stable financial environment in which to work, in return for a more explicit and well managed commitment on the CBC's part as to how it is to administer its budget. The third part of the strategy addresses the role of the Board of Directors and the President of the CBC, particularly as this relates to the Corporation's maintenance of its arm's length relationship to government.

Matching Money to the Mandate

We have outlined our vision of what the national service should be in the 80s and 90s, argued for particular changes in both mandate and operations and calculated the probable cost to the taxpayer of what we wish to see done. It seems to us this is exactly how the government should go about its own long-term planning for the national service. Assumptions and expectations are made explicit, and their merits and flaws can be openly debated. The measures that flow from these premises can then be seen not only for what they are but also for how much they cost. And both the taxpayers and their elected representatives can comment on whether one set of proposals is good but just too expensive, given other national priorities, or affordable but less good than some other set.

The world, alas, can never be this neat and tidy. But the funding of Canadian public broadcasting certainly leaves much room for improvement. Even if there can be no perfect match between the duties imposed on the CBC through its mandate and the resources made available to discharge these duties, we believe a much greater effort can be made to treat each of these as though they were related.

We have approached this question with a number of principles in mind. The government of the day must determine both the general nature of the services the CBC is to provide and the general level of resources it is willing to make available. At the same time, the CRTC plays a crucial role in ensuring that the coherence of the broadcasting system as a whole is maintained. Given that the CBC is the largest and most important element of the system and must answer to the CRTC in its periodic licence renewals, the CRTC is well positioned to facilitate public discussion on the CBC's programming role. Members of the public, for their part, have a right to make their views known on how well they feel they have been served by the broadcaster which operates on their taxes. They also have a right, which is perhaps less readily exercised than the preceding one, to let the government know how they feel about the federal policies which guide the CBC.

The basic elements of a more coherent process for determining the CBC's long-term strategy are already in place. What remains is to bring them together at one focal point. We feel this focal point ought to be the public hearings at which the CBC is asked to defend its record and reveal its plan for the next five-year period — the CRTC licence renewal hearings. For all this has been a lively forum for public discussion in the past, the missing element has always been any basis for judging what it would be reasonable to ask the CBC to do over the next licence period.

When the CBC goes before the Commission now for the renewal of its licence for the next five years, it has not received any indication from the Minister, the Government or Parliament that the funds required for the CBC to carry out its five year plan and to meet its promise of performance will be available. This situation derives from the informal and irregular way in which the government announces its views on the CBC's role, and from the fact that the appropriation for CBC is made on an annual basis. It has very distinct disadvantages and weakens every aspect of the accountability process.

One result is that a profound sense of unreality now surrounds the CRTC's licence renewal process and any conditions the CRTC may decide to attach to the CBC's licences. In these circumstances, public scrutiny of the CBC, which occurs in no other government forum, is rendered far less valuable and effective.

We have concluded that the system should be changed. Prior to the filing of the CBC's application for its licence renewal, the government should indicate what level of financing it intends to provide to the Corporation for its next five-year period. The government's plans for the financing of the CBC would be based on an examination of the Corporation's five-year plan, which reflects the CBC interpretation of its mandate and expresses its intentions as to the general allocation of resources. On the basis of both the CBC's five-year plan and the indication of the government's intended level of financing, the CRTC hearing would then take place. Based on public comments on the CBC's plans and its overall view of the context of Canadian broadcasting, the Commission would decide whether any adjustments were necessary to the CBC's plans and would attach such conditions of licence as it deemed appropriate.

The CBC licences in question would be granted for five years or some other appropriate period. The licence conditions would comprise both operational and financial elements. Provision might also be made for any modification proposed by the government, the CRTC or the CBC to be subject to another round of public discussions. Otherwise, between these regularly scheduled forums, the Corporation should be left free to carry out its publicly announced mandate as it sees fit — without fear of the unanticipated disruptions created by new policies, budget cuts or task forces, but in the expectation that it will be responsible on an annual basis for a financial accounting to the government and at the end of the licence period will be accountable to the CRTC and the public through the licence renewal process. The CBC would have a duty not to propose any disruptive and costly expansions in its services, or to request additional funds for unanticipated expenditures during the licence period.

Recommendation

The CBC licence renewal process should be preceded by a statement from the government on the extent of funding it intends to provide over the pending CBC licence period. It should also be preceded by the CBC's plans for the licence period, including its promise of performance to the Commission. On this basis, as well as the public comment provided through a full licence renewal hearing and its overall view of the content of the Canadian broadcasting system as a whole, the CRTC would then attach to the CBC's licence such conditions as it deemed appropriate.

Long-term Resourcing: from Platitude to Organizing Principle

In the history of public enquiries into Canadian broadcasting, there can be few more famous sentiments — after the beloved distinction between programming and 'housekeeping' — than the perennial urging that the federal government provide long-term, fixed financing to our beleaguered national broadcaster. As often as this idea has been put forward, so often has it been ignored or rejected by successive governments. The enquiries which have preceded us have carried on this tradition of espousing long-term funding, despite what must have seemed to each one like the utter futility of a long-ago lost cause.

This Task Force is in the same tradition: we think the CBC needs its resourcing framework settled for a period of up to five years in advance. Are we thus destined to have the policy-makers nod politely at our reformulation of a platitude and then move on to more serious matters? We hope otherwise; and we hope a brief comment on why this idea has never been embraced by government will set the stage for a more convincing version.

Our reading is that long-term funding has always been presented as a measure owed to the Corporation or that is exclusively in the Corporation's vested interest. This is a misguided assumption, for two reasons. It ignores the resistance in certain political quarters to the notion of making what are perceived to be financial 'concessions' to the CBC. In more substantive terms, it also ignores the problems created by financial instability not for the Corporation, but for those in government who must oversee its spending. There is, in other words, another side to the coin of stable resourcing. Yet to our knowledge, the idea of stable or long-term financing has never been presented in a way that suggested opportunities for a more orderly accountability régime, in addition to opportunities for better planning strategies on the part of the CBC.

Our recommendation should therefore be considered within the problematic budget context described above. We believe the long-term resourcing framework should operate on several assumptions:

- Both capital budgets and earned revenues would be excluded from the operating resource framework.
- Earned revenues would be subject to a 'shelter' arrangement, allowing the Corporation to keep surplus earned revenues, in recognition of the *de facto* current practice, but with no commitment to offset revenue shortfalls.
- Fluctuations in the price of goods and services utilized by the Corporation would be absorbed by the CBC, although the cost of providing special event coverage, as well as certain other extraordinary expenditures, could be subject to a specially negotiated annual additional subsidy.

- The resourcing framework would reflect the CBC's historic capacity for revenue generation, as well as the decision to provide the necessary funds over the next five years to finance the implementation of our recommendations;
- The framework would be subject to adjustments to offset the rate of inflation.
- The CBC would be obliged to provide Treasury Board and DOC with appropriate long-term corporate financial plans which would complement the programming plans for the period filed with the CRTC. These would also provide an acceptable level of financial reporting on a regular and systematic basis.

We believe that if these and other appropriate conditions are respected, both the Corporation and the central agencies will stand to benefit from improved working relations and improved productivity.

Recommendation

The public subsidy granted CBC should be calculated and publicly announced to cover the same period as the CBC's station and network licences. In return the CBC should be expected to manage its resource base over this financing period without requesting any adjustments for either earned revenue shortfalls or fluctuations in the cost of doing business.

The Role of the President and the Board

The issues relating to the accountability of the CBC discussed thus far have been external and confined to the relationship with government. They may be the most visible or controversial, but they are certainly not the only ones. How the CBC is expected to relate to government has an important bearing on the structure of senior management and its relationship to the Board of Directors. On the other hand, if accountability means taking responsibility for one's actions and keeping open lines of communication, then the CBC's sense of accountability certainly ought to extend beyond the confines of a small group of Ottawa bureaucrats. To us, those who manage the CBC have an equally important responsibility to both the creative and support staff who make it function and the public who pay the bills. Our concerns begin with whether the chief executive of the CBC — the President — should also be the Chairman of the Board, as is now the case.

One of the disadvantages of having the two most senior corporate positions filled by one incumbent is the perception that Board functions are not sufficiently distanced from the operational side. This would not pose such a sensitive problem were it not for the creative and journalistic nature of CBC operations, and the great premium placed on keeping them at arm's length from outside influence. Because the board and its chairman are appointed by the governor in council, the legitimate fear exists that direct political pressure can be brought to bear on the chairman and board members — however cheerfully and subtly this may be achieved.

This issue is one of institutional arrangements, not personalities. It is one of public perception and of the sense of priorities a chief executive is likely to bring to the function. Creative autonomy in a publicly funded broadcasting organization is a precious commodity that must be protected not only from real compromise but also from the slightest hint or appearance of compromise. There is more than just symmetry or balance at stake in the separation of powers between the policy-making functions of the chairman and the board, and the day-to-day operational responsibilities of a president.

A president who is appointed for the express purpose of heading the daily management of the Corporation's affairs will inevitably place less priority on participation in the board's policy-making functions than on becoming a full-time advocate for programmers and program-makers. The present arrangements already provide for an Executive Vice-President whose area of responsibility is described by the Act as the "management of broadcasting operations".

We believe the nature of this position must now be modified, for two reasons. First, the executive vice-president is currently responsible not to the board but to the president, who may assign him duties from time to time as he sees fit. Second, although the executive vice-president is technically appointed by the board, the appointment is made on the recommendation of the president with the approval of the governor in council. We are convinced that both policy and operational functions will be better served if the executive vice-president position is changed to reflect a division of the duties now performed by the president.

Recommendation

> The offices of the Chairman of the Board of Directors and the President and Chief Executive Officer of the CBC should be separate and clearly defined. The Chairman of the Board should be primarily concerned with policy, while the President and Chief Executive Officer should be empowered to implement policies determined by the Board of Directors. The Chairman of the Board, like other Board members, should be appointed by the Governor in Council. The President and Chief Executive Officer should be appointed by and be responsible to the Board of Directors, in recognition of the principle of arm's length.

Accountability Revisited: Dealing with Public Complaints about CBC

We have already registered our concern about the responsibility which the CBC has to the tax-paying public. Canadians already enjoy certain privileged democratic channels for expressing their views on the performance of bodies like the CBC: communication with their MPs and letters to the editors of newspapers and magazines are perhaps two of the most important. Canadians have always been vocal about the CBC, both for what it broadcasts and for how it manages its affairs.

But if channels for the expression of opinion have always been available, mechanisms for responding to criticism have never been able to keep up. The CBC itself has worked diligently through its audience and press relations departments to maintain a dialogue with the public. Sometimes, however, a legitimate grievance arises that requires redress and neither the editorial pages nor for that matter the courts are likely to provide resolutions held to be fair and appropriate by all concerned.

Our suggestion is that an ombudsman be appointed as a 'people's agent' for fair and balanced programming on CBC. The ombudsman would respond to public complaints about journalistic fairness and balance, sexual and ethnic stereotyping, fair representation of Canada's multicultural nature and any other matter on which individual members of the public might wish to be heard about CBC practices. The ombudsman could also respond to complaints referred by Parliament or its committees.

The ombudsman should be appointed by the CBC Board, and should in fact be a two-person office, one appointee being francophone, the other anglophone. The appointees should have the full resources of the Corporation at their disposal for investigating complaints and then publicizing results, including access to broadcast time on the appropriate network or networks. The special nature of broadcasting in Canada makes it as important to protect the CBC from unfair criticism and pressure as it is to protect the public from unfair programs or practices.

Recommendation

The statutory mandate of the CBC should provide for an Office of the Ombudsman, to be appointed by and responsible to the CBC Board. Two appointees should be named to the office, one anglophone, one francophone, who should investigate public complaints about the CBC and publicize their results.

Labour Relations

In order to produce and broadcast thousands of hours of radio and television programming every year, the CBC must employ a large number of people having very diverse skills. While the CBC has approximately 11,000 staff employees, it also draws on a talent pool of some 30,000 contract employees and freelancers. There are many different kinds of relations between the Corporation and this large group of individuals and they are governed by no fewer than 29 separate collective agreements.

Basically CBC employees belong to one of two types of bargaining unit: professional or freelance associations, or staff employee unions. The first type includes writers, performers, musicians and producers divided among half-a-dozen particular units. Their members are normally not staff employees but freelance professionals who are hired for the purposes of a specific project or to provide a particular service. Although these are not accredited units, they negotiate collective agreements with the CBC which, among other things, require that the CBC use only members in good standing to carry out certain specified tasks.

The other grouping comprises unions accredited under the Canada Labour Code, who enjoy the exclusive right to represent certain employees. Two of the largest of these units are NABET, which represents most of CBC's technical staff, and the Canadian Union of Public Employees, which represents office and professional staff. Many of the CBC's bargaining units operate in only one language, i.e. within either French or English services, and the jurisdictional structure is quite different on each of the two sides of the Corporation.

It has often been noted that the complexities of the CBC's labour relations have made adapting to technological change somewhat difficult. The Task Force has no intention of commenting directly on the substance of the contract negotiations underway between CBC and its numerous bargaining units at the time of writing. But certain remarks of a general nature are appropriate.

First of all, it is important that the impact on labour relations be taken into consideration in any major policy decision affecting the CBC. To suggest, for example, that the CBC ought to withdraw from production activities without examining the implications for labour relations seems to us to be very unwise. Second, the CBC and its unions have much to gain by acting co-operatively during any period of rapid technological change or great uncertainty concerning the CBC's mandate and resources.

Further, we believe that an inappropriate labour relations regime, which flows from the Canada Labour Code and North American practice in general, is largely responsible for the contentious atmosphere surrounding labour relations at the CBC. Our research indicates that the problem is that an industrial labour relations model has been applied to an organization that is essentially creative in nature.[21] The challenges posed by the creation of cultural products on a massive scale are only intensified by the burdens of the CBC's far-reaching mandate and the need to justify its use of public funds. The question, then, is how to go about finding a labour relations model that is suited to the peculiar structure and activities of this complex, sprawling organization.

We are also convinced that the Labour Relations Board has taken a much too legalistic approach in its decisions concerning accreditation and jurisdictional issues at the CBC. Be that as it may, management and labour must be urged to discuss the Corporation's problems openly, even though their narrower interests are naturally divergent. If the CBC is to assume its full creative responsibilities in the provision of the national service, an atmosphere of co-operation must prevail.

Most of the parties in question recognize that the present system has been too closely modeled after industrial organizations. They also recognize that the challenges facing the CBC will not be overcome without the full co-operation of the unionized staff. Most of these staff undoubtedly support the public service ideals of the CBC and would like to see it become a more efficient organization. Neither the ideals nor the goals of efficiency are enhanced by poor labour relations.

Given the fundamental role of labour relations in the evolution of the CBC, we believe a clear need exists for a specially commissioned examination of all aspects of the CBC's labour relations and collective bargaining. This independent inquiry should have as its chief aim a wholly preconceived labour relations structure appropriate to a creative organization along with a set of measures for its implementation. The members of the inquiry should be instructed to consult widely with all parties involved and should be given access to all pertinent documentary information, whether held by the CBC, the Labour Relations Board or another public agency.

Recommendation

The Ministers of Communication and Labour should jointly establish a committee of inquiry to conduct a thorough examination of the labour relations practices and structures of the CBC, with a view to ensuring that the CBC's human resources are allowed to work to their full potential in the realization of the national service mandate.

Notes

1. Canada, House of Commons *Debates*, Official Report, 3rd Sess., 17th Parl., 22-23 George V, Vol. 111, 1932, p. 3035.
2. Letter from Allan Slaight to André Bureau, December 20, 1984.Peter C. Newman, "A Take-Over Bid for CBC-TV", *Maclean's* 97 (53) (December 31, 1984), p. 4.
3. Allan Slaight, address to *Financial Post* Conference on Crown Corporations and Regulated Industries, April 11, 1985.
4. François Baby, "La politique canadienne de la radiodiffusion: analyse et propositions de modification", brief submitted to the Task Force on Broadcasting Policy, Ottawa, 1986.
5. Conrad Winn, "The Relative Accessibility of Canadians to American Commercial Programming", research for the Task Force on Broadcasting Policy, Ottawa, 1986.
6. Most of the facts and figures about CBC operations in this section and throughout the chapter are drawn from published CBC documents or from information made available to the Task Force by CBC staff in oral or written form. Individual references are not given to these CBC sources, with the exception of quotations from the Corporation's brief to the Task Force, *Let's Do It*! The analysis and recommendations in this chapter are also based on various external sources, including existing research reports, studies commissioned by the Task Force and expert briefings. These other sources of CBC-related information are cited where appropriate, both in this chapter and elsewhere in the present Report.
7. The Toronto production figure of 1000 hours for 1985-86 includes nearly 300 hours for one local program alone, namely *CBLT Morning*. It was discontinued at the end of that fiscal year in the budget-cutting exercise.
8. Canada, Department of Communications, *Building for the Future: Towards a Distinctive CBC* (Ottawa: The Department, 1983) p. 16.
9. Walter I. Romanow, Stuart H. Surlin, Walter C. Soderlund, "Analysis of Local TV News Broadcasts", study prepared for the Task Force on Broadcasting Policy, Ottawa, 1986.
10. BBM Bureau of Broadcast Measurement, "A Review of Trends in Canadian Radio Listening, 1976–1985", study prepared for the Task Force on Broadcasting Policy, Ottawa, 1986.
11. James F. Sward, "The Future of Canadianism on Radio", address to the Canadian Conference of the Arts, Conference on the Future of the Canadian Broadcasting System, Ottawa, October 16, 1985.
12. Canadian Broadcasting Corporation, *Let's Do It! A Vision of Canadian Broadcasting*, brief submitted to the Task Force on Broadcasting Policy, (Ottawa: CBC, 1985), p. 18.
13. School of Physical and Health Education, University of Toronto, brief submitted to the Task Force on Broadcasting Policy, Ottawa, 1986.
14. Canadian Broadcasting Corporation, *Let's Do It*, p. 34.

15. Canada, Special Joint Committee of the Senate and the House of Commons on Canada's International Relations, *Minutes of Proceedings and Evidence*, Issue no. 20, (October 30, 1985), pp. 9 and 42.
16. Background information on the CBC's television affiliates came from two existing studies, one commissioned by the National Affiliate Committee of the CBC, the other by the Corporation. The first is *CBC Private Affiliate Television Stations*, May 1985, Currie, Coopers & Lybrand. The second is *Financial and Substantive Relationships between the Canadian Broadcasting Corporation and its Television Affiliates* by John McKay, Phase I, April 1984, Phase II, August 1984.
17. CRTC Decision 1974-70, *Radio Frequencies are Public Property*, (Ottawa: CRTC, 1974), p. 36.
18. Robert Fulford, "The Management Myth", in *Saturday Night*, June 1986, p. 7.
19. Laurent Picard, *Problèmes de gestion en radiotélévision*, address to L'Union Européenne de Radiodiffusion, Conference on Modern Management in Broadcasting, Brussels, May 1972. Quoted in Marc Thibault, *Radio-Canada, des structures et des hommes*, study prepared for the Task Force on Broadcasting Policy, Ottawa, 1986.
20. Canada, Department of Communications, *Building for the Future*, p. 13.
21. Gérard Hébert, "Les relations de travail dans la radiodiffusion canadienne", study prepared for the Task Force on Broadcasting Policy, Ottawa, 1986.

Chapter 11

Provincial Broadcasting

Provincial Broadcasting

Overview

Provincial governments played only a marginal role in the first half century of broadcasting, since public broadcasting and its regulation were a jealously guarded federal preserve. In the past 15 years, however, provincial broadcasters have gained in both status and stature. We believe their role should be further strengthened.

No experience during our year-long work touched us as deeply as hearing the submissions on our tours of eastern, western and northern Canada. The notion of regional alienation so often invoked as a bloodless, abstract cliché in Toronto, Ottawa and Montreal, came alive with passion and visceral reality. Canadians who live outside the central regions want desperately to have their lives reflected in our national broadcasting media. This will be no easy chore. But its achievement cannot even be contemplated without the participation of provincial broadcasters.

Manitoba took pride of place in provincial broadcasting, putting CKY, Winnipeg on the air in 1923. The longest continuing provincial involvement in educational broadcasting has been in Alberta, where Radio Station CKUA, originally licensed to the University of Alberta, has been broadcasting continuously since 1927.

Today, Radio-Québec, TVOntario, Access Alberta and, on a more modest scale, British Columbia's Knowledge Network of The West, are making a substantial contribution to Canadian broadcasting providing educational, cultural and regional services. Other provinces are examining broadcasting possibilities and some are preparing to play a greater role in educational communications. In the Atlantic region, for example, all four provinces are co-operating in providing a schedule of educational programs broadcast via the Atlantic Satellite Network.[1]

The emergence of provincial broadcasters was based on provincial jurisdiction over education in Canada's constitutional arrangements. However, there has always been tension between federal and provincial governments over broadcasting and, more generally, communications. When the 1980 constitutional discussions began they followed almost a decade of negotiations on communication matters that had included six federal-provincial and five interprovincial conferences which reached no comprehensive agreement.

In 1966 the Ontario Ministry of Education, under its minister, William Davis, applied to the Board of Broadcast Governors for a licence to operate an educational television station. The federal government refused, citing a 1946 policy statement by C.D. Howe, one of the powerful cabinet ministers of the day, which said:

> the government has decided that, since broadcasting is the sole responsibility of the Dominion government, broadcasting licenses shall not be issued to other governments or to corporations owned by other governments.[2]

Ottawa itself developed an interest in entering educational broadcasting in the mid-sixties. The 1967 Speech from the Throne promised that "Legislation will be placed before Parliament concerning the provision of broadcasting facilities for educational purposes".[3] In December that year Secretary of State Judy Lamarsh announced establishment of a Canadian Educational Broadcasting Agency allowing for the operation of broadcasting services on behalf of provincial organizations.

The reaction from the provinces was uniformly hostile. In the spring of 1968 a federal task force was established to advise on problems surrounding the introduction of a Canadian Educational Broadcasting Act. The problems included strenuous protests led by Ontario and Quebec, which objected to federal intrusion on provincial responsibilities in education. The proposed legislation died.

The federal and provincial governments had agreed in 1969, after long negotiations, to the following definition of educational broadcasting:

> programming . . . to provide a continuity of learning opportunity aimed at the acquisition or improvement of knowledge or the enlargement of understanding of members of the audience.[4]

TVOntario began operating on Channel 19 in Toronto in 1970. Radio-Québec, established in 1968, began operating on cable in 1972 and over the air in 1975. The existence of CKUA Alberta, for years Canada's only provincially operated educational broadcaster, was regularized. The station had been virtually unnoticed in central Canada until Quebec cited it during the Quiet Revolution as a precedent for provincial entry into broadcasting.[5]

In 1972, an agreement was finally negotiated which gave the provinces full control over the types of programming carried on educational stations within the agreed definition of educational broadcasting, but licensing power was retained by the CRTC. This settlement left ambiguous and unresolved the critical question of the independence of the provincial broadcaster from the provincial government funding it.

Despite federal-provincial agreement on the definition of educational broadcasting, each provincial authority in fact defined its mandate largely as it saw fit. By 1979, the Clyne Committee was recommending that the reality of provincial independence in type of programming be formally recognized. The Committee proposed that the government abandon the fiction about education programming because the definition was so broad that provincial broadcasters could fill their evening hours with entertainment of a very general nature. It recommended the CRTC issue licences to provincially funded broadcasting corporations for stations whose programming would be general rather than strictly educational.

Only Alberta, Ontario and Quebec operate federally-licensed systems, while British Columbia's unlicensed service functions in some similar ways. In Alberta, where on-air educational television began in March 1970, the Alberta Educational Communications Corporation, known as The Access Network, operates a satellite-to-cable network reaching 85 per cent of the province's population. Access also operates radio station CKUA.

TVOntario, the broadcasting arm of the Ontario Educational Communications Authority, provides a wide range of educational programming defined broadly enough to include Elwy Yost's popular *Saturday Night at the Movies*. The service is provided by a combination of on-air transmitters and satellite-to-cable delivery reaching most Ontarians. TVOntario has become a world leader in the production of innovative educational programs and earns income from the sale of programs abroad. It has won recognition for its contribution to the sadly neglected field of children's programming.

In Quebec, Radio-Québec offers programming that stretches the definition of 'educational' to make it a more general tool to support and strengthen francophone culture in Canada. It is at times difficult to discern much difference between programming offered by Radio-Québec and Radio-Canada. Under a special arrangement with the CRTC, Radio-Québec, for a two-year trial period, carries commercials like those seen on conventional television. A 1985 accord between the Ottawa and Quebec governments provided for the extension of the Radio-Québec service to francophone communities across Canada by satellite-to-cable, but arrangements to do so are still under study. In Quebec, CANAL, La Corporation pour l'avancement de nouvelles applications des langages, a non-profit corporation grouping various educational institutions, has recently been licensed to provide more formal educational television services throughout the province.

British Columbia's Knowledge Network of the West Communications Authority is not licensed by the CRTC, nor enshrined in provincial legislation. It is not considered by the B.C. Government to be a broadcasting service, but rather a telecommunications service. It is funded by the province. Its satellite-to-cable service provides almost entirely instructional programming. Having no production facilities, it acquires programs from member educational institutions.

The Atlantic provinces have begun to develop educational programming. Manitoba provides an hour of educational television each weekday through the facilities of a private sector television station in Winnipeg. Saskatchewan has announced plans to proceed with the Saskatchewan Communications Advanced Network (SCAN) which will deliver education and other television services over the provincially-owned SaskTel optical fibre and coaxial cable network.

Quebec, Ontario, Alberta and British Columbia have formed an organization to promote and facilitate educational broadcasting, the Agency for Tele-Education in Canada (ATEC). It is designed to foster co-operation in the economic exchange, utilization and evaluation of educational broadcast materials and may become the basis for the larger co-operative activities we hope will emerge.

Programming

The Task Force recognizes that it is inappropriate for federal authorities to define the meaning and scope of educational broadcasting since the content of education clearly falls within provincial jurisdiction. Different provinces have defined educational broadcasting in different ways, with Quebec, for example, interpreting the subject in much broader terms than British Columbia. Indeed, to repeat the words of the Clyne Committee, it is time "the fiction about educational programming" was abandoned.

We believe Provincial Government broadcasting operations make a significant contribution to the Canadian broadcasting system, both in developing and encouraging regional production and in reflecting Canada's regions, and that contribution may well be more general than simply educational programming, however it is defined.

Recommendation

The CRTC should continue to license provincial broadcasting entities, but the provinces should determine the nature of such broadcasting, including the balance between educational and more general programming.

Jurisdiction

It is desirable for Ottawa and the provinces to settle the long-standing contention over jurisdiction in the fields of broadcasting and telecommunication. Up to and during the constitutional debate, several provinces vied with Ottawa for control over cable television distribution, which they saw as closed circuit communications within the province, different from over-the-air-broadcasting and therefore not subject to federal regulation. The B.C. Knowledge Network's satellite-to-cable network public service is unlicensed either provincially or federally while Alberta's Access Network, with a similar delivery system, is licensed by the CRTC.

The Task Force believes provincial broadcasting in Canada should be considered part of the broadcasting universe encompassed in the definition of broadcasting we are recommending.

Recommendation

The Government of Canada should initiate negotiations with provincial governments to bring all provincial broadcasting under the general regulatory structure of the CRTC, taking into account the previous recommendation.

Broadcaster's Autonomy

Given the ambiguity that continues to characterize the relationship between provincial governments and their broadcasting authorities, the Task Force reaffirms the principle that such authorities should no more be under the direct control of provincial governments than federal public broadcasters should be under the control of the federal government. The best mechanism to assure this result is the model we have already recommended for the CBC. In the provincial case, the provincial government would, every five years, outline to the CRTC its expectations for the provincial broadcasting system and establish a funding level adequate to fulfil those expectations.

Recommendation

Broadcasting entities licensed by the CRTC and funded by provincial governments should be operated at arm's length through autonomous broadcasting authorities or corporations. Every five years, during licence renewal hearings, the provincial government should outline to the CRTC its expectations for the provincial broadcasting system and establish a funding level adequate for their fulfilment.

Distribution

The Task Force considers it important that programming by provincial broadcasting organizations should be as broadly distributed as possible within their jurisdictions.

Recommendation

Provincial broadcasting services should be given priority carriage on the basic tier of all cable systems operating within a province whether or not the programs are broadcast from traditional, over-the-air-transmitters.

Consultation

We believe that broadcasting and communications policy should recognize and support the distinctive and dynamic educational communications organizations and activities that are developing in the provinces. The cultural, social and educational development of a region can best be reflected by people who live and work there and this is a legitimate and increasingly important role for public broadcasting at the provincial level.

We also believe it important that provincial broadcasting authorities have some influence in determining which educational broadcasting licences are approved in their jurisdictions.

Recommendation

The CRTC should consult with appropriate provincial authorities before awarding any licence for program signals to be broadcast within their province that could be viewed as a competitive educational service.

National Role

Finally, it is the view of the Task Force that educational broadcasters in the provinces have a significant contribution to make to the Canadian broadcasting system beyond their borders. As recommended elsewhere in this Report, they would be invited to participate in TV Canada, a new satellite-to-cable public service. But we also encourage educational broadcasters to initiate other co-operative ventures to enrich Canadian broadcasting. To that end, provincial broadcasters must have full access to the support system put in place at the federal level to foster production of Canadian programs.

Recommendation

There should be no impediment to provincial broadcasting organizations' participating in national or regional broadcasting networks. Provincial broadcasting corporations should have full access to the Broadcast Fund and other incentives to the production of Canadian programs.

Notes

1. Ronald G. Keast, "The Role of the Provinces in Public Broadcasting", study prepared for the Task Force on Broadcasting Policy, Ottawa, 1986.
2. C.D. Howe, *Federal Debates*, May 3, 1946 as quoted in Keast, "Role of the Provinces".
3. Canada, House of Commons, *Debates* Official Report, Volume 1, 2nd Sess. 27th Parl. 16 Elizabeth II, 1967.
4. Direction to the CRTC (Reservation of Cable Channels).
5. Consultative Committee on the Implications of Telecommunications for Canadian Sovereignty: *Telecommunications and Canada* (Ottawa, Minister of Supply and Services Canada, 1979) p. 33.

Chapter 12

National Film Board

National Film Board

The Task Force's interest in the National Film Board is its place in the broadcasting system — or, as it happens, its anomalously insignificant role in Canadian television programming compared with its capacity to contribute.

This venerable Canadian institution is at a precarious moment, its future highly uncertain. It is buffeted on all sides, its enemies clamorous, its defenders uncertain, its board and staff divided, its paymaster — the government of Canada — anxious for assorted reasons to reduce its budget. The question of how the NFB becomes more relevant, or relevant again, is pressing, since hardly anyone, friend or foe, is satisfied with the status quo. Many wonder whether the Board has not simply outlived its usefulness.

In some ways it is paradoxical for the NFB to be in such crisis. It has after all played an important role in the self-affirmation of the Québécois at the time of the Quiet Revolution through the documentaries prepared by its francophone arm, and it has rarely attracted such large audiences and lavish praise as it has done recently in English Canada. Not entirely by chance, its current prominence in English Canada results from the appearance on national television of NFB productions. Nor perhaps is it mere coincidence that two of its most recently acclaimed films — *Canada's Sweetheart: Hal Banks* and *Final Offer: Bob White and the UAW* — were co-productions with the CBC, which showed both.

It seems logical to us that in a Canadian world starved for quality Canadian programming, the NFB has proved that it continues to have a strong and distinctive contribution to make.

Established in 1939, well before the age of Canadian television, the Board has never quite given production for the tube the same attention as its work for school classrooms and other non-commercial institutions such as government departments, trade unions, church groups, cultural organizations and the like. Yet its vague but provocative mandate stands: to interpret Canada to Canadians — not merely to reflect, but to interpret, make judgements, take stands, have opinions. The execution of this mandate has inevitably changed over the generations, but the creative spirit has largely endured. Today part of its purpose remains a commitment to being a feisty advocate of the public interest on controversial issues like equality, the environment and disarmament, among others.

Of course NFB management would like a greater presence on television and is hoping appropriate access routes may materialize; the NFB has, for example, been a senior partner in the proposed children's TV network, Young Canada TV. It has after all much to offer television: NFB French and English productions average 90 original films a year, many of them of suitable length for television. On the other hand, it must be recognized that most NFB films are produced with non-TV audiences in mind, and the adult world may too casually forget the Board's highly successful film productions for classrooms — productions no one should wish to see terminated.

Even though they complain of the cost of making Canadian programs, private broadcasters generally make scanty use of the type of film produced by the NFB. TVA and CTV, for example, have each telecast only one NFB film in the past half-dozen years. Some CTV affiliates purchase them as a cheap source of Canadian content, often in 1000-minute (16 ½-hour) contracts to be shown well outside peak viewing hours. Educational broadcasters, not surprisingly, are important users of NFB films, although their audiences are relatively small.[1]

No one, certainly not the CBC, has any obligation to use NFB productions. Nor are all their films necessarily worth telecasting. Still, as one might expect, the English and French networks of the CBC are the primary means for the NFB to reach sizeable Canadian audiences. Broadcasts on both the English and French networks represent some 25 percent to 30 percent of all hours of Board films telecast, including educational television, although most of this time is represented by 15 owned and operated stations. And while, as we have seen, some of the well-known English programs were NFB-CBC co-productions, the greatest quantitative access for Board films to CBC happens to be spot bookings by CBC O and O stations, especially for fillers or to solve some other local scheduling problem.

In fact, while the French network's record of co-operation with the Board is stronger than the English network's, both networks decline to broadcast almost as many NFB titles as they accept. Network prime time original broadcasts of NFB films over the past six years represent 36 percent of the Board's production during the period, while rejections represent 33 percent. On the other hand, the French network telecast far more NFB films than it rejected, while the English network rejected more than it used.

The English network attributes its relatively limited use of NFB films primarily to limited air time. The NFB has long been told there is no dramatic solution to this problem except second French and English networks. These are, however, questions of choosing priorities; the CBC has always carried popular American programs in its network schedule as money spinners.

Other reasons CBC offers for rejecting NFB films include poor quality, inappropriateness for TV audiences for which they were not designed and, perhaps most controversially, contravention of CBC's 'journalistic standards'. This last issue has clearly hurt Studio D, the NFB women's arm, none of whose avowedly partisan documentaries has been shown as a feature film on English CBC, although the Oscar-winning *If You Love This Planet* was eventually telecast on *The Journal* because it 'made news' by receiving the Academy Award. Indeed, in the CBC's submission to this Task Force, the Corporation makes it clear that while its proposed extra channels would solve the problem of availability of airtime for NFB productions, the Board would still have to "recognize the CBC's special responsibilities in . . . the treatment of controversial subjects".[2]

We wonder. Why provide the NFB with disincentives for doing what it does best? Surely a reinvigorated Board depends on a rededication to its original mandate, and a truly Canadian broadcasting system would find ample room for provocative subjects presented with little pretence to balance and impartiality. As we have redefined balance in this Report, it need not be present in each and every program so long as it is provided over time by the CBC. Although the Task Force has tried to eschew the temptation to become a programmer, it is in our view a loss to all Canadians that CBC no longer dedicates a regularly-scheduled time-slot to NFB films.

We are persuaded that the Board has a significant contribution to make to Canadian television — in particular to the new public TV network we are recommending — in its proven fields of excellence: social-issue documentaries and educational films. We would be disappointed if its participation in the broadcasting system proved to be at the price of watering down its advocacy role. At the same time, some of the films that the NFB's existing mandate calls on it to produce may well prove to be suitable for television as well. It was suggested to us, for example, that although certain NFB productions may well work best when viewed collectively by a community group, they can also make sense as television programs.

Recommendation

The NFB should be seen as a significant producer of television documentaries featuring contemporary social issues, as well as of educational and children's programming for the proposed new public television network, TV Canada. Legislation governing the NFB should be amended to extend its mandate from films to broadcasting and to assure it an arm's length relationship from government for that purpose. While TV Canada would pay appropriate licence fees for the use of NFB productions, the Board should nevertheless receive sufficient government funding to enable it to make its contribution to Canadian television programming.

Moreover, the NFB can continue making a significant contribution both to regional aspirations and to creative local talent outside major centres. While the NFB has not yet achieved its stated objective of undertaking 50 percent of English production in the regions, its track record on regional involvement is impressive. The English regional production system appears to be successfully developing new talent and local film-making communities, and often producing work with a clear-cut regional viewpoint for national exposure.

As for French production, it had already achieved its autonomy during the heady nationalist days of the 1960s, which francophone film makers both benefited from and contributed to. Regionally, French production is quite different from English. In New Brunswick, the cultural milieu of the Acadians permits a contribution which the dispersal of francophones through the Western provinces makes difficult. In the West and Ontario, for example, French production functions more as a training operation serving relatively small local francophone populations in the centres where they operate. For that reason, French production may well enhance the sense of cultural future within these francophone communities.

Recommendation

The NFB should be encouraged to continue its regional role, using local talent to make films for television that reflect a regional point of view for national audiences.

We are also convinced there exists an audience both in Canada and abroad for the important and innovative films of Studio D. Its size is necessarily indeterminate, but clearly it includes leaders in the global movement for the enhancement of women's equality. Most Canadians will learn with surprise that Canada has developed a unique training and production capacity in women's films. It began in Quebec in the 1970s, when films produced under the title "En tant que femmes" constituted a breakthrough for documentaries produced by women for women, and culminated in Studio D's leadership at the International Women's Film Festival and Forum at the End of the Decade Conference in Nairobi, Kenya. Unhappily, this noteworthy event received barely any attention in Canada itself. Indeed, one might say that, like the NFB in general, Studio D receives more attention and honour abroad than at home.

Recommendation

Studio D, the women's arm of the NFB, should be seen as an important player in the NFB's contribution to TV Canada, its expertise in producing women's films serving as a model to the entire broadcasting industry.

Notes

1. Kirwan Cox, "The National Film Board and Television", study prepared for the Task Force on Broadcasting Policy, Ottawa, 1986.
2. Canadian Broadcasting Corporation, *Let's Do It! A Vision of Canadian Broadcasting*, brief submitted to the Task Force on Broadcasting Policy, (Ottawa: CBC, 1985), p. 46.

Chapter 13

TV Canada

TV Canada

The challenge of redressing the present imbalance of American over Canadian programs on the Canadian television broadcasting system cannot be met effectively by any one broadcaster. In this Report we call on all parts of the broadcast system — public, private and community — to play a greater role in the creation of Canadian television programs. Further, we have concluded that even with existing broadcasters doing all they can, an additional vehicle which we call TV Canada in English and Télé-Canada in French is needed to distribute television programs made specifically for Canadians.

The Task Force considered carefully the CBC proposals for a multiplicity of television and radio services. We fear the plan would divert the Corporation's resources, energy and attention from the main responsibility we propose for it: to be the major broadcaster of Canadian programming, serving both mainstream and minority tastes more effectively. But this means the Corporation will never have sufficient resources to serve all legitimate minority needs satisfactorily — those of the regions, those of children and youth, or those with a preference for arts programming and documentaries.

The Task Force believes that these needs are important, not only to the many minorities who have a passionate and continuing interest in non-mainstream programming, but also to the cultural life of our country. While the CBC should participate in the development of the proposed new programming services, their operation should be separate and independent (see Chapter 10).

At every meeting we held across the country we were met by supporters of Young Canada Television, advocating that we endorse a proposal for a special satellite-to-cable children's channel financed by subscriber fees collected and passed back by cable owners. We heard other proposals for a children's channel as well.

We agree with the premise that both English-speaking and French-speaking Canadian children are inadequately served by our broadcasting system (see Chapter 5 for a description of the present availability of children's programming). Clearly, there is a serious need which should be filled as quickly as possible.

However, we are not able to support the notion of a channel dedicated exclusively to young people. In our view, as legitimate as the need for children's programming is, there is also a need for more outlets for regional programming, for documentaries, for NFB productions, for many other sorts of specialized programming. The Canadian system simply does not have the resources to accomodate many new Canadian channels, unless they serve simply as vehicles to import more foreign programming. It is our judgement that the most viable and equitable way of providing more quality children's programming is through a sharing arrangement as part of the new public sector networks we are recommending.

We also understand the National Film Board's desire for better access to Canada's television delivery system. As we show in Chapter 12, we are confident that the NFB has a meaningful role to play in the kind of TV Canada channel we envision. Not only are their educational programs to be welcomed, but their documentaries are an art form sadly lacking in our present broadcasting system. While the Film Board has over $35 million to fund production in 1986-1987, little of that production is likely to become available to Canadians on television, particularly in the mid-evening hours when most Canadians could watch.

It is true that programs like *Le Point* and *The Journal* have given new life to a kind of documentary film, but as Mark Starowicz, the executive producer of *The Journal*, has said: "*The Journal* never represented an argument against the NFB; far from it. We all lament the decrease in 60-90 minute documentaries . . . We should have 52 such documentaries a year, every Sunday night. . . ."[1]

The role of documentaries was eloquently expressed in a manifesto titled *Appel en faveur du cinéma documentaire*, which was circulated in Quebec in January 1986 at Le Rendez-vous du cinéma québécois. The existence of a vigorous and independent documentary production capacity, the authors wrote, "open to diverse points of view, is an essential condition for the respect of freedom of expression in a society where the influence of television has tended to reduce information to capsules".

Both French and English Canada excel in the making of documentaries. Yet increasingly, independent producers who wish to make such films face two problems: public subsidy programs usually allocate little money for documentaries, and outlets for showing such films are scarce. We believe the new non-commercial television networks we envision can help re-invigorate Canadian documentary production, giving it a place on television screens at attractive viewing hours.

Again, the Task Force took very seriously the persuasive arguments we heard in all parts of the country for more regional access to the system, for something better than transitory opportunities to reflect the special qualities of the regions to themselves and to other Canadians. After decades of television in Canada the creative potential we are convinced resides in each of our regions remains substantially underdeveloped.

We found the debate about centres of excellence and the critical mass said to be required to produce high quality television to be the source of passionate contention. On the one hand, citing New York and Los Angeles in the American context, advocates of the critical-mass philosophy argue that Canada cannot mount world class television productions unless it concentrates its resources in a few places — Toronto, Montreal, and possibly Vancouver — usually in that order. On the other hand, advocates of increased regional production argue that with the miniaturization and lower cost of production equipment and today's mobility of production specialists, television programs can be made anywhere. Furthermore, they state, programs made for Canadians by Canadians do not always need to meet the standard of expensive, elaborate American productions. There are many different kinds of television programs with widely varying budgets and excellence is not always predicated on a large budget or expensive production techniques.

The Task Force believes that there is no need to choose sides in the debate. A sound broadcasting policy and structure will provide for Canadian programming done both in the main centres like Montreal and Toronto and in the regions. The real issue is one of balance. There is production talent in smaller centres now and it can and should be developed.

We were told frequently by creators and their audiences in regional centres that even when they can marshall the resources to produce programs they cannot get access to the broadcast schedule. Networks leave little room in their schedules for local or regional production, and what room is left is far from prime time. Further, we were told, the trend in recent years has been toward less rather than more access to the networks for regional and local productions. Thus, what little non-news programming is produced in the regions is too often accessible only to the small audiences available in low-viewing periods and is rarely seen outside its own area.

With the growth of provincial broadcasting services described in Chapter 11, it has also become obvious that the country is not reaping the full benefit of these sources of programming by sharing them among all the provinces. There is now a substantial volume of Canadian programming produced for the provincial broadcasting services which would be of interest to all Canadians but which remains unavailable to most Canadians.

The Canadian broadcasting system seems to have been biased against local and regional production. Although historically there may have been sound economic reasons for centralization, the Task Force believes that today's technology creates opportunities to adjust the balance and we have attempted to do so in several significant ways. A number of the provincial governments have already begun to support their resident production communities in an effort to develop the existing potential. Such measures need to be complemented by federal initiatives.

The Task Force proposes that a new, omnibus, public-sector, satellite-to-cable service be established to contribute substantially to redressing the present imbalance that favours foreign programs on Canada's television broadcasting system. The service would be non-commercial. It would not carry sports or, in English, news and current affairs programs. It would be symbolically important, we believe, for the headquarters of the English and French divisions of the network to be in cities other than Toronto and Montreal.

The kind of programming TV Canada would show would include the following:

- Programming for children and young people, of the variety proposed by Young Canada Television, broadcast at times appropriate to those audiences.
- Repeats of the best Canadian programs originally broadcast by national and provincial public broadcasters, or by broadcasters in the private and community sectors.
- National Film Board productions and co-productions, which need not have been designed specifically to be shown on television.
- Arts productions and documentaries by independent producers.
- Francophone programs in English Canada and anglophone programs in French Canada, with sub-titles or dubbing.
- Selected foreign arts, children's and youth programs not usually available on other stations.

- Programs created by regionally based independent producers in any of the categories mentioned above.

TV Canada services could adopt a block schedule. The morning and afternoon could, for example, be reserved for children's programs, perhaps running as late as 7 p.m. The evening would be primarily for documentary, arts or dramatic programming, but might include some regular time slots for programs for teen-age audiences. The extent of use of repeat Canadian programming or foreign shows would depend on the resources available and could change over time.

To the extent that TV Canada would be involved with independent producers of children's, arts, drama, variety and documentary productions, programs produced for these services could benefit from support from both the Broadcast Fund and provincial government agencies. Four of the provincial governments already provide support progams and at least two others are developing policies of support. TV Canada would work with producers in all regions of Canada and would provide a national vehicle for the exhibition of regional productions in attractive viewing periods.

TV Canada could increase significantly the availability of Canadian children's programs during most of the time periods when children watch television. In addition, it could increase very substantially the availability of Canadian programs in the mid-evening viewing hours when, particularly in English, remarkably little Canadian programming is available. Moreover, it could provide the regions with the access to national television exhibition in prime time which they have never had and which the mainstream CBC networks can provide only to a limited degree.

The French network, Télé-Canada, would have a somewhat different balance since it would include news and public affairs and could show programs from the international TV-5 network. As we note in Chapter 2, Canada and Quebec are participating, through a consortium of representatives of public and private broadcasting, in the French-language TV-5 network, whose programs are broadcast by satellite-to-cable in a number of countries of Europe and North Africa. The development in Canada of this network, which was initiated by France, Belgium, and Switzerland, is at present under study.

The TV-5 programming format of six-and-a-half hours a day, with each participating country presenting 'national evenings' of programs in turn, appears ill-suited to the North American context. The Task Force believes, however, that such programming might very well be fitted into Télé-Canada, with TV-5 programs that best meet the needs and requirements of the francophone Canadian audience being chosen for its schedules.

Over the years, the evolution of TV-5, which some hope to make into the TV channel of the worldwide francophone community, and of Télé-Canada could lead to the creation of two independent networks in Canada, but for the moment cooperation between TV-5 and Télé-Canada seems to us the best solution.

For TV Canada to succeed it will need the co-operation and collaborative efforts of many organizations. As the CBC said in its submission to this Task

Force, "Partnership is what is needed to build the Canadian broadcasting system we would all like to see".[2] In addition to public broadcasters, the new service will need the active support of independent producers, creators and their association and unions, and of distributors and other copyright holders.

We propose that the English and French TV Canada be operated by a consortium which might include all public broadcasters — the CBC English and French networks as well as the provincial services — and the National Film Board.

TV Canada would operate no studios or production facilities. It would develop its schedule in part by purchasing the rights to repeat programs originally broadcast by others, and by commissioning some original productions from independent producers. New and less costly terms will need to be negotiated with rights holders for 'second window' broadcasts of programs originally seen on other outlets. Several years ago, at the time of the application for CBC-2, some performers' associations were prepared to negotiate such terms.

TV Canada's relations with independent producers could well be modeled on the practices of Britain's Channel Four. While the terms vary significantly, much of Channel Four's programming is produced on the basis of the network paying producers the full cost of production, plus a reasonable producers' fee. The network then usually owns all domestic rights to such programs and shares with the producer the proceeds from foreign sales. On these terms Britain's Channel Four has had considerable success in marketing its programs to television systems in North America and elsewhere.

In the Canadian context, however, historical realities call for some modification. The existence of Telefilm Canada's Broadcast Fund at the national level, and provincial funding programs for film and television production in Quebec, Alberta, Manitoba and Ontario, are a reaction to the fact that Canadian independent producers have not been able to rely on sales to Canadian broadcasters as their main source of funding. As we note in the next chapter, the Canadian television production industry lacks a stable domestic market. In principle the Task Force would like to see the licence fees paid by Canadian broadcasters, including TV Canada, approach the level of those paid in other industrialized countries so that the bulk of the costs of production could be recovered in Canada. But we recognize that the Broadcast Fund must play an important role by matching broadcaster licence fees. Our recommendations in Chapter 14, on the Canadian Broadcast Program Development Fund, deal in more detail with this challenge.

Producers and others in English Canada made it clear to the Task Force that in the real world relatively few TV programs made for Canadians will earn substantial revenues from foreign sales, even when such sales are made. When our producers earn a major share of their revenues from foreign sales it is usually because the programs sold are made to look like American products. The programs we would like to see on TV Canada would be quite the opposite — programs made for Canadians by Canadians with the expectation that their producers would recover the bulk of their costs in the domestic market, and would have no need to 'internationalize' their programs.

The new English and French TV Canada channels would be delivered by satellite to Canadian cable systems and carried on basic or extended basic service. All cable systems which now offer discretionary services, such as MuchMusic or the movie channels, would be required to carry the channel appropriate to the language of their majority audience on basic service at a per-subscriber charge to the cable system operator. As we note in Chapter 24, cable rates would be adjusted by an appropriate amount to reflect these costs. We would expect systems that offer the TV Canada service to provide the network in the minorities' official language of the area on the extended basic or augmented channel service in all cases where such carriage arrangements are reasonable. At a minimum the TV Canada minority language service should be included in a discretionary tier without an increase in price. By linking the carriage of TV Canada on basic cable service to the carriage of disretionary services, small systems with few channels would be exempt from the carriage requirement, which in such systems might prove difficult.

Distribution arrangements should take account of viewer convenience in the different time zones and in northern and southern Canada. They should also provide for the possibility of direct-to-home service where satellite-to-cable is not feasible. These decisions ought properly, of course, to be dealt with as part of the detailed planning process for the new services.

As noted above funding for the service would come from a direct charge to cable system operators. There are some 5.7 million cable subscribers in Canada so it is easy to determine the yield for various fee levels. By using a base of roughly five million subscribers, we would exclude those in systems whose technical capacity precludes them offering discretionary services or TV Canada. A monthly charge of 75 cents would yield $45 million annually. This would rise to $60 million at a charge of $1.00, $75 million at $1.25, and $90 million at $1.50, although as the number of subscribers reached increased, revenues would also increase. We propose that the new service begin with a charge of 75¢ per subscriber, which would rise by 25¢ annually to a maximum of $1.50. Thereafter adjustments would be made periodically to reflect inflation.

A systematic national study of cable rates in relation to inflation in systems with high and low subscription rate levels done for the Task Force concluded that ". . . high cable rates have had no significant effect on subscriber growth". In fact, "Growth in high-rate systems exceeds average growth in all areas except Alberta and B.C." The study also analyzed the market response to rate increases of between 25 percent and 33 percent which were granted between June 1983 and September 1985 in the large urban systems of Montreal, Toronto and Vancouver-Victoria. They concluded that ". . . in no case were these associated with a decline in subscriptions". In fact, in the Rogers systems serving Toronto, Vancouver and Victoria ". . . the subscriber bases were progressively increased during this period". In Montreal the rate changes were associated with major changes in service structure which made more services and programming available on the basic cable service. The resulting increase in Montreal market penetration from 7 percent to over 20 percent led to the conclusion that "This illustrates the market tolerance for rate increases which are associated with improvements in the perceived value of the services provided."[3]

The relative price insensitivity of basic cable rates has been acknowledged by the cable industry itself. In a cable operator survey carried out in 1985 for the Canadian Cable Television Association's Project 90, operators were asked what rate increases they thought could be made without any loss of subscribers (with no increase in service). The operators' consensus was that immediate increases of $1.50 would be accepted without difficulty, even if no additional services were being added to provide increased value. Our own study, based on the rates in effect in November, 1985, concluded that rate increases of as much as $2.00 would have little effect on subscription levels. In part this reflects the fact that in constant dollars the cost of cable service declined by 22 percent between 1972 and 1984.

Canada's cable television industry plays an important role in our broadcasting system. Like other parts of the system it benefits from regulations which protect its territory and otherwise regulate its marketplace to create a profitable environment. In return for these benefits the cable television industry is expected to make available facilities for a community channel and to render other services to the system. In addition to these services the Task Force expects that the cable industry will ensure that the new TV Canada channels are made available to Canadians on the basic or extended service, and will make payments for the service on a per-subscriber basis. Appropriate rate adjustments would be made, as we indicate more fully in Chapter 24 and Chapter 29.

With a substantial and predictable source of funding and no large administrative or production infrastructure to maintain, the new channels, in English and in French, will offer Canadians programming which many have long wanted. Although the programs for children, for youth and for those who enjoy dance and opera and certain kinds of drama and music will serve minorities, we believe that, taken together with repeats of high quality Canadian programs and with programs originating in centres in all regions of Canada, the new service will reach a substantial and important part of the Canadian population. The aspirations which originally led to the establishment of C-Channel, specializing in arts entertainment, the support for the Young Canada Television licence applications, and the flow of Canadian viewers' dollars to PBS stations across the border all point to needs that TV Canada can meet.

The Government of Canada, like the provincial governments, plays a substantial and critical role in the funding of many arts organizations, particularly in performing arts that lend themselves to television exhibition. Some of this federal funding is delivered directly through the Canada Council and other agencies, some of it through the CBC networks which have always scheduled a certain amount of arts programming, although this is true more of their radio than of their television schedule. We believe that the Government of Canada should consider delivering some of its support to the arts in Canada through TV Canada. Additionally, provincial governments which have substantial programs of support for the arts might consider using TV Canada as a means of delivering support to artists in their jurisdictions.

The Government of Canada should lead the way in creating the new service. First, it should hold discussions with the likely participants in the consortium that would run TV Canada and seek agreement on a more detailed plan for the new service. Based on this and other input an application would then be made to the CRTC to license the service to operate new networks in French and English.

Recommendation

> Canada needs a new non-commercial, satellite-to-cable television service in the public sector, in English and French, with a programming emphasis on regional production, programs for young people, performing arts, documentaries and the best programs shown by other Canadian broadcasters. The French, but not the English, network would also carry news and information programs. The government should convene a meeting of public broadcasters from the federal and provincial levels, together with the National Film Board, to consider the establishment of such a service under a board of directors representative of the interested parties.

The headquarters of the English and French networks of the new service should be in centres other than Toronto and Montreal. All cable systems which offer discretionary pay television services should be required to carry the new channel on the basic service in the language of the majority population served, and to make it available, where appropriate, in the minority language.

Recommendation

> Funding should be through a charge by the new service to cable system operators based on a per-subscriber rate, with the cost reflected in appropriate adjustments to cable rates.

Notes

1. National Film Board, *Setting the Record Straight* (Montreal: Syndicat général du cinéma et de la télévision, 1985), p. 24.
2. Canadian Broadcasting Corporation, *Let's Do It! A Vision of Canadian Broadcasting*, brief submitted to the Task Force on Broadcasting Policy (Ottawa: CBC, 1985), p. 43.
3. Moss, Roberts and Associates Inc., "An Economic Profile of the Canadian Cable Industry", study prepared for the Task Force on Broadcasting Policy, Ottawa, 1986.

Chapter 14

The Broadcast Fund

The Broadcast Fund

When the Canadian Film Development Corporation (CFDC) was formed in 1968 to stimulate the development of a feature film industry in Canada it was not an unusual initiative. Most industrial nations, with the notable exception of the United States, have, or have had, state-funded programs to support a domestic film industry. But Canada, with the Broadcast Fund established in 1983, is almost alone in having a special fund to assist the producers of television programs.

The decision implicit in the establishment of the Fund to develop television production independent of broadcasting networks and stations was not in itself unusual. In Canada as in many countries excluding the United States the early, almost exclusive, reliance of television broadcasters on in-house production was changing and conscious efforts were being made by many governments to change the balance between the making and buying of television programs. In Canada itself the 'make or buy' theme appeared as early as the 1965 report of the Fowler Committee. However, what was different in Canada was the decision to rely primarily on a new program of public support to the independent producers rather than to ask the broadcasters to shift some of their production budgets to external producers or, as Britain decided to do, to set up a new network, Channel Four, which would buy from independent producers and pay up to 100 percent of the cost of production of the programs acquired.

Within Canada, the emergence of independent producers as a group meriting special attention in broadcasting policy is a recent phenomenon. (We use the term independent producer to identify production companies not linked by ownership or affiliation to broadcasters). For most of the history of Canadian television,it was simply assumed that it was a desirable thing for broadcasters to develop their own production facilities and their own in-house production capacity to achieve economies of scale and a sufficient critical mass for efficient high quality production.

An independent production industry began to develop after the establishment of the Canadian Film Development Corporation in 1968. However, it focused most of its attention through the 1970s on making feature films for release in movie theatres. With the collapse of Canadian feature film production after 1980, the independent production industry was relatively idle. Pressure increased to give it greater opportunities to produce for television. Generally speaking, the resulting shift toward independent production occurred without much analysis of the possible implications.

The independent producers argued that they could offer better value for production budgets than in-house producers, particularly those working within the CBC. In-house production, they asserted, was too often unnecessarily expensive, bureaucratic and uncreative, a function of such factors as burdensome union agreements and excessive job security. Reliance on in-house production was also said to reduce the opportunities for creative new producers to get started.

We accept only a part of this argument. As we note in our discussion of the CBC we could not find any evidence to support claims either that in-house production is more expensive than independent or that the reverse is generally true. Decisions about the balance that should be struck between in-house and independent production should, therefore, not be based even in part on assumptions about the relative costs of each. We also did not accept the view that the creativity of in-house producers is generally lower than that of the independents, and we found merit in the idea that the maintenance of a critical mass of production activity within the CBC is important and helpful.

We would be particularly concerned by any extreme shift to independent production since there is a non-commercial, public sector programming philosophy that has its roots within the CBC and is vital to meeting many of our programming needs. This is linked to the mandate of the CBC to provide programs that are Canadian in content and character and to serve minority needs. Many of the independent producers themselves recognize this and share our view that a balance between in-house and independent production is desirable.

However, we believe the opportunity to draw upon a wider range of talent is a persuasive argument for greater use of independent production. An equilibrium between in-house and independent producers also broadens the choice of approaches to programming and provides the opportunity to compare the two sources. We have therefore agreed with the decision to develop independent production and in this chapter have focused our attention on recommending policy changes to allow independent producers to contribute more effectively to meeting the goals we recommend for the *Broadcasting Act*. We had to look carefully, however, at whether the Broadcast Fund was the best way to achieve this goal. In doing so we had to take into account the unusual situation in Canadian broadcasting at the time the Fund was created.

First, at least in English Canada, there was relatively little in-house production being done in private-sector broadcasting in the categories the Fund was set up to support, particularly in drama programming. Private English broadcasters were spending little on Canadian drama production, in-house or independent. To the limited extent that they did, vertically integrated production companies were used. In the CBC and in French private broadcasting, where drama production did occur in significant volume, it was done in-house.

In most developed countries, as independent television production grew, producers were able to earn the lion's share of their production costs, if not a profit, from domestic television licence fees which are the payments broadcasters make to producers to telecast their programs. The range, as Telefilm Canada stated in its submission to this Task Force, is between 75 percent to 80 percent in Australia and 100 percent in Britain and France. In the United States producers can earn a substantial profit in their home market. Canada, however, does not now have a viable domestic marketplace for independent television production. Before 1983, such production was done mainly for the CBC; producers were rarely able to earn more than 20 percent of their costs of production from CBC licence fees. With the Broadcast Fund in place and with private as well as public broadcasters now buying independent productions, the average size of Canadian licence fees has not changed. The fact that independent producers rarely recover more than 20 percent of their costs from sales in their home market remains the key problem that must be addressed.

In setting up the Canadian Broadcast Program Development Fund, commonly known as the Broadcast Fund, as part of its 1983 broadcasting strategy, the government chose to use public funds to compensate for the limited licence fees earned in Canada. The fund was made part of the operation of the Canadian Film Development Corporation, which subsequently became known as Telefilm Canada, in conjunction with its new role of aiding the production of TV programs. While the Fund was to provide support in the form of loans, loan guarantees or equity investment, it was clear from the beginning that owing to the weakness of the Canadian market for independent productions, the loans and investments would rarely result in a financial return to Telefilm. This has proved to be the case. Telefilm, in fact, receives an annual allocation for the fund which is set at a level that assumes little reliance can be placed on receiving a return from earlier investments.

This Task Force agrees that public funds should be used to support the production of Canadian television programs. It has long been recognized that Canada cannot create its own entertainment, its own mythology, its own culture, without government support. In the fine and performing arts, in publishing and in broadcasting, taxpayers at one level or another and through one means or another have footed a significant part of the bill. In the case of the Broadcast Fund, however, the form of the assistance has created serious tensions and ambiguities. We will return to this theme later. First, let us briefly recall the rationale for the Fund's existence.

In Chapters 4 and 5 we see that while Canada has one of the world's most advanced broadcasting systems in the technological sense, this country does not generate enough of its own Canadian programs in some important categories, especially dramatic entertainment. As we note in our first chapter, the way for privately owned television stations to make money is to import American programs at a fraction of the cost of production. This creates a problem since it is the acquisition cost of American programs that determines the licence fees that both public and private broadcasters expect to pay for Canadian as well as foreign programs. In their in-house production, of course, public and private broadcasters must pay the full cost of production and they therefore concentrate, particularly in the case of private broadcasters, on less expensive categories of programming. Prior to the creation of the Broadcast Fund, independent producers, to the extent they could function as producers of TV programs at all, had to try to satisfy the program needs of foreign rather than Canadian broadcasters because the bulk of their revenue had to come from abroad.

It is clear, then, that the need for indigenous Canadian programs cannot be met in our limited market without additional government support. The growing group of competent independent producers working outside both public and private networks is an important source of new programming. However, for the reasons given above, these producers need the support of the Broadcast Fund if they are to produce programs tailored to the Canadian market.

No new legislative basis has been established for the operation of the

Broadcast Fund. It is administered under the *Canadian Film Development Corporation Act*, 1966-1967, which does not provide authority for the CFDC to support anything but feature film production. The Fund thus operates on the basis of a Memorandum of Understanding between the Minister of Communications and the CFDC, rather than under a mandate from Parliament.

The Memorandum guidelines state that, as a condition for receiving assistance through the Fund, creative control over productions should rest with Canadians and employment opportunities, to the maximum extent possible, should be provided for Canadians in all stages of production. To gain access to the Fund, producers require a prior commitment by an over-the-air broadcaster to run the programs in the most attractive viewing hours, 7 p.m. to 11 p.m. Children's programs may be broadcast at other times.

Telefilm Canada was authorized under the 1983 policy to cover up to one-third of the cost of projects, by way of loans, loan guarantees, equity, or some combination of the three. The agency was asked to seek "an appropriate balance in its investments so as to foster program production in all regions of Canada".[1] One-third of the Fund was to be directed toward French-language production.

As part of the strategy connected with the Fund, it was announced in October 1983 that the CBC would increase its prime time Canadian content level from about 70 percent to 80 percent over the five years ending in 1988. The increase was to come mainly from the purchase of programs from independent producers. It was expected that by 1989 the CBC would be purchasing some 230 hours annually in additional programming through the Fund, with the emphasis on drama.

The Broadcast Fund was launched with significant funding: $35 million in the first year, rising to $50 million in the second and to $60 million by 1987-88, when it was to expire. Up to half the money from the Fund was earmarked for projects broadcast on the CBC, the remainder for the private sector. A six-percent tax on cable television industry revenue was imposed to offset the cost of the new program, although this is not a dedicated tax, as there is no direct link between the revenues generated and the Broadcast Fund. This tax has since been increased to 8 percent.

So far as private broadcasters were concerned the policy statement announcing the Fund noted that

> Precise targets in each program category and the responsibilities of particular broadcasters with respect to hours and quality, will, of course, be defined by the CRTC. . . .
>
> The direction taken by the commission in its January 31, 1983 announcement of proposed changes in its Canadian content regulations lays the groundwork very well for the development of such targets.[2]

In the CRTC policy document referred to, the Commission had repeated a statement it had made earlier in 1979 noting that it was "even more valid today":

> With the exception of the Canadian Broadcasting Corporation, Canadian English-language broadcasters offer Canadian audiences virtually no Canadian entertainment programming in peak viewing periods and next to no Canadian drama — light or serious — at any period in their schedules.[3]

The statement did point out, however, that private French-language broadcasters had generally performed better, allocating more resources to variety and musical programs as well as providing about two hours of Canadian drama each week.

The CRTC stated it would use conditions of licence for individual broadcasters to ensure that in future they made a contribution to drama programming commensurate with their resources. This issue is examined in Chapter 17. The recommendations made there for the regulation of private television should be seen as complementary to the analysis and recommendations in this chapter.

The crucial assumptions made when the Broadcast Fund was established were that the CBC's schedules would become more Canadian, based on private-sector production, and that the CRTC would increase its demands on private broadcasters to purchase and exhibit Canadian programs for exhibition in prime time. Both the CBC and private broadcasters were expected to free up air time between 7 p.m. and 11 p.m. for the resulting Canadian programs. Equally important, they were expected to pay enough for the programs to provide independent producers — in combination with the Fund — with the domestic financial base they had always lacked. Meeting these two essential requirements for the development of a private-sector production capacity in Canada would, however, require major changes in the way both public and private broadcasters had functioned for decades.

The Broadcast Fund began operation on July 1, 1983. Over the first 18 months it stimulated $156 million worth of production, a significant accomplishment in light of the fact that in 1984-85 the CBC and private television broadcasters spent $832 million on all production and acquisition of Canadian programs. Production stimulated by the Fund included feature films, drama series, variety and children's programs. During the year of the Task Force's deliberations, many of these programs went on the air achieving popular success.

By the end of 1984, however, production had stalled and a review of the operations of the Fund was undertaken in an atmosphere of crisis. In September of that year the CBC, facing budget restrictions, froze its participation in the Fund. It was by then clear that the CBC had been the major player in Fund-related production; without its participation expectations would not be fulfilled. In French-language production, 97 percent of all of the money that broadcasters had made available for Fund projects had come from Radio-Canada. In English-language production, 68 percent had come from the CBC. On a national basis the CBC accounted for just over 75 percent. Private broadcaster support had been disappointingly low in the first 18 months. CTV, for example, accounted for barely one percent of the broadcasters' financial commitments to Fund-related production. Among French-language broadcasters, while private French stations continued to be involved significantly in drama and variety production, they continued to rely on in-house production rather than independent production supported by the Broadcast Fund. With a well established in-house production capacity and an efficient system for volume production, the shift to significant use of independent production would be a slow process.

Telefilm Canada had made available $44.8 million during the first

18 months of its operation. But Canadian broadcasters, through licence fees, committed only $20.8 million, just 13 percent of the $156 million worth of production, to buy the rights to put the programs on the air.

Clearly, the plan was not working, and with the effective withdrawal of the CBC, Telefilm Canada was projecting in January 1985 that it would have $33 million in unspent funds by the March 31 end of its fiscal year, fully 40 percent of the total amount that had been allocated. Further, the Fund had been unable to reach its target for French-language production, with just over 25 percent of its support having gone to French-language productions, compared to the proposed 33 percent. Regional production, or support for productions originating outside Ontario and Quebec, which essentially meant Toronto and Montreal, accounted at that time for just 4.6 percent of the monies that Telefilm had provided for Broadcast Fund projects.

The review precipitated a number of changes. A revised Memorandum of Understanding was signed in March 1985, which allowed the Broadcast Fund to assume where necessary a larger share of the costs of production. The changes also had the effect of allowing money spent by the CBC to go further. The terms of reference of the Fund were expanded to include documentaries and more clearly define the eligibility of performing arts productions. Telefilm was allowed, on a discretionary basis, to increase its participation from one-third to 49 percent in the case of wholly Canadian productions, partly as a means of addressing the imbalance between French-language and English-language production and between regions. In announcing the revisions to the Memorandum, the Minister of Communications stated:

> The Fund must support a genuinely national production industry, drawing effectively on the creativity and the resources of all parts of the country. The revised criteria also reflect an awareness that it has always been more difficult for independent producers to arrange the necessary financing for projects that are fully Canadian, however important those projects may be culturally.[4]

Production accelerated by the end of 1985. Between April 1 and October 31 Telefilm committed $52 million to production, more than it had allocated in its first 18 months. French-language production rose to the targeted 33 percent of committed funds and production outside Ontario and Quebec increased from less than 5 percent to about 12 percent. Private French broadcasters, however, accounted for only 7 percent of French-language broadcaster support, while Radio-Quebec which had been made eligible under the revised guidelines began to play a significant role, providing 20 percent. In English Canada, CTV increased its level of participation from less than 1 percent to 17 percent, with its affiliates providing a further 7 percent. Global's share rose from 6 percent to 15 percent. TVOntario contributed 4 percent.

While the upsurge in production was dramatic, one thing did not change. Licence fees paid by Canadian broadcasters to air the productions remained disappointingly low, continuing to account for an average of just 10 percent in French production and 18 percent in English.

When announcing the revisions to the Memorandum of Understanding the Minister of Communications had said:

> I want to stress the fact that the review of the Broadcast Fund has raised many issues that cannot properly be resolved either by changes to the criteria which govern access to the Fund or changes in the way that Telefilm administers the fund. Without a strong domestic market, a financially stable Canadian television production industry will not develop.[5]

Telefilm Canada made the same point in its submission to us. Its presentation was concerned exclusively with the Canadian broadcasters' financial participation in Canadian productions, and with comparisons with the United States, France and Britain. Noting "that the situation in Canada is at odds with the way other broadcasters and independent producers approach financing of . . . independent productions", Telefilm concluded that "only by making fundamental changes . . . will Canadian producers have a chance to succeed financially as well as they do creatively".[6]

In the three countries Telefilm selected for comparison they made the observation we referred to earlier, that "independent producers recover 80 percent to 100 percent of their costs of production from broadcast networks in their own domestic market". In fact, as Telefilm noted, television production the world over tends to be national in its financing, in this important respect differing from feature film financing, where revenues from foreign sales are typically much more important. Telefilm noted that when the Broadcast Fund was established, "the assumption was that Canadian broadcasters would license Canadian independent production for a minimum of approximately one-third of the production costs". Their brief went on to note, however, that this did not happen. In fact, "Total financing available from eligible Canadian broadcasters — both in the form of licence fees and equity — has averaged only 15.6% overall, and only 14.9% to date in 1985–1986."[7]

Telefilm agreed, however, that there were legitimate limits to what private Canadian broadcasters could be expected to pay. "Canadian broadcasters have quite rightly argued that they cannot pay as much to license Canadian productions from Canadian independent producers as other broadcasters", in large part because of the small size of the market.[8]

Telefilm recommended that "Canadian broadcasters should increase their licence fees to approximately 50% of the cost of production." Its brief noted that "with supplementary financing from other private and government sources (Telefilm Canada, la Société générale du cinéma du Québec, etc.), other Canadian markets (theatrical, video cassette, pay, syndication), Canadian producers could anticipate financing 80% of their production costs within Canada".[9]

Telefilm was also concerned with the amount of air time to be given to Broadcast Fund projects. It recommended that broadcasters be encouraged to provide greater access to their schedules, particularly in prime time.

This Task Force shares the view that the present pattern of financing of independent production is unworkable, and that substantial changes are required if the Broadcast Fund is to achieve its purpose. One option that must be considered is to phase out the Broadcast Fund and put in place a different strategy to ensure the independent production industry's development as a source of Canadian television programs. Many producers, for example, expressed their admiration for the basic approach represented by Britain's Channel Four. In effect, what the British did was give independent producers a major new domestic buyer for their programs, rather than providing them with direct financial assistance.

Within the Canadian context it would be possible to take initiatives to achieve the purpose of establishing buyers for independent Canadian productions. The CBC could, for example, be given the funds through a separate vote and could operate on the basis of a licence fee payment that covered an average of perhaps 75 or 80 percent of production costs. Private broadcasters could be relieved of their responsibilities for Canadian content and taxed to provide money for production elsewhere. In the simplest model the money could be added to the CBC budget. In a more sophisticated model a new agency, perhaps along the lines of Britain's Channel Four, could be established to produce or commission programming.

The Task Force has, however, not been persuaded that a radical change should be made. Instead we have concentrated our attention on the mandate and operating guidelines of the Broadcast Fund, on the essential changes required to find adequate access for independent productions to the schedules of established Canadian broadcasters, and on an increased return from these broadcasters.

Implicit in our approach is the judgement that a healthy independent production industry is vital to increase indigenous programming and that, under the appropriate conditions, independent producers can contribute in an expanded way to providing Canadians with their own television programs. But we also believe that in-house production is important and we call on all broadcasters to help meet the challenge. The energy and creativity of both are needed if we are to reflect and strengthen Canadian identity in our broadcasting system.

It should be said, parenthetically, that in a strict sense there is no 'private sector' production industry in our country. With very rare exceptions independent television producers receive some, often the majority, of their funding from public sources. For example, Clément Richard, former Quebec Minister of Cultural Affairs, noted that the market in Quebec is so small that government support will always be needed, and it is not appropriate to call the independent producers 'private sector' producers. Or as SARDEC (Société des Auteurs, Recherchistes, Documentalistes et Compositeurs) put it in an open letter sent to the French newspaper *La Presse* and repeated with emphasis to the Task Force in a meeting:

> Apart from the TVA network, which has always managed to finance production of its programs on its own, there isn't a real private film or program producer for television in French Canada. Without the considerable financial role of Telefilm Canada and the Société Générale du Cinéma, without the financial participation of CBC, Radio-Québec or the NFB, almost no programs would be produced. It must therefore be concluded that the so-called private industry doesn't exist and that it should be defined, rather, as private management of a majority public undertaking.[10] (translation)

Licence Fees

As we have seen, licence fees, the money paid to producers or their agents for the right to show a program, have become a central issue. The low fees paid by broadcasters in Canada are partly the result of a persistent myth that Canadian productions can recover most of their production costs beyond our borders, particularly in the United States, and that against potential profits from foreign sales the Canadian market is of limited significance. Every producer wants to crack the big time — the big time being Los Angeles, the hub of world distribution.

With rare exceptions, however, Canadian programs do not sell to the major networks in the United States. What does sell, when we succeed in the big time, is in most instances American programs made in Canada. The actors and production personnel may be more-or-less Canadian, the locations, usually neutralized by altering licence plates and taking down flags, may be Canadian, but the programs, in their style and substance, are American. Almost anyone involved in Canadian television can provide examples.

When truly Canadian programs are sold abroad, and they often are, the unhappy truth is that their producers usually don't get much for them. This is true not just for Canada's sales abroad but for every country's. Foreign sales of American programs, in addition to profoundly influencing world tastes and standards for entertainment, also set the international prices for sales of television programs, including Canadian programs. *Variety* magazine, for example, shows American prime-time, half-hour television series selling at prices that range from a low of several hundred dollars to a high of $48,000 per episode, depending on the size of the country making the purchase and the audience reached by the broadcaster. Canadian broadcasters typically pay $15,000 to $20,000 per half hour in English and $6,000 to $9,000 in French for American productions which will have cost at least ten times as much to produce.

A study of Telefilm Canada prepared for this Task Force by Colin Hoskins and Stuart McFadyen[11] showed that a Canadian documentary made for $250,000 was sold to the U.K., France and West Germany for a meagre $15,000 apiece. A half-hour television drama can be expected to deliver foreign sales revenue of $30,000 to $40,000 per episode over three years. Total international sales by the CBC in 1985 are estimated at $6 million. The private sector managed $5 million.

Important conclusions follow from the fact that a substantial majority of the financing of Canadian television productions must come from the domestic market. At the same time, we are equally convinced that there is an urgent need to clarify, in policy terms, and to indicate in the enabling legislation under which Telefilm operates, what ultimate goals the Broadcast Fund is intended to serve.

The 1983 announcement of the Broadcast Fund was unclear about ultimate ends, mentioning job creation, industry development and export sales as well as the crucial need to reinforce Canadian identity and to have an expanded

Canadian presence on the screen in prime time. Priorities among these aims were not established.

There would be no problem here if there were no potential conflicts between the various goals which might be pursued by the Fund. If maximizing revenue from foreign sales and maximizing a return to the Fund were perfectly compatible with the expression of Canadian identity and with achieving linguistic and regional balance in production activity, Telefilm would not be faced with the need to choose which goals should have priority. But this is clearly not the case. There are, for example, a significant number of programs produced in Canada now with a reasonable expectation of profit and no need for public support. Most such productions are designed explicitly for American broadcasters and are produced here in Canada largely because of the low value of the Canadian dollar. If Telefilm wished to maximize its revenues and to invest in projects which would achieve maximum success outside Canada, it would be wise to encourage the producers of these shows to meet its minimum point requirements, as set out in Chapter 5, for acceptance as Canadian programs and invest in them. Most Canadians, however, would be unable to identify any of these productions as having anything at all to do with Canada or Canadians, for the simple reason that they were designed to satisfy American broadcasters and audiences.

In practice, Telefilm has put much of its money into genuinely Canadian productions. It has tempered purely industrial assessment of funding decisions by concern with the character of the productions. Most of the projects Telefilm has participated in do not try to disguise their Canadian origin. Owing to the minimal licence fees Canadian producers are earning from Canadian sales of their productions, however, and in the absence of a clear mandate for the operation of the Fund, the Task Force believes that there has been and will be steadily increasing pressure on independent producers and, as a result, on Telefilm to tailor the projects that receive support better to satisfy foreign broadcasters. At the same time there will be more pressure to ignore anything but mainstream Canadian productions, at the expense of regional programs, performing arts programs and other kinds of production that would be part of a balanced pattern designed to fit the schedules of both public and private broadcasters, in both French and English.

In their study Hoskins and McFadyen reported that they had found that there

> . . . had been reason for concern that in recent months Telefilm Canada had been over-emphasizing rate of return considerations and under-emphasizing cultural significance. In our discussions with Telefilm Canada officials, fiscal responsibility and the need to get a good return on taxpayers' money was emphasized.[12]

Our purpose here is not to be critical of Telefilm Canada's administration of the Broadcast Fund, but to respond in a comprehensive way to the considerable problems connected to the operation of the Fund. The Task Force believes that in addition to addressing the licence fee issue identified by Telefilm Canada, there is a need to be clear about the nature of the productions that should be encouraged. This is not easy. However, Hoskins and MacFadyen make a useful distinction between defining 'inputs' such as actors, editors, writers, directors and so on as Canadian and defining production 'output' as Canadian. In our view it is clearly important to try to identify the nature of the programming that Telefilm should support, and not simply to count up the inputs. The Task Force believes the primary role of the Fund should be to support productions that are under the creative control of Canadians and that are made primarily for Canadian television audiences, both popular mainstream audiences and minority audiences. It should not be to support programs that are designed essentially for export, with Canadian 'inputs' and a Canadian broadcast window built in only as a means of obtaining support from the Fund. While the economic and industrial benefits that flow from the development of Canadian production activity are clearly important, the pursuit of these goals should be seen as secondary.

There is no intention here of reducing support for the marketing of Canadian productions outside Canada; quite the contrary. We believe that Canadian programs that are true to themselves and express universal values through Canadian experience can in the long run find greater success abroad than what Michael MacMillan of Atlantis Films calls "American clone programming". More important, it is such programs that we as Canadians need and that require and merit support through public funding.

Nor is it our intention to suggest that the government ought not to sign co-production treaties with other countries. Under a co-production treaty, projects involving producers in both countries are treated as though they are domestic productions, thus qualifying for many of the benefits available to domestic productions in both countries. While no one would want international co-productions to do more than complement national production activity, they do provide the potential to carry out ambitious projects. So long as such treaties ensure a real balance of both cultural and economic benefits to both countries involved, they can be of real value.

Priority for genuinely Canadian programs will have to be accompanied by action on the licence-fee problem. While we look at this issue in Chapters 10 and 17, we need to discuss here how Telefilm's support might be changed. We accept the view that Canadian productions will usually have to recover at least 70 to 80 percent of their financing from the Canadian market, as is the case in other countries.

If, as Telefilm itself recommended, 50 percent of production costs were covered by Canadian broadcaster licence fees, it would still be necessary for the average project to earn a great deal from other sources, and especially from foreign sales, before it could show a profit. However, we share Telefilm's view, as did both Canadian producers and broadcasters, that it is not reasonable to base a standard financing formula for Canadian TV productions on earning more than 20 percent of costs from foreign sales. We also recognize that the 50 percent Telefilm proposes would represent an enormous increase from present levels.

In our view it would be more reasonable to consider the combination of Canadian broadcaster licence fees and Broadcast Fund support as providing the domestic base Canadian television production requires. A number of Canadian broadcasters cited in the Task Force's research study suggested that Fund support should match licence fee payments of Canadian broadcasters. If this principle were accepted, a minimum licence fee payment might be set as a basis for triggering access to the Fund; perhaps 15 percent would be a reasonable level at least initially. Telefilm could then match the broadcaster on a dollar-for-dollar basis up to a maximum of 35 percent, so that 70 percent of costs would be covered.

Under this approach, Telefilm's participation would not be that of a simple equity investor. We are not in a position to suggest the precise technical form Broadcast Fund support should take under this arrangement. The aim would be to achieve the equivalent of increasing the producers' return from the domestic market. The form of aid could be a financial contribution, a loan forgiveable if certain criteria were met, an investment recoverable in last position after other investors, or some combination of these methods. A matching basis of support would provide a strong incentive to Canadian broadcasters to increase their licence fee payments. If a Canadian producer could thus recoup 70 percent of the costs of production, chances of recovering the remaining 30 percent from ancillary markets such as video cassettes, additional plays on pay-TV and other media, and some foreign sales become realistic.

The Task Force believes that Telefilm Canada should move in the direction of providing its support to programs made for Canadian audiences by matching the licence fees provided by both private and public broadcasters. With the realities of our market in clear perspective, there is little justification for the Broadcast Fund to be operated as though it were just a public venture capital fund, which exists essentially to follow market forces.

The mix of equity and licence fees provided by Canadian broadcasters, public and private, to Broadcast Fund projects is a directly related issue. In its submission to the Task Force, Telefilm Canada expressed concern that the total level of financing provided by Canadian broadcasters was very low, and "some Canadian broadcasters (notably English and French CBC) are insisting on dividing their participation in Canadian production between licence fees and equity investment".[13] The result is that Canadian broadcasters are not only paying far less than their counterparts in other countries to exhibit domestic productions but also wanting to own a piece of each production. We share Telefilm's view that "While such a policy might be defensible, if tied to licence fees nearer 80 percent of production costs, it seems . . . unreasonable, given the extremely low licence fees offered".[14] In the case of the CBC we consider such policies particularly inappropriate. In the case of the private broadcasters we believe the approach of matching licence fees we recommend will encourage broadcasters to provide their financing through licence fee payments. We also note in Chapter 17 that the CRTC should focus its own approach on encouraging broadcasters to commit reasonable funds to the acquisition of the right to show Canadian productions.

If Canadian broadcasters are to increase the licence fees they pay, it is reasonable to expect that they will want to have more say about the programs they buy. Once a broadcaster and a producer have agreed on the nature of the program to be broadcast, however, creative control should remain with the producer, subject to the terms of his agreement with the broadcaster. Telefilm's role should be to decide whether the project is consistent with the objectives of the Fund and what level of support is appropriate under its guidelines.

It should be understood that the emphasis we recommend may well involve a trade-off between the goals of generating programs made primarily for Canadians and the maximizing of the Broadcast Fund's leveraging potential. If we say that Canadian productions should recover most of their costs in Canada, then there may well be fewer than if productions were designed mainly to satisfy an American buyer. In speaking to our researchers, producer Stephen Roth, who served as co-chairman of the 1985 federal film industry Task Force, made this point, noting that:

> If Telefilm concentrates on the commercial viability of projects and attempts to minimize its financial involvement in each of them, it could quickly find itself in the position of being a minority partner in a large number of projects over which it had little creative control and was therefore completely unable to achieve the cultural goals originally set out for the program.[15]

The implications of systematically seeking the maximum possible leveraging of Broadcast Fund dollars are now well understood. An earlier study of the potential market in the United States for Canadian production, prepared for the Department of Communications in March 1983 by the consulting firm Grieve Horner and Associates, concluded that "if Canadian-made programs are to generate meaningful revenues from the United States, such programs must be developed in co-operation with U.S. program buyers, producers and distributors and on the basis of pre-commitments from U.S. buyers and distributors".[16]

The Grieve Horner study was quite clear in its findings, insisting that "Canadian producers must involve potential American buyers in the development of their programs from the very beginning of the development process". The conclusion they reached was that if revenue from the American market was to be maximized, then "the international potential of Canadian programs should not be hobbled by making Canadian specificity a compulsory ingredient of Canadian content".[17]

In the CBC's 1984 application for renewal of its English-language television licence, the Corporation made the same point, noting that "popularity — if it is expressed in terms of international saleability — may be at variance with distinctiveness". The application went on to note that "the notion of distinctiveness or 'Canadianness' bears particularly on the percentage of the production budget which the CBC may have to contribute", and concluded that "it may, in some cases, be necessary for the CBC to contribute . . . as much as 50 or 60 percent in order to obtain a program with the characteristics it wants" and "to provide a reasonable return to the producer".[18]

If we have demonstrated that the problem in Canadian television, a problem that is at crisis level in English Canada, is a market not robust enough on its own to meet the challenge of readily available foreign programs, then the role of the Broadcast Fund is clear. To be an engine of Canadian television production, the Broadcast Fund must not be based on an industrial investment policy predicated on the myth that there is a pot of gold at the end of the American rainbow, but be based instead on a policy of creating a viable domestic market for Canadian producers, taking account of both broadcaster licence fees and Telefilm Canada. In relation to the United States, Canada will never be able to produce as much television programming as it needs or would like. But the Task Force believes that it is critical to the survival of Canada as a distinctive and separate country that our own programs have a significant presence in our broadcast system.

And so, we repeat, licence fees are the central issue. Canadian producers will succeed best when they are paid for what they produce, with a reasonable chance of profiting from their creativity. Owing to the realities of our market, that means the expenditure of public funds and we can only point out that it is entirely consistent with our history, in broadcasting, in film, and in the arts in general. As we indicate in Chapter 29, the level of support which could be provided through the Fund in a second five-year term would be $75 million initially and could rise at least in line with inflation over the five-year period. This calculation is based on the level of offsetting tax revenue which would result if the tax on basic cable service is reduced to 5 percent, with a 10 percent tax levied on discretionary services, as proposed elsewhere in this Report.

Canada must join other industrialized countries in providing a strong return from its domestic market if it wishes to have indigenous production. The Task Force believes that the future role of a renewed Broadcast Fund must be to work with broadcasters to increase their licence fees and that Fund policies should be revised to reflect this purpose.

Recommendations

The Broadcast Fund should be extended beyond the 1988 expiry of its first five-year term. One third of the support should continue to go toward French-language programming.

Legislation should be passed formally establishing Telefilm Canada as an arm's length agency of government and providing it with a mandate on which to base its administration of the Broadcast Fund. The legislation should make it clear that Telefilm Canada's support for television programs has as its primary objective the furthering of the goals of the Broadcast Act through increased production of television programs made under the creative control of Canadians and primarily for Canadian television audiences, both popular mainstream and minority audiences.

The guidelines for the operation of the fund should be designed to help achieve the goal of developing a sound domestic market for indigenous production. Broadcast Fund involvement in television production should change so that by the end of 1987-88 support will be provided principally in the form of matching the licence fee payments made by Canadian broadcasters. (This recommendation is linked to our recommendations concerning the CBC and to our proposals concerning private broadcasting, including those related to the conditions of licence established by the CRTC for private broadcasters.)

By the end of 1987-88, support from the Fund should be provided principally to programs made primarily for Canadian by Canadians, and based on the expectation that such productions must recover most of their revenues in the Canadian market.

In future, support through the Broadcast Fund for programs that are designed primarily for sale in foreign markets should be provided on the basis of profit-motivated investment, and the Fund's involvement in such projects should not account for a major portion of expenditures.

Telefilm should determine that projects supported are consistent with its mandate and eligibility criteria, and have the required commitment from a Canadian broadcaster to exhibit them. Creative control should rest with the producer, subject only to the terms of the producer's agreement with the broadcaster.

Telefilm Canada should continue to assist in developing the financial and managerial capabilities of production companies and in supporting the marketing of Canadian television programs.

Notes

1. *Memorandum of Understanding Concerning the Establishment of the Canadian Broadcast Program Development Fund*, Ottawa, February 21, 1983, p. 4.
2. Canada, Department of Communications, *Towards a New National Broadcasting Policy* (Ottawa: Minister of Supply and Services Canada, 1983), p. 9.
3. Canadian Radio-television Telecommunications Commission, *Policy Statement on Canadian Content in Television*, CRTC Public Notice 83-18, (Ottawa: CRTC, 1983), p. 6.
4. Hon. Marcel Masse, *Statement Concerning Changes to the Canadian Broadcasting Program Development Fund*, Toronto, March 15, 1983 (Ottawa: Department of Communications, 1983), p. 3.
5. Ibid., p. 14.
6. Telefilm Canada, "Financing Canadian Television Production," brief prepared for the Task Force on Broadcasting Policy, Ottawa, 1986.
7. Ibid.
8. Ibid.
9. Ibid.
10. S.A.R.D.E.C. (Société des auteurs, recherchistes, documentalistes et compositeurs), "L'industrie privée de l'audiovisuel", quoted in Société Radio-Canada, *Un aperçu du réseau de la télévision française*, brief prepared for the Task Force on Broadcasting Policy, Ottawa, 1986.
11. Colin Hoskins and Stuart McFadyen, "The Canadian Broadcast Program Development Fund: Past Experience and Future Options", study prepared for the Task Force on Broadcasting Policy, Ottawa, 1986.
12. Hoskins and McFadyen, "Program Development Fund".
13. Telefilm Canada, "Financing Canadian Television Production".
14. Ibid.
15. Hoskins and McFadyen, "Program Development Fund".
16. Grieve, Horner & Associates Inc., *A Study of the United States Market for Television Programs*, part 2 (Ottawa: Department of Communications, 1983), p. 2.
17. Ibid., p. 11.
18. Canadian Broadcasting Corporation, *Application for the Renewal of the Television Networks Licences of the Canadian Broadcasting Corporation*, vol. 1 (Ottawa: CBC, 1984), pp. 36 — 37.

Part V

THE PRIVATE SECTOR

Chapter 15

Public Policy and the Business of Broadcasting

Public Policy and the Business of Broadcasting

Public Policy and the Private Sector

Although the Aird Commission of 1929 hoped broadcasting in Canada could be delivered entirely by the public sector, private broadcasters continued to play a significant role in the system as they had from the outset. In fact the private sector is now dominant in its share of audiences and financial resources in both radio and television.

Private broadcasters in Canada have long agreed that in return for the genuine — and often lucrative — privilege of being granted a broadcasting licence, they are obligated to perform certain services for the system that are not necessarily in the best immediate self-interest of their enterprise. The question has always been, however, the balance that should be struck between their private needs and their public responsibilities.

In our meetings with private sector representatives we were happy to take at face value their frequent and unsolicited commitments to fulfilling their role in meeting Canadian broadcasting objectives. Nevertheless, it would be unreasonable to expect the private sector to meet its obligations unless public policy makes clear what they are.

The 1968 *Broadcasting Act* requires both public and private broadcasters to provide programming that is "of high standard, using predominantly Canadian creative and other resources". Apart from that provision, what is expected from private broadcasters under existing legislation is defined under objectives that are set out for the Canadian broadcasting system as a whole. The Act calls for programming to be "varied and comprehensive" and to "provide reasonable, balanced opportunity for the expression of differing views on matters of public concern".[1]

The only additional statement contained in the Act is a requirement that the system "should be owned and effectively controlled by Canadians". The rationale provided for Canadian ownership and control is "to safeguard, enrich and strengthen the cultural, political, social and economic fabric of Canada",[2] although the Act does not now state directly that the Canadian broadcasting system should assist in meeting these objectives.

The requirement to provide programming of high standard and to use predominantly Canada creative and other resources has been interpreted by the CRTC as being consistent with the presence in the Canadian broadcasting system of individual broadcasting signals provided by American broadcasters which use no Canadian creative resources. Further, the CRTC considers this provision to be consistent with Canadian content requirements for private Canadian broadcasting services which are substantially lower than the 50 percent which would flow from the commonly-understood meaning of "predominantly".

In Part II of this Report we present a revised set of objectives for Canadian broadcasting that are intended to achieve two basic goals. First, we recommend objectives which will be more realistic and avoid contradictions between the intention of the Act and the reality of the regulatory requirements, such as the anomaly just noted. Second, we recommend that clearer objectives be set for the system as a whole, with each component being expected to make a contribution compatible with its resources. The public broadcasting service — the CBC — would, however, continue to be expected to carry out functions not assigned to the system as a whole.

Our proposed changes would eliminate the requirement that the programming provided by each broadcaster should use predominantly Canadian creative and other resources. Instead, the revised legislation proposed in Chapter 6 would establish the following objectives for the system:

1. Only Canadians may own and control broadcasting undertakings in Canada.
2. In both its organization and operation, the Canadian broadcasting system should serve the interests of all Canadians and their need to express themselves, in order to safeguard, enrich and strengthen the cultural, political, social and economic fabric of Canada.
3. The Canadian broadcasting system should play an active role in developing an awareness of Canada, reflect the cultural diversity of Canadians and make available a wide range of programming that is Canadian in content and character and that provides for a continuing expression of Canadian identity. It should serve the special needs of the geographic regions and actively contribute to the flow and exchange of information and expression among the regions of Canada.
4. The Canadian broadcasting system should offer a range of programming that is varied and comprehensive, providing a balance of information, enlightenment and entertainment for people of differing ages, interests and tastes.
5. The overall programming of each broadcaster, in keeping with its status in the community served, should provide a balanced opportunity for the expression of differing views on matters of public interest.
6. The programs provided by Canadian broadcasters should be of high standard, reflecting commitments made by broadcasters and recognized professional standards appropriate to the category of the broadcaster.

The CRTC would be expected to regulate the broadcasting system as a whole and to establish for each component of the system requirements consistent with the achievement of these objectives. We also recommend that broadcasting policy recognize the different environment and circumstances in which Quebec broadcasters operate and their special place in French-language broadcasting in Canada.

The terms of reference of this Task Force require that we present recommendations for an industrial and cultural strategy for broadcasting, as well as review the mandate of private broadcasting. For those reasons, we have examined carefully the capacity of private radio and television broadcasters to contribute to meeting the above objectives. In particular we have given considerable attention in our research and consultations to understanding the various factors which affect the financial strength of Canadian radio and television stations and networks. In the case of television broadcasting this has included an examination of measures such as Bill C-58 and the CRTC's simultaneous program substitution rules.

The Task Force has also reviewed present measures to encourage private broadcasters to make a reasonable contribution to broadcasting goals. We have taken advantage of our research and discussions with industry participants and interested parties to develop recommendations to improve those measures.

We will now look in general terms at the nature of private broadcasting as a business.

Broadcasting as a Business

Broadcasting in all its forms is the largest of the cultural industries. The private sector of broadcasting obtains nearly all its revenue from advertising, and is of course even more dependent than the print media on advertising for its business health.

Although we speak of separate private and public broadcasting sectors, they overlap. The private sector, for instance, includes both radio and television affiliates of the publicly-owned CBC. The CBC, in its television services, competes with the private sector for advertising revenue. Even the community sector sometimes fills a role close to that of the private sector when it provides the only radio station in a small community which lacks the resources to support a private station.

The business of private radio and television, addressed in the following two chapters, is to sell audiences to advertisers, thereby earning the revenue which enables them to broadcast programs and make a profit. As we see in the chapter on programs and audiences, elaborate means of measuring audiences have been developed so that the advertiser will know the size, location and a good deal about the social makeup of the audience which is to be exposed to the advertising message.

Among the major factors which have affected Canadian television broadcasting are the development and increasing carriage capacity of cable television and the application of satellite technology to the delivery of broadcast services. Over the past three years new television services which rely on payments from subscribers or the cable industry — either instead of, or in addition to, advertising — have been added to the Canadian broadcasting system. While pay television and specialty programming services still account for only a small percentage of television audiences in Canada, they are becoming an important additional source of revenue. These services are examined in Chapter 18. Cable is not extensively used to carry radio, although it could be.

Taking the private and public systems together, English and French, Canada has 514 radio and 114 television originating stations, exclusive of the community sector. If their revenues, including CBC, are combined with cable revenues, the total turnover in 1984 was well over $3 billion, of which the private sector share was about $2.15 billion. Private radio and television stations had revenue of just under $1.5 billion in 1984.

Radio and television stations compete not just with one another but with all the media for advertising dollars. The way the advertising dollar has been divided over the past 25 years can be seen from the figures in Table 15.1

Table 15.1 Share of Net Advertising Revenues (percent)[a]

	1960	1970	1984[b]
Television	9.1	13.1	17.3
Radio	9.2	10.7	9.7
Daily newspaper	30.9	28.4	24.7
General magazines	3.8	2.5	4.4
Community newspapers	4.3	4.9	5.7
Catalogues and direct mail	21.4	20.5	21.9
Billboard, other outdoor	6.7	9.1	5.9

Note: a. May not sum to 100 as minor categories have been omitted.
b. The figures for 1984 are estimates.
Source: Maclean Hunter Research Bureau

After rising significantly in the 1960s, private radio held an extremely steady share (approximately 11 percent) of all media advertising revenue through the next decade. Since 1980, however, radio's share has declined slightly. At the same time, the television industry's (private and public) share of total advertising revenue for all media has been increasing steadily. In 1960 its share was 9.1 percent; by 1984 it had reached 17.3 percent.

As a proportion of gross national product, radio advertising revenue held steady at about 0.13 percent from 1970 to 1984, while the TV advertising climbed from 0.15 percent to 0.23 percent.

Radio and television combined have fared well in competing with non-broadcast media for advertising revenue, increasing their share of total media advertising from 18.3 percent in 1960 to 27 percent in 1984. This means two things: the broadcast media have gained tens of millions of dollars of revenue against their non-broadcast competitors and, by implication, Canadians turn to the broadcast media more and more as a source of information and entertainment.

While the broadcast media combined have gained ground against non-broadcast media, radio and television also compete directly with one another for revenue. As Table 15.1 indicates, radio still received almost as much advertising revenue in 1970 as television — 46 percent of the combined radio-television total compared with 54 percent. By 1984, however, radio had dropped to 36 percent and TV had risen to 64 percent. The financial position of radio can be more clearly appreciated by looking at the revenue shares in the two different categories of advertising: national and local. Television has not only strengthened its dominance in national advertising, it has also moved strongly into local advertising, increasing its share from 25 percent in 1970 to 34 percent in 1984.

Historically, advertising for retail goods and services has been carried in the local newspaper. Increasingly, however, radio is being caught in a squeeze between the old strength of the newspaper and the new strength of television in carrying this type of advertising.

The impression emerging from this analysis of the relative strengths of the radio and television must be adjusted slightly, however, by looking to comparisons outside Canada. On a per capita basis, for example, the revenues of radio in Canada are roughly the same as those for radio in the United States. However, as we shall see below in the chapter on private television, the revenues of Canadian television stations and networks are approximately half the level in the United States. In other words there is a far wider gap between the revenues of radio and television in the United States than there is in Canada.

Within Canada there are two distinct broadcasting systems, one English, the other French, though they have much in common. As the Tables in Chapter 16 and Chapter 17 indicate, there are more radio and television stations in proportion to the number of anglophones than there are in proportion to the number of francophones. While French is the language of the home for 24.6 percent of Canadians, according to the 1981 census, only 18.4 percent of radio stations and 18.5 percent of television stations broadcast in French.

Again looking at the Tables in Chapter 16 and Chapter 17, comparisons can also be made between the shares of audience of French stations and their shares of advertising revenue. In 1984, for example, 24.6 percent of all listening to private Canadian radio stations was to French-language private stations, but the French stations earned only 18.2 percent of advertising revenues in the private radio industry. Similarly in television 23.5 percent of the viewing of private Canadian stations was of private French stations, but they earned only 16.3 percent of the commercial revenues.

The small number of French stations in proportion to population may be explained in part by the difference between French and English population distribution. The French population tends to be either concentrated in two big cities — more than half of it in Montreal and Quebec City — or spread out in places too small to have a TV station, or even a radio station. There are far more middle-size urban areas in proportion to population in English Canada.

A number of reasons have been suggested for the differential between audience share and advertising share. We will discuss them in the appropriate places in the two following chapters.

Notes

1. *Broadcasting Act* (1968), R.S.C., Chapter B-11, Section 3(d).
2. *Broadcasting Act* (1968), R.S.C., Chapter B-11, Section 3(b).

Chapter 16

Private Radio

Private Radio

Introduction

Beginning almost sixty years ago, private radio was the seedbed for all that was to come in the expanding world of broadcasting. The pioneers of those early days now seem legendary figures: entrepreneurs such as Roy Thomson who started stations on a shoestring; announcers such as Roger Baulu for 55 years a voice of Montreal and still on the air, or hockey's Foster Hewitt who held the nation on the edge of its chairs for sports events and had his own radio station; and a whole succession of colourful personalities who have loomed large in their home towns as stars of local music, talk, and open-line shows.

Canadian private radio has been programmed primarily at the local level, since until recently networking was the domain of the public sector, and has had a strong local orientation. However, since the arrival of television in the 1950s the mainstay of radio programming has been recorded music which is obtained almost entirely from national and international sources.

The powerful intimacy and homey appeal of private radio in combination with its close, interdependent relationship with the sound recording industry has carried it through all the upsets and innovations caused by the arrival of television and the competition of other media. Its share of the advertising dollar has remained relatively constant over the past several decades even though there are many more stations now than there were. 'Listening pleasure' still sells.

Through their association, the Canadian Association of Broadcasters, private stations undertake a number of projects to improve their service. The Golden Ribbon Awards were inaugurated in 1982 to replace existing awards and to honour stations for community service, Canadian talent development, public affairs programming, news programming, distinguished service, and engineering achievement. In the past 18 months Association radio members have been engaged in an extensive campaign to promote and sell Canadian music. Satellite networking and commercial operations this year took over from the Association its 24-year-old free service of exchanging programs among stations in different parts of Canada.

We heard from several worried people representing both the public and private sectors who feared the Task Force might overlook radio owing to the conspicuous, glamorous and economically more important place of television. But we agree with their view that it is in the public interest for Canada to have a healthy private radio sector which will continue to attract millions of people to entertainment and information programming with strong Canadian content, a worldwide reach of interest and withal a down-home flavour. Generally, we concluded that radical policy changes would be disruptive to the private radio industry and what the public has come to expect of it. Rather, we will put forward for the most part a policy of gradual adaptation to change.

Before proceeding to a more careful examination of policy issues, we will look first at the development of radio, giving particular attention to changes during the past decade. As we see in Chapter 5 the private sector holds a larger share of the audience in radio than in television. Or, to put it another way, publicly-owned CBC looms larger in the TV business than in the radio business.

Private radio is thus a more important industry in relation to private television than might be expected — its turnover of $559 million in 1984, almost entirely in advertising sales, was equal to almost two-thirds of the turnover in the private television industry. The 446 private radio stations actually provided more direct employment than private TV — 10,000 jobs compared with slightly over 7,000 jobs.

Industry Profile

The surge of FM and the relative decline of AM are reflected in the business story of private radio over the past decade, as illustrated in Figure 16.1. The number of FM stations almost doubled, increasing from 62 to 120, or from 17 percent to 27 percent of the total number of private radio stations. Listening to FM has increased to a much greater degree, from 17 percent of radio listening in 1976 to 41 percent in 1985, including both private and public sectors. The provincial distribution of AM and FM stations in 1979 and in 1984 are shown in Table 16.1. Since 1975 the number of hours of AM listening dropped by an estimated 14 percent, while hours of FM listening rose by over 190 percent.

FM's revenue share in private radio went from 7 percent in 1974 to 25 percent in 1984, and its share of the profits has increased even more sharply. In 1984 FM stations earned almost half of radio's pre-tax profits.

While total radio listenership has increased by 20 percent over the decade, a substantial part of the FM advance has come at the expense of AM. However, half of the largest stations in the country are still AM. The substantial growth in listenership, revenues and profits that has occurred in FM radio has been achieved in spite of the heavier regulatory expectations for FM.

As we see in Chapter 5, the CRTC allows AM an omnibus programming schedule while restricting FM stations to specialized roles and one program format in popular music. It allows AM 250 minutes of advertising a day, FM only 150 minutes. By these means, the regulator has sought to differentiate between different types of station in order to assure the public a variety of programming and to protect each type of station's financial ability to fulfil its obligations under the *Broadcasting Act* and its promise of performance.

The high point for private AM stations was reached in 1977 when they numbered 334. The number dropped to 316 but recovered somewhat and over the past five years has been about 325. As shown in Table 16.1, however, of the net increase of 46 which occurred for private radio stations between 1979 and 1984 only 10 of the stations were AM, the other 36 were FM. Quebec, the Prairies and British Columbia accounted for 28 of the 36 new FM stations, representing a doubling of FM stations in these regions during the five years. Ontario, which had its surge of FM openings in the 1970s, gained only four new private FM stations in the five-year period; but a third of its 135 private radio stations are FM, the highest proportion of any province.

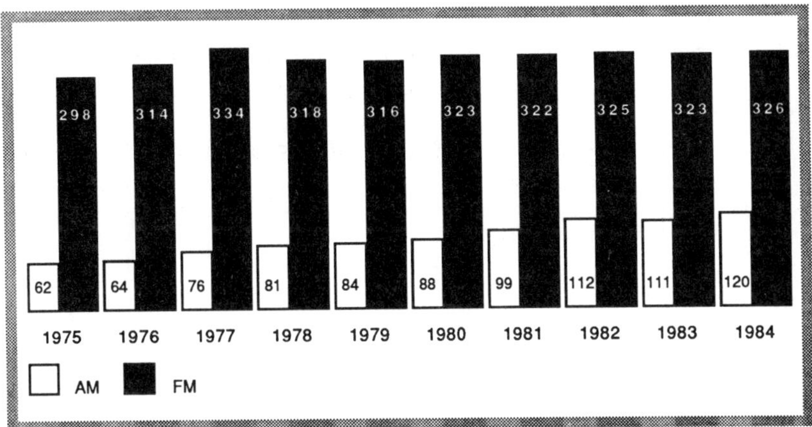

Figure 16.1 Number of AM and FM Radio Stations in Canada, 1975–1984

Quebec was the only province in which the number of private AM stations dropped between 1979 and 1984 — from 67 to 63 stations. The number of AM stations increased during the period in Ontario, British Columbia and, especially, Alberta with an increase from 29 to 33 stations.

Francophone Canada, with a quarter of the population, accounted for 82 stations in 1984, just over 18 percent of the total. Outside Quebec there were four private French-language AM stations in Ontario and two in New Brunswick during the five-year period. There are no French-language private FM stations outside Quebec. The increase in private French-language stations in Canada between 1979 and 1984 — from 77 to 82 — was entirely due to the increase of FM stations in Quebec, which more than offset the loss of AM stations in that province.

Revenues and Expenses

Private radio station revenue comes almost exclusively from advertising. In 1984, advertising accounted for more than 97 percent of total revenues, or $545 million.

In Table 16.2 we can trace the contrast between strong growth in revenue for FM radio and relative stagnation for AM between 1974 and 1984, with FM's share of radio revenues rising from 7 percent to 25 percent over this period. Allowing for inflation and expressing revenue in constant dollars, the increase in overall industry revenue was only 32 percent for the period. While FM sailed through the 1981-1983 recession with strong revenue growth, AM experienced reduced revenue growth in each of the four years preceding 1984 when it finally pulled out of the slump. FM revenues, even expressed in constant dollars, nearly quintupled between 1974 and 1984. The real value of AM revenue in 1984, expressed in constant dollars, was only six percent higher than in 1974.

Radio's share of the advertising dollar has diminished slightly over the past decade, dropping from close to 11 percent to a little under 10 percent. As we saw in the previous chapter, however, radio's share of advertising revenue was still

Table 16.1 Number of Private Stations in Operation, 1979 and 1984[a]

		AM Stations				FM Stations				Total			
		Eng.	Fr.	Other	Total	Eng.	Fr.	Other	Total	Eng.	Fr.	Other	Total
NFLD.	1979	15	0	0	15	1	0	0	1	16	0	0	16
	1984	15	0	0	15	2	0	0	2	17	0	0	17
P.E.I.	1979	3	0	0	3	0	0	0	0	3	0	0	3
	1984	3	0	0	3	1	0	0	1	4	0	0	4
N.S.	1979	15	0	0	15	5	0	0	5	20	0	0	20
	1984	16	0	0	16	6	0	0	6	22	0	0	22
N.B.	1979	10	2	0	12	2	0	0	2	12	2	0	14
	1984	10	2	0	12	3	0	0	3	13	2	0	15
Que.	1979	6	61	0	67	3	10	0	13	9	71	0	80
	1984	6	57	0	63	3	19	0	22	9	76	0	85
Ont.	1979	80	4	1	85	40	0	1	41	120	4	2	126
	1984	85	4	1	90	44	0	1	45	129	4	2	135
Man.	1979	14	0	1	15	4	0	0	4	18	0	1	19
	1984	15	0	1	16	6	0	0	6	21	0	1	22
Sask.	1979	17	0	0	17	2	0	0	2	19	0	0	19
	1984	17	0	0	17	6	0	0	6	23	0	0	23
Alta.	1979	29	0	0	29	8	0	0	8	37	0	0	37
	1984	33	0	0	33	13	0	0	13	46	0	0	46
B.C., Yukon, N.W.T.	1979	58	0	0	58	8	0	0	8	66	0	0	66
	1984	61	0	0	61	16	0	0	16	77	0	0	77
Total	1979	247	67	2	316	73	10	1	84	320	77	3	400
	1984	261	63	2	326	100	19	1	120	361	82	3	446

Note: a. These stations are required to declare their revenues to the CRTC. Rebroadcasting stations are excluded as the originating stations file combined revenue reports to the CRTC.
Source: CRTC, Industry Statistics and Analysis Division.

slightly larger than the 9 percent it was in 1960. Radio has also become more dependent on local advertising where it is challenged by both television and newspapers. Today about three-quarters of radio advertising revenue comes from local advertising, compared with 64 percent 15 years ago. Many of the new TV stations offered reduced advertising rates, especially in their first few years, bringing TV advertising within reach of clients who could previously only afford radio advertising.

French-language stations (AM and FM) earned $99.3 million in advertising revenue, only 18.2 percent of total advertising revenue; English-language stations earned $445.8 million, or (81.8 percent). The percentages do not reflect the proportional size of the English-speaking and French-speaking population of Canada, nor the percentage of all tuning to private radio which is accounted for by French-language private stations. They are, however, almost identical to the relative numbers of English-language and French-language stations.

The disparity in advertising revenue is largely attributable to French-language AM stations, which earn only 16.9 percent of Canadian AM station advertising revenue; French-language FM stations earn 22 percent of the total.

French-language stations were less dependent on local advertising than English, perhaps in part because so much of the listenership is accounted for by the huge Montreal urban area. A second factor is the existence of private French-language radio networks which do not at present have a counterpart in English. Nevertheless, even in national advertising the share of revenue earned by private French-language stations, at 21.5 percent, is less than their 24.6 percent share of all listening to private Canadian radio stations. The breakdown of advertising revenue for English and French stations can be seen in some detail in Table 16.3.

The expenses that private radio must meet from its revenue are shown by broad category and different types of station in Table 16.4. The largest single share of expenditures — 36 percent — goes to programming, while 33 percent goes to overhead and administration, 25 percent to sales and advertising, and 5 percent to technical expenses. The cost structure is quite different from television, where nearly 60 percent of expenditure goes to programming. In fact, radio's success is dependent on relatively inexpensive programming — about 50 percent of it recorded music.

There is little difference in the allocation of expenditures between radio stations in different parts of the country, or between AM and FM stations. One notable difference is the 31 percent of total expenditures accounted for by programming by French-language FM stations compared to the 39 percent by English FM stations. This discrepancy does not exist in AM.

The profitability of radio stations as a whole declined slowly but steadily between 1974 and 1981, with profit margins (ratio of pre-tax profit to revenue) dropping from 16.2 percent to 11.6 percent. As the recession took hold profits fell more sharply in 1982 and 1983 before recovering slightly in 1984.

Profitability of radio stations also varied by station category. Over the last six years for which figures are available AM profit margins dropped steadily, from 14.2 percent in 1979 to 2.9 percent in 1984. The performance of FM stations for the same period improved in inverse proportion — from –2.5 percent in 1979 to 8.3 percent in 1984. For a close look at the evolution of profits and profitability in recent years see Tables 16.5 through 16.8.

Table 16.2 Growth in Revenue of the Private Radio Industry, 1974-1984[a]

	AM and FM Stations			AM Stations			FM Stations			FM share of total revenue
	Revenue ($ millions)	Annual Growth Rate		Revenue ($ millions)	Annual Growth Rate		Revenue ($ millions)	Annual Growth Rate		
		Current $	Constant $		Current $	Constant $		Current $	Constant $	
		%	%		%	%		%	%	%
1974	182.8			169.9			12.9			7.1
1975	207.8	13.7	2.6	191.5	12.7	1.7	16.3	26.4	14.0	7.8
1976	243.8	17.3	9.2	223.6	16.8	8.6	20.2	23.9	15.6	8.3
1977	271.5	11.4	3.1	246.3	10.2	2.0	25.2	24.8	15.3	9.3
1978	309.1	13.8	4.6	275.6	11.9	2.8	33.5	32.9	21.9	10.8
1979	355.4	15.0	5.3	312.9	13.5	4.0	42.5	26.9	16.3	12.0
1980	396.3	11.5	1.4	342.6	9.5	−0.4	53.7	26.4	15.1	13.6
1981	445.8	12.5	−0.2	373.8	9.1	−3.2	72.0	34.1	18.8	16.2
1982	475.7	6.7	−3.7	386.3	3.3	−6.7	89.4	24.2	12.1	18.8
1983	489.7	2.9	−2.7	380.8	−1.4	−6.8	108.9	21.8	15.3	22.2
1984	559.3	14.2	9.5	417.4	9.6	5.1	141.9	30.3	24.8	25.4
Compound Annual Growth Rate 1974-1979		14.2	4.9		13.0	3.8		26.9	16.6	
Compound Annual Growth Rate 1979-1984		9.5	0.8		5.9	−2.5		27.3	17.1	

Note: a. Including revenues from network operations.
Source: CRTC, Industry Statistics and Analysis Division.

Table 16.3 Private Radio Station Advertising Revenue, 1984[a]

	AM & FM			AM			FM		
	($ thousands)	%	%	($ thousands)	%	%	($ thousands)	%	%
English Stations									
Local advertising	331,702	**74.4**		252,639	**75.1**		79,063	**72.2**	
National advertising	114,054	**25.6**		83,630	**24.9**		30,424	**27.8**	
Advertising revenue	445,756	**100.0**	98.2	336,269	**100.0**	98.0	109,741	**100.0**	98.9
Total Revenue	454,061		100.0	343,320		100.0	110,741		100.0
French Stations									
Local advertising	68,062	**68.5**		48,411	**70.9**		19,651	**63.7**	
National advertising	31,253	**31.5**		20,077	**29.3**		11,176	**36.3**	
Advertising revenue	99,315	**100.0**	94.4	68,488	**100.0**	92.5	30,827	**100.0**	98.9
Total Revenue	105,244		100.0	74,065		100.0	31,179		100.0
All Stations									
Local advertising	399,765	**73.3**		301,051	**74.4**		98,714	**70.4**	
National advertising	145,308	**26.7**		103,709	**25.6**		41,599	**29.6**	
Advertising revenue	545,073	**100.0**	97.4	404,760	**100.0**	97.0	140,313	**100.0**	98.9
Total Revenue	559,306		100.0	417,386		100.0	141,920		100.0

Note: a. Including revenues from network operations.
Source: CRTC, Industry Statistics and Analysis Division

Table 16.4 Revenue, Expenses and Profits of Private Radio Stations, 1984[a] ($ millions)

	AM Radio[b]						FM Radio					
	English		French		Total		English		French		Total	
	$	%	$	%	$	%	$	%	$	%	$	%
Revenue	344.8		73.8		418.6		109.6		31.2		140.7	
Expenses	299.3	100.0	70.2	100.0	369.6	100.0	95.5	100.0	24.9	100.0	120.4	100.0
Programs	106.3	35.5	25.9	36.9	132.3	35.9	36.9	38.6	7.7	30.9	44.6	37.0
Technical	15.9	5.3	3.3	4.7	19.2	5.3	4.8	5.0	1.0	4.0	5.8	4.8
Sales and Promotion	76.0	25.4	15.1	21.5	91.0	24.6	26.3	27.5	6.7	26.9	32.9	27.3
Administration	101.1	33.8	25.9	36.9	127.0	34.4	27.5	28.8	9.6	38.6	37.1	30.8
Operating Profit	45.5		3.6		49.0		14.1		6.3		20.3	
Profit before tax[c]	14.7		-2.4		12.3		6.6		5.0		11.6	
Profit before tax as a percent of revenue		4.3		-3.3		2.9		6.0		16.0		8.2

Notes: a. Including network operations.
b. As some radio stations are licensed for both AM and FM operations and file a combined financial report to the CRTC, AM station data include some FM station data. In terms of revenue, these FM stations accounted for $1,174,690 ($1,168,450 from English-language stations and $6,240 from French-language stations) which is less than 0.3 percent of the AM total revenue.
c. Obtained by subtracting standardized depreciation, interest expense and adjustments from the operating profit.

Source: CRTC, Industry Statistics and Analysis Division.

Table 16.5 Operating Profit and Profit Before Tax of Private Radio Stations, 1974-1984[a]

	1974	1975	1976	1977	1978	1979	1980	1981	1982	1983	1984
Operating profit ($ millions)	37.2	39.9	46.0	45.2	49.1	58.3	63.8	69.1	54.4	54.6	69.3
Operating profit as a percent of revenue	20.3	19.2	18.9	16.6	15.9	16.4	16.1	15.5	11.4	11.2	12.4
Profit before tax[b] ($ millions)	29.6	33.5	37.6	35.4	37.7	44.8	48.0	51.5	36.7	19.7	23.9
Profit before tax as a percent of revenue	16.2	16.1	15.4	13.0	12.2	12.6	12.1	11.6	7.7	4.0	4.3

Notes: a. Including network operations.
b. Obtained by subtracting standardized depreciation, interest expense and adjustments from the operating profit.

AM Radio & FM Radio						FM as % of AM & FM
English		French		Total		
$	%	$	%	$	%	%
454.3		105.0		559.3		25.2
394.9	100.0	95.1	100.0	490.0	100.0	24.6
143.3	36.3	33.6	35.3	176.9	36.1	25.2
20.8	5.3	4.2	4.4	25.0	5.1	23.2
102.2	25.9	21.8	22.9	124.0	25.3	26.5
128.6	32.6	35.5	37.3	164.1	33.5	22.6
59.4		9.9		69.3		29.3
21.3		2.6		23.9		48.5
	4.7		2.4	4.3		

Table 16.6 Profit Margin of Private Radio Stations by Category, 1979-1984[a] (%)

	1979	1980	1981	1982	1983	1984
AM Stations[b]						
English	14.2	13.9	14.2	11.4	4.9	4.3
French	14.6	10.9	2.6	–5.6	–0.8	–3.3
Total	**14.2**	**13.5**	**12.3**	**8.6**	**4.0**	**2.9**
FM Stations						
English	–1.9	5.1	7.2	2.3	3.1	6.1
French	–4.6	–5.4	8.6	7.8	8.6	15.9
Total	**–2.5**	**2.9**	**7.5**	**3.4**	**4.3**	**8.3**
AM & FM Stations						
English	12.6	12.9	13.2	9.9	4.6	4.7
French	12.4	8.6	3.6	–3.0	1.5	2.4
Total	**12.6**	**12.1**	**11.6**	**7.7**	**4.0**	**4.3**

Notes: a. Including network operations.
b. Includes information on some FM stations that have filed combined reports with the CRTC. The revenue of these stations does not exceed 2.3 percent of total AM station revenues.

Table 16.7 Profitability of Private Radio Stations, 1979-1984

	1979	1980	1981	1982	1983	1984
Number of reporting units[a]	361	374	384	396	394	437
Total revenue ($ millions)	355.4	396.3	445.8	475.7	489.7	559.3
Profit before tax ($ millions)	44.8	48.0	51.5	36.7	19.7	23.9
Profit as percent of revenue	12.6	12.1	11.6	7.7	4.0	4.3
Number of units showing losses	111	137	148	185	173	176
Total revenue of units with losses ($ millions)	52.2	79.3	102.3	159.9	150.5	167.1
Total losses of units with losses ($ millions)	(13.9)	(15.5)	(23.0)	(41.6)	(38.9)	(45.1)
Number of units showing profits	250	237	236	211	221	261
Total revenue of units with profits ($ millions)	303.2	317.0	343.5	315.8	339.2	392.2
Total profit of units with profits ($ millions)	58.6	63.6	74.5	78.2	58.6	69.0

Note: a. Generally, a declaring unit is described as a radio station in operation. However, some units include two or three stations, filing combined financial reports. Also, each network constitutes a different reporting unit; in 1984, the 437 reporting units account for 446 operating stations and seven networks.
Source: CRTC, Industry statistics and analysis division.

The decline in profitability in radio also hit smaller stations particularly hard, with most of them continuing to show losses in 1984. Of the stations with revenues under $1.3 million annually almost half still reported losses in 1984, while only 16 of the 71 with revenues of over $2 million were still reporting losses. The average profit margin of the large stations (revenues of over $2 million) was 11.2 percent by comparison with the industry average of 4.3 percent.

During the five years from 1979 to 1984 French FM stations did exceptionally well while French AM stations did exceptionally poorly especially during the latter part of the period. English AM stations actually did better than FM stations until 1984.

To a quite remarkable degree radio is an industry of winners and losers. As Table 16.7 indicates the 261 reporting units which showed profits in 1984 had pre-tax profits of $69 million, or 17.6 percent of revenue. This figure, as we shall see later, is in fact quite comparable to the profits earned in television. However, these handsome earnings while down somewhat from the comparable level of

Table 16.8 Profitability of Private Radio Stations by Revenue, 1984

Station Revenue	1 Less than $200,000	2 $200,000 to $300,000	3 $300,000 to $400,000	4 $400,000 to $500,000	5 $500,000 to $800,000	6 $800,000 to $1,300,000	7 $1,300,000 to $2,000,000	8 More than $2,000,000	**Total**
Number of reporting units[a]	43	32	43	30	74	80	64	71	**437**
Total Revenue ($ thousands)	5,094	7,868	15,140	13,859	48,655	83,440	99,860	285,391	**559,306**
Profit before taxes ($ thousands)	(1,956)	(1,492)	(3,113)	(1,203)	(4,524)	(2,647)	6,944	31,875	**23,884**
Profit as a percent of revenue	–38.4	–19.0	–20.6	–8.7	–9.3	–3.2	7.0	11.2	**4.3**
Number of units showing losses	30	17	24	12	34	25	18	16	**176**
Total revenue of units with losses ($ thousands)	3,032	4,167	8,416	5,530	22,806	26,637	27,466	69,023	**167,077**
Total losses of units with losses ($ thousands)	(2,244)	(1,956)	(3,946)	(2,169)	(7,833)	(9,926)	(2,629)	(14,430)	**(45,134)**
Number of units showing profits	13	15	19	18	40	55	46	55	**261**
Total revenue of units with profits ($ thousands)	2,062	3,701	6,724	8,329	25,849	56,803	72,394	216,368	**392,229**
Total profits of units with profits ($ thousands)	288	464	834	966	3,309	7,279	9,573	46,305	**69,018**

Note: a. Generally, a declaring unit is described as a radio station in operation. However, some units include two or three stations, filing combined financial reports. Also, each network constitutes a different reporting unit; in 1984, the 437 reporting units account for 446 operating stations and seven networks.

Source: CRTC, Industry Statistics and Analysis Division.

24.8 percent in 1982 are in stark contrast to the losses of $45 million registered by the 176 losing stations in 1984.

During 1982 almost half of all stations reported losses. Over the period 1979 to 1984 reported losses totaled $178 million; however, over the same years the profitable stations realized profits of $402 million.

Retaining the Objectives

As the above analysis suggests there are a significant number of problems in the private radio sector. There is increased competition for local advertising, including competition from television; the growing strength of FM is creating difficulties for many AM stations; and many small independent stations, especially those in smaller communities, are experiencing serious difficulties. During our consultations we also heard considerable concern with the output of the Canadian music industry and the number of French-language recordings available for broadcast, and there were frequent unflattering comments about the burdensome and demanding nature of the regulatory regime developed by the CRTC.

We had to ask ourselves what the rationale is for the state to be interested in whether television or radio is attracting most advertising dollars. Why is it the business of government that some AM stations, or some rural stations, are suffering financially? Is it sensible to describe as Canadian content — as a contribution to Canadian culture — pop music that is deliberately intended to be indistinguishable from American in the hope it will be popular in the United States? And even if it were, has the government an obligation to support it, or to expect private broadcasters to support it?

In short, the issue of the appropriateness of state intervention in the broadcasting system and the difficulties of sorting out what is culture as distinct from industry were never more central to our deliberations than on the topic of private radio. Why, asked one spokesperson for a successful radio chain, should the right to go broke not apply to the world of private radio? Since listeners had the option of choosing public radio if they wished, why should the market not prevail in determining what private radio offered?

In fact, almost none of the radio broadcasters who appeared before us advocated a pure market alternative to the present system. Certainly, there was a universal desire for simplification of CRTC regulations. Few submissions, however, asked for deregulation and few broadcasters failed to approve of Canadian content rules for Canadian music.

One FM operator complained to us that "The programmers of Canada have become bookkeepers. We spend countless hours on interpretation and implementation of broadcast regulations." Yet the same person, who wished to remain anonymous, went on to explain to us that regulation "permitted AM radio in Canada to remain healthy, strong, and to provide tremendous service in markets all across Canada". Moreover, he concluded to our considerable surprise,

> It is my contention that unless the regulations are quite detailed, then they are not regulations at all and provide no control as entrepreneurial broadcasters will find ways around regulations that are not very detailed and extensive.

We are satisfied that the CRTC's general approach and objectives relating to private radio broadcasting make sense. We do not want radio to be everywhere standardized and homogeneous, playing to the lowest common denominator as established by regular audience preference surveys. We reject for Canadian private radio the role of private radio in the United States as little more than a marketing tool to sell large blocks of consumers to advertisers.

To hold a radio licence in Canada is to hold a public trust. In return for the privilege of holding a licence, private broadcasters can appropriately be required by public policy to contribute — as parts of the system — to providing balance and diversity to the listening audience. They can also appropriately be required to avoid excessive standardization and excessive commercialization, and to provide a reasonable amount of Canadian programming, especially music. The American experience tends to demonstrate that none of these objectives would be achieved if market forces were permitted free play. Since the private sector has to make a profit, it would be unrealistic to expect it to fulfil the listening demands of all Canadians. The government must therefore provide ample funding for a public radio sector with programming uninfluenced by commercial considerations.

Canadians who make their livelihood from Canadian music face problems owing to the small size of the Canadian market by comparison with the American. It is therefore sensible for public policy to support the music industry directly as well as by ensuring private sector support.

The Task Force has not been requested save for a very few exceptions to revise the principle of Canadian content. But Canadian music can only be heard if there are stations to play it and we are thus against a deregulated system in which a number of smaller and more specialized stations might go to the wall.

We are also persuaded of the value of preserving and protecting radio's particular role as a local medium at least in terms of news and information programming.

Finally, we hope effective regulations can be substantially less cumbersome than those adopted in recent years. If more of the burden of regulatory obligation were imposed through individual conditions of licence rather than general rules, it should be possible for each station to contribute to the cultural goals of the system according to its capacity without jeopardizing its economic survival. This means tailoring similar conditions of licence for comparable licensees, not discriminating among licensees. Smaller and poorer stations could be treated sympathetically while wealthy operators would be expected to contribute more significantly to the objectives of the system.

We believe the CRTC expressed the objectives well when it said in introducing the 1975 FM radio policy:

> The disparate groups in Canada's society deserve to have available on their airwaves a clear choice of different kinds of programming which recognize their particular needs and concerns. Radio should serve the public when it wants to be entertained, and also when it wants to be informed or enlightened.[1]

Recently, the CRTC aptly summarized the new context in which these objectives must be implemented. Introducing proposed regulations on AM and FM broadcasting, it said:

> Currently, Canada is experiencing substantial change which exerts a profound influence upon the broadcasting system. In radio, a variety of technological, social, and economic forces are converging to stimulate new competition, new audio service concepts, improved and more efficient delivery options, and new patterns of consumer utilization. Furthermore, the Commission notes that many of its radio licensees have experienced financial difficulties over the past few years. An increasing number of stations have not had significant growth in their revenues at a time when their operating costs have increased dramatically.
>
> In addition, the Commission notes the concerns expressed by broadcasters, record industry representatives, and the federal and some provincial governments over the difficulties encountered by the Canadian recording industry in supplying sufficient Canadian recordings for broadcast in all formats.[2]

Our own studies have borne out the truth of the main points made in this observation. While recognizing that policy adjustments may well be needed to deal with technological and other changes, we believe only a limited number of steps are justified and necessary at this time. It is as yet unclear what technological possibilities are most promising or most likely to excite public demand. Will AM stereo, for example, rescue AM radio from its current doldrums? If so, it may be possible to consider an approach that is based less on the current distinction between AM and FM stations.

We believe our recommendations here and elsewhere will help along the road leading to a strengthened policy toward radio. But we do not have all of the answers now and it would be wrong to pretend we do. Public policy cannot respond to every technological novelty, nor should it ever be determined by what may turn out to be temporary trends. We should have a grasp of strong cumulative development before making policy changes that would be bound to be disruptive to those who have participated in good faith in the present system.

Recommendation

> Continued regulation of radio is necessary to ensure diversity, and to promote the use of Canadian creative and journalistic resources. Regulatory tools should be flexible and — through conditions of licence — appropriate to the resources and operating environment of each licensed radio station and network.

Differentiation of AM and FM

Artificial differences have been designed for AM and FM mandates. As FM radio developed, it was seen as a means of serving more specialized audiences. FM's freedom from technical interference and its capacity for high fidelity sound gave it an enormous advantage, as we see both in the chapters on programming and technology and in our discussion of the economics of radio. The remarkable success of FM radio and its growth rate lead us to believe that AM radio may suffer additional losses of audience. As we see in the chapter on the Evolution of Broadcasting Technology, AM stereo is barely past the experimental stage.

The public policy question is whether the artificial distinction between AM and FM should be eliminated. At first sight the proposal is attractive; there is a logic to it — radio is radio — and it would dramatically simplify regulation. But the economic impact on AM stations could be devastating.

Reading and understanding the various regulations and policy statements, including the CRTC's recent proposed amendments, is admittedly a complex exercise in intellectual gymnastics. The caricature of an FM station operator needing to use a calculator to ensure that he respects the regulations is not exaggerated: it appears to be a convincing example of truth being stranger than fiction. An operator who wishes to remain anonymous has described for us the type of accounting exercise he must engage in to satisfy current regulation:

> The FM broadcaster is, during the licence application and renewal process and indeed in day-to-day programming, required to accomplish the following:
>
> 1. Break down every 126-hour week into specific percentages of programming content by news, surveillance, enrichment, spoken word actualities, music, traditional and special interest music, production, advertising and station contests.
> 2. Set out clearly the ratio of vocal to instrumental.
> 3. Record the number of distinct musical selections.
> 4. Record the maximum number of times any record will be played.
>
> Most ludicrous is the approximate number of hits (heaven knows who this satisfies except the AM operator who has the opportunity to play as many hits as he wants! — hits here defined as popular music or the music the audience prefers to hear most). The AM broadcasters can therefore be satisfied in the knowledge that FM will remain a marginal competitor as a result of playing marginal material and more unpopular material.

This broadcaster summed up his statement by saying that he considers broadcasting to be a creative business, that broadcasters must be allowed to express creativity through flexibility and must be able to respond to the changing conditions of the market place.

Broadcasters also told the Task Force about the positive aspects of existing regulation, however, and emphasized that there was a need for their activities to be regulated and protected. The following testimony is an example:

> The benefit of the current FM regulations is that they have permitted AM radio in Canada to remain healthy, strong and to continue to provide tremendous service in markets all across Canada. While I agree that the FM regulations may have retarded in some ways the growth of FM in Canada, we still have a situation in Toronto, Montreal and Ottawa where FM tuning approximates 50 per cent of total radio tuning in those markets. As well, there is a big demand to acquire new FM licences in Canada and the number 1 station in Canada in the Fall '85 BBM was an FM station.

> The situation in Canada should be contrasted with that in the United States, where FM and AM have been virtually totally deregulated, with the result being that in most major markets over 70 per cent of the tuning is to FM stations, and in some cases, as high as 80 per cent or more. This results in a serious deterioration in the quality of AM radio without contributing to diversity in the market place.[3]

We see again the intermingling of cultural and industrial issues. By implementing cultural diversity on FM, the regulator has allowed AM to survive but perhaps retarded the growth of FM.

Aside from mostly American music — the majority of its programming — AM radio carries essentially local content. It is a mass medium for the general audience while FM radio aims at rather more specialized audiences. Though we believe that FM's regulatory burden could be lightened to allow it to fulfil its primary role of music programming, with information playing only a supplementary role, we are satisfied that regulation should continue to ensure the programming distinction between AM and FM, which limits direct competition between the two services. To abolish such a distinction would mean a revolution in the present broadcasting structure, the consequences of which the Task Force cannot foresee. If AM should slide further, however, policy would have to be reviewed at some point since the ability of AM stations to carry out their role in radio programming, particularly in local news and information, would become too limited. But policy should not continue to be based on protecting AM if it appears to be declining as a commercial medium.

Recommendation

> The present differentiation between AM and FM should be maintained with close monitoring of the evolution of both services. The status of AM radio in particular should be reviewed periodically.

Music Formats

The CRTC has developed a number of instruments over the years to achieve its objectives in AM and FM. The Commission adopted the format concept which had been devised in the U.S. in order to sell air-time to advertisers and which, of course, had spilled over into Canada. Formats were developed to handle the evolution of various types of music in the United States and track the market approach of the U.S. to providing FM services in various areas.[4] Formats used in Canada are described in Chapter 5 on Programs and Audiences.

The challenge of identifying types of music leads to difficulties in defining musical genres in order to create market niches different from one operator to the other. To protect less popular kinds of programming, the CRTC has licensed stations to provide particular kinds of music, thereby reducing the potential for head-to-head competition between stations.

The Task Force has not attempted to carry out the exercise of distinguishing between progressive rock and dance music, blues or soul and rhythm and blues, or country and western. The American-inspired format approach adopted by the CRTC seems not as well suited, however, to the Canadian situation as it could be, especially in the case of music in French-language broadcasting. In 1984, when the CRTC simplified FM radio formats into four groups for a number of types of stations, formats no longer resembled the American model quite so closely. Nevertheless, the 'group' stations, as they are now called, are still related to American formats.

Still, this approach appears to be a lesser evil, for the Task Force remains convinced that the objectives of the *Broadcasting Act* require a variety of sounds in radio and hence different types of station. This can only be achieved by regulation for many reasons. The first is economic: private radio is an industry whose purpose is profit. To be profitable the station must obtain advertising revenue by attracting listeners. In order to attract large numbers of listeners the station will attempt to offer a sound and programming that will please the greatest possible number. It is obvious that without format regulation there is likely to be a duplication of services; minority tastes are likely to be neglected, if not forgotten altogether. Formats must, of course, evolve along with sociocultural and demographic changes and take into account market demand. (See Chapter 8 for a discussion of this point relating to francophone broadcasting.)

Recommendation

The format approach should be maintained for cultural diversity but should be flexible enough to reflect the evolution of music and market characteristics.

The second reason to keep regulation is the necessity to preserve a distinctively Canadian private broadcasting industry. Formats are an important means to reach that goal; so are Canadian content requirements. Canadian radio has a distinctive sound beside American radio. Before there were Canadian content quotas substantially fewer Canadian musical selections were aired, although many Canadian recording artists proved very popular both in Canada and abroad once Canadian artists received this exposure. While radio listeners typically tune to a few preferred stations and indeed 'shopping the dial' may be becoming more prevalent, there nonetheless tends to be a core loyalty to one particular station. People become attached to a disc jockey or a host who personifies the station. An example of this attachment occurred recently in Quebec city when station morning man André Arthur took his large and loyal following of listeners from one station to another and then back again. There is fierce competition among stations to tie down listener loyalty. High tuning percentages and ratings in radio are achieved slowly; any loss is slow and difficult to repair.

Regulation is undertaken to ensure a diversity of sounds that will reflect the cultural diversity of potential listeners in a given market — what one American writer has called "representative diversity".[5] The goal is to ensure that the programming in a market meets the needs of the community without stifling creativity. An approach which would allow broadcasters to define their own niche in a given market does not appear to us to be sufficiently well developed to represent an alternative to the existing system.

The Task Force agrees with the intention of the CRTC in its proposed radio regulations of March 19, 1986,[6] that AM radio should have the same definition of content categories and sub-categories, and the same definition of format groups for popular-music stations, as those laid down for FM stations in 1983.[7] But AM would remain free to choose from these categories and formats.

FM 'group' stations should, however, be maintained to implement diversity. Such groups should not be rigid pigeon-holes constraining all creativity; they should rather be labels for the sound of the stations and their target audiences. AM stations should be free to propose a mixture chosen from the four groups. It is a matter of à-la-carte programming for AM and table-d'hôte programming for FM.

Spoken-word Programming

The requirement to produce segments of programming in the foreground format illustrates the complexity of the FM regulations.

The purpose of foreground and mosaic formats is again to differentiate between AM and FM. FM stations are required to devote a portion of their schedules to thematic programming entailing a greater amount of preparation, known as foreground or mosaic programming, as outlined in Chapter 5.

As stated by the CRTC in its proposed regulations, many licensees tend to respect the letter, not the spirit, of this regulation. The CAB contended that a broadcaster is tempted, if not forced, to stretch a good seven-minute program into a less appealing fifteen-minute one, or to spread a good fifteen-minute segment over two or three.[8] Every thematic thread, however slender, is used to hang a foreground segment on. Foreground programming is often mere idle chatter. It goes against the needs of most listeners, 64 percent of whom would like less talk on FM, as shown in research conducted for the Ontario Ministry of Transportation and Communications in June 1984.[9]

As they are drafted, the spoken-word or foreground and mosaic requirements are cumbersome; they restrain the industry. The objective of a revised policy should be to focus attention on ensuring that individual radio licensees commit a reasonable share of their resources to providing such programs and that the air time they are expected to devote to such programs reflects their ability to provide high quality spoken-word programming. Naturally, the broadcasters themselves will decide what the program content should be.

Recommendation

The CRTC should drop blanket spoken-word requirements on FM radio but continue to pursue its objective in spoken word programming through conditions of licence tailored to local circumstances. Such requirements should provide for the commitment of a reasonable share of available resources to such programs and for adequate air time, consistent with maintaining high quality.

Economic Resources and Conditions of Licence

Much earlier than television, radio experienced market fragmentation, its share of the advertising dollar staying fairly steady but being divided among more and more stations. Today private radio is facing increased competition from television and daily and community newspapers for the local advertising on which it most relies. During the consultations held with various industry representatives, the Task Force was frequently told about problems being encountered by station operators in secondary and tertiary markets, and in non-urban markets.

It is our view that conditions of licence for station operators in non-urban markets should reflect regional and local demographic, geographic, social and economic conditions. Severe difficulties are being experienced by station operators in some markets. A regulatory approach with conditions of licence based on the characteristics of a licensee in a particular market would help the broadcaster to contribute to the objectives of the system. For example, in smaller markets an exclusive AM operator should be allowed more flexibility in advertising and the clustering of ads. We have more to say on advertising later in this chapter. However, the content requirements related to the playing of Canadian musical selections and — for French-language stations — to francophone music would apply to all licensees, with exceptions approved by the CRTC.

Recommendation

The CRTC should use conditions of licence to allow broadcasters to offer a service better tailored to their markets, taking into consideration the size of the station, the characteristics of the market and the kind of radio services provided.

Networking

Measures to facilitate the development of radio networks would be another means of relief from economic hardship. The CRTC's proposed radio regulations, opening the door wider to the establishment of Canadian private networks, would be a positive step. The orderly development of such networks would be facilitated if the Commission were to establish clear policy guidelines for their operation, based on the objectives of broadcasting policy.

The pooling of resources would ease the financial burden for smaller operators. Such a measure could, however, curtail the local programming considered essential for a radio station to reflect the needs of its community. Thus Canadian networks should be encouraged only to the extent they do not jeopardize local content. This problem is considered in Chapter 8 on French-language broadcasting where radio networks have played a prominent role for many years.

Network programming of good quality, by sharing costs among many stations, could represent a worthwhile saving. For example, networks can provide national and regional news, announcer-and-music programs according to format requirements, common talk-show formats, in-depth news, cultural, lifestyle and other informational features, special coverage of events like elections, budgets and other news specials, play-by-play accounts of sports, and entertainment series or events. It will be the task of the CRTC to lay down a clear policy to accommodate the expansion of network programming while retaining appropriate emphasis on Canadian content and ensuring that network time does not encroach excessively on local programming.

Recommendation

Networks should be encouraged as long as they are Canadian networks. Restrictions will be required to protect Canadian content in network programming, to ensure network programs do not enroach excessively on local programming and to ensure that radio networks operate in a way consistent with achieving the objectives proposed for the broadcasting system.

Canadian Content and the Music Industry

The Canadian private radio industry depends on the use of recorded music in the case of most AM and FM stations for at least 50 percent of its programming. To the extent that Canadian radio is expected under the existing *Broadcasting Act* and CRTC regulations to play Canadian recordings, the stations depend on the existence of an adequate supply of Canadian recordings appropriate to the format of each particular category of station.

Content quotas to assure Canadians of opportunity for both expression of, and access to, their own musical creative and performing talent on private radio have been developed in considerable detail and are described in Chapter 5. The rules differ for AM and FM.

Content quotas are the foundation stone for the development of Canadian musical expression. In order that quotas be fulfilled, however, there must be a strong Canadian musical production industry. Broadcast content quotas alone will be ineffective if they are not accompanied by effective government policies for the development of Canadian sound recordings and the Canadian sound recording industry.

The regulatory requirement to play Canadian recordings at present imposes no direct extra financial burden on the stations. Radio broadcasters pay no more to play Canadian recordings than foreign — in each case only relatively small copyright payments. In television, by contrast, the requirement to show Canadian programs involves substantial additional cost. Radio broadcasters have therefore never been as dissatisfied as television broadcasters with Canadian content obligations.

Data vary greatly on the adequacy of the supply of Canadian recordings and even on whether the supply is increasing or decreasing. But the balance of opinion appears to be that there is a decreasing supply of discrete titles for radio programming not only in Canada but internationally. Some broadcasters told us there was a shortage of recordings to meet content quotas in both French and

English and the quotas should be lowered; others said quotas should be left at present levels. Part of the concern seems to stem from the limited supply of Canadian music videos, which are a key mechanism to promote recordings.

Meanwhile, the CRTC has begun to reduce the content requirement. A major campaign by the Canadian Independent Record Production Association (CIRPA), the Association of Canadian Television and Radio Artists (ACTRA) and Union des artistes has been mounted to halt this trend. CIRPA appealed the reductions to Cabinet in 1985.

The Task Force believes that Canadian content levels should be maintained. Continuing with the existing quotas is essential to the development of Canadian music, including both the creation and performance of music by Canadians.

Recommendation

The existing Canadian content requirements for radio broadcasters should at a minimum be maintained, including the 30 percent quota for AM licensees.

Many radio operators recognize that in return for the right to use a frequency they should contribute to the development of the industry that provides their raw materials. In 1982 some station operators put this principle into practice by establishing a group called FACTOR — and later a francophone counterpart called MusicAction — to stimulate Canadian record production. This important initiative created a body of Canadian broadcasters who contribute to a fund intended to produce records in Canada using Canadian talent. FACTOR has thus far spent more than $800,000 to support Canadian recordings. Because of the merger in 1985 of FACTOR and the Canadian Talent Library (CTL), which was formerly responsible for distributing music catalogues to broadcasters, the production of records in categories of music other than rock, which are less popular and less profitable, may decline. Initiatives such as FACTOR are important in order to revitalize the Canadian music and record industry.

The Task Force believes the contribution of FACTOR-CTL and MusicAction to the Canadian music industry should be encouraged by concrete measures. The CRTC should include in a more systematic way as one of the conditions of licence that appropriate licence holders must make a financial contribution to these two organizations. Standard Broadcasting Corporation suggested to us "a tax-like regulation whereby stations contribute 0.75 per cent of gross revenue" to FACTOR-CTL. We will refrain from suggesting a figure. The level of participation should be established on the basis of each licensee's operating environment and financial position. The various contributors to FACTOR-CTL and MusicAction would then presumably want to ensure that the funds they contribute would be used for producing records appropriate to the formats within which the stations operate and in proportion to their respective investments.

Recommendation

Public policy should strengthen the position of FACTOR-CTL and MusicAction under the control as at present of a private board com-

> posed of radio industry and music industry representatives. The CRTC should use conditions of licence to require more adequate funding of FACTOR-CTL with the level of contribution reflecting individual stations' ability to pay.

Programs financed by the radio industry itself will inevitably focus on the support of the most popular kinds of music. It will, therefore, be necessary to provide a substantial level of support from public sources if a diverse range of Canadian music is to be available.

Recently the government announced that a $5 million per year program will be provided over a five-year period to support Canadian record production and provide financial assistance to the music industry. Included in the program is $2.6 million per year to fund the production of commercial sound recordings, $300,000 to fund the recording of specialized Canadian music, and $500,000 for Canadian music videos. The remaining funds will be used for export market development and management assistance.

The Task Force believes that the industry can and should through FACTOR-CTL and MusicAction provide an increasing amount of support for mainstream Canadian sound recordings. As the support programs established by the industry itself are expanded, public support should be concentrated increasingly on the many minority musics which will benefit little, if at all from industry-financed assistance. These include not just classical music, but jazz, the music of ethnic groups, folk music, the music of native Canadians, and perhaps some forms of popular music which may otherwise be neglected. In the case of classical music such support seems an essential counterpart to the quite substantial levels of support for composition and live performance which are provided by the Canada Council and provincial arts funding agencies. Substantial funds will be required to support the production of such recordings, perhaps as much as $5 million annually, if classical music and other minority musics are to be recorded in reasonable variety and made available for use by radio broadcasters in Canada.

There will, of course, be a need as well for the Department of Communications to continue to develop and pursue integrated policies for strengthening the Canadian music industry. However, it is beyond the mandate of this Task Force to make recommendations concerning sound recording industry policy.

Other Issues

Advertising

At present AM stations are limited to a maximum of 250 advertising minutes between 6 a.m. and midnight each day but a maximum weekly total of 1500 minutes.

AM radio is undergoing an extremely difficult time which imperils its very viability. Making advertising restrictions more flexible would allow AM radio to compensate for the listeners it loses as the programming day advances and to maximize its revenues at peak listening periods. Easing restrictions on types of products and services that can be advertised might also be desirable.

Because most radio revenue comes from local retail advertisers, this measure would allow smaller stations to generate additional revenue at certain times during their operating months, such as before Christmas, and to do better during low listening periods. It would give broadcasters greater flexibility in preparing advertising messages for certain time periods. Broadcasters believe the market would act as a deterrent to operators tempted to abuse the measures.

Operators should also improve their sales strategies by offering improved research services to radio advertisers, thus allowing them to target their listening audiences more accurately and offer better performance per dollar invested.

Despite their general financial health, a number of FM stations are also experiencing problems, especially in small markets. The Task Force believes that, for FM as for AM, the record-keeping burden should be lightened and that monthly maximums should be established to allow broadcasters to have greater autonomy in organizing their programming and making optimum use of the advertising minutes available to them.

Recommendation

Advertising regulations for radio should be relaxed and maximums set on a monthly basis, taking into account the operating environment of a station in its own market, the type of service offered, the size of the station and competition within the market.

Cable Carriage

The Task Force believes the present regulations on carriage of radio on cable fail to recognize the importance of Canadian and local stations. The rules omit Canadian AM stations and permit the carriage of American FM stations. Since American commercial stations do not add significantly to the diversity of programming available, there is no reason to give them valuable positions on cable.

Recommendation

Cable operators should carry all local AM and FM audio services including transmission of AM stereo and any FM subcarrier. The carriage of American FM stations and subcarriers, with the exception of public broadcasters, should be prohibited.

Program Logs

Section 5 of the FM regulations and section 4 of the AM regulations request that a program log with many items of information be written each day, filed with the CRTC each week, and kept by the station for a minimum of four weeks. This imposition on licensees is an administrative headache yielding poor results.

Recommendation

Station operators should be required to keep simplified logs for four weeks, without filing with the CRTC. Other means of monitoring should be used.

Long-term Policy

The challenge of policy-making for private radio is to reconcile culture and industry, diversity and competition.

It is a tricky business to devise a regime which will respect both the private firm's imperative of being profitable and the cultural goals which society feels entitled to demand from those accorded the privilege of a radio frequency.

One of the goals for the whole broadcasting system is a free flow of entertainment, information and opinion from the widest possible diversity of sources. Sometimes it is argued that the provisions to ensure a free competitive market will look after the diversity issue. But as we have noted in this chapter, the situation is rather the reverse: competition for the biggest audiences that can be sold for most dollars to advertisers tends to reduce choice. While a certain amount of competition keeps broadcasters on their toes, too much is likely to drive those who serve segments of the market, rather than the whole mass market, out of business.

The delicate art of balancing cultural and industrial goals, and of encouraging both competition and diversity, requires the continuous attention of the regulatory body. The regulatory structure for private radio is something like a house of cards; remove one card and the others collapse.

We have not thought it wise to recommend a thoroughgoing change of private radio policy at this time. The problems of private radio need to be dealt with by gradual alteration rather than the once-only prescription of a task force. We endorse the CRTC's policy of moving toward relaxation of annoying or too-onerous regulation. We also support some shifting of emphasis from blanket regulation to conditions of licence that recognize local conditions and circumstances. Our recommendations are intended to contribute to this fine-tuning and to urge ever greater efforts in building the support base for Canadian content, especially in music.

Notes

1. Canadian Radio-television and Telecommunications Commission, *FM Radio in Canada: A Policy to Ensure a Varied and Comprehensive Radio Service* (Ottawa: CRTC, 1975), p. 3.
2. Canadian Radio-television and Telecommunications Commission, *Proposed Regulations Respecting Radio (AM) and Radio (FM) Broadcasting*, CRTC Public Notice 1986-66 (Ottawa: CRTC, 1986), p. 2.
3. Gordon Rawlinson, President, Rawlco Communications Limited, Regina, Saskatchewan in a letter to the Task Force on Broadcasting Policy, Ottawa, December 13, 1985.
4. Edd Routt, James B. McGrath, and Frederic A. Weiss, *The Radio Format Conundrum* (New York: Hastings House Publishers, Communications Arts Books, 1978).

5. Theodore L. Glasser, "Competition and Diversity Among Radio Formats: Legal and Structural Issues", *Journal of Broadcasting* 2 (Spring 1984), p. 127.
6. CRTC, *Proposed Regulations*, p. 6.
7. Canadian Radio-television and Telecommunications Commission, *Policy Statement on the Review on Radio*, CRTC Public Notice 1983-43 (Ottawa: CRTC, 1983), p. 8.
8. Canadian Association of Broadcasters, *A New Approach for Canada's AM and FM Broadcasters: Revised Regulations and Policies* (Ottawa: The Association, 1985), p. 26.
9. Paul Audley & Associates, *Viewer Choice of TV Services in Ontario*, *Part 2, A Report on the Attitudes of Ontario Residents Towards Television Service Levels Costs, and Programming* (Toronto: Ministry of Transport and Communications, 1984).

Chapter 17

Private Television

Private Television

Introduction

Private television in Canada is ubiquitous. With strong encouragement from the CRTC, private broadcasters have extended their coverage to reach every part of the country, however uneconomical it was to do so.

Private television is also popular. Helped enormously by the practice of simultaneous program substitution, conventional private Canadian TV stations, including the CBC's private affiliates, accounted for 53 percent of English-language TV viewing in 1985. In French-language viewing private Canadian broadcasters, including CBC's affiliates, accounted for a substantial 62 percent of viewing of French-language television.

Private television has the lion's share of resources in Canadian broadcasting. English private television had revenues of $748 million in 1984. By comparison CBC television had an operating budget of $430 million in fiscal 1983-84, including both the network and its owned and operated stations. CBC's budget, of course, reflects its appropriation from Parliament as well as commercial revenues. On the French-language side the situation is the reverse, with private broadcasters earning revenues of $150.3 million in 1984 while Radio-Canada television had an operating budget of $242 million.

From an economic point of view private television is an indispensable advertising vehicle for Canadian businesses. It is an important source, both directly and indirectly, of employment for Canadians.

Compared with private radio, private TV breezed through the recession. While revenue growth in real terms was only slight in 1983, the industry rebounded sharply in 1984, posting an increase of just under 10 percent in constant dollars. Moreover, the television broadcasters continued to show a high level of profitability throughout the recession.

As we see in Chapter 5, most viewing of private Canadian stations in English television is of foreign programs. It varied in 1984 from 73 percent of viewing of independent stations to 54 percent of viewing of the private stations affiliated to CBC. In French-language broadcasting, by comparison, just under half of the viewing of TVA's affiliated stations was of foreign programs, and only 40 percent of viewing of CBC's private affiliates was of foreign programs. Clearly there are reasons in a review such as ours to be concerned with the degree to which adequately funded Canadian programs are available on private television and available at times when they can attract substantial audiences.

In this chapter we outline carefully the role the Task Force believes private television can and should play. The contribution of private broadcasters to Canadian performance programming has been less than impressive over the past 25 years. Some earlier inquiries have made harsh judgements of the private broadcasters' contribution. The CRTC made known its own considerable dissatisfaction in its 1983 *Policy Statement on Canadian Content in Television*:

> An examination of the stations' logs during the last three years indicates an unacceptable decline in the amount of Canadian programming scheduled by a number of private television broadcasters serving major markets during the hours of heavy viewing, between 7:30 and 10:30 p.m. In addition, there is an underrepresentation of some forms of programming, particularly in the areas of entertainment and children's programming. Canadian dramatic productions are virtually non-existent on private English television, which is dominated by foreign entertainment programs, and this is particularly the case during the mid-evening hours.[1]

We agree. True, private broadcasters have for many years been providing well-produced and popular news and supper-hour shows. True too, government funds through Telefilm Canada are starting to increase the amount of Canadian drama on private English-Canadian TV screens. The ATV system in the Maritimes, for example, drew to our attention a series of six half-hour dramas written by Maritime playrights which were produced for The Atlantic Television Network (ATV) by CHUM Atlantic Programs Ltd. in co-operation with Telefilm Canada.[2] The programs were shown in peak viewing time at 8 p.m. Friday evenings.

The prairie province affiliates of CTV have also joined forces to produce a number of new Canadian entertainment programs. CKND in Winnipeg has developed a reputation for its involvement in new Canadian drama, while Global Television has exhibited a series of dramas produced by Atlantis Films based on Canadian short stories.

CTV, by far the most important institution in private English television, has also begun to improve on its record. "Three years ago", a spokesperson for the network noted, "we were looking at a variety show, a situation comedy and licensing theatrical Canadian movies. Now there is a profound change, largely as a result of the Broadcast Fund. CTV was looking", he said, "for first rate [Canadian] programming in competitive time periods. I'm looking at two drama series a week, an average of two mini-series and eight movies a year". While he declined to talk about precise amounts he said that: "We're spending significant dollars ... infinitely greater than three years ago."[3]

In spite of these encouraging signs, there continues to be relatively little Canadian programming or children's programming in the schedules of English-language broadcasters. Equally important, the financial commitments of private broadcasters, as we see in Chapter 14, are limited. We believe it is fair to ask them to do more and to do more in a continuing and systematic way.

First, however, we turn to a review of the present situation in private television broadcasting.

Industry Profile

The private television industry is made up of stations affiliated with the English and French networks, CTV and TVA; the private affiliates of the two public networks, CBC and Radio-Canada; and a number of independent stations, all English-language. Table 17.1 shows the distribution of private TV stations by affiliation throughout the country.

Table 17.1 Distribution of Private Television Stations by Affiliation, 1979 and 1984[a]

		Independent Stations	TVA Affiliates	CTV Affiliates	CBC Affiliates	Radio-Canada Affiliates	Total
Nfld.	1979			3			3
	1984			3			3
P.E.I.	1979						
	1984						
N.S.	1979	0		2			2
	1984	1		2			3
N.B.	1979			1	1		2
	1984			1	1		2
Que.	1979		9	1	1	6	17
	1984		10	1	1	5	17
Ont.	1979	4		8	11		23
	1984	4		9	11		24
Man.	1979	1		3	1		5
	1984	1		3	1		5
Sask.	1979			4	5		9
	1984			5	5		10
Alta.	1979	3		3	3		9
	1984	3		3	3		9
B.C., Yukon & N.W.T.	1979	1		1	6		8
	1984	1		2	5		8
Canada	1979	9	9	26	28	6	78
	1984	10	10	29	27	5	81

Note: a. The stations in this Table are those required to declare their revenues to the CRTC. Rebroadcasting stations are excluded as the originating station files combined revenue reports with the CRTC, with the exception of eight CTV rebroadcasting stations that carry some local advertising.

Source: CRTC, Industry Statistics and Analysis Division.

In 1984 there were 81 originating stations in the private sector, most of them network affiliates. Of these, 27 were English-language CBC affiliates nationwide and five were French-language CBC affiliates in Quebec; the CTV network had 21 affiliated stations (16 'full affiliates' and five 'supplementary affiliates') in addition to eight rebroadcasting stations which carry some local advertising spread through all Canadian provinces except Prince Edward Island; and TVA had ten stations in Quebec. The remaining stations were independents.

Private French-language stations accounted for 15 of the 81, or 18.5 percent, the same share as French-language private radio stations, compared with close to 25 percent of the population for which French is the language of the home. No French-language private TV station operates outside Quebec. The CBC provides the only originating stations serving francophone minorities in the predominantly anglophone provinces. By contrast, two private stations broadcast

English programming within Quebec: CFCF, the CTV affiliate in Montreal whose English minority constitutes one of the largest English urban areas in the country, and CKMI in Quebec City, a CBC affiliate serving the far smaller English minority in the provincial capital and neighbouring region.

Three new originating stations were established in Canada between 1979 and 1984. No new private station has joined the CBC network since 1979. In 1981 station CHEK in Victoria, owned by Western Broadcasting Co. Ltd., switched from CBC to CTV. In 1983, station CHAU in Carleton, Quebec, owned by Claude Pratte and Paul Desmarais, switched from Radio-Canada to TVA.

In 1983 a new television service, the Atlantic Satellite Network (ASN) in Halifax controlled by CHUM, began operation. Two new stations became associated with CTV: CIEW in Carlyle, Saskatchewan, operated by Skinner Holdings; and CJBN-TV in Kenora, Ontario, became a CTV affiliate. In September of 1986 a second private French station, CFJP will begin broadcasting in Montreal. The Commission has also licensed the Quatre Saisons network to rebroadcast the programs of the new Montreal station in the major regional markets of Quebec.

Among the markets that Quatre Saisons will reach are Sherbrooke, Quebec City, Hull, Trois Rivières, Jonquière and Val d'Or. Except for a very small amount of local programming in two or three of the markets reached, the Quatre Saisons network will essentially rebroadcast the Montreal station's programming. The closest parallel among existing broadcasting services is Global Television, which is licensed as a Southern Ontario network with only one station which originates programming, but has rebroadcast transmitters in other markets.

The CTV network includes both affiliate stations and supplementary affiliates. The former are located in medium and large markets; the latter are all in small markets. Some of the stations have been allowed to affiliate to CTV as well as CBC. Such operations are usually referred to as 'twin-sticks'. In similar circumstances, twin-stick French-language licensees were established affiliated to both Radio-Canada and TVA. In April 1986, with the licensing of the Quatre Saisons network, the CRTC licensed Radio-Nord Inc. to operate in Rouyn, Quebec as the first 'triple-stick' in Canada, rebroadcasting the programs of the Radio-Canada, TVA and Quatre Saisons networks.

Almost all the private affiliates of the CBC English and French networks are in small cities. This fact is reflected in relatively low revenues but not, as we shall see later, in low profitability.

Evolution of Viewing Habits and Audience Fragmentation

The size of the audiences they attract is fundamental to the financial position of private broadcasters. A station's viewing share dictates its share of commercial revenue, which in turn affects its ability to produce or acquire attractive programs, which — to complete the circle — generates viewing and revenue shares.

Table 17.2 Audience Share Trends by Station Group, 1971-1985[a] (percent)

Station Groups	1971	1972	1973	1974	1975[b]	1976	1977	1978	1979	1980	1981	1982	1983	1984	1985
English-language															
CBC	29.9	28.5	27.3	24.6	22.4	20.2	19.8	20.7	19.8	18.1	16.0	17.1	17.3	17.4	16.8
Owned	14.4	14.6	13.7	12.2	12.1	11.3	11.2	11.7	11.4	10.3	9.5	10.4	10.7	10.7	10.5
Affiliates	15.5	13.9	13.6	12.4	10.3	8.9	8.6	9.0	8.4	7.8	6.5	6.7	6.6	6.6	6.3
CTV	23.5	23.3	24.4	24.1	24.9	25.1	25.2	24.8	25.6	23.1	26.7	25.9	25.5	22.9	23.0
Independents[c]	3.2	3.3	2.7	5.8	6.9	8.9	9.5	9.6	9.3	11.3	11.7	11.4	13.2	12.8	11.5
Pay television	–	–	–	–	–	–	–	–	–	–	–	–	–	1.3	1.5
TVO/KNOW	#	#	#	#	0.3	0.4	0.4	0.5	0.6	0.6	0.8	0.8	1.0	0.9	1.0
United States	19.0	19.3	21.0	20.9	21.8	22.1	22.2	22.6	22.7	24.5	23.9	24.6	24.0	23.7	23.6
TOTAL	75.6	74.7	75.4	75.4	76.3	76.7	77.1	78.2	78.0	77.7	79.0	79.6	80.9	79.0	77.4
French-language															
CBC	13.9	14.4	14.1	12.6	12.5	11.8	11.0	10.3	9.9	8.3	8.4	9.1	9.0	9.1	9.2
Owned	7.2	8.3	8.0	7.4	7.6	7.5	6.9	7.0	6.5	5.6	5.7	5.8	6.3	6.4	6.6
Affiliates	6.7	6.1	6.1	5.2	4.9	4.3	4.1	3.3	3.4	2.7	2.7	3.3	2.7	2.7	2.6
TVA	10.5	10.9	10.5	12.0	11.0	11.3	11.6	11.2	11.7	13.3	11.9	10.5	8.3	10.3	11.5
Radio-Québec	–	–	–	–	0.2	0.2	0.3	0.3	0.4	0.6	0.6	0.7	0.9	1.1	1.2
Pay television	–	–	–	–	–	–	–	–	–	–	–	–	–	0.2	0.3
TVFQ	–	–	–	–	–	–	–	–	#	0.1	0.1	0.1	0.1	0.1	0.1
Others[d]	–	–	–	–	–	–	–	–	–	–	–	–	0.8	0.3	0.3
TOTAL	24.4	25.3	24.6	24.6	23.7	23.3	22.9	21.8	22.0	22.3	21.0	20.4	19.1	21.0	22.6
All Stations	100.0	100.0	100.0	100.0	100.0	100.0	100.0	100.0	100.0	100.0	100.0	100.0	100.0	100.0	100.0

Notes: a. In average fall weeks.
b. No comparable survey in November 1975. Figures relate to January 1976.
c. Includes House of Commons and Global.
d. Includes House of Commons. In fall 1983 CHAU was also included.

Key: – not on air
less than 0.05 percent

Source: Canadian Broadcasting Corporation, CBC Research, raw data from BBM Bureau of Broadcast Measurement.

Since the beginning of the 1970s, the private television industry has had to contend with dramatic increases in the number of potential channels, owing to the development of cable. Many new services, starting with American channels, have in fact been introduced. Most recently pay-TV and specialty channels in Canada and the United States have been added. However, as Table 17.2 indicates the result has not yet been a proportionate fragmentation of television audiences.

The important audience developments over the past 15 years have been the jump from 3 percent to 11.5 percent of total TV audiences achieved by independent Canadian stations and the large decline in viewing of CBC's private affiliates — from 22 percent to 9 percent. Smaller but still significant changes also occurred. The American stations available in Canada increased their share of audiences from 19 percent to 24 percent. The share of total viewing achieved by the CBC's own English stations declined by 4 percentage points.

Both the CTV and TVA stations were remarkably successful in maintaining their share of the national television audience throughout this period. By 1985, pay-TV and specialty services had taken only a small share of audiences from off-air broadcasters. As Table 17.2 indicates, there has been something approaching a new equilibrium in the period after 1980. Viewing share figures indicate the way the money in the system will be divided.

Revenues and Expenses

Private television revenues of $899 million in 1984 were almost double the figure of five years earlier, $474 million, measured in current dollars. In constant dollars the industry revenues grew at a compound annual rate of 4.6 percent between 1979 and 1984. The revenue growth rate varied considerably, however, between different industry segments as Table 17.3 illustrates.

Independent TV stations showed the highest average annual growth between 1979 and 1984 at 7.4 percent. CTV affiliates were not far behind at 6 percent. The members of the TVA French-language network had revenue growth of only 0.9 percent. English CBC affiliates actually had a negative growth rate of −0.9 percent, while French affiliates' revenue declined by an average 2.7 percent per year.

The TVA stations' revenue performance may have been due partly to the impact on viewing share of a long technicians' strike at Télé-Métropole, the network's flagship station, in 1983. The decline in the revenues of CBC's English affiliates occurred almost entirely in 1981, reflecting the switch of CHEK in Victoria from CBC to CTV. Slower growth of the CBC's French and English affiliates may also have reflected the fact they were smaller stations and were hit hardest by the contraction of advertising budgets and concentration of advertising in big markets during the recession. The affiliates' revenues recovered somewhat in 1984; and as we shall see below, profitability was little affected by slumping revenues.

Advertising revenues do not account for quite as high a percentage of total revenue in television as in private radio, but still account for more than 90 percent, or $817 million of the $899 million total in 1984. The distribution of ad

Table 17.3 Private Television: Growth in Revenue by Affiliation, 1979-1984[a]

	Independents			TVA			CTV		
	Revenue ($ millions)	Annual growth rate (%)		Revenue ($ millions)	Annual growth rate (%)		Revenue ($ millions)	Annual growth rate (%)	
		current $	constant $		current $	constant $		current $	constant $
1979	110.2	—	—	83.4	—	—	213.2	—	—
1980	137.8	25.0	13.7	97.9	17.4	6.8	244.4	14.6	4.3
1981	169.2	22.8	8.9	109.5	11.8	–0.9	292.1	19.5	6.0
1982	202.9	19.9	8.3	116.1	6.0	–4.3	337.9	15.7	4.5
1983	212.3	4.6	–1.1	117.4	1.1	–4.3	367.1	8.6	2.7
1984	238.3	12.2	7.6	132.5	12.9	8.1	432.2	17.7	12.8
Annual Compound Growth Rate (%)		16.7	7.4		9.7	0.9		15.2	6.0

Table 17.3 (cont'd)

	CBC Affiliates			Radio-Canada Affiliates			Total		
	Revenue ($ millions)	Annual growth rate (%)		Revenue ($ millions)	Annual growth rate (%)		Revenue ($ millions)	Annual growth rate (%)	
		current $	constant $		current $	constant $		current $	constant $
1979	53.9	—	—	13.5	—	—	474.3	—	—
1980	62.9	16.7	5.9	14.7	8.9	–0.6	557.7	17.6	7.0
1981	61.4	–2.4	–13.4	13.4	–8.8	–18.9	645.7	15.8	2.7
1982	68.5	11.6	–0.9	12.7	–5.2	–14.1	738.1	14.3	3.2
1983	72.6	6.0	0.0	14.5	14.2	6.6	783.9	6.2	0.4
1984	78.0	7.4	3.1	17.8	22.8	18.5	898.8	14.7	9.9
Annual Compound Growth Rate (%)		7.7	–0.9		5.7	–2.7		13.6	4.6

Note: a. Including revenue from network operations.
Source: CRTC, Industry Statistics and Analysis Division.

revenues, broken down into national and local, is seen in relation to station affiliation, region, and English and French sectors in Tables 17.4 to 17.6. Television advertising revenue in Canada is at only half the level per capita of population that it is in the United States and constitutes a much smaller proportion of gross national product.

Between 1979 and 1984, revenue from sales of national advertising rose far more sharply, at 96 percent, than revenue from local advertising, at 58 percent. The increases were much greater for independent stations and CTV members than for TVA members and CBC affiliates. The independent stations' share of total advertising revenue rose from 23 to 26 percent during the five-year period, and for CTV members ad revenue rose from 44 percent to 48 percent. The TVA network stations' share dropped from 18 percent to 14 percent, and that of CBC French and English private affiliates from 15 percent to 12 percent.

While the independent stations' gains were mainly in local advertising, CTV stations gained mainly in national advertising. The TVA and CBC affiliate stations' losses were more at the local than the national level.

Looking at the French-English breakdown we see that the share of private television's total advertising revenue earned by French stations dropped from 20.5 to 16 percent. Over the five-year period, the ad revenues of French stations rose by only 48 percent while those of English stations almost doubled. The French loss of share was about equal in national and local advertising.

As we have seen, French-language commercial broadcasters accounted for just under 24 percent of all viewing of private sector commercially funded Canadian stations and networks in 1984. The fact that private French-language stations that sell commercial time nevertheless earned just 14 percent of national TV advertising revenues is difficult to explain. The principal factor behind this wide discrepancy could well be the absence of a third French station in the large Montreal market, which has to a significant degree left unsatisfied the demand by national advertisers for access to francophone viewers. We return to this issue below in discussing policies affecting French-language television. The essential point to make here is that the proportion of national television advertising that flows to commercial French-language television broadcasters does not, at present, reflect their share of TV audiences.

About 75 percent of private television's total advertising revenue come from national advertising and the share has been rising over the past few years. This ratio is the reverse of the ratio for private radio where roughly 75 percent of ad revenue is local.

A far higher proportion (79 percent) of English station and network revenues come from national advertising than is the case for French TV broadcasters (66 percent).

In order to get a full picture of the distribution of advertising revenues, we must include the CBC network and its owned and operated stations, because CBC television competes for advertising. The CBC's inclusion, shown in Table 17.7, brings total advertising revenue to $970 million in 1984.

Table 17.7, covering a ten-year period, shows that while CBC advertising revenues in current dollars tripled between 1975 and 1984, those of private

Table 17.4 Private Television: Share and Growth of Advertising Revenue by Affiliation, 1979 and 1984 ($ millions)

	1979						1984						Growth 1979-1984		
	Local		National and Network		Total		Local		National and Network		Total		Local	National and Network	Total
	$	%	$	%	$	%	$	%	$	%	$	%	%	%	%
Independent Stations	18.9	15.6	82.9	26.0	101.8	23.2	43.2	22.5	168.6	27.0	211.8	25.9	128.6	103.4	108.1
TVA Affiliates	30.9	25.5	47.0	14.8	77.9	17.7	39.5	20.6	77.4	12.4	117.0	14.3	27.8	64.7	50.2
CTV Affiliates	44.1	36.3	150.9	47.4	194.9	44.3	76.0	39.5	319.3	51.1	395.3	48.4	72.3	111.6	102.8
CBC Affiliates	22.7	18.7	30.0	9.4	52.7	12.0	27.2	14.2	49.1	7.9	76.3	9.3	19.8	63.7	44.8
Radio-Canada Affiliates	5.0	4.1	7.5	2.4	12.5	2.8	6.2	3.2	10.2	1.6	16.4	2.0	24.0	36.0	31.2
All Stations	121.4	100.0	318.3	100.0	439.7	100.0	192.2	100.0	624.5	100.0	816.7	100.0	58.3	96.2	85.7

Source: CRTC, Industry Statistics and Analysis Division.

Table 17.5 Private Television: Share and Growth of Advertising Revenue by Region, 1979 and 1984[a]
($ millions)

	1979						1984						Percent Growth 1979-1984		
	Local		National and Network		Total		Local		National and Network		Total		Local	National and Network	Total
	$	%	$	%	$	%	$	%	$	%	$	%	%	%	%
Atlantic	9.4	7.7	16.1	5.1	25.5	5.8	14.3	7.4	31.2	5.0	45.6	5.6	52.1	93.8	78.8
Quebec	41.3	34.0	73.1	23.0	114.9	26.1	57.7	30.0	125.5	20.0	183.3	22.4	39.7	71.7	59.5
Ontario	18.0	14.8	146.8	46.1	164.8	37.5	37.6	19.6	277.6	44.5	315.2	38.6	108.9	89.1	91.3
Manitoba and Saskatchewan	14.6	12.0	21.8	6.8	36.5	8.3	21.4	11.1	47.3	7.6	68.8	8.4	46.6	117.0	89.0
Alberta	22.1	18.2	31.1	9.8	53.3	12.1	38.8	20.2	77.4	12.4	116.2	14.2	75.6	148.9	118.0
British Columbia	16.0	13.2	28.8	9.0	44.9	10.2	22.3	11.6	65.5	10.5	87.7	10.7	39.4	127.4	95.3
Canada	121.4	100.0	318.3	100.0	439.7	100.0	192.2	100.0	624.5	100.0	816.7	100.0	58.3	96.2	85.7

Note: a. The CTV Network advertising revenues have been distributed among the affiliates using a method established by the CTV Network and used by the CRTC.
Source: CRTC, Industry Statistics and Analysis Division.

Table 17.6 Private Television: Share and Growth of Advertising Revenue by Language of Broadcast, 1979 and 1984 ($ millions)

	1979						1984						Growth 1978-1984		
	Local		National and Network		Total		Local		National and Network		Total		Local	National and Network	Total
	$	%	$	%	$	%	$	%	$	%	$	%	%	%	%
English Stations	85.6	70.5	263.8	82.9	349.3	79.5	146.5	76.2	537.0	86.0	683.5	83.7	71.1	103.6	95.7
French Stations	35.8	29.5	54.5	17.1	90.3	20.5	45.7	23.8	87.6	14.0	133.3	16.3	27.7	60.7	47.6
All Stations	121.4	100.0	318.3	100.0	439.7	100.0	192.2	100.0	624.6	100.0	816.8	100.0	58.3	96.2	85.8

Source: CRTC, Industry Statistics and Analysis Division.

television nearly quadrupled. Thus the CBC's share of advertising revenue dipped from more than 19 percent in 1975 to less than 16 percent in 1984. The CBC holds a much more significant place in national advertising, with a share of 18 percent, than in local advertising, with 6.5 percent. This reflects, among other factors, the fact that the CBC network provides more hours of network programming to its O and O stations than does CTV.

On the expenditure side, Table 17.8 shows the expenses of private television stations at $676 million in 1984, 75 percent of total revenues. Programming accounted for the largest proportion of revenues, at 46 percent, compared with the 32 percent share of private radio revenues that go to programming. Other private TV revenue shares were: general expenses and administration, 15 percent; sales and promotion, 9 percent; and technical expenses, 6 percent.

In order to understand the differences in the breakdown of revenues among the various categories of stations, it is important to bear in mind the reality behind the numbers. In the case of the CBC and Radio Canada affiliates most of the stations are quite small. The breakdown therefore reflects differences in size of the stations in each category. There are also special affiliation agreements in place for small affiliates of CBC and Radio Canada, as there are for the small CTV affiliates, which affect the expenditure breakdown and expenditures on programming.

Programming Expenditures

A special survey was carried out for the Task Force by Statistics Canada to determine the degree to which different categories of Canadian television broadcasters finance particular kinds of program. The results are summarized in Tables 17.9 to 17.11. The Canadian Association of Broadcasters (CAB) and the CBC made this survey possible through their prompt and active co-operation.

As Table 17.9 indicates, in the year that ended August 31, 1985 the CBC and private television broadcasters together spent just under $1 billion on television programming. Private broadcasters spent $434 million or 44 percent, while the CBC spent $563 million. Of the combined total, 83 percent, or $832 million, was spent on Canadian programming, the remaining $165 million on foreign programming.

While private broadcasters accounted for 44 percent of all programming expenditures, they accounted for a significantly lower percentage of spending on Canadian programs, at 35 percent. Private broadcasters, French and English, spent $292 million on Canadian programming, while the CBC spent $540 million. Of the $165 million spent on foreign programs, private broadcasters accounted for $142 million, or 86 percent.

There are, however, substantial differences in the pattern of expenditures between French and English language broadcasters. While French broadcasters, public and private, account for 29 percent of all expenditure, they account for 32 percent of expenditures on Canadian programs, but just 10 percent of spending on foreign programs. To make the point differently, while English-language broadcasters spent 21 percent of their programming budgets on foreign programs, French-language broadcasters spent just 6 percent. Naturally, these

Table 17.7 Advertising Revenue of Private and Public Television Stations, 1975-1984 ($ millions)

	1975		1979		1980		1981		1982	
	$	%	$	%	$	%	$	%	$	%
Private Stations										
Local	62.0	29.4	121.4	27.6	139.9	27.5	157.5	26.6	166.8	24.9
National and Network	149.0	70.6	318.3	72.4	369.5	72.5	433.7	73.4	503.0	75.1
Total	211.1	100.0	439.7	100.0	509.4	100.0	591.2	100.0	669.8	100.0
CBC Owned and Operated										
Local	6.2	12.2	10.3	11.9	10.7	107.0	11.4	11.2	12.7	11.9
National and Network	44.6	87.8	76.4	88.1	89.7	89.3	90.4	88.8	93.7	88.1
Total	50.8	100.0	86.7	100.0	100.4	100.0	101.8	100.0	106.4	100.0
Private and Public Stations Combined										
Local	68.2	26.0	131.7	25.0	150.6	24.7	168.9	24.4	179.5	23.1
National and Network	193.7	74.0	394.7	75.0	459.2	75.3	524.1	75.6	596.7	76.9
Total	261.9	100.0	526.4	100.0	609.8	100.0	693.0	100.0	776.2	100.0
CBC Share (%)										
Local	9.1		7.8		7.1		6.7		7.1	
National and Network	23.0		19.4		19.5		17.2		15.7	
Total	19.4		16.5		16.5		14.7		13.7	

	1983		1984		Growth Rate 1975-1984 (%)	Growth Rate 1979-1984 (%)
	$	%	$	%		
Private Stations						
Local	172.1	24.2	192.2	23.5	210.0	58.3
National and Network	540.4	75.8	624.5	76.5	318.8	96.2
Total	712.5	100.0	816.7	100.0	286.8	85.7
CBC Owned and Operated						
Local	11.4	9.3	13.4	8.7	116.0	30.1
National and Network	111.8	90.7	140.3	91.3	214.6	83.6
Total	123.2	100.0	153.7	100.0	202.6	77.3
Private and Public Stations Combined						
Local	183.5	22.0	205.6	21.2	201.5	56.1
National and Network	652.2	78.0	764.8	78.8	294.8	93.8
Total	835.7	100.0	970.4	100.0	270.0	84.3
CBC Share (%)						
Local		6.2		6.5		
National and Network		17.1		18.3		
Total		14.7		15.8		

Source: CRTC, Industry Statistics and Analysis Division.

Table 17.8 Revenue, Expenses and Profits of Stations by Affiliation, 1984[a] ($ millions)

	CBC Affiliates		Radio-Canada Affiliates		CTV Affiliates		TVA Affiliates		Independents		All Stations	
	$	%	$	%	$	%	$	%	$	%	$	%
Revenue	77.8	100.0	17.8	100.0	432.2	100.0	132.5	100.0	238.3	100.0	898.8	100.0
Expenses	53.7	69.0	13.2	74.2	320.5	74.2	99.4	75.0	189.3	79.4	676.1	75.2
Programming	21.7	27.9	3.6	20.2	209.6	48.5	45.7	34.5	131.6	55.2	412.2	45.9
Technical	5.8	7.5	2.3	12.9	24.4	5.6	11.0	8.3	8.6	3.6	52.1	5.8
Sales and promotion	10.4	13.4	3.1	17.4	32.9	7.6	13.1	9.9	19.4	8.1	79.0	8.8
Administration	15.7	20.2	4.3	24.2	53.6	12.4	29.5	22.3	29.7	12.5	132.8	14.8
Operating profit	24.2	31.1	4.6	25.8	111.7	25.8	33.2	25.1	49.1	20.6	222.7	24.8
Profit before income tax	19.4	24.9	4.1	23.0	85.7	19.8	20.7	15.6	33.4	14.0	163.3	18.2

Note: a. Including network operations.
Source: CRTC, Industry Statistics and Analysis Division.

figures reflect not only the amount of foreign programming being purchased but also the fact that French-language broadcasters would pay much less on a per-hour basis for that programming.

Within English-language broadcasting there are substantial differences between the way the CBC and the private broadcasters spent their program budgets. While the private broadcasters spent $133 million or 37 percent of their program budget on foreign programs, the CBC spent $16 million or 4 percent.

In order to understand these figures it should be remembered that foreign programs are purchased at a small fraction of what it costs to produce them, usually less then 5 percent for a TV series and 1 or 2 percent for feature films. Hence, for an expenditure of $133 million, English private broadcasters bought the right to show programs that probably cost at least $3 billion to produce, and might easily have cost $4 billion or $5 billion. It is not surprising that private broadcasters find this an attractive proposition, particularly when these shows come with the backing of extensive publicity and advertising that spills into the Canadian market.

As Table 17.9 indicates, most of the spending on foreign programs by English-language broadcasters was for entertainment programs. Within the entertainment category the major expenditures, accounting for $125 million, were for foreign feature films and TV series. While the spending on foreign programs by French-language broadcasters was much lower, here too most of the money went to buy feature films and TV series, $15.3 million out of a total of $16.6 million.

As we see in Chapter 5, these foreign drama programs account for almost half of English-language TV viewing in Canada. Revenues earned from selling commercials on these shows in turn represent by a wide margin the major source of revenue for English-language broadcasters.

Table 17.10 sets out in a more condensed form than Table 17.9 the pattern of expenditures on Canadian programs according to four general program categories. As Table 17.10 indicates, private TV broadcasters accounted for a minority of expenditures in every category except English-language sports. Private broadcasters accounted for 24 percent of all spending on Canadian programs in the French-language sector and for 40 percent among English broadcasters.

The private broadcasters' share of total spending on Canadian programs varies greatly, however, by program category. In English broadcasting they made a substantial contribution in news and information programming and in sports, but only a small one in children's programming.

In the broad categories of entertainment and arts, and letters and science, private English-language broadcasters accounted for just over one-quarter (27 percent) of total spending in 1985. Under one-half, or roughly $18 million in this category was spent on Canadian feature films and TV series. As we see in our examination of performance programming in Chapter 5, most of the programs offered by private English-language broadcasters in these categories are talk shows or quiz and game shows.

The situation is significantly different in French broadcasting. While private broadcasters account for a smaller share of total expenditures on Canadian

Table 17.9 Analysis of Cost of Programs Telecast by Television Stations in Canada for Year Ended 31 August 1985 ($ millions)

ENGLISH STATIONS	Canadian Programs						Foreign Programs						All Programs					
	C B C		Private		Total		C B C		Private		Total		C B C		Private		Total	
	$	%	$	%	$	%	$	%	$	%	$	%	$	%	$	%	$	%
Information																		
News	98.9	28.1	104.4	29.1	203.3	28.6	—	—	2.2	0.6	2.2	0.3	98.9	28.1	106.6	29.7	205.5	28.9
Public Affairs	64.9	18.4	28.0	7.8	92.9	13.1	—	—	2.7	0.7	2.7	0.4	64.9	18.4	30.7	8.5	95.6	13.4
Other	21.4	6.1	18.8	5.2	40.2	5.6	—	—	0.3	0.1	0.3	a	21.4	6.1	19.1	5.3	40.5	5.7
Total	185.2	52.6	151.2	42.1	336.4	47.3	—	—	5.2	1.4	5.2	0.7	185.2	52.6	156.4	43.5	341.6	48.0
Children's	14.2	4.0	1.9	0.6	16.1	2.3	—	—	1.4	0.4	1.4	0.2	14.2	4.0	3.3	1.0	17.5	2.5
Entertainment																		
Feature	2.4	0.7	2.1	0.6	4.5	0.6	2.4	0.7	37.4	10.5	39.8	5.6	4.8	1.4	39.5	11.1	44.3	6.2
TV Series	5.7	1.6	15.5	4.3	21.2	3.0	12.7	3.6	72.9	20.3	85.6	12.0	18.4	5.2	88.4	24.6	106.8	15.0
Quiz/Game	—	—	3.4	1.0	3.4	0.5	—	—	2.9	0.8	2.9	0.4	—	—	6.3	1.8	6.3	0.9
Other	41.0	11.7	15.9	4.4	56.9	8.0	0.5	0.1	7.6	2.1	8.1	1.1	41.5	11.8	23.6	6.5	65.1	9.2
Total	49.2	14.0	36.9	10.3	86.1	12.1	15.6	4.4	120.9	33.7	136.4	19.1	64.8	18.4	157.7	44.0	222.5	31.3
Arts, Letters & Sciences	57.2	16.3	3.4	1.0	60.6	8.5	—	—	0.7	0.2	0.7	0.1	57.2	16.3	4.1	1.2	61.3	8.6
Sports	30.7	8.7	32.4	9.0	63.1	8.9	—	—	4.8	1.3	4.8	0.7	30.7	8.7	37.3	10.3	68.0	9.6
Total	336.6	95.6	225.9	63.0	562.5	79.1	15.6	4.4	132.9	37.0	148.5	20.9	352.2	100.0	358.8	100.0	711.0	100.0

FRENCH STATIONS	Canadian Programs						Foreign Programs						All Programs					
	C B C		Private		Total		C B C		Private		Total		C B C		Private		Total	
	$	%	$	%	$	%	$	%	$	%	$	%	$	%	$	%	$	%
Information																		
News	50.7	24.0	17.5	23.4	68.2	23.8	—	—	—	—	—	—	50.7	24.0	17.5	23.4	68.2	23.8
Public Affairs	16.3	7.7	4.0	5.3	20.3	7.1	—	—	—	—	—	—	16.3	7.7	4.0	5.3	20.3	7.1
Other	32.5	15.4	8.6	11.4	41.1	14.4	—	—	—	—	—	—	32.5	15.4	8.6	11.4	41.1	14.4
Total	99.5	47.1	30.0	40.1	129.5	45.3	—	—	—	—	—	—	99.5	47.1	30.0	40.1	129.5	45.3
Children's	13.1	6.2	0.1	0.2	13.2	4.6	—	—	—	—	—	—	13.1	6.2	0.1	0.2	13.2	4.6
Entertainment																		
Feature	0.6	0.3	0.9	1.2	1.5	0.5	2.7	1.3	3.3	4.4	6.0	2.1	3.3	1.6	4.2	5.6	7.5	2.6
TV Series	7.7	3.7	9.9	13.3	17.6	6.2	4.5	2.1	4.8	6.5	9.3	3.3	12.3	5.8	14.8	19.7	27.1	9.5
Quiz/Game	—	—	3.5	4.7	3.5	1.2	—	—	—	—	—	—	—	—	3.5	4.7	3.5	0.5
Other	36.8	17.4	18.4	24.6	55.2	19.3	0.4	0.2	0.8	1.0	1.2	0.4	37.1	17.6	19.2	25.7	56.3	19.7
Total	45.1	21.4	32.8	43.8	77.9	27.2	7.6	3.6	8.9	11.9	16.5	5.8	52.7	25.0	41.7	55.7	94.4	33.0
Arts, Letters & Sciences	24.4	11.5	—	—	24.4	8.5	—	—	—	—	—	—	24.4	11.5	—	—	24.4	8.6
Sports	21.5	10.2	2.9	3.9	24.4	8.5	—	—	0.1	0.1	0.1	a	21.5	10.2	3.0	4.0	24.5	8.6
Total	203.6	96.4	65.8	88.0	269.4	94.1	7.6	3.6	9.0	12.0	16.6	5.8	211.2	100.0	74.8	100.0	286.0	100.0

Note: a. Value less than 0.05.

Table 17.9 (cont'd)

ALL STATIONS	Canadian Programs						Foreign Programs						All Programs					
	C B C		Private		Total		C B C		Private		Total		C B C		Private		Total	
	$	%	$	%	$	%	$	%	$	%	$	%	$	%	$	%	$	%
Information																		
News	149.7	26.6	121.9	28.1	271.5	27.2	—	—	2.2	0.5	2.2	0.2	149.7	26.6	124.1	28.6	273.8	27.5
Public Affairs	81.2	14.4	32.0	7.4	113.2	11.4	—	—	2.7	0.6	2.7	0.3	81.2	14.4	34.7	8.0	115.9	11.6
Other	53.9	9.5	27.3	6.3	81.2	8.1	—	—	0.3	0.1	0.3	a	53.9	9.2	27.7	6.4	81.8	8.2
Total	284.7	50.5	181.2	41.8	465.9	46.7	—	—	5.2	1.2	5.2	0.5	284.7	50.5	186.4	43.0	471.1	47.3
Children's	27.3	4.8	2.1	0.5	29.4	2.9	—	—	1.4	0.3	1.4	0.1	27.3	4.8	3.4	0.8	30.7	3.1
Entertainment																		
Feature	3.0	0.5	3.0	0.7	6.0	0.6	5.2	0.9	40.7	9.4	45.8	4.6	8.1	1.4	43.8	10.1	51.8	5.2
TV Series	13.5	2.4	25.4	5.9	38.8	3.9	17.2	3.1	77.8	17.9	95.0	9.5	30.7	5.5	103.2	23.8	133.9	13.4
Quiz/Game	—	—	6.9	1.6	6.8	0.7	—	—	2.9	0.7	2.9	0.3	—	—	9.7	2.2	9.7	1.0
Other	77.8	13.8	34.4	7.9	112.2	11.3	0.8	0.2	8.4	1.9	9.3	0.9	78.6	14.0	42.8	9.9	121.4	12.2
Total	94.2	16.7	69.7	16.1	164.0	16.4	23.3	4.2	129.8	29.9	153.1	15.4	117.5	20.9	199.4	46.0	316.9	31.8
Arts, Letters & Sciences	81.7	14.5	3.4	0.8	85.0	8.6	—	—	0.7	0.2	0.7	0.1	81.7	14.5	4.1	0.9	85.7	8.6
Sports	52.2	9.3	35.4	8.1	87.5	8.8	—	—	4.9	1.1	4.9	0.5	52.2	9.3	40.3	9.3	92.5	9.3
Total	540.2	95.9	291.7	67.3	831.9	83.4	23.3	4.2	141.9	32.7	165.1	16.6	563.4	100.0	433.6	100.0	997.0	100.0

Note: a. Value less than 0.05.
Source: Statistics Canada Supplementary Survey.

Table 17.10 Canadian Programming Expenditures for CBC and Private Broadcasters, 1985

	CBC		Private Broadcasting		Total	
	$ millions	% of total	$ millions	% of total	$ millions	% of total
English Stations						
News and Information	185.2	(55)	151.2	(45)	336.4	59.8
Sports	30.7	(49)	32.4	(51)	63.1	11.2
Children's	14.2	(88)	1.9	(12)	16.1	2.9
Entertainment, Arts, etc.	106.4	(73)	40.3	(27)	146.7	26.1
TOTAL	336.6	(60)	225.9	(40)	562.5	100.0
French Stations						
News and Information	99.5	(77)	30.0	(23)	129.5	48.1
Sports	21.5	(88)	2.9	(12)	24.4	9.1
Children's	13.1	(99)	.1	(1)	13.2	4.9
Entertainment, Arts, etc.	69.5	(68)	32.8	(32)	102.3	38.0
TOTAL	203.6	(76)	65.8	(24)	269.4	100.0

Source: Statistics Canada Supplementary Survey.

programming in news and information, sports, and children's programming, they account for a larger share of expenditure than their English counterparts in entertainment programming. While French private broadcasters, like their English counterparts, are extensively involved in providing talk and quiz shows, they also present a significant amount of drama. Their reported expenditures on Canadian feature films and TV series were $11 million in 1985.

In 1985 private English-language broadcasters spent over seven times as much on foreign feature films and TV series as they spent on Canadian programs in these categories, or $110.3 million by comparison with $17.6 million. The situation was significantly different in French-language broadcasting, where 57 percent of all expenditures on programs in these categories were for Canadian programs, by comparison with 14 percent in English.

The patterns of expenditure also vary widely among the different categories of private English-language television broadcasters, as shown in Table 17.11. The independent stations spent a higher percentage of their revenues on programming than did CTV, 56 percent by comparison with 49 percent. This difference seems mainly to reflect the far higher percentage of revenue the independents spend on foreign programs, 27 percent by comparison with 15 percent, for CTV. With revenues of just over half those of CTV and its affiliates, the independents, nevertheless, actually spent more on foreign programs than CTV, $67 million by comparison with $63 million. The difference presumably reflects the collective buying power of the CTV network acting on behalf of its affiliated stations.

The independent stations also spent far less of their programming budget on Canadian programming than CTV, 51 percent for the independents, 69 percent for CTV. If expenditures on Canadian programming are seen as a percentage of revenue, however, the difference is less substantial. The independents spent 29 percent of their revenues on Canadian programs, CTV and its affiliates combined spent 33 percent.

Both the independent stations and CTV and its affiliates made substantial expenditures on news programming. They committed significant funding to public affairs shows, but it was still far less than CBC. Although CTV expenditures in both categories were proportionately a little greater, the difference was not large.

While news and information programs accounted for only 18 percent of English television viewing, they represented 72 percent of the expenditures independent stations make on Canadian programs and 62 percent for CTV and its affiliates. CTV and its affiliates committed a proportionately higher percentage of the Canadian programming budget to sports, at 17 percent, than the independent stations, at 10 percent.

The remaining proportion of the Canadian programming budget represents what is left for the other categories of programming, which account for over two-thirds of English television viewing. In the case of Canadian programming for children total expenditures by all private English broadcasters were $1.9 million, roughly one-fifth of one percent of revenues, and 1 percent of their combined expenditures on Canadian programs. Expenditures by private English broadcasters on programs categorized as arts, letters and sciences were $3.2 million, roughly 1.5 percent of their total spending on Canadian programs.

The independent stations committed 15 percent of their Canadian programming budgets to entertainment programs, including feature films, TV series of all kinds, and quiz and game shows. By comparison, 18 percent of the Canadian programming expenditures of CTV were on these categories, which attract the core of television's audiences. In the important category of TV series production, the independent broadcasters spent $2.7 million, while CTV spent almost five times as much, or $12.7 million.

By way of comparison, the independent stations spent 14 times as much on foreign TV series as on Canadian, or $37.4 million. CTV and its affiliates spent almost three times as much on foreign TV series as on Canadian — $34.0 million by comparison with $12.7 million. It should be noted here that the expenditure reported on Canadian programs included the financial commitments private Canadian broadcasters made to co-productions and co-ventures, including co-ventures with American broadcasters and producers that qualify as Canadian under the CRTC's definition of a Canadian program.

Now we turn to French-language television where as we saw earlier the expenditure patterns are quite different. First, private French-language broadcasters spent a much smaller percentage of their programming budget on foreign programs than did private English TV stations and networks, 12 percent by comparison with 37 percent. Secondly, they committed a somewhat smaller percentage of their programming budgets to news programming than their English counterparts, 23 percent by comparison with 30 percent. Total expenditures on information programming, however, did not differ much, representing 40 percent of the program budget in private French television and 43 percent in English.

Table 17.11 Program Expenditures by Category for English Private Network and Station Groups Year Ended 31 August 1985

($ millions)

Independents[c]	Canadian Programs			Foreign Programs			All Programs		
	$	%[a]	%[b]	$	%[a]	%[b]	$	%[a]	%[b]
Information									
News	33.2	13.6	24.3	2.1	0.9	1.5	35.3	14.5	25.8
Public Affairs	8.9	3.7	6.5	2.5	1.0	1.9	11.4	4.7	8.4
Other	8.4	3.5	6.1	.1	0.1	0.1	8.5	3.6	6.2
Sub-total	50.5	20.8	36.9	4.7	2.0	3.5	55.2	22.8	40.4
Children's	.6	0.2	0.4	.8	0.3	0.6	1.4	0.5	1.0
Entertainment									
Feature Films	.5	0.2	0.4	16.4	6.7	11.9	16.9	6.9	12.3
TV Series	2.7	1.1	2.0	37.4	15.4	27.3	40.0	16.5	29.3
Quiz & Games	2.4	1.0	1.7	2.0	0.8	1.5	4.4	1.8	3.2
Other	4.9	2.0	3.5	4.3	1.8	3.2	9.1	3.8	6.7
Sub-total	10.4	4.3	7.6	60.0	24.7	43.9	70.5	29.0	51.5
Arts, Letters & Sciences	1.6	0.7	1.2	.6	0.2	0.4	2.2	0.9	1.6
Sports	7.1	2.9	5.2	.6	0.2	0.3	7.6	3.1	5.5
Total	70.2	28.9	51.3	66.7	27.4	48.7	136.9	56.3	100.0

Table 17.11 (cont'd)

CTV	Canadian Programs			Foreign Programs			All Programs		
	$	%[a]	%[b]	$	%[a]	%[b]	$	%[a]	%[b]
Information									
News	61.5	14.6	30.1	—	—	—	61.5	14.7	30.1
Public Affairs	17.6	4.2	8.6	.04	—	—	17.6	4.2	8.6
Other	8.7	2.1	4.3	.2	—	0.1	8.9	2.1	4.4
Sub-total	87.8	20.9	43.0	.2	—	0.1	88.0	21.0	43.1
Children's	1.2	0.3	0.6	.5	0.1	0.3	1.8	0.4	0.9
Entertainment									
Feature Films	1.5	0.4	0.7	20.1	4.8	9.8	21.6	5.1	10.6
TV Series	12.7	3.0	6.2	34.0	8.1	16.7	46.7	11.1	22.8
Quiz & Games	.9	0.2	0.4	.6	0.2	0.3	1.5	0.4	0.7
Other	11.0	2.6	5.4	3.1	0.7	1.5	14.1	3.4	6.9
Sub-total	26.0	6.2	12.7	57.9	13.8	28.3	83.9	20.0	41.0
Arts, Letters & Sciences	1.6	0.4	0.8	.1	—	—	1.7	0.4	0.8
Sports	24.8	5.9	12.1	4.3	1.1	2.1	29.1	6.9	14.2
Total	144.4	32.7	69.2	63.0	15.0	30.8	204.4	48.7	100.0

Numbers may not sum to 100 due to rounding.

Notes: a. Cost as a percentage of airtime revenue.
b. Cost as a percentage of total program costs.
c. Includes multilingual station in Toronto.

CBC Private Affiliates	Canadian Programs			Foreign Programs			All Programs		
	$	%[a]	%[b]	$	%[a]	%[b]	$	%[a]	%[b]
Information									
News	9.7	14.3	55.8	.1	0.1	0.3	9.8	14.4	56.1
Public Affairs	1.5	2.2	8.5	.1	0.2	0.7	1.6	2.4	9.2
Other	1.7	2.5	9.6	.04	0.1	0.3	1.7	2.5	9.9
Sub-total	12.9	17.0	73.9	.2	0.4	1.3	13.1	19.3	75.2
Children's	.1	0.2	0.7	.04	—	0.2	.2	0.2	0.9
Entertainment									
Feature Films	.1	0.2	0.8	1.0	1.4	5.3	1.1	1.6	6.1
TV Series	.1	0.2	0.7	1.5	2.2	8.7	1.7	2.4	9.4
Quiz & Games	.1	0.1	0.5	.2	0.3	1.2	.3	0.4	1.7
Other	.1	0.1	0.5	.3	0.4	1.6	.4	0.6	2.1
Sub-total	.4	0.6	2.5	2.9	4.3	16.8	3.4	5.0	19.3
Arts, Letters & Sciences	.2	0.3	1.2	—	—	—	.2	0.3	1.2
Sports	.6	0.9	3.4	—	—	—	.6	0.9	3.4
Total	14.3	21.0	81.7	3.2	4.7	18.3	17.5	25.7	100.0

Table 17.11 (cont'd)

All Private English Stations	Canadian Programs			Foreign Programs			All Programs		
	$	%[a]	%[b]	$	%[a]	%[b]	$	%[a]	%[b]
Information									
News	104.4	14.3	29.1	2.2	0.3	0.6	106.6	14.6	29.7
Public Affairs	28.0	3.8	7.8	2.7	0.4	0.7	30.7	4.2	8.5
Other	18.8	2.6	5.2	0.3	—	0.1	19.1	2.6	5.3
Sub-total	151.2	20.7	42.1	5.2	0.7	1.4	156.4	21.4	43.5
Children's	1.9	0.3	0.6	1.4	0.2	0.4	3.3	0.5	1.0
Entertainment									
Feature Films	2.1	0.3	0.6	37.4	5.1	10.5	39.5	5.4	11.1
TV Series	15.5	2.1	4.3	73.0	10.0	20.3	88.4	12.1	24.6
Quiz & Games	3.4	0.5	1.0	2.9	0.4	0.8	6.3	0.9	1.8
Other	15.9	2.1	4.4	7.6	1.0	2.1	23.6	3.1	6.5
Sub-total	36.9	5.0	10.3	120.9	16.5	33.7	157.7	21.5	44.0
Arts, Letters & Sciences	3.4	0.5	1.0	0.7	0.1	0.2	4.1	0.6	1.2
Sports	32.4	4.4	9.0	4.8	0.7	1.3	37.3	5.1	10.3
Total	225.9	30.9	63.0	132.9	18.2	37.0	358.8	49.1	100.0

Numbers may not sum to 100 due to rounding.

Notes: a. Cost as a percentage of airtime revenue.
b. Cost as a percentage of total program costs.
c. Includes multilingual station in Toronto.

Source: Statistics Canada Supplementary Survey.

What is different is the fact that private French broadcasters spent 44 percent of their total programming expenditures on domestic entertainment programs, while their English counterparts spent 10 percent. Although the revenues of private French stations and networks are just one-fifth of the total for private English TV broadcasters, $150 million by comparison with $749 million, they actually spent almost as much on domestic entertainment programs, $33 million by comparison with $37 million. French-language private broadcasters spent next to nothing on children's programs and substantially less than their English counterparts on sports.

All these facts about program spending reflect two fundamental realities. First, they show what kinds of programs private broadcasters screen to attract viewers and ad revenue. Secondly, they show the cost of the various kinds of programs that attract audiences. The balancing of these dual concerns constitutes the business of broadcasting.

There is no question that the environments in which English and French broadcasters operate are quite different. At least up to the present time it has been possible to produce domestic French-language entertainment programs with substantially smaller budgets than would be necessary in English television and still attract large audiences. As the penetration of cable television in Quebec increases and as competition increases owing to the second French-language private network, this advantage may be reduced. The differences in production costs of attractive entertainment in French and English television must be balanced against significant differences in the resources available to each. Private English broadcasters have revenues five times larger than those of their French counterparts. While English broadcasters may have to spend more on domestic programs to attract audiences, they have far more to spend.

The overriding factor for English television is, however, the fact that viewers and ad revenue can be attracted at far lower cost with foreign (almost entirely American) TV shows than with Canadian. A general rule of thumb is that it costs ten times as much to produce a Canadian show as it costs to buy an American show. The Canadian program might well be just as, or even more, successful with Canadian viewers; it might even attract as much, or more, advertising revenue, although this is not usually the case. But the gap between the cost of the Canadian and American shows is so great that the business-like thing to do is to import.

Over 86 percent of all spending by private English broadcasters on TV series and feature films — or $110 million — is on foreign programs. Less than $18 million is spent on Canadian programs. Canadian viewers are not being offered Canadian choices in these important categories because it would not be in the commercial interest of private broadcasters to offer them. It is not, and never has been, a question of English Canadians being offered their own attractive and well-financed Canadian programs and rejecting them.

The key regulatory issue in Canada is where the balance is to be struck between the business-like decision and the public's right to a return in Canadian programming for the private broadcaster's use of public frequencies and protection from undue competition under the licensing process. Where that balance has been struck in the past is indicated by the degree of profitability achieved in the industry.

Table 17.12 Program Expenditures by Category for French Private Network and Station Groups Year Ended 31 August 1985

($ millions)

TVA	Canadian Programs			Foreign Programs			All Programs		
	$	%[a]	%[b]	$	%[a]	%[b]	$	%[a]	%[b]
Information									
News	15.6	13.5	22.8	—	—	—	15.6	13.5	22.8
Public Affairs	2.7	2.4	4.0	—	—	—	2.7	2.4	4.0
Other	8.5	7.4	12.5	—	—	—	8.5	7.4	12.5
Sub-total	26.9	23.3	37.3	—	—	—	26.9	23.3	39.3
Children's	.1	0.1	0.2	—	—	—	.1	0.1	0.2
Entertainment									
Feature Films	.9	0.8	1.3	2.6	2.3	3.9	3.6	3.1	5.2
TV Series	9.9	8.6	14.5	4.7	4.1	6.9	14.6	12.7	21.4
Quiz & Games	3.5	3.0	5.1	—	—	—	3.5	3.0	5.1
Other	16.1	13.9	23.6	.8	0.6	1.1	16.9	14.5	24.7
Sub-total	30.5	26.3	44.5	8.1	7.0	11.9	38.6	33.3	56.4
Arts, Letters & Sciences	—	—	—	—	—	—	—	—	—
Sports	2.8	2.4	4.0	.1	0.1	0.1	2.9	2.5	4.1
Total	60.3	52.1	88.0	8.2	7.1	12.0	68.4	59.2	100.0

Radio-Canada Private Affiliates	Canadian Programs			Foreign Programs			All Programs		
	$	%[a]	%[b]	$	%[a]	%[b]	$	%[a]	%[b]
Information									
News	1.9	13.8	29.1	—	—	—	1.9	13.8	29.1
Public Affairs	1.3	9.3	19.8	—	—	—	1.3	9.3	19.8
Other	.01	0.1	0.2	—	—	—	.01	0.1	0.2
Sub-total	3.1	23.2	49.1	—	—	—	3.1	23.2	49.1
Children's	—	—	—	—	—	—	—	—	—
Entertainment									
Feature Films	—	—	—	.7	5.0	10.5	.7	5.0	10.5
TV Series	.01	0.1	0.2	.1	0.9	1.9	.1	1.0	2.2
Quiz & Games	—	—	—	—	—	—	—	—	—
Other	2.3	17.1	36.2	.02	0.1	0.3	2.3	17.2	36.4
Sub-total	2.3	17.2	36.4	.8	6.0	12.7	3.1	23.2	49.1
Arts, Letters & Sciences	—	—	—	—	—	—	—	—	—
Sports	.1	0.9	1.8	—	—	—	.1	0.9	1.8
Total	5.6	41.3	87.3	.8	6.0	12.7	6.4	47.3	100.0

Numbers may not sum to 100 due to rounding.

Notes: a. Cost as a percentage of airtime revenue.
b. Cost as a percentage of total program costs.
c. Includes multilingual station in Toronto.

Table 17.12 (cont'd)

All Private French Stations	Canadian Programs			Foreign Programs			All Programs		
	$	%[a]	%[b]	$	%[a]	%[b]	$	%[a]	%[b]
Information									
News	17.5	13.5	23.4	—	—	—	17.5	13.5	23.4
Public Affairs	4.0	3.1	5.3	—	—	—	4.0	3.1	5.3
Other	8.6	6.6	11.4	—	—	—	8.6	6.6	11.4
Sub-total	30.0	23.2	40.1	—	—	—	30.0	23.2	40.1
Children's	.1	0.1	0.2	—	—	—	.1	0.1	0.2
Entertainment									
Feature Films	.9	0.7	1.2	3.3	2.6	4.4	4.2	3.3	5.6
TV Series	9.9	7.7	13.3	4.8	3.7	6.5	14.8	11.4	19.7
Quiz & Games	3.5	2.7	4.7	—	—	—	3.5	2.7	4.7
Other	18.4	14.3	24.6	.7	0.6	1.0	19.2	14.7	25.7
Sub-total	32.8	25.4	43.8	8.9	6.9	11.9	41.7	32.3	55.7
Arts, Letters & Sciences	—	—	—	—	—	—	—	—	—
Sports	2.9	2.3	3.9	.1	0.7	0.1	3.0	2.4	4.0
Total	65.8	51.0	88.0	9.0	7.0	12.0	74.8	58.0	100.0

All Private Canadian Stations	Canadian Programs			Foreign Programs			All Programs		
	$	%[a]	%[b]	$	%[a]	%[b]	$	%[a]	%[b]
Information									
News	121.9	14.2	28.1	2.2	0.3	0.5	124.1	14.4	23.6
Public Affairs	32.0	3.7	7.4	2.7	0.3	0.6	34.7	4.0	8.0
Other	27.3	3.2	6.3	.3	—	0.1	27.7	3.3	6.4
Sub-total	181.2	21.1	41.8	5.2	0.6	1.2	186.4	21.7	43.0
Children's	2.1	0.2	0.5	1.4	0.2	0.3	3.4	0.4	0.8
Entertainment									
Feature Films	3.0	0.4	0.7	40.7	4.7	9.4	43.8	5.1	10.1
TV Series	25.4	2.9	5.9	77.8	9.0	17.9	103.2	12.0	23.8
Quiz & Games	6.9	0.8	1.6	2.9	0.3	0.7	9.7	1.1	2.2
Other	34.4	4.0	7.9	8.4	1.0	1.9	42.8	5.0	9.9
Sub-total	69.7	8.1	16.1	129.8	15.0	29.9	199.4	23.2	46.0
Arts, Letters & Sciences	3.4	0.4	0.8	.7	0.1	0.2	4.1	0.5	0.9
Sports	35.4	4.1	8.1	4.9	0.6	1.1	40.3	4.6	9.3
Total	291.7	33.9	67.3	141.9	16.5	32.7	433.6	50.4	100.0

Numbers may not sum to 100 due to rounding.
Notes: a. Cost as a percentage of airtime revenue.
b. Cost as a percentage of total program costs.
c. Includes multilingual station in Toronto.
Source: Statistics Canada Supplementary Survey.

Profitability

Margins of operating income and profit before taxes remained high and stable in private television over the past 10 years, as shown in Table 17.13. Operating income ranged between 22 percent and 25 percent of revenue, while profit before taxes ranged between 17 percent and 20 percent.

Profitability varied among the various groups of stations although every category operated with substantial profitability. The most pronounced difference was the extraordinarily high level of profitability of TVA stations up to 1982. Thereafter, TVA stations' profits and those of French-language broadcasters moved down to the level of profit achieved by English TV broadcasters, although this decline may reflect the influence in 1983 and 1984 of the long TVA technicians' strike.

The CBC's affiliated stations operate mainly in small markets, but their profits are at least as large proportionately as those of other broadcasters. Table 17.14 shows profit margins by station group. The level of profitability of independent stations through this period has typically been below average for the industry as a whole. This may reflect the higher percentage of revenue that independent stations must spend to acquire programming.

Television, unlike radio, is not an industry characterized by winners and losers. In fact, over the period 1979 to 1984 the reported profits of profit-making stations totalled $770 million, while the losses of stations with losses were less than $20 million.

Medium-size and large stations realized the highest profit margins in 1984, the medium doing better than the large. Smaller stations' profit margins were much lower, as shown in Table 17.15. Still, winners outnumbered losers in all revenue categories. The few losers were almost all small stations with under $4 million in revenue annually.

Structure and Performance

Television is primarily not a local but a national medium. The key to national programming is effective Canadian network structures or other mechanisms that would enable production resources to be aggregated at the national level in both French and English broadcasting. Without effective, national mechanisms, no amount of regulatory pressure will achieve the programming goals we recommend in this Report.

This is so in all countries because individual stations generally lack the resources to finance programs other than local news and information. All countries rely on networks for domestic entertainment programs, and national news and information programs. In the typical North American network structure the local affiliated station fills part of its daily schedule, especially the supper hour, with local programs; many — outside peak time — also schedule syndicated programs, largely old movies or reruns of earlier network series. The core of the schedule of all affiliated stations, however, is filled by the network, based on the much larger revenues that flow from selling advertising on a large number of stations. The bulk of viewing is of programs that originate with the network, not locally. The figures are in Chapter 5.

Table 17.13 Operating Profits and Profit Before Tax of Private Television Stations 1974-1984[a]

	1975	1976	1977	1978	1979	1980	1981	1982	1983	1984
Operating Profit ($ millions)	50.3	73.5	77.6	96.7	113.3	125.5	161.0	189.0	197.9	222.7
Operating Profit, as a % of Revenue	22.2	26.1	23.5	24.1	23.9	22.5	24.9	25.6	25.2	24.8
Profit Before Tax ($ millions)	37.9	57.9	59.6	77.5	91.3	98.5	123.5	145.5	145.7	163.3
Profit Before Tax, as a % of Revenue	16.7	20.6	18.0	19.3	19.2	17.7	19.1	19.7	18.6	18.1

Note: a. Including network operations.
Source: CRTC, Industry Statistics and Analysis Division.

Table 17.14 Profit Margins of Private Television by Category, 1979-1984[a]

(percent)

	1979	1980	1981	1982	1983	1984
English Stations						
CBC Affiliates	21.0	18.9	19.9	20.1	21.8	24.8
CTV Affiliates	18.2	18.9	21.0	22.0	21.4	19.8
Independents	11.3	7.1	9.3	11.6	12.0	14.0
TOTAL	16.6	15.2	17.0	18.3	18.4	18.5
French Stations						
Radio-Canada Affiliates	17.8	24.5	7.4	13.4	16.8	23.0
TVA Affiliates	31.5	27.6	30.5	27.7	20.1	15.6
TOTAL	29.6	27.2	28.0	26.3	19.7	16.5
All Stations	19.3	17.7	19.1	19.7	18.6	18.2

Note: a. Including network operations.
Source: CRTC, Industry Statistics and Analysis Division.

Table 17.15 Profitability of Private Television Stations by Revenue, 1984

Revenue	Less than $1,500,000	$1,500,000 to 2,500,000	$2,500,000 to 4,000,000	$4,000,000 to 7,000,000	$7,000,000 to 15,000,000	$15,000,000 to 25,000,000	$25,000,000 and over	All Stations
Number of reporting units[a]	20	11	10	13	6	6	13	79
Total revenue ($ millions)	16.9	22.9	32.7	63.9	71.4	105.0	585.9	898.8
Profit before income tax ($ millions)	2.2	2.5	5.7	13.4	16.6	18.5	104.5	163.3
Profit as a % of revenue	13.0	10.9	17.4	21.0	23.2	17.6	17.8	18.2
Number of units showing losses	5	1	1	1	0	0	1	9
Revenue of units with losses ($ millions)	3.5	2.2	3.7	5.4	0	0	29.3	44.1
Amount of losses ($ millions)	(0.237)	(1.4)	(0.024)	(0.018)	0	0	(1.8)	(3.5)
Number of units showing profit	15	10	9	12	6	6	12	70
Revenue of units with profits ($ millions)	13.4	20.7	29.0	58.5	71.4	105.0	556.6	854.7
Amount of profit ($ millions)	2.4	3.9	5.7	13.4	16.6	18.5	106.3	166.9

Note: a. Generally, a reporting unit is described as a television station in operation. However, some units include more than one station that files combined financial reports. The CTV network operations have been distributed among the affiliates.

Source: CRTC, Industry Statistics and Analysis Division.

In a recent interview, David Jones, until 1985 the chairman of the Australian Broadcasting Tribunal, stated that: "Networking is essential in a country that wants high local (meaning domestic) content."[4] That understanding is reflected in the structure of British television, and in the United States, where the three powerful national networks have dominated TV for decades.

In Canada, too, most stations operate as network affiliates, but the flow of advertising into network organizations is relatively limited. In 1984, just 22 percent of the Canadian industry's revenue flowed into networks, compared with 45 percent in the United States.[5] The relative strength of American networks is most apparent in national advertising revenues, from which one would expect networks to derive their support. In the U.S., 60 percent of national television advertising revenue goes to the networks, compared with 28 percent in Canada. If Canadian networks had received the same share of national advertising as their American counterparts, they would have had revenues of $454 million in 1984, more than double their actual $215 million. The combined effect of the low per capita spending on TV advertising in Canada and the low aggregation of advertising revenue on networks is that Canadian networks have revenues that are only 2.5 percent of those of the American networks.

The Canadian television broadcasting industry is able to get away with the current lack of aggregation of resources because, unlike its American counterpart, it has available the option of buying foreign programs instead of paying for domestic content in the most expensive categories of programming. If private television in Canada, which has continued to grow rapidly over the past 25 years, is going to begin to make a commensurate contribution to financing prime-time Canadian entertainment, the resources of the industry will have to be pulled together at the national level to a much greater degree than at present. In present circumstances, it is hardly surprising that the main burden of producing Canadian programming nationally has been borne in both French and English by the CBC networks. This is not to say that in those areas of programming in which CTV and TVA stations have been active they have not made a significant contribution. Still, the contribution of the private networks to meeting national programming objectives has been distinctly limited. After a period in which the emphasis in English-language private television has been principally on extending the reach of private TV services and providing national and local news and information programming, the next stage in the development of English private TV should include a substantial contribution to Canadian performance programming. French-language priorities, discussed in Chapter 8, are somewhat different.

The division of commercial revenues between the individual stations and their networks is determined by affiliation agreements. The agreements specify the amount of time each station will allocate to network programming and the way station and network will divide revenues from selling air-time on network programs. The CRTC decides how many stations and networks should be licensed and attaches conditions to both types of licence. Affiliates cannot disaffiliate without the Commission's approval. The affiliation agreements between stations and networks require the Commission's approval to see that they meet its policy goals.

CTV

Private television networks in Canada began in 1961, the year CTV began distributing programs to the network. Originally, CTV distributed Canadian Football League games and the eight affiliated stations also combined to offer a daily national newscast at 10:30 p.m. In late 1961 CTV was distributing just nine hours of programming a week.

Since then, the CTV network feed to its affiliates has expanded to 66 hours a week, including the national news. The CTV Network News, which operates out of CTV's Toronto headquarters, maintains bureaus in Montreal and Ottawa, and has national news reporters in six other Canadian cities as well as foreign bureaus in Washington, London and Peking. The network's Daily News Service (DNS) collects items principally from affiliated stations and regional bureaus. Material is provided to affiliated stations through the network's leased microwave facilities.

CTV also provides extensive coverage of national sports events, the popular morning show *Canada AM*, and the weekly public affairs show *W5*, which has been on the air for 20 years. While the role of the CTV network has expanded over the past 25 years, the study the Task Force commissioned on radio and television news noted that: "The difficulty of acquiring operating funds from the member stations has been a constant theme in the development of CTV news and current affairs programming."[6] The same difficulty has been experienced in acquiring funds for performance programming, although as we saw earlier in this chapter, the performance of CTV and its affiliates in funding Canadian programming of all kinds compares favourably with that of the independent stations.

Difficulties in developing effective, English Canadian network structures in private TV go back almost to the beginning. In 1965, just four years after CTV began operations, the Fowler Committee on Broadcasting noted that: "The CTV network has had a difficult time financially." The Committee concluded that

> The commercial power of the affiliates has been such that they have been able to negotiate arrangements which give little hope of financial success for the network itself. The essential trouble is that the CTV affiliates do not want CTV to be a success.[7]

The Fowler *Report* further noted that in signing agreements that gave up as little revenue as possible to the networks, the affiliates "have curtailed the means for CTV to provide an adequate national service". The Fowler Committee believed, however, that "the private stations have national as well as local responsibilities". To achieve those national objectives "there is a need for a private, national television network".[8]

The CTV structure examined by Fowler was quite different from today's. Private investors held a controlling interest in the network, with the affiliates holding just 23 or 24 percent of the stock. Although the Fowler Committee had recommended against it, the Board of Broadcast Governors allowed the affiliates to acquire control of the network shortly after the Fowler Report was tabled. Since then, the CTV network has been run as a non-profit co-operative. Today, Baton Broadcasting of Toronto holds a 24.1 percent interest and owns the Regina, Toronto and Saskatoon affiliates. British Columbia Television (BCTV), owned and controlled by Western International Communications, holds 16 percent. CFCF Inc., owned and controlled by Jean Pouliot and family, holds 13.8 percent. The remaining shares are divided among the owners of the remainder of the 16 full affiliates with no one station holding more than 8.2 percent of them.

The CTV network structure makes provision for three classes of affiliates: the 16 owner stations, which are "full affiliates"; "affiliates", which are stations with revenues of under $2 million annually; and "supplementary affiliates". There are at present five supplementary affiliates, a category set up primarily to facilitate the extension of CTV service into small markets that already had CBC affiliates. They are not expected to contribute financially to the network operation.

The standard CTV agreement, last filed with the Commission in 1979, states that the network "shall pay to the Full Affiliates a Time Payment, being a percentage of the margin from Network Sales Time, after deducting distribution and program costs and guaranteed Time Payments to affiliates" and that the percentage "shall be 75 percent or any other percentage as may be determined by the Directors". Based on this formula, the CTV shareholders receive 75 percent of the net revenues earned by the network from the sale of air time to advertisers within network reserve time, leaving 25 percent of net revenue as the operating fund for the network.

A number of other factors affect the way revenues are split between the network and its affiliates. First, there is the number of hours the network may require its affiliates to carry. At present, the figure is a minimum of 60 hours each week or an average of just under nine hours daily. This time is divided into 36 hours and 20 minutes weekly of "regular network sales time", or just over five hours daily, and "special network sales time", that includes specials, continuous news coverage, and sports.

The CTV affiliation agreement setting out minimum hours of regular network sales time that the network must be allowed to program requires only 12 hours weekly in peak hours (7 p.m. to 11 p.m.). In general, the agreement does not place onerous demands on the stations for network time.

Within these constraints, the allocation to the network of time in affiliate schedules is determined by CTV's board of directors or executive committee, representing the network's owner affiliates. CTV's total network sales time includes an average of over 10 hours weekly of sports and almost 20 hours of news and current affairs. The responsibility for sale of commercials in this time rests with the network although unsold commercial time may be used by the stations.

CTV's network service includes what is referred to as "station service", in addition to the 60 hours of network sales time described above. Station service is made up largely of foreign programming that the network buys for its affiliate stations. Within the CTV station service, roughly 25 hours per week of additional programming is provided by the network. The affiliated stations rather than the network sell the commercials on station service programming. The network is reimbursed for acquiring the programs.

Within the 60 hours of CTV's network sales time, about two-thirds of the programming the network provides its affiliates, or about 40 hours each week, is of Canadian origin. Just under 90 percent of that is news and information or sports programming. The remainder is entertainment programming, including feature films, drama series, variety and music programming, talk shows, and so on. A profile of the CTV network's Canadian programming is provided in Chapter 5.

Of the one-third of network sales time made up of foreign programs, the bulk is performance programming, although a substantial minority of sports programs are also of foreign origin. About 80 percent of all the performance programming CTV provides its affiliates within network sales time is of foreign origin.

Information is not available on network spending on programs, but only on the combined program spending of both CTV and its affiliated stations as we saw in Table 17.11. The Table shows that expenditures were divided roughly 70:30 between Canadian and foreign programs. However, 78 percent of all expenditures on Canadian programming were for news, information, and sports programming.

Of the $68.3 million the network and its affiliates spent on feature films and TV series, $54.1 million, or 79 percent, went for the acquisition of foreign programs in the year that ended August 31, 1985. The $14.2 million spent on Canadian programming by the network and its affiliates included expenditures on in-house production, co-productions, investment in independent productions, and licence fee payments.

As we note in our discussion of the Broadcast Fund in Chapter 14, broadcasters have not provided the level of financial support to its projects that was anticipated when the fund was planned. Licence fees paid by broadcasters to producers for the right to exhibit their programs remain low. Because CTV is the most important programmer in private television, its capacity to make a greater contribution is critical to the fulfilment of broadcasting goals.

The continuing strength of the CTV affiliates is, in fact, remarkable. The affiliates accounted for 30 percent of all English-language television viewing in 1985, little different from the 31 percent they held in 1971. CTV and its affiliates earned 51.5 percent of all national television advertising revenues in 1984, up from 47.4 percent five years earlier. While the CTV share of all television advertising also increased over this period from 44 percent to 48 percent, the affiliates' profits before interest and taxes of $85.7 million in 1984 represented 25.3 percent of their total revenues of $339 million. The network functions as a co-operative with virtually all of its net income distributed to the affiliate-owners.

The strength of CTV is even more apparent if one looks at the network structure simply in terms of its position in English-language television. Combining network and affiliates, revenues from advertising sales alone were

$395.3 million in 1984, or 58 percent of the English television industry's total commercial revenues, an increase from 56 percent in 1979. Among the factors reflected in that increase was the shift of the Victoria station, CHEK, from CBC to CTV in 1981.

For its affiliates, CTV is able to exercise concentrated buying power in the purchase of American network programs and movie rights, and to facilitate national advertising placement. At the same time it functions to some extent as an instrument of cross-subsidization between the group of larger stations that are full affiliates and the small stations that function as supplementary affiliates. Almost all of the major private television broadcasting companies in Canada are part of the CTV ownership structure. Most of those companies are involved in radio as well as in television. Six are involved as well in cable television, and three in some aspect of satellite services.

All of the companies in the CTV ownership structure have program production facilities that are used for their own and for network production, and also by independent producers. The CTV network itself, however, has very limited production facilities and is not technically a broadcaster. Unlike the CBC networks or the American networks, CTV owns no stations. Its network programming is delivered over leased microwave circuits.

In earlier years, the bulk of CTV's programming was produced in the production facilities of its owner-affiliates. But now, more is coming from independent producers owing to the Broadcast Fund. More than half of CTV's domestic programming continues, however, to come from the affiliates, most of it from a single source, Glen Warren productions in Toronto, a subsidiary of Baton Broadcasting.

The principal owner-affiliates of CTV now have many other interests in Canadian broadcasting. CHUM, for example, owns and controls two satellite-to-cable networks: MuchMusic, the national music video channel, and the Atlantic Satellite Network (ASN), a regional satellite service, as well as the independent Toronto station, CITY-TV. MuchMusic depends primarily and ASN and CITY-TV depend entirely, on advertising revenues. Two other owners, BCTV and Selkirk, are both financial participants in CANCOM, the satellite service that delivers eight television signals nationally. The Pouliot family has recently been licensed to run a new French-language television station in Montreal and the Quatre Saisons network.

The CTV network now competes to some degree for national advertising revenue with new national services such as MuchMusic, and the regional services such as the ASN network, which are owned by the network's owner-affiliates. Moreover, seven of the eight television channels carried by CANCOM are entirely advertiser supported and, as these channels carry advertising into the markets of some of CTV's affiliated stations, there has been and still is a strong concern over their impact on the revenues of the network and its affiliated stations. While CANCOM naturally wishes to extend its services into new markets, CTV and most of its affiliates are just as naturally concerned about the impact. This gives rise to one of many examples of the conflicts in the broadcasting system that must be reconciled within a structure with many interlocking elements. Thus, the same person is chairman of the CTV network's board of directors and chairman of the board of CANCOM as well as president of Western International Communications (WIC) and chairman of the board of BCTV. Because Canadian broadcasting has grown, the operations of CTV's owner-affiliates have expanded into a complex structure of potentially conflicting interests.

At the level of the affiliate stations and the network, comparable issues of conflicting interest arise, as the Fowler Committee *Report* concluded. The owner affiliates, for example, decide how large a share of the network's advertising revenues should stay with the network, where it might be spent on developing Canadian programming, and how much should go to the stations, where it may either enhance their profits or be used to develop other interests. Similarly, it is the affiliate-owners alone who decide what time slots to allocate to the network, and whether the total network service should expand through increasing network sales time or station service. Their decisions determine the balance between network earnings of national advertising revenues and the earnings of the affiliated stations, particularly those in large markets, through their own sales of commercial time to national advertisers. Both the network and the affiliated stations have separate commercial sales staffs which sell time to national advertisers; both have an interest in having the best programs and the best time slots to sell.

In our judgement, the fundamental issue is the extent to which commercial TV revenues are used to support broadcasting policy. In the year ended August 31, 1985 only 3.4 percent of the revenues of CTV and its affiliated stations went into investments and licence fees for Canadian feature-length films and television series. Yet, such programs account for the majority of TV viewing.

If the CTV network had allocated an additional $15 million to $20 million annually to buying independent productions produced with Broadcast Fund support over the Fund's first three years, there would have been many more opportunities to view genuinely Canadian television programs. However, that did not happen and without regulatory intervention there is little reason to expect that it will.

Any effective policy must consider the network and the affiliates together as a single entity, and take account of the division of both air time and revenue between them. We were pleased by the CRTC's March 11, 1986 Decision (CRTC 86-203) which extended the licences of a number of CTV affiliates so that the Commission could consider their renewal at the same time as that of the network.

Recommendation

The CRTC should consider the licence renewals of the CTV network and its affiliated stations at the same time, and should thoroughly review the structural and financial relationships between the network and its affiliates to ensure that these arrangements permit the entire CTV structure to make an appropriate contribution to the broadcasting system, including the acquisition and exhibition of Canadian performance programming.

The Independents

The independent TV stations in Canada, all English-language, had revenues of $238.3 million in 1984, $211.8 million from the sale of commercial time. The rate of growth of the revenues of independent stations between 1979 and 1984 was 16.6 percent annually, or 7.4 percent in constant dollars. In fact, the independents are growing more rapidly than any other part of the television industry in Canada, and their advertising revenues are 31 percent of the private English TV total.

Between 1979 and 1984, the independent stations increased their share of English-language television viewing from 12 percent to 16 percent; in 1974 it had been just eight percent. Table 17.16 shows that viewing of Canadian programming is lower on the independents than on any other category.

Table 17.16 Percent of TV Viewing of Canadian Programming by Station Category, 1984

CBC French O and O Stations	72
Radio-Québec	72
CBC English O and O Stations	65
CBC French Affiliates	60
TVA Affiliates	52
CBC English Affiliates	46
TV Ontario/Knowledge Net (combined)	39
CTV Affiliates	37
Global Network	32
Independent English Stations	27

Source: Harrison, Young, Pesonen and Newell Inc., "Canadian TV Viewing Habits", a report prepared for the Task Force on Broadcasting Policy, Ottawa, January, 1986.

The licensing of more and more independent stations, therefore, seems to be the policy least likely to achieve the goal of attracting larger audiences to Canadian programming. However successful the independent stations may be in providing local programming, their capacity to generate Canadian entertainment programming is distinctly limited. The aggregation of funds from a substantial number of stations is needed for that. In the United States, independents generate little national programming, but purchase syndicated programming that appeared originally on the commercial networks. In Canada, independent stations have no pool of syndicated Canadian programming to draw on and, instead, join their American counterparts in the market for syndicated American programs.

Our financial data for independent stations include the Global Television Network, although Global has only one originating station with rebroadcast transmitters networking its signal into most of Southern Ontario. Because Global is licensed as a regional Ontario service, it is prevented under conditions of licence from soliciting local advertising in the Toronto market. Because local television stations depend mainly on national advertising, however, the prohibition does little to protect local broadcasting services. Global competes for national advertising with local stations in the markets in which its service is available. Global Network's nightly newscast is shown by independent stations in Western Canada. But it has no responsibility under its licence to provide national programming. To some extent services such as Global Television's can be viewed as regional superstations. Without being asked to take on the responsibilities of a national broadcaster they nevertheless are given access to an expanded pool of advertising revenue.

The Task Force believes that the conclusion is unavoidable, that the less the pooling of resources in the private TV industry is organized into effective structures for aggregating resources, the less the industry will be able to contribute to restoring reasonable balance between Canadian and foreign programming.

Recommendation

> CRTC policy should be designed to enhance the aggregation of the resources of those English-language television stations that are outside the structure of the CBC and CTV networks, in order to stimulate the development of domestic performance programming.

French-language Television

In French-language television, there exist two network structures, CBC and TVA, plus the recently licensed Quatre Saisons. The French broadcasters, however, could not resort as easily, quickly and profitably as the English ones to showing imported programs. The French stations have, therefore, looked to cost-sharing arrangements and resource aggregation to give them a substantial volume of popular domestic programming, including drama and other entertainment programs. However, dubbed American programs or programming imported from France can be acquired at less cost.

French broadcasting may in future encounter increasing difficulty in meeting the need for Canadian programs. More market fragmentation may result from increasing competition, with smaller revenue shares for each competitor. Quatre Saisons will begin to compete in September 1986. In 1985 Radio-Québec, which had previously operated as a non-commercial network, was allowed to begin competing for commercial revenue; under pressure of budget cuts in 1986 it surely will do so more resolutely. Similarly, in part as a result of budget cuts, the CBC's French television service has become a more aggressive competitor for commercial revenues.

The revenues of French-language television are not growing significantly in constant dollars. Between 1979 and 1984 the revenues of TVA's affiliates increased at a rate of 0.9 percent in constant dollars while the revenues of CBC's French affiliates declined by 0.9 percent annually over the same period.

Furthermore, French-language private stations appear to earn less commercial revenue than might be expected based on their 23.5 percent share of viewing of private Canadian stations. Their share of private TV revenues was only 16.3 percent in 1984, a decline from 20.5 percent in 1979. The shortfall is not at the local level, where they earned 23.8 percent, but in national advertising, where they earned just 14 percent, a drop from 17.1 percent in 1979.

During the period from 1979 to 1984, the profit margin of French-language stations also declined steadily from an extraordinarily high 29.6 percent (much higher than the industry average) to 16.5 percent, which, while still high by comparison with other industries, was slightly lower than the industry average.

The licensing of the Quatre Saisons network is predicated on the view that national advertisers, most of them English-language companies, can be brought back to using French-language private stations and networks to a much greater degree. Until the licensing of Quatre Saisons, there were only two French-language stations selling commercials in the large Montreal market, whereas in most large English cities there were at least three, and Toronto had four English-language stations selling commercials. Because the level of national advertising going to French private television is just over 60 percent of what one would expect in relation to their share of viewing, there is clearly room for improvement. The shortfall in 1984 alone was worth over $55 million in revenue.

In the next section we recommend a tax measure to make advertising on French-language programs more attractive. The flow of ad revenues, and in particular of national advertising revenues, to French-language television broadcasters should be followed carefully to determine whether their share is increasing to a level closer to their share of television viewing.

Protecting Private Broadcasters

C-58 and Simultaneous Substitution

It has not always been evident how the protection and incentives given to broadcasters could have been inspired by the objectives of the *Broadcasting Act*. For example, the CRTC will hear no competing bids for licences when they come up for renewal. No television licence has ever been terminated, whatever the record of the broadcaster in meeting promises of performance. If a broadcaster wishes to sell a licence, the Commission will accept applications only from the party designated by the seller. These are all tremendous safeguards to private broadcasters, though they tend to contradict the *Broadcasting Act* by recognizing de facto private-property rights over frequencies.

The CRTC has also protected private broadcasters against potential competition. The number of network and station licences has been limited for that very purpose. Has this protection been justified by the contribution of the licensees? What contribution in the future would justify continued protection?

Finally, there are two measures — one regulatory, the other legislative — that reward Canadian broadcasters greatly but do not necessarily do anything for Canadian programming. First, Bill C-58 of 1976 amended the Canadian *Income Tax Act* to allow the cost of advertisements directed to Canadians to be deducted as legitimate business expenses only if placed on Canadian stations or networks. The measure makes it less attractive to Canadian advertisers to reach Canadian consumers through American stations imported into Canada by cable or, more recently, by satellite. But while Bill C-58 benefitted Canadian broadcasters, it did not reduce the incentive to Canadian stations to obtain the rights to the most popular American programs which, shown during peak viewing hours, would attract substantial Canadian audiences and advertiser interest. Perhaps policy makers assumed that the CRTC would ensure that an appropriate share of the protected revenues would go into Canadian programming.

The CRTC regulations on simultaneous program substitution, however, actually contributed to the tendency to schedule American shows in peak viewing time. Upon demand, a local cable company must substitute a local station's broadcast of a program and its commercials for the delivery of the same program from a distant station at the same time. Designed to protect the program rights of local stations, this rule has a devastating impact on Canadian programming. What really happens is that broadcasters purchase popular American programs and schedule them to run at the same time as they are shown on the American network. They then have their own signal substituted on cable in their market, increasing significantly the size of their audience and, above all, the interest of their advertisers.

Task Force researchers estimated that in 1984 Bill C-58 had the effect of increasing the net revenues of Canadian television stations and networks by $35.8 million to $41.8 million, and simulcast regulations increased them by about $53 million.[9] The combined effect was revenue 8.9 percent to 9.5 percent higher than it would otherwise have been. Had these two measures not been in place Canadian advertisers would have made substantially more use of stations in the United States to reach Canadian consumers. In addition, the commercials placed on American stations and networks essentially to reach consumers in the United States would have reached many more Canadians as well, thereby reducing the need for multinational companies with business in both countries to spend funds in Canada on television advertising to reach Canadians.

Even with Bill C-58 and the simulcast policy in place, Canadians are heavily exposed to the advertising on American television stations. The per capita advertising revenues earned by Canadian television stations and networks are far lower than in the United States. American stations and networks would account for much more than one-third of all viewing of English-language television in Canada if the simulcasting policy were not in place. While American television broadcasters had revenues of $19.4 billion in 1984, the Canadian television industry revenues of $970.3 million in 1984 were not 10 percent of U.S. revenues in proportion to population, but rather just 5 percent.

The reduction of commercial revenues attributable to the spillover of American television advertising into Canada is extremely difficult to calculate. Our research looked at this issue from several perspectives. If, for example, the same percentage of GNP went into television advertising in Canada as in the United States, Canadian television broadcasters would have had $953 million in additional revenues. Alternatively, if on a per capita basis expenditures had been the same as in the United States — or in Australia — revenues would have been $750 million higher.

There are many differences, obviously, between Canada and the United States, including differences in industrial structure, standards of living, the mix of marketing and advertising and the like. Furthermore, some of the American advertising that spills into Canada is either of a purely local nature or is for American products that are not available in Canada, but these programs account for little of the viewing of American stations in Canada.

A research study carried out for this Task Force estimated that, despite the effect of C-58 and simulcasting, the loss of advertising to Canadian television broadcasters attributable to the remaining spillover of American TV ads was between $50 million and $149 million in 1984. A restricted sample of specific companies led to an estimated impact of $124 million.

Some Canadian broadcasters view the estimate of the impact of simulcasting used above, $53 million in 1984, as too low. Global Television, for example, told our interviewers that the estimate used in our study for the benefit to their own operation was much too low. They would put it twice as high. Such calculations are extremely difficult.

The Task Force shares the views expressed by the Clyne Committee on the fundamental principle on which both the simulcast policy and Bill C-58 are based. Referring to the American stations imported into Canada by cable as transplants, the Clyne Committee observed in 1978 that:

> The existence of the transplant system is inherently unfair to Canadian private stations and CBC. The showing of U.S. programs on the transplants detracts from the commercial value of those programs to Canadian stations, even though the Canadian stations have bought Canadian rights to them.[10]

Much as we regret the counter-productive impact on Canadian programming of Bill C-58 and simultaneous substitution, we endorse their maintenance. Their legitimate purpose is the protection of an orderly market based on the property rights duly purchased and held by Canadian broadcasters. By having their commercial needs protected, broadcasters are better able to contribute to Canadian programming objectives.

Recommendation

To enhance the capacity of private broadcasters to contribute to the objectives of a new broadcasting act, both Bill C-58 and the CRTC policy on simultaneous program substitution should be maintained.

Simulcasting leaves us in the position, however, where Canadian broadcasters can protect their rights only by showing the American programs they purchased at the same time as they are shown on an American station in their market. In effect, the schedules of Canadian broadcasters are determined by American schedules, thereby hindering the showing of Canadian programs in peak time. But Canadian broadcasters must not be allowed to renege on their obligations under the *Broadcasting Act* in exploiting the benefits of simulcasting. In Chapter 28 we propose study of an alternative approach to the import of American signals that would obviate the need for simulcasting.

Recommendation

The CRTC must develop measures to ensure that its program substitution policies do not have the effect of reducing exhibition of Canadian programs in peak viewing time.

Our detailed recommendation on the Canadian programming responsibilities of private broadcasters is found in the last section of this chapter. As long as they are protected by policies such as Bill C-58 and simulcasting, and as long as the CRTC guarantees them licence renewals effectively in perpetuity, then it is appropriate to ask that they make some substantial contributions to the goals of the *Broadcasting Act*.

Private Television and Foreign Programming

Before the Broadcast Fund was established, private broadcasters had little or no financial incentive for replacing popular foreign programming with Canadian fare. Many of our recommendations aim at improvements in financing and scheduling Canadian programs. This does not mean that we favour a reduction in the amount of foreign programming available to Canadians, or any drastic change in the way such programming is delivered. On the contrary, we believe there are two compelling reasons for allowing private television broadcasters to continue as suppliers of American programs. One stems from a general goal of broadcasting policy, the other from a concern with the economic well-being of the industry.

First, we endorse the policy of varied and comprehensive programming. Domestic production, important as it is, must remain part of a balanced supply that includes foreign content, both commercial and non-commercial and, ideally, from many countries.

We approach foreign programming with the question of how it can be delivered so as to enhance the national interest. Television is the single most important vehicle for national advertising and is important for local advertisers too. It is also an important source of employment, accounting directly for 7,215 jobs and over $240 million in wages and salaries in the private sector in 1984.

If the foreign programs on Canadian channels were instead only on foreign channels, Canadian broadcasters would lose an enormous amount of revenue, with no compensating gains elsewhere in the system. Estimates provided to the Task Force indicate that at least 70 percent of nearly $1 billion in television ad revenues in 1984 was realized through the sale of commercial time on non-Canadian, almost entirely American, programs.

The essential point is that American programs aired on private Canadian television act to subsidize the Canadian programs shown on these same channels. Revenues earned from foreign programs allow the private broadcasters to finance domestic production, through licensing or other arrangements. Any substantial impairment of the ability of private television to earn such commercial revenue would harm its ability to increase the quality and quantity of Canadian programs.

Recommendation

Broadcasting policy and regulations should assure to the extent possible that foreign programs are distributed in Canada by Canadian television stations and networks holding exhibition rights for the Canadian market, in order to maximize their available resources to present a wide range of Canadian programming and to ensure that they can be an effective advertising vehicle for Canadian businesses.

Maintaining Local Television Service

Among the goals of broadcasting policy are equalization of broadcasting services throughout Canada and the increase of the range of choice in television. Because everything cannot be done at once, these goals inevitably come into conflict with the equally legitimate objective of responding to local needs and interests.

These conflicts go back to the early days of television in Canada. Once the CBC's network of off-air affiliates was in place, private stations were licensed and private networks developed. In smaller markets the arrival of the signal of the new private network in some cases threatened the survival of the existing local station and its local programming in that market. To avoid such loss of local service, the 'twin-stick' option emerged; the broadcaster already in the market as a CBC affiliate became an affiliate of the private network as well.

The rapid cabling of Canadian cities beginning in the early 1970s created a greater challenge to local stations and programming, by introducing competing Canadian and American signals. The resulting fragmentation of audiences in these communities was much greater than in the United States, where stations had to compete only with other American stations.

Local programming is almost exclusively news and current affairs. The studies of news programming carried out for this Task Force under the direction of Peter Desbarats indicate that over the past 15 years private broadcasters have improved such programming substantially.[11] The core of local programming is the supper hour show. In many markets, private broadcasters operate with the latest production equipment and local popular stars anchor their supper hours. Audiences are large.

The emphasis broadcasters place on local programs reflects their belief that a strong performance creates a positive local image that helps the station and attracts audiences to the evening entertainment programs.

The Task Force believes that local coverage of news and current affairs is a fundamental element of television programming. The protection of local programming is one reason we favour program substitution rules, protecting stations' exclusive rights to show programs in their local markets.

For the millions of Canadians who do not subscribe to cable television, off-air local broadcast service is all that is available. Cable importation of distant signals does not help them, and care must be exercised that it does not reduce the service available to them. Also, local stations are the necessary foundation of the Canadian networks.

The opening-up of local markets to increased competition from distant Canadian broadcasting signals has been under review in recent years. In January 1984, the CRTC (in Public Notice 1984-13) invited comments on its proposal to reduce the existing restrictions on the cable carriage of distant Canadian signals, noting that increased use of satellite distribution and the expanded capacity of cable systems to distribute new services offer a means to increase the choice of programming available to Canadians. The Commission noted in its 1984 Public Notice that "the distribution of existing Canadian signals beyond their licensed service areas may be one means to ensure that the broadcasting system as a whole remains predominantly Canadian".

The CRTC held hearings on the issue in late November 1984. The Canadian Motion Picture Distributors Association argued against any change on the grounds that imported distant stations did not hold the rights to show their programming in any market but the local one they had been licensed to serve. The Canadian Association of Broadcasters argued that importing distant Canadian signals would add little to the extent of local Canadian programming in any particular market while it would reduce the advertising revenues available to local stations. The CBC and CTV argued that there were "too many practical and economical arguments against importing distant signals and too few benefits to be derived from it".[12]

The Canadian Cable Television Association, on the other hand, argued that proposals to permit distant Canadian signals would increase consumer choice, including choice of Canadian programs. Ontario's Minister of Communications also supported the proposals, arguing that the benefits of increased choice outweighed the fact that "the introduction of Canadian superstations may cause some financial and programming adjustments on the part of local broadcasters".

In March 1985 the CRTC announced a new policy on the carriage of distant Canadian television signals. The Commission argued that it was consistent with the objectives of the *Broadcasting Act*, representing "one means of ensuring that the broadcasting system as a whole remain predominantly Canadian and that overall long-term benefits accrue to the Canadian broadcasting system by extending alternative Canadian viewing choices to all parts of Canada, by enhancing the diversity and variety of Canadian programs distributed by cable systems".[13] The Commission noted that it would be "particularly desirable to provide an additional Canadian service in those communities which do not have access to a third Canadian service".[14]

The CRTC announced that it would view favourably applications from cable companies to carry distant Canadian television signals on an additional, discretionary tier of cable service, for which cable subscribers pay an extra fee. The Commission said "there should be no objection on the part of the originating station whose signal is being extended" and "the originating station whose signal enters a distant market should not accept local advertising from such a market".

The Commission added, however, that it would also examine case-by-case applications to carry distant Canadian signals on the basic cable service. In such cases the two above conditions for carriage on a discretionary tier would have to be met and the station imported would be required to both adhere to the local programming commitments in its original licence and add to the diversity of Canadian programming in the applicant's market. Under similar conditions, it said, over-the-air distribution of distant signals could also be considered. Public hearings would be held on each application for carriage on basic service. The Commission further stipulated that: "A licensee proposing to extend its service for the cable distribution of its signal to distant markets may be required to file an application for a network licence", but did not at the time elaborate on this point.[15]

Despite these conditions, the central premise of the commission's decision was that expanded carriage of Canadian signals into distant markets would help to ensure that the broadcasting system remains predominantly Canadian. We believe there are two serious flaws in the CRTC's argument that accommodating distant signals will help make the system predominantly Canadian. First, as our analysis in Chapter 5 indicates, the Canadian broadcasting system is not now predominantly Canadian, if this is measured in terms of the balance of Canadian and foreign programming rather than the number of Canadian and foreign channels. Secondly, the stations most likely to take advantage of the opportunity to be distributed outside their local markets are not the network affiliates, but the independents that have heavy American content and light viewing of Canadian programs. Furthermore, because a substantial share of the viewing of Canadian programs on independent stations is of their local programming, their Canadian programming in distant markets would be likely to account for an even smaller share of viewing. They would almost certainly function primarily as an additional source of American programming, particularly in peak viewing time. In addition, however, with the policy of importing the three-plus-one American services, the carriage of additional distant Canadian signals will generally add relatively little to the range of American programs available.

Except in special circumstances in some small communities, distant signals are unlikely to contribute to expanded viewing of Canadian programs. They will further fragment a television market already more fragmented than any other in the world. They will threaten the viability of local programming and the availability of off-air service to households without cable.

Recommendations

The CRTC should continue to recognize the basic importance of local television programming and pursue policies designed to avoid or minimize threats to local television stations and local programming. Policies which will tend to transform local independent stations into regional or national superstations should therefore be avoided.

The CRTC should consider allowing existing local broadcasters to become new 'twin' or 'triple' stick operators rather than allowing distant Canadian signals into local markets if they threaten the viability of local broadcasters.

In communities where no local television service is now provided, the Task Force concurs with the proposal to allow the importation of distant signals either by way of cable or low-power, off-air rebroadcasting transmitters where frequencies are available.

The CRTC should continue to require licensees to make a contribution to local programming consistent with their financial capacity as well as an appropriate contribution to meeting the broader Canadian programming objectives of the whole system.

Private Broadcasters and Canadian Programming

If a new Broadcasting Act increases the obligations of private broadcasters and if, as this Report insists, Canadians have a right to be able to choose more quality

Canadian performance programming on private Canadian stations in peak viewing hours, the CRTC must have a regulatory approach to ensure these objectives are met. As it happens, much of the appropriate approach has already been developed; what is required is rigorous application.

Canadian content rules were first set in 1959 when the Board of Broadcast Governors (BBG) required that 55 percent of programming broadcast be Canadian. After the BBG was succeeded by the CRTC, the Commission raised the requirement in 1970 to 60 percent, but set it at only 50 percent between 6 p.m. and midnight. After the policy was reviewed in 1979, the CRTC ruled that CTV was to provide 26 hours of new and original drama in the 1980-81 season and 39 hours the following season. CTV appealed the decision to the Supreme Court, which upheld the right of the CRTC to set such regulations.

In 1983, the CRTC released its *Policy Statement on Canadian Content in Television* which essentially recognized the failure of Commission policy between 1970 and 1983 in relation to English television drama and entertainment programming. It concluded that "simple compliance with the minimum quantitative requirements under the current regulation has not been enough" and that: "Widespread practices have evolved which are at odds with the spirit of the Canadian content regulation."[16]

The 1983 policy set as a goal that: "An adequate quantity of Canadian television programs must be available in all major program categories." Specifically, it noted that "children's programs, variety, and particularly drama, are seriously underrepresented in Canadian television schedules". Drama was defined as including "feature films, situation comedies, adventure series, plays and serials".[17]

The Commission went on to state that: "It is essential that Canadian programming attract a significant Canadian viewing audience [and] that a substantial quantity and variety of Canadian programs of quality be scheduled during popular viewing hours and that they be reasonably distributed over all periods throughout the year".[18]

The CRTC stressed the fact that "Canadian programs must, in general, reflect Canadian experience and the social, visual and linguistic idioms of this country", while at the same time speaking to universal themes and resulting in programs of widespread appeal. The CRTC concluded:

> If Canadians do not use what is one of the world's most extensive and sophisticated communications systems to speak to themselves — if it serves only for the importation of foreign programs — there is a real and legitimate concern that the country will ultimately lose the means of expressing its identity. Developing a strong Canadian program production industry is no longer a matter of desirability but of necessity.[19]

Ironically, since 1979 when the review began, the Commission acknowledged there had been "an unacceptable decline in the amount of Canadian programming scheduled by a number of broadcasters serving major markets during the hours of heavy viewing, between 7:30 p.m. and 10:30 p.m.". Although private broadcasters now accounted for the lion's share of TV viewing, the Commission found that "Canadian dramatic productions are virtually non-existent on private English-language television".

Because adequate funding was essential to improvement, the Commission stated as a premise of its revised policy that: "The regulation of Canadian content should therefore be designed to stimulate, to the greatest extent possible, increased expenditures by broadcasters on Canadian programming." In its 1983 policy statement, the Commission proposed three key changes to its regulations:

1) The point system to define Canadian content which is described in Chapter 5.
2) A change in the reporting period for Canadian content, from annual to semi-annual, the reporting periods to be October 1 to March 31, and April 1 to September 30.
3) The use of conditions of licence as a complement to the general regulations, so that the particular resources available to each licensee could be taken into account in establishing requirements for purchasing, producing and scheduling Canadian programs.

The proposed policy would have allowed the Commission to determine whether licensees should provide more Canadian programs in particular categories and whether more resources should be allocated to them. The Commission would have reserved the right to specify a minimum percentage of revenues or of total program budget to be spent on such programming.

The Commission recognized that for the new policy to be implemented, there would be a need "to develop uniform accounting procedures for the reporting of all revenues and expenses, including production operations that are integrally related to the licensed operation but are actually carried on through affiliated or associated companies".[20] The latter problem is not a trivial one if implementation is to be fair and balanced because it is essential that the resources available to individual broadcasters be assessed on a consistent basis.

The government responded to the Commission's policy initiative by establishing the Broadcast Fund in 1983, as described in Chapter 14, to put up one-third of the cost of Canadian programs. In setting up the fund, the government assumed the CRTC would act on the new policy, noting in its announcement that the CRTC would define appropriate targets in each program category and establish the responsibilities of particular broadcasters with respect to hours and expenditures.

The Task Force is in full and enthusiastic agreement with the CRTC's policy. But is the CRTC? As this Report is being written, some six years after the CRTC decided that the 1970 approach was extremely deficient and initiated a review, very little of the new approach suggested after the 1979 review has been implemented.

The CRTC's 1984 policy for defining a Canadian program, including a point system described in Chapter 5, is central to its Canadian content regulation. Because the social and cultural goals of Canadian broadcasting can be met only through quality Canadian programs, the achievement of broadcast policy goals in the case of private broadcasters is dependent to a large degree on the way the Commission defines such programs and, in particular, on the minimum standard set. The CRTC will fall short if it accepts Canadian productions that fail to meet the objectives proposed for the new Broadcasting Act.

The present Canadian content definition has the advantage of being objective, as it must be. In our judgment, however, it has the disadvantage of appearing likely to allow Canadian accreditation of programs that television viewers would not recognize as being made by, for, or about Canadians. We recognize that this is a difficult issue and to some extent within the province of Telefilm Canada to help resolve, if Telefilm is given a clear mandate to operate the Broadcast Fund so as to achieve the progamming goals of broadcasting policy. But CRTC policies must serve the same purpose and define Canadian programs so that they are not conducive to systematic evasion of broadcasting objectives.

In Chapter 14 we set out our view that 'Canadian' programs are those which are creatively controlled by Canadians and made primarily for Canadians. Implicit in that definition was the exclusion of programs that were simply made in Canada but were tailored essentially for sale to foreign broadcasters. As we said there, the central determinant of the market for which a production is being made is where the bulk of the money is coming from. We concluded that the combination of Broadcast Fund support and Canadian broadcaster licence fees must cover a substantial majority of the cost of programs if they were really to be made under Canadian control and with an eye on Canadian viewers' interests. While the Commission's definition of a Canadian program must be an objective one, it should be designed to be consistent with the cultural intent of Canadian content regulation, which certainly goes beyond economic and industrial concerns. Just as important, however, to the achievement of these Canadian programming goals will be the actions the Commission takes to see that Canadian broadcasters, like broadcasters in other countries, commit significant resources to pay for their domestic programs. In the case of the independent productions they carry, the licence fees paid will be of fundamental importance.

Moreover, because the Commission's definition is technical only, it can speak in no way to the question of programming quality. We ourselves have tried intermittently throughout our deliberations to find criteria that could distinguish between productions of greater or lesser quality. We are clear among ourselves that we have little interest in simply substituting mediocre Canadian programming for mediocre — or indeed, good — American programming. We find little intrinsic redeeming value in programming made in Canada for its own sake.

After all, it is not the overriding goal of Canadian broadcasting policy to build an industry or create jobs but rather to establish a Canadian presence on television through programs that are made by Canadians, chiefly for Canadians and good enough to attract Canadian viewers. There is no reason, in our view, why the important secondary benefits of broadcasting — job creation and industry growth — cannot be realized through the production of high-quality Canadian programs. However, these objectives cannot be met through the

Commission's definition of what will qualify as Canadian under the Canadian content quota. The pursuit of quality programming will be more dependent on the resources individual broadcasters are expected to commit to the Canadian programs they produce and show.

Recommendation

> The CRTC must ensure that its definition of a Canadian program will result in Canadian performance programming that reflects the objectives of Canadian broadcasting policy.

The Task Force heard from many parties who believed private broadcasters had not made an adequate contribution to the social and cultural goals of Canadian broadcasting. But they disagreed about the remedies. Al Johnson, former president of the CBC, made an impassioned plea that the number of hours of Canadian programming be at least equal to the hours of American programming on the Canadian system. Former CBC vice-president Peter Herrndorf suggested that the system be required to exhibit some 400 hours of Canadian drama in peak viewing time, a figure that was necessarily arbitrary but, he argued, made both programming and financial sense.

Finally, the Friends of Public Broadcasting in English Canada strongly suggested that all such attempts to enhance the contribution of private broadcasters to the social goals of the system are unrealistic and should be abandoned. After all, the Friends pointed out, it is clearly not in the financial interest of the private broadcasters to provide quality Canadian drama and entertainment programs; it is little wonder, therefore, that even after 25 years of constant pressure, repeated exhortations and verbal warnings, they have never done so in a serious way.

Under the alternative favoured by the Friends of Public Broadcasting, private broadcasters would pay a rental fee for the public property they are licensed to use. Revenues would be assessed at a rate of 15 percent, with an exemption for small stations. Over $150 million would be generated in 1987, it was estimated, and this could be used to fund Canadian programming. Reductions in the fees assessed under this licence arrangement could be earned by broadcasters airing certain amounts of Canadian programming in defined categories.

The Task Force has chosen not to recommend any of these proposals. The 'equal time for Canada' concept seems to us difficult to apply and unnecessarily burdensome for the broadcasting system; we believe Canadians must be able to choose to watch some good Canadian programming each night but there seems no need that it be equal in quantity to foreign shows. Similarly, while Herrndorf's 400 hours may be the appropriate number, we would rather leave it to the regulatory agency to work out in practice the hourly implications of our principles.

As for the Friends of Public Broadcasting, while its cynical view of the contribution of private broadcasters may be understandable, we think their proposal has two serious flaws. First, it is notoriously difficult to determine a generally applicable licence fee which would be appropriate and fair for the purpose of assessing all broadcasters. Second, even with the addition to the system of TV Canada, we believe the quantity of good Canadian performance programming that we wish to see in peak time can only be achieved with the participation of private broadcasters. If the Telefilm Broadcast Fund is amended as we recommend to make it a more effective element in a strategy for achieving the programming objectives of the broadcasting system, and if the CRTC revises certain of its regulations and implements others, we are confident that private broadcasters will soon make that contribution that has been expected of them for so long. Indeed, as they themselves have stated, thanks to the Broadcast Fund they have already begun to do so.

The CRTC delayed the six-month reporting period for Canadian content until October 1, 1986, two years after it was originally proposed. The Task Force supports the Commission's concern that broadcasters spread their Canadian programming more evenly through the broadcast year and therefore believes that policies to achieve this goal are essential.

The Task Force has considered the question of whether the minimum time requirements for Canadian programming should be reduced. But in our many meetings with broadcasters, we heard little or no desire that the 60-percent overall or the 50-percent prime-time requirement be watered down.

However, we are concerned, as the Commission has been at least since 1979, with the limited amount of Canadian programming private broadcasters show during peak viewing hours. So frustrated was the Commission at the dominance of American programming on Canadian stations in mid-evening viewing hours that it stated in its 1983 policy on Canadian content that it had considered introducing a minimum 35 percent average Canadian content rule during the 7:30 p.m. to 10:30 p.m. period. An obligation to run an average of an hour a night of Canadian content in this time period would not necessarily be onerous: one good sports event would neatly cover off two or three evenings.

Nevertheless, the Commission failed to turn this idea into a firm policy, even a postponable policy. However, there have been substantial changes since the Commission's 1983 decision not to proceed with the 35-percent quota, most notably the creation of the Broadcast Fund to put millions of dollars of public money into Canadian programs. Initiatives to ensure that private broadcasters make a greater contribution to achieving the goals of broadcasting policy are surely even more reasonable now because of government support through the Fund. Therefore, we believe the time has come to establish a requirement that more of the mid-evening viewing hours be given to Canadian programs.

The existing CRTC "prime time" requirement really does not cover what the industry regards as prime time. Private broadcasters are required to provide 50 percent Canadian content between 6 p.m. and midnight. Most run an hour between 6 p.m. and 7 p.m. and a half hour at 11 p.m. This leaves them with one and a half hours additional to provide nightly, which is usually done between 7 p.m. and 11 p.m., resulting in an average of 37.5 percent Canadian content in this time slot or 10.5 hours weekly. If an average of two additional weekly hours of Canadian programming were added in the 7 p.m. to 11 p.m. time period, the resulting Canadian content level would be 45 percent. The Task Force believes that such a requirement is reasonable. Moreover, a requirement based on this time period would reflect the Broadcast Fund's general requirement that the Canadian productions it supports be shown in this time period. This regulatory requirement would help to resolve the problem of inadequate access to air time in this period, which both independent producers and Telefilm identified in their presentations to the Task Force.

Recommendations

> The CRTC should, for conventional off-air broadcasters, maintain the requirement that 60 percent of all programming and 50 percent of the programming scheduled between 6 p.m. and midnight must be Canadian. It should adopt a minimum 45 percent Canadian content quota for private broadcasters in the evening viewing hours from 7 p.m. to 11 p.m.
>
> The CRTC should ensure that the productions private broadcasters telecast to meet their Canadian content requirements are of high quality and include a substantial proportion of programs in the categories now most inadequately represented on private Canadian television.

The Task Force believes program expenditure requirements should be set specifying minimum levels of expenditures to produce Canadian programs in-house or to acquire the right to exhibit them. We make this recommendation out of a conviction that Canadian programs must be paid for primarily in Canada, just as domestic programs are in other countries. A regulatory policy based only on quantitative quotas proved its inadequacy long ago. Only a more integrated and comprehensive policy which deals with financing as well as airtime can hope to succeed.

Recommendation

> Private television stations and networks must be required to commit greater resources to Canadian programs. The CRTC should use conditions of licence to require that stations and networks make expenditures for internal production of, or acquisition of, the right to exhibit Canadian programs consistent with their financial and other resources.

The contribution of private Canadian broadcasters to quality Canadian performance programming has not been among the great elevating successes of the Canadian broadcasting system. But there are already signs that, thanks in good part to government support through the Broadcast Fund, the record has begun to improve. We were heartened by the repeated expressions of good intentions on the part of the broadcasters with whom we met. We are confident that they will co-operate in a new era of development of quality Canadian performance programming for peak time viewing. Canadians have a right to expect that they will do no less, and the CRTC must at last insist upon it.

Notes

1. Canadian Radio-television and Telecommunications Commission, *Policy Statement on Canadian Content in Television*, CRTC Public Notice 83-18 (Ottawa: CRTC, 1983), p. 6.
2. Joseph Irvine. Letter to Gerry Caplan from Mr. Irvine, V.P. Programming, ATV, June 3, 1986.
3. Arthur Weinthal, as reported in a column by Sid Adilman in *The Toronto Star*, November 18, 1985.
4. David Jones, as reported in an article by Barbara A. Moes in *Broadcaster* magazine, March 1986, p. 13.
5. The combined result of the lower level of TV advertising per capita in Canada and the lower level of aggregation of ad revenue at the network level is that Canadian networks have revenues equal to just 2.5 percent of American network revenues. Data used here were compiled for *Television Digest* by the Television Bureau of Advertising Inc. in the United States based on official Federal Communications Commission figures. Network revenues were $8.5 billion in 1984 out of total TV ad revenues of $19 billion.
6. Peter Desbarats, "Radio and Television News: The Roles of Public and Private Broadcasters, and Some Other Critical Issues", study prepared for the Task Force on Broadcasting Policy, Ottawa, 1986.
7. Canada; Committee on Broadcasting, (Fowler Committee) *Report* (Ottawa: Queen's Printer, 1965), p. 236.
8. Ibid., p. 237.
9. Arthur, W. Donner, "An Analysis of the Importance of U.S. Television Spillover, Bill C-58, and Simulcasting Policies for the Revenues of Canadian TV Broadcasters", study prepared for the Task Force on Broadcasting Policy, Ottawa, 1986.
10. Consultative Committee on the Implications of Telecommunications for Canadian Sovereignty. *Telecommunications and Canada* (Ottawa: Minister of Supply and Services Canada, 1979), p. 44.
11. Desbarats, "Radio and Television News".
12. Canadian Radio-television and Telecommunications Commission, *Distant Canadian Television Signals*, CRTC Public Notice 1985-61 (Ottawa: CRTC, 1985), p. 6.
13. CRTC, Public Notice 1985-61, p. 17.
14. CRTC, Public Notice 1985-61, p. 18.
15. CRTC, Public Notice 1985-61, p. 23.
16. Canadian Radio-television and Telecommunications Commission, *Policy Statement on Canadian Content in Television*, CRTC Public Notice 1983-18, (Ottawa: CRTC, 1983), p. 3.
17. CRTC, Public Notice 1983-18, p. 3–4.
18. CRTC, Public Notice 1983-18, p. 4.
19. CRTC, Public Notice 1983-18, p. 27.
20. CRTC, Public Notice 1983-18, p. 19.

Chapter 18

Pay-TV and Specialty Services

Pay-TV and Specialty Services

Over the past decade the nature, variety and number of television broadcasting services have changed dramatically. Most of the new services are delivered by satellite to cable television systems. The cable system functions, in effect, as the affiliate of the network at the local level.

By comparison, conventional networks deliver their programming through affiliated local stations which broadcast over-the-air both network and local programming. While conventional over-the-air network programming is available at no direct cost to all local residents within reach of its transmitters, the new satellite networks are available only to those in each market who subscribe to cable. The exception is those individuals who, like the cable system operators, own a satellite receiving dish.

In the United States an increasing number of the existing satellite networks are transmitted using a scrambled or encoded signal because their financing requires that they receive payments on a per-subscriber basis from cable system operators or individuals. Satellite networks which are sold on a per subscriber basis and which could previously be received free by individual satellite dish owners, are being made available to dish owners at a monthly charge.

It is only with satellite-to-cable television that the possibilities of retail or user-pay broadcasting have been extensively exploited. While over-the-air subscription television was introduced in the United States, it has never been accepted in Canada and seems not to have been missed. Multipoint distribution systems (MDS), using scrambled microwave signals, are also a possibility for pay-TV. But the ease of controlling, metering and billing for the television services received over cable has made cable the preferred vehicle of pay television in this country.

Operating with a significantly smaller potential audience than over-the-air broadcast networks, the new satellite networks characteristically offer their viewers only national programming, rather than a combination of local and national. This has contributed to a development pattern in which such services have been used to complement or fill gaps in the existing broadcasting system, either by making available certain kinds of programs that were in short supply or by making particular kinds of programs available at hours when conventional broadcasters were not likely to air them.

As we see in Chapter 5, less than three percent of English-language television viewing in Canada can now be attributed to pay and specialty services, and even less of French TV viewing. This is partly because these services were introduced only recently — in 1983 and 1984. However, in the case of the pay-TV movie channels particularly, it also reflects lower demand in Canada for these additional services. In the case of the specialty services their viewing share also reflects their carriage on a discretionary tier of cable service. As we see in Chapter 8, there have been until very recently no French-language specialty services licensed by the CRTC. By contrast, in the United States both pay television and specialty services have a much larger share of television viewing.

There are a number of options for introducing new pay and specialty services into the Canadian system. They are similar to the options in conventional television. The first is simply to allow direct import from the United States. The second is to license new Canadian services that can purchase rights for the best of the new foreign programming and combine it with Canadian programming in an economically viable service. The third is to develop new public services, with an essentially Canadian programming mandate.

The existing movie channels fall clearly in the second option, as do all of the Canadian specialty channels licensed so far. Canadian cable systems, however, have also been allowed to affiliate to American specialty services, acting as the importers and marketing agents for them. This application of the first option in the case of specialty services has different implications than in conventional television. Because these American networks have formal agreements with Canadian cable companies and are being paid for the carriage of their channels in Canada, they are obliged to purchase the right to show their programs in Canada, as well as in the United States. As we saw earlier, this is not the case in conventional television, where the American networks do not hold exhibition rights for Canada.

We will have occasion to return to these options in recommendations flowing from a closer look at the development of pay and specialty services. The situations in both French-language and English-language broadcasting must be considered in order to arrive at a balanced policy.

Satellite-to-cable networks began to develop in the United States in the late 1970s, following the success achieved by the American movie service, Home Box Office, when it began in 1976 to deliver its programming by satellite to American cable systems. The satellite-to-cable services in the U.S. are usually divided into three categories: cable networks, superstations and pay or premium services. The cable networks carry advertising and are the equivalent of specialty services in Canada. They include separate channels devoted to sports, news, various kinds of music, religious denominations, children's interests, health, the U.S. Congress and public affairs, financial news and information, black Americans, arts, Spanish-language programming, and so on.

Superstation programming is made up primarily of reruns of conventional network shows. Finally, the pay or premium services do not carry advertising and are paid for entirely by subscribers. Most pay services in the United States run movies. Home Box Office, with over 14 million subscribers, is by far the most successful.

In the United States the pay television services accounted for six percent of television viewing (including viewers without cable) in 1985, little changed from the five percent of viewing in 1984. The viewing of the cable networks grew from seven percent in 1984 to eight percent in 1985, with superstations accounting for an additional six percent of viewing in each year.

What is more significant, however, is the levels of viewing being achieved by the American satellite-to-cable networks in American households with cable television. In cabled households pay services accounted for 12 percent of viewing in 1985, up from 11 percent the previous year. The cable networks, which are the counterparts of Canadian specialty services, attracted 15 percent of viewing in 1985, an increase from 13 percent the previous year.

In Canada, although the debate over pay television began in the early 1970s, pay services were not licensed until 1982. Applications to provide specialty programming services were invited by the CRTC in 1983. The term specialty service has been used in Canada to describe satellite networks which usually concentrate on providing a particular kind or format of televison programming.

After almost a decade the jury is still out in the United States on the important issue of the extent to which pay and specialty services are likely to displace conventional networks and local stations. Conventional broadcasters maintain by far the largest share of viewing and of industry revenues. Further, the most successful satellite channels still include the superstations WTBS and multiformat services such as the U.S.A. Network and CBN (Christian Broadcasting Network) which attract their audiences largely with reruns of conventional network programming. The viewing of the premium and primarily movie channels has stabilized. Moreover, the videocassette recorder (VCR), by enabling viewers to reschedule conventional network programs, has provided an alternative to the narrowcasting method of bringing to viewers the kind of program they want when they want it. The VCR is also a competitor as a delivery vehicle of movies and programs from other non-broadcast sources.

Many American services have failed or merged with competing services. Nevertheless, a number have now been in operation for more than five years, the audiences for all satellite services combined are growing and, as cable penetration increases, growth appears likely to continue.

In responding to the challenge of the new services in Canada, the CRTC has had to bear in mind that they compete with conventional Canadian broadcasters who already face more competition than their American counterparts in a much smaller market serving two language groups.

Pay Television

In Canada, pay-TV has played to, at best, mixed reviews. In less than four years it has gone through massive restructuring and a number of failures, it has cost its investors millions, failed to keep its promise on Canadian programming, and been greeted by Canadians with far less enthusiasm than its boosters predicted.

The CRTC delayed the introduction of pay-TV in Canada until 1982. It was concerned that no predominantly Canadian service could be provided that would itself contribute to achieving the goals of the *Broadcasting Act*, and that any such service would weaken the capacity of existing Canadian broadcasters to fulfil their obligations under the Act. CRTC research also indicated that

Canadians were much less interested than Americans in subscribing to pay television, in part because the average Canadian with cable already had a wider choice of television channels than the average American.

When the CRTC bowed to a decade of pressure — part of it from the government — and decided in April 1981 to call for applications, it set out a number of objectives. The pay television services were to contribute to the realization of the objectives of the *Broadcasting Act*, increase the diversity of programming in Canada, and make available high quality Canadian programming from new sources by providing opportunities and revenue sources for Canadian producers otherwise unable to gain access to the broadcasting system.

In issuing its call the CRTC chose to open the system to competing services, acting against advice that only a national monopoly was viable. Even though the competitive model and the high expectations for Canadian content were based largely on projections provided by some of the applicants, and even though the Commission had no independent research capacity to set against some of the claims it heard, it licensed the six applicants which, in its view, best responded to its call. (We recommend in Chapter 6 that the CRTC expand its research and analysis capability to allow it to check the bidding escalation phenomenon inherent in the competitive licensing process.)

Several pay-TV channels were licensed by the CRTC. First Choice, as the national general interest service, was to provide separate programming in both official languages. There were three regional general interest services, one each in Atlantic Canada, Ontario and Alberta. An English-language national performing arts service called C-Channel was licensed, and a regional multilingual service was licensed in British Columbia. An additional call was issued to fill in the English regional network for Manitoba, Saskatchewan and British Columbia, and for a French-language regional service.

For the first time, Canadian content levels were set according to both time and money. The general interest pay television licensees were asked to provide up to 30 percent Canadian content overall and in particular from 7 p.m. to 11 p.m., rising to 50 percent in the last 15 months of the licence. Drama programs were to account for at least half of the Canadian content provided by the general interest channels. At least 45 percent of the national licensees' total revenues — and 60 percent of programming budgets — were to be spent on Canadian programs. Slightly lower requirements were set for the regional channels. The performing arts licencee was to provide 40 percent Canadian content over the full day and in the evening; 30 percent of its daily and evening schedule was to consist of performing arts programming. The CRTC chose not to regulate wholesale and retail prices. This left three essentially competing services — the national, the regionals, and the arts service — dependent upon and competing for the favours of a monopoly, the cable companies.

The misgivings felt by many were reflected in the dissenting opinion of two commissioners, Jean-Louis Gagnon and John Grace, who called the licensing decisions "system overload". They asked, "How many of these birds will fly?" They added:

> The arguments in support of a full system of regional pay television systems we

> find unconvincing, and the financial impact of such a system on a national pay operation insufficiently recognized, particularly with respect to the real possiblity of 'cream skimming' by certain regional pay systems in the more lucrative markets.[1]

The launch of pay-TV was a disaster. Confused consumers were barraged by the conflicting claims of three competing services in deciding whether they wanted pay-TV at all. The licensees badly oversold their product. First Choice signed a notorious deal with the Playboy Channel in the U.S., which boosted sales in the short-run, but the ensuing debate over pornography and the media eventually hurt pay-TV in general, particularly in the important family market. The early collapse of C-Channel also shook investor confidence and had a profound effect on the smaller regional networks which were fighting the additional burden of higher satellite costs per capita.

The industry went through a high 'churn' period, subscribers either switching services or switching off entirely. With average penetration rates for individual services rarely rising above 5 percent and with break-even operation dependent on levels of at least 10 percent, the investors in pay-TV quickly ate through their initial capital. Failures and consolidation of competing services inevitably followed.

In July 1984, after a year-and-a-half of operation and more than $50 million in combined losses, Allarcom was given the right to market Super Channel west of Ontario and in the Yukon and the Northwest Territories. First Choice, now controlled by Astral-Bellevue, was given Ontario, Quebec and the Atlantic provinces. The regional French channel was merged with the French national service, Premier Choix, to form Super-Écran in eastern Canada.

Since the restructuring the pay channels have enjoyed at least a slow but steady growth. At the end of April 1986, First Choice had 446,000 subscribers, Super Channel had 180,000 and Super-Écran 120,000. The growth is due in part to offering the 'pay' movie service along with the 'specialty' music and sports channels for $15.95 as part of the "Canadian Pack". This packaging agreement, designed to serve the mutual interests of the Canadian pay and specialty service licensees, is not a formal requirement of the CRTC.

This encouraging development was the result of the initiative of the pay and specialty services, with the co-operation of the cable industry and judiciously exercised moral suasion by the CRTC. (Carriage and linkage requirements are considered in greater detail in the section on specialty services [below] and in Chapter 24.)

Recommendation

> Pay and specialty services should be free of CRTC regulation in making joint marketing and distribution arrangements with the cable companies, provided such packaging arrangements favour the development of Canadian services.

At time of writing, the CRTC was considering an application by the pay operators to reduce Canadian content for the remainder of the first licence period, which will end in 1987. It would be inappropriate for the Task Force to comment on their specific application, but our general view is that their obligations should be commensurate with their resources.

Recommendation

In setting Canadian content requirements for the second licence term the CRTC should consider the realistic and appropriate contribution that pay operators can make as their subscription base expands.

Because of the licensing of specialty services that provide sports and music programming, the focus of pay television is now even more on exhibition of feature films, primarily features already exhibited in movie theatres. Pay television services are a secondary, not the primary, exhibitor of most of their content.

The degree to which pay television services can reasonably be expected to exhibit Canadian movies depends more on film policy than broadcasting policy. Whether pay-TV is willing or required to show Canadian movies will certainly not decide whether Canadian movies are made.

A Canadian Feature Film Fund has been established, administered by Telefilm Canada, with annual funding of $33 million following the recommendations of the Task Force on the Canadian Film Industry. The Fund represents an important element in the revitalizing of Canadian feature film production. The CRTC, in addressing the pay television issue at the time of the licence renewals, will have to consider fully the government's film policy. Feature films are important to the objectives of broadcasting.

Recommendation

In establishing conditions of licence for the pay television services, the CRTC should take into account the film policy of the federal government and, in particular, the creation of the Canadian Feature Film Fund.

The conditions of licence for pay television should ensure exhibition of most Canadian feature films especially since pay now operates as a monopoly. Fluctuations in the level of production of Canadian movies make it difficult for the CRTC to project the range of Canadian films that will be available, although the new federal fund and some provincial initiatives mean that there will be increased production. The Commission will need to monitor film production as it now monitors musical record production in reviewing content requirements for radio.

Recommendation

The CRTC's conditions of licence for pay television services should be designed to ensure the exhibition of most of the Canadian feature films being produced. Canadian film production levels should be monitored

> to determine whether adjustments are appropriate, and provision should be made in the conditions of licence for adjustments.

Finally, in view of the experience of what is a new industry and the new directions suggested, we remain reasonably optimistic that at least part of the promise of pay can be realized, especially if undue direct American competition is precluded.

Recommendation

> The CRTC should continue to prohibit the importation of American services that directly affect the viability of comparable Canadian pay channels.

Pay-per-view Television

Pay-per-view is a recent development in the United States which is now being considered in Canada. The system at present permits viewers to choose items from a schedule of movies, concerts, sports events and so on which is offered by the cable company. Viewers do not have to subscribe to the whole schedule to receive a particular program, as they do with regular pay-TV.

The system usually works by phone from the subscriber to the cable headend, with the most up-to-date systems using a coded number to trigger release of the program to the subscriber's TV set. The set must have an addressable decoder. The technology is available but the capital costs are high. Before committing these funds the cable companies must be satisfied the programming will attract sufficient subscribers, which is by no means yet clear. In the United States penetration among local subscribers has ranged from 40 percent with a championship boxing match to four percent for a rock concert. Movie distributors have taken a cautious approach to pay-per-view. However, many operators see it as a potential means of competing against the VCR and the cassette market. If it is licensed its success will likely be determined by whether it is allowed to exhibit new productions prior to their release on video cassette.

There is also the question of who will control pay-per-view. Both the movie studios and cable operators want to eliminate intermediaries, arguing that profit margins are already too precarious. In a Vancouver application Rogers Communications Inc. suggested to the CRTC that any subscriber to pay-per-view first be a subscriber to pay-TV. This would provide extraordinary protection for the pay operators, but other questions of market potential, appropriate levels of Canadian content, types of programming, and structure for pay-per-view remained to be considered at a CRTC hearing at time of writing. By limiting selection to a one-channel schedule, pay-per-view as presently offered is far from the demand-access television that may eventually be possible on interactive, broadband networks. Our view is simply that careful examination is required before pay-per-view in its present form is approved.

Specialty Programming Services

Pay television, relying exclusively on subscriber fees, has become something of an anomaly in the new generation of satellite networks. Most satellite channels in the United States are funded by a combination of advertising revenue and a monthly charge per subscriber to the cable system operator.

In its 1983 call for applications to provide specialty programming services, the CRTC spoke aptly of "the marriage of satellite technology and cable television". It said it was looking for "narrowcast television programming designed to reflect the particular interests and needs of different age, language, cultural, geographic and other groups". By contrast the American satellite channels include services such as the U.S.A. Network which offer a wide range of general interest programs, usually referred to by the CRTC as multi-format services. The Commission saw specialty services "as being complementary to the Canadian services available at present", and emphasized that "it is not now calling for applications based on programming for general audiences, particularly those which include mass appeal feature films or variety specials".[2]

The Commission's intention in defining the scope of specialty service programming was that "new services should complement existing services and not jeopardize the program producing ability of existing licensees".[3] But many of the kinds of service the Commission was anticipating licensing — sports, music, news, and so on — were in fact already part of conventional programming and had wide appeal.

A fundamental contrast with American cable networks practice was the Commission's preference that, rather than being carried as part of basic cable service, the Canadian specialty channels would "be available on a discretionary basis at the option of the subscriber".[4]

The Commission received over 40 applications but, in a controversial move, refused to hear over half, in most cases because the model proposed was not fully discretionary to subscribers. Most applicants argued either that the approach the Commission was insisting on made it impossible for Canadian services to be viable, or that to be viable they would be unable to contribute significantly to providing Canadian programs.

For the Commission, the balance that had to be struck was one that weighed the protection of the already fragmented conventional broadcasting system against the potential contribution of specialty services. The presence of the American three-plus-one channels meant that conventional Canadian broadcasters already faced far more competition for viewing audiences in their domestic market than did American broadcasters in theirs. Per capita advertising levels in Canada were less than half the level in the United States. At the same time, even in the large American market a substantial majority of the satellite channels were losing money. Some American analysts predict that even in the United States the small, special-interest channels will disappear, leaving only the broad-based nationally connected channels. Others, naturally, disagree.

In 1983 the CRTC stuck to its guns and heard just 15 of the 41 original applications, it licensed only two: the music service (MuchMusic), operated by

CHUM Ltd., and The Sports Network (TSN), owned by Labatt's Breweries. Four applications were adjourned, with the applicants given additional time to revise their applications. One of them, a medicine and health care network, The Life Channel, was subsequently licensed in March 1985. The Commission licensed two third-language services, the Tele-latino Network, to provide programming in Italian and Spanish, and Chinavision Canada.

No specialty services were licensed in French at that time. Later the CRTC allowed MuchMusic to distribute a partially French video music service to Quebec and eastern Canada, but the Minister of Communications has asked the Commission to review the entire issue of specialty services in French.

No Canadian news channel was licensed, nor a Canadian children's programming service, nor an arts service. Similarly, none of the licensed services promised any enhanced role in programming for regional creators and producers. Initially, the licensed services were required to meet relatively limited Canadian content requirements: 10 percent for the music channel and 18 percent for TSN (although the requirement for TSN was higher in peak viewing time). These levels were to rise to 30 percent in the fifth year for MuchMusic and to 35 percent for TSN.

Two years after the CRTC's decision, MuchMusic and TSN are subscribed to by some 800,000 households. From the beginning the two services have been marketed with pay television, which made them mutually supportive and enhanced the marketing of all three as a cable 'tier', both to subscribers and advertisers. Their counterparts in the United States, however, reach proportionally more of the American population; Music Television (MTV) goes to 27 million, or 33 times as many as MuchMusic, and the sports service (ESPN) reaches 36 million viewers, or 45 times as many as TSN. The other Canadian services, the Life Channel, Tele-latino and Chinavision have experienced substantial difficulty in making arrangements with cable systems to offer their services to subscribers. The CRTC ruled that the cable companies themselves should decide whether to make the discretionary services available to subscribers, how to package them, what to pay, and what to charge subscribers.

The CRTC's approach has substantially limited the kinds of Canadian service that might be developed and their ability to provide well-funded Canadian programming. The only services that have been developed have low production costs or, in the case of MuchMusic, present music videos which are produced by the record companies as promotions for sound recordings. The CRTC approach has also limited the possibility of specialty services in French. On the other hand, this approach minimized the impact of the new services on conventional television at a time when the CRTC was proposing to ask broadcasters to commit significantly greater resources to Canadian programming. Also, despite the proportionally stronger American advertising market, the experience in the United States indicates that relatively few Canadian channels could have succeeded. Even if they had been based on the American model their contribution to providing Canadian programming would have been very limited.

The Task Force believes the Commission has acted judiciously in approaching specialty services with caution at the beginning. It is our judgement that the time has come, however, to take greater advantage of inexpensive satellite-to-cable distribution for Canadian purposes.

Consistent with Canada's tradition in broadcasting, the Task Force believes that both the public and the private sectors must have a role in satellite-to-cable networks. We are therefore recommending the new non-commercial channel, TV Canada, as part of basic cable service in systems in which discretionary services are available (see Chapter 13), and also a CBC English-language news and current affairs channel (see Chapter 10). At the start, a partial news service should be provided in French as part of the Télé-Canada service.

Apart from these two proposals the Task Force sees growth in satellite networks coming from the private sector with the possible exception of provincial government initiatives. The emphasis should continue to be on services which complement existing broadcast programming.

As we said at the outset, the satellite networks reproduce the issues and options tackled earlier by broadcasting policy in the conventional Canadian television services. In the new struggle to create strong Canadian satellite networks, as in the old struggle for Canadian TV programming, there are two principal objectives: to make sure Canadian services exist and to provide a balance of Canadian and non-Canadian programs.

It is already clear that satellite-delivered networks, unlike conventional stations and networks, will be subject to strict adherence to copyright. Early in 1986, for example, the U.S. State Department blocked WTBS, an American superstation which the CRTC had authorized for carriage on Canadian cable systems in remote areas, from making arrangements for carriage of its signal in Canada. The reason the State Department gave was that the operator of WTBS, Turner Broadcasting, did not hold copyright for Canada to the programs it carried. The State Department has authority over the transborder distribution of American signals by satellite. Similarly, some of the programming carried by the Arts and Entertainment Network in the United States has to be blocked out in Canada because the network holds only American rights. In all cases, of course, where the American networks must sign affiliation agreements with Canadian cable systems for carriage of their signal, they are naturally bound by the terms of their contractual relations with the providers of their programming. If they are to be in Canada they will have to buy Canadian rights.

The CRTC's rule is that Canadian cable operators may not carry American satellite networks if those networks carry programming similar to a Canadian satellite network. At present, 16 American satellite-to-cable services are authorized by the CRTC for distribution by Canadian cable affiliates:

Cable News Network (CNN)
CNN Headline News
The Nashville Network (TNN)
The Arts and Entertainment Network
Financial News Network
The Weather Channel
The Learning Channel
Biznet, the American Business Network
Country Music Television

Cable Satellite Public Affairs Network (C-Span)
The Silent Network
The Professional Education Network (PEN)
AP Newscable
Dow Jones Cable News
Reuters News View
United Press International Custom Cable

What is necessary now is to establish a pattern of development for satellite channels which will serve Canada well in the future when the role of such services may become much more important. The main practical concern must be with American satellite networks which are extended into Canada with no licensing requirement but with a requirement to buy Canadian as well as American rights to all their programming. First, their presence here as a competitor would at the least fragment an already small market. Even in the large American market there tends to be only one participant providing each kind of programming. On this issue the Commission said in its original decision that "should the Commission license, in the future, a Canadian service in a format competitive to an authorized non-Canadian service, the latter will be replaced by a Canadian service".[5] This replacement policy could lead to practical difficulties which will have to be addressed in future examination of the issue.

An assessment of the experience of the major Canadian specialty channels leads us to hope they have learned from the errors of pay-TV. It appears possible that specific Canadian programming needs can be met by the second policy option we mentioned at the outset — the combination of American and Canadian content in a mutually supportive way on specialty channels.

In Chapter 8 we look at the special problems that arise in French-language broadcasting in Canada as a result of the relatively small size of the market and make recommendations concerning the carriage of specialty services. Our recommendation here is applicable to English-language services only.

Recommendation

Pending any radical restructuring of the present cable tiering system, Canadian specialty services should remain on a discretionary cable tier and the carriage of competitive signals from the U.S. should be prohibited. Cable carriage should be arranged at time of licensing between the satellite service and cable operators with the CRTC acting as arbiter in cases of failure to reach agreement.

Religious Programming

A policy for specialty services must include religious programming, because it is only as a specialty service that this type of programming can develop with all the latitude it needs to be compatible with the basic principles that underlie the Canadian broadcasting system.

The problems posed by religious programming have affected Canadian broadcasting policy from the outset. A dispute that arose in the late 1920s when the Minister of Marine and Fisheries refused to renew the broadcasting licence held by a religious sect led to the establishment of the Aird Commission in 1929.[6]

There are in Canada a great many groups professing various religious beliefs and not enough radio frequencies to accommodate all of them. This has in the past consistently led regulatory authorities to refuse to license religious broadcasting organizations. It was argued that a licensee broadcasting religious views would find it difficult to meet the balanced programming requirement.[7]

The Commission nevertheless recognized that it was necessary to include some religious programming in the system to ensure that it provided diversity and comprehensiveness. The CRTC's approach in recent years has been to encourage the development of specialty services offering religious programming if provided by corporations owned by generally representative elements of the various religious denominations and serving diverse religious beliefs.[8]

The question of religious programming is a complex one, touching upon fundamental freedoms guaranteed by the Constitution. It is difficult to envisage creating specialty religious channels for every group in Canada wishing to reach people with their religious beliefs. The interdenominational approach, encouraging various religious groups to work together, remains the best one. It stands the best chance of ensuring the development of religious programming services in a manner that would use Canadian creative resources and at the same time respect the beliefs of fellow citizens.

The Task Force is encouraged to see the work being done to promote interdenominational services. Here as in other areas the special linguistic and regional features of Canada must also be taken into account.

Notes

1. Canadian Radio-television and Telecommunications Commission, *Pay Television*, Decision CRTC 82-240 C.R.T. (Ottawa: CRTC, 1982). Minority Opinion of Commissioners Gagnon and Grace, p. 658.
2. Canadian Radio-television and Telecommunications Commission, *Call for New Specialty Programming Services*, CRTC Public Notice 83-93 (Ottawa: CRTC, 1983), p. 4.
3. CRTC, Public Notice 83-93, p. 10.
4. CRTC, Public Notice 83-93, p. 6.
5. Canadian Radio-television and Telecommunications Commission, *Specialty Programming Services*, CRTC Public Notice 1984-81 (Ottawa: CRTC, 1984), p. 13.
6. John Bennett, "The Licensing of Religious Radio Stations in Canada", *Canadian Communications Law Review* 1 (1969), p. 1.
7. Canadian Radio-television and Telecommunications Commission, *Public Hearing on Religious Broadcasting*, Notice of Public Hearing CRTC 81-54 (Ottawa: CRTC, 1981).
8. CRTC Public Notice 83-112, June 2, 1983.

Part VI

THE COMMUNITY SECTOR

Chapter 19

Community Broadcasting

Community Broadcasting

Today, community radio and television are changing the old idea that access to broadcasting is more difficult than access to the print media. The 1957 Royal Commission on Broadcasting reflected the old view when it observed in its report:

> The right of access to the printed word may take many forms, some more effective than others, but access in some form is open to anyone and does not depend, as in broadcasting, on the decision of some one of the licensees of the relatively few available frequencies in Canada.[1]

Since that time, the CRTC has not only licensed many community radio stations but also required the provision of a community channel on cable television. These stations in turn have opened their doors to the public. Technological advances have increased the availability of channels to community radio and TV thereby giving access to more and more communities. We can look forward to an age of greatly increased access to these media if policies are adopted to accommodate the voluntary initiatives of those who are interested.

The development of community radio and television was one of the results of the trend to democratization and social change which began in the sixties. These new radio and television outlets began as instruments of innovation and community participation in the field of communication. They were designed to fulfil social and cultural needs which the traditional broadcasting systems by their nature could not meet.

Community radio and television began as a social experiment, chiefly in Quebec and in northern and Native communities. Such stations made possible, among other things, the production and broadcasting of programs designed to reflect people's daily concerns. In Native communities, remote areas and small communities, community broadcasting provided local radio and television outlets where otherwise there would have been none. In larger centres, community broadcasting gave opportunities for groups from minority cultural backgrounds, tastes or beliefs to find expression in radio and TV.

The developers of community television broadcasting believed its programming should be as rich and varied as the communities it served. Accordingly, depending on where and when a person tuned in, a community television station might be broadcasting a peewee hockey game, the deliberations of the municipal council, a heritage-language romance or travel film, a forum or debate on multicultural issues, a meeting of teenagers in a baton-twirling competition or — as happened in some instances — a public meeting held by this Task Force.

Community broadcasting, complementing the public and private sectors, must be seen as an essential third sector of broadcasting if we are to realize the objective of reasonable access to the system that is a central theme of this Report. Community broadcasting is part of the voluntary sector of society, in which people help themselves and one another to establish activities ranging from help for the handicapped and less fortunate to sports and outdoor recreation, from arts and crafts to environmental and community planning concerns. Conventional broadcasting includes an element of public service programming, but community broadcasting goes beyond what is possible in a commercial or fully professional system. Like other activities in the voluntary sector, community broadcasting is not-for-profit; indeed, it is usually to be found struggling along on a shoestring and heavily dependent on voluntary labour and financial assistance.

Technological developments in broadcasting are encouraging to the community sector. New transmission possibilities, such as the radio subcarrier channels, low-power television transmitters, and the steady increase in cable channels are providing the means to reach smaller audiences at lower cost. As these new channels of broadcasting are developed, it will be important to ensure that a reasonable proportion of the additional capacity is reserved for the community sector.

Community broadcasters operate under different conditions in radio and in television. Community radio stations are licensed as such by the CRTC and operate independently, though in the future there will be opportunities to use radio or cable subcarriers in co-operation with other operators. On the other hand, all community television broadcasters are on the community cable channel in their area, dependent on the co-operation of the local cable operator. The pioneers of community broadcasting in Canada generally are to be found in four groups: the provincially supported community broadcasting sector in Quebec, the federally supported Native Peoples community broadcasting sector in the North, the student radio services on university campuses, and the dispersed and unorganized community broadcasting sector in most of the southern parts of Canada outside Quebec.

In the sections that follow we will look at the achievements and difficulties of community broadcasting and then consider policies for its future.

Community Radio

In 1985 the Canadian Radio-Television and Telecommunications Commission (CRTC) defined community radio broadcasting as requiring non-profit community ownership and community participation in decisions on programming.[2] The definition also requires programming to be different from that of other stations and to provide access in a way that will reflect the interests and special needs of the community. The CRTC recognized that production standards should not be set at levels that only professionals and the more skilled helpers could attain, intimidating the volunteers on whom community radio must rely for much of its production.

The Commission issues two types of licence — A or B — to community radio stations. Type A is for stations where no other AM or FM station operates in the same language in the same market or part of it. Type B is for stations where there is at least one other AM or FM radio station serving all or part of the same market in the same language. Type A stations are allowed to run more advertising than Type B since, to some extent, they are making up for the absence of a commercial station. Some of them have become scarcely distinguishable from commercial stations. We deal more extensively with these matters in a separate section on finances.

Thanks to provincial government support, both community radio and community television are more advanced in Quebec than in other provinces.

Quebec Community Radio

At the end of 1985, 21 community radio stations were operating in Quebec: six more were being organized. Their total revenue in the fiscal year ending March 31, 1985 was $3.8 million, of which $1.6 million came from grants and over $1.3 million from advertising.

During 1985 the Quebec stations produced an average of 120 hours of programming each week with 200 workers and 2,000 active volunteers. According to the *Association des radiodiffuseurs communautaires du Québec (ARCQ)*, the representative organization of the province's community radio broadcasters, the community stations were backed by 12,000 individual members and 1,000 organizations, including chambers of commerce and labour unions.

Type A stations provide the only local broadcasting in such communities as Fermont and Natashquan. Type B stations are found in larger centres such as Montreal and Quebec City, and regional centres such as Rivière-du-Loup and Sherbrooke.

Community radio programming has become steadily more diversified. The stations usually put emphasis on training people from the community in program production and station operation. Students interested in broadcasting are often able to gain knowledge and experience at the community stations. For example, CIBL-FM in Montreal receives students from the communications department of Université du Québec à Montréal. This has led to a popular comedy program created by a group of students, "Rock et Belles Oreilles", which moved from the community station to a popular commercial station and became a star attraction for the younger generation. Another example is CHOC-FM at Jonquière, which welcomes students and also offers a basic radio course to members of local groups and associations. This station, like others, welcomes all kinds of community groups — housing committees, tenants' associations, unions, women's groups, day-care associations — to discuss their interests and make known their views.

Among the common subjects of programming on Quebec community radio stations are municipal happenings; the state of the environment and wildlife in the area; community services; tips on or how-to approaches to, say, fishing, preparing local recipes, birdwatching, or best trails for hiking; and consumer guidance for helping the aged or living with new technology. Regional history is a popular subject or, in the cities, pieces on local neighbourhoods and their personalities. Local artists — musicians, painters, writers — are interviewed, along with others prominent on the local scene. Help-wanted and other classified ads are popular. Sports events involving local teams — hockey, baseball, basketball, soccer — may be broadcast. Other broadcasts include services from local churches, poetry readings, radio plays, programs put together by or for children aged six to eleven, and programs of special interest to teenagers or produced by teenagers. Regional press reviews and programs of news background are heard on many community stations, as well as fullscale documentaries on important neighbourhood, local, or regional issues, or on the local effect of federal, provincial, municipal, school board, public-utility or other public policies.

Northern and Native Community Radio

There are at present six AM and 55 FM community radio stations serving small and isolated communities, many of them operating transmitters with a range of only a few miles. From such places as Poste-de-la-Baleine in Quebec, Moosonee in Ontario, Fort Chipewyan in Alberta, Old Crow in the Yukon, and Tuktoyaktuk in the Northwest Territories these little stations offer programming tailored to local needs.

Programs include open-line shows on community issues, local weather reports, personal message services, story-telling and music. Such fare is appreciated in communities that otherwise receive all their programs from remote (to them) metropolitan centres in Canada and the United States. The CRTC has simplified application procedures and technical requirements for low power stations in remote communities. (See Chapter 20 for a discussion of aboriginal broadcasting.)

Student Radio

Student broadcasting goes back to the beginnings of radio in Canada, with the establishment of an experimental station at Queen's University in Kingston in 1922. The first campus station of the modern era went on the air in 1964 at the University of Saskatchewan, but it was preceded by campus radio clubs in the fifties and sixties which broadcast on closed circuit to university buildings for a few hours each day.

In 1973 before the CRTC formally adopted a policy on student radio (in 1975), the first FM licence awarded to a campus radio station went to CKRL-FM at Université Laval in Quebec City. Later, in 1976 student organizations at Carleton University in Ottawa and the University of Manitoba at Winnipeg received the first licences for English-language FM campus stations. At present there are 18 student FM stations, one AM, and 14 closed circuit.

An informal national organization of student stations was formed in 1980 and became the National Campus/Community Radio Organization (NCRO). One of the aims of this non-profit organization is to develop a loosely-structured network to exchange programs and information and to share resources.

Campus stations take pride in being open to new ideas. They concentrate on programs of information, discussion and debate, public and community affairs, the arts, and usually a vast and eclectic menu of music not often heard on conventional radio. The stations are heavily dependent on volunteers. Their aims are to give students access to the means of communication, to involve the larger community in university concerns, and to offer an alternative to conventional broadcasting.

Community Radio in Other Provinces

Apart from community radio stations in remote communities and on campus, there are only two outside Quebec, one in Ontario, the other in British Columbia.

Kitchener station CKWR-FM has been on the air since 1974. It is operated by Wired World Inc., a non-profit corporation with charitable status, and raises its budget from subscriber fees and other forms of community support. A Vancouver community radio station, CFRA-FM, has also been on the air since 1974. It is owned by Vancouver Co-operative Radio, a non-profit corporation incorporated under the British Columbia Co-operatives Act. In both cases, the stations rely heavily on volunteers who are active in program production, technical operation and administration.

Community Television

The CRTC opened the way to community television with its requirement that all but the smaller cable systems set aside a community channel. The establishment of a community channel was made the sixth order of priority on the basic service in the 1975 cable regulations, which assured it a place on all but the smallest systems. The CRTC said in a 1975 statement that "the community channel must become a primary social commitment of the cable television licensee".[3] Provision of a community channel is considered to be the cable licensee's return to the public for the advantages of a cable licence.

The CRTC's 1975 statement went on to require programming on the community channel to come from the community itself, with the exception of limited outside content of local relevance. The Commission set out guidelines and criteria for assessing the cable operator's performance upon the occasion of application for renewal of licence.

The CRTC noted that in smaller communities cable systems normally serve the whole community, but in larger urban areas they often cut across neighbourhoods, wards and even whole municipalities. Such systems could nevertheless serve communities of interest "based on cultural background or arising out of common endeavour". In the view of the Commission, "The communications needs of these communities extend to such matters as the exchanging of ideas, increasing of social and political awareness and the dispelling of the sense of isolation so prevalent in large urban centres."[4]

The CRTC expected licensees "to seek out these communities of interest within their service areas and to encourage them to give expression to their interests and concerns". Community channels would be expected to give attention to such matters as the activities of municipal councils and school boards, opportunities for expression of ethnic communities in the area, the provision of mobile equipment to cover events, and the arrangement of interconnections with adjacent cable systems to offer "simultaneous programming of a kind which provides a significant alternative to the programming available in the off-air stations serving their licensed areas".[5]

In proposing amendments to the cable regulations in 1986, the CRTC observed that "there is a well developed core of programmers and volunteers across the country who produce a significant amount of locally oriented programming".[6]

Again, it is in Quebec that the community-channel opportunity has been most extensively developed, thanks to provincial government support for community television associations. At the beginning of 1986, 33 community TV associations were in operation; four more were being organized. (There are 149 cable TV companies in Quebec.) The total revenue of Quebec community TV associations in the fiscal year ending March 31, 1985 was $1,925,000, of which $1,233,600 came from governments.

The associations produced an average 16 hours a week of programming with a total of 68 full-time workers, 180 part-time, and about 2,000 volunteers who participate actively in the work of the associations. Altogether, according to the *Regroupement des organismes communautaires de communication du Québec* (ROCCQ), the representative organization of community TV in Quebec, the associations have about 30,000 supporting members.

The community associations have improved their programming abilities in both content and technical presentation. Like the community radio organizations, they place emphasis on training volunteers in TV production and operation. They also often serve as training grounds for people seeking careers in professional broadcasting. ROCCQ told the Task Force that its members experience occasional difficulties with local cable operators in gaining access to community channels. The organization supported the joint view of the federal and Quebec communications departments, expressed in 1985, that the CRTC should recognize local community television organizations and establish their status and responsibilities in community programming.[7]

Community TV associations in Quebec bring the camera to bear on many of the same subjects and activities as the community radio stations described earlier. News programs are oriented to local social, political, economic and cultural developments. These, too, are the subject of longer documentaries aimed at helping citizens obtain sufficient information to reach decisions on matters of local concern. The participation of teenagers in the conception and production of programs for their own age group is encouraged. Artists and craftspersons and their works are a popular subject, as are local artistic and entertainment groups — choirs, dancers, bands, theatrical companies. Local festivals and celebrations make for good coverage. Sports, on TV as on radio, are important, with special attention paid to all kinds of amateur sport and partial or complete coverage of local matches. There are programs for those interested in specialized activities or hobbies. Coverage of local events may deal with labour-management conflicts, demonstrations and protests, public inquiries and election campaigns. Local associations are given a chance to publicize their activities. Religious programs are arranged in co-operation with local churches.

Another form of community television is provided with low-power transmitters. At present community television organizations serving remote communities make use of nine such transmitters. Like community radio in similar circumstances, these stations rely largely on volunteers. In many underserved areas the CBC has made its transmitters available to community broadcasters during periods on the schedule when network programs would be least likely to appeal to local interests.

Campus television has not been developed to the point of establishing student television stations. Student television production groups use other outlets, such as community cable channels or closed circuit transmission.

As in Quebec, cable operators in other provinces often work with community groups and give them major responsibility for program production. Many cable operators make a substantial contribution to the community channel. However, the extent of local community participation and the standard of programming vary widely from place to place.

Financing Community Broadcasting

Community broadcasters have several sources of financing. In the case of radio, a limited amount of advertising may be carried. In the case of television, they are assisted to varying degrees by the cable system operator but are not allowed to carry advertising. Both community TV and radio can look to a number of federal and provincial sources for various types of aid to their activities, rather than direct aid to community broadcasting as such. In Quebec, however, they can obtain direct aid from the provincial government. Finally, community broadcasting can look to support from the local community through memberships, sponsoring organizations, fund drives and other money-raising ventures. If the broadcaster is registered as a charitable organization because of its educational or social role, donors can deduct their donations from taxable income, which is a form of governmental aid through tax spending.

A reasonably complete picture of the financial support of community broadcasting is available only for Quebec. Figures compiled by the *Association des radiodiffuseurs communautaires du Québec* and supplied to the Task Force show in Table 19.1 the breakdown of revenues for community radio stations in the fiscal years 1981-82 and 1984-85.

A similar breakdown for community television in Quebec is given in Table 19.2 with figures compiled and provided to the Task Force by the *Regroupement des organismes communautaires de communication du Québec*.

The Quebec figures show that the growth of the community broadcasting sector in number of radio stations and TV associations has outstripped the growth in revenue. Let us take a look at each of the main sources of revenue.

Advertising Revenue

Advertising has accounted for an important share of revenue for Quebec's community radio stations — about a third of the total in both years shown in Table 19.1. But the shares between Type A and Type B stations are quite different.

Type A stations are allowed by the CRTC to carry more advertising because they do not compete with private stations. On these stations advertising can occupy up to 250 minutes a day, or 1500 minutes a week for stations broadcasting 18 hours a day (6 a.m. to midnight), seven days a week. Otherwise, advertising is limited to 20 percent of a station's total broadcast time.

Table 19.1 Revenues of Community Radio Stations in Quebec[a]

	1981-82 (13 stations)		1984-85 (26 stations)	
	Amount $	Percent of Total	Amount $	Percent of Total
Operating	794,712	31.5	1,432,732	37.9
Governmental and other grants	1,401,548	55.5	1,654,191	43.7
Community	248,621	9.9	459,391	12.1
Other	77,156	3.1	236,048	6.3
Total	2,522,037	100.0	3,782,362	100.0
Breakdown of operating revenues				
Advertising	733,196	29.1	1,338,885	35.4
Other	61,516	2.4	93,847	2.5
Breakdown of governmental and other grants				
Govt. of Quebec	911,665[b]	36.1	162,801	4.3
COMAP			962,872	25.5
Federal Govt.	386,522	15.3	383,330	10.1
Municipal, school bd, and non-govtl.	103,361	4.1	145,188	3.8

Note: a. Fiscal year ends August 31.
b. Includes grants for 1981-82 from COMAP (Community Media Assistance Program).
Sources: "Guide de la radio communautaire au Québec", Association des radiodiffuseurs communautaires du Québec (ARCQ), 1984.
Data from ARCQ, February-March 1986.

Table 19.2 Revenues of Community Television Associations in Quebec[a]

	1981-82 (20 associations)		1984-85 (37 associations)	
	Amount $	Percent of Total	Amount $	Percent of Total
Non-governmental				
Local fundraising	257,429	21.0	493,000	25.6
Cable contribution	53,862	4.3	198,430	10.3
Total	311,291	25.3	691,430	35.9
Governmental				
Community Media Assistance Program (COMAP)	495,000	40.4	697,000	36.2
Other Quebec govt. programs	169,400	13.8	292,230	15.2
Federal programs	249,760	20.5	244,400	12.7
Total	914,160	74.7	1,233,630	64.1
Combined Total:	1,225,451	100.0	1,925,060	100.0

Note: a. Fiscal year ends 31 March.
Source: Regroupement des organismes communautaires du Québec (ROCCQ), February-March 1986.

Type B stations are permitted an average of only four minutes of advertising an hour, with no more than six minutes in any given hour. These are stations that share their local market with private stations.

While advertising revenues of $1,338,885 were important for the community radio sector in 1984-85, they were the equivalent of only a little more than one percent of the 1984 advertising revenues of private commercial stations in the province, which were $118,300,000. Still, they were the most important source of increased revenue to the expanding community radio sector between 1982 and 1985.

The CRTC only began authorizing advertising on community radio stations in 1972 and at that time limited it to: a mention of the sponsor, with brief description of his products; classified advertisements paid by individuals; and information provided by community non-profit organizations. The restrictions were modified in 1983. In 1985 the Commission lifted the restrictions and allowed broadcasting of ordinary commercial messages, including national advertising. It recommended, however, that community broadcasters

> . . . continue to seek funding for their operations from a diversity of sources, particularly from within the community, as a means to ensure the continued interest and support of the community and to lessen the effect of advertising on programming.[8]

Up to now the CRTC has prohibited advertising altogether on community television channels, though some have been running commercial messages anyway. At the time of this Task Force inquiry, the Commission proposed to permit three types of advertising — sponsorship, credit and contra. A commercial message that mentions the sponsor of an event shown on community TV and the sponsor's products is *sponsorship*; acknowledgement of the providers of direct financial assistance to community programming, together with their products and services, is *credit*; and acknowledgement of goods and services provided free for use in community programming is *contra*.

Cable Operator's Contribution

The cable operator's contribution may be to either audio or television community broadcasting by cable; in practice it is almost entirely to the programming of the local community television channel. In arriving at the 1975 cable regulations, the CRTC first considered the idea of requiring cable operators to commit 10 percent of gross subscriber revenue to the support of the community channel. In the end, the CRTC settled for "a reasonable percentage of their gross revenue", but said it would keep 10 percent in mind as a useful yardstick for assessing performance when licence renewal time came around.[9]

The CRTC recognized that some of the cable company's contribution to the operation of the community channel "will be required for facilities or hardware". But "the Commission will expect the major portion to be spent on the variable cost of producing community programs".[10] Table 19.2 shows that in 1984-85, 10 percent of community TV association revenue in Quebec came from the cable operator contribution. This was an improvement on the four percent in 1981-82. Comparable figures are not available for English-language community channels.

Federal Government Support

Federal financial support for community broadcasting includes aid to Native Peoples' broadcasting, the tax-spending embodied in charitable treatment of community broadcasting organizations, job-creation programs to which those who wish to work in community radio have access, and other federal social and cultural programs which may indirectly aid community broadcasting.

Tables 19.1 and 19.2 show the federal share in support of Quebec community radio and community television respectively. In community radio in Quebec the federal contribution dropped slightly, from $386,522 in 1981-82 to $383,330 in 1984-85.

In community television in Quebec federal programs provided $249,760 in 1981-82 and $244,400 in 1984-85, again a slight reduction by contrast with the increasing support for community television from the Quebec government and other sources.

The federal programs dropped from 20.5 percent of total support in the first year to 12.7 percent in the second.

Provincial Government Support

Quebec is the only province with a development program of aid to community media. Quebec's assistance began with the Community Media Assistance Program (COMAP) of 1973, further elaborated in the 1979 development policy for community media. The program covers community newspapers as well as the electronic media. One of its objectives is "stabilizing the financing of community media".[11]

The program, administered by the Quebec Department of Communications, assists community publishing and broadcasting organizations as well as the associations that support them. Support takes the form of technical advice and expertise as well as grants. The program requires that "applicants must demonstrate a desire to be financially self-sufficient".[12]

Community radio stations and community television associations in Quebec have both roughly doubled in number in the past five years. In the latest year shown in Tables 19.1 and 19.2, the province's direct and indirect programs of aid accounted for 30 percent of community radio station revenue and 51 percent of community television association revenue.

Over the past five years COMAP has provided $6 million to community radio, which was about double the amount given to community television. According to Quebec participants in the community broadcasting sector, the reasons for the preference for radio were: the denial by the courts in 1977 of the Quebec claim to jurisdiction over cable television, the technical and physical flexibility of radio, and lower production costs and larger audiences for community radio.

Funding provided to ARCQ and ROCCQ, the representative organizations of community radio and television in Quebec, has remained at about the same level for the past five years. These organizations serve as intermediaries between community broadcasters and provincial and federal government departments, represent their membership at CRTC hearings, undertake studies on policy issues affecting community broadcasters, provide training courses and facilities, and send participants to international meetings.. Like the federal government and other provincial governments, Quebec also has job-creation and other community and individual assistance programs which provide support to the community broadcasting sector. The number of programs and the amounts paid vary from year to year.

A number of Quebec government departments and agencies occasionally solicit the assistance of community radio and television to co-produce local or regional programs on health, the environment, education, social problems or other areas in which the government provides services.

Community Support

Community broadcasters are essentially voluntary membership organizations and look to membership fees for part of their support. Campaigns for membership and donations take the form of radiothons and telethons, other types of benefit performance and activity, and mail campaigns. Some community broadcasting groups are helped from time to time by the local United Way campaign.

Northern and Native community television and radio stations depend heavily for funds on such local activities as bingos and on-air campaigns. Student radio is usually supported by grants from the Students' Union at each university or a levy collected along with student fees.

Community interest groups which participate in community radio and television often help support programming through service contracts or sponsorship, in the manner of the Quebec government agencies mentioned above which co-produce programs. Sometimes municipal governments and school boards make small grants to community broadcasters who have been encouraged by CRTC guidelines to cover local government and provide a forum for discussion of local issues.

Tables 19.1 and 19.2 indicate that in Quebec about 12 percent of the revenue of community radio and 25 percent of the revenue of community television come from community fundraising of one kind or another.

Policy Issues and Recommendations

The Task Force believes the community sector of broadcasting should play an increasingly important role as a forum of community expression and a primary means of access to the broadcasting system for ethnic, cultural and minority groups. In large centres several groups may be able to operate many community broadcasting services, each focused on a particular range of interests. In smaller centres with limited resources, individual licensees will have to provide for the diverse needs of whole communities. In both cases, the public gains from an increase in the diversity of sources of information, entertainment and opinion in the world of broadcasting.

Community broadcasting has proved its worth to listeners and viewers in many diverse circumstances. It has been encouraged by the regulatory authority, the CRTC, which has helped develop its status as a distinct alternative service. Financially, community broadcasting continues to be a struggle for survival, but a wide range of sources of support has been found. It is our view that the community broadcasting sector has won the right to be accorded formal status alongside the public and private sectors in the Broadcasting Act, and that the public interest would be served by such recognition. Recognition would give new impetus to the growth of community broadcasting and help consolidate its unique position among other broadcasting services.

Recommendation

The Canadian broadcasting system should be recognized as comprising not-for-profit community elements as well as the "public and private elements" already acknowledged in the 1968 *Broadcasting Act*.

Regulatory Regime

The CRTC deserves special recognition for the manner in which it has gradually shaped and fostered the development of the community broadcasting sector in both radio and television. We wish to endorse the Commission's view that the sector should remain not-for-profit (as underlined in our legislative recommendation above), and a source of distinct types of programming so that it will contribute to the 'many voices' of broadcasting. The time has now come for further regulation to put community television on a firmer footing.

The *Regroupement des organismes communautaires de communication du Québec* (ROCCQ), representing some 25 community television organizations in Quebec, made a strong presentation to this Task Force urging a licensing procedure for community television associations. The group made the point that lack of licensing raises questions of legal responsibility for broadcasts. Cable operators have felt inhibited from granting access because of their legal responsibility for content.

The ROCCQ would like to see each community TV association have official beneficial and legal status distinct from that of cable operators. As licensees, they would become repositories of the public trust granted them by the CRTC and would be expected to live up to the responsibilities of community broadcasters set out from time to time by the regulatory authority after public hearings. Cable operators would be expected to assure them appropriate access to the community channel. We concur with the ROCCQ proposal.

Recommendation

The CRTC should license community television associations on terms similar to those developed for community radio stations. As in the case of community radio, with the distinction between Type A and Type B stations, more latitude of operation should be given to associations working in communities where there are no local TV services.

We also agree with ROCCQ's view that there should be regulation governing the relationship between the community TV organizations and the cable operators who provide the community channel. The cable operators provide material assistance in the form of technical and studio facilities, and sometimes in the form of technical staffing.

Recommendation

> The CRTC should regulate the relations between licensed community television broadcasters and cable system operators, recognizing the rights and responsibilities of community broadcasters. Other than those currently exempted by reason of size, the regulations should include the existing obligation of cable system operators to contribute to the communities they are licensed to serve through material support of the community channel. The CRTC should keep a record of the contributions to community channels of operators throughout the country.

In many parts of Canada, the cable system operators themselves provide all or part of the programming on the community channel. The Task Force recognizes the value of this service, but considers it to be a broadcasting operation, distinct from the mere delivery of outside television signals and other services, and bound by the same rules as all other broadcasters.

The Commission should create a special class of licence for the operators of the community channel in cable systems. Regardless of whether the licence is held by the operator of the local cable system or by a community group, there should continue to be special criteria applicable to such licences. Restrictions on access to commercial revenue would, therefore, continue and, more important, the focus would continue to be on the community access role of this channel as a means of complementing existing broadcasting services. Given the special character of the community channel, the licensing procedures should be as simple as possible, consistent with ensuring that licensees are effectively responsible for carrying out this special role in Canadian broadcasting.

Recommendation

> Cable system operators who themselves program community channels should be licensed separately as community broadcasters.

It should be made clear, also, that the cable operator should not enjoy a monopoly of community programming. Situations may arise in which local community organizations are not satisfied with the service offered by the cable system's broadcasting affiliate and may wish to provide their own community-channel services, possibly on a part-time basis.

Recommendation

> The CRTC should when necessary provide for the licensing of community TV associations in addition to the local cable operator in communities where the cable system already offers a community service.

Because of the cultural and ethnic diversity of many of Canada's communities, policy and regulation governing the community sector of both radio and television must be flexible enough to provide fair access and representation to different sectors of the community served by the licensee.

Recommendation

The licences of all community radio and television broadcasters should recognize the need of fair access for various ethnic, cultural, interest and opinion groups. Regulation should cover both the case of large metropolitan centres, where several community broadcast organizations need right of access for their services, and the case of smaller centres where a single licensee may have to provide for the diverse access requirements of the community.

The Task Force agrees with the CRTC policy of licensing low power community radio and television stations in remote areas and believes this practice should continue. The CRTC has also encouraged the establishment of services in these communities by keeping licensing procedure as simple as possible.

Access to CBC Transmitters

Access to CBC transmitters in sparsely settled areas has also been a means for local community radio and television broadcasters to reach audiences. We believe this advantage should be extended to community broadcasting associations of the official-language minorities — francophones outside Quebec and anglophones in Quebec. One of the main complaints these groups have made to the Task Force is that the CBC programming available to the official-language minorities lacks local content and flavour. They could very well supply this for themselves during sections of the CBC network schedule which are of little local interest.

Recommendation

The CBC should provide access, when circumstances permit, to licensed, official-language-minority community broadcasters on terms similar to those established for aboriginal groups in northern areas.

Government Policy and Financial Support

Just as community broadcasting should have recognition in legislation and appropriate support in regulation, so it should receive attention in government administration. At the federal level a number of departments and agencies have, or may have, an interest in encouraging community broadcasting but there should be a focal point for the coordination of policy and for study and research related to community broadcasting policy. The cultural sector of the Department of Communications could well be the most appropriate place to locate such a centre of responsibility. It would also serve as a reference point for members of the public interested in community broadcasting. The establishment of such a focal point should not detract from the substantial responsibilities and interests of other departments in community broadcasting. The approach of provincial and territorial governments and local authorities to community broadcasting is also critical to its success, since it is essentially local broadcasting.

Our role is restricted to making recommendations to the federal government but we commend the Quebec example for study elsewhere. We believe it is desirable for federal and provincial governments and the regulatory authority to co-operate in the development of the community sector, particularly in the matter of trying to obtain adequate financial support.

Our findings make it clear that the community sector is sorely in need of more financial support, indeed cannot hope to achieve the level of public service we feel it should without additional backing. We endorse the proposals of the CRTC to introduce a limited amount of advertising on the community channel. The proposed limitations could perhaps be made more liberal in the case of community TV associations in places where there are no private TV services in the same language. We believe, however, that nationwide study of existing financial arrangements and possible options, followed by intergovernmental consultation, are necessary to try to establish a more adequate financial base for community broadcasting.

Recommendation

The federal government should establish a focal point in the Department of Communications for coordination of funding, grants and programs which have a direct bearing on the aims and objectives we have established for community broadcasting. The federal, provincial and territorial governments should consult on appropriate measures to develop the community broadcasting sector.

Making the Community Sector Flourish

We do not underestimate the difficulties of implementing the principles we have put forward for community radio and television. By definition, this is a sector of voluntary initiative in which individuals and voluntary groups gain access to broadcasting. It will always be dependent for support on sweat equity and knocking on doors. Full subsidization by the state at the federal, provincial or local government levels would be tantamount to a simple extension of the public sector. It would doubtless be rejected by taxpayers and, in any case, it would undermine the self-reliance which is essential to a healthy community broadcasting sector. Complete reliance on advertising, on the other hand, would soon make community broadcasting merely an additional element in the commercial sector.

Nevertheless, sources of support are available. In television, cable operators have a responsibility to support community television as a social premium for their privilege of holding a licence which gives them a monopoly over cable delivery in their area. A number of government support programs at the various levels are available. Businesses and voluntary organizations can often be persuaded of the advantage of supporting community radio or TV programming. Although some permanent staff is needed, volunteers can produce much of the programming — indeed that is what gives community television its special character.

In an era when the "global village" has become a cliché in communications, community broadcasting is at the other end of the scale from the world-spanning vision of communication the phrase implies. We might see it as a form of appropriate technology for the world of broadcasting, providing an antidote to the 'production values' of American broadcasting.

In many small communities, the community station may be the only local media outlet. In these places, there are no daily or weekly or even monthly newspapers, no movie houses, and rarely a theatre where touring companies give live performances. Local broadcasting in small communities is the last link in the economic chain of the system, drawing upon the smallest local resources and enjoying the least amount of regional or national advertising support. While we seek to balance and make more equitable the provision of broadcasting service to all Canadians, regardless of where they live, we also recognize the need to preserve and maintain the provision of indigenous local service. This is one of the major challenges facing our broadcasting system; community broadcasters will have to play a major role in meeting it. However, we recognize the justice of the relaxed rules regarding community channels in the smallest cable television systems, those with fewer than 3,000 subscribers.

Community broadcasting is hardly less important in our growing urban areas where individuals risk being swallowed up in the conformity and anonymity of the mass. Here, community broadcasting can serve to preserve peoples' cultural heritage and sense of belonging to recognizable local communities and interest groups. In a sense, it is a matter of restoring the close and rewarding human relations of the old-fashioned village within the distant and impersonal contacts of the global village.

Since this chapter was completed, the CRTC issued new regulations on cable and their projected new regulations on television. Both documents cover some of the matters discussed here.

Notes

1. Canada, Royal Commission on Broadcasting, (Fowler Commission) *Report* (Ottawa: Queen's Printer, 1957), p. 84.
2. Canadian Radio-television and Telecommunications Commission, *Review of Community Radio*, CRTC Public Notice 1985-194 (Ottawa: CRTC, 1985), p. 9.
3. Canadian Radio-television and Telecommunications Commission, *Policies Respecting Broadcasting Receiving Undertakings (Cable Television)* (Ottawa: CRTC, 1975), p. 3.
4. Ibid., p. 4.
5. Ibid.
6. Canadian Radio-television and Telecommunications Commission, *Proposed Regulations Respecting Cable Television Broadcasting Receiving Undertakings*, CRTC Public Notice 1986-27 (Ottawa: CRTC, 1986), p. 25.
7. Canada, Department of Communications and Quebec, Department of Communications, *The Future of French-Language Television*, Federal-Provincial Committee Report (Ottawa: The Department; Quebec: The Department, May 1985), p. 75.
8. CRTC, Public Notice 1985-194, p. 15.
9. CRTC, *Policies Respecting Broadcasting*, p. 4
10. Ibid.
11. Quebec, Department of Communications, *Community Media Development Policy* (Quebec City: The Department, 1979), p. 20.
12. Quebec, Department of Communications, *COMAP Information File* (Quebec City: The Department, 1985–1986).

Part VII

MINORITY BROADCASTING

Introduction

Any review of Canadian broadcasting requires special attention to the native people of Canada, the francophone and anglophone minorities, and the 3.2 million Canadians of diverse ethnic origin. By its very nature as a mass medium, broadcasting has not served minorities well. This is changing, however, and broadcasting policy must be bold and imaginative in order to stimulate further change.

Already disadvantaged in other spheres, minorities have perhaps the most to lose through exposure to the homogenizing impact of most broadcast programming. If our minorities are not given the opportunity to become full and active participants in broadcasting, all Canadians stand to lose much of what makes the cultural and linguistic fabric of this country distinctive.

We discuss the three major minority groups in the order of their arrival in what is today Canada: aboriginal peoples, official-language minorities, and minorities of diverse linguistic and ethnic origin. Since this Report is essentially about English and French broadcasting, with a special chapter devoted to the particular characteristics of broadcasting in French, we will only touch lightly on the two official-language minorities inside and outside Quebec in this chapter.

Chapter 20

Native Peoples

Native Peoples

There are many reasons why broadcasting policy should recognize the special needs of the more than 500,000 status Indian, non-status Indian, Metis, and Inuit, the aboriginal peoples of Canada. Unlike other minorities, they have no other lands of origin in which their languages and cultures are protected.

Native people have special rights by virtue of their aboriginal status. These rights, now enshrined in the Canadian Constitiution, are a part of the laws, customs and treaties of the land. Although not fully defined, aboriginal rights are certain to include the protection and enhancement of native languages and culture.

Among the more eloquent and passionate briefs to the Task Force were the submissions of northern native broadcasting groups. Those of us who were able to meet with their representatives in Frobisher Bay, Yellowknife, Whitehorse and elsewhere were impressed by their vitality and their recent broadcasting achievements.

We will discuss broadcasting policy in relation to the new native broadcasting initiatives in the North and suggest steps that could be taken to foster a stronger native presence in broadcasting throughout Canada.

Development of Native Broadcasting Policies and Services

Several events in the late 1970s and early 1980s helped shape the direction of native broadcasting. Most significant was the introduction of satellite television to the North after the federal government approved the CBC's Accelerated Coverage Plan (ACP) in 1974. The plan was designed to bring the national service to underserved pockets of Canadians, many in remote areas. The ACP made no provision for local or regional program production. This angered the indigenous northern population and prompted one leader to comment: "The introduction of television has meant the last refuge of Inuit culture, the home, has been invaded by an outside culture."[1] It did not matter to most indigenous northerners whether the programming was Canadian or American — it was all foreign.

Nevertheless, most of the community welcomed southern television, although some protested. Organizations like the Inuit Tapirisat of Canada and the Northern Quebec Inuit Association mounted successful lobbies for native programming services.

Following two highly successful Anik B experiments involving Inuit in Arctic Quebec and the Northwest Territories, the CRTC's Committee on the Extension of Services to Northern and Remote Communities (the Therrien Committee) set the stage for future northern and native broadcasting activities. The Therrien Report recommended that federal funding be provided for the development of native broadcasting networks in order to fulfil Canada's obligation to provide opportunity for its native peoples to preserve the use of their languages and to maintain and develop their cultures. In 1981, the CRTC licensed a federally subsidized Inuit television network sharing a satellite transponder leased by the CBC. Also licensed was a joint application from Yukon Indians and the Dene of the Northwest Territories for a satellite radio network in the northwest. The same year, in order to broaden programming choice for all northerners, the Commission approved a licence for Canadian Satellite Communications Inc. (CANCOM). The CRTC instructed CANCOM to carry native radio and television services and to provide the necessary audio and video uplink facilities in northern locations suitable to the independent native production groups. Today, CANCOM distributes radio programming produced by two native communications societies in Northwestern Canada. However, the company has not fulfilled commitments it made in 1981 as a condition of licence to provide a video uplink suitable for native-produced programming and to substitute up to 10 hours per week of native-produced television programming on its schedule.

In 1983, following consultation with northern broadcasters and representatives from 16 native organizations, the federal government announced the Northern Broadcasting Policy and the Northern Native Broadcast Access Program (NNBAP). The NNBAP, a $40.3 million fund over four years, was designed to stimulate native-language radio and television production in 13 northern regions. The Northern Broadcasting Policy directed existing northern broadcasters to distribute the native-language programming on their systems.

Today, three years after the unveiling of the Northern Broadcasting Policy and the NNBAP, there are 13 independent native societies producing mainly native-language programming in the two territories and the northern regions of seven provinces, as illustrated in Figure 20.1. Together they produce approximately 10 hours of television and 150 hours of radio each week to a total native population of about 200,000. By the time the NNBAP expires in 1987, it will have created employment for more than 300 people, some in communities where unemployment rates average about 50 percent. To date, independent audience surveys have been positive: native people are listening to and watching the programming produced by participating societies, and they are asking for more.

While the NNBAP has begun to foster the development of regional networks, community radio is the mainstay of native broadcasting. Most community stations rely on volunteer labour and local fundraising. Programming, usually in native dialects, has a distinctive local flavour, often a mixture of music, personal messages, local news and radio bingo. There are more than 100 native community radio stations across Canada, many in rural and remote communities with populations of less than 1,000, a few in larger centres in the South. Native community radio is particularly strong in Quebec where funding assistance is provided by the provincial Ministry of Communications.

The only conventional broadcaster producing significant amounts of native-language programming or native-oriented programming is the CBC Northern Service. In the Northwest Territories and northern Quebec, the Northern Service produces radio programming in eight indigenous languages.

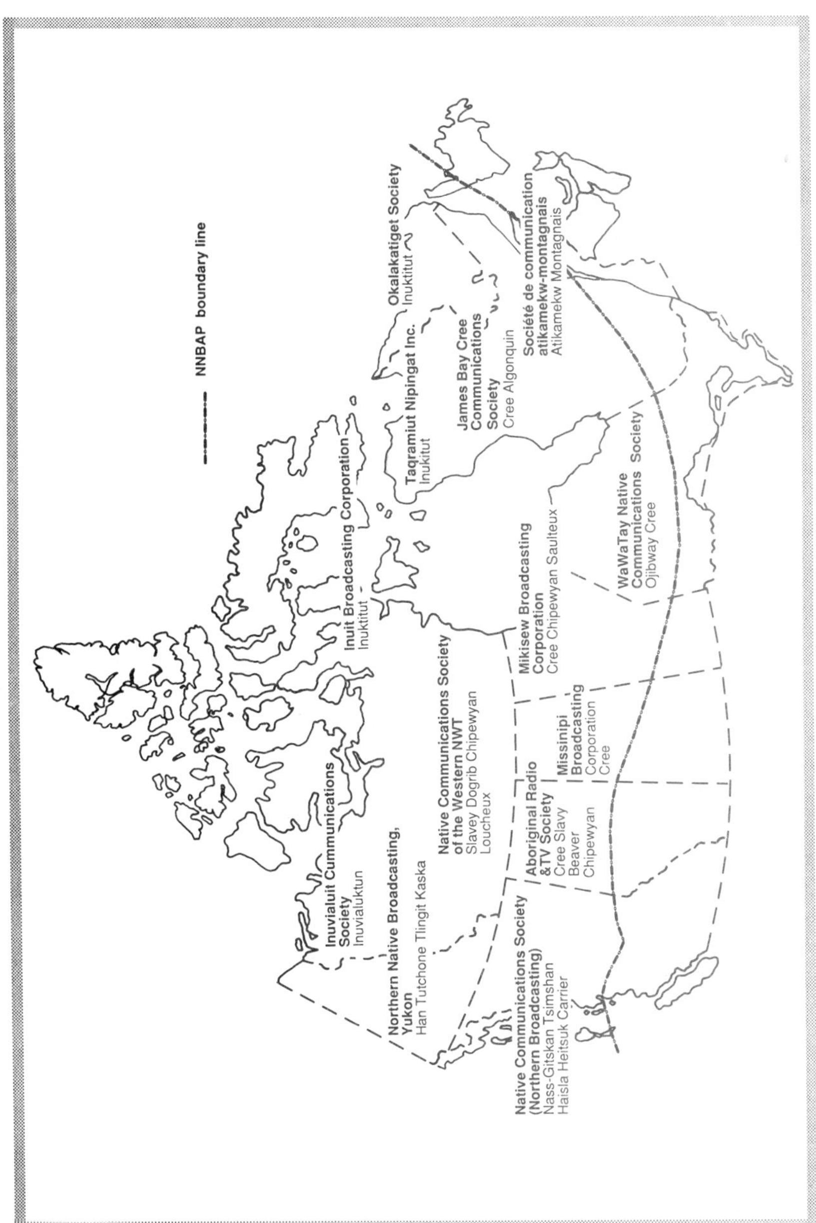

Figure 20.1 Societies and Linguistic Regions Funded by the Northern Native Broadcast Access Program (NNBAP)

Source: Native Citizens Directorate Department of the Secretary of State, Ottawa, 1985

Issues

Native-language Broadcasting Legislation

Language is regarded by many native people as the cornerstone of their culture. Some consider the protection and enhancement of their languages as an aboriginal right.

In their submissions to the Task Force, the majority of native communications societies suggested changing the *Broadcasting Act* to give indigenous languages a status equivalent to that of Canada's two official languages. Their briefs, and research conducted for the Task Force, pointed to a number of precedents in support of this request. For example:

- The Report of the Royal Commission on Bilingualism and Biculturalism defined non-official languages as any language other than English, French, Indian or Eskimo;
- CRTC Public Notice 1984-237 and Public Notice 1985-139 defined ethnic programming as including programming in a language other than English, French and the aboriginal languages;
- The territorial Task Force on Aboriginal Languages has recommended that Chipewyan, Loucheux, Dogrib, Slavey, Inuktitut and Inuvialuktun be recognized as official languages in the Northwest Territories, along with English and French.

Aboriginal groups want to entrench native-language services in a new Broadcasting Act in order to place native-language broadcasting on a solid foundation. They argue that without the weight of legislation coupled with long-term fiscal commitments native-language broadcasting services may not survive, despite well-intentioned federal policies and regulations. They point to cutbacks totalling more than $4.5 million to the NNBAP between 1984 and 1986 as an example of their present vulnerability.

The survival of native identity is at stake in the language issue. The cards have been stacked against native people for some time. Ethnologist Michael Foster estimates that only three of the 53 aboriginal languages spoken in Canada have an excellent chance of survival; 13 are moderately endangered; and eight are on the verge of extinction.[2] Native leaders point to the proliferation of English mass media, especially television, as a major contributor to the decline. Rosemarie Kuptana, now president of the Inuit Broadcasting Corporation, underscored this concern with the following statement at a CRTC public hearing in December 1982:

> We might liken the onslaught of southern television, and the absence of native television, to the neutron bomb. This is the bomb that kills the people but leaves the building standing. Neutron-bomb television is the kind of television that destroys the soul of a people but leaves the shell of a people walking around. The pressure, especially on our children, to join the invading culture and language . . . is explosively powerful.[3]

Native people in many parts of Canada are determined to rejuvenate their languages and cultures through broadcasting and other institutional measures. There are signs of success as native people assume more control over their own education and social and economic programs. As we note in Chapter 6, entrenching native-language services in the Broadcasting Act would be consistent with aboriginal rights principles and with a pluralistic philosophy that encourages the expression of aboriginal identity. Native languages embody a part of the special cultural heritage of Canada to be protected and strengthened.

Recommendation

> The broadcasting act should affirm the right of native peoples to broadcasting services in aboriginal languages considered to be representative where numbers warrant and to the extent public funds permit.

The term 'representative' is used to suggest broadcasting service in the dominant aboriginal dialects of those aboriginal people concerned with the preservation of their languages.

Native Broadcasting and the CBC

The Northern Broadcasting Policy and NNBAP have raised questions about the role of the CBC and its responsibilities in native broadcasting.

The CBC has requested clarification of its mandate here, given high expectations at a time of budgetary restraint and it argues that its present mandate and the limited capacity of its distribution systems severely restrict the amount of native-language radio and television it can carry. The Corporation states that it cannot substitute independently produced native programming for key network and regional programming without compromising the integrity of the national service. In the CBC's view, key programming includes foreign programs on the network as well as CBC-produced native-language services, such as those broadcast in the Northwest Territories and northern Quebec. In a recent submission to the CRTC, the CBC elaborated on this position:

> Ideally, CBC should provide its own native programming proportionate to the population served. Independent native communication societies could provide alternative services so that the public benefits from choice, differing media perspectives and the availability of a full CBC service comparable to other regions of the country.[4]

In submissions to the Task Force, native broadcasters stressed the importance of the CBC's role in the distribution of programs produced by their societies. One suggested that the CBC should leave all native-language production to the independent native societies whose costs are considerably cheaper. Most native societies, however, argue that the CBC should distribute independent native programming as a first priority and, as a second priority, produce native programming of its own that complements programming by independent native broadcasters.

The Inuit Broadcasting Corporation's *Position Paper on Northern Broadcasting (1985)* sheds light on the broader policy implications of the debate over roles:

> IBC is providing, within the public broadcasting system, a service the CBC has admitted it cannot provide. Our role is tied to the devolution of the CBC. We see ourselves not as a private sector production house of the CBC Northern Service, but rather, as an equal partner in the provision of one northern public broadcasting service. Our participation serves to strengthen public broadcasting in our homelands. It is time we received due recognition as an integral element of the public broadcasting system.[5]

The Task Force is sympathetic to the compelling arguments of both the CBC and the native broadcasting societies. Both positions must be accommodated in the long-term.

As a national cultural priority, the provision of native-language services should clearly be a part of the mandate of the national public broadcaster. Furthermore, the Task Force believes that there should be an autonomous native-language service within the CBC, as there are now distinct French and English services. We believe that this would give native-language broadcasting a much higher profile and a stronger foundation within the CBC.

Recommendation

> The broadcasting act should give the CBC a clear mandate to provide broadcasting services in representative aboriginal languages where numbers warrant and as public funds become available. Furthermore, we recommend the CBC establish an autonomous aboriginal-language service, as there are now distinct French and English services.

While the Task Force sees the CBC as an important provider of native-language services, it should not be considered the sole producer. Independent native communications societies should be an integral part of the public broadcasting system with an equally important role in production. Independent and CBC-produced native-language programming should be complementary. The programming strength of the independent native communications societies lies in their close ties to communities — each has its own board and each is responsible to the people of a region. The native broadcasting societies should be independent of native political organizations, as they are now under the Northern Native Broadcast Access Plan (NNBAP).

Distribution of Native Programming

Program distribution is one of the most pressing issues facing northern native broadcasters. The NNBAP, for example, is primarily a production fund for independent native communication societies. Distribution is dependent on northern broadcasters complying with the 'fair access' principle of the Northern Broadcasting Policy, which states: "Northern native people should have fair access to northern broadcasting distribution systems to maintain and develop their cultures and languages."

Although each NNBAP-funded native society has some arrangement for borrowing time on the distribution systems of northern broadcasters, there are major problems. Often, native radio and television producers must contend with poor time slots, pre-emptions, sudden schedule changes, and network coverage that does not reach all the native communities in a particular region. In a brief to the Task Force, Marion Telop of Northern Native Broadcasting, Yukon, voiced the frustration of many:

> There is one continuing obstacle that jeopardizes our success. That is "guaranteed access" by aboriginal broadcasters to existing public and private distribution systems in Northern Canada. The new policies assumed native groups would have access to the nation's distribution systems. . . . We have learned a very hard lesson, what "should be" does not necessarily mean what "shall be".[6]

Broadcasters who have been requested to provide time on their networks have raised legitimate concerns of their own. The CBC, which provides distribution for 10 of the 13 native societies, contends that it has neither the mandate nor the flexibility in its distribution systems to carry more independent native programming than at present. In the provinces, CBC regional distribution systems are almost entirely land-based, serving large geographic areas that contain many more non-native communities than native communities. CBC's terrestrial systems cannot readily be adapted to distribute native-language programming only to predominantly native communities. The CBC's satellite channels serving the Arctic are not dedicated to the North; their primary function is to relay national network television programming across the country for regional distribution. Other northern broadcasters have raised concerns about editorial control over native programming and some fear an outcry from non-native audiences in their service areas. A few private broadcasters want to be compensated for access time.

The CRTC has taken a flexible regulatory approach. It has set benchmark figures of 20 hours per week for radio and five hours per week for television, indicating that it is the responsibility of all broadcasters, private and public, to provide independent native producers with regional access at "appropriate and convenient times for the intended audiences". Preferring industry self-regulation, the CRTC has proposed that an Action Committee deal with native distribution problems as they arise.

The long-term solution is to place all independent and CBC native-language production on a separate satellite distribution system with local transmitters in each predominantly native community. The CBC estimates the minimum cost of a satellite distribution system dedicated to native broadcasting to be approximately $23.3 million capital and $5.5 million in annual operating funds, based on 1984 dollars.[7] However, these costs cannot be justified at this time, given the restricted market and the relatively small volume of programming anticipated even with the most optimistic production projections.

After considering a variety of options, the Task Force supports, as an interim measure, the suggestion made by the majority of northern native broadcasters that a dedicated satellite transponder be shared by northern native communications societies and the CBC Northern Service. When coordinated by the CBC's satellite distribution control centre in Toronto, the service could relieve many of the distribution bottlenecks faced by the societies operating north of 60°. It might also provide an alternative means of distribution for some of the societies serving the northern regions of the western provinces where distribution options are very limited. A dedicated northern transponder would give the CBC Northern Service greater flexibility for expanding northern regional television programming. As suggested by the Northern Native Broadcasting Committee of the CRTC, increased allocations to the NNBAP for distribution are necessary in order to cover the estimated $2 million to $3 million annual costs of the shared-transponder option.

Recommendation

> As production levels warrant and as public funds become available, a separate satellite distribution system should be established to carry native-language programming produced by independent native communications societies and the CBC. As an interim step, we recommend that native communications societies and the CBC Northern Service share a satellite transponder dedicated to serving northern communities. Furthermore, we recommend that the Government of Canada increase allocations to the NNBAP in order to cover costs associated with the shared transponder option.

Until CBC and independent native-language production levels warrant a separate satellite distribution system, the distribution of programming produced by the independent native communication societies will have to follow a patchwork pattern for a number of years. Because these services are a matter of public broadcasting policy and a priority, the CBC must continue to bear the largest share of distribution. Provincial public broadcasters could become more involved following TV Ontario's outstanding example in bringing radio and television programming produced by Wawatay Native Communications Society to the Cree and Ojibway of Northern Ontario. Private broadcasters should be viewed as a last resort in the absence of other options. However, the Task Force concurs with the Committee on Northern Native Broadcasting of the CRTC (Public Notice CRTC 1985-274) in urging CANCOM to fulfil its licence commitment to substitute native-produced television programming on its schedule as it becomes available.

Native Broadcasting in the South

There is little broadcasting activity among the majority of native people who live in the southern regions of the provinces and who do not benefit from any programs on the scale of the NNBAP supporting production. Members of the Task Force are concerned about what may be inequitable treatment.

When the Northern Broadcasting Policy was formulated, it was argued that support should be concentrated in the North where native language use was strongest, where natives were most affected by the introduction of southern television services, and where the native population formed a majority in many communities. The policy has created rifts in some native organizations, however, particularly in the western provinces where the artificial northern boundary line (see Figure 20.1) makes little sense. In British Columbia, for example, there is reason to support the view that 'North' should begin just beyond the first range of mountains north of Vancouver.

The broadcasting needs of native people in the South may well be different from those in the North, requiring an approach different from the NNBAP. According to a recent urban Indian media survey,[8] native people in the South may place a higher priority on representation and portrayal in mainstream English and French media than they do on regional broadcasting services in aboriginal languages. The Government of Manitoba suggests that priority be given to increasing native participation in southern media.

Recommendation

> A research and consultation process should be carried out among aboriginal people in the South in order to identify regional needs and to establish a general policy of native broadcasting for the whole country.

Since local native FM radio is not well developed in the South, except in Quebec where subsidies are available, our recommendations on community radio are particularly relevant to the southern native population (see Chapter 19).

Other Issues

Native representatives have raised several other concerns. Taqramiut Nipingat Inc. pointed to the fact that eight Inuit communities in Arctic Quebec, all with populations of less than 500, were unable to receive CBC services except by short wave or in some instances by means of unreliable, community-owned reception and transmission facilities. Research conducted for the Task Force indicated that there are many other native communities — 18 in northwestern Ontario alone — that are without the national broadcasting service.[9] Equally important, many of these small communities, especially in the western provinces, are also denied the local and regional native access opportunities made possible by the CBC. Owing to cutbacks and budget restraint, the CBC has been forced to curtail activities under its Accelerated Coverage Plan and is therefore unable to extend services to many of the smaller, isolated native communities.

Recommendation

> In extending the Accelerated Coverage Plan, the CBC should give special consideration to serving isolated aboriginal communities that request service, regardless of size.

In their presentation to the Task Force, Native Communications Inc. of Manitoba highlighted another concern expressed by many native broadcasters:

> It is certainly high time that Native people and Native broadcasters be permitted to participate in major communications decision-making which so deeply affects the languages and cultures of the Native aboriginal people of Canada.[10]

In other presentations to the Task Force and in recent briefs to the CRTC, native communication societies were united in their appeals for more effective consultation and native representation at the highest levels of the CRTC, the CBC and other federal bodies that affect broadcasting policy. In this regard, the Task Force itself did not escape criticism for its lack of native representation.

The Task Force agrees that it is desirable to have native representation in federal institutions dealing with broadcasting. As a first priority, however, we have made recommendations to strengthen native broadcasting institutions themselves. We have also made a general recommendation designed to increase representation for women and minority groups, including natives, in mainstream broadcasting.

Native broadcasters said they need more money and cooperation from both federal and provincial authorities in a number of critical areas. Training was singled out as a high priority. Because there are no media schools in the North and few trained native journalists, producers, technicians or managers, the success of present native broadcasting efforts is entirely dependent on grants for training programs. Many native broadcasters expressed fears that recent cutbacks in training funds from the Canada Employment and Immigration Commission would seriously jeopardize present services and future growth.

The Task Force is aware that these problems are being addressed as part of the NNBAP program review. We believe that as long as native-language broadcasting is administered as a departmental program, it will be subject to the vagaries of departmental priorities, budget allocations and bureaucratic bottlenecks.

Recommendation

> Native-language broadcasting should be administered at arm's length from the federal government and should be provided with sufficient funds to cover the cost of all essential related activities such as training. Furthermore, until there are new administrative arrangements, we recommend that no further cutbacks be made to the NNBAP and funding for production training.

The Task Force received many complaints about the cancellation of the English-language native affairs program, *Our Native Land*, after a run of more than 25 years. *Our Native Land* was for many non-native Canadians a window on native affairs and an important bridge to a native perspective on current affairs. The CBC held that, rather than confining native current affairs programming to one time slot each week, it would integrate native stories with its regular programming. But is it a matter of either/or? Would not the native peoples and broadcasting audiences benefit both from special attention to native issues and better aboriginal representation in general programming? The Task Force has decided to refrain from offering program advice but suggests these questions should be considered.

Notes

1. John Amagoalik, *Statement to the Annual Assembly of the Inuit Tapirisat of Canada* (Ottawa: The Inuit Tapirisat, 1980).
2. M. Foster, *Indigenous Languages (by Family) in Canada and Adjoining Areas: Approximative Numbers of Speakers and Chances of Survival*, chart published by the Commissioner of Official Languages (Ottawa: Minister of Supply and Services Canada, 1984).
3. Rosemarie Kuptana, *Inuit Broadcasting Corporation Position Paper on Northern Broadcasting*, Statement made at a CRTC Public Hearing in Hull, December 1, 1982 (Ottawa: Inuit Broadcasting Corporation, 1985), p. 3.
4. Canadian Broadcasting Corporation, *Comments of the Canadian Broadcasting Corporation in Response to CRTC Public Notice 1985-67* (Ottawa: CBC, 1985), p. 11.
5. Inuit Broadcasting Corporation, *Position Paper on Northern Broadcasting*, revised, October 1985 (Ottawa: Inuit Broadcasting Corporation, 1985), p. 19.
6. Northern Native Broadcasting, *Presentation to the Task Force on Broadcasting Policy* (Whitehorse, Yukon: Northern Native Broadcasting, 1985), pp. 5-6.
7. Canadian Broadcasting Corporation, *CBC and Northern Native Access: A Northern Policy and Plan* (Ottawa: CBC, 1984), p. 63.
8. DPA Group Inc., *Native Media Survey* (Ottawa: Department of the Secretary of State, 1985).
9. J. Mark Stiles, "Broadcasting and Canada's Aboriginal Peoples", study prepared for the Task Force on Broadcasting Policy, Ottawa, 1986.
10. Native Communications Inc. and Mikisew Broadcasting Corporation Inc. *CRTC Public Notice 1985-67 Call for Comments Respecting Northern Native Broadcasting* (Thompson, Manitoba: 1985), p. 7.

Chapter 21

Official-language Minorities

Official-language Minorities

According to 1981 census figures, there are about 700,000 French-speaking Canadians outside Quebec and 800,000 English-speaking Canadians in Quebec who comprise the official-language minorities of Canada. In this brief chapter, a number of issues common to both groups are examined. Many of the specific concerns of francophones outside Quebec are reviewed more extensively in Chapter 8.

The term 'official-language minorities' is one of those labels that mean more to government bureaucracy than to the people it is intended to describe. Collectively referred to as official-language minorities, individually they are Franco-Albertans, Franco-Ontarians, Acadians, English Montrealers, Townshippers, English Quebecers, and the like. Their individual identity has much to do with regional cultural heritage as well as with language. What each group wants from broadcasting is more than simply the provision of French-language or English-language services. Each group wants programming that reflects the culture of its community and region. That is the message the official language minorities have delivered to the Task Force.

As a starting point, official-language minorities must have access to public broadcasting services. This is an unresolved problem for many.

The Fédération des franco-colombiens, for example, states that 38 percent of the francophone population in British Columbia is unable to receive Radio-Canada services. Many francophone groups outside the province of Quebec have little or no choice of French-language programming on their cable systems.

Much progress has been made in recent years in extending basic services to official-language minorities across Canada, and this will continue. Radio-Canada reaches about 95 percent of francophone Canadians and, as funds become available to implement the Accelerated Coverage Plan, service will be extended to such communities as Simcoe and Port Elgin in Ontario, Powell River, Vernon and Quesnel in British Columbia and Whitehorse and Yellowknife in the North.

Additional French services are available via satellite and cable systems. Anik C, beaming to Ontario, Quebec, the Maritimes and part of Manitoba, now carries Radio-Québec programming, La Sette (TVFQ-99), TV Ontario and Super-Écran pay television. Anik D, covering the entire country, carries Radio-Canada and the French programming services of CANCOM. Many cable companies, however, argue that the small francophone population does not justify carrying these services. The Fédération des francophones hors Québec is pressing for policy and regulatory changes that would require the cable operators to provide more French services.

Most Quebec anglophones (500,000) live in and around Montreal, where there is a large selection of media available: two television networks, nine radio stations, cable distribution of American networks, TVOntario, an English-language pay-TV channel and four specialized channels. That is, they have a typical metropolitan choice of English-language programming which is considerably greater than the number of French-language choices within Quebec, let alone outside.

But in the case of the CBC, English Montrealers express concern over the flow of talent and budgets away from Montreal to the network headquarters in Toronto. They attribute the decline of CBC drama programming in Montreal to Toronto's appetite for resources. Hence they want the CBC to take greater account of the importance of the anglophone community in Quebec and of its cultural vitality in theatre, music, painting, dance and so on.

The programming choice of anglophone Quebecers outside Montreal is greater than that of francophones outside Quebec. In recent years the CBC has taken steps to improve services to the Eastern Townships and the Gaspé. In briefs to the Task Force, organizations like the Townshippers Association cautioned against further CBC cutbacks that could jeopardize coverage in the region. For them, the CBC provides an essential cultural link with the anglophone community across Canada. The Quebec Farmers Association underscored this point in their submission to the Task Force: "Our need for a sensitive and viable regional English-language CBC is as strong or stronger in 1985 than twenty or forty years ago."[1]

Access to services will be of limited value unless there is local and regional programming to meet the broadcasting needs of the official-language minorities. Both French and English minority groups put forward convincing arguments that this would require much strengthened CBC regional services.

As we have seen in Chapter 8, the Task Force received more than a dozen briefs from francophone groups outside Quebec calling for an end to what they saw as Radio-Canada's almost total disregard of the regions. Brief after brief described Radio-Canada as being dominated by Montreal in programming, resource allocation and decision-making. Citing audience surveys showing a low proportion of francophones tuned to Radio-Canada in the regions, some groups questioned the relevance of Radio-Canada's present service outside Quebec.

Francophone minorities want Radio-Canada to do more to develop talent in the regions rather than importing talent from Quebec. Only with the development of local broadcasters and performers, they argue, can distinctive regional cultures be reflected locally and to the nation.

With its history of volunteerism and local self-help, community radio holds potential for official-language minorities. Groups like the Fédération des jeunes Canadiens français deserve support in their efforts to establish community radio stations across the country. Other provinces would do well to follow Quebec's example by providing capital assistance to local community radio societies. We recommend in Chapter 19 that the CBC provide access to its transmitters to local official-language minority broadcasting organizations. Provincial broadcasters could assist in the same way.

Note

1. Quebec Farmers' Association, brief submitted to the Task Force on Broadcasting Policy, Quebec, September 1985, p. 2.

Chapter 22

Multicultural Minorities

Multicultural Minorities

The term 'multiculturalism' is an ideal, an expression of the cultural and linguistic plurality of Canada. It reflects the mosaic, rather than the melting-pot nature of the country. As stated in the federal policy of multiculturalism and in the Canadian *Charter of Rights and Freedoms*, it embodies a commitment to the preservation and enhancement of the multicultural heritage of Canadians within the nation's bilingual framework. Multicultural broadcasting, therefore, is broadcasting that reflects the cultural and linguistic diversity of Canada.

Multicultural broadcasting includes, but is not restricted to, ethnic or ethno-cultural broadcasting by and for people who are neither aboriginal Canadians nor members of Canada's two official-language groups. Ethnic broadcasting includes what is known as third-language, heritage-language or multilingual broadcasting in Canada. These terms generally refer to languages other than English, French and aboriginal languages.

Today, one in three Canadians have their roots in cultures other than French or British. In spite of the existence of a national policy of multiculturalism, broadcasting for and by Canada's cultural minorities has remained largely focused on the provision of multilingual services by the private sector. In its hearings across Canada, this Task Force welcomed vigorous participation from more than 15 cultural minority organizations, some representing many varied ethnic communities. We agree with their consensus view that broadcasting policy must embrace the principle of multiculturalism in order to encourage needed change in the direction of reflecting the true diversity of the Canadian people.

Evolution of Multilingual Broadcasting

Multilingual broadcasting in Canada began as immigration increased after the Second World War. From the start, the inclusion of 'foreign-language' programming on regular broadcast schedules was a private sector initiative driven by market demand. By 1958, there were 54 radio stations carrying varying amounts of third-language programming, much of it in German and Italian.

The first licence application for a multilingual AM radio station designed specifically to serve minority-language groups was made in 1957. The station, CFMB in Montreal, was eventually licensed five years later after a lengthy debate by the Board of Broadcast Governors. Sometime afterwards, a second application for a multilingual licence came from the Lombardi group, operators of the Toronto station CHIN. Over the years, regulatory permission to increase the amount of foreign-language content was granted and by 1970 the Lombardi group's licence set third-language levels at 40 percent.

The federal government's 1971 policy of cultural pluralism arising from the *Report of the Royal Commission on Bilingualism and Biculturalism* encouraged the development of multilingual broadcasting services. The Canadian Radio-Television Commission, as it was then called, began to direct more attention to multicultural issues, third-language services in particular.

The increase in multilingual services intensified with the introduction of cable. The Cable Policy set by the CRTC in 1975 called for cable licence holders to provide opportunities for expression by the various ethnic communities in their licensed area. In 1979 CFMT-TV, the first multilingual television station, was licensed in Toronto. Ethnic pay-television services followed in 1982, starting with the licensing of World View in British Columbia.

During this period the licensing pattern began to change. Many cable companies were allowed to devote whole channels to multilingual programming. Multilingual broadcast stations were allowed to carry up to 60 percent third-language programming. The ethnic pay-television services were given third-language and Canadian content quotas based on individual applications rather than on general standards.

With the spread of cable came closed-circuit audio services in third languages. Supported by advertising, these services proved popular. In 1984 the CRTC licensed two discretionary satellite-to-cable network services, Chinavision and Telelatino.

In response to the growing demand for ethnic broadcasting services, and in light of the scarcity of broadcast frequencies in many urban centres and the limited channel capacity of some cable systems, the CRTC embarked on a policy review with a series of public hearings on ethnic broadcasting in 1984 and early 1985. In July 1985 it published *A Broadcasting Policy Reflecting Canada's Linguistic and Cultural Diversity*.

CRTC Policy Reflecting Canada's Linguistic and Cultural Diversity

The CRTC's 1985 policy is a landmark for cultural minority audiences and the private broadcasters who provide them with services. The most significant aspect of the new policy is its recognition of the importance of multicultural programming in English and French. Programming quotas are based on three new categories (Types B, C, and D) in English or French and a combination of English, French and a third language, rather than on only third-language programming as in the past. The creation of the new programming categories was in response to the changes that have occurred over the past 15 years in the makeup of Canada's immigrant population. In addition to the previous preponderance of Europeans speaking a variety of languages there are now large groups of immigrants from visible minorities whose common language in the country of origin is French or English.

While the possibility still exists for broadcasters to provide programming only, or mainly, in minority languages the policy encourages the development of more French and English services for cultural minorities. Overall the policy succeeds in providing a rationale for licensing consistency and a framework for licensing procedures. With it the CRTC gives greater legitimacy to an area of broadcasting that developed without significant regulatory intervention or government sanction. Still, a number of pressing concerns to cultural minorities remain.

Issues

Multiculturalism and Conventional Broadcasting

> It's high time Canadian broadcasting reflected the Canadian multicultural reality.[1]

In both public forums and briefs presented to this Task Force cultural minority representatives noted that conventional broadcasters, both private and public, must do more to reflect the multicultural reality of Canada in their programming.

Cultural minorities do not want multicultural programming ghettoized or confined to special ethnic television and radio services. They want the multicultural mosaic of Canada reflected in both the English-language and French-language programming of mainstream, conventional broadcasters. They expect public broadcasters, the CBC in particular, to take the lead. In its brief to the Task Force the Canadian Multicultural Council emphasized this point:

> It is our belief that the CBC should be in the forefront of promoting the equity and fairness principle central to our nation's cultural freedom in order that the development of a multicultural Canada can be truly realized.[2]

Cultural minorities were critical of the CBC for failing to mirror the multicultural dimension of Canada in programming and staffing. In French Canada the problem exists in all media. Jacques Godbout, well known writer and filmmaker, stresses this point:

> If we were to believe the picture that is presented by TVA and Radio-Canada television news, Quebec society would be exclusively composed of the sons and daughters of the members of the founding nation. To find himself reflected on the TV screen, the immigrant must watch English news, as on the French side not a single reporter born outside the great white French family can be found.[3]

The lack of interest by the francophone media in ethnic communities leads immigrants to Quebec to listen to and watch anglophone media. In this way the French community deprives itself of a sorely needed cultural and linguistic contribution, especially in view of its weak population growth.

In a presentation at the CRTC hearings on Ethnic Broadcasting Policy, the CBC argued that its domestic services should be in English and French only but that its programming should consciously reflect Canada's ethno-cultural dimension. This position is reasonable. The national public broadcaster cannot be expected to provide domestic services in languages in addition to English, French and, where warranted, aboriginal languages. There are encouraging signs that the CBC recognizes its shortcomings and is prepared to undertake more programming that reflects Canada's multicultural heritage. For example, on English radio the CBC has established multicultural programming objectives for local, regional and national network shows.

Recommendation

The CBC should establish a policy of multiculturalism and cultural programming objectives throughout the Corporation, similar to those developed for English radio.

The CRTC has introduced limited measures to encourage conventional broadcasters to increase multicultural programming. The Commission has also called on both conventional and ethnic broadcasters to examine the potential of television and radio subcarrier capacity to serve cultural minorities.

Many cultural minority groups want more aggressive action, beyond the regulatory powers of the CRTC. In its presentation to our Task Force the Canadian Ethnocultural Council, a coalition of more than 30 national ethnic organizations, stated:

> The Broadcasting Act of 1968. . .does not reflect the demographic changes in Canada, and does not specifically mandate the public and private broadcasters to program for a multicultural Canadian society and to reflect a Canadian identity which is now bilingual and multicultural in nature. . . .As such, these 8 million Canadians are grossly underserved by the Canadian broadcasting system.[4]

The Canadian Ethnocultural Council would entrench the principle of multiculturalism in legislation, including legislation governing the CBC. Only in this way, it argues, will mainstream broadcasters be committed to multiculturalism.

The distinction between multiculturalism and multilingualism is important. In proposing legislative amendments most cultural minority groups are not suggesting multilingual programming be the responsibility of mainstream broadcasters. They want conventional broadcasters like the CBC to "reflect the cultural diversity of Canada, giving practical expression to the concept of multiculturalism in a bilingual society".[5] The Task Force concurs with this position.

Recommendation

The Broadcasting Act should make reference to the need for programming reflecting the principle of multiculturalism in a bilingual society.

Many authorities on minorities broadcasting see the need to shift more responsibility for multicultural services from the private sector to the public sector, at the municipal, provincial and federal levels. The Ukrainian Canadian Committee (Alberta Provincial Council) argues that the public sector should provide services, including multilingual programming, where they cannot be adequately provided by private broadcasting.

Regardless of legislative changes and other prescriptive measures, the key to the successful implementation of multiculturalism in conventional broadcasting is to win the commitment of broadcast managers to the principle of multiculturalism. The Task Force endorses the National Committee on Cultural Diversity in Broadcasting, proposed by the Minister of State for Multiculturalism and supported by the Minister of Communications and the CRTC, as a vehicle for promoting multiculturalism in the industry. We are pleased to note that the National Committee on Cultural Diversity in Broadcasting is to be action-oriented. As proposed, it will provide information to ethnocultural communities on the operation and regulation of the broadcasting industry and it will encourage opportunities for the production and distribution of programming that reflects Canada's cultural diversity.

Representation and Depiction of Cultural Minorities

The Task Force received many briefs from cultural minorities expressing concern over stereotyping, unbalanced reporting and a lack of minority representation in mainstream broadcasting. Several groups called for increased opportunities for access in both creative and administrative capacities to avert discriminatory portrayal from within. The League for Human Rights of the B'nai Brith Canada (Eastern Division) emphasized this concern in their brief to the Task Force:

> The ethnic communities will look to prime-time television to see their cultures and life styles depicted and accepted without stereotyping. They will look to on-camera representation of their group members as confirmation of both acceptance of the group and as a source for identity-strengthening role models.[6]

In its 1985 policy, the CRTC acknowledged that it had neither the resources nor the legislative mandate to regulate representation and depiction. It urged the industry to regulate its own conduct and referred some of the cultural minority concerns to consultative committees.

Some improvement in depiction of minorities can be achieved through education, public awareness and consultation. The Task Force recognizes the challenge faced by the proposed Committee on Cultural Diversity in Broadcasting on this issue and encourages it to work with members of the industry in developing practical measures to promote awareness and change.

The Task Force believes that one of the most practical measures in combating ethnocultural stereotyping and ethnocentrism is to increase minority representation at all employment levels in the industry. Under new federal legislation (Bill C-62) Crown corporations such as the CBC will be required to report to Parliament each year on progress towards stated employment equity goals for certain groups including cultural minorities. In Chapter 6 we propose stronger measures that would make employment equity programs a condition of licence throughout the industry.

Other Issues

There remain a number of regulatory matters impeding the growth of cultural minority services. While these may be relatively minor issues, members of the Task Force felt that they should be dealt with expeditiously in order to stimulate further development in this sector without delay.

In 1985, the CRTC sanctioned the practice known as brokerage, whereby many independent ethnic program producers purchase blocks of time from radio and television stations. Many popular multilingual programs have been broadcast that otherwise might not have been produced. Brokerage has been limited however, because section 3 of the *Broadcasting Act* makes each licensee responsible for programs on its system, whatever the source. It has been suggested that the Broadcasting Act should permit licensees of cable, satellite or off-air broadcasting stations to lease blocks of time and pass responsibility for the content to the program producers. The broadcaster would function as a common carrier. While the Task Force does not fully support the proposed legislative change, we propose the following recommendation to encourage the brokerage practice.

Recommendation

The CRTC should create a special class of licence for minority groups wanting to use the brokerage practice making them responsible for program content.

Ethnic closed-circuit cable audio services, which are not subject to regulation of content, have been in operation in large metropolitan centres such as Toronto and Montreal for over ten years. They rely on advertising revenues and provide single-language programming, whereas licensed ethnic stations must broadcast in a variety of languages. In its 1985 policy the CRTC decided to allow cable licensees to continue distributing previously authorized ethnic closed-circuit audio services.

Recommendation

In addition to encouraging closed-circuit audio on cable, the regulations governing the redistribution of multilingual broadcast signals should be modified to allow cable operators to construct composite service schedules out of a variety of content sources such as distant broadcast signals and community channels.

Cultural minority representatives have continued to lobby for much lower Canadian content quotas for multilingual programming. They point to a number of practical constraints, such as the dearth of Canadian ethnic programming, high production costs, difficulties in securing studio facilities, and scarcity of Canadian creative resources. The Task Force acknowledges these constraints.

Recommendation

Canadian content rules should be reduced for multicultural broadcasting to give the providers of multicultural services the fullest opportunity to carry revenue-generating material.

Notes

1. Canadian Ethnocultural Council, brief submitted to the Task Force on Broadcasting Policy, Ottawa, August 1985.
2. Canadian Multiculturalism Council, brief submitted to the Task Force on Broadcasting Policy, Ottawa, August 1985, p. 2.
3. Jacques Godbout, *Actualité*, May 1986, p. 182.
4. Canadian Ethnocultural Council, p. 2.
5. Francis Spiller and Kim Smiley, "Multicultural Broadcasting in Canada", study prepared for the Task Force on Broadcasting Policy, Ottawa, 1986.
6. League for Human Rights of B'nai Brith (Eastern Region), Montreal, "An Ethnic Broadcasting Policy for Canada", brief submitted to the Task Force on Broadcasting Policy, Ottawa, September 1985, p. 8.

Part VIII

DISTRIBUTING THE PROGRAMS

Chapter 23

The Evolving Distribution Structure

The Evolving Distribution Structure

Until fairly recently both radio and television broadcasters acted as their own distributors. They not only produced scheduled programming services, but also delivered them directly into the households of their audiences using their own transmitters. While such arrangements are still characteristic of radio, most Canadians now receive television service not from the TV broadcasters themselves but through cable companies which are in the business of retailing many television signals to subscribers. By 1985, 62 percent of Canadians subscribed to cable television service.

The old ways in broadcasting had some clear advantages for program producers and broadcasters. Copyrights could be more effectively exploited by producers and the rights broadcasters held to local, regional or national markets could be protected more easily. By contrast, cable television developed outside the framework of copyright law. The existing, antiquated *Copyright Act* does not apply at all to the retransmission of broadcast signals, whether by cable, satellite or any other means.

For the viewing public, however, this change in the pattern of distribution provided the potential to have available an expanded number of broadcasting services. Cable television was successful to the extent that it provided attractive programming which was not available off-air. Naturally the judgement the public had to make was whether the additional programming they got from cable was worth the monthly cost of subscribing.

In English Canada the public proved to be far more interested in cable television prior to 1975 than was the case in the United States since it was used in Canada to bring in American channels. In 1970, for example, 21 percent of Canadian households subscribed to cable television, while only 7 percent of American households subscribed. Even in 1975 cable penetration in the United States was still just 14 percent, while 42 percent of Canadian households subscribed.

In the United States most of the households cable reached could, of course, already receive the three American commercial networks, CBS, NBC and ABC, as well as the non-commercial PBS service off-air. What cable offered in the United States prior to 1975 was mainly distant conventional stations, and this did not add a substantial amount of attractive additional programming.

By contrast, what cable television offered Canadians was essentially the three American commercial networks plus PBS. Known as 'three-plus-one', this combination proved attractive. The doubling of cable penetration in Canada between 1970 and 1975 reflected a decision made by the CRTC in the early 1970s to allow the four American networks to be imported by microwave to cities distant from the American border.

No comparable success occurred in the American cable industry until after 1975 when, beginning with Home Box Office, cable was linked with satellite transmission to make new services available to its subscribers. These new services, with the American cable industry itself providing part of their financing, gave cable a boost comparable to that achieved earlier by Canadian systems. Over the next decade American cable penetration grew rapidly rising from 14 percent in 1975 to 40 percent in 1985.

For Canadian broadcasters, however, the three-plus-one distribution arrangements presented problems. Most of the advertising revenue of private Canadian TV stations and networks came from buying the rights to show the same programs carried on the three commercial American networks that were now being imported by Canadian cable companies. In effect, Canadian TV stations and networks now faced direct competition from Canadian cable companies to supply American network programs to Canadian viewers. But the Canadian TV stations and networks had to buy the rights to show American network programs in Canada and were obliged by regulation to include Canadian programs in their schedules, while cable companies did neither.

The growing strength of cable television in the 1970s, therefore, presented major challenges to the *Broadcasting Act*. While the CRTC had been directed by Parliament to ensure that each broadcaster provided programs using "predominantly Canadian creative and other resources", the Act did not address distribution services such as cable television directly. With the importation of the three-plus-one American networks, the programming provided by cable companies was clearly predominantly American. In Chapter 5 we see how the viewing habits of Canadians differ depending on whether or not they are cable subscribers. The effect of cable on francophone viewers is described in Chapter 8. Those who have cable watch Canadian TV stations and Canadian programs less than those who do not have cable and this simply reflects the menu of programs that is offered to them.

Through the 1970s a number of initiatives were taken to try to meet the threat to the commercial revenues of Canadian stations and networks and to offset the major shift in the balance of Canadian and foreign programming available to Canadians. The two main initiatives were the passage of Bill C-58 and implementation by the CRTC of a policy of simultaneous program substitution. As we see in Chapter 17 these measures have had considerable success in offsetting potential revenue losses by Canadian television broadcasters. Although Canada's television stations and networks still earn far lower per capita commercial revenues than their counterparts in the United States they have achieved significant real growth over the past fifteen years.

The challenge which in our judgement has still not been met is the cultural one. Canadian households with cable are not offered an adequate range of well-funded programs made by and for Canadians. Throughout this Report we focus on shifting the balance, using the strength that exists in the Canadian broadcasting system as a whole, to create and exhibit more and better Canadian programs, particularly in the mid-evening hours when most of us watch television.

To meet these goals there must be a much clearer definition of the role of cable television. There must also be a clear understanding of what Canadian cable companies can and ought reasonably be expected to do. We turn in this part of our Report first to a profile of cable television and then to a review of basic cable policy issues and recommendations.

Let us recall briefly a more recent development in the evolution of the distribution structure: the use of satellites. It is satellite technology, as we note in

Chapter 18 on Pay-TV and Specialty Services, that is the key to inexpensive distribution of new programming services to cable systems and, potentially, to individual satellite dishes. The all-news channel and the TV Canada service we propose are both predicated on satellite technology, as are the existing private sector pay and specialty services. These initiatives exemplify the opportunity to use the increasingly strong and sophisticated distribution structure not simply to import more foreign programming, but to serve the Canadian purpose.

Satellite technology also offers the opportunity, because the costs involved are relatively insensitive to distance, to provide better service to underserved communities. In Chapters 25 and 26 we look at the costs of Canadian satellite distribution, the structures through which satellite services are provided and the degree of success that has been achieved in extending service to underserved communities. We also look in Chapter 26 at the degree to which the operations of CANCOM, the company set up to serve remote and underserved areas, have created policy dilemmas comparable to those raised by the development of cable television.

It must be remembered, however, that copyright continues to be a critically important factor in the evolution of the distribution structure of Canadian broadcasting, dictating what distributors can and cannot do with other people's property. There is little question that Canadian cable and satellite services would have developed differently if copyright protection extended to the retransmission of signals. Our analysis and recommendations concerning copyright in Chapter 28 should therefore be considered an integral part of our comments on the way the distribution system should develop in the future.

Chapter 24

Cable Systems

Cable Systems

It is 35 years since the first Canadian cable TV system was established in London, Ontario, though it was preceded by a Montreal cable system that was used only for audio until 1952 when it began offering television. As late as 1967 there were only half-a-million Canadian cable subscribers. By 1985 there were five-and-a-half million.

After Belgium, Canada is the second most cabled country in the world. The high penetration level, with 62 percent of households subscribing in 1985, was achieved almost entirely through the sale of basic cable service rather than pay and specialty services. In this way the growth pattern and structure of cable television in Canada differs fundamentally from that of the United States.

Only since 1983 has cable service in Canada included the option for individuals to subscribe to additional channels, including both pay television and specialty services. Their advent began a new period for cable television in Canada, raising a whole new set of broadcast policy issues. These are considered in Chapter 8 on the Distinctiveness of French Broadcasting, Chapter 10 on the CBC, Chapter 13 on TV Canada and Chapter 18 on Pay-TV and Specialty Services.

In many respects cable is a unique component of the broadcasting system. While radio and TV stations face increasing competition for audiences and ad revenue, cable is operated as a monopoly. Subscribers can only buy service from the cable company that serves their street. For the vast majority of Canadians with cable, it has been treated as the sole source of a wide range of broadcast signals.

To make this point is not to deny the existence of direct reception by individual dishes or SMATV antennas, but simply to keep these alternative reception methods in perspective. In fact, in Chapter 7 on Policy and Regulation and in Chapter 28 on Copyright Issues, we make recommendations designed to ensure that there is fair and equitable treatment of all existing and potential distribution systems for television programs.

In this chapter we review the state of the cable industry and consider the policy and regulatory framework. First, we turn to a more careful look at the growth pattern of cable television.

Market Penetration

In our examination of both private radio and private television, we consider audience size and commercial revenues to be the key indicators of strength. The parallel yardsticks in cable television are the number of subscribers and the amount of revenue from subscribers.

Cable television service is not available to all Canadians. As Table 24.1 indicates, however, the percentage of Canadians to whom service was available almost doubled between 1970 and 1984, rising from 42 percent to 80 percent. However, not everyone who can subscribe actually does. In fact, just over three-quarters of the Canadians to whom cable is available do subscribe. The proportion of all Canadian households taking cable in 1984 was thus 61 percent, triple the figure of 21 percent in 1970.

Table 24.1 Market Penetration of Cable, 1970 and 1974 to 1984

	1970	1974	1975	1976	1977	1978	1979	1980	1981	1982	1983	1984
Households[a] in cabled areas as a percent of total households	42.4	61.2	63.1	65.8	68.9	74.0	76.6	76.6	77.0	78.2	78.5	80.0
Subscribers as a percent of households in cabled areas	48.7	62.6	66.3	67.0	67.9	67.8	68.8	70.9	74.3	74.8	74.9	75.9
Subscribers as a percent of total households	20.6	38.3	41.8	44.1	46.8	50.2	52.7	54.4	57.2	58.4	58.8	60.8

Note: a. Estimates of number of households include mobile homes but exclude households in the Yukon and Northwest Territories, households on Indian reserves and crown lands, and inmates of institutions. Also excluded are military camps; collective-type households such as those living in hotels, large lodging homes, clubs, logging and construction camps.

Sources of Basic Data: For number of households — Statistics Canada, Household Survey Division; for number of households wired and subscribers — CRTC, Industry Statistics and Analysis Division (1974-1984); Statistics Canada 56-205 (1970).

The rate of cable growth has been uneven. In the early seventies, the number of subscribers increased by about 20 percent annually. At the time many Canadians were simply waiting to subscribe until cable became available in their home towns. In fact, the proportion of Canadian households to which cable was available rose from 42 percent in 1970 to 61 percent in 1974. In the same four years, the proportion of these households that actually chose to subscribe also grew sharply, rising from 49 percent to 63 percent.

The annual growth rate in number of subscribers dropped considerably during the second half of the seventies and in the early eighties cable penetration began to level off. By 1983 annual growth rates for the number of households to which cable was available and the number of subscribers had fallen to approximately 3 percent, roughly the same as the growth rate in the total number of Canadian households, owing primarily to the high penetration level already reached in the 1970s.

Many of the large cities are fully cabled and market penetration rates in some of them are extremely high. Figures obtained from Statistics Canada show the following levels of market penetration — percentage of total households subscribing to cable — in some of Canada's main urban markets at the end of 1984: Victoria — 92 percent; Vancouver — 95 percent; Edmonton — 83 percent; Calgary — 84 percent; Regina — 74 percent; Winnipeg — 90 percent; London — 85 percent; Toronto — 84 percent; and Ottawa-Hull — 80 percent. The situation, however, was different for French-language cities. In 1984 Montreal market penetration was only 55 percent, Quebec City was 60 percent, and Chicoutimi-Jonquière was 57 percent.

There was substantial recovery in the rate of growth of cable subscriptions in 1984, following the introduction of pay television in the spring of 1983 and the end of the recession. The sustained growth of 5.9 percent in the number of cable subscribers in 1985 may reflect the September 1984 introduction of specialty services (MuchMusic, TSN, and some American services).

These innovations are extremely important because of the close links between available services and industry growth. Although the growth in the number of households to which cable is available will never soar as it did in the seventies, 24 percent of households in this category were still not subscribers in 1984. This gives the cable companies a strong incentive to make both their basic and optional services more attractive.

Another recent incentive to growth has been the establishment of satellite-to-cable services for small communities where cable had previously not been economically viable. Increasingly, the progress of cable has been linked to satellite communication as a result of the role of satellites in making available both new satellite-to-cable services and a variety of broadcast signals for distribution in remote communities.

As indicated by our look at major urban markets, the cabling of Canada is quite uneven. In Table 24.2, which is based on 1984 figures, we see, for example, that only 49 percent of households in Newfoundland have cable service available, although 74 percent of those households are connected, which is about the Canadian average. That gives a penetration level of cable for the province of only 36.5 percent of all households, compared to the Canadian nationwide average of 61 percent. The provinces that are both heavily cabled and heavily connected are Ontario, Manitoba, Alberta, and British Columbia.

Table 24.2 Availability of Cable and Subscription Levels by Province, 1984

	NFLD	PEI	NS	NB	Que	Ont	Man	Sask	Alta	B.C.	CANADA
Households[a] in cabled areas as a percent of total households	49.1	45.0	62.0	58.1	79.6	82.4	76.5	59.4	85.4	92.5	80.0
Subscribers as a percent of households in cabled areas	74.4	88.9	85.6	87.2	59.6	82.3	83.4	68.2	72.6	88.0	75.9
Subscribers as a percent of total households	36.5	40.0	53.1	50.7	47.5	67.8	63.9	40.6	62.0	81.4	60.8

Note: a. Estimates of number of households include mobile homes but exclude households in the Yukon and Northwest Territories, households on Indian reserves and crown lands, and inmates of institutions. Also excluded are military camps; collective-type households such as those living in hotels, large lodging homes, clubs, logging and construction camps.

Sources of Basic Data: For number of households — Statistics Canada, Household Survey Division; for number of households wired and subscribers — CRTC, Industry Statistics and Analysis Division.

Cable penetration in Quebec has followed a pattern different from that in any other part of the country. Although the proportion of Quebec households that have access to a cable system is virtually the same as in Ontario (80 percent compared to 82 percent), the proportion of subscribers is far lower (48 percent compared to 68 percent). Of all Canadian provinces, Quebec has the lowest proportion of households to which cable is available that opt to subscribe (60 percent). The Quebec pattern is mainly a result of linguistic and cultural factors.

Revenues and Expenses

Until 1983 the cable industry earned nearly all its revenues from subscriber payments for reception of basic cable television service. Cable industry revenue therefore depended fundamentally on the number of subscribers and the monthly rate that they were charged. Because cable companies do not compete with one another for subscribers, the rates were set by the CRTC. Hence, the Commission's policies on rate increases were a fundamental determinant of cable revenues and, indirectly, of profitability.

The Commission's responsibility is to ensure that the amounts charged consumers are fair and reasonable and that they reflect the costs of providing service and a profit consistent with the risk.

New discretionary services have recently changed the revenue structure of cable. Cable companies may now get $10 from one subscriber but $30 from another. The principal effect on industry revenue is that the average revenue per subscriber increases. A substantial effect was felt as early as 1984, with 16 percent of the industry's revenue coming from discretionary services. In 1985 just 14 percent of all cable subscribers were receiving discretionary services. While this was far from the success that had been hoped for, it represented a substantial increase in industry revenue.

The industry also earns smaller amounts of revenue from installing cable service, as well as from the sale or rental of the converters necessary to receive channels additional to the 12 that most television sets are equipped to receive. The non-pay channels provided through the use of a converter are usually referred to as the expanded basic service. These channels are received, however, as part of the service available for the basic monthly rate approved by the CRTC.

In Figure 24.1 we can follow for the years 1974 to 1984 the annual growth rate of cable revenues from subscriptions to basic service in relation to the rate of growth of number of subscribers, subscription rates, households to which cable is available, and new household formation. Here we see graphically the slowdown of cable growth just described. The revenue picture for basic service from 1974 to 1984 is shown in Table 24.3. Preliminary data available for 1985 now indicate that the industry's revenue from basic service grew substantially in 1985, rising by 12.1 percent in current dollars and by 8.1 percent in constant dollars.

Excluding discretionary services, the revenues of the cable industry grew sharply from 1974 to 1984, rising from $132 million to $594 million. Over the

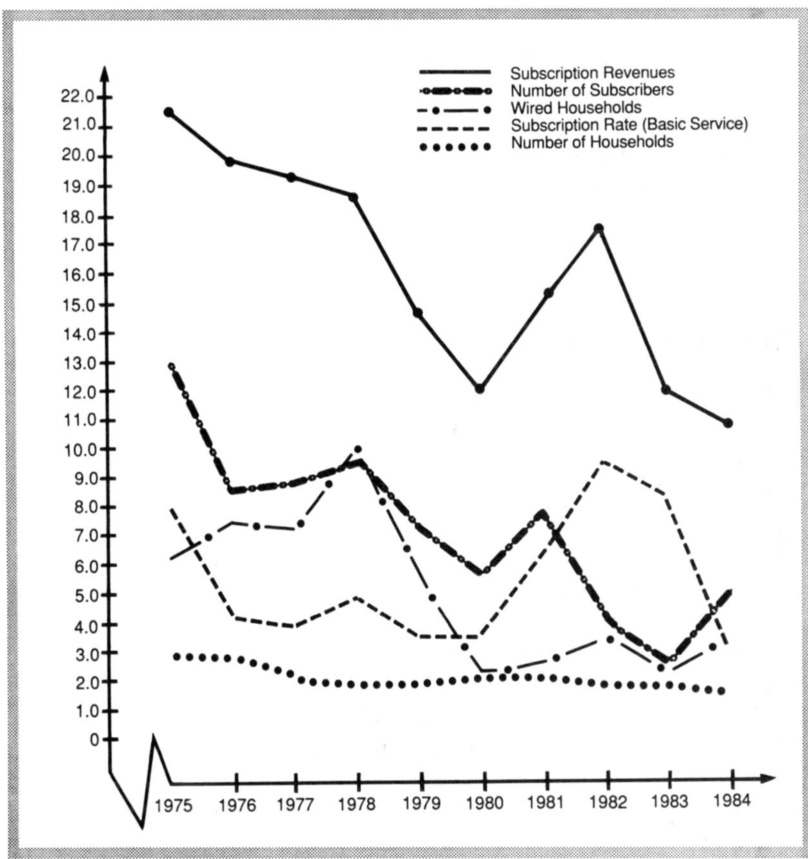

Figure 24.1 Annual Growth of the Cable Industry

Source: CRTC, Industry Statistics and Analysis Division and Statistics Canada, Household Surveys Division

decade subscription revenues accounted for about 94 percent of total revenue from basic service with installation charges and converter rentals making up the remainder.

The compound annual rate of growth in cable's revenue from basic service was 9.1 percent in constant dollars from 1974 to 1979 but dropped to an average of 4.6 percent over the next five years. There were two main reasons for the decline: the slowdown in growth in the number of subscribers as the cable industry in larger centres matured, and the application of the federal anti-inflation guidelines. Under the restraint program the CRTC was obliged to limit rate increases for cable companies to 6 percent, 5 percent, and 4 percent in the three years beginning in June 1982 when the guidelines were announced. A substantial number of catch-up increases have since been approved and have begun to show up in the 8 percent real growth reported for 1985.

Table 24.3 Revenue Growth for Basic Service of Cable Companies between 1974 and 1984

		Atlantic			Quebec			Ontario	
	Revenue ($ millions)	Annual growth rate (%)		Revenue ($ millions)	Annual growth rate (%)		Revenue ($ millions)	Annual growth rate (%)	
		current $	constant $		current $	constant $		current $	constant $
1974	3.9	—	—	24.7	—	—	60.0	—	—
1975	6.0	53.8	39.2	28.9	17.0	5.6	72.6	21.0	9.2
1976	8.2	36.7	26.2	36.3	25.6	16.8	85.7	18.0	9.8
1977	10.9	32.9	23.8	48.2	32.8	23.1	96.8	13.0	4.7
1978	14.7	34.8	23.6	56.5	17.3	7.6	113.8	17.5	8.0
1979	20.3	38.5	26.6	62.9	11.3	2.0	127.5	12.0	2.6
1980	23.8	17.2	6.3	69.4	10.4	0.3	139.2	9.0	−0.9
1981	27.5	15.6	2.6	85.3	22.9	9.2	153.7	10.4	−1.9
1982	30.3	10.1	−0.7	104.6	22.6	10.7	176.0	14.5	3.3
1983	32.4	7.0	1.1	119.5	14.3	8.1	194.8	10.7	4.7
1984	41.4	27.5	22.8	136.8	14.5	9.7	217.0	11.4	6.7
Compound Annual Growth Rate	1974-79	39.1	27.8		20.6	10.7		16.3	4.9
	1979-84	15.3	6.1		16.8	7.5		11.2	2.3

Note: a. Including revenue from Yukon and Northwest Territories.
Source: CRTC, Industry Statistics and Analysis Division.

	Prairies			British Columbia			Canada[a]		
	Revenue ($ millions)	Annual growth rate (%) current $	Annual growth rate (%) constant $	Revenue ($ millions)	Annual growth rate (%) current $	Annual growth rate (%) constant $	Revenue ($ millions)	Annual growth rate (%) current $	Annual growth rate (%) constant $
1974	17.5	—	—	26.3	—	—	132.3	—	—
1975	22.5	28.6	16.3	29.9	13.7	2.6	160.0	20.9	9.1
1976	26.8	19.1	10.6	35.2	17.7	9.6	192.3	20.2	11.8
1977	31.4	17.2	8.5	42.5	20.7	11.8	229.8	19.5	10.7
1978	38.8	23.3	13.6	48.6	14.4	5.1	272.4	18.5	8.9
1979	49.0	26.4	15.6	52.5	10.0	−1.1	313.2	15.0	5.3
1980	58.6	19.6	8.6	59.5	12.9	2.8	351.5	12.1	1.9
1981	69.5	18.6	5.5	7.4	13.3	0.7	404.6	15.1	2.3
1982	82.2	18.4	7.0	77.3	14.6	3.6	472.0	16.6	5.3
1983	96.2	17.0	10.6	6.2	11.6	5.3	531.3	12.6	6.4
1984	104.2	8.3	3.8	92.3	7.1	2.7	593.5	11.7	7.1
Compound Annual Growth Rate 1974-79		22.9	12.9		14.8	5.5		18.8	9.1
Compound Annual Growth Rate 1979-84		16.3	7.0		11.9	3.0		13.6	4.6

Note: a. Including revenue from Yukon and Northwest Territories.
Source: CRTC, Industry Statistics and Analysis Division.

What should be kept in mind, then, in assessing the revenue growth as well as the profitability of the cable industry, is the major effect of the federal restraint guidelines since 1983. In addition it must be remembered that beginning in February 1983 with the initiation of pay television services, the cable industry has been earning revenues from discretionary services as well. As Table 24.4 shows, these revenues amounted to $109 million in 1984, bringing total revenues to $703 million, more than five times what they had been in 1974. In constant dollars this represents an increase of 119 percent between 1974 and 1984.

Cable Rate Levels

The basic influence on the financial performance of cable companies is the rates approved by the CRTC. The economic profile of the industry prepared for the

Table 24.4 Revenue, Expenses and Profits: Basic and Discretionary Services, 1984[a] ($ millions)

	Basic Service	Discretionary Services	Total
Revenue	587.1	108.8	695.9
Expenses	362.2	78.7	440.9
Operating Profit	224.9	30.0	254.9
Depreciation	89.9	13.0	102.9
Interest expense	67.0	2.2	69.2
Adjustments	(2.6)	0.1	2.5
Profit before income tax	70.5	14.2	84.7
Provision for income tax	33.8	2.7	36.5
Profit after income tax	36.8	11.4	48.2
Profit before income tax, as a percent of revenue	12.0	13.1	12.2

Note: a. The basic service results given here do not correspond entirely to those in the other Tables in this chapter. The main reason for the difference is the use of each company's depreciation method in this Table compared to the use of standardized depreciation in the other Tables. Moreover, the results on basic service as well as on discretionary services are those of corporations with more than 1,000 subscribers. Corporations with fewer than 1,000 subscribers have earned revenues of $6.4 million with basic service and of $280,000 with discretionary services.

Source: CRTC, Industry Statistics and Analysis Division.

Task Force by Moss, Roberts and Associates drew attention to "the lack of any formalized, explicit policy for rate setting, and the rather arbitrary system which results".[1] We return to this matter later in this chapter.

Table 24.5 shows the results of the CRTC's rate setting policies between 1972 and 1985. In assessing these rate levels it is important to recall that cable companies rarely, if ever, rebuild a system. Once an area is cabled, the operator may upgrade it and must maintain it, but nevertheless continues to use the basic plant initially installed. As a result, rate increases would not necessarily be expected to keep pace with inflation, except to reflect increases in the value of the service being provided to subscribers. A further vitally important factor is market penetration, because it is the number of subscribing households per mile of cable that constitutes the measure of the efficiency of a cable system.

Table 24.5 Average Rates for Basic Cable Service, 1972-1985

Year	Approved Rate	Realized Rate	
	Current $	Current $	Constant $
1972[a]	4.81	4.36	4.36
1975	5.43	5.02	3.79
1980	6.87	6.89	3.43
1985[b]	9.76	9.87	3.39

Notes: a. 1972 is the first year for which the CRTC calculated such figures.
b. Preliminary.
Source: CRTC, Industry Statistics and Analysis Division.

The cost of basic cable service in real terms was 22 percent lower in 1985 than it was in 1972. The Task Force asked Moss, Roberts and Associates to examine the price elasticity of basic cable service in order to evaluate the likely market reaction to any increase in the price level of cable services. Their study concluded that basic cable service is "relatively price insensitive, at least up to monthly rates of $12.00" and that there could be considerable flexibility in repricing the service.[2] The average price at that time (September 1985) was $10.02, roughly $2 lower.

The price of cable service in Canada varies, depending on the size of the cable system. Table 24.6 shows the breakdown in September 1985.

Table 24.6 Canadian Basic Cable Rates by System Size

Number of Subscribers	Weighted Average Monthly Basic Cable Rate ($)
Up to 3,000	12.49
3,000 – 10,000	10.64
10,000 – 25,000	9.72
25,000 – 50,000	9.58
50,000 – 100,000	9.24
over 100,000	10.14

Source: Moss, Roberts and Associates, Inc. "An Economic Profile of the Canadian Cable Industry", study prepared for the Task Force on Broadcasting Policy, Ottawa, 1986

Table 24.7 Revenue, Expenses and Profits for Basic Service of Cable Companies between 1975 and 1984

($ millions)	1975	1976	1977	1978	1979	1980	1981	1982	1983	1984
Revenue	160.0	192.3	229.8	272.4	313.2	351.5	404.6	472.0	531.3	593.5
Expenses	85.5	106.9	125.7	150.8	182.4	201.9	246.1	288.4	322.5	365.6
Operating Profit	74.5	85.4	104.1	121.6	130.8	149.7	158.5	183.5	208.8	227.8
Standard Depreciation	33.5	39.6	46.5	52.7	58.6	65.6	77.9	86.3	95.8	106.0
Interest Expense	13.9	17.5	20.3	23.6	28.0	34.4	59.2	66.0	65.8	68.2
Others	(1.6)	(2.6)	(3.6)	(4.5)	(1.9)	0.9	(5.0)	(4.2)	(1.5)	(2.6)
Profit Before Income Tax	28.6	30.9	40.9	49.8	46.0	48.8	26.5	35.5	48.7	56.2

(as a percent of revenue)

Revenue	100.0	100.0	100.0	100.0	100.0	100.0	100.0	100.0	100.0	100.0
Expenses	53.4	55.6	54.7	55.4	58.2	57.4	60.8	61.1	60.7	61.6
Operating Profit	46.6	44.4	45.3	44.6	41.8	42.6	39.2	38.9	39.3	38.4
Standard Depreciation	20.9	20.6	20.2	19.3	18.7	18.7	19.3	18.3	18.0	17.9
Interest Expense	8.7	9.1	8.8	8.7	8.9	9.8	14.6	14.0	12.4	11.5
Others	(1.0)	(1.4)	(1.6)	(1.7)	(0.6)	0.3	(1.2)	(0.9)	(0.3)	(0.4)
Profit Before Income Tax	17.9	16.1	17.8	18.3	14.7	13.9	6.5	7.5	9.2	9.5

Source: CRTC, Industry Statistics and Analysis Division.

The Task Force considered the question of whether cable is at present underpriced in order to assess the effect of either further taxes or allowing the companies to add to basic service new TV channels for which they would make payments out of subscriber revenues. In the United States most of the recent expansion of basic cable channels available to subscribers has been a result of new networks distributed to cable systems by satellite. These new television networks in the United States have in most cases been supported by a combination of advertising revenues and a monthly charge to the cable system operator that usually ranges from $0.01 to $0.30 a month per subscriber for each network. These monthly charges represent part of the cost to cable companies of the basic service they are marketing and are therefore reflected in the rates charged to subscribers.

In this Report, we recommend the creation of two new Canadian satellite-to-cable services, TV Canada and a news and current affairs channel, that would be carried as part of basic cable service. At the level of charges we recommend for these services, the Task Force is confident that the resulting rate increases will not be onerous, especially if combined with the reduction of tax for basic service from 8 percent to 5 percent as we recommend in Chapter 29.

Profitability

Cable is a capital-intensive industry and one in which assets are usually financed using a high percentage of debt rather than equity capital. Hence the industry is extremely sensitive to interest rate changes. As Table 24.7 indicates, rapidly escalating interest rates and galloping inflation at the end of the 1970s and in the early 1980s combined to erode the profit performance of the cable industry in Canada. The proportion of revenue spent by Canadian cable companies on interest charges rose from 9 percent to 15 percent between 1978 and 1981, with profit margins dropping from 18 percent in 1978 to 6.5 percent in 1981. The same thing happened during this period in the United States, where pre-tax profit margins fell even further, dropping to under 4 percent in 1981 from 15 percent in 1978. The Canadian industry's profits, in spite of the 6-5-4 anti-inflation program, recovered to 9.5 percent by 1984. Preliminary 1985 CRTC data indicate a further recovery to 11.2 percent.

The industry figures in the early 1980s reflect the fact that two of the largest companies in the industry, Rogers and Vidéotron, took on particularly heavy debt in this period as they financed major expansion and restructuring of their services. This was also a period in which inflation pushed operating expenditures up faster than revenues, partly because of the anti-inflation guidelines and partly because in a regulated industry, charges to customers, cable subscribers in this case, cannot be instantly increased to reflect increased costs.

The rise in the profit margin between 1981 and 1984 was due to the stabilization of the proportion of revenue absorbed by operating expenses and a drop in the proportion absorbed by interest charges. The figures in Table 24.7, however, do not tell the whole story. The industry also reported significant profits from discretionary services, as Table 24.4 indicates, at a slightly higher profit margin than for basic service. It should be noted, however, that the allocation of expenditures between discretionary and basic service is not based on any systematic or rigorous cost separation and may be misleading.

As Table 24.8 indicates, there were some significant differences in profitability based on company size in 1984. Pre-tax profit margins tended to grow with size for companies with more than 150,000 subscribers. The lower profits of companies in this category reflect the heavy debt burden assumed by some large cable firms, particularly Rogers Communications Inc., as they undertook ambitious acquisitions and expansions. More recent figures would almost certainly show a marked improvement in the financial performance of the large companies.

In examining profitability it is also important to look at operating profits. Companies in all size categories show substantial operating profits, ranging from 29 percent of revenue to 44 percent. These variations, like those in pre-tax profit margins, are an indicator of the effects of the CRTC's current approach to rate regulation. The largest category of companies, despite its lower pre-tax profits, is near the top in operating profits. The principal factors that produce these differences between operating profits and pre-tax profit margins are the amounts allocated to depreciation and to interest payments.

The 19 largest cable companies, those with over 50,000 subscribers, accounted for just over two-thirds of cable industry revenues in 1984. By contrast the 230 companies with fewer than 5,000 subscribers, while they represented over two-thirds of the cable companies reporting, accounted for only 7 percent of industry revenue, and just 6 percent of subscribers.

Among the most significant changes in the cable industry between 1974 and 1984 were changes in the financing structure. As Table 24.9 shows, the proportion of assets financed by share capital dropped by almost half, from 30 percent in 1975 to 17 percent in 1984. At the same time, the non-current liabilities of the industry climbed sharply, from 47 percent to 63 percent of total liabilities and equity. What this means is that increasingly, cable companies were financing their growth, including acquisitions, new ventures and the upgrading of their systems, by borrowing rather than through increased investment or out of retained earnings. As part of this pattern, a growing share of long-term liabilities was accounted for by liabilities to associated companies.

Table 24.10 shows the evolution of the return on net fixed assets for basic tier services of cable television between 1975 and 1984, based on both the ratio of operating profits to net fixed assets and pre-tax profit as a percentage of net fixed assets. The average pre-tax return on net fixed assets employed dropped from an average of 14 percent between 1975 and 1980 to 7 percent between 1981 and 1984.

Table 24.8 Profit and Loss for Basic Service by Cable Corporation Size, 1984 **($ millions)**

Size of Corporations[a] (Number of Subscribers)	Up to 5,000	5,000 – 10,000	10,000 – 20,000	20,000 – 50,000	50,000 – 100,000	100,000–150,000	More than 150,000	All Corporations
Number of Companies	230	41	25	21	5	7	7	336
Number of subscribers (000)	347.1	288.8	340.4	676.4	366.4	898.2	2,465.8	5,383.1
Revenue	43.8	36.1	39.1	77.0	39.2	93.5	264.7	593.5
Operating profit	13.0	10.3	12.5	30.9	14.5	41.4	105.3	227.8
Profit before income tax	4.0	3.2	4.2	9.9	5.5	17.7	11.8	56.2
Profit as a percent of revenue	9.0	8.9	10.7	12.9	14.1	18.9	4.5	9.5
Number of corporations showing losses	66	3	4	4	1	0	2	80
Revenue of corporations showing losses	10.2	3.0	8.4	13.6	10.1	—	111.5	156.8
Operating profit	1.5	0.2	1.4	5.3	3.3	—	38.2	49.8
Losses before income tax	(1.9)	(1.1)	(0.3)	(1.0)	(1.1)	—	(15.6)	20.9
Number of corporations showing profit	164	38	21	17	4	7	5	256
Revenue of corporations showing profit	33.6	33.1	30.6	63.5	29.1	93.5	153.3	436.7
Operating profit	11.5	10.1	11.1	25.6	11.1	41.5	67.2	178.0
Profit before income tax	5.8	4.3	4.4	11.0	6.6	17.7	27.4	77.1

Note: a. The "Corporation" is the economic unit which holds the CRTC licence. Several "corporations" may be owned by one holding company.
Source: CRTC, Industry Analysis and Statistics Division.

Table 24.9 Assets, Liabilities and Shareholders' Equity of Cable Corporations, 1975, 1979 and 1984[a]

	1975		1979		1984	
	$	%	$	%	$	%
Assets	318.1	100.0	537.0	100.0	1,189.7	100.0
Current	28.0	8.8	49.5	9.2	94.5	7.9
Investments and Advances	48.4	15.2	52.5	9.8	242.1	20.3
Fixed and other assets	241.7	76.0	435.0	81.0	853.1	71.7
Net fixed assets (basic service)	201.4	63.3	347.3	64.7	642.2	54.0
Net fixed assets (non basic service)	4.9	1.5	9.1	1.7	50.5	4.2
Intangible fixed assets	13.7	4.3	58.5	10.9	123.5	10.4
Other	21.7	6.8	20.2	3.8	36.9	3.1
Liabilities	222.7	70.1	400.7	74.6	992.1	83.4
Current	73.8	23.2	146.2	27.2	244.2	20.5
Non-current liabilities	148.9	46.9	254.5	47.4	747.8	62.9
Long-term debt	114.1	35.9	170.1	31.7	354.4	29.8
Associated companies, deferred income tax and other liabilities	34.7	10.9	84.4	15.7	393.4	33.1
Shareholders' equity	95.0	29.9	136.3	25.4	197.6	16.6
Total liabilities and equity	318.1	100.0	537.0	100.0	1,189.7	100.0

Note: a. Corporations with more than 1,000 subscribers.
Source: CRTC, Industry Statistics and Analysis Division.

Table 24.10 Changes in the Pattern of Cable Industry Financing Between 1975 and 1984[a] ($ millions)

	Operating Profit (basic services)	Ratio of Operating Profit to Net Fixed Assets (%) (basic services)	Net Fixed Assets (basic services)	Non-current Liabilities	Interest Expense (basic services)	Shareholders' Equity	Dividends Declared	Pre-tax Profit (basic services)	Ratio of Pre-tax Profit to Net Fixed Assets (%) (basic services)
1975	73.6	36.5	201.4	148.9	13.7	95.0	8.5	28.6	14.2
1976	85.1	36.3	234.2	179.9	17.3	105.7	16.3	31.2	13.3
1977	103.0	38.2	269.8	199.7	20.0	109.7	19.8	40.9	15.2
1978	120.4	39.1	308.0	223.1	23.2	117.0	21.6	49.8	16.2
1979	129.7	37.3	347.3	254.5	27.7	136.3	13.4	45.9	13.2
1980	148.4	38.1	389.5	311.9	34.0	174.1	13.7	48.7	12.5
1981	157.4	33.0	476.6	478.6	58.8	118.1	64.5	26.4	5.5
1982	181.1	34.1	530.5	536.4	65.4	218.8	19.7	35.3	6.7
1983	205.9	35.2	584.6	706.4	65.2	154.0	103.0	48.1	8.2
1984	224.9	35.0	642.2	747.8	67.0	197.6	1[illegible].7	56.1	8.7
Average Return 1975-1980		37.7							14.1
Average Return 1981-1984		34.3							7.3

Note: a. Corporations with more than 1,000 subscribers.
Source: CRTC, Industry Statistics and Analysis Division.

Changes in cable industry operations were only partially responsible for this drop with the ratio of operating profit to net fixed assets declining only slightly from an average of 38 percent between 1975 and 1980 to 34 percent between 1981 and 1984. The decline in the pre-tax return on net fixed assets in fact reflected the sharp growth in indebtedness.

Table 24.11 shows the growth in net fixed assets for the basic cable television service and the changes that occurred in the pattern of industry financing. The average growth in net fixed assets did not change greatly, declining from an average of 14 percent between 1975 to 1980 to an average of 13 percent between 1981 to 1984. However, annual growth in shareholders' equity dropped very sharply, from 13 percent to three percent, while non-current liabilities grew by an average of 24 percent between 1981 and 1984, up from 16 percent between 1975 and 1980.

The changes in the return on net fixed assets that occurred over this period need to be set in the context of sustained net fixed asset growth, very slight increases in shareholders' equity and steadily escalating reliance on debt capital. Of necessity the result is an acceleration of interest payments and the soaring interest rates in 1981 and 1982 intensified the problem.

1981 was a critically important year for the cable industry. The combined effect of a 22 percent increase in net fixed assets and a 245 percent increase in dividend payments produced a 53 percent rise in long-term liabilities and 73 percent increase in interest payments. As a result, the industry's pre-tax return on net fixed assets fell from 12.5 percent in 1980 to 5.5 percent.

The dividends that cable industry shareholders took out of the industry in 1981 were almost two-and-a-half times their pre-tax profit, $65 million compared to $26 million. Shareholders' equity in the industry fell by one-third. The same unusual situation occurred in 1983 with shareholders taking $103 million in dividends, more than double the $48 million in pre-tax profit reported. Again, shareholders' equity fell by almost one-third.

After 1982, declining interest rates resulted in an increase in the pre-tax return on net fixed assets in the industry from 5.5 percent in 1981 to 8.7 percent in 1984. The preliminary 1985 data available to the Task Force suggest a further significant increase in 1985.

In order to allow the Task Force to better understand the profit performance of the cable industry we asked Moss, Roberts to develop financial projections for cable for the next 15 years. Part of the study was a comparison of the cable industry's rate of return with that of regulated common carriers. Based on the conservative assumption that cable rate increases were held at 80 percent of inflation in the future, the study indicated an average return on equity of 16 percent over the 15 years for which the projection was made. The analysis suggested that on this basis, the rate of return for cable would be 2.1 percentage points higher than the rate allowed Bell Canada at the present time.

Table 24.11 Annual Rates of Growth in Key Areas Relating to Cable Industry Financing Between 1975 and 1984[a]

		Net Fixed Assets (basic services)	Non-current Liabilities	Interest Expense (basic services)	Shareholders' Equity	Dividends Declared
1976		16.3	20.8	26.3	11.3	91.8
1977		15.2	11.0	15.6	3.8	21.5
1978		14.2	11.7	16.0	6.7	9.1
1979		12.8	14.1	19.4	16.5	–14.8
1980		12.2	22.6	22.7	27.7	1.6
1981		22.4	53.4	72.9	–32.2	244.9
1982		11.3	12.1	11.2	85.3	–69.5
1983		10.2	31.7	0.0	–29.6	422.8
1984		9.8	5.9	2.8	28.3	–88.6
Compound Annual Growth Rate	1975-1980	14.1	15.9		12.9	
	1980-1984	13.3	24.4		3.2	

Note: a. Corporations with more than 1,000 subscribers.
Source: CRTC, Industry Statistics and Analysis Division.

There was a marked contrast, however, if it were assumed that rates moved up in line with inflation. The average return on equity would then be 25.7 percent, by comparison with the 13.9 percent now allowed Bell Canada. While such analyses are never precise, they indicate in a general way what can be expected. Perhaps more important, they indicate the close interrelationship between the rate-setting policies of the CRTC and the profits of the cable industry.

Current Legal Status of Cable

The 1968 *Broadcasting Act* provided little guidance to the CRTC as to the way in which the objectives of the Act were intended to affect the regulation of cable television. While the programming provided by each broadcaster was to be predominantly Canadian and the mandate of the CBC was to be predominantly Canadian in content and character, it was not at all clear how, or even if, these goals had a parallel in what was expected of cable television companies. The closest the Act comes to indicating what is expected from cable is in the general requirement that the system — which includes cable — be owned and controlled by Canadians in order to safeguard, enrich and strengthen the cultural, political, social and economic fabric of Canada.

With cable television now serving over 60 percent of Canadian households, it has become essential to the effective functioning of the Canadian broadcasting system that the role of cable be more clearly defined. For Canadian television broadcasters in particular, the questions of whether they must be carried by cable companies and in what order of priority are crucial to their success in attracting viewers and generating advertising revenues. The higher priority a broadcaster has, the more households will be reached. As satellite-to-cable networks develop, it has become important whether a new service can be offered as a basic or discretionary service, and if discretionary, whether or not it can be left out of the services offered by cable companies or must be combined with others according to linkage rules such as those on pay television and specialty services.

As we see in Chapter 17 on Private Television it also makes a great deal of difference to Canadian broadcasters whether the signals of directly competing foreign broadcasters can also be carried. In the case of the existing policy on the importation of the three-plus-one, policy-makers have spent the past 15 years trying to compensate through other measures for the loss of exclusivity in program rights and the reduced viewing of Canadian channels that results. In the case of specialty channels, as we see in Chapter 18, there is simply no possibility that Canadian services can co-exist with directly competing American specialty channels or pay television. Even in the very large American market there is almost no direct competition among the existing cable networks.

Cable policy, then, will be fundamental to achieving the objectives we have recommended for a revised broadcasting act. It will be essential to understand clearly, however, what the Canadian cable television industry can and cannot do.

Cable operators are regulated by the CRTC as broadcasting receiving undertakings. The 1932 Privy Council decision mentioned in Chapter 1, which established that Parliament has jurisdiction in broadcasting, provided that this jurisdiction extends to both the transmitting and receiving of signals.[3] Parliament was thus in a position to include cable in the 1968 Act as a broadcasting receiving undertaking, as confirmed by a later judgement. Assigned the responsibility for regulating the Canadian broadcasting system, the CRTC attempted from 1969 onward to incorporate cable television in the system. This was not easy, both because the statutory basis for doing so was unclear and because there was substantial tension and conflict of interest between the cable industry and Canadian broadcasters.

Following its early policy statements,[4] the CRTC published its first comprehensive Cable Television Regulations in 1975,[5] and they are still in force today. About two years ago, the CRTC began consultations to revise the regulations. It issued proposed new regulations in February 1986. (New regulations were in fact introduced after the deliberations of this Task Force were concluded.)

Treating cable undertakings in the same fashion as conventional broadcasters raises a number of problems because they are involved in different activities. While broadcasters produce or purchase programs and, if they are commercial, sell time in their schedules to advertisers, cable companies are primarily retailers of broadcasting services from other sources. They differ from most retailers in that the law does not require that they get permission either to market or pay for broadcasters' signals.

While conventional broadcasters transmit their programs by means of signals that may be received by any individual with a receiving set in the area, cable services are available only to subscribers. Although cable operators produce and distribute some programs, they principally retransmit signals received from conventional broadcasters in Canada and abroad.

The inclusion of cable services in the Canadian broadcasting system under the present Act can be disputed. Cable operators do not send signals using Hertzian waves; they receive them and, after converting them, redistribute them by means of cable to those who decide to subscribe to the system, not to any person equipped with a radio or television receiver. The cables used by the undertakings are not, except in Manitoba and Saskatchewan, public property.[6] The cable network's transmission capacity is becoming even greater than the available natural frequency spectrum. This combination of facts has led a number of experts to describe cable networks as being analogous to print media; in 1971, for example, the Sloan Commission stated that: "cable television, by freeing television from the limitations of radiated electromagnetic waves, creates . . . a situation more nearly analogous to that of the press".[7] In the United States, it was considered important that cable services did not require the use of Hertzian waves over the air. It was this fact that led to court and administrative decisions tending to consider cable operators as similar to publishers and granting them immunity based on freedom of the press similar to that which had previously been extended to newspapers.[8]

This came about because in the United States, the scarcity of frequencies available for over-the-air broadcasting was the factor on which legislation was based to give the government control over the use of radio frequencies. Cable in the U.S. did not, however, develop outside a regulatory framework, as we shall see, partly because of its monopoly status. In Canada, it was not just the scarcity of frequencies that primarily justified the regulation of broadcasting. Other considerations, such as the need to affirm national sovereignty and to create opportunities for Canadian expression, motivated the regulation of broadcasting from the outset.

The contribution of cable television to the achievement of the objectives of the Canadian broadcasting system is linked fundamentally to its increasing pervasiveness as a carrier of broadcasting services. Although cable is regulated as a receiver of broadcasting signals, it is nevertheless obvious that what is regulated is essentially the distribution, rather than the reception, of signals. Thus, section 6 of the *Cable Television Regulations* establishes the order of priority for the distribution of broadcast services within the constraints of the available channels. Cable operators may be licensed to distribute other services as well, once they have satisfied their obligation to distribute the signals prescribed in the regulations.

Although cable is mainly an industry that retails broadcasting signals it also assumes other responsibilities including the operation of the community channel. The various activities of cable undertakings make them hybrids, with some activities similar to those of broadcasters and others similar to those of common carriers, but not analogous to them in all respects. Unlike the broadcasters, they are not at present subject to copyright law or Canadian content regulations. Unlike the telecommunications carriers, they are not subject to rate-of-return regulation.

At the moment, the main regulatory obligations imposed upon cable operators concern the rates they may charge subscribers, the signals and services they can or must provide, the rules relating to substitution of identical signals (simulcasting), and the community channel.

The rates charged for basic cable service are established through conditions of licence, and may be changed only with CRTC approval. The Commission assesses applications for increases on the basis of a number of variables such as the quality of service provided by the operator, additional services proposed, the difference between the projected rate and the rates charged by other operators in the region, the intent of the operator to share the cost involved in providing the service, and financial need.[9]

In the rules on the distribution of signals and the provision of services, the Commission distinguishes between tiers containing the basic service, discretionary services, and non-programming services.

The basic services are those offered to all cable subscribers in a system for a single monthly rate. Cable operators must include in basic service priority Canadian signals and services under the Cable Television Regulations, and can only add services that have been approved by the CTRC. Basic service includes the basic band VHF service of channels 2 to 13. Together with augmented channel service provided by means of a converter, this is the service provided for a flat monthly rate. In this Report, we use the term 'basic service' to include both basic-band and converter channels.

Discretionary services are not offered in all systems. This tier may include channels offered for payment of fees in addition to the basic service rate. It is in this tier that pay TV, specialty, and any other Canadian and foreign services not included in the basic tier are included. These services can be grouped in various ways subject to the linkage rules established by the Commission when it licensed specialty services in 1984.

Cable operators may also offer non-programming services such as emergency and burglar alarms, utility monitoring or computer-assisted entertainment and similar services. Cable operators need the authorization of the CRTC to offer these services because section 5 of the *Cable Television Regulations* prohibits any licensee from using its undertaking except as required or authorized by its licence or by the regulations. The provision of non-programming services must be free of advertising and must not compromise priority and local programming.

In principle, cable operators may not themselves alter or curtail signals during distribution, but the CRTC may require them to do so in particular instances. For example, cable operators who hold a class A licence, which means 6,000 or more subscribers, are required to carry out simultaneous program substitution, or simulcasting. This means that when two or more stations are broadcasting identical signals that a cable undertaking is required or permitted to carry, it must curtail the signal of the station or stations farthest away from its locality — usually American stations — and replace them with the signals of the local or regional station. Substitution is subject to a number of other more detailed conditions as well. (Class B licensees are those with fewer than 3,000 subscribers; Class C are between 3,000 and 6,000.)

Cable operators are required to provide a community channel as part of their basic service. The content to be broadcast on this channel should consist of programs produced by the cable operators themselves or by members of the local communities. Although in principle the selection of programs to be broadcast is up to the operators, they cannot use the community channel to distribute any feature motion pictures, any signal or reproduction of any signal or any advertising material.[10] The CRTC order of priorities for cable operators is shown in Table 24.12.

A New Regulatory Framework for Cable

The framework that we describe in the following pages is essentially intended to ensure that Canadian cable television should develop within a clearer regulatory structure. As Yves Mayrand, Secretary of Allarcom Limited, noted, "regulation, deregulation or re-regulation of cable television, depending on the point of view, is not a simple matter".[11] Fortunately, the situation in Canada is simpler than that in the United States. Although the federal regulatory burden on cable television in the U.S. has been lightened somewhat, it remains extremely complex. The following comment appeared in the February 1986 edition of *Marketer: Rogers Marketing Newsletter*:

> For those not familiar with cable operations in the U.S., it is a commonly held belief that operations there are carried on in a climate devoid of regulation and subject only to the competitive forces of the marketplace. This perception is

further reinforced by 'rumors' that the Cable Communications Act of 1984 completely deregulated cable in the U.S. In fact, cable regulation in the U.S. is highly complex.

In Canada, the regulation is at a federal level, and it is predictable in that it involves a large and experienced bureaucracy with a good sense of what its mandate is towards broadcasting and communications. U.S. regulation is primarily at the local level. The city ordinances governing the operation of a cable system are not only detailed and complex, but they are also regulated in an exceedingly political environment. Then there are state and federal agencies whose actions impact directly on the operator.[12]

It is not enough, however, to rejoice over the fact that cable television regulation in Canada is somewhat simpler than in the United States. It must be made clear that Canadian cable television should contribute to the achievement of the objectives of Canada's broadcasting policy. The regulatory and policy framework for the cable industry must state what is required and expected of it. The regulation must also be flexible and avoid imposing unnecessary burdens.

Table 24.12 CRTC Carriage Priorities for Television Signals on Cable

<table>
<tr><th>Basic Service[a]</th><th>Augmented Channel Service</th></tr>
<tr><td>– signals of all local television stations
– owned and operated by the CBC
– owned and operated by a provincial broadcaster
– signals of all local television stations not affiliated with the preceding
– regional stations not affiliated with the networks described above
– a community channel
– signals of any extra-regional CBC television station, broadcasting in a language other than the CBC stations described above</td><td>– signals of the remaining priority stations if there are not enough channels available on basic service
– signals of "optional television stations" (stations to which the cable company can, but has no obligation to, assign a channel)
– special programming channels</td></tr>
<tr><th colspan="2">Discretionary Services</th></tr>
<tr><td colspan="2">– Canadian pay-TV services
– Canadian specialty programming services
– Foreign services, subject to linkage rules related to carriage of Canadian services (maximum five channels for non-Canadian discretionary services)</td></tr>
<tr><th colspan="2">Non-programming Services</th></tr>
</table>

Sources: CRTC Cable Television Regulations.
CRTC Public Announcement, March 26, 1979.
CRTC Public Notice 1984-81.

Note: a. This reflects the major carriage priorities, but is not a comprehensive list.

A Clear Status as a Carrier of Broadcasting

Cable television is a hybrid because it delivers signals and is also a programmer, both in the same operation. Although their programming activity remains limited, cable operators are nevertheless both carriers and programmers. This dual role presents a number of challenges. The Clyne Committee put it this way:

> The Persian general ordered the execution of the messenger who brought bad news: The lesson is that a carrier should not be held responsible for the content of the information he receives and delivers; conversely a carrier must not be permitted to tamper with the information entrusted to him for transmission.[13]

The CRTC has also identified problems stemming from the hybrid nature of cable television. In a 1979 review of Cable programming issues, the CRTC said:

> If cable television were to assume the characteristics of traditional over-the-air broadcasting operations then it could be argued by broadcasters that cable television licensees should have to comply with all the regulatory requirements of over-the-air broadcasting, including compliance with Canadian content regulations. In addition, it could be argued that cable licensees should not expect to benefit from both subscriber revenue and commercial advertising in competition with broadcasters. Alternatively, broadcasters could argue that they should be granted relief from present content regulations in order to compete, which would, in the Commission's view, be a serious setback to the implementation of the broadcasting policy as outlined in the Broadcasting Act.[14]

Cable operators have tended to invoke their programming role to justify a loosening of the transmission rules, and a continued exemption from rate-of-return regulation.

Under the present Act, cable operators are responsible for the content of all programs they carry even though they had nothing to do with the production of them. This applies, for instance, to programming supplied for the community channel by community broadcasting organizations. Similarly, many cable undertakings distribute programs from la SETTE that provides a selection of programs from France.[15] The broadcasts are distributed by cable operators, each of which is liable, although the cable undertakings do not control the content of the programs. The same situation arises in connection with programming services originating with one cable operator that are made available to others.

It is not reasonable, we believe, to require that undertakings with no real control over programming be held liable for it. To establish a clearer status for cable operators, their basic role as transmitters of broadcast programming needs to be separated from their other functions. The best way to achieve this is to acknowledge the mixed status of such undertakings and to distinguish clearly among the three major functions they perform: the transmission of programming services; the creation, assembly and marketing of programming; and the provision of non-programming services.

Recommendation

Cable undertakings must be clearly identified as undertakings that receive and retransmit broadcasting signals. The activities of creation, assembly and marketing of programming, other than that which is simply retransmitted, or of providing non-programming services, should be entrusted to separate organizations.

Transmission

A cable undertaking must be redefined to encompass only the activities of receiving broadcasting signals and retransmitting them to its subscribers. It ought not as such to be responsible for the content retransmitted. Its role is to retransmit content in a specified order of priority based on existing broadcasting policy objectives and regulations.

Clearly, the cable operator has the right to be paid and to earn a fair return for the services offered to subscribers, such as signal-receiving operations, retransmission, system maintenance and replacement, and administration and marketing. Should a retransmission right be established in revised copyright law, the cable system operator would also be expected to make any required copyright payments.

The involvement of cable as a transmission undertaking in dealing with the programming of the broadcasters whose services are carried should be limited to simulcasting, as required by regulation. Such substitution only involves replacing the programming of one broadcaster with that of another, without altering content.

Decisions as to what may be retransmitted by cable companies must, of course, continue to be subject to regulation by the CRTC, based on the objectives set out in the broadcasting legislation. These objectives should be clearly articulated in broadcasting policies, which can be the subject of public discussion and industry review. We propose detailed priority rules later in this chapter.

Programming Services

Community programming and any programming services in which the owners of a cable system may be involved should require separate licences.

Community programming could be provided through a subsidiary of the cable undertaking or by independent organizations. It would thus be the responsibility of an organization distinct from the cable operator, as would other programming now originating with cable undertakings.

By clearly stating the principle that responsibility for programming lies with organizations that are distinct from the cable undertaking, cable is made a true carrier that does not intervene in content (except for simulcasting).

Cable systems must obviously continue to carry community programming but, as we recommend in Chapter 19, this programming is the responsibility of the organizations licensed to produce it. There is nothing to prevent a cable operator from being the holder of such a community broadcasting licence producing local programming. Such an organization or entity could obtain a licence pursuant to the terms and conditions set by the regulatory authority. We recommend in Chapter 19 that the licensing procedure be reduced to a minimum. The underlying objective is to ensure a clear status for the cable companies without limiting the supply of local and community programming.

Recommendation

> Community programming and any other programming services in which the owners of a cable transmission undertaking may be involved should be the responsibility of separately licensed entities.

Non-Programming Services

The development of non-programming services could be fostered by the new status proposed for cable undertakings. Subject to priority obligations to distribute Canadian programming, the operator would be free to rent channels on an equitable basis to anyone wishing to offer non-programming services. The cable undertaking would not be authorized to offer such services itself, but it could establish subsidiaries to do so. The CRTC should restrict its role to that of an arbitrator when disputes arise over conditions of access to non-programming service channels.

Recommendation

> Cable undertakings should be free to offer non-programming services as long as they meet their obligations to distribute Canadian programming as specified in the regulations or the licence conditions. Non-programming services should be offered by undertakings distinct from the cable undertakings.

Advertising

Because under our proposals cable operators must not be involved in program content, they should not compete for advertising revenues.

Under the CRTC's proposed cable regulations published in February 1986 the community channel could carry contra (exchange for services) advertising as well as the names and messages of sponsors. Such advertising, described in Chapter 19 on Community Broadcasting, could help to finance organizations responsible for community programming. But in view of the principle of the separation of content and carriage that we advocate, it could not be used to increase the revenues of cable operators.

Advertising revenue should be used to support programming and thus be available only to undertakings involved in programming. Carriers that do not produce content should not be allowed to receive advertising revenue. Moreover the right of cable operators to fair and reasonable rates makes it completely unnecessary for them to sell advertising.

Recommendation

Cable television undertakings should not be allowed to compete for advertising revenue with licensed Canadian broadcasters.

The Role of Cable in the Canadian Broadcasting System

The Task Force believes that the role of the Canadian cable television industry is to be first and foremost a carrier of Canadian radio and television services, both public and private. First priority for carriage should go to Canadian public sector services, followed by the Canadian private sector. To the extent that foreign broadcasting signals are carried, they should complement programming from Canadian sources. We recognize that an exception must be made for foreign television signals that are already an established part of the system, especially the three-plus-one. Even here we suggest in Chapter 28 a careful exploration of alternative approaches to the provision of these services. The presence of a particular foreign signal in the system should never be allowed to preclude the development of new Canadian services. Priority must always be given to the development of our own broadcasting services.

We believe it is evident that Canada's own broadcasting industry, both the public and private sectors, can do most of the job of providing programming that is varied and comprehensive, including both foreign and Canadian programs. If the rights to show American programs in Canada were retained and exploited by American broadcasters rather than being sold to Canadian broadcasters, it would be destructive of Canada's broadcasting system, particularly of private broadcasting. More important, it would create an even greater imbalance between foreign and Canadian programs and reduce Canada's ability to produce programs. The carriage rules that apply to cable television will have a powerful influence on the degree to which Canadian broadcasting services develop and the revenues that they earn.

Special problems arise in designing regulations that effectively meet the needs of Canada's French-language population. In Chapter 8 we examine the tailoring of broadcast policy to satisfy the requirement that broadcasting be available in both French and English. This objective may well necessitate special carriage regulations giving priority to French-language services for cable systems that serve primarily French-language subscribers.

Recommendation

The essential role of cable television is to be a carrier of Canadian radio and television broadcasting services, both public and private. First priority should be given to public-sector Canadian services followed by private Canadian services. To the extent that foreign radio and television services are carried, they should represent a source of programming complementary to that available from Canadian broadcasters. Priority should be given to services in French on systems that serve primarily francophone subscribers.

Regulation of Cable Service Structure and Carriage Priorities

Cable television in Canada developed above all as a method of distributing American signals to Canadian households. Such signals were available free of charge to cable companies and represented a ready source of additional attractive programming. This approach, approved by the CRTC, made it possible for cable operators to compete directly with broadcasters as distributors of American programming. In English Canada, a high percentage of programs carried on American commercial networks is available on Canadian stations, as shown more fully in Chapter 28 on Copyright Issues. The cable import policy has provided a greater choice of channels, but not a proportionately greater choice of programs. By importing signals, which to a great extent contain the same programs acquired by Canadian broadcasters, the cable television industry exacerbated the competition between American networks and Canadian stations.

The price of increasing American choice on cable was a decrease in viewing of Canadian channels which occasionally meant the disappearance of a station, especially in peripheral areas. Canada had to face the challenge of the entire network television output of another country in all its major markets.

Signals from American television stations have always been within reach of Canadian households in communities near the border. Cable merely improved the quality of reception. Later, the threat of individual dishes receiving satellite signals was put forward to justify importing more American signals.

The first assumption underlying policies that allowed virtually unrestricted import was that because the technical capacity existed to carry both the American and Canadian broadcasting services, that was what should be done. The second and related assumption was that copyright was irrelevant to the operation of Canadian cable systems. In fact, Canadian cable systems have been free of copyright restrictions and able to import signals without paying for programs.

Today the legal environment is changing. In the United States copyright extends to cable rediffusion, albeit under a compulsory licensing requirement. Criticism in the U.S. of the unauthorized carriage of American signals on Canadian cable and satellite systems has mounted. The Canadian Cable Television Association (CCTA) noted in a brief to the Task Force that cable companies in the United States have dropped many of the signals they carried when no payment was required. According to a study prepared for the CCTA by Nordicity Group Ltd., the average American cable system carries two distant signals, while the average Canadian system carries 3.5 distant signals.[16] In Canada we are moving toward the application of copyright law to cable, an issue we examine in Chapter 28.

As we move toward applying copyright law to cable television the tensions within the Canadian broadcasting system become more acute. Canada's broadcasters have always argued that the rights they purchase to show American TV programs in Canada should be respected. To a significant degree the CRTC substitution rules do protect those rights. The question of who will hold the rights to show American programs to Canadians can be expected to become more controversial, however, in relation to both conventional broadcasting and pay and specialty television services.

It is true that Canadians want a wider range of high-quality programs and that the possibility is open to obtain them outside the Canadian broadcasting system. That is why something must be done to ensure that Canadian broadcasters themselves provide an appropriate selection of high quality programs both foreign and Canadian, with appropriate protection of the rights they acquire to foreign programs.

Because cable companies in Canada now reach a growing majority of Canadians, their carriage of new Canadian satellite-to-cable channels provides an inexpensive means of national distribution and can contribute significantly to strengthening Canadian broadcasting. To the extent that the Canadian signals carried require payment by cable system operators, they, like their counterparts in the United States, can also contribute financially to the development of new national programming services.

While there will be an ongoing need to revise the details of carriage regulation to reflect the objectives of the *Broadcasting Act* and the role of cable in the Canadian system, we suggest a number of basic principles. Many are either identical or close to existing priority carriage regulations, or reflect changes proposed by the CRTC in February 1986. These principles would apply to carriage on the basic service:

1. Cable operators must carry all CBC services. This obligation should be extended to include all available signals, including both mono and stereo radio. Cable services should carry CBC radio services available via satellite where they are not available locally.
2. In each province cable operators should carry all provincial public radio and television services licensed by the CRTC, whether they are available over-the-air or only by satellite.
3. The recommended TV Canada services and the proposed CBC news channel should both be carried on basic service in all cable systems that offer discretionary services. (See Chapter 10 and Chapter 15).
4. Priority carriage should be extended to apply to the channel broadcasting the proceedings of the House of Commons and, where appropriate, to similar services covering the provincial legislatures.
5. Cable operators should carry all available local and, where appropriate, regional Canadian television services with such priority extended to licensed services received by satellite as well as off-air services.

   Cable operators clearly should continue to carry the local signals of Canadian broadcasters as well as the regional signals to the extent needed to give Canadians access to the widest possible range of Canadian programming. Extra-regional Canadian signals should not be carried unless it is clear that they would not compromise the viability of local regional broadcasting services.

   The obligation to carry available Canadian services should not be limited to the signals from conventional transmitters, but where appropriate, be extended to satellite networks such as ASN (Atlantic Satellite Network).

This type of service is not discretionary; it is related to traditional broadcasting services and subject to the same obligations. There is no reason to deny priority to the carriage of this type of service simply because it is available only by satellite. This should be interpreted in light of recommendations in Chapter 17 on private television concerning distant Canadian signals and Canadian superstations.

6. Cable operators should carry all local AM and FM audio services including transmission of AM stereo and any FM subcarrier and, with the exception of public sector services, should not carry foreign radio services. There is no valid reason why commercial American radio signals should be carried because there is an extremely wide range of programming available from Canadian commercial radio services.

The Task Force has also set out in Chapter 18 on Pay-TV and Specialty Services certain criteria for the carriage of these and other discretionary services.

The Tiering of Cable Television Service

Virtually all broadcasting services available to Canadians can be fitted into three general categories.

1. Services essentially Canadian in character providing mainly Canadian programs. These are mostly public-sector services exempt from the pressure to maximize financial return to shareholders. Characteristically, such services exist entirely because of their role in Canadian programming.
2. Services owned by Canadians and providing both Canadian and foreign programs, but relying, on the anglophone side, for most of their audience appeal and revenue on lower-cost foreign programs. Virtually all private-sector Canadian services fall into this category. All are exposed to the inevitable commercial incentive to use foreign programs that can be bought for far less than the cost of producing Canadian programs.
3. Foreign broadcasting services naturally offering almost entirely foreign programs.

The relative importance of each of these types of service in providing Canadian-origin programming is clear. Our recommendations on carriage of signals in Canadian cable systems reflect the view that the highest priority should be given to essentially Canadian services, then to other Canadian services that may be driven commercially by foreign programming but nevertheless offer Canadian programs as well, and finally to complementary foreign broadcasting services.

Based on these criteria we considered whether it might be possible to re-tier Canadian cable service, at least in English language systems, better to reflect these priorities. A model was developed and tested by Moss, Roberts to determine whether such a system could also be consistent with the interests of the cable industry. The model is set out in schematic form in Table 24.13.

Table 24.13 Current and Alternative Cable Tiering Structure

Current Structure[a]	Alternative Structure
Basic Tier (including augmented channel service)	**Alternative Basic Tier**
– Canadian channels, public and private, which qualify for priority carriage under CRTC regulations	– Canadian channels, public and private, which qualify for priority carriage under CRTC regulations
– Community channel where required	– Community channel
– Parliamentary channel	– The proposed TVCanada services
– Optional channels as permitted by the CRTC, including the American 3 + 1 and, in some cases, independent U.S. stations	– Proposed Canadian all-news channel.
– "Barker" channel, which promotes discretionary tier	– Optional conventional Canadian channels, as permitted by CRTC
Discretionary Services	**Second Tier**
– Canadian movie channel (First Choice/Superchannel/Super Ecran)	– Canadian specialty channels (subject to higher Canadian content requirements than at present)
– Canadian specialty channels (The Sports Network, MuchMusic, Life Channel)	– Optional conventional American signals including 3 + 1 and any additional American signals now carried on basic
– American specialty channels approved for carriage by CRTC	**Premium Tier**
	– Canadian movie channels
	– Canadian specialty channels (i.e. those which choose not to meet requirements for carriage on second tier)
	– American specialty channels which are complementary to licensed Canadian services

Note: a. This is a general schematic picture applicable mainly to English-language systems. As the text of the chapter indicates, not all systems carry all the services enumerated.

The major change tested in the model was the reconfiguration of the present two tiers into three. Placement on each of the tiers would reflect a tiering allocation based on Canadian content. The new basic tier would be all-Canadian. The new second tier (which would be received for a fee with removal of a block-trap scrambling device), would carry the American three-plus-one and other American independents now on the basic tier, as well as any licensed Canadian discretionary services willing to increase their Canadian content to reflect their enhanced position.

The new premium services tier would carry licensed Canadian pay-TV services, any Canadian discretionary services that chose not to move to the second tier, as well as complementary American discretionary services. The carriage of additional services from the United States on this tier would be based on the requirement that cable not carry any American service if the CRTC had licensed a similar Canadian service.

The model fulfils a number of policy objectives for cable that are recommended by the Task Force, including:

- the highest Canadian content services will have priority tier positioning;
- the moving of Canadian discretionary services to a lower tier (lowering their price) will offer Canadian viewers more choices of Canadian programming;
- cable operators will be offered greater flexibility to offer more services to Canadian subscribers.

The Task Force feels that much additional research is required before adopting such a model. Market research is needed to determine if our assumptions, in particular our estimate of the anticipated penetration of the new second tier, are correct.

The Task Force also feels that a number of broad policy questions about the proposed re-tiering would need to be answered before implementation. For example, will our model really create and offer more Canadian programming? Would moving MuchMusic or The Sports Network (TSN) to the expanded basic tier mean an increase in Canadian content for these services?

Is the national Canadian advertising pool large enough to support new and transferred services on the 'expanded basic' tier? What is the potential effect on the ad revenues of off-air broadcasters? It would probably be necessary to continue to restrict these satellite-delivered services to non-local advertising as well as to maintain the limit of eight commercial minutes per hour of programming.

Then again, would the additional revenues earned by the discretionary services from moving to the 'expanded basic' tier be sufficient to offset the increased programming costs of such a move?

Economic analysis of the re-tiered service indicates that it has the potential of producing growth for both cable systems and Canadian broadcasters. If market research indicates that the assumptions are correct, the re-tiered cable service would continue to provide a fair and reasonable return to Canadian cable system operators.

Recommendation

Further study should be undertaken to determine the feasibility of re-tiering cable service on the basis of the principles and model set out in this Report.

The Obligation to Comply with Rebroadcast Rights

Because the determination by the Exchequer Court in 1953 that the retransmission by cable of a television program was not covered by the *Copyright Act*,[17] there has been controversy on whether or not cable operators should be responsible for paying fees to authors and other creators of program content they carry.

While some have claimed that the development of cable television was based on piracy, the cable companies have in fact complied with existing law. The industry has argued against the establishment of rebroadcast rights on the ground that they would not lead to any significant inflow of additional funds for the production of Canadian works. Because the cable industry imports American signals on a massive scale, it is obvious that the payment of rebroadcast rights, especially for the rebroadcast of American signals to regions where they cannot be received over-the-air, might lead to substantial payments to American broadcasters.

The existence of a market assumes recognition of the rights of those who invested in program creation and production. Policies to accommodate fair markets will not be achieved if these rights are denied. Thus, it would not be surprising if massive imports of foreign content led to substantial payments to foreign copyright holders. This happens whenever foreign products are imported. If copyright payments had been required, cable operators might have imported less. It must be noted that Canadian television broadcasters paid $165 million in 1985 for the rights to exhibit foreign programs, almost all American. The amounts that would have to be paid by cable operators for foreign rebroadcast rights should not, however, be exaggerated. The House of Commons Subcommittee felt that the probable amounts had been overestimated.[18]

The granting of a rebroadcast right would make it possible to establish a more market-related system for importing foreign signals. A market system that works well can effectively complement the regulatory system because it generates behavioural incentives. A market-related system could well reduce incentives to import distant foreign signals. That is why in Chapter 28 the Task Force recommends adopting the principle of a rebroadcasting right.

Rate Regulation

From the hearings the CRTC held recently on its proposals for revision of the existing cable regulations, it is evident that many, perhaps most, Canadians believe that cable television has become an essential service, provided on what is in fact a monopoly basis. The Task Force does not believe that VCRs, computers or video games or even TVROs, which are popular mainly in non-urban areas, can be construed as direct alternatives to cable service. While SMATV service is a more direct competitor for part of cable's market, the expanded range of channels that cable is now authorized to carry, combined with the scrambling of the most attractive signals previously received by SMATV, reduces competition substantially.

The reality is that a steadily increasing proportion of Canadians rely on the cable industry for television service. In 1985 there were 5.7 million Canadian households subscribing to cable service, an increase of 5.9 percent over 1984 and more than ten percent over 1983. By contrast there are, for example, an estimated 175,000 TVROs spread throughout Canada. In many large communities with cable service, as much as 80 or 90 percent of the population are subscribers. For most urban dwellers there is no practical alternative.

The Task Force concludes that the monopolistic nature of cable television makes it essential to continue to regulate cable subscription rates for basic service. We are concerned, however, that as cable systems have become larger and more sophisticated no satisfactory process has been established to determine fair and reasonable rates. The Moss, Roberts study prepared for this Task Force noted that "there is no explicit rationale for rate setting".[19] Nevertheless, the rates that may be charged are regulated by the CRTC as part of the conditions of licence.

Rate setting should be seen as a process through which the regulator acts as an arbitrator between the interests of consumers and the interests of the cable companies. The goal should be a process fair to both parties and should be seen to be fair as well.

At present, the financial data reported to the CRTC is inadequate. For example, the Commission does not require that cable licensees provide balance-sheet information system by system. The financial arrangements between parent and subsidiary companies also require close monitoring. Finally, within individual systems, there is no full separation of costs in order to allocate reasonable shares to basic or enhanced services. It is only with the rapidly expanding revenues earned from discretionary services since 1983 that the proper allocation of costs has become a serious issue, and it will become even more important.

Because rate setting is done system by system, it will not be possible to make anything but an arbitrary decision about what constitutes reasonable rates unless there is reliable balance-sheet and operating data available for each system. For systems offering discretionary services, it will be equally important that proper cost separation be carried out. At present the basic approach seems to be to allocate to discretionary services only the direct incremental costs associated with them. This approach will become more and more unsatisfactory.

The increasing sophistication and precision of the CRTC's approach to the regulation of telephone rates contrasts with the increasingly generalized approach to regulating cable rates. We acknowledge the lack of resources available to the CRTC, but it remains a serious policy matter to determine what is in the public interest. Canadians will pay just under $1 billion in 1986 for cable services. For its part, the cable industry will continue to invest hundreds of millions of dollars in upgrading plant to deliver those services. The public has a right to be assured that it is paying rates that fairly reflect the costs. At the same time the cable companies merit equitable treatment for all systems operating in the industry, both large and small, as well as a reasonable rate of return.

To permit the public to intervene effectively, the Task Force believes that the CRTC must require that cable companies disclose financial information on their operations. Otherwise, there is little purpose in providing the public with an opportunity to comment on proposed rate increases. Because the cable systems, like the telephone companies, provide service on a monopoly basis, there seems to be no public policy reason why disclosure should be required in the one case but not in the other.

Recommendations

The rates charged by cable companies for basic service should continue to be regulated by the CRTC. As a basis for rate regulation, the Commission should require that both balance-sheet and operating data be maintained on a system-by-system basis, and that financial transactions between parent companies and their subsidiaries be monitored.

Cable companies should be required to carry out full cost separations as a basis for the fair allocation of costs to basic, discretionary, and any other services.

Financial data on a system-by-system basis should be disclosed as a basis for public involvement in rate setting.

The rates allowed cable companies should reflect the costs of upgrading their basic services, including the cost of the proposed new Canadian television services, and also allow them a fair and reasonable return on their investment.

Notes

1. Moss, Roberts, and Associates Inc., "An Economic Profile of Canadian Cable Industry", study prepared for the Task Force on Broadcasting Policy, Ottawa, 1986.
2. Ibid.
3. *In Re Regulation and Control of Radio Communication in Canada*, (1932) A.C. 304.
4. In particular, Canadian Radio-television and Telecommunications Commission, *Canadian Broadcasting — A Single System — Policy Statement on Cable Television* (Ottawa: CRTC, 1971).
5. *Cable Television Regulations*, C.R.C. 374, enacted on November 14, 1975. At the same time, the Commission issued another major policy statement entitled *Policies Respecting Broadcasting Receiving Undertakings* (Cable Television), 16 December 1975.
6. In Manitoba and Saskatchewan, cable undertakings rent the infrastructures of telecommunications undertakings that are owned by the Province.
7. Sloan Commission on Cable Communications, *On The Cable, The Television of Abundance* (New York: McGraw-Hill, 1971). p. 92.
8. See *Quincy Cable TV v. F.C.C.*, 768 F 2d 1434 (1985).
9. Canadian Radio-television and Telecommunications Commission, *Applications by Cable TV Licensees for Changes in Fees Charged to Subscribers*, Public Announcement (Ottawa: September 1974); and, CRTC, *Cable Television Undertakings — Class "A" and "C" Licensees, Issues Related to the Regulation of Cable Rates* (Ottawa: CRTC, June 1984). See also Marie-Philippe Bouchard, Michèle Gamache, Mireille Beaudet, "Étude du statut juridique des entreprises de radiodiffusion au Canada", study prepared for the Task Force on Broadcasting Policy, Ottawa, 1986.
10. *Cable Television Regulations*, C.R.C. 374, s. 11.
11. Yves Mayrand, presentation to the Conference on Canadian Communications Law, Toronto, April 1986.
12. *Marketer: Rogers Marketing Newsletter* 2 (9) (February 1986).
13. Canada, Consultative Committee on the Implications of Telecommunications for Canadian Sovereignty (Clyne Committee), *Telecommunications and Canada* (Ottawa: Minister of Supply and Services Canada, 1979), p. 17.
14. Canadian Radio-television and Telecommunications Commission, *A Review of Certain Cable Television Programming Issues*, Public Announcement (Ottawa: CRTC, 1979).

15. The Commission approved applications submitted by cable undertakings, members of the *Société d'édition et de Transcodage T.E. Ltée (SETTE)*, with respect to the broadcasting of programs from all three television channels in France. It considered that this service would contribute to improving the balance between services offered in the French and English languages by Quebec cable undertakings. The Commission is of the opinion that this service does not enter into direct competition with traditional broadcasting services. It is prohibited, in its licensing conditions, from all advertising content and its programming is subject to rules intended to reserve existing or future production rights to broadcasting undertakings. SETTE is not a network under the Act. There is, therefore no delegation of liability with respect to program content. See CRTC Decision 79-460, 8 August 1979.
16. Nordicity Group Ltd., "Economic Analysis of Cable Copyright Liabilities in Canada", study prepared for the Canadian Cable Television Association (Ottawa: Corporation, 1985).
17. *Canadian Admiral c. Rediffusion*, 1954 Ex. C.R. 362.
18. Canada, House of Commons, Standing Committee on Communications and Culture, *A Charter of Rights for Creators: Report of the Sub-Committee on the Revision of Copyright* (Ottawa: Minister of Supply and Services Canada, 1985), p. 79. and; SECOR INC., *Probable Cost of a Retransmission Right in Canada: An Adaptation of the American System to Canada*, study prepared for the Sub-committee on the Revision of Copyright, September 1985.
19. Moss et al., "An Economic Profile".

Chapter 25

Satellite Distribution

Satellite Distribution

Development of a Domestic Satellite Communication System

Communication satellites became the centrepiece of Canada's space program following the Chapman report of 1967.

Dr. John Chapman was the scientist-administrator who played the leading part in Canada's pioneering space-age project, the study of the ionosphere by means of the Alouette 1 satellite, which was launched in 1962. In 1966 the government appointed him chairman of a study group to examine the country's upper atmosphere and space programs. The group recommended that the prime objective of space technology in Canada be its application to telecommunications (including broadcasting) and survey problems. This was a space age role naturally suited to the demands of Canadian geography, climate and sparse settlement in many regions. It was a means of affirming Canadian occupation and control in the vast northern reaches of land and sea where Canadian sovereignty might be challenged if not effectively exercised.

A 1968 White Paper upheld the Chapman vision. The next year Parliament adopted legislation establishing Telesat Canada as a monopoly owner and operator of Canadian domestic satellite communication systems. The company was owned in equal shares by the federal government and the main telecommunication common carriers, most of whom were members of the Trans-Canada Telephone System (TCTS), which became Telecom Canada in 1983.[1] The government's intention was that Telesat Canada would eventually be owned roughly one-third by the government, one-third by the carriers and one-third by the general public. But the company never achieved sufficient profitability to make a public share issue feasible.

The public-private, multi-service solution embodied in Telesat Canada came after a debate in the sixties over single-use or multi-use communication satellites. In 1966 Power Corporation and Niagara Television proposed the establishment of a national satellite television network. In 1967 the Trans-Canada Telephone System and CN-CP joined in a proposal for a telecommunication satellite designed primarily to provide communication services to the far north. The government decided, however, that the national interest in strategic and social communication services to be provided by satellite was too great to leave entirely in private hands. Communications Minister Eric Kierans, putting the Telesat Canada bill before the House of Commons in 1969, said:

> The project serves a national purpose. Outer space, carrying with it major considerations of international policy, should not, in the government's judgment, become the preserve of a privately-owned corporation.[2]

The government wanted the participation of the telecommunication carriers in Telesat Canada, however, because they "have acquired an outstanding expertise in the economic development of telecommunications". Mr. Kierans said the government foresaw a domestic satellite communications system fulfilling four needs: (1) television coverage in the north and underdeveloped regions; (2) telephone and message communications service to the north and underdeveloped regions; (3) extension of television service in both languages to all Canadians; and (4) establishment of a second and supplementary service to the existing east-west microwave network.

The government assured the carriers that Telesat Canada services were intended to be complementary to, not competitive with their own. It was to be a carriers' carrier except in the case of leasing full television channels to broadcasters. Mr. Kierans also stressed that the government wished Telesat's operation to be commercially viable, not dependent on government support.

The TCTS said satellite communication might be a serious competitive threat if it were allowed to undermine Canadian long distance rates, which historically had been used along with business rates to subsidize local residential rates. The TCTS also told the Commons committee studying the Telesat Canada bill that experiments with wave guides and lasers were more likely than satellites to represent the wave of the future in telecommunications. The prediction turned out to be wrong, but other technological developments did lessen the role of satellites. Mr. Kierans told the committee:

> Inescapably, in almost anything connected with communications, there is a troubling vagueness. To put the problem at its simplest, we do not know precisely what future communications technology will be and we do not know with any precision what the effects of that technology will be.[3]

Telesat Canada had its first Anik A satellite in orbit in November 1972 and inaugurated telecommunication service at the beginning of 1973. The CBC began leasing three transponders in 1973 after being pressed to do so by the government of the day. It was Telesat Canada's only full-time broadcasting customer until 1981, when Canadian Satellite Communications Inc. (CANCOM) was licensed to provide service to underserved and remote areas. Since then pay-TV and specialty services have also been added to satellite traffic. The CTV network is expected to go to satellite transmission when its present terrestrial transmission contracts expire. CBC and CANCOM use transponders not only for TV transmission but also for radio.

In the early years of Telesat Canada, however, CRTC reluctance to license pay television and other specialty services suited to satellite-to-cable transmission was a factor in delaying the expected accession of TV customers. Also, in broadcasting as well as general east-west telecommunications, the common carriers were not anxious to transfer traffic from the 50,000-mile microwave networks to the satellite. Failure to use Telesat extensively for telephone traffic was not simply a matter of protecting vested interests. Satellite two-way communication, as mentioned in our chapter on technology, has a serious flaw owing to the 0.30-second time required — even at the speed of light — for a signal to go out to a geostationary satellite and back. This destroys the effect of instantaneous exchange given by transmission at the speed of light over terrestrial distances. The split-second delay splinters telephone conversations and raises problems for exchange between computers. People in northern and remote areas who otherwise would be dependent on less reliable radio service are willing to put up with the problem, but those with terrestrial means of transmission available to them are not.

Telesat's services to the north and remote areas were a great, if expensive, success; but its east-west services were under-used, supported by the common carriers' commitments to lease transponders. Then came fibre optics — the better technology for most point-to-point long distance operations. Today Telesat Canada's system is operating at less than half capacity. As most of Telesat's costs are fixed, a higher rate of utilisation would lower per-channel cost to individual users, including broadcasters. One of its satellites, Anik C-1, was put up for sale in 1985 but has not been sold.

Broadcast and satellite-to-cable networking involving the point-to-multi-point, one-way transmission for which satellites are well suited, have become important users. Use of satellites for information gathering in program production and for syndicating programs is also increasing. A representative of Telesat Canada told us that today about 60 percent of Telesat revenues in the space segment — that is, excluding ground stations — come from broadcasting. If Telesat revenue from ground stations is included, the broadcasters' share of revenues is about 50 percent, since most broadcasters own their own ground stations.

The Anik A and B communication satellites were launched in the 1970s, the Anik C and D satellites in the 1980s. Telesat Canada is now completing the planning for the Anik E satellites which will take over in the 1990s. Its forecast of demand is that the requirement for broadcasting channels will at least double by 1995.[4]

The satellites used today for broadcast purposes are the Anik C and Anik D series. The three Anik C satellites operate in the Ku-band, at 14/12 GHz, with either half-Canada or quarter-Canada spotbeams which do not reach the Yukon or the Northwest Territories as shown in Figure 25.1. They are used about equally for broadcasting and other telecommunications. The spotbeams enable broadcasters to schedule satellite transmissions for regional time zones. Owing to their high gigahertz frequency and power, these satellites can be received with relatively small dishes, about 1.2 metres in diametre, which makes them suitable for direct-to-home broadcasting. Anik C-3 is used by broadcasters primarily for the distribution of a number of regional services, provincial educational services and Canadian pay-TV services. Anik C can be received in the lower parts of the territories with outsize dishes, or could be tilted to give regular northern coverage.

The two Anik D satellites operate in the C-band, at 6/4 GHz, with a footprint that gives all-Canada coverage as shown in Figure 25.2. Reception requires dishes of two metres or more in diametre. Anik D-1 is the only fully used Canadian communication satellite. Broadcasters account for 90 percent of 6/4 GHz satellite use. Among the services Anik D-1 delivers are CBC French and English proceedings of the House of Commons, the CANCOM service of four Canadian and four American stations, and Canadian specialty services such as MuchMusic and The Sports Network (TSN).

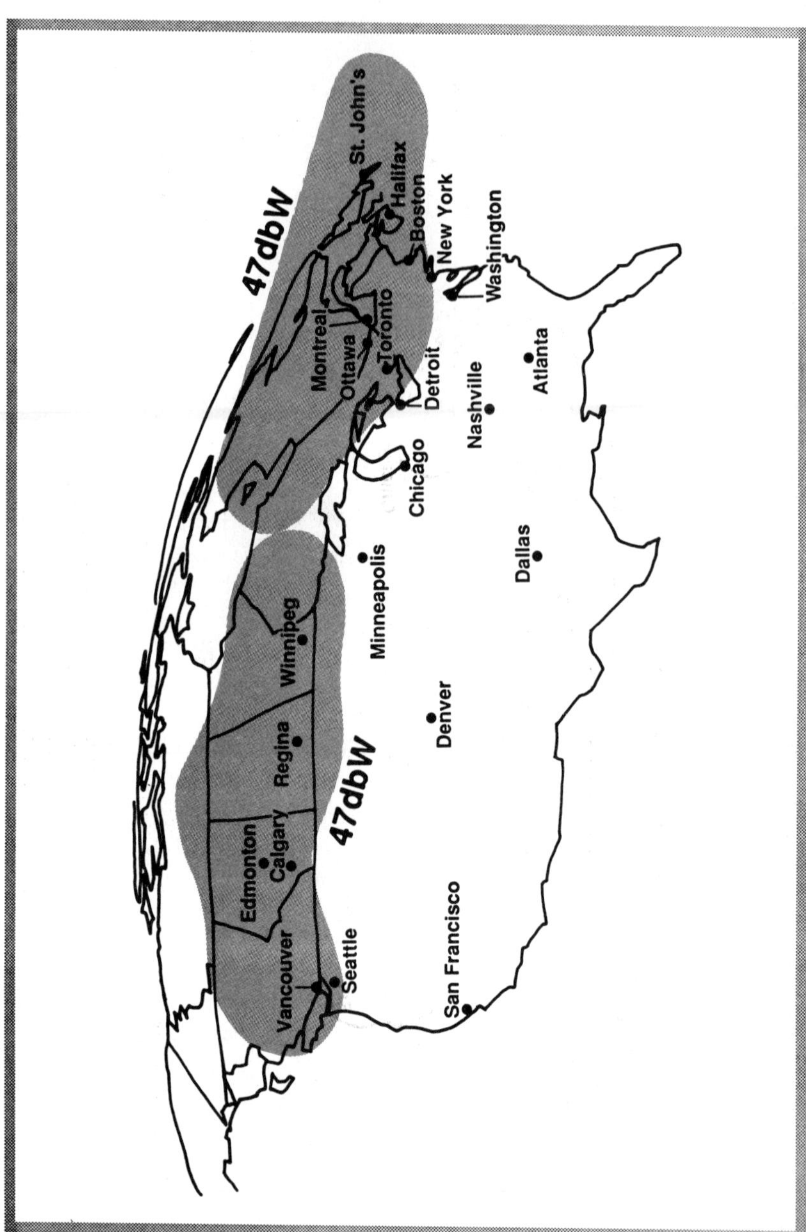

Figure 25.1 Anik C Footprint

Note: This is the area covered by Anik C's half-Canada spotbeams with full-power (47 dbW) radiation. Beyond the footprint, larger-than-standard dish antennas are needed for reception.

Source: Telesat Canada

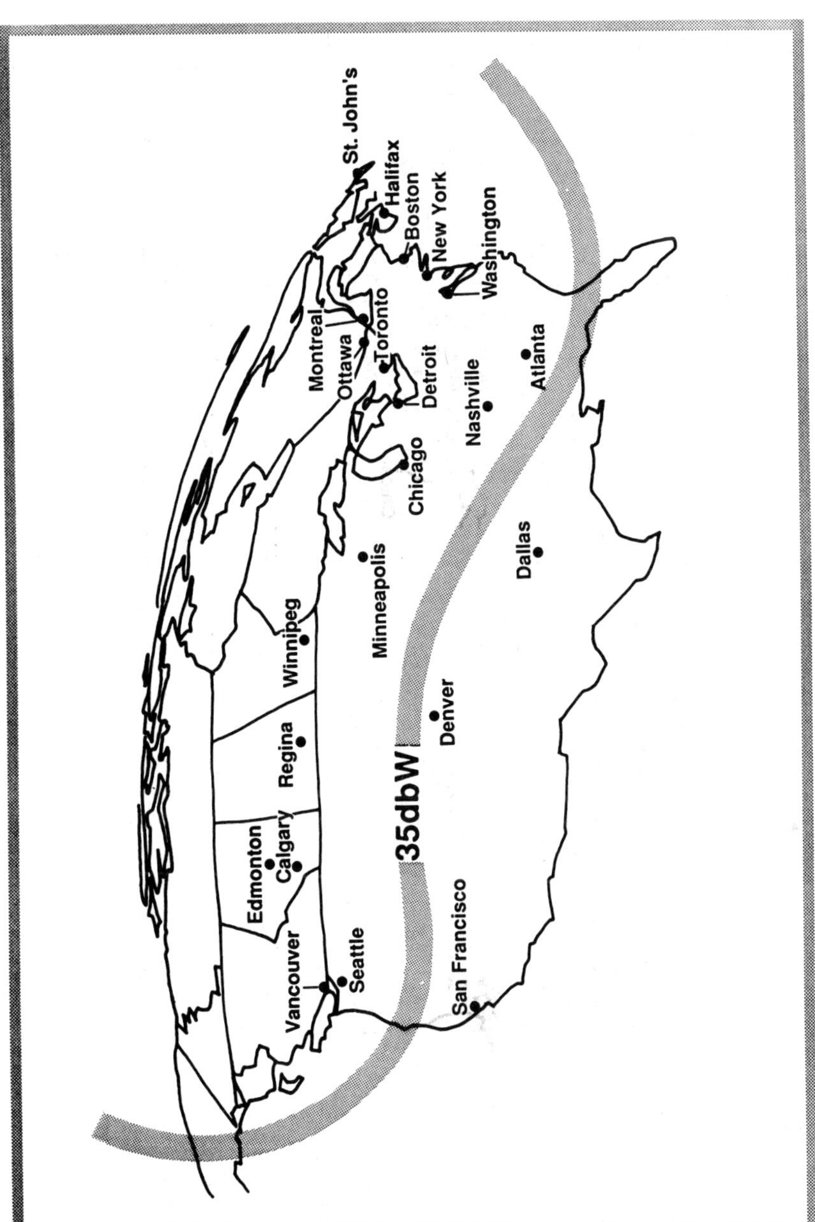

Figure 25.2 Anik D Footprint

Note: This is the area covered by Anik D with full-power (35 dbW) radiation, including all of Canada and part of the U.S.

Source: Telesat Canada

As described in our chapter on broadcasting technology, the C-band has turned out to be the popular one for transmission of network broadcasts and home-dish reception. The direct-to-home broadcasting that had been expected to develop on the Ku-band, designated for direct broadcasting satellites (DBS), has so far failed to come about in Canada or other countries. It is estimated that of the 175,000 or so TVROs (television receive-only earth stations) in Canada, about 95 percent are capable of receiving only C-band signals. The more C-band use has grown, the greater the potential resistance from C-band users to being put to the expense of buying additional equipment to bring in the Ku-band as well. Most of the individually owned TVROs are aligned to receive signals from American satellites only. One advantage of the Ku-band is that its frequencies are free from interference with terrestrial microwave frequencies. The two proposed Anik E satellites will be dual-band, each one capable of either C-band or Ku-band transmission.

The Telesat Canada legislation gave the company the objective of using "to the extent practicable and consistent with its commercial nature, Canadian research, design and industrial personnel, technology and facilities in research and development connected with its satellite communications systems and in the design and construction of the systems".[5] The building of the Anik A, B, and C series was contracted outside Canada, though with some provision for use of Canadian content.

The Anik Ds were built in Canada at a premium of $28 million above the cost of purchase abroad. The Department of Communications made a payment of $22 million to help Telesat Canada to defray one-time development costs of the prime contractor, Spar Aerospace Limited, and Telesat made up the remaining $6 million. In the case of the Anik Es, there is to be no premium. In February 1986 the government announced its intention of entering a five-year agreement with Spar Aerospace for a space development program, part of which is intended to assist the company in becoming an independent contractor for major satellite procurement.

Institutional and Financial Arrangements

Telesat Canada was launched with $60 million in equity split equally between the federal government and the common carriers. The amount, together with government-guaranteed borrowing, covered the costs of planning, building and placing in orbit the first generation of satellites. By 1976 it was clear that Telesat Canada would be in serious financial difficulties when it came time to launch the second generation of satellites in the early 1980s.

Telesat Canada and the Trans-Canada Telephone System proposed that the satellite corporation should become a full member of TCTS under a new interconnection agreement. This would give the carriers more control in the planning and management of Telesat Canada, in return for which the satellite corporation was to benefit from commitments to give it more traffic, from the TCTS revenue settlement plan for sharing long distance revenue, and also from other TCTS support.

In 1977 the CRTC disapproved of Telesat's becoming a member of TCTS. It would "compound the difficulties of identifying the costs and economics of satellite facilities offered to the public". It would "significantly reduce incentives to efficiency". It would also "raise a substantial likelihood of undue preference to TCTS". The Commission also foresaw an "erosion of Telesat's decision-making capacity" if the interconnect agreement were approved.[6]

The government, however, reversed the Commission's decision for policy reasons which it said lay outside the purview of the CRTC. Communications Minister Jeanne Sauvé, in a news release explaining the decision, said:

> Satellites are essential elements in communications service in the North and in other isolated areas. It is expected that new technology satellites will permit new health, educational and social services to become available on an economic basis. In the absence of the increased utilization envisaged under the proposed agreement, and the revenues arising therefrom, service to these areas would become very much more costly. Moreover, to abandon the next series of satellites, or to delay them, would mean the loss of contracts for Canada's space industries, with resultant adverse effects on employment in this sector.[7]

The minister also said it was important to get the Anik Cs into orbit in order to protect the orbital positions obtained by Canada under international agreement. The projected new technology satellites did not come about.

The TCTS provided financial guarantees to Telesat to obtain a $60 million debt issue and a $150 million line of credit. Telesat was now in the position of being simply one of the transmission routes available to customers of TCTS. In 1981 the CRTC again ruled that Telesat Canada could not remain a carriers' carrier. Again the government overruled the CRTC, although an exception was made to allow the corporation to deal directly with broadcasters for full radio frequency channels, as it had in the early years. By this time the broadcasters had become Telesat Canada's major customers.

In the early eighties the outlook for satellite traffic build-up did not look promising; Satellite Business Systems suffered cumulative losses of $300 million in the United States. Telesat Canada was overtaken by a number of setbacks. The 6/5 anti-inflation guidelines limited its rates for two years to far below what it felt it needed. An expected contract for American traffic did not materialize. It experienced delay in obtaining CRTC approval for Anik C rates on the 14/12 GHz band.

In these conditions, the transfer payments promised by Telecom Canada (formerly TCTS) to bring Telesat's return up to the weighted average of the Bell Canada-B.C. Tel rate of return became higher than expected, and the likelihood of reversing the flow during the lifetime of Anik C diminished.

Telesat Canada received $1.8 million in transfer payments in 1981, $5.2 million in 1982, a whopping $28 million in 1983, and $18.8 million in 1984. This led in 1985 to renegotiation of the 1976 interconnection agreement between Telesat and Telecom Canada: Telesat remained a member of Telecom Canada but Telecom payments to Telesat were to be limited to $20 million in each of the years 1985, 1986 and 1987, ceasing with the last year. In return, Telesat Canada was to gain freedom in marketing its services and Telecom Canada guaranteed to lease four transponders until the mid-1990s. The agreement received final CRTC approval in May 1986.

If Telesat Canada's new freedom to market directly to customers were carried to its logical conclusion, the company could go into competition with telephone companies for long distance traffic. It might be able to offer rates so low that customers would accept the inconvenience of the quarter-second delay in satellite communication.

This type of direct service to customers is authorized for satellite communication companies in the United States by the Federal Communications Commission. Local telephone companies throughout the country are required to provide interconnection to satellite carriage. The United States has two-tier regulation: the FCC regulates all interstate telecommunication and can order companies throughout the country to interconnect; the individual states only control telecommunication within the state.

In Canada, jurisdiction is divided between the federal government and the provincial governments. There is in fact no national regulation of telecommunication in Canada. The CRTC regulates in Quebec, Ontario, British Columbia, the Territories, and part of Newfoundland owing to particular historical circumstances. Elsewhere, however, provincial authorities regulate and can decide whether or not Telesat Canada has the right to serve customers directly through interconnection with the provincial telephone companies.

Many provinces would oppose direct competition from Telesat Canada in long distance because it would bypass their own telephone companies, which receive lucrative revenues from long distance transmission and use these revenues to keep down local telephone rates. The federal government and the CRTC are also sensitive to public opinion on anything that would tend to increase local telephone rates by removing the long-distance cross subsidy.

Broadcasting Policy Issues and Recommendations

Policy concerning Telesat Canada cannot be approached from either the telecommunication carriers' side alone or the broadcasters' side alone. Up to now, however, although Telesat's services have become predominantly broadcasting services, the company has been governed by policies and regulations based upon common-carrier principles, regulations, and commercial obligations. This should change. Telesat Canada ought in future to be seen primarily as a communication service to broadcasters and as an instrument of broadcasting policy. We believe this change would be consistent with the new principles put forward in this Report for broadcast delivery services.

We recognize, however, that our treatment of these issues and our recommendations will have to be tempered by the government's findings in its telecommunications policy review, since there remain important non-broadcast functions of Telesat Canada. In the far north, particularly, satellites must be used for most telecommunication services. In respect to both broadcasting and general carriage, Telesat Canada has a vital role to play in the servicing of the north and the affirmation of Canadian sovereignty over the Northwest Passage and other Arctic areas within Canadian jurisdiction.

Terrestrial microwave service cannot be extended out over the seas. The islands beyond the Northwest Passage are dependent on satellites for high-tech communications. Telesat Canada services are important to both the new defence warning system in the north and the extraction of resources in such areas as the Beaufort Sea. These important strategic roles are added to the social role of making the North more habitable in the modern age, a desirable goal in itself and also a support for the strategic objectives.

Many departments of government are concerned with effective northern and Arctic communications provided by Telesat Canada, which in future will include the new MSAT satellite for mobile communications. These departments include Defence, External Affairs, Transport, Energy Mines and Resources, Environment, Indian and Northern Affairs, Regional Industrial Expansion, and the Ministry of State for Science and Technology, in addition to the Department of Communications. While the departmental interests in northern communications are vital to the country, they in fact involve only a comparatively small amount of carriage capacity.

It would be generally agreed, however, that if these national objectives require subsidy it should come from the country as a whole rather than as a cross subsidy from the broadcasters' use of Telesat Canada services. Members of Telecom Canada would argue that they are already subsidizing Telesat services, including broadcast transmission, through their transfer payments to Telesat.

Rate Structure

Whether as common carrier or broadcast carrier, Telesat Canada must have its rates controlled in the public interest owing to its monopoly position in satellite communications. It has already been noted by the CRTC Task Force on Access to Television in Underserved Communities (Klingle) in its 1985 report, however, that Telesat Canada is under too tight a rein. As a common carrier subject to the authority of Parliament its rates for satellite transponder services are regulated by the CRTC under the Railway Act. The Klingle report noted that under this regulatory regime Telesat rates must not only recover the cost of providing a specific satellite service but also cover general administration and contribute to the company's overall rate of return. Preferential discount rates for certain services or users are not permitted, even for new services which may have few subscribers during the start-up phase.

The Klingle report found that rates per transponder were not out of line with rates for equivalent American satellite service. But there is a much higher effective charge *per subscriber* in Canada owing to this country's smaller population. The Klingle Task Force recommended that Telesat be regulated in "a more flexible way, in order to give it greater opportunity to ensure maximum use of its excess capacity".[8]

The view of this Task Force is that Telesat Canada should be regulated primarily on the broadcasting side of the CRTC rather than on the telecommunications side. Subject to CRTC approval, Telesat Canada should be in a position to offer reduced rates to attract potential customers to unused transponders, as on its 'spare' satellites — Anik D-2 and Anik C-2 — or to build up the Ku-band as well as the C-band. The rigidity of *Railway Act* pricing prevents vigorous marketing of Telesat services and adaptation of rates to broadcasting, rather than common-carrier needs. Fuller loading of the satellites will permit lower individual rates.

In the course of our consultations we have heard complaints of Telesat Canada's refusal or inability to offer services, time slots and rates which would meet regional needs. The Atlantic Television System (ATV) news departments objected to having to lease minimum half-hour transmission blocks when shorter periods were needed.[9] Telesat has apparently told ATV that blocks of 10 to 15 minutes are being considered and it is to be hoped the company will take action on this long-standing complaint. ATV also desired freer choice of satellite routing and the possibility, which came into effect in April 1986, of owning its own fixed or portable uplink facilities.

Unless "value of service" as well as "cost of service" can be taken into account in rate-making, the less populated areas of the country will always suffer from having to recover rates from a smaller subscription base. A measure of cross-subsidization in the rate structure would be justified to meet the social and cultural aims of broadcasting policy and make full use of satellite capabilities. Such a policy would, of course, be reached through the CRTC's public-hearing process.

Recommendation

New legislation should provide a special regime of broadcast-carriage rate-setting for Telesat Canada. It should protect the consumer interest in fair and reasonable rates. It should permit economic pricing for the marketing of information and entertainment services. If necessary, broadcast services of public interest using Telesat Canada should be federally subsidized to provide for the viability of satellite communications in Canada.

Industrial Policy

Care must be taken to keep industrial policy separate from broadcasting and cultural policy in connection with Telesat Canada.

We have no fault to find with the aim of fostering the Canadian areospace industry, which has outstanding achievements to its credit and is important to national policy in many ways. Nevertheless, the aim of encouraging industry should not be at the expense of broadcasters who are already faced with heavy network transmission expenses in most parts of Canada owing to the country's geography and population pattern.

In the past Telesat Canada has been enabled to place orders in Canada through government support. This course should be continued to assure that the rates charged by Telesat Canada for broadcast carriage will never reflect an extra cost of buying its equipment in Canada rather than abroad.

Ownership Policy

The ownership of Telesat Canada has not fulfilled the original intention of a rough three-way split among government, telecommunication carriers, and the general public (including other users). The ownership question has recently been under review in the course of the government's policy of transferring crown holdings to the private sector where feasible.

The government's role as half-owner appears to have been one of pressing Telesat to support the Canadian space industry and making sufficient concessions to the telecommunication carriers to ensure that they will operate the system without government subsidy. From the point of view of broadcasting the government has been an indifferent owner.

The position of the telecommunication carriers as co-owner of Telesat Canada is bound to be influenced by their other major interests in copper wire, microwave facilities, cable and optical fibre networks, as well as the shortcomings of satellite voice transmission. The development of technology has been such that the carriers have continued to meet their needs by improved microwave networks and, more recently, by fibre-optic systems. In the mid to late 1970s improved technology, including digital transmission, made it possible to double the carrying capacity of existing microwave networks.

At present, however, satellites still appear likely to be favoured for network broadcast transmission, satellite-to-cable, information gathering, syndication and a limited amount of DBS transmission where other means of delivery to the home are not practical. There are vast areas of Canada which will continue to depend on satellite transmission for the closest approximation possible to the high-tech telecommunication and broadcasting services in the more populous parts of the country.

The time appears ripe for a re-examination of the Telesat Canada ownership question in light of the goals which satellite communications are intended to fulfil for Canada in the future. This Task Force cannot resolve the issue on the basis of broadcasting interests alone. The whole gamut of interests and the related questions of ownership and regulation will have to be considered at the same time.

Recommendation

> In connection with Arctic sovereignty, telecommunication policy, broadcasting policy, the interests of user groups and the general public interest, the government should review the ownership of Telesat Canada with a view to recognizing more adequately the corporation's special role in providing carriage for broadcasting and telecommunication services to underserved areas. The broadcasting industry should be consulted to determine its agreed common interests in satellite communication policy.

Future Satellites and Services

The changes we have suggested, particularly the recommendation that broadcasting be given primacy in the regulatory regime for satellite communications, will probably alter the market forecast on which Telesat's planning for the Anik E satellites in the 1990s is based.

The dual-band Anik Es are planned to have the same coverage as the present Anik Ds in the 6/4 GHz band (C band), as shown in Figure 25.1, and the same coverage as the two half-Canada spotbeams of Anik C in the 14/12 GHz band (Ku band), as shown in Figure 25.2. As a design objective, however, Telesat has requested provision of extended coverage to the north at 14/12 GHz if this can be accomplished in a cost-effective way without reducing performance levels in the areas now covered by Anik C. Telesat Canada told the Task Force that dual-band satellites had been chosen because they will provide improvements in performance and have the lowest cost per unit of capacity. Dual-band receivers to work with dual-band satellites such as Anik E have already started to appear on the market.

We believe a new basis for rate-making, as we recommend, could well encourage broadcasters to plan for a greater use of satellites because of an expectation of generally lower rates. Such major users as the Canadian Broadcasting Corporation might in these new circumstances find it economical to distribute a larger proportion of their programming by satellite. At present the Corporation uses satellites for national networking, but uses terrestrial transmission for regional networking.

As we see in Chapter 4 on Broadcasting Technology there is a movement toward higher definition digital transmission which requires the kind of high-capacity bandwidth that is found on satellite and cable but is lacking in present over-the-air broadcasting channels. This is an added reason to expect that broadcast carriage will become a more important part of satellite business. Radio and television production have also been increasing their use of satellites in information gathering and program feeds.

The future of DBS remains in doubt. Telesat Canada has its own proposal to sponsor such a service through its Anikasting subsidiary. Anikasting would bring a number of broadcasters together on the 14/12 GHz band for small-dish reception in areas receiving the quarter-Canada or half-Canada beams in the southern part of the country. The proposal raises a number of regulatory questions. It also appears doubtful that remote and underserved areas could support both the Anikasting DBS service and the Cancom Service, which can be received as a DBS service by individual owners of 6/4 GHz band dishes with descramblers. Further deliberation among interested parties and the regulator is needed on these matters.

> Cable companies should be required to carry out full cost separations as a basis for the fair allocation of costs to basic, discretionary, and any other services. Financial data on a system-by-system basis should be disclosed as a basis for public involvement in rate setting.

Notes

1. For general background, see Video World Inc, "The Role of Satellites in the Canadian Broadcasting System", study prepared for the Task Force on Broadcasting Policy, Ottawa, 1986.
2. Canada, House of Commons, *Debates*, Official Report, 1st Sess. 28th Parl., 18 Elizabeth II, vol. 7, 1969, (April 14th, 1969), p. 7495
3. Canada, House of Commons, Standing Committee on Broadcasting, Films, and Assistance to the Arts, *Minutes of Proceedings and Evidence*, 1st Sess. 28th Parl. (May 20th, 1969), p. 2051.
4. Econotec Inc., "Satellites and the Broadcasting Industry: Additional Considerations", study prepared for the Task Force on Broadcasting Policy, Ottawa, 1986.
5. *Telesat Canada Act*, R.S.C. 1970, c. T-4, s. 5(2).
6. Canadian Radio-television and Telecommunications Commission, *Telesat Canada, Proposed Agreement with Trans-Canada Telephone System*, Telecom Decision 77-10 (Ottawa: CRTC, 1977), pp. 265, 266.
7. Statement by Minister of Communications Jeanne Sauvé in Respect of an Order-in-Council to Vary CRTC Decision 77-10 and to approve a proposed agreement for membership by Telesat Canada in the Trans-Canada Telephone System, Thursday November 3, 1977.
8. Canadian Radio-television and Telecommunications Commission, Task Force on Access to Television in Underserved Communities, *The Cost of Choice* (Ottawa: Minister of Supply and Services Canada, 1985), p. 22.
9. News departments of the Atlantic Television System and the Atlantic Satellite Network, brief submitted to the Task Force on Broadcasting Policy, Halifax, December, 1985.

Chapter 26

Underserved Areas

Underserved Areas

For some years the issue in broadcasting has not been coverage itself, since virtually all Canadians have access to at least one or two radio and television channels. The issue has become the quantity, quality and content of coverage in what are usually called the "remote and underserved" areas.

First, a word about those two words — remote and underserved. Remoteness, like beauty, lies in the eye of the beholder. Tuktoyaktuk looks remote from Toronto; Toronto looks equally remote from Tuktoyaktuk. Ottawa is often felt to be remote from all other parts of Canada. The point is made because remoteness involves not only the problem of bringing in programming from the metropolis but also the problem of installing some indigenous broadcasting capacity. This is a major concern of the Native Peoples — to make possible communication outward as well as inward. The term 'underserved', on the other hand, does not necessarily mean 'remote'. Some of the lonely crowds in the metropolis may be as ill-served as the lighthouse keeper. Many areas of Canada that are fairly close to large cities have been — and some still are — underserved in the sense of having only a few channels compared with the variety available on cable in more heavily settled urban areas nearby.

Recognizing the Problem

In retrospect we can see that the seventies, especially the second half of that decade, were a period of insensitivity on the part of public authorities toward the problem of inequality in broadcasting services in Canada. It was a time when people in TV-starved areas took broadcasting technology — and the law — into their own hands and erected dish antennas to tap the satellite downlinks and obtain a better quality of picture reception than most home TV sets in urban centres. The government beat a retreat before the do-it-yourself movement and in its 1983 policy statement licensing requirements were dropped for TVRO (televison receive only) earth stations serving individual homes.

In the meantime, home-dish reception of satellite signals meant mostly American programming. People in the remote and underserved areas were therefore confronted with a choice between CBC and CTV programs transmitted by either terrestrial microwave or satellite networks to rebroadcast transmitters on the one hand, and the increasing number of satellite services available from the United States on the other.

In responding to the satellite challenge to the Canadian broadcasting system and to the problem of promoting equality of broadcasting service in remote and underserved communities, the public authorities found it impossible to keep urban and remote-area problems separate. But the economics and organization of extending service to sparsely settled areas raise particular problems; these are in danger of being overridden by pressures to serve the greater number in the heavily settled parts of the country.

Thus the CRTC's 1980 Committee on Extension of Service to Northern and Remote Communities, under CRTC vice-chairman Réal Therrien, became involved in setting guidelines for the general extension and expansion of television services, including pay-TV, no matter where.[1] Three years later the Department of Communications issued a report based on a series of studies of direct-to-home satellite communications, or direct broadcast satellites (DBS), with the view that "satellite communications is an ideal technology for overcoming the tyranny of distance and population dispersion".[2] This exercise, too, kept returning to satellite services for the built-up areas and the possibility of a whole distinct satellite broadcasting system. The reaction of most broadcasters was swift and strong to the effect that satellite services should be a complementary part of the broadcasting system rather than a competitive system.

In this chapter we will see how CANCOM, the main private-sector instrument for extension of services to underserved areas, has steadily become more involved in the general broadcasting system, including services for built-up areas.

Licensing CANCOM

Increasingly and understandably individuals, community groups and finally cable companies began in the late 1970s to receive and distribute American satellite signals, most of them unauthorized by the CRTC because they competed with comparable Canadian services. Further, most did not hold copyright for Canada in the programs they carried. This outright defiance of the authority of the CRTC threatened the credibility of the whole system. The Therrien committee said:

> Our first unanimous conclusion is that immediate action must be taken to meet the needs of the many Canadians who believe that, as regards broadcasting, they are being treated as second class citizens . . . In short, there are several million Canadians who have reasonable cause for complaint and, in rapidly increasing numbers, they are seeking to satisfy their needs by the unauthorized reception of broadcast signals from American satellites. We cannot stress too strongly the immediacy of the problem: alternative television programming must be provided from Canadian satellites with no further delay.[3]

On the recommendation of the Therrien Committee the CRTC called for applications to supply the service. It chose the response from Ralph Hougen, a Whitehorse entrepreneur with long-time interests in broadcasting. The Canadian Satellite Communications Corporation (CANCOM) was licensed and a satellite service launched in 1981. The initial authorization was for eight radio signals, including two native language stations, and four Canadian television signals. The English-language TV input came from three of the key investors brought in by Hougen: CHAN Vancouver, a CTV affiliate owned by WIC (Western International Communications); CHCH Hamilton, an independent owned by Selkirk and CITV Edmonton, an independent owned by Allarcom, with the French-language TVA signal also provided. The company has gone through restructuring in which Hougen's stake has been substantially reduced and WIC's has risen to 49 percent.

Besides carrying the four Canadian TV stations, CANCOM was authorized by the CRTC in 1983 to add the three-plus-one — the three main American commercial networks plus the Public Broadcasting System (PBS). To minimize time zone differences and distance from source, CANCOM said it would rely for the three-plus-one on Detroit signals to feed central and eastern Canada and on Seattle signals for its western service. In the event, however, CANCOM, deeply in debt, relied on Detroit for its service to all areas and never added Seattle. The CRTC decision gave rise to renewed complaints from the government of the United States and the American networks about the unauthorized marketing of the American signals. This is discussed in our chapter on copyright issues.

CANCOM's scrambled signals are uplinked to Telesat Canada's Anik D satellite from six locations in Canada. CANCOM supplies addressable decoders to those authorized to receive the service. Each decoder possesses a unique electronic code which can be addressed from the company's control centre at Oka, Quebec.

CANCOM leases eight transponders from Telesat Canada for $12.3 million a year (including uplink facilities) and earns revenue by charging cable affiliates a monthly fee for each television signal taken, multiplied by the number of the affiliate's subscribers. The radio signals are offered free of charge. Where there is no cable CANCOM rents decoders to satellite dish owners. The maximum charge per subscriber to the cable operator, regulated by the CRTC, is $7 a month for the whole package but varies greatly at different places below that ceiling. At the end of August 1985 (CANCOM's last fiscal year), the company was serving 604 communities with about 850,000 households. The company's deficit was $32.8 million. Today, however, the company has made a public share offering and is deemed by many analysts to have a bright future.

CANCOM explains its heavy debt by noting that it had to pay full satellite fees from the outset before the terrestrial receiving and distribution infrastructure for subscribers was established. We have discussed the high cost of satellite transponders in the previous chapter and a number of our recommendations might improve CANCOM's long-term viability. But the company has added to its potential by finding business in regular broadcasting markets as well as its 'core' market in the underserved areas.

CANCOM'S Mandate and Markets

CANCOM's original mandate was to extend Canadian broadcasting services to the remote and underserved regions of Canada.

Although CANCOM is not a broadcaster, it is licensed as a network. Its service is really analogous to cable, as it is a distributor of other people's broadcasting signals and not directly involved in the content. Whereas cable companies are retailers, however, CANCOM is essentially a wholesaler, marketing its signals to cable systems which sell them to subscribers and must be licensed by the CRTC.

Early in 1985 in response to consumers' impatience and the general tensions being felt in the system, the CRTC created the Klingle Task Force to update the five-year old Therrien Report. The new study, called *The Costs of*

Choice, identified high per capita terrestrial costs as one of the impediments to the extension of service to remote areas. It also noted that "CANCOM rates would have to come down if it is to increase the number of systems subscribing to its service in the core market".[4] It recommended, among other things, the establishment and licensing of regional cable companies. Small communities within a region could be grouped together or become part of a single enterprise and take advantage of economies of scale through co-ordinated purchasing and operating. With CANCOM encouraging and assisting the establishment of these regional companies, economies of scale have reduced the price of headend equipment from over $50,000 not long ago to under $20,000 today. The cost per cable mile has dropped from a range of between $10,000 and $12,000 to below $9,000. It is now possible to build a viable system for a community of 75 households.

These developments, along with the marketing of the CANCOM service on a direct-to-home basis where cable is not feasible, have brightened CANCOM'S prospects in the underserved market. Scrambling of the most popular American signals, which has begun in a serious way, will also improve CANCOM's position. We support the Klingle recommendations to give copyright holders increased rights to prevent unauthorized use of American signals.

The core-market communities were originally uncabled because they were considered too small or their density too low to make cable service viable. The average size was in the 100-to-300 household range. This market is now estimated at 600,000 potential households. CANCOM expects a penetration level of 66 percent or 400,000 households.

CANCOM charges represent an additional cost to cable operators above the already high per capita cost of the plant and equipment required to provide cable service in small communities. The capital costs are the same for legal and illegal systems. However, in the case of the licensed legal system which gets its signals from CANCOM, there is a substantial additional cost of paying CANCOM up to $7 per subscriber monthly to receive its signals. By contrast, the illegal systems receive free signals directly off the American satellites. The degree of attractiveness of being an illegal, of course, depends on the range and quality of the American signals which continue to be available in an unscrambled form.

There have also been substantial complaints over the way the CRTC regulates CANCOM's price structure, which at present is simply by setting maximum prices. In a December 1985 submission to the CRTC, for example, Saskatchewan's Minister of Justice, Garry Lane, stated that CANCOM's policies involved price discrimination. His concern was over the rates CANCOM charged in remote and underserved communities compared with rates charged in communities designated as the 'replacement' market, i.e. those communities in which CANCOM signals were being used to replace microwave imports of the three-plus-one American signals. Lane noted that in 22 communities in the province, 3,100 subscribers are required to pay $5.10 per subscriber per month for four channels, while for the 136,000 subscribers in the larger markets that constitute the replacement market in Saskatchewan the cost for the same package was 62¢.

The same complaint was expressed to this Task Force in its public meetings and consultations. For example, the Manitoba Government's Minister responsible for telecommunication policy, Al Mackling, drew our attention to the fact that:

> The CANCOM signals are being offered to the (cable) operators in Winnipeg . . . for as little as sixteen cents per channel/month/subscriber, while northern and remote systems in Manitoba continue paying an average of one dollar per channel/month/subscriber.[5]

The Minister went on to observe that it was difficult to find a defence on technical grounds because, "it is no more costly to deliver CANCOM signals to a northern or remote system than to an urban system".

The report of the Klingle Task Force drew attention to the fact that this problem must be viewed in the context of the reception of unauthorized U.S. satellite signals which are perceived by some as being "free".[6] If small systems have a choice between Canadian signals which are perceived to be both expensive and perhaps unfairly priced, and American signals which are perceived to be free, the outcome will continue to be troubling.

If public policy results in the creation of an economic obstacle to small communities availing themselves of the licensed CANCOM service, then there will continue to be a tremendous incentive to operate outside the law and outside the licensed Canadian broadcasting system. The result inevitably is reduced legitimacy for the regulatory process and the broadcasting system itself.

While this Task Force has no simple recommendation to make, we share the view of the Klingle Task Force that it is essential to make changes in public policy that will reduce the additional costs that must be borne by licensed cable systems serving small communities. The government could, for example, provide an exemption from the 8 percent cable tax for cable systems with fewer than 500 subscribers, limiting the exemption to systems licensed by the CRTC. In a system with per-subscriber charges of $25, this would reduce the cost to subscribers by $2.

Alternatively, it would be possible to provide direct support to reduce the cost of receiving CANCOM signals in the core underserved community. If, for example, public support were available to reduce the cost of CANCOM signals to a maximum of 25¢ per signal per subscriber, then the maximum cost to these systems for the CANCOM signals would be $2 rather than $7. While this is still more than it costs large systems to buy signals from CANCOM in the south, it would nevertheless not be an unreasonable price to expect people to pay to be part of the legitimately licensed Canadian broadcasting system.

There is also, as the Klingle Task Force recommended, the potential to make federal programs of support to industry open to small legitimate cable systems to offset part of the capital costs of such services. Programs under the Department of Regional Industrial Expansion (DRIE), such as small business support, or the assistance provided under ERDA, could be used. It would also be possible to consider allowing cable systems in the core underserved market to benefit from an accelerated write-off of capital expenditures.

Finally, there appears to be good reason to review the way in which

CANCOM's rate structure is now regulated by the CRTC. It is not clear that, as CANCOM rapidly expands its service in urban communities, there will ever be a reduction in the great disparity in prices charged to its customers in underserved communities.

Since CANCOM has a national monopoly, it will continue to be necessary to regulate its rate structure. There are precedents, however, for other approaches. In the Manitoba government's brief to the Task Force, for example, it was noted that:

> . . . through a CRTC-approved agreement developed by the Association of Cable Operators of Manitoba, the annual cost of operating the ICBN (Intercity Broadband Network) is divided by all subscribers receiving the signals.[7]

With CANCOM now operating profitably it is important to consider whether changes to its approved rate structure are desirable to reduce the cost of service in the underserved market. Action should be taken promptly.

Recommendation

Action should be taken to reduce as much as possible the cost of CANCOM's service to the remote and underserved communities that constitute its core markets.

At present only one of the eight television signals carried by CANCOM provides programming in French. However, we recommend in Chapter 6 that the Canadian broadcasting system should provide programming services to Canadians in both French and English and we believe that this objective must apply equally to service in underserved communities. The development of policies on this issue must bear in mind that there are underserved francophone communities, both in Quebec and across the country, whose need for a reasonable diversity of programming in their own language ought to be met through the CANCOM service.

With the commencement of the Quatre Saisons service, there will be an additional service available in French which would be appropriate for carriage nationally to underserved areas. If the proposed TV Canada service is licensed, it could also provide an additional French service. There has already been discussion of possible carriage of the Radio-Québec service to francophones across the country.

From a purely commercial perspective, however, carriage of a balanced menu of French-language services to underserved communities is not an attractive proposition. The Task Force believes that it would be appropriate to consider whether financial assistance from public sources is necessary to achieve this purpose.

Recommendation

In developing further broadcasting services for underserved communities, special attention should be given to measures that will ensure the availability of a reasonable number of attractive broadcasting signals in French.

CANCOM also now serves the so-called extra-cable market and the replacement market. Extra-cable means that CANCOM supplies those of the three-plus-one services not available on a local cable service. Replacement means that CANCOM can supply one or more of the three-plus-one when they are of poor technical quality if imported by cable systems from a border station. The CRTC has allowed CANCOM to replace American border signals in Saskatchewan and Manitoba. CANCOM estimates this market in the range of 500,000 households out of approximately 5.4 million cabled households in Canada. Conventional broadcasters oppose the move on the ground that the creation of Detroit superstations for Canada, with their advertising reaching *all* parts of the country, will adversely affect Canadian advertising revenue for local stations where CANCOM delivers the superstations to cable. CANCOM argues there should be no appreciable loss of revenue and the replacement market is limited.

CANCOM competes with microwave for the replacement market with cut-rate prices. As noted, remote markets protest paying as much as five times more than the south for the same Detroit signals. CANCOM argues that southern revenues cross-subsidize northern costs.

Broadcasters also argue against CANCOM's being allowed to import distant Canadian stations to medium-size markets where the revenues of local broadcasters may be damaged by such competition.

The Task Force believes the viability of CANCOM and its service to remote and northern communities would best be served by the expansion of its core base and the long-term reduction of satellite costs, rather than by its intrusion into the markets of conventional broadcasters. We have opted to continue protecting private broadcasters in return for a significantly greater contribution to Canadian programming and we affirm that strategy again here.

On the other hand, we acknowledge the difficulty of taking sides on an issue in which so much information remains to be determined. Does CANCOM pose dangerous competition to broadcasters or does it not? In the absence of solid data on which to build a coherent policy, the CRTC has allowed CANCOM to expand through a series of *ad hoc* decisions.

Recommendation

> The CRTC should call a new policy hearing to determine the economic consequences of CANCOM expanding into extra-cable and replacement markets, and enunciate a definitive policy for service to those markets on the basis of its findings.

Whatever the outcome of such a hearing, we believe there could well be a useful role for CANCOM in the gateway concept for obtaining and paying for residual rights on American programs not already owned by Canadians. Under this concept, which is described in the chapter on copyright, there would be one non-profit company that would hold all these residual copyrights for delivery in Canada. CANCOM could be the delivery vehicle for the gateway company, marketing American program packages in this country.

CANCOM's DBS package which we mentioned above is available in all parts of Canada, since the CANCOM signals are on Anik D, a C-band satellite — that is, one that operates in the 6/4 gigahertz band and has a full-Canada footprint. CANCOM markets the eight-channel DBS package for $21.95 a month. The decoder costs about $500. At time of writing it had about a thousand DBS customers and hoped to attract more of the some 175,000 Canadian dish owners who now have their antennas trained on American satellites. In addition to the CANCOM channels subscribers can also pick up the unscrambled channels on Anik D which is the main satellite TV carrier in Canada.

At the same time, through its Anikasting subsidiary Telesat Canada is planning to package the broadcast programs it carries and market them as a DBS service from Anik C. This is the Ku-band satellite in the 14/12 gigahertz range with higher power: its signals may be received on a smaller, less costly dish. It has the advantage of quarter-Canada or half-Canada spotbeams to target time zones, but the disadvantage of not being received in the northern territories with the normal size dish. CANCOM's view is that the underserved market cannot support two DBS services and that it would be a costly inconvenience for dish-owners to adapt their antennas to receive Ku-band as well as C-band signals. But Telesat Canada points to eventual advantages of a shift of DBS services to the Ku-band and states that the Ku-band component of its next-generation satellite may have a more northward footprint.

The DBS market for Canadian services which CANCOM is pioneering thus involves a number of complex technical issues as well as conflicting interests. Nevertheless, DBS service will become important in the effort to provide expanded services to areas that are at present underserved. Government and regulator alike will have to pay close attention to DBS issues.

CANCOM has found an additional source of revenue as a distributor of radio networks on the subcarriers of the eight satellite transponders it rents from Telesat Canada to carry its video signals. Since the CRTC's decision to permit resale and sharing of satellite services, CANCOM has moved aggressively to sub-lease 18 of its audio subcarriers to six different radio entertainment programmers or news services. Our recommendation on networking contained in the chapter on private radio will increase such opportunities.

While the sub-leasing contracts have helped CANCOM to become viable, there is concern that there will be competition between it and Telesat in the sale of carriage and that their respective mandates will become blurred. In the chapter on satellites we recommend that the federal government identify its often conflicting and overlapping interests in satellite communication. The next step will be to sort out the roles of CANCOM and Telesat Canada in the fields of both carriage and content.

Recommendation

The federal government should undertake discussions with CANCOM and Telesat Canada concerning their respective functions and their regulatory and ownership structure. Discussions should also include CANCOM's role in the establishment of a distribution system for native broadcasting recommended in the chapter on Native People's broadcasting.

Equality of Broadcasting Services

Equality of broadcasting services is becoming a possibility to an extent only dreamed of by the prophets of satellite communications a generation ago. But it is not only satellites that are creating a new world of possibilities for the underserved. New cable capacity and various types of subcarrier capacity are also making it possible to serve underserved minorities in the midst of our built-up areas.

We touch on the issues that concern underserved communities and groups in several other chapters of this report, dealing with services to Native Peoples, multicultural minorities, and the official-language minorities. In our chapter on community broadcasting we note its possibilities for reaching the underserved — through community radio stations, TV channels, low-power transmitters, and partial use of CBC rebroadcast transmitters.

With the era of possibilities for reaching underserved areas come new challenges and problems. At a time when broadcasting systems are developing interactive or two-way capability so that people can exercise greater selectivity and become their own programmers, there is the danger that this will be deemed a luxury too expensive for minority markets, thereby perpetuating privileged and underprivileged levels of service.

There will always be the concern we mentioned at the beginning of this chapter: consideration of the problems of the underserved will be diverted to consideration of services for the majority. Instead, we must build into our method of approaching broadcasting the proviso that whenever we consider the question of services for the majority we also make a point of considering the minority who would be deprived of those services unless special provision were made for them.

Notes

1. Canadian Radio-television and Telecommunications Commission, Report of the Committe on Extension of Service to Northern and Remote Communities, *The 1980s: A Decade of Diversity: Broadcasting, Satellites, and Pay-TV* (Ottawa: Minister of Supply and Services Canada, 1980).
2. Canada, Department of Communications, *Direct-to-Home Satellite Broadcasting for Canada* (Ottawa: Minister of Supply and Services Canada, 1983); p. 1.
3. CRTC, *The 1980s*, p. 1.
4. Canadian Radio-television and Telecommunications Commission, Task Force on Access to Television in Underserved Communities, *The Costs of Choice* (Ottawa: Minister of Supply and Services Canada, 1985).
5. Government of Manitoba, *The Extension of Cable Television Services in Manitoba*, brief (Part II) submitted to the Task Force on Broadcasting Policy, Winnipeg, November 1985, p. 8.
6. CRTC, *The Costs of Choice*, p. 24.
7. Government of Manitoba, op. cit., p. 6.

Part IX

OWNERSHIP AND COPYRIGHT

Chapter 27

Patterns of Ownership

Patterns of Ownership

Ownership issues in broadcasting were the subject of considerable debate during the year of the Task Force inquiry. In Quebec, there were the application by Power Corporation to acquire Télé-Métropole, the proposed merger of Télé-Capitale with Pathonic Communications, and the eventual proposed acquisition of Télé-Métropole by Videotron after the CRTC rejected the Power Corporation bid. In Saskatchewan discussion centred on the acquisition by Baton Broadcasting of controlling interest in CTV's Regina affiliate, CKCK-TV, and of CKOS-TV in Yorkton and CKBI in Prince Albert. Baton already owns CFQC-TV, the CTV network's Saskatoon affiliate.

Concentration of ownership in broadcasting and other cultural industries raises cultural and civil liberties issues, rather than the economic issues — the danger of excessively high prices — raised by concentration in other areas. Broadcasters are usually in vigorous competition with other media in the prices they charge advertisers. The prices charged subscribers on cable are under CRTC surveillance and control owing to the monopoly status of cable companies. The principal concentration issue in the cultural industries is usually considered to be the public's right to a free flow of information, opinion, and entertainment from the broadest possible array of sources. Knowledge and enjoyment do not come from allowing only a few to dictate broadcast schedules of news, viewpoints and entertainment. The maintenance of different sectors of broadcasting — public, private, and community — is one way of assuring diversity. Within the private sector excessive concentration needs to be avoided so that no particular interest group or alliance of interests can get a stranglehold on broadcast content.

The Task Force has reviewed the present degree of concentration of ownership in radio, television and cable, as well as cross-media ownership. In addition, the Task Force commissioned a study of policy issues related to broadcast ownership.

In this chapter we look first at the degree of concentration of ownership in each component of broadcasting and at the major companies with investments in more than one part of the Canadian media system. Then we examine the policy issues and make our recommendations.

Ownership in Radio Broadcasting

Ownership patterns indicate the degree of concentration of economic power in broadcasting. Many radio stations today belong to large corporations that own several stations and have interests in other sectors of broadcasting. Often their activities encompass far more than broadcasting.

Although concentration has been increasing, ownership is still quite widely dispersed, as shown in Tables 27.1 and 27.2. Table 27.1 shows the number of originating radio stations belonging to the 13 groups with the largest number. These groups own a little more than 30 percent of all private radio stations. CHUM is the largest with 24 stations, or 5.4 percent of the total.

Table 27.1 Numbers of Private Radio Stations Owned by the 13 Most Important Groups, 1985

Groups	Atlantic	Quebec	Ontario	Prairies	British Columbia	Canada	Stations Share %
CHUM	8	2	8	5	1	**24**	5.4
Telemedia	—	10	10	—	—	**20**	4.9
Selkirk	—	—	1	7	4	**12**	2.7
Maclean Hunter[a]	2	—	6	3	—	**11**	2.7
C U C Group	—	—	11	—	—	**11**	2.7
Moffat	—	—	1	6	2	**9**	2.0
WIC	—	—	4	3	2	**9**	2.0
AGRA Industries	1	1	3	2	1	**8**	1.8
Claude Pratte & Paul Desmarais Groupe	—	2	6	—	—	**8**	1.8
Eastern Broadcasting	7	—	—	—	—	**7**	1.6
Radiomutuel	—	7	—	—	—	**7**	1.6
Gordon Rawlinson Group	—	—	—	7	—	**7**	1.6
Standard Broadcasting	—	2	5	—	—	**7**	1.6
Number of Stations Owned by the 13 Groups	**11**	**24**	**55**	**33**	**10**	**133**	**31.4**
Total Number of Originating Stations in Operation	**58**	**85**	**135**	**91**	**74**	**446**	**100.0**
Relative Share of Total of the 13 Groups in Each Region (%)	**19.0**	**28.2**	**40.7**	**36.3**	**13.5**	**29.8**	

Note: a. Excluding short wave stations.
Source of Basic Data: CRTC, Financial Statistics and Analysis Division, Financial and Corporate Analysis.

The 13 corporations do not have the same impact in all areas: they own 40 percent of the stations in Ontario, but only 13 percent in British Columbia. Most of the 13 corporations operate stations in Ontario; few of them can be considered as truly national. Apart from CHUM, their holdings in radio are limited to one or a few regions of the country. Télémédia and Standard Broadcasting concentrate their activities in Quebec and Ontario; Selkirk and Moffat operate primarily in Western Canada. Canadian Utilities Communications (CUC) and Radiomutuel are strictly provincial companies; CUC in Ontario, Radiomutuel in Quebec. Some of these companies have recently acquired stations in regions where they did not previously operate, suggesting a tendency to expand to cover the country. The recent acquisition of CKGM and CHOM-FM in Montreal by CHUM is an example.

The real competition between radio broadcasters is for listeners in each market. Table 27.2 gives the share of listening hours for stations of the largest owners in six of Canada's large markets. In 1985, the group captured at least 57 percent of listening hours in those markets. For Toronto, their share is 66 percent; for Winnipeg, 69 percent. Some of the owners capture nearly one-third of a market's listening hours, such as CHUM in Halifax and WIC in Winnipeg.

Study of these six markets, important as they may be, does not provide a full picture of the impact of the 13 large groups. Ninety-four of their 140 stations are in other places, some in smaller markets. For example, Radiomutuel owns stations in Quebec City and Trois-Rivières, Selkirk owns stations both in Blairmore and in Edmonton. CUC does not operate in any of the six large cities shown in Table 27.2.

CRTC policy on radio ownership has been to limit a single company to one AM station and one FM station in each market. The Commission has not considered it necessary or desirable to be concerned about a single company owning several radio stations in different markets.

We can report that in a general way, at the national level, ownership concentration in the private radio industry has not reached a high level. But detailed study of each market, and consideration of the question of cross-ownership of radio and other media and non-media interests, would be required to make a judgement on concentration. We look at the issue of cross-ownership later.

Table 27.2 Audience Share of the 13 Largest Radio Groups in Fall 1985 in Some Major Canadian Markets[a]

Markets		CHUM		Telemedia		Selkirk		Maclean Hunter		Moffat		WIC	
		Number of Stations	Audience Share (%)	Number of Stations	Audience Share (%)	Number of Stations	Audience Share (%)	Number of Stations	Audience Share (%)	Number of Stations	Audience Share (%)	Number of Stations	Audience Share (%)
Halifax		2	32.0	—	—	—	—	2	25.0	—	—	—	—
Montreal		2	10.0	2	20.0	—	—	—	—	—	—	—	—
Toronto		2	12.0	1	10.0	1	5.0	1	5.0	—	—	2	9.0
Winnipeg		2	20.0	—	—	—	—	—	—	2	20.0	2	29.0
Calgary		—	—	—	—	1	14.0	2	13.0	2	21.0	1	8.0
Vancouver		1	8.0	—	—	2	13.0	—	—	2	17.0	2	19.0
Number of stations owned by the 13 groups	in the major markets	9		3		4		5		6		7	
	in total	24		20		12		11		9		9	

Markets		AGRA		Radiomutuel		G. Rawlinson		Standard Broadcasting		Total		Total Stations capturing more than .05 of listening audience
		Number of Stations	Audience Share (%)	Number of Stations	Audience Share (%)	Number of Stations	Audience Share (%)	Number of Stations	Audience Share (%)	Number of Stations	Audience Share (%)	
Halifax		1	1.0	—	—	—	—	—	—	5	58.0	9
Montreal		1	0.0	2	15.0	—	—	2	12.0	9	57.0	21
Toronto		1	2.0	—	—	—	—	2	23.0	10	66.0	26
Winnipeg		—	—	—	—	—	—	—	0.0	—	69.0	16
Calgary		1	20.0	—	—	1	9.0	—	—	8	67.0	15
Vancouver		1	1.0	—	—	—	—	—	—	8	58.0	20
Number of stations owned by the 13 groups	in the major markets	5		2		1		4		46		
	in total	8		7		7		7		114		

Note: a. The CUC Group, Eastern Broadcasting and the Pratte-Desmarais Group control 26 radio stations among them. However, none is situated in the markets shown here. "Group" is defined as owner of seven or more stations.

Ownership in Television Broadcasting

Nearly 80 percent of private television stations in Canada are operated by business groups that own more than one station, nearly 50 percent by groups that control three stations or more. The 21 groups owning two or more television stations are shown in Table 27.4.

Many of 40 stations owned by firms with three or more stations (shown in the upper part of Table 27.3) are small undertakings. Only six of these stations are among the 25 stations having the largest audience in Canada.

Some of the large firms in the upper part of Table 27.3 are also in radio and/or cable television, and program production, with operations covering several regions, including the largest Canadian markets. Selkirk is a prime example. In addition to controlling four television stations in medium and large markets (Hamilton, Lethbridge, Calgary, and Kelowna), the company operates 12 radio stations in Canada, and cable television systems in Canada and the United States. It also owns its own sales organization (eight offices in Canada, four in the United States), has an interest in Canadian Satellite Communications Inc. (CANCOM), and is a minority shareholder in the CTV network. Moffat Communications Limited and CHUM also have substantial broadcasting holdings outside the television sector.

Other firms are provincial or regional in scope. In some cases, like Pathonic and Skinner Holdings, they have little or no interest in other aspects of broadcasting. Some others, like CUC, have substantial holdings outside the television sector.

The 12 Canadian interests that own two television stations (bottom of table), have little in common. Baton Broadcasting Inc., Western Broadcasting Company Limited and Canwest Communications Corporation own television stations that broadcast to the largest Canadian markets, such as Toronto, Vancouver and Winnipeg. They are also involved in other aspects of broadcasting. Western, for example, owns nine radio stations, a sales organization and an interest in CANCOM. Another important firm, Télé-Métropole Inc., operates CFTM, the largest Montreal television station and produces most of the Canadian programs broadcast by the TVA network, of which CFTM is the flagship station.

Almost all of the other firms with two stations broadcast in smaller markets and have few interests in other aspects of broadcasting. Several have twin-stick operations; that is, a company uses the same facilities to broadcast both CBC and CTV or CBC French-language and TVA programs to a single market. The two stations of Shortell Limited in Lloydminster, Alberta are an example. CKSA is affiliated to CBC, CITL to CTV. Three more of the 12 firms in this group have similar operations: Huron Broadcasting Limited in Sault Ste-Marie (CBC, CTV), Marc and Luc Simard in Rivière-du-Loup (TVA and Radio-Canada) and Thunder Bay Electronics in Thunder Bay (CBC and CTV).

The television firms with two or more stations are predominant in Quebec and Ontario, with 88 and 83 percent of the stations respectively, as shown in Table 27.3. Télé-Métropole and Pathonic Inc. own most of the TVA network stations and also control almost half of the private stations in Quebec. CUC is the largest television broadcasting undertaking in Ontario by number of stations but they are mostly small, twin-stick operations. It operates four CBC affiliates and three CTV affiliates in the province, giving it almost 30 percent of the province's 24 stations.

Seventeen private television stations are owned by single-station firms, but five of them engage extensively in other aspects of broadcasting. CITV in Edmonton is the only station owned by Allarcom Limited, which is the principal shareholder in Allarcom Pay-TV (Super Channel). CFMT in Toronto is the only TV station owned by Rogers Communications Inc., the largest cable television owner in the country. Standard Broadcasting Corporation owns a single television station, CJOH in Ottawa, but controls seven radio stations in Quebec and Ontario. Similarly, Maclean Hunter, the media giant, operates a single television station (CFCN in Calgary) but also has 11 radio stations and is the third largest cable company in Canada. CFCF Inc. the owner of the CTV affiliate in Montreal, also controls one of the largest cable systems in Canada. Most private television stations are thus affiliated to firms extensively involved in some other aspect of broadcasting.

Television audiences in the largest Canadian markets are not dominated by stations owned by "groups" as much as radio audiences. It is important to note here that "group" is defined somewhat arbitrarily as owners of two or more stations in television and seven or more in radio. The situation for TV is illustrated in Table 27.4 which shows the listening share of private and public stations in some of the largest Canadian markets. In no case do stations operated by private-sector groups capture more than 52 percent of the television audience in a market; for radio, the comparable figure is 69 percent, largely because CBC stations count for a much smaller part of radio listening than of TV viewing, and listening to American stations is negligible. In Montreal, notably, the French- and English-language CBC networks capture 30 percent of the television audience. The CBC network captures 20 percent of Halifax and Winnipeg viewing and about 15 percent of viewing in Toronto, Vancouver and Calgary.

Some stations owned by single-station owners have a large share in their market, like Maclean Hunters' CFCN-TV which captures 27 percent of the audience in Calgary. Six of those 17 stations are among the 25 most popular in Canada.

We can report that in private television, as in private radio, there continues to be considerable dispersal of ownership especially of the largest stations, both nationwide and in the major markets we have studied.

Table 27.3 Number of Private Television Stations Owned by the 21 Most Important Groups, 1985[a]

Groups	Atlantic	Quebec	Ontario	Prairie	British Columbia	CANADA	Share of all Canadian stations (%)
CUC Ltd.	—	—	7	—	—	7	8.6
CHUM Ltd.	4	—	2	—	—	6	7.4
Skinner Holdings	—	—	—	6	—	6	7.4
Pathonic Inc.	—	5	—	—	—	5	6.2
Selkirk Communications Ltd.	—	—	1	2	1	4	4.9
Moffat Communications Ltd.[b]	—	—	—	3	—	3	3.7
Newfoundland Broadcasting Co.	3	—	—	—	—	3	3.7
Radio Nord	—	3	—	—	—	3	3.7
Claude Pratte and Paul Desmarais Group	—	1	2	—	—	3	3.7
Number of stations controlled by nine largest groups	7	9	12	11	1	40	49.4

Baton Broadcasting	—	—	1	1	—	2	2.5
Canwest Communications	—	—	1	1	—	2	2.5
Cogeco	—	2	—	—	—	2	2.5
Harvard Developments	—	—	—	2	—	2	2.5
Huron Broadcasting	—	—	2	—	—	2	2.5
London Free Press Holdings	—	—	2	—	—	2	2.5
Monarch Broadcasting	—	—	—	2	—	2	2.5
Shortell Ltd.	—	—	—	2	—	2	2.5
"Marc and Luc Simard" Group	—	2	—	—	—	2	2.5
Télé-Métropole	—	2	—	—	—	2	2.5
Thunder Bay Electronics	—	—	2	—	—	2	2.5
WIC	—	—	—	—	2	2	2.5
Number of stations controlled by by the 21 television industry groups.	7	15	20	19	3	64	79.0
Total number of private stations in operation	8	17	24	24	8	81	100.0
Regional holdings by 21 groups (%)	87.5	88.2	83.3	79.2	37.5	79.0	

Notes: a. Some of these stations may be termed rebroadcaster stations with a small amount of local programming and/or advertising sold locally, they file revenue reports with the CRTC and in this way are considered separate entities.
b. Two of Moffat's three TV stations are 50 percent owned through Relay Communications Ltd.

Source: CRTC, Industry Statistics and Analysis Division, Financial and Corporate Analysis.

Table 27.4 Audience Share of the Largest Television Groups in Fall 1985 in Some Major Canadian Markets[a]

Halifax	
CJCH (CHUM)	37.0
ASN (CHUM)	7.0
CBHT (CBC-O)	20.0
U.S.A.	30.0
Others	6.0
Groups	44.0

Montreal	
CFTM (Télé-Métropole)	26.0
CHLT (Télé-Métropole) Sherbrooke	2.0
CBFT (CBC)	23.0
Radio-Québec	5.0
CFCF (CFCF Inc.)	16.0
CBMT (CBC)	7.0
U.S.A.	15.0
Others	6.0
Groups	28.0

Toronto	
CFTO (Baton)	19.0
CHCH (Selkirk)	7.0
CITY (CHUM)	9.0
CKVR (CHUM) Barrie	3.0
CHEX (Pratte-Demarais) Peterborough	1.0
Global (CANWEST)	13.0
CBLT (CBC)	12.0
TVO	2.0
CFMT (Rogers)	2.0
U.S.A.	24.0
Others	8.0
Groups	52.0

Winnipeg	
CKND (Canwest)	21.0
CKY (Moffat)	26.0
CBWT (CBC)	19.0
U.S.A.	30.0
Others	4.0
Groups	47.0

Calgary	
CFAC (Selkirk)	24.0
CFCN (Maclean Hunter)	27.0
CBRT (CBC)	15.0
U.S.A.	25.0
Others	9.0
Groups	24.0

Vancouver	
CHAN (WIC)	23.0
CHEK (WIC) Victoria	6.0
CKVU (Western Approaches)	10.0
CBUT (CBC)	16.0
U.S.A.	38.0
Others	7.0
Groups	29.0

Note: a. "Group" is defined as owner of two or more stations. Their audience shares are shown above in boxes.
Source: BBM Bureau of Broadcast Measurement.

Ownership in Cable Television

Cable ownership has tended to follow the historical pattern of the early days of the telephone — a multitude of companies at the outset followed by steadily increasing consolidation. As regulated monopolies in their area, the cable companies are in a similar position to telephone companies. The CRTC has looked favourably on the creation of larger units as the industry has grown in both coverage and sophistication. In 1985, 75 percent of subscribers were hooked up to the 12 largest cable companies, and more than half of the subscribers (53 percent) were connected to only five companies, as shown in Table 27.5.

Concentration of ownership was in some ways actually higher at the end of the sixties, when two American companies controlled or held interests in systems accounting for more than half (51 percent) of subscriptions. At that time, Quebec, Ontario and British Columbia accounted for nearly 95 percent of subscribers. All cable systems were shifted to Canadian ownership in the early 1970s following the recommendations of the 1965 Committee on Broadcasting (second Fowler report), which were reflected in the 1968 Broadcasting Act. The result of the Canadianization of the interests owned by the two American companies was a breakup of their cable holdings on a regional basis.

Later, when cable growth began to level off at the end of the seventies, some companies turned to acquisitions to keep up their pace of expansion. Three major transactions radically altered the industry's ownership structure, substantially increasing the concentration level.

In 1979, Rogers Cablesystems, now Rogers Communications Inc., took over Canadian Cablesystems, the company which had acquired most of the Ontario holdings of Famous Players (a subsidiary of Paramount Pictures in the U.S.) when it was forced to sell under the 1968 Act. In 1980, Rogers acquired Premier Cablevision, which had obtained the CBS cablesystems in British Columbia when their sale was forced. As a result, Rogers held 30 percent of Canadian subscriptions. This had dropped to 23.5 percent by 1985.

In 1980, Vidéotron, a middle-size but dynamic company like Rogers, took control of Cablevision Nationale, the main Quebec company, which had transferred from CBS ownership to Quebec interests at the time of the forced sale. This gave Vidéotron 63 percent of Quebec subscribers and 12 percent of the national total. Its national share in 1985 was 11.4 percent.

All the other cable companies have shares of less than 10 percent of total subscriptions. Some of the 12 largest companies operate in only one province: CFCF in Quebec, Maclean Hunter and the CUC group in Ontario and Moffat in Manitoba. Others operate in two or three provinces: Rogers and Cablenet (Agra) in Ontario, Alberta, and British Columbia; Selkirk in Ontario and Manitoba, Cablecasting in Ontario and Alberta; Bushnell (owned by Standard Broadcasting) in Quebec and Ontario. None of the 12 companies is truly national in scope.

Concentration of cable ownership, under regulation, may well be desirable in many parts of the country to foster the capital development that is needed to provide additional services and better quality through the installation of new technology.

Table 27.5 Cable Ownership Patterns (1973, 1980, 1985)

Year	Holding/Cable Company	Province	Subscribers	% of Canadian Total	Cumulative %
1973	1. Premier Cablevision	Ont., B.C.	300,200	14.2	14.2
	2. Canadian Cablesystems	Ont., B.C.	291,700	13.4	27.6
	3. Cablevision Nationale	Que.	189,000	8.9	36.5
	4. Maclean Hunter	Ont.	187,000	8.8	45.3
	5. Selkirk Holdings	Ont., Man., Alta.	100,800	4.8	50.1
	6. Cablecasting Ltd.	Ont., Man., Alta.	91,500	4.3	54.4
	7. Bushnell Communications	Ont.	67,700	3.2	57.6
		Total Canadian Subscribers:	2,116,000		

Year	Holding/Cable Company	Province	Subscribers	% of Canadian Total	Cumulative %
	1. Rogers Cablesystems	Ont., Alta., B.C.	1,270,300	29.6	29.6
1980	2. Vidéotron Ltée	Que.	500,100	11.7	41.3
	3. Maclean Hunter	Ont.	339,600	7.9	49.2
	4. Cablecasting Ltd.	Ont., Man., Alta.	156,800	3.7	52.9
	5. Moffat Communications	Man.	133,300	3.1	56.0
	6. Agra Industries	Ont., Sask., Alta., B.C.	131,300	3.0	59.0
	7. Cable TV (CFCF)	Que.	130,000	3.0	62.0
	8. Selkirk Communications	Ont., Man	127,100	2.9	64.9
	9. Cable West	Alta., B.C.	105,600	2.5	67.4
	10. Bushnell Communications	Ont., Que.	104,800	2.4	69.8
	11. Capital Cable	Alta., B.C.	96,200	2.2	72.0
		Total Canadian Subscribers:	4,293,000		

1985

Holding/Cable Company	Province	Subscribers	% of Canadian Total	Cumulative %
1. Rogers Cablesystems	Ont., Alta., B.C.	1,280,400	23.5	23.5
2. Vidéotron Ltée[a]	Que.	621,700	11.4	34.9
3. Maclean Hunter	Ont.	370,100	6.8	41.7
4. Shaw Cablesystems	Alta., B.C., N.S., Nfld.	319,300	5.9	47.6
5. CUC Holdings	Ont.	290,800	5.4	53.0
6. Cablecasting (excluding Greater Winnipeg)	Ont., Alta.	210,400	3.9	56.9
7. Selkirk Communications	Ont., Man.	177,100	3.3	60.2
8. CFCF	Que.	167,300	3.1	63.3
9. Cablenet (AGRA)	Ont., Alta., B.C.	161,600	3.0	66.3
10. Moffat Communications	Man.	142,900	2.7	69.0
11. Bushnell Communications (Standard)	Que., Ont.	141,500	2.0	71.0
12. QCTV Limited[a]	Alta.	110,700	2.0	73.0
	Total Canadian Subscribers:	5,438,000		

Note: a. QCTV has been acquired by Vidéotron, CRTC approval pending.

Source: For 1973 and 1980, Jean-Guy Larcroix, Robert Pilon, "Cablodistribution et télématique grand-public : historique du développement de la câblodistribution au Canada (1950-1980)", research study, Université du Québec à Montréal, 1984, pp. 60-61, p. 64. For 1985, *Cable Communications Magazine*, vol. 51 (10), November 1985.

Selected Profiles of Ownership Groups

Many ownership policy issues arise out of cross-media ownership or vertical integration. The Task Force prepared profiles of a number of important companies with multiple holdings in Canadian broadcasting. The summaries which follow illustrate both the differences between companies and the various patterns of ownership that are emerging.

Agra Industries Limited

Communications is one of a wide range of interests of Agra Industries of Saskatoon, others being engineering, medical services and food processing. Agra's communications interests include, radio broadcasting and cable television services as well as wholesale magazine distribution.

Agra controls CKO, an eight-station, all-news radio network operating across the country. It also controls Cablenet Limited, which operates cable systems in Ontario, Alberta and British Columbia with a total of 162,000 subscribers and, jointly with Tele-Communications Inc. of Denver, Colorado, operates cable systems in Chicago suburbs with 61,000 subscribers. It also operates General News, a magazine wholesale distributor in Southern Alberta.

CKO Inc. operates a radio stations in Vancouver, Edmonton, Calgary, London, Toronto, Montreal, Ottawa and Halifax. At licence renewal time in 1986, CKO executives promised to open four other long-delayed CKO stations across Canada, but the financial health of the network is uncertain. A CRTC decision renewed the CKO licence for only 18 months instead of the customary five years because of a fuzzy financial picture, unacceptably low levels of local news coverage and failure to open the four new stations.

Baton Broadcasting Inc.

Baton Broadcasting Inc. of Toronto owns CFTO-TV, the flagship station of the CTV network and produces much of the Canadian programming on the network through its subsidiary, Glen-Warren Productions.

Baton had its origins in 1961 when CFTO-TV was opened in Toronto. Later that year the newly-formed CTV Television Network chose CFTO as its anchor station. In 1972 Baton purchased radio station CFQC-AM and CFQC-TV (the CTV affiliate) in Saskatoon and a controlling interest in station CFGO-AM in Ottawa. In 1976 Baton diversified with acquisition of C.F. Haughton Limited, a printing company in Scarborough, Ontario.

Baton's bid to purchase control of CFCF-TV in Montreal in 1978 was denied by the CRTC because it would have resulted in undue influence by one party over the CTV television network. Applications to extend Baton's Saskatchewan TV holdings were under consideration during our inquiry.

Through subsidiaries, Glen-Warren Productions engages in the production of motion pictures, owns the rights to specials such as the annual Miss Canada program and sells advertising time to national advertisers.

Blackburn Group

In the cities of London and nearby Wingham, the Blackburn family owns London's only daily newspaper, *The London Free Press*, four radio stations and two television stations, both CBC affiliates. The group is regionally integrated and a force in the economy of both cities.

CFCF Inc.

CFCF Inc. of Montreal, controlled by Jean A. Pouliot, is a major player in the Montreal area market, with a television station, two radio stations and a production house, major cable operations, and two-thirds ownership of the new French-language Quatre Saisons television network. The broadcasting business of CFCF began as Canada's first radio station in 1919. CFQR-FM began operations in 1947 and CFCF-TV, the CTV affiliate in Montreal, in 1961. While CFCF-TV is the third largest CTV affiliate in Canada, its viewing share has been slipping from an impressive 22 percent in the fall of 1983 to 16 percent in the fall of 1985.

CFCF is involved in television production through Champlain Productions which produces both national and local television commercials and programs for both CFCF-TV and CTV. It also provides facilities and staff for use by other networks and independent producers. In 1982, CFCF Inc. acquired CF Cable TV which is the second largest system in Quebec and the fourth largest in the country.

CHUM Limited

CHUM Limited of Toronto has grown from one radio station in Toronto in 1954 into the country's largest private radio station owner with 24 stations as well as six television stations, the MuchMusic discretionary service, a production company and a Muzak franchise.

In the late 1950s and through the 1960s CHUM expanded its radio interests in Ontario and Nova Scotia. As CHUM attempted to move into the Montreal market, bids were also being made to acquire radio stations in the West. Involvement in television began in 1965 in Barrie, Ontario and in the Maritimes in the early 1970s. CHUM broke into the British Columbia market in 1973 and the Manitoba scene the following year. A Toronto television station, CITY-TV, came under CHUM's control in 1978. In 1984, CHUM received a licence for MuchMusic, a discretionary satellite-to-cable music channel.

Today, CHUM's radio group operates in seven provinces and is Canada's only truly national private radio business. The company's sixth attempt to enter Quebec succeeded with the acquisition of CHOM-FM and CKGM-AM from Maisonneuve Broadcasting.

CUC Limited

CUC Limited of Scarborough, Ontario is mainly a regional broadcaster occupying the dominant position in radio, television and cable in Northeastern Ontario.

Through its subsidiaries, CUC's television twin-stick operations hold the six private television licences in Sudbury, Timmins and North Bay. CUC also owns the CBC affiliate in Pembroke. Northeastern Ontario is also home to CUC's six wholly-owned AM radio stations and one FM station, as well as a partly-owned AM outlet. CUC has another AM station in Pembroke and a 50 percent interest in two stations in Windsor.

Through cable subsidiaries, CUC serves 52 communities in Ontario, including Scarborough, which is one of the largest systems in the country with nearly 140,000 subscribers. It has minority interests in a number of other cable systems in Ontario.

In a joint venture with Key Publishers Company Limited, CUC publishes *Toronto Life* magazine. CUC is also one of the original investors in The Life Channel, a discretionary satellite-to-cable service.

Irving Group

The New Brunswick Irving family, led by K.C. Irving, controls a vast corporate empire which includes mass media interests in the province. A company controlled by two of K.C. Irving's sons owns CHSJ-TV in Saint John and its seven rebroadcasting stations throughout the province, radio station CHSJ in Saint John, and the morning and evening newspapers in the city. Another son controls the company which owns the English-language daily newspapers in Fredericton and Moncton. In 1984 the television station had the largest audience of any CBC English-language affiliate and is still the only source of CBC English TV service in the province.

The fact that Irving family members own a large television station broadcasting all over the province, all the province's English-language dailies, and a Saint John radio station warranted a look into the family's cross-media holdings at CHSJ-TV's licence renewal hearing in 1983, owing to the former Liberal government's *Direction to the CRTC on Issue and Renewal of Broadcasting Licenses to Daily Newspaper Proprietors*. The directive, dated July 29, 1982, stipulated that the CRTC may not issue or renew licences to applicants effectively controlled, directly or indirectly, by a proprietor of a daily newspaper "where the major circulation area of the daily newspaper substantially encompasses the major market area served or to be served by the broadcasting undertaking, unless the Commission is satisfied that refusal to do so would be contrary to overriding public interest . . . ".[1] The CRTC, in its decision 83-656, found N.B. Broadcasting ineligible for licence renewal. In the public interest, the CRTC did extend CHSJ-TV's licence for a period so that sudden cessation of CBC programming to the area would not occur and "to provide sufficient time for N.B. Broadcasting to rearrange its affairs or for other arrangements to be made which will ensure that the people of New Brunswick are not deprived of the CBC network service".[2]

Before a review of the situation was to take place in 1985, the cross-ownership directive was repealed by the present government under Order-in-Council 85-1735. The CRTC renewed the licence for a year in January 1986.

The Irving Group's non-media interests embrace everything from oil (Irving Oil Limited), to pulp and paper (Saint John Pulp and Paper Limited), transportation (Interprovincial Coach Lines Limited), and printing (Unipress Limited). The family remains a powerful economic force in the province.

Maclean Hunter Limited

Maclean Hunter of Toronto is one of Canada's leading media conglomerates, with interests in magazines, newspapers, television, radio and cable. It has important interests in the United States and Europe as well as Canada. In 1985 it had revenues of almost $1 billion and employed nearly 9,000 people.

As Canada's major publisher of both consumer and trade magazines, Maclean Hunter is well known for *Maclean's*, *l'Actualité*, *Chatelaine* (in French and English), and the *Financial Post*. The company acquired control of Toronto Sun Publishing Corp. in 1982. It publishes *Sun* newspapers in Toronto, Edmonton, and Calgary, and the *Houston Post* in the United States.

Maclean Hunter owns 11 radio stations serving a total population of 7.2 million in three provinces: three in Alberta, six in Ontario, and two in Nova Scotia. It has one television station, CFCN-TV in Calgary, a full affiliate of the CTV network, serving a population area of about 1.2 million.

Maclean Hunter's Canadian cable operations, all in Ontario, served 385,000 subscribers at the end of 1985, about 7 percent of the Canadian total, making it the third largest cable company after Rogers and Vidéotron. The company's cable operations in the United States in New Jersey and Michigan have 234,000 basic-service subscribers, who also take an average 1.3 pay-TV channels, and cable earned twice the revenues of its Canadian operations.

Aside from its mass circulation magazines Maclean Hunter has a particularly strong media presence in certain cities, notably Calgary (television and radio stations and the *Calgary Sun*), Edmonton (radio station and the *Edmonton Sun*), and Toronto (radio station, major cable presence, and the *Toronto Sun*).

Moffat Communications

Most of the Moffat interests in broadcasting are concentrated in the Prairies, especially in Winnipeg where they own CKY, the CTV local affiliate, two radio stations and a major cable system. They also own half interests in stations in Brandon & Dauphin which, together with CKY reach 97 percent of the Manitoba population. Moffat is the sixth largest radio business in Canada with nine radio stations in all.

Recently, the company has tried unsuccessfully to expand in the East. The CRTC has turned down its bid to open an FM station in Toronto. Moffat was also a minory shareholder with the Quebec company COGECO in an unsuccessful bid to open a new station in Montreal.

Pathonic Inc.

With five television stations, Pathonic Inc. is the largest owner of private TV stations in Quebec, and accounts for half the stations in the TVA network. Its stations are CHEM in Trois-Rivières, CHLT in Sherbrooke, CFCM in Québec City and CFER in Rimouski. The fifth station is an English-language CBC-affiliate in Quebec City serving the anglophone minority. Pathonic also has a minority interest in Télé-Inter Rives Ltée. which operates CIMT, another TVA affiliate, in Rivière-du-Loup.

An important minority shareholder in Pathonic Communications is Télé-Métropole, owner of CFTM-TV, flagship station of the TVA network and the station with the largest audience in Canada.

Communications Radiomutuel Inc.

After Télémédia, Radiomutuel of Montreal is the second largest radio station and network owner in Quebec. The network provides almost 38 hours of entertainment programming weekly to 15 (five of which are owned by Radiomutuel) AM stations throughout the province of Quebec. Radiomutuel owns and operates radio stations in Montreal, Québec City, Trois-Rivières and Gatineau (Hull). The company is also involved in music publishing.

Rogers Communications Inc.

Rogers Communications Inc. of Toronto is Canada's largest cable operator, accounting for close to a quarter of all Canadian cable subscribers and controlling major cable systems in the United States. It also has television and radio interests.

With nearly 2 billion subscribers, Rogers is the fourth largest cable company in North America. In Canada, cable systems controlled by Rogers have 1,280,000 subscribers in three provinces: Ontario, Alberta and British Columbia. Rogers has minority interests in two other cable companies with 90,000 subscribers. One-third of the Canadian systems with more than 50,000 subscribers are owned by Rogers. The Toronto system alone has 370,000 subscribers. Rogers' two Amercian subsidiaries operate systems with a total of 561,000 subscribers, of whom 60 percent are in Texas and California. Although only 30 percent of Rogers' subscribers are in the United States, the American operations account for more than 45 percent of revenues of the combined systems. Because of substantial pay-TV revenues, the rapid growth of Rogers cable systems left the company with heavy long-term debt. The company has recently begun to divest itself of substantial holdings in the United States.

Rogers has two radio stations in Toronto, two in Sarnia, and one in Leamington, Ontario. In 1986 its broadcasting subsidiary also acquired the multilingual Toronto television station, CFMT.

Selkirk Communications Limited

Selkirk Communications of Toronto is Canada's third largest private radio-station owner. It also owns television stations, cable television systems and broadcast sales companies in three Canadian provinces, the United States and Britain, as well as a large record and tape marketing firm.

Southam Inc., a large print-media owner, holds a 20 percent voting interest in Selkirk. The Southam interest originated with Calgary Herald radio station, CFAC-AM in 1922.

Through wholly-owned Selkirk Broadcasting Limited, Selkirk Communications operates 12 radio stations, the majority in major markets. Except for the recently acquired CFNY-FM in Toronto, all are in Alberta and British Columbia, including the leading stations in Calgary and Edmonton.

Of the ten independent television stations in Canada, three are controlled by Selkirk: CFAC-7-TV and CFAC-TV in Calgary and CHCH-TV in Hamilton, Canada's most popular independent station. A CBC affiliate in Kelowna, British Columbia is 50 percent owned by Selkirk.

Selkirk's cable interests have also been increasing. They include Ottawa Cablevision Limited, and 50 percent of Greater Winnipeg Cablevision Limited. These cable systems in Ottawa and Winnipeg are two of the largest in Canada. Selkirk Communications also has substantial cable interests in Florida and holds an eight percent share of Canadian Satellite Communications Inc. (CANCOM).

Standard Broadcasting Corporation

From its start with radio station CFRB in 1927, Standard Broadcasting of Toronto has become an important owner of electronic media — radio, television, cable, program production and videocassette reproduction.

In addition to CFRB, for years Toronto's most popular station, Standard Broadcasting now owns radio stations CKFM in Toronto, CJAD and CJFM in Montreal, a station in Ottawa, and two stations in St. Catharines, Ontario. CFRB has the largest audience of any radio station in Canada. Standard Broadcast News was established in 1966 and now serves Standard's own stations and 42 others. The company has minority interests in several radio stations in Britain.

In 1975 Standard obtained control of Bushnell Communications, thus acquiring CJOH-TV in Ottawa one of the main CTV affiliates. Standard has major program production facilities in Ottawa and Toronto.

Standard Broadcasting has substantial cable distribution interests in Canada (Hull and Ottawa) and California. In 1984 its subsidiary, VTR Production of Toronto, built the largest videocassette reproduction plant in Canada.

The company now belongs to Slaight Broadcasting, which had to sell its two radio stations in Toronto in order to obtain CRTC approval for the purchase of Standard from Hollinger Argus in 1985. Otherwise Slaight would have owned four radio stations in Toronto.

Télémédia

With 20 wholly-owned radio stations in Ontario and Quebec, Télémédia of Montreal is the second largest radio-station owner in Canada after CHUM Limited. Télémédia is also a growing force in the Canadian magazine publishing industry.

The company began as the grouping of the radio broadcasting interests of Power Corporation in Quebec, purchased by Philippe de Gaspé Beaubien in

1970. The company was comprised at the time of two television stations and eight radio stations. Since then it has sold the TV stations and added two radio stations in Quebec.

Télémédia owns ten radio stations in Quebec, six AM and four FM, all in major markets. Its CKAC-AM, for years the dominant station in the Montreal market, is the second most popular station in the country after CFRB in Toronto. Like Radiomutuel, Télémédia operates a French-language network which exploits the economic advantages of network programming. In 1985 news, entertainment and sports were provided to five of its own AM stations and 32 other AM stations throughout Quebec and New Brunswick. The 37 AM network stations receive over 18 hours of programming each week. One source of this programming is CKAC, known for its news presentation. The network is Canada's largest after the CBC. Télémédia is also involved in networking sports events like Expos and Blue Jays baseball games to a large number of stations.

Télémédia extended its radio operations into Ontario in the early 1980s, building a chain of ten stations primarily in smaller centres throughout the province. Its only Ontario station in a major market is Toronto's CJCL-AM, now second only to CFRB after a history of poor ratings.

Télémédia was one of five founding shareholders of Canadian Satellite Communications Inc. (CANCOM). Its equity position has dwindled from 25 percent to 8.07 percent.

An interest in Cantel, a national cellular radio service of which Télémédia was one of the founders, has been reduced from 30 percent to 11.5 percent. The publishing arm of the Télémedia group, newly named TV Guide Inc., publishes the leading TV-listing magazines in English and French, *TV Guide* and *TV Hebdo*, as well as *Canadian Living* and *Coup de Pouce*. In 1985, Télémédia-Procom Inc. was established in a joint venture as a print media sales and promotion company.

WIC Western International Communications

The WIC (Western International Communications) group of Vancouver controls or has interests in three TV stations in British Columbia which, with the help of repeaters, reach 98 percent of the province's population. The group is also a major player in the radio business with nine radio stations (Western Radio Group) and is the leading shareholder in Canadian Satellite Communications Inc. (CANCOM).

The company's television interests are held through British Columbia Broadcasting Company, in which it has 63 percent control, the remaining shares belonging to Selkirk Communications. The TV subsidiary owns the CTV affiliates CHAN in Vancouver and CHEK in Victoria, and has a half share of CHBC, the CBC affiliate in Kelowna. British Columbia Broadcasting also holds the WIC interest in CANCOM, which was increased from 25 to 49 percent during 1985 and 1986.

Five of the WIC radio stations are in western Canada: two in New Westminster in the Vancouver area, one in Calgary and two in Winnipeg; they include the leading AM stations in the Vancouver and Winnipeg markets. The four other

WIC stations are in Ontario, two in Hamilton and two in Toronto. The latter two are the ones Slaight Communications had to sell when it acquired Standard Broadcasting in 1985. One of these, CILQ-FM, had the fifth largest audience in Canada in the fall of 1985.

Ownership Policy Issues

Since 1968 ownership policies in the Canadian broadcasting system have reflected public concern with ownership by non-Canadians, chain ownership, vertical integration, multiple media ownership in a single market, media conglomerates, and media ownership by non-media conglomerates. We discuss each of these issues below.

Ownership by Non-Canadians

Until 1968, there was substantial foreign ownership and control of Canadian broadcasting interests, mostly in cable television. After the 1968 *Broadcasting Act* was passed, foreign ownership in all broadcasting entities was reduced to a minority and non-controlling position.

The purpose is to protect Canada's cultural sovereignty by ensuring that decision-making is in Canadian hands. We recommend in this Report that any revised legislation continue to require that all broadcasting undertakings be owned and effectively controlled by Canadians.

Chain Ownership in One Component of the Industry.

No explicit rules have ever been set to limit the number of radio or television stations or cable systems any company may own. No measure has ever been established to determine how much of the Canadian radio, television or cable industry should be in the hands of a single owner, such as the percentage of national listening or viewing, or the percentage of all cable subscribers. In the United States, by contrast, the number of radio or television stations any single company may own continues to be limited by the Federal Communications Commission (FCC). The FCC invited comments recently on whether there should also be limits on the number of cable systems any one company can own, although the Commission rejected a similar proposal in 1982. The cable inquiry has been undertaken because the American production industry and small cable systems expressed concern that a few big cable companies might gain too much power over selection and price of television services for exhibition.

Chain ownership in Canada has been a concern primarily in the newspaper industry, rather than in broadcasting. In television broadcasting, there are nine owners, each controlling three or more stations, representing half of the total number of stations, although in most cases the stations are small. In radio, two companies own 20 or more stations, led by CHUM Ltd. with 24 stations and Télémédia with 20 stations. The next three companies each own more than ten stations. While the overall level of concentration within the Canadian cable industry is much higher than in radio and television, the level of concentration has not increased over the past 12 years. Although the largest company, Rogers

Communications, accounted for almost a quarter of all subscribers in 1985 by comparison with the 14 percent of subscribers accounted for by the largest firm in 1973, the share of the five largest firms has changed very little. The potential significance of having a few dominant companies may well have changed, however, with the advent of discretionary services carried on cable. Since the CRTC has, to a considerable degree, left the carriage and pricing of discretionary services to be negotiated between the service providers and the cable companies, the market share of any single multiple-system operator may come to be viewed somewhat differently.

In chain ownership, public policy has always considered not just the number of stations under common ownership, but how concentrated those stations are geographically and how large their audience share is. If, for example, a single owner accumulates ten television stations scattered across the country, there is potential impact on the public than concentrated control of, say, ten French-language stations in Quebec, or ten English stations in Western Canada.

Vertical Integration

Vertical integration may take many forms since a wide range of different kinds of business engage in radio and television broadcasting. In television, for example, ownership of a network such as CTV by its affiliated stations merges the source of programs with the stations that purchase and carry them. In radio, common ownership of a record company and radio stations is another example of vertical integration. Many broadcasters in both radio and television set up subsidiaries to produce audio or video programming, to produce commercials and audio or video production, or to syndicate or network programs.

Vertical integration usually represents efficient operating practices that need be of no concern to policy-makers. In some cases, however, important public policy concerns arise and measures have been taken to deal with them.

Ownership of production facilities by television licensees to the possible detriment of independent production companies has been a frequent subject of concern. The CRTC's original pay-TV regulations, for example, stated: "A licensee . . . shall not distribute on its programming, any programming, other than filler programming, produced . . . by itself or by a related production company."[3] Similarly, the Commission's 1985 decision licensing the Quatre Saisons network raised the issue, noting the assurance given by the network that its affiliated production house, Champlain Productions Inc. "will not act as an independent producer of programs for the Four Seasons network".[4] When the pay-TV regulations were revised in 1984, the restrictions on vertical integration between production and broadcasting were relaxed to allow the pay licensees to show programs from their own production and post-production facilities. The same exception was made for Quatre Saisons.

The Commission's concerns about the integration of production and distribution have been predicated on the view that if control over program production and distribution is in the same hands the effect will be to limit seriously or freeze out entirely independently produced programming. Recognizing that such vertical integration is extensive, the Commission, in many of its licensing decisions since 1980, has tried to ensure that new licensees in particular were open to acquiring programs from independent sources.

Common ownership of television stations or networks and their exhibition systems has also received attention. Until recently cable companies were not allowed to hold television-station or network licences. In calling for applications to provide pay-TV in 1981, for example, the Commission expressed concern that "if licensees of undertakings that exhibit a pay television service also distribute the service, the opportunity for other pay television distributors to have their product exhibited on such undertakings may be reduced".[5] Since then, however, the Commission has licensed a specialty programming service, the Life Channel, with cable industry ownership, as well as allowing the takeover by Rogers Communications Inc. of the multilingual TV station in Toronto. Again, in the Commission's 1983 decision to license CANCOM it allowed common ownership of broadcast services and the satellite distribution vehicle which was to carry them.

In 1982 the owner of Montreal's CFCF-TV acquired control of a large cable system in that city. More recently, as the Task Force was completing its Report, the proposed takeover of Télé-Métropole, which owns the largest television station in Canada, Montreal's CFTM, by Videotron, the second largest cable system in Canada, raises the issue of vertical integration in a more substantial way.

Ownership of Multiple Media Enterprises in a Single Market

The CRTC has traditionally been unwilling to allow a broadcaster to own more than one television station, AM radio station or FM radio station in the same market, although a single owner might — and in many cases does — own one of each. An exception was made in the licensing of the French-language Quatre Saisons in Montreal. It is owned by CFCF, the English-language Montreal affiliate of CTV. Of the other exceptions almost all have been the acceptance of twin-stick ownership in small television markets as essential to the survival of a local station.

Cross-media ownership has also been a concern. Should the local newspaper owner also be allowed to own the local radio and television stations? Should cross-ownership of a local newspaper and the local cable system be allowed?

Cross-media ownership is an issue not only in local markets but also in provincial or regional markets. The profiles of Maclean Hunter's Calgary holdings, the Irving family interests in New Brunswick or the Blackburn family holdings in London, Ontario illustrate some existing patterns of cross-media ownership.

In the United States the rules of the FCC on cross-media ownership are detailed and restrictive. The ownership by cable companies of television networks, telephone companies, broadcasting outlets, or newspapers serving the same market is prohibited. No single owner can have an interest in more than one AM-FM radio combination or television station in a single market; nor can a single owner hold an interest in a newspaper in a particular market and also have a broadcast licence to serve that market. The effect is to limit participation to one media outlet in a market. In the vast American market these rules have still left the possibility for large media corporations to develop.

Media Conglomerates

In addition to cross-media ownership in a single market, there is a growing number of large companies with holdings in several media at the national level, such as Southam and Maclean Hunter. These conglomerates, which specialize in the media, are of increasing importance in Canada. They have the capacity to bring substantial financial resources and expertise to bear on new development in broadcasting, as well as other media. At the same time, their strength and influence have resulted in public concern that a few media companies will exercise too pervasive and powerful an influence on media expression in Canada and on public opinion.

Media Ownership by Non-media Conglomerates

Particular attention has been given in earlier studies, including the *Reports* of the Special Senate Committee on Mass Media (Davey), The Royal Commission on Corporate Concentration (Bryce), and the Royal Commission on Newspapers (Kent), to the potential influence on freedom of expression and democracy in Canada that can flow from the control of the media being in the hands of predominantly non-media interests.

The Bryce Commission did not find evidence of corporate interference in editorial matters in the cases it studied but said that "potential editorial bias is created by any kind of concentrated ownership". It noted that a CRTC statement of policy had said, in approving ownership of broadcasting outlets, that it would consider "the extent of ownership of other commercial undertakings which might influence the performance of broadcasting stations". In fact, however, "There have been few cases where this point seems to have been given much, if any weight in decisions." The Bryce Commission's conclusions were cautiously framed. While they said that their finding provided no knowledge that would justify "a general exclusion" of media ownership by non-media interests,

> It is the trend of one medium expanded into other media areas and of ownership media interests by industrial or commercial interests that seem to us the most significant to the public interest at this time and the areas where greatest concern should be focussed.[6]

Views on Media Ownership Policy

The CRTC has always recognized that a degree of diversity of ownership should be maintained to fulfil the stipulation of the 1968 *Broadcasting Act* that "the programming provided by the Canadian broadcasting system should be varied and comprehensive and should provide reasonable, balanced opportunity for the expression of differing views on matters of public concern".[7]

The Davey Committee, which reported in 1970, found that both broadcasting and the daily newspaper industry have many of the characteristics of a natural monopoly, since the costs of reaching additional listeners, viewers and readers decline as the total circulation or audience served increases. While the Committee saw little that would constrain such trends in the newspaper industry, they noted distinct differences in broadcasting which would make for a somewhat more competitive marketplace. In particular, the Commission noted that although newspapers could handle theoretically limitless advertising, the amount of advertising any single broadcaster could sell was limited by regulation.

While the Davey Committee did not recommend strict rules it reached a judgement that the potential dangers to the public interest from corporate concentration were significant. Particular concern was expressed about increasing cross-ownership within the media and media ownership by non-media conglomerates. The Committee's greatest concern, however, was that the large and powerful media entities which dominate the system were failing to channel their substantial resources toward the achievement of public policy objectives, such as the production of Canadian programming. The Davey *Report* did not, however, find that the large media entities abused their power by charging too much, rather "it was not a case of charging too much, but of spending too little". While the Committee rejected adoption of the United States rules to limit cross-media ownership and concentration, it recommended that the *Broadcasting Act* incorporate a more explicit provision to protect the public interest against excessive ownership concentration.[8]

The 1978 Bryce *Report* looked at media concentration in the much broader context of concentration in the economy as a whole. Its emphasis was primarily on the implications of large media conglomerates, cross-ownership, and non-media ownership of broadcasting and publishing enterprises. The general finding, as we have noted, was that such ownership created the potential for abuse and should be taken into account. The Commissioners found that while competition law might occasionally be a useful check, "there are no practical legislative or regulatory instruments available or in prospect to deal with this problem comprehensively". They further noted that, "The CRTC has the power to control the ownership of broadcasting outlets but it is apparent that their decisions are much more heavily influenced by other considerations." Nevertheless, they recommended that "the CRTC be empowered to prevent the owners of broadcasting stations from also owning newspapers and other print media that circulate in the same market".[9]

In the same year that the Royal Commission on Corporate Concentration reported to the government, the CRTC released a report from its own Ownership Study Group. This study found that group ownership of broadcasting undertakings was associated with higher profitability, particularly in television, and that it had no significant impact on advertising rates, even in cases of cross-ownership in the same market. The study found that group-owned stations spent a smaller proportion of revenues on program production than did non-group stations. Non-group stations were found to spend relatively more on news programming than did group-owned stations. In addition, as the number of stations in an ownership group increased the proportion of prime-time hours devoted to news and information decreased in favour of more light entertainment.

While broadcasting was obviously not an explicit part of the mandate of the Kent Commission, which reported in 1981, the Commission did take up cross-ownership of newspapers and broadcasting outlets. The Kent *Report* also dealt with the importance of content and carriage separation in the ownership structure of such new media as electronic publising.

The report concluded that, as long as the different media operate in geographically distinct markets, cross-media ownership does not raise public policy concerns. But common ownership in the same market was found to reduce the diversity of information sources. The Commission recommended that newspaper interests not be allowed to own a cable system, radio or television station if 50 percent of the population with good reception of the broadcasting service lived in the area where the newspaper was generally available.[10]

Based on the recommendations of the Kent Commission, the government issued the direction to the CRTC which we noted earlier in the profile of the Irving interests in New Brunswick. The companies potentially affected included Southam and Selkirk, since Southam had an important minority interest in Selkirk and published daily papers in five cities where Selkirk had broadcast operations; Maclean Hunter, which through its control of Sun Publishing was involved in dailies in three centres where it held broadcast licences; the Irving family which had all the English-language daily papers in the province, Saint John's only local television station, (covering the whole province through repeaters), and a Saint John radio station; and the Blackburn family, which owned the London Free Press, as well as radio and television stations in London and nearby Wingham.

The direction appears to have been without effect except for a temporary limitation on the Irving TV licence and, as we have mentioned, was eventually withdrawn.

The way in which the CRTC acted in response to the 1982 direction reflected the Commission's traditional reliance on a case-by-case approach to ownership issues. The approach has the virtue of flexibility but permits no reference to firm criteria against which all cases will be fairly judged. The study undertaken for this Task Force on the ownership structure of the broadcasting industry drew attention to "the absence of a comprehensive policy framework", observing that, "As might be expected, given the case-by-case nature of the process, regulatory decisions on transfers of ownership were not always consistent."[11]

Evolution of the CRTC's Approach

While the Commission has not laid down rules, it has observed some general and applied standards fairly consistently. For example, the Commission generally held the view that television undertakings in a community should be under separate ownership from cable systems, except in special circumstances. Similarly, the Commission generally discouraged local cross-ownership of newspapers and broadcasting stations, and acted on the general, if necessarily somewhat ambiguous principle that corporate concentration should be limited, except to the degree that it was determined to be clearly in the public interest.[12]

As early as 1976, however, opposition to cross-ownership began to be questioned as a hindrance to ensuring a strong Canadian industry. Then Communications Minister Jeanne Sauvé proposed a re-examination of policies on cross-ownership, based on the need to make more capital available for extension of service and improved programming.[13]

On February 9, 1979, the CRTC released a notice of public hearing, recognizing the need for a formal evaluation of the Commission's ownership policies, particularly on cross-ownership. The public hearing, which would have been the first explicitly on ownership and control, was later cancelled.

More recently, the Commission's emphasis has been on the need to strengthen the industry. CRTC Chairman André Bureau said in a speech in April 1985 that the Commission was prepared to take "a completely flexible approach" to the cross-ownership issue "in order to strengthen and expand the Canadian broadcasting system". The renewed emphasis on industry strength was put in the context of increased competition and new services. Mr. Bureau noted that "Canada has not got the luxury of being able to afford failure in these areas".[14]

Many were hoping that the CRTC would clarify its position on concentration of ownership in connection with the application of Power Corp. to acquire Télé-Métropole. But such was not to be; although Power Corp., with its major newspaper holdings and vast interests in non-media businesses, raised several of the concentration issues we have mentioned, the CRTC turned down its application on other grounds.

The Need for a Comprehensive Policy

The mandate of the Task Force asks that we recommend an industrial strategy taking account of the increasingly competitive environment in which Canadian broadcasters function; and that we propose means of "reducing the structural impediments to the broadcasting system's contribution to the Canadian economy". There is a legitimate need to have Canadian companies in the broadcast sector with financial strength to compete effectively.

Concentration in Canadian broadcasting and the media generally must also be seen in the context of growing concentration in other countries. If the trend is toward large companies outside Canada, then within Canada our goal of Canadian ownership of the system needs to be pursued in a manner that results in Canadian broadcasting companies strong enough to keep abreast of new technologies such as stereo sound for television, to finance new services, and to help finance high quality Canadian programs. Program objectives, as we note in Chapter 17 on Private Television, will depend on the degree to which programming resources are aggregated within Canada, at least as much as on the strength of individual companies in the industry.

The Task Force was also asked, however, to recommend a cultural strategy and to take into account the role of the broadcasting system in Canadian society. From that perspective we share the concern expressed over 15 years ago by the

Davey Committee and in later reports that there continue to be a diversity of sources of information, opinion and entertainment for Canadians and a number of alternative opportunities for journalists, creators and producers to pursue their work.

The *Broadcasting Act* itself, both as it stands and as we recommend it be revised, incorporates a concern for balance and diversity. The Task Force believes that there clearly is a point beyond which concentration of ownership and control is not compatible with these objectives. What will continue to be necessary in the future is to balance the need for strong corporate structures with the need to ensure the expression of divergent opinions and a climate that is open to the work of our creators and producers.

The recommendations we make reflect an acceptance of more media concentration. Both the industry and the public need to know, however, the acceptable limits to concentration. The Task Force's research study suggested clearly defined and explicit limits should be established to the degree of ownership that may be held by a single firm, expressed in market share. The Task Force believes a more precise public policy must be developed and that there would indeed be merit in basing that policy in part on limits to the share of particular markets that an individual broadcaster or media owner might hold. Such an approach would require definition of the markets to which it would apply, taking into account linguistic and geographical factors and the degree of overlap of the media from one market to another.

That is to say, the CRTC should go back to the drawing board on this issue, as it originally planned to do in 1979, undertaking thorough research and a full public hearing in order to arrive at clear and explicit guidelines on ownership concentration. To proceed case by case without clear guidelines will surely raise difficulties and, indeed, confusion and controversy. For the industry, new guideposts will prevent wasted expenditures on applications to the CRTC or on planning takeover bids likely to be rejected. For the public, they would clearly indicate that the inevitable increases in industry concentration which will occur are occuring within a framework that protects the diversity of voices within Canadian broadcasting and the media generally.

Recommendations

The CRTC should hold a policy hearing to review the issues related to ownership concentration in broadcasting.

Based on the public input provided through the hearing process the Commission should publish a statement of its policies on broadcast ownership.

Commission ownership policy should recognize the need to consider French and English language broadcasting as separate components of the system which serve relatively distinct audiences, and should give particular attention to the development of policy guidelines concerning cross-ownership within individual broadcast and media markets.

Notes

1. Canadian Radio-television and Telecommunications Commission, Direction to the CRTC, *Directive to the CRTC on Issue and Renewal of Broadcasting Licenses to Daily Newspaper Proprietors*, July 29, 1982 as quoted in CRTC *Decision 83-656* (Ottawa: CRTC, 1983), p. 7.
2. Ibid., p. 11.
3. Canadian Radio-television and Telecommunications Commission, *Regulations Respecting Pay Television Broadcasting*, CRTC, Public Notice 82-123 (Ottawa: CRTC, 1982), p. 8.
4. Canadian Radio-television and Telecommunications Commission, Decision 85-733 (Ottawa: CRTC, 1980), p. 24.
5. Canadian Radio-television and Telecommunications Commission, *Call for Applications for Pay Television Service*, Public Notice 81-33 (Ottawa: CRTC, 1981), p. 10.
6. Canada, Royal Commission on Corporate Concentration, (Bryce Commission) *Report* (Ottawa: Minister of Supply and Services Canada, 1978), p. 350 — 53.
7. *Broadcasting Act* 1968, R.S.C. Chapter B-11, Section 3(d).
8. Canada, Special Senate Committee on Mass Media, *The Uncertain Mirror*, Vol. 1. (Ottawa: Queen's Printer, 1970).
9. Royal Commission on Corporate Concentration, *Report*, p. 411.
10. Canada, Royal Commission on Newspapers, (Kent Commission) *Report* (Ottawa: Minister of Supply and Services Canada, 1981), pp. 223 — 27.
11. Stratavision Inc. "Ownership Structure and Behavior in the Canadian Broadcasting System", study prepared for the Task Force on Broadcasting Policy, Ottawa, 1986.
12. Ibid., p. 18.
13. Sauvé, Jeanne, "Increase in Cross Ownership Possible, Sauvé Says", *Broadcaster*, May 1976, p. 6 as quoted in Stratavision, op. cit., p. 21.
14. Bureau, André, "CRTC: – Economics and Regulations", Speech to the Montreal Association of Financial Analysts (Ottawa: CRTC, April 3, 1985), p. 23.

Chapter 28

Copyright Issues

Copyright Issues

Without programs to broadcast, broadcasting could not exist; without creators, there would be no programs worth broadcasting. It is the creators who give life to the system and that is why their rights must be recognized in any broadcasting policy.

The basic right of creators is the right to receive fair remuneration for their creative work. It is not only a matter of equity, but also in the interest of the broadcasting system itself, because one cannot expect the Canadian broadcasting system to present Canadian works of high standard if steps are not taken to pay creators properly. We have already indicated our preference for a broadcasting policy which emphasizes programming content rather than technical considerations. Hence fair remuneration for creative work becomes a basic organizational principle. The question then becomes how and under what conditions creators should be paid.

We are not the first to argue that the antiquated *Copyright Act*[1] needs to be updated to deal with the era of modern communications. Following numerous studies[2] the government tabled its 1984 White Paper on copyright entitled *From Gutenberg to Telidon*.[3] More recently, in October 1985, a sub-committee of the Standing Committee on Communications and Culture made public its report called *A Charter of Rights for Creators*.[4]

By recognizing rights for writers, performers and even broadcasters, copyright legislation would allow a cultural products market to develop, and radio and television programs would certainly be among the products traded. It is most unlikely that the cable television industry would have developed in the same way if copyright legislation had recognized a right to broadcasters over the retransmission of their programs.

It would also include foreign works because Canada, as a signatory to international conventions on copyright, is required to treat nationals of other signatory countries on the same basis as Canadians. This has caused some consternation because Canada, as a net importer of cultural products, would no doubt find an increase in the outflow of payments instead of more money going to its own creators.

The *Report* of the Sub-Committee on the Revision of Copyright recommends a number of measures designed to give greater recognition and rewards to creative endeavour, to extend the scope of copyright protection and to specify the scope of moral rights. The sub-committee recommended updating the types of works protected to include those produced using the new technologies. It was also recommended that protection for sound recordings, radio and television programs, and all forms of performance be protected as a category separate from the original works themselves. These are what are called "subsidiary rights", i.e. rights over recordings or performances that exist independently of the content of the recording or performance. These subsidiary rights have a considerable impact on broadcasting.

We generally agree with the Standing Committee's conclusions on broadcasting-related issues. Further comment is nevertheless in order on a number of the problems that relate to broadcasting policy:

- copyright in sound recordings and performances;
- copyright in radio and television programs, including retransmission rights;
- measures to deal with piracy of audio-visual works.

Sound Recordings and Performances

Under the current Act, composers and writers of lyrics have the right to royalties for the performance, transmission and retransmission of their works. The sub-committee recommends granting analogous rights to performers over performances and to producers over sound recordings.

The government has stated its agreement in principle with these recommendations.[5] A number of arguments have been put forward against such a right for producers because it would lead to increased costs for the use of Canadian sound recordings which would harm the distribution of these works, primarily because such a right does not exist in the United States. It is also argued that producers of sound recordings derive adequate indirect compensation from the publicity which results from the broadcast of their products on radio and television.

These objections are aimed at the implementation of the principle and not at the principle itself. The amount producers would earn from fees remains to be negotiated; the Act provides only that such a right should exist. Broadcasters use sound recordings to attract and to keep audiences and it is fair that producers should derive compensation as well.

The recognition of performers' rights will not have a very dramatic impact on broadcasters. They are already established by means of collective agreements signed with performers' associations like ACTRA and the Union des artistes and including them in the Act would merely confirm existing practices.

Broadcast Programs

The recognition of a distinct right in broadcasts will have serious consequences for Canadian broadcasting policy. Broadcasters maintain that their signals should be protected as such, independently of the already protected works that are included in them. The sub-committee agreed "that there is surely as much creative input in arranging a broadcast, or a 'broadcast day' as it is referred to by broadcasters, as there is in compilations",[6] and that this form of creative endeavour should be protected as are, for example, telephone directories.

They therefore recommended granting four broadcast-related rights: a right of reproduction, a right of transmission, a right of retransmission and a right to authorize reproduction and retransmission. The retransmission right should, according to the sub-committee, consist simply of a right to payment and not a right to authorize or refuse to authorize retransmission. These rights are also to be provided to foreign broadcasters on the basis of reciprocity pursuant to international agreements.

In its response to the report of the copyright sub-committee, the government took the position that the Act should provide for special treatment in specific cases such as the recording of ephemeral works with a view to their eventual distribution and retransmission rights in programs from local stations.

Currently, cable operators that simultaneously retransmit radio and television programs need not ask permission nor pay compensation for the works in question. This is because of a 1954 decision by the Exchequer Court,[7] which ruled that the simultaneous retransmission of signals to households is not radiocommunication of the work or equivalent to a public performance. Hence the simultaneous retransmission of programs by cable does not bring with it any copyright obligations.[8] The decision is generally considered to apply also to point-to-point retransmission by satellite.[9]

Copyright holders of course argue that the current situation is unfair to them. Simultaneous retransmission without either permission or compensation deprives them of control over much of the audience to whom their works are distributed.

Neither cable operators, who retransmit programs, nor broadcasters, whose programs are being retransmitted, pay any royalties on the new territories opened up for the works these programs contain. Broadcasters claim that they have exclusive rights because they have acquired rights to broadcast works over specified territories. But if these same works are retransmitted in these territories by cable or satellite, they obviously lose any advantage they may have gained from such exclusive rights. This is why the American networks claim compensation for the additional audiences reached by Canadian cable operators and CANCOM, who retransmit their programs in this country.

The cable television industry is strongly opposed to the establishment of a retransmission right over broadcast programs. Because of the many U.S. programs carried, it would mean having to pay substantial amounts of money to American broadcasters, which would further aggravate the Canadian balance of payments deficit; cable subscribers, who are already taxed,[10] would also end up bearing the burden of the resulting additional costs. CANCOM adds that the introduction of a retransmission right would threaten its unique mission to provide service to underserved regions.

The fact is that few contest the legitimacy of compensation for the retransmission of programs. Any objections stem primarily from the anticipated financial impact. We believe all these factors should be taken into account and that there would be a number of advantages to recognizing a retransmission right like the one recommended by the sub-committee. It would give copyright holders the right to receive compensation but would not prevent retransmission. This approach would strike a balance between the creators' right to receive fair compensation for their work and the legitimate aspirations of the public to have access to the programs in question, because broadcasters would not be able to prevent retransmission. Of course the CRTC would continue to have the general power to authorize any form of retransmission.

We have not forgotten the special problems of remote communities. Because of their isolation, the provision of broadcasting services is more essential than elsewhere, and at the same time the financial burden of providing service to such communities is heavier. The Sub-committee on the Revision of Copyright, following the American lead, recommends that small cable television undertakings serving isolated communities should only be required to pay a token royalty, an ingenious suggestion with which we agree. In the United States, cable systems with fewer than 500 subscribers pay one cent per month per subscriber.[11] This approach shows concern for the rights of both parties. It does not follow that creators and only creators should be required to bear the burden of paying for retransmission to isolated communities. Negotiated retransmission payments would make it possible to spread such costs over the whole audience through appropriately adjusted rates.

We now come to the effects of the retransmission right on programs retransmitted from the United States. It is true that in border areas where American broadcasting signals may be received directly the value of retransmission rights would not be significantly higher. In Canada, the copyright subcommittee reminds us that most cable undertakings can receive the signals of American networks directly. Also when American programs are broadcast at the same time on Canadian networks, the rules on simultaneous substitution mean that there is no real retransmission of a foreign signal because the cable operator is required to substitute the Canadian signal. Here again the overall economic impact of a retransmission right would not be very considerable.

The problem becomes more complex when distant American signals are retransmitted without substitution, a practice which has given rise to much controversy in both Canada and the United States.[12]

Wishing to extend the program choice available in border regions to other parts of the country, the CRTC began in 1971 to allow the importing of signals from the three major American commercial networks (NBC, CBS, ABC) and the American public television network (PBS). The three-plus-one policy was extended in 1983 to CANCOM, a company which the CRTC licensed in 1981 to serve remote communities. The CRTC's CANCOM decision revived the controversy over the 3 + 1 policy.

American producers and broadcasters holding copyright on the retransmitted programs complained that this kind of retransmission made it difficult for them to sell rights to these programs in the Canadian market. Canadian broadcasters complained that the exclusive right they were supposed to have when they bought broadcast rights for Canada for a number of American programs could no longer be guaranteed.

In April 1985 the Chairman of the Federal Communications Commission (FCC) which regulates American television, and a spokesperson for the U.S. Department of Commerce, wrote to the CRTC to object to CANCOM's inclusion in the 3 + 1 policy. Noting that cable retransmission of American broadcast services "has long been of serious U.S. concern", the letter urged the CRTC "to consider the implications of its policy for the communications relationship between our two countries". Expressing strong support of initiatives to resolve "this important issue of unauthorized and uncompensated retransmission of U.S. originated broadcasts", they went on to observe that in their 1985 summit conference, Prime Minister Mulroney and President Reagan had pledged "co-operation to protect intellectual property rights, including trade in counterfeit goods and other abuses of copyright and patent law". Recognizing that it is difficult to withdraw any service once it has been made available, the Americans noted that "if there is any expectation of a near term change in Canadian copyright law, it may be unwise to cause expectations to be created and investments to be made where a change in the law may shortly disturb their expectations and investments".[13]

There is no doubt that the massive importation of American signals was made possible by the absence in Canadian copyright law of a requirement to pay copyright holders for retransmissions beyond the coverage area for which they had agreed to assign their rights.

The 3 + 1 policy was the key to the tremendous success of cable television in Canada, improving the reception of U.S. signals where they had previously been available off-air, and making them available in communities distant from the border where they had previously been unavailable. As soon as the policy was extended to CANCOM, however, CANCOM sold the U.S. network signals at a per-subscriber charge for each signal. This practice, deemed by the Commission to be vitally important to the economic success of CANCOM, has led to particularly strong complaints from the United States with CBS, NBC and ABC, as well as the Canadian Motion Picture Distributors Association, which represents U.S. producers, appearing frequently before the CRTC to oppose the policy.

Simultaneous substitution and tax measures were in fact regulatory responses to counter the trend towards imported signals which had developed in part because there was no charge for retransmission of foreign signals. If a price had been attached to the importing and retransmission of signals it is likely that the efforts of the cable operators and the CRTC would have been directed to other methods for increasing program choice besides the importing of foreign signals. It is from this standpoint that the issue of retransmission rights should be viewed, not as an historical exercise, but rather to guide Canadian broadcasting in the coming years.

We recommend that a retransmission right should be recognized in order, first, to protect the interests of Canadian broadcasters and second, to foster the dissemination of Canadian works.

Canadian broadcasters hold broadcast rights over a good many American programs. Allowing cable operators and CANCOM to retransmit such programs free of charge is a denial of the exclusive right that Canadian broadcasters have paid for. Mandatory simultaneous substitution allows Canadian broadcasters to recover the advertising value of programs retransmitted from the United States by placing their own commercials in these programs. This mechanism is nevertheless only a partial response to the problem of free signal retransmission because it applies only when such programs are broadcast at the same time in both countries. It also encourages Canadian broadcasters to arrange their programming schedules to coincide with the schedules of the American networks.

If costs had been attached to retransmission, cable operators would have questioned the wisdom of a decision to import signals consisting primarily of programs for which broadcast rights were already owned in Canada. The existence of a mechanism to cover retransmission rights would perhaps have lessened the need to introduce regulations like simultaneous substitution because retransmission royalties would have been paid to the Canadian companies that acquired the rights on the retransmitted programs. As Table 28.1 shows, a substantial percentage of programs broadcast by the American networks are available on Canadian networks.

Table 28.1 Proportion of U.S. Network Programs Currently Available on Canadian Stations

	U.S. Program Schedule	
	12:30–4 p.m.	8–11 p.m.
Toronto	71%	80%
Montreal	29%	38%

Source: Coopers Lybrand Consulting Group, "Impact of Selected Policy Changes in the Canadian Broadcasting System", study prepared for the Task Force on Broadcasting Policy, May 1986, p. 58.

The purpose of the substitution policy was to correct the imbalance of a situation that could be set right by the recognition of broadcast program rights. It has also become a bone of contention between Canada and the United States. Although this second reason is not a determining factor, a better policy would ease the concerns not only of the Americans, who rightly feel that their interests are being harmed, but also of those Canadians who believe unrestricted imports make it more difficult to Canadianize the airwaves.

Recognizing a retransmission right makes the obligation to pay for all television product, including foreign product, an established policy principle. Once the principle is established, consideration can be given to determining the form of payment, an exercise that no one wishes to engage in while retransmission is free.

In many ways, the retransmission right proposed by the Commons subcommittee is unsatisfactory. Producers would certainly prefer to exercise their rights more freely. A retransmission right as here defined does provide them with compensation but does not allow copyright holders to prevent retransmission. That is why there would be a need to keep regulatory measures designed to protect the rights of Canadian broadcasters, such as simultaneous substitution rules. What the retransmission right provides is an obligation to take all the costs involved in retransmission into account. We shall now examine a more effective method for so doing.

Although in the past the primary method for importing American signals was microwave relays, it is now possible to receive American signals at a single point in Canada and to retransmit them by satellite across the country. This technological development allows us to envisage a mechanism based on acquiring all rights to the programs carried on these imported signals, except those already held by Canadians.

Here, in summary, is the concept we propose be considered:

a) A non-profit corporation, jointly owned by Canada's public and private broadcasters would be established.
b) The corporation would make arrangements to clear Canadian rights for all American network programs not already purchased on the open market by Canadian broadcasters.
c) Arrangements would be made to uplink the 3 + 1 U.S. channels by satellite from a number of points along the Canada-U.S. border.
d) Because Canadian distribution rights would be held for all network programming, commercials would be eliminated and the corporation would be free to sell commercial time to advertisers in Canada, or to make such other use of that air time as they deem appropriate.
e) The simultaneous substitution rules already in place to protect Canadian broadcasters could be continued or strengthened. Free network air time could be filled as deemed appropriate by the CRTC, after consulting both Canadian broadcasters and the general public.
f) The uplinked signals would be substituted within all Canadian cable systems over a reasonable period of time for the stations now imported by microwave, at a cost determined by the CRTC.
g) Any revenues of the Corporation in excess of costs would be used to finance Canadian programming to be carried on existing Canadian broadcasting services, thereby helping to restore balance between Canadian and American programming in the broadcasting system.

Following this approach, the Corporation could contract with CANCOM to handle arrangements with cable operators to purchase the four signals and to deal with any technical matters related to satellite distribution of the signals. CANCOM is already equipped for this and could include the signals in its DBS service. They would be scrambled to prevent unauthorized reception and spillover back into the U.S.

Arrangements along the lines described above would be more desirable from many standpoints than the current 3 + 1 arrangements and would take advantage of Canada's satellite distribution capacity. First, and perhaps most important, they would continue to satisfy the established expectations of Canadians that all four U.S. networks should be available to them but without the negative consequences of the existing arrangements. All rights to the American programs would be purchased legitimately, thereby responding to American complaints about the pirating of their signals. Because no American commercials would be carried, the problems created for Canadian broadcasters by the spillover of U.S. ads into their market would be largely resolved. Bill C-58, which discouraged Canadian businesses from advertising in the United States, would no longer be necessary because Canadian commercials would be broadcast with American programs. Instead of simply adding a number of 100 percent foreign signals to the broadcasting system, there would be the potential for a balancing contribution to be made to the financing of Canadian programming. Since satellite distribution, unlike cable, has the advantage of being insensitive to distance, the costs of receiving the 3 + 1 signals could be significantly reduced in smaller and more remote communities. Costs could be equalized across the whole of the Canadian system.

In a fundamental way, the arrangements suggested above would greatly enhance Canada's cultural sovereignty. They would reinforce the pattern whereby program exhibition rights for Canada are held by Canadian broadcasters and encourage advertisers to treat Canada as a separate market. They would increase the authority of the CRTC over the Canadian broadcasting system, but would do so in a way that is sensitive to the expectations of Canadian television viewers.

The Task Force has carried out only an initial assessment of the feasibility of this alternative approach to the 3 + 1 dilemma. We are confident that from a technical point of view the approach is feasible. To test the concept further it would be necessary to carry out a thorough study which would assess more carefully the problems that would have to be overcome in order to implement such a plan. We believe that the potential benefits of such arrangements are so substantial that a thorough study should be done.

Recommendations

The principle of independent protection for sound recordings as a category distinct from the original works they contain should be recognized in the *Copyright Act*.

The right of performers over their performances of a creative work should be recognized in the Copyright Act.

The principle of a retransmission right should be recognized in the Copyright Act. The terms and conditions for the amounts of such rights should take into account the cost of retransmission and the limitations involved in broadcasting in remote regions.

Retransmission payments for programs on which rights are already held in Canada should be made to the Canadian owners of such rights.

The Department of Communications should study the feasibility of introducing the following system in place of the existing 3 + 1 policy: a non-profit corporation, owned jointly by Canada's public and private broadcasters which would purchase the distribution rights to American programming in order to retransmit throughout Canada via satellite the programs of the four American networks now made available in Canada by means of microwave relay.

Provisions against Piracy

The unauthorized reception of signals cannot be entirely prevented without very elaborate policing methods. Canadian broadcasting policy must nevertheless stop piracy of pay-TV networks.

The CRTC Task Force on access to television services for underserved communities noted that most broadcasters and cable operators that appeared before the Task Force requested a more vigorous compliance policy for legislation prohibiting unauthorized reception of signals. As the Task Force chaired by Paul Klingle noted:

> It must be made clear to all that this activity negates the proprietor rights of the owners of the programming and in turn erodes the ability of individuals in the artistic community to receive compensation for their labours.[14]

We agree that the legislation should emphasize the protection of creators rather than the tracking down of those who do not respect the rules. Thus, although there are provisions in the *Criminal Code* and in the *Radio Act* that can be used to take legal action against pirates, we believe it would be more appropriate to provide remedies for copyright holders. This approach was adopted in the United States, where the *Cable Communications Policy Act*[15] protects the ownership rights in signals by establishing a clear distinction between signals intended for individual reception without payment and others.

Section 633 of the American *Cable Communications Policy Act* prohibits not only piracy but also the manufacturing and distribution of unauthorized decoders. Section 705 of the U.S. Act concerns the unauthorized reception of satellite signals but provides an exception for individual private use. This exception to the principle that prohibits the reception of unauthorized reception of signals applies only if the programming is not scrambled or if there is no marketing system available to allow individuals to acquire the right to receive such programming, or where there is such a system, that the individual has obtained permission to receive the programming in question.

We recommend that Parliament should pass similar provisions to take into account the specific conditions surrounding Canadian broadcasting while at the same time strengthening existing criminal remedies.

This would reserve the right to market legitimate programming services in Canada to those authorized by the owners of the rights in question and licensed by the regulatory authorities; it would also provide remedies for copyright holders to allow them to protect their interests. Controls over piracy are necessary for any market-based system of ownership rights.

Recommendations

Cable operators should have the right to civil remedies to prevent unauthorized reception of their signals or the manufacture and sale of illegal decoders, and a right to be compensated for damages caused thereby.

Holders of copyrights on programs relayed by satellite and primarily intended for direct reception by cable operators with a view to retransmission to cable subscribers should have the right to go before the courts to prevent unauthorized reception of their signals and to prevent the manufacture and sale of illegal decoders. Further, they should have a right to be compensated for damages caused thereby. An exception should be allowed when the programming in question is not scrambled and has not yet been marketed.

Notes

1. *Copyright Act* R.S.C. 1970, c. C-30.
2. See Canada, Royal Commission on Patents, Copyright, Trade Marks and Industrial Design, (Isley Commission), *Report on Copyright* (Ottawa: Queen's Printer, 1958); Economic Council of Canada, *Report on Intellectual and Industrial Property* (Ottawa: Information Canada, 1971); and, A.A. Keyes and C. Brunet, *Copyright in Canada: Proposals for a Revision of the Law* (Ottawa: Queen's Printer, 1977).
3. Canada, Department of Communications and Department of Consumer and Corporate Affairs, *From Gutenberg to Telidon: White Paper on Copyright* (Ottawa: Ministry of Supply and Services Canada, 1984).
4. Canada, House of Commons, Standing Committee on Communications and Culture, *A Charter of Rights for Creators: Report of the Sub-Committee on the Revision of Copyright* (Ottawa: Minister of Supply and Services Canada, 1985).
5. Canada, Department of Communications, "Government Response to the Report of the Sub-Committee on Copyright" (Ottawa: The Department, 1985).
6. Standing Committee, *Charter of Rights for Creators*, p. 62.
7. See Canadian Admiral Corporation Ltd. v. Rediffusion Inc., (1954), Ex. C.R. 382.
8. Victor Nabhan, "La télévision par câble et le droit d'auteur au Canada", *Revue canadienne du droit d'auteur*, (1982), p. 8.
9. Victor Nabhan "Les satellites et le droit d'auteur au Canada", *Revue canadienne du droit d'auteur*, 1983, p. 9; David W. Tarbet "Use of American Broadcast Signals By Canadian Cable Networks: The CANCOM Decision", (1983) 32 *Buffalo Law Review*, 731-747, and John D. Hylton, Gary Maavara, "The Interaction of Copyright Law and Broadcasting Policy", study prepared for the Task Force on Broadcasting Policy, Ottawa, December, 1985.
10. Cable subscribers pay an 8 per cent subscription tax. This tax was established to help fund Telefilm Canada's television production fund.
11. Standing Committee, *A Charter of Rights for Creators*, p. 83.
12. See Thomas J. Ryan and James S. Crane "International Telecommunications pirates: Protecting U.S. Satellite Signals from Unauthorised Reception Abroad" (1985) 17 New York University, *Journal of International Law and Politics*, p. 851.
13. Video World Inc., "The Role of Satellites in the Canadian Broadcasting System", study prepared for the Task Force on Broadcasting Policy, February 1986, p. 111.
14. Canadian Radio-television and Telecommunications Commission, Task Force on Access to Underserved Communities, (Klingle Committee) *The Costs of Choice* (Ottawa: Minister of Supply and Services Canada, 1985), p. 46.
15. Sections 633 and 705 of the *Cable Communications Policy Act of 1984* contain provisions prohibiting the illegal reception of unauthorized cable or satellite signals and also provide that the injured parties may go before the courts to stop unauthorized reception as well as to stop the manufacture and sale of illegal decoding equipment. See Anthony F. LoFrisco, *Television Piracy* (New York: Practising Law Institute, 1985) and George R. Borsari Jr., Gary L. Christensen, *A Practical Guide to the Cable Communications Policy Act of 1984* (New York: Practising Law Institute, 1985).

Part X

CONCLUSIONS

Chapter 29

Financing the Task Force Proposals

Financing the Task Force Proposals

Introduction

Throughout our deliberations we were very much aware that improving the Canadian broadcasting system will require money. This is especially so if more high quality Canadian drama and entertainment programming is to be shown. While the funds might come from many sources, including reallocation of existing revenues, there is no effective solution that does not cost money. Certainly no amount of rhetoric about cultural sovereignty, Canadian identity or cultural expression will in itself accomplish anything.

We have operated on the premise that we must be able to indicate, at least in general terms, what it would cost to implement our recommendations and where the money might come from. We have proposed some quite significant changes but we have tried to be realistic about three things. First, we have sought to avoid any pretence that redressing the growing imbalance between Canadian and foreign programming in our domestic broadcasting system can be accomplished without substantial additional funds being committed to Canadian programming. Second, wherever possible we have looked for the necessary funds from within the broadcasting system itself, through reallocation of resources, better organization, or changes in structure and operating practices likely to produce greater efficiencies. Third, we have not pretended that our estimates for either costs or sources of funding are precise, although they do represent informed and reasonable estimates.

We have been hampered in achieving clear and precise analysis by the limited and sometimes inconsistent information available. For example, there was simply no information concerning annual expenditures by public and private broadcasters on Canadian drama or children's programming, so we did not know what the trend had been. We therefore asked Statistics Canada to assist us by carrying out a special survey. The results are summarized in Chapter 17 and referred to in the analysis that follows.

It was also difficult to establish consistent real costs for the component parts and activities of the CBC. While the Corporation was generally open in its dealings with the Task Force, our policy review took place at a time when it was adopting new financial and management information systems. We believe, however, that the available information makes it possible to estimate the financial implications of our CBC recommendations with reasonable accuracy.

Finally, we found the same difficulties in costing our proposals as a political party does in costing its election platform. Even assuming the best will in the world, access to pertinent information is always incomplete. More important, until a proposal is fleshed out in full detail, its true costs can only be estimated. Nevertheless, we are satisfied that by combining the information in our own commissioned research with other sources we have been as scrupulous as possible in our estimates and we are confident they at least indicate the scale of costs and revenues involved.

In the light of the serious deficiencies which now exist in the annual survey of television broadcasters, the Task Force considers it essential that the survey be amended to provide precise information on expenditures in each program category. Then it would be possible to monitor changes in expenditure patterns against the base year ending August 31, 1985, which is covered in the special supplementary survey prepared for the Task Force.

Recommendation

The annual statistical survey of Canadian television broadcasters by Statistics Canada should be amended to provide data on expenditures on Canadian and foreign programming for each program category.

The Cost of Implementation

Most of our recommendations involve costs, whether to provide better news coverage of regions of Quebec now neglected, to distribute CBC's stereo radio service to more Canadians, or to establish new French-language and English-language television channels.

We have itemized in Table 29.1 all proposed expenditures, together with cost estimates, and comments on financial implications. Where we have had difficulty estimating cost, the reasons are explained.

CBC Expenditures

Our central CBC recommendation is that the Corporation's mandate be more focussed. Instead of providing balanced programming drawing on both foreign and Canadian production, the CBC should become essentially a source of Canadian programs. We want to see the CBC in its information programming continuing to serve the widest possible range of Canadian interests, while carrying on its service as broadcaster of last resort for official-language minority groups, for native Canadians, for farmers and for a wide range of Canadian communities with particular interests.

Our recommendations on CBC broadcasting of news and information will not save money. The proposal for small 'storefront' CBC news operations in parts of Canada which have no CBC station and are not covered by CBC news will add costs, depending on the number. Similarly, in recommending a new CBC news and current affairs channel, we do not see the resulting revenue helping to finance existing CBC services, but rather providing funding for vitally needed additional coverage by Canadians of foreign news stories.

The one area where our recommendations call for a curtailment of CBC program production and expenditure is in some television stations. On the English-language side we wish to see all but five of the CBC's owned and operated stations reduced to producing information programming, including local news and supper hour programs and — principally in stations in provincial capitals — additional current affairs programs. As the recommendations in Chapter 10 indicate, however, it is our intention that any money thus freed up should be reallocated for production within the regions. We wish to see an expansion of production activity in the regions both for the regions themselves and for the network.

Table 29.1 Implementation Costs of Task Force Recommendations

Expenditure Item	Estimated Cost	Comment
1. **Native Broadcasting** – Increased allocation of funds to the Northern Native Broadcast Access Program (NNBAP) to cover costs associated with sharing a satellite transponder with CBC.	$2 million – $3 million	The option of a shared transponder to carry native programming is proposed as an interim step toward separate satellite arrangements for carriage of native-language programming.
2. **CBC Programming** A. **News and Information** – Establishing of 'store-front' radio news gathering service in regions of Canada not now covered by the CBC's English radio news service.	CBC has estimated the costs at $13 million over a 5-year phase-in period to bring local radio service to 19 unserved communities (just over $2 million annually). The cost of serving each community through a 'store-front' service is an average capital expenditure of about $300,000 and average operating costs of about $160,000 annually.	Such service could be extended at any rate, based on the extent of funding available. The Task Force endorses the principle that the gaps in CBC's news coverage of Canada should be filled as efficiently as possible.
– Open offices in a number of key regions of Quebec where the CBC has no staff journalists (Abitibi, Eastern Townships, St. Maurice, etc.)	The cost of operating each such office would be approximately $400,000 annually. If three such offices were opened annual costs would be $1.2 million.	The recommendation to establish these offices is linked to our recommendations concerning the reorganization of CBC service in Eastern Quebec.

Table 29.1 Implementation Costs of Task Force Recommendations (cont'd)

– Produce on a trial basis for 3 to 5 years a regional French-language television newscast in Chicoutimi for carriage on the local CBC affiliate.	The estimated cost is $700,000 annually.	This recommendation is also linked to a reorganization of CBC French-language services in Quebec.
– Establish a dedicated news and current affairs channel in English and program a partial channel in French. Link to establishing additional news bureaus outside Canada.	The costs involved depend on how ambitious an approach is taken, but could vary from $20 million to $35 million. The cost of each foreign correspondent is estimated at $300,000.	Revenues would be derived from a per-subscriber charge collected from cable television companies and from national advertising. At a charge of 25¢ per subscriber with carriage on basic or extended basic service in systems offering discretionary services to their subscribers, the cable revenue combined with advertising would cover the cost of providing a strong service.
B. **Performance Programming: Prime Time**		
– Concentrate responsibility for English-language production of programming other than news, information and sports in Halifax, Montreal, Toronto, Winnipeg and Vancouver and strengthen such production in these centres. Do the same for French-language production in Montreal, Ottawa, Quebec and Moncton.	In part this involves a reallocation of expenditure within each region. However, to the extent that production in the regions for the network is strengthened, it would be linked to network expenditures on Canadian programs.	The Task Force's recommendation is that the CBC's television production in the regions should be strengthened, but with production of performance programming concentrated in a single station in each region. This recommendation should be considered in conjunction with the role recommended for TV Canada in the regions.

– Increase the licence fees now paid by CBC to exhibit independent Canadian productions.	The incremental cost of this change is estimated at $15 million.	The result of this change would be to increase the average licence fee payment made by the CBC to 40 percent. It is assumed that on average the Broadcast Fund would match this amount.
– Increase the percentage of Canadian programming exhibited on the CBC's French and English television networks between 7 p.m. and 11 p.m.	The costs to CBC involved in increasing Canadian programming in this time period from the present level of 80 percent are estimated as follows: to 85 percent: $10 – $12 million to 90 percent: $20 – $24 million to 95 percent: $30 – $36 million The costs to Telefilm would be equivalent to the above figures, thereby doubling the total costs (see Item 8 below). The CBC estimates that it might also lose between $30 million and $50 million in advertising revenue if it increased Canadian content to 95 percent, although the proposed tax incentive should substantially reduce these losses.	There is now little Canadian performance programming available in the mid-evening hours. The focus the Task Force has recommended for the CBC would be reflected in increased Canadian content. If the continuation of the Broadcast Fund is assumed beyond 1987, then Telefilm's share of the required funding would already be committed.

Table 29.1 Implementation Costs of Task Force Recommendations (cont'd)

	The CBC estimates that it might also lose between \$30 million and \$50 million in advertising revenue if it increased Canadian content to 95 percent, although the proposed tax incentive should substantially reduce these losses.	
– Increase the percentage of Canadian programming exhibited outside prime time on CBC's French and English television networks.	The estimated cost to the CBC is between \$10 and \$15 million. Only to the extent that the CBC used independently produced children's programs as part of this Canadianization would part of the cost be born by the Broadcast Fund.	Greater or lesser degrees of Canadianization of non-prime time CBC schedules might be considered, with varying costs.
3. **Distribution of CBC Services**		
– Extension of CBC service to cover isolated aboriginal communities – Extension of CBC services to francophone minorities outside Quebec.	As funds become available the extension of coverage by CBC signals should continue.	The extension of CBC services to underserved communities and regions should continue, reflecting an ongoing commitment to CBC's role as broadcaster of last resort serving Canadians who would otherwise receive no service.
– Complete replacement of the remaining 14 CBC radio affiliates.	\$5 million – \$6 million in capital expenditures for new transmitters.	This expenditure could be spread over several years.

– Extend coverage of CBC's English and French stereo radio service.	For the English stereo service expenditures of $37 million would increase coverage from the current level of 72 percent to over 96 percent. In the short term, expenditures of $10 million would increase coverage to 82 percent. Costs for extension of French service would be $3 million to cover communities of 40,000 population.	At present, centres as large as Victoria, Sudbury and Charlottetown cannot receive the CBC's stereo service. Extension of service could be spread over a number of years.
– Negotiate with CBC's French and English TV affiliates to ensure carriage of virtually the full network service.	Costs will vary depending on the degree to which any affiliates are replaced by CBC re-broadcast transmitters or the extent to which renegotiated affiliation agreements can be struck. The net effect on CBC's costs, however, is not expected to be substantial.	This review of the CBC's affiliation agreements is under way. Its outcome will be affected by any further Canadianization of CBC schedules and by any action taken to make advertising on Canadian programs more attractive. While there is no immediate net loss financially, there is the potential for network programs to attract a smaller share of viewing to the CBC when it is no longer linked to local programming.
– Establish an English-language CBC television station in New Brunswick.	CBC is already spending a significant amount of money on programming in N.B. under its agreement with its N.B. affiliate. The incremental costs of establishing a station are estimated at an initial capital cost of $25 to $28 million, with additional operating cost of $1.5 million annually.	N.B. is now the only province without an English language CBC television station. The establishing of a station would ensure carriage of the full network service in N.B.

Table 29.1 Implementation Costs of Task Force Recommendations (cont'd)

4. **CBC Ombudsman** – Establish an internally appointed office of CBC ombudsman, with dual appointees responsible for English and French services respectively.	$500,000 to $750,000 annually.	Incremental funding for this purpose should be provided out of government appropriations.
5. **Private Radio and Sound Recording** – Additional support by private radio broadcasters to FACTOR/CTL and MUSICACTION.	It is expected that the approach recommended would lead to additional funds being available to support Canadian sound recordings.	The emphasis of these two industry agencies will be on mainstream commercial categories of recordings.
– Additional direct support by government to finance Canadian sound recordings, with the focus on minority recording interests not served by FACTOR/CTL or MUSICACTION.	The Task Force believes there is a need for at least $5 million annually in public funds to support the production of Canadian sound recordings, with emphasis on non-mainstream music unlikely to receive support through the industry agencies.	Some additional funds have now been committed under the program announced recently by the Minister of Communications.
6. **Private Television** – Conditions of licence should be used to ensure that private broadcasters make a greater contribution to financing Canadian programming.	The objective should include having expenditures by the Broadcast Fund to finance Canadian programs for private broadcasters matched by licence fees paid by private broadcasters. If Telefilm commits $35 million in 1987-1988, for example,	Telefilm should only support productions if a designated percentage (15 percent is suggested to start) of the budget is committed as a licence fee. The balance of emphasis will vary from broadcaster to broadcaster and between the French and

	$35 million should be paid in licence fees by private broadcasters. This should not come at the expense of news and information programming to which adequate resources should also be committed.	English sectors. At present news and information is stronger in English broadcasting than in French; Canadian entertainment programming is the greatest weakness of English television.
7. **TV Canada** – New non-commercial services should be established in French and English with an emphasis on children's, documentary and arts programs, and on independent productions originating in the regions. The services will also repeat existing programs from other broadcasters.	First year budget would be $45 to $50 million, rising to $100 million over 5 years. Service would benefit from complementary NFB funding, provincial governments, Telefilm Canada, and repeating Canadian programs.	Per-subscriber payments from cable companies would start at 75¢ and rise by 25¢ annually to $1.50. Thereafter adjustments would reflect inflation. Appropriate cable rate adjustments would be made, as indicated in Chapter 24.
8. **The Broadcast Fund** – The Broadcast Fund should be extended for a second 5-year period from 1988 to 1993.	The level of funding we consider appropriate for the Broadcast Fund would be $75 million in 1987-88, and would rise at least in line with inflation over the next five years.	The cost of the Broadcast Fund would be offset by the tax revenues generated by a continuation of the tax on basic cable subscriptions at a reduced rate of 5 percent and a tax of 10 percent on discretionary cable services.

Table 29.1 Implementation Costs of Task Force Recommendations (cont'd)

9. **Tax Incentive to Advertisers** – Establish a 150 percent deduction for the cost of all advertisements placed on Canadian children's programs, drama, variety, performing arts and documentary programs which qualify for 10 points under the CRTC's criteria for defining Canadian programs.	Maximum cost estimate is $29 million. To the extent this measure attracts more advertising to Canadian programs it will generate offsetting economic benefits.	The proposal will complement the Broadcast Fund policy, CBC's increased Canadian content, and CRTC's recent initiatives to strengthen Canadian programming in these categories.
10. **Research and Regulation** – The CRTC should implement a compliance strategy for its regulations and conditions of licence, and both DOC and the CRTC should substantially increase research resources.	Without detailed knowledge of CRTC operations, costs are difficult to determine for the compliance strategy. Our estimate is an additional $5 million to $7 million.	The CRTC collects in licence fees from broadcasters much more than it spends on regulating the industry. The costs are, therefore, fully covered within the activity itself and there is scope for additional expenditures. Some of the increase may be offset by increased use of self-regulation.
– Establish a data bank of CRTC decisions, assist various groups of citizens to monitor and be involved in developing broadcast policy and decision-making, and establish a public participation officer in each regional CRTC office.	Costs are estimated at between $1 million and $1.5 million.	As noted above, revenues from broadcast licence fees exceed CRTC expenditures.

Some reallocation of CBC's French-language television resources within the regional service may be possible owing to the reorganization proposed in Chapter 8. It would reduce all but four of the French stations to news and information production. We have argued, however, that the CBC's French-language services outside Montreal have to be improved in many respects.

If our recommendations on the CBC are acted upon the principal expenditures will be on increasing Canadian programming on the CBC's French-language and English-language television networks. At present both are providing roughly 80 percent Canadian programming in peak viewing time. Based on information provided by independent producers, Telefilm and the CBC, the net additional costs to the CBC of increasing Canadian content on both networks between 7 p.m. and 11 p.m. are estimated as follows:

– to 85 percent: $10-12 million.
– to 90 percent: $20-24 million.
– to 95 percent: $30-36 million.

These costs ignore the possibility that CBC will lose advertising revenue as it replaces big budget American network productions with Canadian programs. Estimates of the losses CBC might sustain if it were to increase Canadian programming in peak viewing time to 95 percent range from $30 million to $50 million, at least initially. If the tax incentive we recommend is implemented, however, this revenue loss should be reduced substantially.

While the Broadcast Fund costs are considered later in this chapter and represent the continuation of an existing program for which money is already allocated, it should be understood that the total cost of increasing Canadian content on CBC is higher than the figures cited above. Taking account of the cost to Telefilm Canada of Broadcast Fund costs and the possible loss of commercial revenue, the costs could be as high as $30 to $40 million to increase Canadian content to 85 percent, $60 to $80 million to increase to 90 percent, and $90 to $120 million to increase to 95 percent. The assumptions made in this costing are that the average cost of the additional Canadian programming is $750,000 an hour and that on the average CBC licence fees cover 40 percent of the total budget and include two plays of each program. On average, the Broadcast Fund would match CBC expenditures. There would be some offsetting reduction in CBC costs, however, owing to reduced purchase of foreign programs.

The Task Force believes that the CBC should not focus only on peak viewing time in Canadianizing its network schedules. In other periods including, for example, the hours of 4 p.m. to 6 p.m. when many children watch television, the CBC should also be offering more Canadian programs, given the paucity of such programs in the system. The net cost of substantial Canadianization of daytime programming in all time periods on the English and French television networks is estimated to be from $10 million to $15 million. Again, there might be a decline in advertising revenue, with total costs possibly ranging from $15 million to $20 million.

In our consultations we heard complaints from private producers that CBC's licence fee payments were inadequate. We address this issue in Chapter 14. The Task Force believes that, even with Canadian content in peak viewing time at the present level of 80 percent, the CBC should commit an additional

$15 million to Broadcast Fund projects. Moreover, this money should be provided entirely in licence fee payments. In our calculation of the cost of a further Canadianization of CBC schedules we have assumed that licence fees will on average be significantly higher than at present.

The total cost to the CBC itself of the proposed Canadianization of CBC television could be from $75 to $100 million, including direct costs to CBC and the maximum estimate of the loss of advertising revenue. In our view that expenditure would be amply justified and is vital to any serious effort to begin to redress the programming imbalance that now exists in English television and to build for the future in French television on the strong existing base of Canadian production. CBC should make no commitment to any level of Canadianization, however, without being certain that the funds are available. The worst thing that could be done would be to spread resources too thinly to produce attractive programs. It would be better to have Canadian programming on CBC at 80 percent with proper funding than to move to a higher level with inadequate resources.

The ability of the CBC to meet programming objectives and to plan for the future depends on its knowing what resources will be available. In our chapter on the CBC we have addressed the need for a five-year financial framework. This is made more urgent now by the need for both Telefilm Canada and the independent producers to know what can be expected from the CBC.

As Tables 29.2 and 29.3 indicate, the level of funding provided to the CBC by Parliament has fluctuated over the past 10 years. Although the CBC has taken on some additional responsibilities, its government appropriation in 1985-1986 was slightly lower in real terms than it was in 1977-1978, and 12 percent lower than in 1978-1979. On the other hand, CBC's earned revenues in constant dollars from advertising have increased between 1978 and 1986 by 25 percent and are projected by CBC to rise roughly in line with inflation this year.

CBC's parliamentary appropriation was cut sharply twice in the past decade, by $70 million in 1979-1980 and by $85 million in 1985-1986. As Table 29.2 indicates, CBC funding was cut further in 1986-1987.

While the CBC admits that some of the expenditure reductions in the past two years have simply involved improvements to the Corporation's efficiency, there have also been cutbacks in the resources available for programming and production and the plan to Canadianize prime time. The Task Force has two main concerns about the changes that resulted from the reduced CBC appropriation. First, there was a disproportionate reduction in the funds for regional operations. Second, the CBC reduced its already limited commitment of funds to Canadianize its peak time TV network schedules using independent production supported by Telefilm.

It is possible to see why the regional cuts were made, as the regions had limited access to the TV networks and were overstaffed for the production they were actually doing. We recommend strongly, however, that this trend be reversed and that more network production come from the designated key stations in each region. We deal with this issue more fully in Chapter 10.

Table 29.2 CBC Revenue, 1977-78 to 1986-87 in Current Dollars

	Government Appropriation		Earned Revenue		Total Revenue	
	$ millions	percent change	$ millions	percent change	$ millions	percent change
1977-78	467.5	–	96.0	–	563.5	–
1978-79	569.2	+21.8	113.6	+18.3	682.8	+21.2
1979-80	522.4	−8.2	129.5	+14.0	651.9	−4.5
1980-81	585.3	+12.0	141.9	+ 9.6	727.1	+11.5
1981-82	658.5	+12.5	143.7	+ 1.3	802.2	+10.3
1982-83	744.3	+13.0	166.7	+16.0	911.0	+13.6
1983-84	815.3	+ 9.5	192.4	+15.4	1,007.7	+10.6
1984-85	904.7	+11.0	228.5	+18.8	1,133.1	+12.4
1985-86	857.3	−5.2	240.1	+ 5.1	1,097.4	−3.2
1986-87	848.5	−1.0	244.1	+ 1.7	1,092.6	−0.4

Source: Information provided to the Task Force by Treasury Board.

Table 29.3 CBC Revenue, 1977-78 to 1986-87 in Constant Dollars

	Government Appropriation		Earned Revenue		Total Revenue	
	$ millions	percent change	$ millions	percent change	$ millions	percent change
1977-78	467.5	–	96.0	–	563.5	–
1978-79	522.2	+11.7	104.2	+ 8.5	626.4	+11.2
1979-80	439.4	−15.9	108.9	+ 4.5	548.3	−12.5
1980-81	447.1	+ 1.8	108.4	−0.5	555.5	+ 1.3
1981-82	447.0	0.0	97.6	−10.0	544.6	−2.0
1982-83	456.1	+ 2.0	102.1	+ 4.6	558.2	+ 2.5
1983-84	472.4	+ 3.6	111.5	+ 9.2	583.8	+ 4.6
1984-85	502.3	+ 6.3	126.9	+13.8	629.2	+ 7.8
1985-86	457.7	−8.9	128.2	+ 1.0	585.9	−6.9
1986-87	n/a	n/a	n/a	n/a	n/a	n/a

Source: Information provided to the Task Force by Treasury Board.

The Task Force did not have the responsibility to carry out an in-depth examination of the efficiency of the CBC. Moreover, we recognize the special problems that arise in deciding precisely what is efficient behaviour in the creative or production component of CBC operations. It is our judgement, however, that programming capacity has already begun to suffer and that continuing cuts would certainly not be compatible with the recommendations we make. The information available to us suggests that there are only limited gains to be made through further reducing CBC's administration. In addition, the reallocation of funds we propose in the regions will fund only a limited share of the strengthening of regional production we propose.

What is essential now is for the CBC and the government to agree on what should be done over the next five years and what that will cost. This financial plan should then be the basis for the CBC's proposals concerning its programming role which will be put before the CRTC for public comment during the Corporation's licence renewal. CBC should then be held fully accountable for the execution of its plan — accountable to the government and to Parliament particularly on the financial side and to the CRTC for fulfilling effectively its programming role in the Canadian broadcasting system.

The Task Force recognizes that adequate financial disclosure is required for agreement between the government and the CBC on a five-year financial plan. Strict interpretation of the arm's length principle dictates that full disclosure would violate the principle. On the other hand, in the real world we are describing an exchange of such information is indispensable. The arm's length principle must still, however, govern all matters relating to CBC programming Philosophy and strategy, as well as all programming decisions.

Source of Funds

The Canadian broadcasting system has three general sources of funds from which new services or program production can be financed. The first is the revenues received from advertisers. The second is the government, using tax revenues. The third is subscribers making direct payments to receive broadcast signals. (It was also suggested to us by the Friends of Public Broadcasting that private broadcasters should be charged a rental fee in exchange for using the public airwaves but, for reasons explored in Chapter 17, the Task Force did not accept this proposal.)

We have made it unmistakably clear that we expect private television broadcasters to provide more quality Canadian programming and private radio broadcasters to contribute to Canadian sound recording production. But our estimates for expenditures by private TV are only rough, based mainly on the matching of licence fee payments which we recommend in Chapter 14. It is up to the CRTC to decide the precise contribution of each broadcaster, consistent with its resources.

Canada's capacity to achieve its national objectives for the broadcasting system depends on both the amount of revenue flowing into the system and the degree to which those revenues are used for the production of more high quality Canadian programming. We will now consider:

- the role of private television broadcasters
- the role of private radio broadcasters
- the Broadcast Fund
- licence fee payments
- cable subscription rates
- the tax on cable television
- a tax on the sales and rentals of audio and video cassettes
- a tax on the sales and rentals of VCRs
- a tax on satellite receiving dishes
- Government of Canada advertising
- tax incentives to stimulate investment in Canadian production
- a tax incentive to encourage advertising on Canadian television programming

Clearly, substantial resources to achieve our objectives are available through these various means.

Advertising

The advertising revenues of Canada's television broadcasters have always been low by comparison with those in other western countries. As we have seen, revenues from advertising are less than half the per capita level of American or Australian broadcasters and there is evidence that the gap between American and Canadian levels is widening.

There has, nevertheless, been substantial real growth in the revenues of Canadian television stations and networks over the past decade. This reflects the passage of Bill C-58 in 1976 and the CRTC's policy on simultaneous program substitution which, as we show in Chapter 17, may have been worth as much as $100 million to English-language broadcasters in 1984, although the measures had little or no impact on French-language broadcasters. The increased revenues have facilitated the establishment by private broadcasters of effective local, regional and national news coverage and information programming. As Chapter 17 indicates, private television broadcasters have the financial capacity to provide more Canadian entertainment programming and improve Canadian programming in other categories.

In radio, as we see in Chapter 16, many stations experience losses but the profitable ones are very profitable indeed. Here, too, we find that there is scope for private radio to make a greater direct contribution out of advertising revenues to producing Canadian sound recordings. In both radio and television we believe this greater contribution should be sought through conditions of licence, not general regulation. Using licence conditions to supplement general regulation, the CRTC can ensure that conditions for each licensee reflect individual capacity.

Revenues from Taxes

We see no alternative to relying chiefly on public broadcasting for Canadian programming, mainly because the Canadian market is relatively small and divided into French-language and English-language segments. Canada needs public television not just to provide non-commercial programming but also to provide popular entertainment — programs produced by Canadians for Canadians.

In addition, the Broadcast Fund is a departure in the way government revenues have been used to support Canadian program production. The Task Force believes that as long as the funds are spent in accordance with clear objectives, this approach can strengthen Canadian programming.

The creation of the Broadcast Fund was linked indirectly to taxation of cable television subscriptions. The Task Force does not oppose this user-pay approach, but it examined and rejected a proposal that new taxes or rental fees be imposed on broadcasters to support Canadian program production. Radio and television stations and networks should, rather, make their contribution to Canadian programming through their own direct expenditures.

Subscriber-based Revenues

Whether Canadians pay for their television through taxes, charges added to the cost of goods and services to cover their advertisement, or charges levied by cable companies, the money ultimately comes out of the same pocket. A distinction is normally made, however, between services paid for indirectly — through taxation or through advertising — and directly. Direct payments provide the financial base of operations for basic cable, pay-TV and specialty services.

Subscriber services have grown more rapidly than others over the past two decades. The revenues of the cable television industry increased from $22 million in 1967 to $352 million in 1980. More recently, with the introduction of pay-TV and specialty programming services, the gross revenues of cable television companies rose to an estimated $853 million in 1985.[1]

In the United States the revenues of growing cable systems have become an additional source of funding for a new generation of satellite-to-cable programming services often described as cable networks (discussed in Chapter 18). Most are financed by a combination of advertising revenues and payments by cable system operators and are provided to cable subscribers in the United States as part of basic cable service. Payments for each service vary greatly, ranging from 1¢ to roughly 30¢ per subscriber per month. These payments are an important part of the financing of many new services in the U.S. In Canada, however, there are not yet any directly comparable Canadian services; no Canadian satellite-to-cable services draw on cable revenue from basic service. Nevertheless, we recommend that two such services be created. Broadcasting policy must meet the challenge of integrating cable and other subscription services into a strategic plan to put Canadian policy into effect.

Private Broadcasters

In radio, both private broadcasters and government must play expanded roles in supporting the production of additional Canadian sound recordings if there is to be adequate output. We recommend in Chapter 16 that the CRTC build on the established practice of industry support of FACTOR/CTL and MUSICACTION. We suggest that the CRTC call upon radio stations with the means to put an appropriate portion of their revenue into these agencies. Inevitably this support will be concentrated on the most popular kinds of music. It is therefore essential that substantial complementary support be provided through one or more of the cultural agencies. We have suggested that at least $5 million should be provided annually to support production unlikely to receive assistance through industry-financed programs, including folk music, jazz, ethnic music, music of the native peoples, and some forms of popular music, as well as classical music.

Use of the industry and government support programs should be monitored carefully to determine their impact on record output and variety. This will provide the CRTC with a basis for judging whether adjustments in funding levels are required.

We also support strongly the CRTC's intention to use licence conditions to require greater spending on Canadian programs by private Canadian TV stations and networks. In the year ended August 31, 1985 private English-language broadcasters spent just 2.4 percent or $17.5 million of their gross revenues on Canadian films and TV entertainment series, including both in-house and independent productions and both investment and licence fee payments. Just $1.9 million or .3 percent was spent on Canadian children's programs. By comparison, they spent $132.4 million or 18.1 percent of their revenues on Canadian news and public affairs programs, and $32.4 million or 4.4 percent on sports programs. More important, they spent over $110 million or 15.1 percent of their revenue on purchase of foreign films and TV entertainment series.

In French television, broadcasters spent $10.9 million (8.4 percent of revenue) on Canadian films and TV entertainment series. By comparison, 16.6 percent of revenue was spent on Canadian news and public affairs and 2.3 percent on Canadian sports programs. A substantially lower proportion of revenue, 6.3 percent, was spent on foreign films and TV series than was the case in English television.

Based on the analysis contained in Chapter 17, the Task Force considers it reasonable to expect, through conditions of licence, that private (especially English-language) broadcasters greatly increase their spending on Canadian television entertainment programs over the next five years.

The Task Force believes it essential that private broadcasters' participation in Broadcast Fund projects be primarily through licence fee payments. The CRTC must bear this in mind when establishing conditions of licence if the proposed development strategy for private sector producers is to be successful.

Cable and Subscriber Revenues

The Task Force recommends that new Canadian satellite-to-cable services be established to provide both a CBC news and current affairs channel in English and two new non-commercial Canadian television networks — TV Canada in English and Télé-Canada in French. The new services would involve payment by cable system operators on a per-subscriber basis. They would be carried on basic cable service in systems already carrying discretionary services. The rates for basic cable service would then be adjusted to reflect the charges for the new services. Rates would also reflect our proposals for changes in the taxation of cable subscribers and the revised approach to rate regulation which we recommend in Chapter 24.

For the proposed CBC news and current affairs channel, we suggest a subscriber rate of 25¢ per month. This rate combined with expected national advertising revenue would cover costs of at least $20 million annually. For the proposed TV Canada service, our recommendation is that the rate be set initially at 75¢ per subscriber and rise by 25¢ annually until it reaches $1.50. The result would be revenues of roughly $45 million in the first year, rising to $100 million in the fifth. Thereafter the charge should simply be adjusted to reflect inflation.

TV Canada will benefit from the relatively low costs of nationwide satellite distribution. With no in-house production, administrative costs will be low. For both the French and English channels it is estimated that technical and transmission costs combined with administrative expense will not exceed $10 million annually. Remaining expenditures could be on purchasing Canadian programming. Detailed schedules and costing for TV Canada and Télé-Canada should be developed through consultations among the potential participants and program suppliers in each case.

The Task Force commissioned extensive research on the cable television industry and is satisfied that at the rates proposed these new services are no threat to cable subscription levels and impose no unreasonable burden on the cable television industry. Comparable costs are already borne by cable system operators in the United States to help finance American programming services. If the full cost is passed through at the proposed levels, the cost of cable service in constant dollars will still be lower than it was 15 years ago. If, as we recommend, the rate of taxation of basic cable subscriptions is reduced from eight percent to five percent, the impact will be significantly lightened.

The Broadcast Fund

The Task Force recommends that the Broadcast Fund be extended beyond its initial five years. The Fund began initially with $35 million and has now risen to $66 million for 1986-87. There will be additional demands on the Fund if our recommendations are adopted. At the level of taxation recommended below, the level of support for the second five years could begin at $75 million in 1988-89 and rise at least in line with inflation over the following five years.

Recommendation

The Broadcast Fund should receive $75 million in 1988-89, with the amount increased over the five-year period to at least reflect inflation.

Taxation

The Tax on Cable Television

At present, the federal government levies a tax of 8 percent on cable television service, which offsets the cost of the Broadcast Fund. The Task Force recommends the rate be dropped to 5 percent on basic service and increased to at least 10 percent on discretionary services. At these rates the projections from our cable industry research study indicate that revenue will offset the cost of the Broadcast Fund at the levels of funding proposed above.

Recommendation

The rate of tax on basic cable service should be decreased from 8 percent to 5 percent, with the tax on discretionary services increased to at least 10 percent.

Generating Additional Tax Revenues

The Task Force does not see why in principle cable services should be subject to federal taxation while other industries which deliver films and television programs are not. While there is now a federal tax on cable television subscriptions, there is no comparable tax on audio or video cassette sales and rentals, on the sale and rental of VCRs, or on the sale of satellite receiving dishes. At a five-percent rate, such taxes would have generated over $110 million in 1984. At the eight-percent rate now applied to cable service, which is a regulated service, the revenue generated would have been $180 million. In fact, there is a valid case to be made for taxing these other delivery vehicles of film and television programs at the ten-percent rate we recommend for discretionary services on cable. The rate of tax should not be excessive, however, and should take into account the existence of some provincial taxes in this area. With appropriate levels for the taxes we propose, the result in the 1987-88 fiscal year would be revenues which would substantially exceed the cost of implementing all of the Task Force recommendations.

Government of Canada Advertising

We have also considered incentives that might offset the risks and costs of greater Canadian content on television. Might changes make it more attractive for advertisers to place commercials on Canadian programs? Before addressing this issue, however, it is important to recognize the potential for the Government of Canada itself to assist in strengthening the commercial revenues earned by Canadian programs. The government spent $71.3 million on advertising in 1985-86, including expenditures of over $25 million on television, and has the potential to support Canadian programming through its advertising policies.

Recommendation

> In its own advertising expenditures the Government of Canada should place its commercials on domestic television programs.

150-percent Write-off of Cost of Advertising on Canadian Programs

As the productions helped by the Broadcast Fund come to air it is essential they attract at least their proportionate share of television advertising revenue to the broadcasters showing them. This applies to both the CBC as it continues its Canadianization of prime time and the private broadcasters. To this end, we believe that section 19 of the *Income Tax Act* should be amended to provide advertisers with a 150-percent deduction for the cost of advertising on Canadian programs in the categories of children's, drama, documentary, variety and performing arts. These are the same categories that qualify for support through the Broadcast Fund, although the proposed incentive would apply to 'in-house' productions as well as Broadcast Fund projects.

The incentive would apply to any Canadian production which qualifies for a full 10 points under the CRTC's Canadian content definition. According to Telefilm Canada this would include the overwhelming majority of Broadcast Fund projects.

The Task Force sought advice from Clarkson Gordon on the implementation of this incentive. The firm advised that it is feasible technically and administratively and it estimated the cost would not exceed $29 million.

Television has annual advertising revenues of over $1 billion. A successful strategy to strengthen Canadian programming must include an initiative to encourage the shifting of a significant portion of that advertising to time slots on Canadian programs. Roughly 70 percent of expenditure on television advertising is now on ads placed on foreign programs. A significant portion of the remainder is represented by ads on Canadian sports programs and Canadian information programs.

It has not always been recognized that there are significant differences between the effects on magazines and on television of what is usually referred to as Bill C-58. This provision of the *Income Tax Act*, section 19, including the original 1965 changes, resulted in Canadian advertising being placed in magazines that are both owned by Canadians and contain a substantial majority of Canadian editorial content in order for the expenditure to be considered a deductible expense for tax purposes. Magazine advertisers normally buy space in the magazine rather than in conjunction with a particular article in the magazine. In television, however, while section 19 provides a valuable incentive for Canadian advertisers to advertise on Canadian rather than American stations and networks, it does not preclude most or even all of the advertisements being placed on the foreign programs scheduled by Canadian broadcasters.

While the existing provisions of section 19 are important (for reasons outlined in Chapter 17), we consider it imperative that it be amended to encourage Canadian programming in accordance with the objectives of the *Broadcasting Act*.

The CBC has advised us that it did well in holding audiences as the schedule was Canadianized. This is confirmed by the information presented in Chapter 5 on programs and audiences, indicating that the Corporation's share of television viewing has remained close to constant over the past three years, while the percentage of Canadian content in prime time increased from 70 percent to 80 percent. CBC management has nevertheless expressed concern that they may reach a stage in Canadianization at which advertisers will object to losing a schedule package which has a mix of American and Canadian programs. Traditionally CBC has packaged Canadian and American shows together to sell to advertisers.

Our discussions with advertisers, broadcasters and advertising agencies indicate that there is in fact reason for CBC to be concerned. There is a psychological block characterized by the systematic assumption that Canadian programs will not do as well as foreign ones, whatever the evidence to the contrary. Behind the block is the fact that foreign shows usually have larger production budgets, come with the benefit of spillover advertising and media hype from the United States and, because of the simulcast policy, will be offered to viewers in major markets on more than one channel while Canadian shows will usually be offered on only one. While attitudes may eventually change, these facts will not. Hence we recommend a revision to the *Income Tax Act* which will encourage advertisers to trust Canadian programs as a means of reaching TV viewers with their messages.

The proposed incentive can help ensure that the CBC's earned revenues remain substantial as it continues to Canadianize prime time. It should also reduce the concerns of CBC's private affiliates with the impact of Canadianization on revenues. For English-language private broadcasters, it will provide important encouragement as they try Canadian shows for the first time in the most attractive spots in their program schedules. For private French-language broadcasters, the incentive will help expand scheduling of Canadian programming in prime time in an environment made more fragmented and competitive by the licensing of a new network.

Recommendation

Section 19 of the *Income Tax Act* should be amended to allow Canadian advertisers to deduct as a business expense 150 percent of the cost of advertisements purchased on Canadian children's programs and on Canadian drama, variety, performing arts, and documentary programs, subject to the condition that each program qualify for 10 points under the CRTC's criteria for defining Canadian programs.

Private Investment in Canadian Production

The strategy for the development of Canadian program production that has evolved over the past few years gives private-sector producers a much more important role. Since 1976, federal policy has relied primarily on the Capital Cost Allowance to stimulate private investment in Canadian film and video productions. In the late 1970s and in 1980 and 1981 the result was a substantial flow of funds. In the absence of a strong domestic market, however, investment declined sharply after 1980. Moreover, the Capital Cost Allowance directed money into individual productions rather than into the production companies.

While it is not exclusively a broadcasting concern, there is evidence of the need to attract equity investment in Canadian production companies. These companies need to be able to finance new projects from their own resources and maintain a continuing volume of production. It is also important to continue to provide an effective incentive to private investment in Canadian production projects.

The Task Force received a number of tax proposals from the private-sector production associations. The Canadian Film and Television Association recommended that the Capital Cost Allowance for Canadian productions be increased to 150 percent for those productions which qualify for the full 10 Canadian content points. The Association of Canadian Film and Television Producers and l'Association des producteurs de films et de vidéos du Québec recommended a review of the Capital Cost Allowance, focusing on the barriers that exist to its expanded use. These two associations also recommended that an incentive be developed to stimulate private investment in Canadian-owned independent production companies. We see merit in these proposals. They deserve careful consideration, taking into account their potential to complement existing measures and their importance to film policy, as well as broadcasting.

Summary of Costs and Sources of Funds

Without pretending to a precision our calculations do not justify, we estimate the additional expenditures our recommendations would incur at roughly $175 million in the first year, using the lowest estimates, rising to about $270 million with full implementation. Most of the difference between these two figures reflects the phasing in of TV Canada, with its revenues rising from $45 million in the first year to roughly $100 million annually. The difference also reflects the high and low estimates, $20 million and $35 million, for the proposed news channel.

The vast majority of these additional expenditures, or over 80 percent of the total, would go into additional financing of Canadian programming. A significant part of the remainder would go toward the cost of distributing that programming.

We also recommend that the Broadcast Fund continue to receive support beyond the initial five-year term. Virtually all of these expenditures — $75 million initially, rising at least in line with inflation — would go to support the production of Canadian programs. The cost of the program would continue to be offset by revenues from the tax on cable television subscriptions.

Not all of the additional spending to implement our recommendations would come from government. The costs of TV Canada and part of the cost of the Canadian news channel would come from cable television. The Canadian news channel would also have advertising revenues, while additional expenditures by private broadcasters on Canadian programming would also come out of advertising revenue.

Our recommendations would involve additional annual expenditures of public funds of between $80 million and $100 million, excluding the cost of continuing the Broadcast Fund. Included in this amount are the costs associated with the CBC, and particularly with the further Canadianization of CBC television schedules, the cost in lost revenue resulting from the proposed tax incentive, the recommended additional CRTC expenditures, and the recommendation on native broadcasting. Excluded from the estimate is the potential loss of advertising revenue which might be associated with the Canadianization of CBC television schedules, particularly in English television. However, the tax incentive which is included in the costs could well offset these potential losses to a substantial degree.

Our recommendations would also require significant capital expenditure in addition to the increased annual spending noted above. Capital costs primarily related to establishing CBC television facilities in New Brunswick and increasing audience coverage of CBC's radio services would total $50 million. We have assumed, however, that they would be spread over five years, resulting in average annual capital expenditures of $10 million. This is not a large amount in relation to CBC's capital budget of just under $70 million in 1986-87, but needs to be seen in the context of the Corporation's existing problems with outdated equipment and facilities. Unless explicit provision is made to cover such expenditures they tend to be deferred indefinitely, leaving many Canadians without proper access to the CBC services their taxes help to provide.

Increased CRTC expenditures on regulation recommended in Chapter 7 and estimated at between $6 million and $8.5 million per year could be more than adequately covered by the revenues which flow to government from the licence fees paid by broadcasters. The remaining costs, as we have suggested, could easily be offset by placing a tax of at least five percent on the sale and rental of video cassettes, video cassette recorders, and satellite receiving dishes. Such a tax would be equitable since a comparable tax already applies to cable television services.

Conclusion

We would like to underline two crucial points established by the data cited in this chapter. First, the costs of funding the changes to the Canadian broadcasting system for which this Report has provided a blueprint are, while not low, at least not extravagant. Certainly they seem to be in a range that we believe many Canadians would find acceptable for the objectives they will fulfil.

Second, potential sources of revenue to flesh out the rejuvenated system are by no means lacking. Clearly, if even some of them were exploited, many of our recommendations could be implemented relatively quickly.

In a real sense, then, paying for the new system is the easy part of the problem. The more difficult question is whether we have the will, whether we care enough about the role Canadian broadcasting plays, to do so.

Note

1. Moss, Roberts and Associates Inc., "An Economic Profile of the Canadian Cable Industry", study prepared for the Task Force on Broadcasting Policy, Ottawa, 1986.

Chapter 30

The Future of Canadian Broadcasting

The Future of Canadian Broadcasting

We began this Report by praising the Canadian broadcasting system and those who have contributed so much to its success over the past half-century. We also noted, however, that our task was to assess the present broadcasting system in Canada — to determine where it is inadequate and which of its accomplishments are incomplete — and to recommend appropriate changes for its improvement which might be adopted as public policy.

Although it is easy to name the achievements of Canadian broadcasting, it is just as easy to identify deficiencies. Indeed, every one of our several predecessors has recognized precisely the same major areas of weakness. As Sir John Aird's commission reported to the government in 1929, when radio alone was at issue, Canada was fast becoming a mere satellite of American broadcasting. It is truly astonishing that in the ensuing 57 years, despite two broadcasting acts, the BBG, the CRTC, the CBC, black and white television, colour television, public television, private television, pay television, provincial television, community broadcasting, cable, téléromans, superstations, satellites, satellite dishes, VCRs, and Telefilm — we continue to be dogged by the same overriding problem Sir John pointed to so long ago.

In the light of the information we have amassed and the work we have done, the nature and magnitude of the present crisis — for crisis we see it to be, above all in television — can be summarized as follows:

- Of the 52,000 hours of English television programming available to the average Canadian annually, barely 370 hours are Canadian drama, including sitcoms, movies, mini-series, etc. Of the 27,000 hours of French-language television available to the average francophone viewer, barely 630 hours are Canadian drama.
- 98 percent of all drama on English television is foreign, while 90 percent of all drama on French television is foreign.
- Only 28 percent of all the programming available on English television is Canadian; of the total time Canadians spend watching English-language television, less than one-third is devoted to Canadian programming.
- Francophone teenagers spend more than half of their viewing time watching foreign programs; anglophone teenagers spend 80 percent of their viewing time watching foreign programs.

The problems are clear enough: inadequate Canadian programming; inadequate high-quality programming; insufficient performance programming by the private sector in English Canada, insufficient attention paid to information and public affairs programming in the private sector in Quebec; and a general reluctance to give priority to the social goals of the broadcasting system.

The reasons for these problems are equally clear: the public sector, which must be the chief purveyor of quality Canadian programming, is inadequately scaled and funded; the private sector, which should complement the public sector at least to the extent of contributing to the fulfilment of the social objectives of the Broadcasting Act, is not contributing enough.

Two groups are responsible for these problems: for the inadequate funding, successive federal governments of whatever political stripe; for the private sector's unimpressive role, a regulatory agency which has failed to interpret its mandate under the 1968 *Broadcasting Act* with sufficient rigour.

Directly or indirectly, nearly every one of our recommendations address the issues which flow from this analysis.

We are aware of the economic and financial implications of our mandate. We recognize both the limitations of the public purse and the legitimate need of private broadcasters to earn reasonable profits. But we are satisfied that our recommendations are consistent with the capacities and responsibilities of government and private sector alike.

We are not naïve about the potential consequences of new satellite technology. We are under no illusion as to its capacity to flood our country (and the rest of the world) with more and more American programs, obliterating cultural distinctions between countries. There is no doubt that the quantitative domination of Canadian television by American programming will remain an inexorable fact. Only our response — how we choose to cope with the inevitable onslaught — is in question.

Our recommendations are not being put forward merely as a chimerical attempt to resist reality. Rather, our purpose is to ensure that Canadians have a greater choice of high quality Canadian programming. Satellite technology offers the opportunity for new distribution methods to carry such programming throughout the country, as Chapter 4 on Broadcasting Technology and Chapter 25 on Satellite Distribution demonstrate. Canadian programming does attract audiences. What is now required is the political will to provide Canada with a fully Canadian broadcasting system — or, at least, as Canadian as possible under the circumstances.

While we consider that system to be a composite, continuing to be licensed and regulated by a single entity, the CRTC, with each discrete component contributing to the achievement of certain common objectives, we believe it no longer makes sense to perpetuate the myth that we have a single broadcasting system in Canada. The significant differences in the way broadcasting operates in the two national languages belie such a claim. Generalizations about the broadcasting system, we discovered over and over again, have really been about English-speaking television. There is also a world of difference between broadcasting inside and outside Quebec, and our Report attempts to reflect this signal fact. Nonetheless, it appears that both French and English in Canada are moving toward a common crisis in their broadcasting system. We note that the crisis in English television programming now has a comparable equivalent in French radio, especially with respect to the musical tastes of young Quebecois. The same phenomenon is appearing on the horizon for French television as well. The happy conviction that téléromans immunized Quebecois from the lure of American production values is now being dispelled by new evidence showing that, increasingly, younger Quebecois are joining the rest of the world in turning away from local programming to watch American. While we hope some of our recommendations deal thoughtfully with this unanticipated and unwelcome development, we also want to make it clear that the distinctiveness of the French-language and English-language components of the system should be recognized in law and be taken into account by the appropriate decision-makers.

We propose a new broadcasting act in which the responsibilities of the broadcasting system as a whole are clearly defined. This does not mean that every component of the system must fulfil every responsibility to an equal extent. We recognize, for example, that broadcasters with fewer financial resources can hardly be expected to make the same commitment to Canadian programming that large, more profitable enterprises are able to make. We also acknowledge the appropriateness of the public sector's carrying significantly greater obligations than the private sector. The universal truth in public broadcasting, after all, as the head of BBC Scotland pithily remarked at the 1986 Banff Television Festival, is that "We make programs, they make profits".[1]

In fact, public broadcasting, especially the CBC, has long been the most significant single source not merely of Canadian programming but of Canadian culture in this country. In Chapter 5 we showed how much of the Canadian performance programming available to Canadian viewers today comes from the CBC. For all its faults and deficiencies, and all the valid complaints (as opposed to baseless myths and spurious gossip) with which we were regaled, that truth has always been constant. Two Canadians sometimes associated with the CBC recently spelled out that role in unusually vivid terms. Pierre Gauvreau, author of the sucessful téléroman, *Le Temps d'une Paix*, said to one of our researchers,

> Have a look at the credits of the films that have been made for the past 20 years. Look at theatres like le Théatre du Nouveau Monde or le Rideau Vert. You will see the background of the set designers, the special effects people, the technicians. Even the American productions made here show the same thing. It has been in Radio Canada that they have all learned their craft and their skills.[2]

Peter Herrndorf, a former vice-president of the CBC's English-language network, made a comparable point another way:

- *Charley Grant's War* had a larger audience in a single night than all of the top 10 grossing Canadian feature films in 1985 combined.
- One episode of the Canadian mini-series *Empire* had a larger audience in a single night than all of Canadian theatre in an entire year.
- The CBC broadcast of the Stratford Theatre's 1986 production of *Twelfth Night* will be seen by more Canadians in one night than attended all of Stratford's productions the previous season.

In other words, the CBC is not only the major instrument of Canadian culture, but also of culture in Canada. Yet the institution has been under attack of greater or lesser severity since its very inception. In the words of one former president, Alphonse Ouimet, the CBC is "the most dammed, slurred, supported, inquired into, ignored, blamed, upheld, detested, praised organization I know".[3]

Certainly an atmosphere of crisis has pervaded the Corporation throughout the year in which we have operated; its uncertain mandate and future dominate any discussion of the Canadian broadcasting system. It was in this climate that we began our work, and it persists even now as we conclude. In late 1984 the CBC and its supporters were shocked by the government's demand that it cut $85 million from its budget; in the spring of 1986 further significant and alarming reductions were announced.

The CBC has long lived in a world of uncertainty. Some periods have been worse than others and the last decade has been particularly nerve-wracking. The Trudeau government began cutting back on the CBC budget in the mid-1970s in reaction to its angry belief that Radio-Canada had been taken over by separatists. Subsequently, the Applebaum-Hébert report of 1982 recommended that all CBC program production other than news programming be turned over to private enterprise. Fortunately, this recommendation was not implemented. In 1983, the Minister of Communications issued a policy statement advocating a re-definition of CBC's mission in the new high-tech era: "In the new, multi-channel broadcasting environment, it is imperative that the CBC provide a more distinctive and Canadian programming service which *complements* that provided by the private sector."[4] The impact of such a proposal on the roles of the major players in Canadian broadcasting would be far-reaching. Even though the 'dominant' position of the CBC was taken over by the private broadcasters through the 1960s and 1970s, the proposal to make the CBC the complement to the private sector, rather than the reverse, was of fundamental import.

Although the government denied any such intentions, the consequences of its statements would likely have meant that the CBC would no longer have the major responsibility for protecting a Canadian identity besieged by a relentless flow of American programming on both American and Canadian channels. It is by no means an exaggeration, therefore, to speak of these policies as marking a turning-point in Canadian broadcasting history.

One of the early steps taken by the Conservative government when it came to office in 1984 was to cut back the CBC's budget significantly. Our Task Force was created in this context of apparent bi-partisan antagonism toward the traditional role of the CBC. It is not surprising, therefore, that notwithstanding our broad mandate many perceived ours to be a Task Force on the CBC. Indeed, some feared we were a Task Force *against* the CBC, a political instrument designed to undermine and diminish the national public broadcaster.

Nothing could be further from the truth. Neither our own predispositions, nor the research we carried out, nor the consultations we organized, has led us to play such a role. It would not, moreover, seem to be consistent with the intention of the present government.

In that context, no clearer statement is available than the one made by Marcel Masse, then Minister of Communications, to the 1986 Banff Television Festival. Mr. Masse said the CBC

> is one of the great links in the Canadian community. . . . For fifty years now, a strong and vibrant CBC has been central to the health of the Canadian broadcasting system, indeed, to the Canadian community as a whole. That was true in the 1930s. . . . It is especially true today, now that the cascade of technological change has gained such momentum. All these events have presented to the Corporation a series of great challenges. It has met these challenges triumphantly.[5]

Like every one of our predecessors, we concur. Our recommendations call for the CBC to continue playing a central role in assuring that Canadians have a truly Canadian broadcasting system. For us the CBC is not a complementary broadcasting agency; it is the central one. It must be the main Canadian presence on television. The role of the private system is to complement the CBC in the area of quality Canadian programming and to supplement it by providing American programming.

But it is also our view that the programming crisis is of such magnitude that it cannot be met by the CBC alone. To provide Canadian programming which satisfies both the mainstream and the minorities, which is both popular and innovative, which reflects an inevitable concentration of resources in central Canada yet provides access to the voice of the regions, is a great task that demands a second significant player in the public sector to complement the work of the CBC. Accordingly, we recommend a second non-commercial public network which will broadcast in both French and English and have its headquarters outside Toronto and Montreal. This new network would both complement and supplement the CBC by providing more of certain kinds of Canadian programming than the CBC is capable of organizing and scheduling on its own.

As described in detail in Chapter 13, our new TV Canada would have several applications. It would be a vehicle for children's programs, NFB documentaries, and regional productions and arts productions. It would also provide a window for repeats of the best productions from CBC, provincial educational systems, and private and community sector broadcasters. Finally, it would carry selected foreign arts and children's programs as well as francophone programs in English Canada and anglophone programs in French Canada. On the French side, Télé-Canada would reflect a somewhat different balance including the carriage of some news and public affairs programming plus programs from TV-5, the consortium in which Canada participates along with several European nations.

We recommend a new network to play this role because, in our judgement, the CBC will be fully occupied carrying out the mandate we recommend for it. The CBC will have one additional major responsibility — a predominantly Canadian all-news and public affairs channel in English Canada. We are convinced that an all-news channel of one kind or another is inevitable north of the border and it would be inconsistent with the spirit of our work if such a channel were substantially dependent on American sources.

One of the serious defects of Canadian news coverage is the shortage of Canadian correspondents reporting back to Canada from abroad. We believe that such a channel is the proper instrument to remedy the situation and we are confident that sufficient numbers of top-notch bilingual journalists are available to ensure that both French-speaking and English-speaking Canadians will benefit from its establishment. It seems unlikely to us that a full all-news service is feasible in Quebec at this time, but we would expect that the reports from these Canadian foreign correspondents could be made available to the radio and television services of Radio-Canada.

There is still more to be done, however, if we are to respond meaningfully to the many requests we received from Canadians in every part of the country for greater access to the broadcasting system. Clearly, Canadians want to be better reflected by the system and they want more opportunity to participate in it. The

Task Force was both moved and persuaded by their admonitions. There is widespread feeling that our broadcasting system, like so many other Canadian institutions, reflects reality largely as it is understood in Toronto and Montreal. Similarly, there is strong belief it also reflects the mainstream elites of central Canada. As a result, westerners, easterners, northerners, women, natives, ethnic groups and minority groups in general feel that Canadian broadcasting neither belongs to them nor reflects them.

The number of Canadians who feel alienated from one of the country's key instruments for enhancing national awareness is disturbingly large and we sympathize with their plight. We believe there are means to satisfy some of their legitimate expectations although there is no panacea for the problem. Nonetheless, we can do far more than is now being done.

In this connection, we have looked essentially to an expanded public sector as the only instrument that can realistically be expected to do the job. We have re-emphasized the regional obligations of the CBC and have recommended its re-structuring — which we expect will result in a more concentrated focus on regional progamming. Since the idea of a region is not the same in French Canada as in English, the re-structuring of CBC's French services would be different from the restructuring of its English services and would have to take into account the needs of francophones inside and outside Quebec.

We welcome an expanded role for provincial broadcasting and contend that it is time to end the pretence that it is concerned only with educational programming. We commend the NFB for its commitment to regional production and we advocate that the Broadcast Fund make a serious regional commitment. Further, we expect both the proposed TV Canada and all-news channel to carry substantial amounts of regional fare.

We also see TV Canada as an opportunity to give women a more significant place in the broadcasting sytem. We have, therefore, singled out the NFB's women's arm, Studio D, as an example for others. We call on the CRTC to assure that programming on private and public-sector stations does not depict overall patterns of stereotyped representations (although we firmly resist any temptation to interfere in the specific programs of any broadcaster); and we call for employment equity programs to be imposed as a condition of licence.

For those who wish to participate more fully in the broadcasting system we recommend the institutionalization of an expanded and activist community sector. This will by no means satisfy every interest group that made an appeal to us but it seems a reasonable first step. Our earnest hope is that this experiment works well enough to merit further development. We also recommend what is frankly a picayune extra cost to provide the sophisticated broadcasting undertakings of native Canadians in the north with a dedicated transponder, to be shared with the CBC. We further recommend that both aboriginal Canadians and multicultural groups receive greater recognition of their right to have access to the broadcasting system. Indeed, we ask that the right of access to the system be entrenched in a new broadcasting act.

It is no accident that so much of this conclusion is devoted to issues of a public nature, since it is evident that the greatest burden of social obligation we have assigned to the broadcasting system as a whole must be borne by not-for-profit broadcasting. We do not, however, exempt the private sector from a signficant role; it must carry a fair share of these obligations. To us, compliance with both the spirit and intent of a new act is an idea whose time has finally come; we hope that by shifting the burden of compliance from general regulations to specific conditions of licence, the work of the CRTC in ensuring that all components of the system contribute to its larger goals will be facilitated.

The Government may have at its disposal Bill C-20 which would give it the right to provide general policy directives to the CRTC. We endorse this right, even though we believe it should be used with much greater safeguards than are provided by the bill. Such legislation should be used by the Government to indicate in no uncertain terms that the CRTC must not only assign specific responsibilities to each part of the system but also ensure that those responsibilities are carried out.

The CRTC will continue to have great power over the world of broadcasting; indeed, it is a veritable parliament of broadcasting. Like other parliaments, it must remember that its mandate requires it to represent the general interests of *all* Canadians and not primarily the interests of the giant industry that it regulates. To focus on supervision rather than regulation, as the CRTC has done over the past several years, makes good sense only if the public benefits in return for the lightening of the regulatory burden. In our recommendations we endorse the CRTC's present priorities so long as they are forcefully executed, calling for conditions of licence to ensure that due contributions to the objectives of the *Broadcasting Act* are made by all, while other lesser regulatory matters can be dealt with by fewer bureaucratic requirements and more supervision and self-regulation.

In order to allow the components of the private sector to perform their newly-assigned roles properly, we have systematically attempted to ensure that they are well-positioned to do so. We largely concur with the CRTC in the matter of private radio. We are satisfied that the regulatory burdens of private FM radio should be reduced and that AM radio needs protection from the advances of FM in order to continue providing its local services. In return, we expect Canadian content quotas on music to remain and to be adhered to, and we expect the CRTC to elicit from each station a contribution to the development of Canadian popular music appropriate to its resources.

Similarly, we endorse for private television broadcasters a wide range of regulatory protection and legislative support worth many tens of millions of dollars in direct advertising revenues and infinitely more in industrial stability. Bill C-58 and simulcasting are the two most prominent measures in question; they provide major incentives for broadcasters to schedule American programs in prime time in order to attract large advertising revenues. We argue that such measures are only justifiable from the point of view of the goals of the broadcasting system if the broadcasters in return make significant contributions to those goals. As we have stressed repeatedly, it is much cheaper to purchase American programs than to produce even half-decent Canadian ones. But broadcasters understand that Canadian broadcasting must operate by criteria beyond simply maximizing profits.

A similar formula has been applied to the cable industry. Cable has played a controversial role in the broadcasting system, especially given its strong lobby to bring more and more American signals into Canada. Nonetheless, we agree that the cable industry has a legitimate need to develop in a more orderly fashion and with some protection from its unregulated competitors. We therefore attempt to provide cable undertakings with a clearer status under the proposed Act, to guarantee them fair and reasonable levels of rates, and to suggest anti-piracy rules which offer them civil recourse to protect their signals and prevent unauthorized reception of those signals. In return, we expect the cable industry to assume its proper role by giving priority to the transmission of Canadian signals instead of continuing to seek further expansion through the carriage of more and more American signals.

In short, we propose that the entire private sector in broadcasting receive some degree of state support and protection in return for which each component of the private sector will contribute to the objectives of the broadcasting system. Sometimes that support can be seen as a direct benefit to something called Canadian culture, as in the obligation of the cable companies to provide a community channel. We endorse simulcasting as a means of enriching television broadcasters using American programming so they can be asked to provide Canadian programming. Private AM radio needs protection from its FM competition in order to continue playing a great deal of American popular music and a certain stipulated amount of Canadian popular music, which seems to be considered a contribution to Canadian culture! As a result, we have frequently in our deliberations stopped to ask ourselves if such a substantial amount of state protection to the private broadcasting system can really be justified, or if much of what passes for cultural protectionism is not, in reality, simple commercial protectionism. The answer can only be that in return for such generous state support, serious benefit to the public interest must be demonstrably forthcoming.

For these reasons, our Report is positively awash with recommendations on every conceivable aspect of the Canadian broadcasting system. While that system already stands as a monument to the ingenuity of the Canadian way of doing things, especially in terms of the ever-controversial balance between the roles of the public and the private sectors, it can be improved. From the beginning Canadians have looked to broadcasting to play much more profound social roles than have ever been expected of the American system. For example, the enhancement of national consciousness has always been considered a responsibility of the broadcasting system. The preservation and extension of Canadian culture is, to a significant extent, dependent on that system. From our point of view it is through the pursuit of individual and human goals of expression and enjoyment that we attain the nation-building goals; it is not at all a matter of creating what some have called a state culture. The goals, therefore, are to provide Canadian listeners and viewers with more and better Canadian programming that will inform, entertain or enlighten, and to provide Canadian creators with significant opportunities to express themselves by producing such programming. The magnitude of that task can hardly be exaggerated. And it will cost. There are no free lunches and certainly no inexpensive ways by which Canadians can foster their cultural development.

There are three ways in which broadcasting is financed. The first is from direct government appropriations, which means indirectly from the taxpayer through general taxes and taxes linked to broadcasting services. The second is directly from consumers, through such measures as payments for home cable services or for the unscrambling of signals. The third is indirectly from consumers through the extra costs to meet advertising expenses that J.K. Galbraith taught us long ago are hidden in the prices of commodities that are advertised on television and radio; we pay for the wash even if we don't watch. If the private sector contributes more to the social objectives of the *Broadcasting Act*, sooner or later the increased costs will be passed on to the taxpayer and the consumer.

Obviously we can do nothing about mark-ups on consumer purchases. But we make recommendations which will to some degree add to individual and government costs in order to pay for a higher quality, more accessible and *Canadianized* broadcasting system. In the nature of things our estimates of the costs of our recommendations and the potential sources of revenue to pay for them are somewhat tentative, and there is a big difference between our lowest estimates and our highest. Sometimes this reflects the difficulty of estimating hypothetical situations. In other cases the gulf reflects the extent to which a recommendation is followed; whether, for example, one or 100 store-front news operations are to be funded. There can be a TV-Canada and an all-news channel and more children's programming at a rudimentary level or at more generous levels. The consequences of making choices are made clear: we can have a little more or a little less of the new system whose blueprint we have provided.

In the end, decisions must be made by those who form public policy: the CRTC, provincial governments and, above all, the government of Canada. It is those bodies that must gauge the extent of the commitment of Canadians to a Canadian broadcasting policy. They must determine how serious they themselves are about demanding a substantial contribution from the private sector to the goals of the new Broadcasting Act that we hope to see introduced. They must decide the proper level of government spending on broadcasting. They must determine, for example, whether Canadians are prepared to pay higher cable fees or sales taxes to pay for a new public sector broadcasting network. We do not underestimate how difficult it will be to make these decisions; but it is perhaps not excessive to assert that a great deal of the future of this country, and the kind of country we will be in the future, rests on those decisions.

We do not expect every component of the broadcasting system to be enthusiastic about every recommendation in our Report, any more than each of us is. But there are irreducible costs to being Canadian, and certainly participation in the Canadian broadcasting system is one of them. We have attempted to apportion those costs in an equitable and balanced way in the hope that we have been as realistic about the self-interest of the various players as about the overriding general interest of the Canadian public.

It is fortuitous that 1986 is an historic year for Canadian broadcasting. It is the diamond jubilee of the Canadian Association of Broadcasters. It is the golden anniversary of the CBC, the very heart of our broadcasting system and the primary instrument in this century for furthering Canadian culture. It is the silver anniversary of Télé-Métropole and CTV. It is the perfect year for a government to re-commit itself to a truly Canadian broadcasting system.

Notes

1. Patrick Chalmers, "Public Television: Who Cares?", speech at the Banff Television Festival, May 26th, 1986.
2. See interview with Pierre Gauvreau, in Normand Cloutier, "La télévision au jour le jour: (entrevues avec artisans)", study prepared for the Task Force on Broadcasting Policy, January 1986.
3. Herschel Hardin, *Closed Circuits, The Sellout of Canadian Television* (Vancouver: Douglas & McIntyre, 1985), p. 117.
4. Canada, Department of Communications, *Building for the Future: Towards a Distinctive CBC* (Ottawa: The Department, 1983) p. 12.
5. Hon. Marcel Masse, speech at the Banff Television Festival, May 25th, 1986 (Ottawa: Department of Communications, 1986).

Appendices

Appendix A

Terms of Reference for the Task Force

I. The Task Force shall make recommendations to the Minister of Communications on an industrial and cultural strategy to govern the future evolution of the Canadian broadcasting system through the remainder of this century, recognizing the importance of broadcasting to Canadian life. The strategy will take full account of the overall social and economic goals of the government, of government policies and priorities, including the need for fiscal restraint, increased reliance on private sector initiatives and federal-provincial co-operation, and of the policies of the government in other related economic and cultural sectors. It will also take full account of the challenges and opportunities in the increasingly competitive broadcasting environment presented by ongoing technological developments.

II. The Task Force will examine and make recommendations to the Minister on:

a) appropriate public policy objectives for the Canadian broadcasting system in the environment of the 1980s and 1990s, addressing specifically the government's cultural and economic priorities;
b) the role and mandate of the national public broadcasting service and the private broadcasting sector, the scope of provincial broadcasting services and the nature of their interrelationships in the current and future economic context;
c) the demands and desires of the public with respect to the services provided by the broadcasting system including, but not limited to, the balance to be sought among national, regional and local services; the particular needs of anglophone and francophone audiences across the country; the needs of ethnic audiences; the needs of native audiences; and the specialized needs of other Canadians;
d) the role of regulation and other policy instruments including, in particular, expenditures of public funds, as effective and efficient means of achieving the objectives; and
e) the means of reducing structural impediments to the broadcasting system's contribution to the Canadian economy and society.

III. In formulating its evaluation of the key factors and trends in the environment, the Task Force will consult with, and take into account the views of a wide range of interested groups and individuals.

IV. The Task Force will submit its report to the Minister of Communications within nine months.

Appendix B

Schedule of Written Submissions

Access Network, The Alberta Educational Communications Corporation *Alberta*

Advisory Committee on Film, Video and Audio *Manitoba*

Agence de Presse et de Communications M.M.C. Inc., Multinational Media Communication *Quebec*

Yves Alavo *Quebec*

Alcohol and Drug Dependency Commission of Newfoundland and Labrador *Newfoundland*

Allarcom Limited *Alberta*

Alliance Française d'Edmonton *Alberta*

Alliance of Canadian Cinema, Television and Radio Artists *Ontario*

Alliance of Canadian Cinema, Television and Radio Artists Maritimes Branch *Nova Scotia*

Alliance of Canadian Cinema, Television and Radio Artists Maritimes Branch, Cape Breton *Nova Scotia*

Alliance of Canadian Cinema, Television and Radio Artists Maritimes Branch, Prince Edward Island *Prince Edward Island*

Alliance of Canadian Cinema, Television and Radio Artists Newfoundland and Labrador Branch *Newfoundland*

Alliance of Canadian Cinema, Television and Radio Artists Performers' Guild, Northern Alberta and the Southern Alberta Composit Branch *Alberta*

Alliance of Canadian Cinema, Television and Radio Artists Perfomers Guild, Toronto Branch *Ontario*

Alliance of Canadian Cinema, Television and Radio Artists Saskatchewan Branch *Saskatchewan*

Alliance of Canadian Cinema, Television and Radio Artists Writers Guild, Alberta Branch *Alberta*

Alliance of Canadian Cinema, Television and Radio Artists Writers Guild, Toronto Branch *Ontario*

Alliance Québec *Quebec*

Assembly of B.C. Arts Councils *British Columbia*

Association canadienne de communication *Quebec*

Association canadienne-française de l'Alberta *Alberta*

Association canadienne-française de l'Ontario *Ontario*

Association culturelle franco-canadienne de la Saskatchewan *Saskatchewan*

Association Culturelle Franco-TeNoise *Northwest Territories*

Association des Franco-Yukonnais *Yukon*

Association de la recherche en communication du Québec Inc. *Quebec*

Association des producteurs de films et de vidéo du Québec and Association of Canadian Film and Television Producers *Quebec*

Association des réalisateurs, CBC *Quebec*

Association des réalisateurs et réalisatrices de film du Québec *Quebec*

Association jeunesse fransaskoise inc. *Saskatchewan*

Association nationale des Téléspectateurs *Quebec*
Association of Canadian Advertisers Incorporated *Ontario*
Association of Canadian Film and Television Producers and Association des producteurs de films et de viédo du Québec *Quebec*
Association of Canadian Film and Television Producers, Toronto *Ontario*
Association of Roman Catholic Communications of Canada *Alberta*
Atlantic Association of Broadcasters *Nova Scotia*
Atlantic Film and Video Association *Nova Scotia*
Atlantic Satellite Network (ATV/ASN) and Atlantic Television System *Nova Scotia*
François Baby *Quebec*
Filipe Batista, Henri Yatrou & Roger Mondoloni *Quebec*
Baton Broadcasting Incorporated *Ontario*
B.C. Coalition for the Arts *British Columbia*
Rob Beamish, Hart Cantelon, Bruce Kidd, Rick Gruneau & David Whitson *Ontario*
Bob Bossin *British Columbia*
Sid Boyling *Manitoba*
British Columbia Association of Broadcasters *British Columbia*
British Columbia Film and Video Industry Association *British Columbia*
Broadcast News Limited *Ontario*
Howard Broomfield *British Columbia*
Cable Television Association of Alberta *Alberta*
Campbell River TV Association *British Columbia*
Canadian Advisory Council on the Status of Women *Ontario*
Canadian Association for Adult Education *Ontario*
Canadian Association for Free Expression Inc. *Ontario*
Canadian Association of Broadcasters *Ontario*
Canadian Broadcasting Corporation *Ontario*
Canadian Broadcasting Corporation, Advisory Committee on Agriculture and Food, English Services *Nova Scotia*
Canadian Broadcasting Corporation, Advisory Committee on Religion, English Services *Ontario*
Canadian Broadcasting Corporation, Advisory Committee on Science and Technology, English Services *Ontario*
Canadian Broadcasting Corporation/Société Radio-Canada, Comité consultatif sur les sciences et la technologie, *Quebec*
Canadian Broadcasting Corporation, Northern Service *Northwest Territories and Yukon*
Canadian Broadcasting Corporation, Radio *Ontario*
Canadian Broadcasting Corporation/Société Radio-Canada, Radio, *Quebec*
Canadian Broadcasting League *Ontario*
Canadian Cable Television Association and Fundy Cablevision Ltd. *New Brunswick*
Canadian Captioning Development Agency *Ontario*
Canadian Coalition Against Media Pornography *Ontario*
Canadian Coalition for Peace through Strength Inc. *Ontario*
Canadian Council on Children and Youth *Ontario*
Canadian Ethnocultural Council *Ontario*
Canadian Film & Television Association *Ontario*
Canadian League of Composers *Ontario*

Canadian Multiculturalism Council, Media Committee *Manitoba*
Canadian Music Centre *Ontario*
Canadian National Institute for the Blind, Newfoundland and Labrador Division *Newfoundland*
Canadian Satellite Communications Inc. *Ontario*
Canadian Television Producers and Directors Association *Ontario*
Canadian Television Producers and Directors Association, Regina *Saskatchewan*
Canadian Union of Public Employes, Broadcast Council *Ontario*
Canadian Union of Public Employees, Broadcast Council, Local 696, Charlottetown *Prince Edward Island*
Canadian Union of Public Employees, Broadcast Council, Local 692, Halifax *Nova Scotia*
Canadian Union of Public Employees, Broadcast Council, Local 676, Ottawa *Ontario*
Canadian Union of Public Employees, Broadcast Council, Local 669, Regina *Saskatchewan*
Canadian Union of Public Employees, Broadcast Council, Local 670, St. John's *Newfoundland*
Canadian Union of Public Employees, Broadcast Council, Local 697, Sydney *Nova Scotia*
Canadian Union of Public Employees, Broadcast Council, Local 667, Toronto *Ontario*
Canadian Union of Public Employees, Broadcast Council, Local 694, Winnipeg *Manitoba*
Canadian Union of Public Employees, Broadcast Council, Locals 678 and 679, Windsor *Ontario*
Canadian Union of Public Employees, Council of Local Sections, Local 672, Moncton *New Brunswick*
Canadian Union of Public Employees, Council of Local Section, Local 683, Ste-Foy *Quebec*
Centre culturel franco-manitobain *Manitoba*
CFMX-FM *Ontario*
Chinavision Canada Corporation *Ontario*
CISN Radio Ltd. *Alberta*
Citizens for Foreign Aid Reform *Ontario*
Club Richelieu d'Edmonton *Alberta*
COGECO Inc. *Quebec*
Commission culturelle Fransaskoise *Saskatchewan*
Commissioner of Official Languages *Ontario*
Committee on Broadcasting for the Nineteen Nineties *Ontario*
Communist Party of Canada *Ontario*
Conseil de la coopération de la Saskatchewan *Saskatchewan*
Conseil de presse du Québec *Quebec*
Conseil des usagers des médias de la Sagamie *Quebec*
Conseil populaire des communications de l'Est du Québec Inc. *Quebec*
Consumers' Association of Canada *Ontario*
Consumers' Association of Canada, Yellowknife *Northwest Territories*
Guy Corbeil *Quebec*
Council of Canadians *Ontario*
Council of Canadians, Ontario Chapter *Ontario*

Roger Cousins *Northwest Territories and Yukon*
Crossroads Christian Communications Inc. *Ontario*
CTV Television Network Limited *Ontario*
Delta Cable Television Ltd. *British Columbia*
Léo J. Deveau *Nova Scotia*
Claude-Jean Devirieux *Quebec*
Easter Seal Society of Ontario *Ontario*
Education Advisory for Parents *British Columbia*
Kenneth Emberly *Manitoba*
Fédération acadienne de la Nouvelle-Écosse *Nova Scotia*
Fédération des Franco-Colombiens *British Columbia*
Fédération des Francophones de Terre-Neuve et du Labrador *Newfoundland*
Fédération des Francophones Hors Québec Inc. *Ontario*
Fédération nationale des communications, C.S.N. *Quebec*
First Choice Canadian Communications Corporation *Ontario*
Barry Fox *Nova Scotia*
Friends of Public Broadcasting *Ontario*
Fundy Cablevision Ltd. and Canadian Cable Television Association *New Brunswick*
Harold Geltman *Quebec*
German-Canadian Congress, Manitoba *Manitoba*
Government of Manitoba, Department of Culture, Heritage and Recreation *Manitoba*
Government of Manitoba, Department of Culture, Heritage and Recreation Telecommunications Policy *Manitoba*
Government of New Brunswick, Department of Transportation, Transportation and Communications Policy *New Brunswick*
Government of Newfoundland, Department of Forest Resources and Lands *Newfoundland*
Government of Nova Scotia *Nova Scotia*
Government of Northwest Territories, Department of Education *Northwest Territories*
Government of Northwest Territories, Department of Information *Northwest Territories*
Government of Ontario, Ministry of Transportation and Communications *Ontario*
Greater Winnipeg Cablevision Limited *Manitoba*
Lawrence Hall *Ontario*
Hamilton-Dante Centre for Italian Language and Culture Inc. *Ontario*
Heritage Christian Ministries *Alberta*
James Hester *Quebec*
David M. Hunter *Ontario*
Indian and Inuit Support Group of Newfoundland and Labrador *Newfoundland*
Institut canadien d'éducation des adultes *Quebec*
Inuit Broadcasting Corporation *Ontario*
Inuvialut Communications Society *Northwest Territories and Yukon*
Island Cablevision Ltd. *Prince Edward Island*
Island Media Arts Co-op *Prince Edward Island*
Italo-Canadian Advertising and Publicity Services *Ontario*
James Bay Cree Communications Society *Quebec*
Judicial Action *British Columbia*
Paul Kahnert *Ontario*

Gordon Keeble *Ontario*
Sheila Knowlton-MacRury *Northwest Territories*
League for Human Rights of B'Nai B'Rith, Canada, Eastern Region *Quebec*
Liberal Party of New Brunswick *New Brunswick*
Life Channel *Ontario*
Shelagh Mackenzie *Nova Scotia*
Maclean Hunter (Cable) Ltd. *Ontario*
Maclean Hunter Limited *Ontario*
Makivik Corporation *Quebec*
Manitoba Association for the Promotion of Ancestral Languages *Manitoba*
Tom Marzotto *Ontario*
Media Club of Ottawa *Ontario*
Monarch Communications Group *Alberta*
Multicultural Association of Nova Scotia *Nova Scotia*
National Association of Broadcast Employees and Technicians *Ontario*
National Council of Women of Canada *Quebec*
National Film Board of Canada *Quebec*
National Radio Producers' Association *Ontario*
National Watch on Images of Women in the Media Inc. (MediaWatch) *British Columbia*
National Watch on Images of Women in the Media Inc. (MediaWatch), Manitoba Branch and Forum for the Awareness of Minority Electorate *Manitoba*
Native Communications' Society of the Western N.W.T. *Northwest Territories*
New Democratic Party Caucus *Saskatchewan*
Newfoundland and Labrador Crafts Development Association *Newfoundland*
Newfoundland Writers Guild *Newfoundland*
Northern Native Broadcasting *Yukon*
Northwest Research & Consulting *Alberta*
NTV, Newfoundland Television *Newfoundland*
N.W.T. Advisory Council on the Status of Women *Northwest Territories*
Oceola Arts Council *British Columbia*
Office des communications sociales *Quebec*
John G. Packer *Alberta*
Michael H. Parsons *Ontario*
Pathonic Communications Inc., CHEM-TV-8 *Quebec*
Performing Rights Organization of Canada Ltd. *Ontario*
Prince Edward Island Federation of Agriculture *Prince Edward Island*
Progressive Conservative Caucus *Ontario*
QCTV Ltd. *Alberta*
Quebec Farmers' Association *Quebec*
Quebec Region Religious Advisory Council to the Canadian Broadcasting Corporation *Quebec*
Marc Raboy *Quebec*
Radio Television News Directors Association of Canada *Ontario*
Ralph C. Ellis Enterprises Ltd. *Ontario*
John Reeves *Ontario*
Regina Cablevision Co-operative, Sascable Services Inc. and Saskatchewan Telecable *Saskatchewan*

Regroupement des organismes communautaires de communication du Québec *Quebec*

Regroupement pour la défense de la télévision publique *Quebec*

Blair Rhodes *Nova Scotia*

Roman Catholic Diocese of Charlottetown, Social Action Commission *Prince Edward Island*

St. John's Board of Trade *Newfoundland*

Saskatchewan Writers Guild *Saskatchewan*

Satellite Television Association of Canada *Alberta*

Satellite Communications Association of Canada *Ontario*

Simon Fraser University Media Group *British Columbia*

Société de la Maison française de Calgary *Alberta*

Société des Acadiens du Nouveau-Brunswick *New Brunswick*

Société Franco-Manitobaine *Manitoba*

Société nationale des Acadiens *New Brunswick*

Société Saint-Thomas D'Aquin *Prince Edward Island*

Standard Broadcasting Corporation Limited *Ontario*

Steering Committee on National Broadcast Reading Service *Ontario*

Studio East Limited *Nova Scotia*

W.A. Sullivan *Quebec*

Suncoast Television Society *British Columbia*

Sunwapta Broadcasting Limited *Alberta*

Syndicat des employés de production du Québec et de l'Acadie *Quebec*

Taqramiut Nipingat Inc. *Quebec*

Teaching English as a Second Language Across Canada *Ontario*

Telefilm Canada *Quebec*

Telemedia Communications Inc., Ontario Division *Ontario*

Télémédia Communications Inc., Division Québec *Quebec*

Telesat Canada *Ontario*

The Sports Network *Ontario*

Major F.R. Thomas *Ontario*

Town of Inuvik *Northwest Territories*

Townshippers' Association *Quebec*

TVOntario *Ontario*

Ukrainian Canadian Committee *Alberta*

Union des producteurs agricoles *Quebec*

University of Alberta, CJSR *Alberta*

University of Alberta, Faculté Saint-Jean *Alberta*

Vancouver Co-Operative Radio *British Columbia*

Wawatay Native Communications Society *Ontario*

Dr. John Weinzweig *Ontario*

West Coast Media Society *British Columbia*

Western International Communications Ltd. *British Columbia*

Writers Federation of Nova Scotia and Writers' Union of Canada, Atlantic Region *Nova Scotia*

Writers Union of Canada *Ontario*

Young Canada Television-Saskatchewan Youth Advisory Council *Saskatchewan*

Appendix C

Schedule of Public Meetings

Ottawa, August 14, 1985

Alliance of Canadian Cinema, Television and Radio Artists, Performers' Guild, National Office
Alliance of Canadian Cinema, Television and Radio Artists, Ottawa Branch
Canadian Broadcasting Corporation, Radio, English Services
Canadian Ethnocultural Council
Canadian Union of Public Employees, Broadcast Council, National Representation
Council of Canadians
Trudy LaCaine
Brian Maracle
Mr. Morrison
Greg Vezina
Oscar Werthorst

Vancouver, August 19, 1985

Alliance of Canadian Cinema, Television and Radio Artists, British Columbia Branch
Alliance of Canadian Cinema, Television and Radio Artists, Performers' Guild, British Columbia Branch
Alliance of Canadian Cinema, Television and Radio Artists, Writers' Guild, British Columbia Branch
Peter Anderson
Assembly of British Columbia Arts Council
Steve Beauwold
Bob Bossin
British Columbia Public Interest Advocacy Centre
Howard Broomfield
Campbell River TV Association
Canadian Union of Public Employees, Broadcast Council, National Communications
Bob Chown
Council of Canada, British Columbia Chapter
Reinhart Darrahs
Education Advisory for Parents
German Canadian Congress, British Columbia
Eleanor Hadley
Judicial Action
Beverley Larsen
Mr. McAlister
Irène McAllister
Daw-Rae McLaren & Brad McCannell
Ian McLennan

Leslie Millin
Oceola Arts Council
Ruth Schiller
Simon Fraser University Media Group
Jim Styles
Symmetric Technologies Inc.
Sigred-Ann Thors-Vernon
Vancouver Co-operative Radio
Debbie Warren
West Coast Media Society
Karen Wilson
Barbara Wutzki

Edmonton, August 21, 1985

Alberta Handicapped Communications Society
Alliance of Canadian Cinema, Television and Radio Artists, Performers' Guild, Edmonton Branch
Cable Television Association of Alberta
Canadian Television Producers and Directors Association, Edmonton Local
Canadian Union of Public Employees, Broadcast Council, National Representation
CHOT
Tom Dodd
Douglas Communications
Carl Hare
Heritage Christian Ministries
Inuvialut Communications Society
National Radio Producers' Association, CBC, Edmonton Local
Northern Native Broadcasting, CHON, Yukon
Ukrainian Canadian Committee, Alberta Branch
University of Alberta
University of Alberta, CJSR-FM
Young Canada Television, Advisory Council of Alberta

Regina, August 22, 1985

Alliance of Canadian Cinema, Television and Radio Artists, Saskatchewan Branch
Alliance of Canadian Cinema, Television and Radio Artists, Writers' Guild, Saskatchewan Branch
Association culturelle franco-canadienne de la Saskatchewan
Association jeunesse fransaskoise inc.
Dr. Lewis Brandt
Canadian Crafts Council
Canadian Television Producers and Directors Association, Regina Local
Canadian Union of Public Employees, Broadcast Council, Local 669, Regina
Commission culturelle fransaskoise
Conseil de la coopération de la Saskatchewan

Globe Theatre
Mr. Leblanc
National Watch on Images of Women in the Media Inc. (MediaWatch)
New Democratic Party Caucus, Saskatchewan
Dave White
Young Canada Television, Advisory Council of Saskatchewan

Halifax, August 26, 1985

Alliance of Canadian Cinema, Television and Radio Artists, Maritimes Branch
Alliance of Canadian Cinema, Television and Radio Artists, Maritimes Branch, Cape Breton
Atlantic Film and Video Association
Canadian Broadcasting Corporation, Advisory Committee on Agriculture and Food
Canadian Television Producers and Directors Association Maritimes Local
Canadian Union of Public Employees, Broadcast Council, Local 692, Halifax
Canadian Union of Public Employees, Broadcast Council, Local 697, Sydney
Leo J. Deveau
Barry Fox
Shelagh Mackenzie
Joan Melanson
Multicultural Association of Nova Scotia
Nova Scotia Coalition on Arts and Culture
Writers' Federation of Nova Scotia and Writers' Union of Canada, Atlantic Region
Young Canada Television, Advisory Council of Maritimes

Winnipeg, August 26, 1985

Alliance of Canadian Cinema, Television and Radio Artists, Winnipeg Branch
Julie Blais
Sid Boyling
Canadian Multiculturalism Council, Media Committee
Canadian Television Producers and Directors Association, Winnipeg Local
Canadian Union of Public Employees, Broadcast Council, Local 694, Winnipeg
Council of Canadians, Manitoba Chapter
Fred Debrecen
Henry Elias
Kenneth Emberley
Jack Eyre
Forum for the Awareness of Minority Electorate
Vivian Fresen
German Canadian Congress, Manitoba
Government of Manitoba, Department of Culture, Heritage and Recreation, Telecommunications Policy
Barbara Holst
Fred Kelbert
David Kidd

Howard Loewen
Manitoba Association for the Promotion of Ancestral Languages
Manitoba Intercultural Council
Multicultural Council of Canada
Doreen Myers
National Watch on Images of Women in the Media Inc. (MediaWatch), Manitoba
Native Communications Inc.
Richard Simoens
Société Franco-Manitobaine
South East Resource Development Council
Winnipeg Chinatown Development Corporation

St. John's, August 27, 1985

Advisory Council on Status of Women
Alcohol and Drug Dependency Commission of Newfoundland and Labrador
Alliance of Canadian Cinema, Television and Radio Artists, Newfoundland and Labrador Branch
Canadian National Institute for the Blind, Newfoundland and Labrador Branch
Canadian Union of Public Employees, Broadcast Council, Local 670, St. John's
Citizens Coalition Versus Pornography
Walter H. Davis
Elysian Theatre Company
Fédération des Francophones de Terre-Neuve et du Labrador
Native People Support Group of Newfoundland and Labrador
Newfoundland and Labrador Crafts Development Association
Newfoundland Writers Guild
Ploughshare Youth
St. John's Board of Trade
St. John's Native Friendship Centre
Dr. John Scott
Teaching English as a Second Language Across Canada, Canada
David Thompson
Harvey Weir

Moncton, August 28, 1985

Canadian Union of Public Employees, Council of Local Sections, Local 672, Moncton
Shirley Dobson
Fundy Cablevision and Canadian Cable Television Association
Martha Jackman
Frank McKenna, Leader of Liberal Party of New Brunswick
Radio-Acadie
Télé-Acadie

Charlottetown, August 29, 1985

Alliance of Canadian Cinema, Television and Radio Artists, Prince Edward Island Branch
Canadian Union of Public Employees, Broadcast Council, Local 696, Charlottetown
Island Cablevision Ltd.
Island Media Arts Co-op
Carl Mathis
Prince Edward Island Council of the Arts
Prince Edward Island, Federation of Agriculture
Roman Catholic Diocese of Charlottetown, Social Action Commission
Société St-Thomas d'Aquin
Technical Arts Co-op

Quebec, September 4, 1985

François Baby
Canadian Union of Public Employees, Council of Local Sections, Local 683, Ste-Foy
Conseil des usagers des médias de la Sagamie
Conseil populaire des communications de l'Est du Québec Inc.
Robert Elias
Laurent Laplante
Regroupement des TV communautaires
Société de Musique de Chambre de Ste-Pétronille
Téléjeunesse Canada, Comité consultatif du Québec
Vidéo-femmes

Montreal, September 5, 1985

Alliance Québec
Alliance of Canadian Cinema, Television and Radio Artists, Montreal Branch
Association des réalisateurs et réalisatrices de film du Québec
Association des réalisateurs, Société Radio-Canada
Association nationale des téléspectateurs
Ateliers Super-Jeunesse
Black Theater Workshop Inc.
Canadian Broadcasting Corporation/Société Radio-Canada, Comité consultatif sur les sciences et la technologie
Canadian Captioning Development Agency
Canadian Union of Public Employees, Broadcast Council, Local 676, Ottawa
Claude-Jean Devirieux
Harold Geltman
James Hester
James Bay Cree Communications Society
League for Human Rights of B'Nai B'Rith, Canada, Eastern Region
Makivik Corporation
P.M.E. Productions

Quebec Farmers' Association
Quebec Region Religious Advisory Council
to the Canadian Broadcasting Corporation
Regroupement pour la défense de la télévision publique
Roman Serbyn
W.A. Sullivan
Taqramiut Nipingat Inc.
Townshippers Association
Union des producteurs agricoles
Basil Vasilio

Toronto, September 16, 1985

Neil Aberle
African Canadian Cultural Association
Alliance of Canadian Cinema, Television and Radio Artists, Performers' Guild, Toronto Branch
Alliance of Canadian Cinema, Television and Radio Artists, Writers' Guild, Toronto Branch
Association of Television Producers and Directors
Jean Augustine
Gloria Bishop
Vladimir Bubrin
Canadian Association for Adult Education
Canadian Association for Free Expression Inc.
Canadian Black Performers Association
Canadian Captioning Development Agency
Canadian Catalogue Interchange Systems
Canadian Coalition Against Media Pornography
Canadian Coalition for Peace through Strength Inc.
Canadian Independant Film Caucus
Canadian League of Composers
Canadian Union of Public Employees, Broadcast Council, National Office
Canadian Union of Public Employees, Broadcast Council, Local 667, Toronto
Canadian Union of Public Employees, Broadcast Council, Locals 678 and 679, Windsor
Frank Carenza
Citizens for Foreign Aid Reform
Committee Against Pornography
Committee on Broadcasting for the Nineteen Nineties
Committee to Procure the Chinavision Service on Maclean Hunter
Council of Canadians, Ontario Chapter
Clive Court
Duane Crandall
Crossroads Christian Communications
Friends of Public Broadcasting
Norm Guilfoyle
Hamilton-Dante Centre for Italian Language and Culture Inc.
Max Hemsol

David M. Hunter
Paul Kahnert
Bruce Kidd
Life Channel
Lynn MacDonald, M.P., New Democratic Party Critic on Culture
Jamshed Mavalwala
Dr. Mary Jane Miller
Performing Rights Organisation Ltd. (PROCAN)
Ralph C. Ellis Enterprises Ltd.
School Trustee "Self"
Bruce Steele
Toronto Chinese Business Community
Universal African Improvement Association
Dr. Bhausaheb Vbale
Richard Wattam
Sheila Weller-Gall
Wyndham Wise
Writers Union of Canada

Yellowknife, October 30, 1985

Advisory Council of the Status of Women, Northwest Territories
Association culturelle Franco-TeNoise
Pearl Binnick
Canadian Broadcasting Corporation, Northern Service
Consumers' Association of Canada, Yellowknife Local
Vince Hill
Litha MacLachlan
Bill Powlitz
Art Sorensen

Whitehorse, October 30, 1985

Canadian Broadcasting Corporation, Northern Service
Hougens Entreprises, Cable and Radio
Northern Native Broadcasting Society

Frobisher Bay, November 12, 1985

Roger Cousins
Geetaloo Kakkik
Cynthia Mallon
Mick Mallon
Abe Oopik
Elija Papatsie
Jose Papatsie
Bryan Pearson

Appendix D

Schedule of Private Meetings

Toronto

July 15 to 18, July 22 to 24,
and **August 12 and 13, 1985**

Alliance of Canadian Cinema, Television and Radio Artists, National Office
Andrew Cochran Associates Ltd.
Association of Canadian Advertisers Incorporated
Association of Canadian Film and Television Producers
Association of Canadian Film and Video Producers
Association of Television Producers and Directors
Baton Broadcasting Incorporated
Broadcast News Limited
BBM Bureau of Broadcast Measurement
Canadian Broadcasting Corporation, Advisory Committee on Religion, English Services
Canadian Broadcasting Corporation, Advisory Committee on Science and Technology, English Services
Canadian Broadcasting Corporation, Radio, English Services
Canadian Broadcasting Corporation, Television, English Services
Canadian Film and Television Association
Canadian Independant Records Producers Association
Canadian Media Directors Council
Children's Broadcast Institute
Chinavision Canada Corporation
CHUM Group Limited
CTV Television Network Ltd.
First Choice Canadian Communications Corporation
Friends of Public Broadcasting
Global Television Network
Lynn MacDonald, M.P., N.D.P. Communication Critic
Maclean Hunter (Cable) Ltd.
Maclean Hunter Limited (Broadcasting)
MuchMusic
National Association of Broadcast Employees and Technicians
National Radio Producers Association, CBC
Public Interest Advocacy Centre
Radio Bureau of Canada
John Reeves
Rogers Broadcasting Limited
Rogers Cablevision Inc.
Selkirk Communications

The Sports Network
Television Bureau of Canada Inc.
TVOntario
TV Bureau

Ottawa

August 14, October 15 to 23, November 27 to 29 and **December 5, 1985**

Affiliate Stations to the Canadian Broadcasting Corporation
American Federation of Musicians, Canadian Office
Association canadienne-française de l'Ontario
Association des radiodiffuseurs communautaires du Québec
Canadian Broadcasting Corporation, Ontario Regional Broadcasting
Canadian Broadcasting Corporation, Ottawa Area
Canadian Council of Children and Youth
Canadian Ethnocultural Council
Canadian Motion Picture Distributors Association
Canadian Music Centre and Canadian League of Composers
Canadian Television Producers and Directors Association
Canadian Union of Public Employees, Broadcast Council, National Office
Consumers' Association of Canada, Regulated Industries Program Council
EN Network
Fédération des Francophones Hors Québec Inc.
Government of Ontario, Ministry of Transportation and Communications
Inuit Broadcasting Corporation
Al Johnson, Canadian Broadcasting League
Progressive Conservative Party Caucus
Telesat Canada
Wawatay Native Communications Society

Montreal

August 6 to 9, September 5 and 6, and **October 3 and 4, 1985**

Alliance Québec
Association canadienne de la radio et de la télévision de langue française
Association des cablôdistributeurs du Québec Inc.
Association des producteurs de films et de vidéo du Québec
Association des réalisateurs, Société Radio-Canada
Canadian Broadcasting Corporation, Quebec Region, English Services
Canadian Broadcasting Corporation/Société Radio-Canada, Radio
Canadian Broadcasting Corporation/Société Radio-Canada, Television
Canadian Satellite Communications Inc.
Canadian Union of Public Employees, Council of Locals Sections
CFCF
CJAD Radio and CJFM-FM Inc., Standard Broadcasting

CKOI-FM, CKVL-AM
COGECO Inc.
Confédération générale des entreprises de publicité
Corporation pour l'Avancement de Nouvelles Applications des Langages
Fédération nationale des communications, CSN
Institut canadien d'éducation des adultes
National Council of Women of Canada
National Film Board
Pathonic Communications Inc., CHEM-TV-8
Radiomutuel Inc.
Radio-Québec
Réseau TVA
Société des auteurs, recherchistes, documentalistes et compositeurs
Super Ecran
Syndicat des employés de production du Québec et de l'Acadie
Téléfilm Canada
Télémédia Communications Inc.
Union des Artistes
Vidéotron Ltée

Vancouver

August 19 and 20, 1985

Association for Public Broadcasting in British Columbia
British Columbia Association of Broadcasters
British Columbia Cable Association
British Columbia Coalition for the Arts
British Columbia Film and Video Industry Association
Canadian Broadcasting Corporation, British Columbia Region
Cowichan Cablevision Ltd.
Fédération des Franco-Colombiens
Government of British Columbia, Department of Universities, Science and Communications
Knowledge Network
National Watch on Images of Women in the Media Inc. (MediaWatch)
Vancouver French Chamber of Commerce
Western International Communications Ltd. (WIC)

Edmonton

August 21 and 22, 1985

Access Network, The Alberta Educational Communications Corporation
Allarcom Limited
Canadian Broadcasting Corporation, Alberta Region
CISN Radio Ltd.
Government of Alberta, Department of Utilities and Telecommunications
Monarch Communications Group

Northern Cablevision Ltd.
QCTV Ltd.
Sunwapta Broadcasting Limited

Regina

August 23, 1985

Canadian Broadcasting Corporation, Saskatchewan Region
CKCK TV
Co-op Com Ltd., Zenon Park
Government of Saskatchewan
Regina Cablevision Co-operative and Sascable Services Inc., Saskatchewan Telecable

Halifax

August 26, 1985

Atlantic Association of Broadcasters
Atlantic Film and Video Association
Canadian Broadcasting Corporation, Halifax Region
Fédération des francophones de la Nouvelle-Écosse
Government of Nova Scotia
Studio East Limited

Winnipeg

August 26 and 27, 1985

Advisory Committee on Film, Video and Audio
Canadian Broadcasting Corporation, Manitoba Region
CanWest Broadcasting Inc., CKND
Fédération culturelle des Canadiens-français
Government of Manitoba, Department of Culture, Heritage and Recreation, Telecommunications Policy
Greater Winnipeg Cablevision Limited
Moffatt Communications

St. John's

August 27 and 28, 1985

Canadian Broadcasting Corporation, Newfoundland Region
Newfoundland Broadcasting Company Limited
Newfoundland's Independant Film Makers Co-op
VOCM, Radio

Moncton

August 29, 1985

Canadian Broadcasting Corporation, Radio, Atlantic Provinces, French Services
Government of New Brunswick, Department of Transportation,
  Transportation and Communications Policy
New Brunswick Broadcasting Company
Société des Acadiens du Nouveau-Brunswick

Charlottetown

August 30, 1985

Government of Prince Edward Island
Island Media Arts Co-op
Point East Productions

Quebec

September 4, 1985

Canadian Broadcasting Corporation, Radio and Television, Quebec Region
André Arthur, CHRC
CJMF
Gouvernement du Québec, Ministère des Affaires culturelles
Gouvernement du Québec, Ministère des Communications*
Jean-Paul L'Allier
Regroupement des organismes communautaires de communications du Québec
Téléjeunesse Canada, Conseil d'administration

Yellowknife

October 30, 1985

Business and Professional Women's Association of Yellowknife
Canadian Broadcasting Corporation, Northern Service
CJCD, Radio and Northwest Territories Association of Municipalities
Consumers' Association of Canada, Yellowknife Local
Government of Northwest Territories, Department of Culture and Communications
Mackenzie Media, Cable
Native Communications' Society of the Western N.W.T.

*Members of the Task Force met privately with Jean-François Bertrand, Quebec Minister of Communications in May 1985, and with Richard French, the new Minister, in January 1986.

Whitehorse

October 31, 1985

Association des Franco-Yukonnais
Canadian Broadcasting Corporation, Northern Service
Hougen Entreprises, CKRW Radio and Northern Television Systems Limited, WHTV Cable
Northern Native Broadcasting, CHON

Frobisher Bay

November 13, 1985

Baffin Regional Inuit Association
Canadian Broadcasting Corporation, Northern Service
Eastern Artic Television
Government of Northwest Territories, Department of Education
Inuit Broadcasting Corporation

Appendix E

List of Research Reports and Other Commissioned Material

Sheila McLeod Arnopoulos
Broadcasting for the Official Language Minorities: The Need for a Community Development Approach

Robert E. Babe Associates
A Study of Radio: Economic/Financial Profile of Private Sector Radio Broadcasting in Canada

Henri Brun
Opinion juridique concernant le pouvoir du CRTC d'assortir les licences qu'il émet de certains types de conditions.

BBM Bureau of Broadcast Measurement
A Review of Trends in Canadian Radio Listening 1976-1985

Mireille Beaudet, Marie-Philippe Bouchard et Michèle Gamache
Centre de recherche en droit public, Université de Montréal
Étude du statut juridique des entreprises de radiodiffusion au Canada

Peter A. Bruck, Jay R. Weston, Patricia L. Bennett & E. Jill Vardy, Centre for Communication, Culture and Society
Bibliography on Canadian Broadcasting

Peter A. Bruck, Will Straw & Dennis O'Sullivan,
Centre for Communication, Culture and Society
Performance Programming in the Canadian Television Broadcasting System

Clarkson Gordon
Technical Feasibility and Estimated Cost of a 150-percent Deduction for Costs of Commercial Time on Canadian Television Programs.

Bernard Cleary & Michel Cormier
La presse électronique au Québec

Normand Cloutier
La télévision au jour le jour (entrevues avec artisans)

Kirwan Cox
The National Film Board and Television

Coopers & Lybrand Consulting Group
Impact of Selected Policy Changes in the Canadian Broadcasting System

Mark Czarnecki
The Creation of Program Material

Marc Deschênes, Viviane Haeberle et Nicole Tremblay
Radiodiffusion et État : Bibliographie des documents en langue française établie à l'intention du Groupe de travail sur la politique de la radiodiffusion

Peter Desbarats
Radio and Television News: The Roles of Public and Private Broadcasters, and Some Other Critical Issues

Arthur Donner
An Analysis of the Importance of U.S. Television Spillover, Bill C-58, and Simulcasting Policies for the Revenues of Canadian TV Broadcasters

Econotec Inc.
Satellites and the Broadcasting Industry

Marie Alison Finkelstein
Selected Social Issues in Programming: The Legal, Constitutional and Policy

Implications of the Equality Provision in Bill C-20

Jacques Frémont
Étude des objectifs et des principes proposés et adoptés relativement au système de la radiodiffusion canadienne

Laura Gaggi
Advertising Revenue Trends in Canada

Richard Hahn
A Study of the Supply of English Language Sound Recordings to Canadian Private Radio Stations

Harrison, Young, Pesonen and Newell Inc.
Canadian TV Viewing Habits: A Study of How Canadians Use the Television Medium, Which Concentrates on How Canadians View Canadian Programming

Gérard Hébert
Les relations du travail dans la radiodiffusion canadienne

Jay A. Herringer, R.S. Jakhu & Cliff Arnold
Options for a New Legal Definition of Broadcasting for Canada

Colin Hoskins & Stuart McFadyen
Review and Evaluation of the Canadian Broadcast Program Development Fund

John D. Hylton & Gary Maavara
The Interaction of Copyright Law and Broadcasting Policy

Jean-Paul Lafrance
La juxtaposition des territoires : étude-synthèse de l'évolution des systèmes de communication en Europe et en Amérique

Jean-Paul L'Allier & Associés Inc.
La spécificité québécoise et les médias électroniques

Alain Lapointe & Jean-Pierre LeGoff
La télévision au Canada : une analyse économique

Vincent Lemieux
Le rôle des différents acteurs dans les politiques de radiodiffusion. Présentation de trois scénarios.

Peter J. Lown
A Reflection on the Roles and Responsibilities of the Major Actors in the Broadcasting System

Kathleen E. Mahoney & Sheilah L. Martin
Broadcasting and the Canadian Charter of Human Rights and Freedoms: Justifications for Restricting Freedom of Expression

McCarthy and McCarthy
Satellite Services, Network Licensing and The Broadcasting Act

Moss, Roberts and Associates Inc.
An Economic Profile of the Canadian Cable Industry

David Nostbakken & André Caron
Children and Television: Programs, People, Policies

Maurice Patry
La télévision éducative au Québec : développements récents et perspectives d'avenir

Frank W. Peers
CBC: The Big Picture

Frank W. Peers
Canadian Broadcasting as "A Single System"

Nathalie Petrowski
Du Canadien errant au Chanteur sans frontières: profil de la musique québécoise et de ses rapports avec l'industrie du disque, les diffuseurs et la société

Rose Potvin & Bonnie Diamond
Women and the Broadcast Media

John Roberts, Brian Chater & Denis Bergeron
Music and the Electronic Media in Canada

Walter I. Romanow, Stuart H. Surlin & W.C. Soderlund
Analysis of Local TV News Broadcasts

Abraham Rotstein
The Use and Misuse of Economics in Cultural and Broadcasting Policy

Liora Salter
Issues in Broadcasting

Liora Salter
Methods of Regulation

Liora Salter
The Regulatory Structure for Broadcasting

Francis Spiller Associates
Multicultural Broadcasting in Canada

Stan Staple
Supply and Demand: English-language Television in Canada During 1984

J. Mark Stiles & Associates
Broadcasting and Canada's Aboriginal Peoples

Stratavision Inc.
Ownership Structure and Behaviour in the Canadian Broadcasting System

Stratégem, Coopers & Lybrand
Factors Affecting the Advertising Revenues of the Broadcasting System in Québec

Marc Thibault
Radio-Canada: des structures et des hommes

Gaétan Tremblay
Le service public : principe fondamental de la radiodiffusion canadienne

Video World Inc. (Ronald G. Keast)
The Role of the Provinces in Public Broadcasting

Video World Inc. (Ronald G. Keast)
The Role of Satellites in the Canadian Broadcasting System

Richard Vigneault
Enquête téléphonique auprès des artisans de la radio et de la télévision au Nouveau-Brunswick

Copies of the commissioned material listed above may be obtained through Information Services, Department of Communications, Government of Canada.

Appendix F

Members of the Task Force

Gerald Lewis Caplan, holds a Masters degree in Canadian history from the University of Toronto and a Doctorate in African history from the University of London. He was the national campaign director for the New Democratic Party of Canada during the 1984 general election. Mr. Caplan's professional background includes employment as national director of the New Democratic Party in 1982-84, director of the Health Advocacy Unit for the City of Toronto in 1980-82, director for the Canadian University Service Overseas (CUSO) in Nigeria in 1977-79, and as a professor in history and philosophy of education with the Ontario Institute for Studies in Education (OISE) and the University of Toronto from 1967 to 1977. Mr. Caplan, who is a frequent public speaker, has also acted as a radio and television interviewer and analyst. He writes a weekly newspaper column on public affairs, and is also the author of books, articles and book reviews on such subjects as politics, education, Canadian history and African and Third World development.

Florian Sauvageau, holds a degree in Law from Laval University and a Masters degree in Journalism from the University of Illinois. A lawyer, journalist and university professor, Mr. Sauvageau has worked as a radio and television public affairs journalist and host with Radio-Canada since 1969. A teacher at Laval University for a number of years, he has been a full professor with Laval's Information and Communication Department since 1982. In addition to work as a script writer and co-producer of several National Film Board documentary productions, Mr. Sauvageau has been a news editor and managing editor with *Le Soleil* in Quebec city. Co-author of *Droit et journalisme au Québec*, he has published articles and co-edited books on journalism and freedom of the press.

Felix Randolph Blache-Fraser (Fil Fraser) is a writer, producer, consultant and broadcast executive in Edmonton with the Alberta Educational Communications Corporation (ACCESS) station. Mr. Fraser has many years experience in communications, particularly in radio and television, as a producer, news director and editor, open-line host and announcer. In 1970 he was program director of MEETA, the first educational television service in Canada. He produced three feature films including *Why Shoot the Teacher*. He has produced, directed and been the host of many television programs for the CBC, and educational television outlets and private stations. He was the founding Chairman of the Banff Television Festival, the Commonwealth Games Festival and the Alberta Film Awards.

Francine Côté, who graduated in Law from the University of Montreal, has been a member of the Quebec Bar since 1975. She is currently associated with Lafleur, Brown, de Grandpré, where she specializes in communications and administrative law. From 1981 to 1984 she worked in the fields of labour, communications and copyright law. She was employed by Cablevision Nationale Ltée from 1975 to 1980 and acted as its representative before administrative tribunals dealing with licence applications and renewals, rates, tariffs and programming changes. In 1980 she was chairperson of the Canadian Bar Association's section on information and communications law. Ms Côté is a member of a number of professional associations.

Mimi Fullerton who holds Masters degrees in Arts and Business Administration, is currently Director-General of TVOntario, responsible for all aspects of programming and acts for the Chairman in his absence. Ms Fullerton's previous professional experience includes Manager of Planning and Development with Telemedia Inc., Communications Industry Analyst with Burns Fry Limited and Vice-President, Special Projects, with Richmond Advertising. From 1975 to 1979 she was employed by *Saturday Night Magazine* where she was Manager, Market Development. Ms Fullerton was formerly a member of the Canadian Association of Broadcasters' Strategic Planning Committee.

J. Conrad Lavigne is a broadcast consultant with considerable experience in radio and television. Mr. Lavigne, who is President of JCL Corporation Broadcast Consultants, has served as Chairman of Northern Telephone Co. Ltd. and as a director of several companies, including Ontario Hydro, Télé-Capitale Ltée, Intercity Gas, the National Bank of Canada and *Le Droit* newspaper. In 1950, he established radio station CFCL in Timmins, the first private French-language station in Ontario. In 1956 he added the first English-language television station in Northern Ontario, CFCL-TV, which became part of the Mid-Canada Television Network, one of the largest privately owned TV networks. Mr. Lavigne, who received the Colonel Keith S. Rogers Outstanding Engineering Award in both 1971 and 1979, was also named Canadian Broadcaster of the Year in 1979. He was a founding member of the Board of Governors of Laurentian University and received the Canada Medal in 1982.

Finlay MacDonald, Jr., a native Nova Scotian, is a Halifax-based television consultant and producer. Parliamentary correspondent for Ottawa's CJOH-TV from 1971 to 1976 and Atlantic correspondent for the CTV network national news from 1976 to 1979, Mr. MacDonald obtained a degree in Law from Dalhousie University in 1971. He was President of the maritime regional pay television service, Star Channel, Chairman of the 1980 Federal Task Force on the Atlantic Production Industry and, during 1981, taught at the King's College School of Journalism in Halifax. In 1984-1985, Mr. MacDonald was a member of the CRTC Task Force on Access to Television in Underserved Communities.

Appendix G

Staff of the Task Force

Executive Director
Paul Audley

Chief, Administration and Finance
Victoria Russ

Director of Publishing
Eunice Thorne

Administrative Assistants
Hélène Bussière
Wanda Hamilton

Special Assistant
Phil Smith

Contracts Administrator
Raymonde Turcotte

Central Registry
Danielle Coates

Word Processing
Christine Briand
Anne Groulx
Suzanne Réhel
Jeanne Séguin

Director of Research
Pierre Trudel

Senior Consultants
Tim Creery
David Ellis
Robert Pilon
Gisèle Tremblay

Research Assistants
Susan Alexander
Joanne Baldassi
Gilles Saint-Gelais
Michel Saint-Laurent
Michel Solis

Departmental Comptroller
Sherril Minns

Public Meetings
Nicole Duschesneau
Richard McLelland